DATE DUE

War and Press Freedom

Office of Censorship poster, World War II. Courtesy of National Archives.

War &

The Problem of

Press

Prerogative Power

Freedom

Jeffery A. Smith

New York   Oxford

Oxford University Press

1999

Oxford University Press

Oxford   New York
Athens   Auckland   Bangkok   Bogotá   Buenos Aires   Calcutta
Cape Town   Chennai   Dar es Salaam   Delhi   Florence   Hong Kong   Istanbul
Karachi   Kuala Lumpur   Madrid   Melbourne   Mexico City   Mumbai
Nairobi   Paris   São Paulo   Singapore   Taipei   Tokyo   Toronto   Warsaw

and associated companies in
Berlin   Ibadan

Library of Congress Cataloging-in-Publication Data
Smith, Jeffery Alan.
War and press freedom : the problem of
prerogative power / Jeffery A. Smith.
p. cm.
Includes index.
ISBN 0-19-509945-1; ISBN 0-19-509946-X (pbk.)
1. Freedom of the press—United States—History.
2. War and emergency legislation—United States—History.
3. War—Press coverage—United States—History.
I. Title.
KF4774.S644   1998
342.73'0853—dc21   97-37755

1   3   5   7   9   8   6   4   2

Printed in the United States of America
on acid-free paper

For Geneviève Prévot Smith

Preface

The theory of democracy suggests that if citizens and their lawmakers are well informed and able to debate issues, they will make better decisions. Yet, often in war, the most serious test of reasoning and sacrifice any society faces, freedom of expression contracts while uncritical acceptance of government decisions expands. Authorities provide their own versions of events, frequently without an adequate opportunity for independent verification. Official and unofficial attempts are made to restrict the flow of information and to rouse public emotions. Dissenting views are condemned and may be punished. For reasons ranging from panic to self-interest, politicians, military officers, and others seek to limit public discourse and to direct public opinion.

This book ponders the extent to which such largely closed systems of communication have been attempted in United States history and have gone beyond justifiable wartime security needs and invited the abuses long associated with autocratic, secretive government. I had originally planned to write a general history of the gradual demise of the country's founding principles of press freedom, but, realizing how many instances of the "death of a thousand cuts" had come from war, I decided to focus on how broad notions of "self-preservation" and "national security" have weakened the most important liberty in the Bill of Rights. I contend that suppressive policies in times of armed conflict usually have been unconstitutional, unjust, and impractical. Part One (chapters 1, 2, and 3) examines the friction between the absolute press clause of the First Amendment and the prerogatives assumed by the executive and legislative branches to restrict statements of fact and opinion about war. Part Two (chapters 4, 5, 6, and 7) considers the impact of wartime politics and paranoia on freedom of expression from the ratification of the First Amendment in 1791 through the Gulf War in 1991. Part Three (chapter 8 and the conclusion) analyzes the roles played by the media in wartime and discusses the risks that propaganda and secrecy create for a democratic system.

The following chapters offer evidence that the government, by withholding information, policing thought, and spreading propaganda, frequently acts as if it is necessary to destroy democracy in order to save it. Truth has been said to be the first casualty in war, but perhaps it is more precise to say that the First Amendment has been the first casualty, followed closely by the marketplace of ideas where truths, or at least better understandings, are more likely to emerge than in a system of authoritarian control. Benjamin Franklin may have been exaggerating when he remarked that "there never was a good War, or a bad Peace,"[1] but, in hindsight, no war in America's past has been so sensible or so lacking in any serious regrets that some further thought would not have been beneficial. The mass media themselves, unfortunately, have contributed to the kind of hysterical saber-rattling and paroxysms of patriotic self-righteousness that brought the United States into an undeclared war with France in 1798, into a declared war with Spain in 1898, and, more recently, into the stockpiling of redundant nuclear weapons during the Cold War. Although free and open debate at each stage of a conflict cannot prevent all the blunders the country will make, it could help eliminate many mistakes.

Contrary to a prevalent perception, the combination of wartime policy problems and adversarial journalism did not originate with Vietnam. One aim of this book, therefore, is to provide a historical overview of the altercations that have pitted the press against government power. My central purpose, however, is not to chronicle all of the many episodes of suppression in the nation's past. Instead, this study is mainly concerned with the legality, dynamics, and rationality of wartime decisions affecting freedom of expression. At the heart of the matter is a fundamental legal issue that has been neglected by scholars. Do presidents and their military subordinates have constitutional authority to impose restrictions on press coverage of armed conflicts? If not, then how have commanders in chief and the armed forces managed to reduce the freedom of the press to report on war? How reasonable has their use of unallocated powers been, and how have they exploited the government's ability to impose secrecy and, at the same time, influence public opinion? I seek to challenge "common sense" assumptions about security and to provide an analysis of how the nation's actions have often fallen short of its highly pragmatic ideals, ideals that I have discussed in two previous books, *Printers and Press Freedom: The Ideology of Early American Journalism* and *Franklin and Bache: Envisioning the Enlightened Republic*.

I have not served in the military, but I respect its professed ideals of honor and discipline and hope that they can be applied to future relations with the press and public. My friends and relatives who have been in battle will not be remembered for making any famous remarks, such as General Sherman's observation that war is "hell" or President Eisenhower's warning about the "military-industrial complex."[2] They did, however, see how war is an education in the best and the worst of human behavior. Wars are, indeed, tests of cultural values. They indicate how power can be used in a society and where it actually resides. At crucial points in American history, citizens, courts, and Congress have yielded effective control over the nation's peace and prosperity to a presidential-military protectorate shielded by secrecy and suppression. This book is therefore a history of how concepts of freedom can wither and how arguments can be constructed to promote the erosion of rights. Those who are oblivious to wars being conducted in unconstitutional, unaccountable, and often unthinking ways are neither sufficiently aware of the follies that result nor adequately prepared to participate in humanity's continuing race between civilized life and self-destruction.

J.A.S.

Iowa City
June 1998

Acknowledgments

Historians may appear to work alone, but they rely on collaborations that can extend far back into the past. I am indebted to the people who have written, preserved, and made available the primary and secondary sources I have consulted. Many of them are no longer alive, and most I will never meet. Some of the secondary works were gathered with the research assistance of Aleksander Bogdnaic, Bonnie Brennen, Gerald Davey, Jonathan Game, Cynthia Grabarek, Jay Hamilton, Anne Kevlin, Baruck Opiyo, Luis Rivera-Pérez, Michelle Rubin, Julia Seidler, Gregg Smith, Ki-Yul Uhm, Jian Wang, Joanna Werch, Sonja West, and Kevin Woodward.

I am grateful for a May Brodbeck Humanities Fellowship, a Semester Assignment, an Old Gold Fellowship, and other support provided by the University of Iowa and for John F. Murray Fund grants from the School of Journalism and Mass Communication at the University of Iowa.

I thank my editors at Oxford University Press, who have given me much encouragement and convinced me I could get by with much less footnote material than I originally included in the manuscript.

Some of the ideas offered here were presented in an entirely different way in "Prior Restraint: Original Intentions and Modern Interpretations," an article that appeared in the Spring 1987 issue of *William & Mary Law Review*. Other tasks and projects made it impossible for me to return to this topic until now. Some portions of chapter 1 appeared in an earlier form in the Summer–Fall 1993 issue of *American Journalism*; I appreciate having the editor's permission to use them here. I have been very dependent on the University of Iowa Libraries. I thank the State Historical Society of Wisconsin for permission to quote from the Byron Price papers.

Contents

Part One: Intentions and Interpretations

1 War, Autocracy, and the Constitution

Nothing was more central to the Enlightenment reasoning that produced the United States Constitution than an aversion to the unwanted effects of human aggressiveness. Zeal and ambition, said the *Federalist* papers, rendered people "much more disposed to vex and oppress each other, than to co-operate for their common good."[1] In the eighteenth century, self-interested, hostile actions were regarded as having led not only to disreputable party politics and destructive wars but also to the downfall of past republics. The United States Constitution was an attempt to construct a means of securing all of the ends listed in its preamble: a more perfect union, justice, domestic tranquillity, the common defense, the general welfare, and the blessings of liberty. The French physiocrats, Adam Smith, and the Jeffersonian Republicans advanced credible and often-admired ideas for achieving peaceful, harmonious human relations within and among societies through the political economy. Thomas Paine was thus one of a number of writers who suggested that world commerce could be "a pacific system, operating to unite mankind by rendering nations, as well as individuals, useful to each other."[2] Yet various Enlightenment proposals for preventing wars—plans that involved dispute resolution by international representative bodies—were either ignored or ridiculed as utopian. Although he formulated his own concept of a universal federation to avert war, Immanuel Kant admitted that "such proposals have always been ridiculed by great statesmen, and even more by heads of state, as pedantic, childish and academic ideas."[3]

Historian Peter Gay has noted that Enlightenment libertarian thought regarded warfare as "the most devastating of disasters, which only irresponsible kings can initiate, fanatical priests can encourage, cruel soldiers can love, and the foolish rabble can admire";[4] but philosophers generally did not expect armed conflict to be eliminated, at least as long as the people who paid in lives and taxes were not in control of governments. "The spirit of monarchy is war and expansion," Montesquieu wrote in *The Spirit of Laws*; "the spirit of republics is peace and moderation." Montesquieu, like many Enlightenment theorists, recognized a right of self-defense, but did not think blood should be shed for arbitrary principles of glory, propriety, or utility. "Above all, let one not speak of the prince's glory," he warned, "his glory is his arrogance; it is a passion and not a legitimate right."[5] Kant observed that a head of state could decide on war without significant reasons and at no risk to "his banquets, hunts, pleasure palaces and court festivals." A republican constitution, however, required the consent of the people, Kant noted, and they would naturally hesitate to

3

embark on an enterprise of death, devastation, and "the crowning evil, having to take upon themselves a burden of debt which will embitter peace itself."[6]

James Madison summarized the sentiments of America's Enlightenment republicanism in a 1792 *National Gazette* essay dismissing a world peace plan advocated by Rousseau. Instead of trying to avert war and revolution by setting up international arbitration, Madison stated, Rousseau should have traced "the past frequency of wars to a will in the government independent of the will of the people" and to "the practice by each generation of taxing the principal of its debts on future generations." The disease of warfare was hereditary to hereditary rulers who did not suffer personal consequences, Madison wrote, and would continue even in republics in the absence of "permanent and constitutional maxims of conduct, which may prevail over occasional impressions, and inconsiderate pursuits." Reason and an honest calculation of the expenses of avarice and ambition—rather than reckless borrowing for military expenditures—would help to prevent "wars of folly" and to preserve unwasted resources for "wars of necessity and defence." War, he told the readers of the *Gazette*, should only be declared "by the authority of the people, whose toil and treasure are to support its burdens."[7]

An enduring republican solution to autocratic misrule, Madison and others in the founding generation believed, would require limited government and unlimited citizen debate. The Constitution they wrote and ratified specifically (in the First Amendment) denied Congress, which was given the sole power to legislate (Article 1), any authority to abridge freedom of the press and did not place the president, who was to enforce the laws, above the law. In contrast to later theories of government that would seek safety in legislative and presidential-military suppression in times of war or other crisis, security was associated with a guaranteed right to analyze and evaluate the performance of the citizens' servants in government. Eighteenth-century Americans experienced and sought to preserve a press that could expose the kind of reckless leadership that could occur in war or peace, leadership that could needlessly impoverish and endanger lives. Consequently, the press clause of the First Amendment can be understood as a manifestation of the Enlightenment's emphasis on improving the general condition of humanity and as a carefully considered refusal to recognize any authority of presidents or other government officials over expression that could reveal their faults and failures. No exigency of the nation, not even war, can rewrite the First Amendment and its absolute ban on prior restraint and on subsequent penalties for news coverage and commentary.

I.

By linking wars and the resulting human misery to royalty, Enlightenment philosophers and journalists undermined the traditional theory that a king was an unselfish, unifying force responsible for the people's safety and the common good.[8] Wars, said one Philadelphia newspaper, "however successful, and however advantageous to individuals, are always a losing business to the people."[9] In *The Rights of Man*, Thomas Paine traced the origins of monarchy to the leaders of roving bandits and to plunderers who divided the world into their dominions. "From such beginning of governments, what could be expected, but a continual system of war and extortion?" he asked. War is the gambling table of governments, Paine said, and meant only taxes to the farmers and manufacturers who found their economic outcome the same whether the military conquered or was defeated. "There does not exist within such government sufficient stamina whereon to ingraft reformation," he argued, "and the shortest, easiest, and most effectual remedy, is to begin anew."[10] Those who were proud of living in a benign Age of Reason thus could also see the necessity of being a bellicose Age of Revolution. One fundamental justification for rebellion against royalty was the belief that peace would be more likely where the people themselves ruled.

Both the recognition that people suffered in war and the idea that public opinion was the best guide in the matter were given extensive discussion in early America—especially in the press, where it was possible to convey reactions to events in a relatively timely and convenient way. Journalists saw themselves as participating in the propagation of Enlightenment thought and spoke frequently of their ambitions to impart libertarian wisdom and useful information to the public. To a great extent, original writings in periodicals and pamphlets were responsible for advancing the ideological debates of a nation in the act of creating itself. Books and European philosophers seem to have played less of a direct role in this process than is often assumed. The press allowed large numbers of Americans to contemplate issues simultaneously and to respond to each other rapidly.[11]

Newspapers and magazines, in particular, were in a position to create a shared political culture that extended even into remote rural areas.[12] Their penetration and periodicity allowed them to speak to many people at the same time, shaping first impressions of the news and reinforcing views through repetition. Readers could feel they were connected to governmental affairs and had the information necessary to make assessments of those in authority. Saying that he lived some distance from the city, but had "benefit of the news prints, which I peruse at leisure hours," the author of a 1793 letter to a Boston editor said, "I esteem it a great privilege, and it affords me a secret satisfaction to sit at home and be informed of the affairs of this great and happy country, from one end to the other." "Rusticus," however, added that he was nevertheless sad at seeing so much journalistic abuse of President Washington after he issued a proclamation of neutrality in the war that had erupted between England and the French republic.[13] Specific decisions on war and peace were, of course, always controversial, but the existence of an unfettered periodical press allowed the public an expanded opportunity to examine the work of political and military leaders.

Attention to the brutality of war was evident in the earliest days of American journalism. In the only issue of the first newspaper to be attempted in the colonies, *Publick Occurrences, Both Forreign and Domestick*, Benjamin Harris in 1690 mentioned the upheavals facing Louis XIV and depicted England's Indian allies in a campaign against Canada as "miserable Salvages, in whom we have too much confided." Stating that he wanted to provide accurate news in a time of confusion and promising to correct any mistakes, Harris published accounts of atrocities on all sides, including one in which a Captain Mason "cut the faces, and ript the bellies of two *Indians*, and threw a third over board in sight of the *French*, who informing the other *Indians* of it, they have in revenge barbarously Butcher'd forty Captives of ours that were in their hands." Before another issue could be printed, the governor and council of Massachusetts, noting the strong nature of the pieces, ordered the suppression of the unlicensed newspaper.[14] Harris had not only published without submitting to censorship but also dared to question behavior in the most emotional of all public matters—war.

Prior restraint soon ended in England and America, however, and accounts of armed conflict became a staple of newspapers. In *The Wealth of Nations*, Adam Smith complained about how comfortably people in a great empire could be informed about distant military actions. Seemingly not inconvenienced at all because their government borrowed funds rather than raised the taxes necessary to pay for the war, they had "the amusement of reading in the newspapers the exploits of their own fleets and armies," Smith wrote, and were disappointed when peace ended the entertainment as well as "a thousand visionary hopes of conquest and national glory, from a longer continuance of the war."[15] In situations with more immediate danger, of course, the realities were difficult to ignore. Many of the cases brought by government against eighteenth-century American journalists were responses to critical writings on delicate defense-related matters, from the jailing of James Franklin in 1722 for a snide comment on officials' failure to pursue coastal pirates to the prosecutions under the Sedition Act of 1798, which were, in large part, the result of hostilities with a much more powerful nation, France. These cases, however, were sporadic and typically unpopular as well as ineffectual.[16]

For Americans, war was less a diversion carried out by professional mercenaries and more an actual experience on the frontier and, during the Revolution, throughout the region. Not only soldiers like George Washington, but also Enlightenment sages such as Benjamin Franklin and Thomas Jefferson knew the sufferings of war at close range. Benjamin Franklin's *A Narrative of the Late Massacres*, a fervent pamphlet condemning the Paxton Boys' revenge killings of peaceful Indian men, women, and children, stated that the victims' only crime seemed to be having red skin and black hair. "What had little Boys and Girls done; what could Children of a Year old, Babes at the Breast, what could they do, that they too must be shot and hatcheted?" he asked.[17] Franklin, who often spoke of the waste and sufferings of war, conveyed bitter wisdom when, among his almanac's aphorisms, he wrote, "Wars bring scars." Other Poor Richard sayings—including "Mad Kings and mad Bulls, are not to be held by treaties and packthread" and "The greatest monarch on the proudest throne, is oblig'd to sit upon his own arse"—do not suggest reverence for royalty. Monarchy itself, Americans were concluding, was at the root of the problem, despite all pretenses of grandeur and protection. Old and corrupt European institutions, it appeared, were destroying peace and prosperity—even in North America. "Kings have long Arms, but Misfortune longer," Poor Richard remarked.[18]

The press encouraged such observations by squarely placing the blame for the horrors of war on kings. In 1746, for instance, a Boston magazine provided a graphic description of the aftermath of a battle in Italy with commentary on the senseless slaughter of soldiers who only hours before had been alive and animated. "These reflections may be equally applied to many other occasions, wherein men have been blindly sacrificed by the thousands to the folly or ambition of monarchs," the editor concluded.[19] After news reports arriving early in 1771 indicated that England might be considering war with Spain, Purdie and Dixon's *Virginia Gazette* offered readers Swiftian accounts from London of kings going to battle over a bit of land or an argument about the color of a woman's eyebrows. Accompanying remarks said that centuries of war in Europe had produced little more than misery and that for each great ruler, there were a thousand who disgraced humanity. A letter to the paper signed "D. R." said that the thirst to add to wealth and the desire to distract a country from domestic unrest were the causes of war. War, the correspondent reminded those who were excited at the prospect, meant "the Reign of Violence; the License of Robbery and Murder, the Fatigues, the Dangers, the Sickness, the Wounds, the Death of Thousands, the Desolation of Provinces; the Waste of the human Species; the Mourning of Parents; the Cries and Tears of Widows and Orphans."[20]

America's prerevolutionary press presented loathsome images of the depravity and designs of enemy royalty. After the Duke of Cumberland routed France's Jacobite invaders in Scotland in 1746 and ruthlessly killed the survivors, colonists were given a feast of patriotic propaganda. Readers of the *South-Carolina Gazette* were told, for example, that Charles Edward Stuart, the Young Pretender, who led the invasion, had left behind a model of the Bastille, instructions for sodomy "after the *Italian* Manner," and a "Bundle of Rods, to whip the Nakedness of pretty Maids, with *Spanish* Padlocks for private Uses."[21] During the French and Indian War, colonial writers contrasted French absolutism and cunning with Anglo-American love of liberty and justice. "The King of France has an arbitrary Authority to do what he pleases," said an essay by "Virginia Centinel," "though his Intellects do not enable him, nor his Heart incline him, to do much Good."[22] Ironically, when the alliance was formed with France during the Revolutionary War, patriot journalists, some of whom received pay from the French minister, found themselves in the position of glorifying Louis XVI while loyalist newspapers said that the French had sinister plans for imposing the authority of their king and the pope on the United States.[23]

To denounce a Louis was, of course, only to condemn the evils of an authoritarian adversary rather than all monarchs. British and colonial American libertarians ritualistically congratulated themselves in the press and elsewhere for having a "mixed" political system that balanced the three classic forms of government—monarchy, aristocracy, and democracy—in the king, Lords, and Commons. In theory, the nation would thus have the advantages of the three forms and expect each to prevent excesses in the others. The monarch could provide leadership without sliding into despotism, the nobility could supply wisdom without fomenting factions, and the people could protect liberty without creating anarchy. At the time of the French and Indian War, the colonial press may have dispensed blistering criticism of official policies and behavior;[24] but even the caustic "Virginia Centinel," whose depiction of "Vice and Debauchery" in the Virginia regiment brought Colonel George Washington and fellow officers close to resignation, hailed mixed government where each part "may be a proper Check on the other, on any Appearance of Deviation from the public Good."[25]

Praised by Montesquieu and others as having successfully combined stability, sense, and freedom, the British constitution was a source of enormous pride for Americans. "How must it swell the Breast of every BRITON with Transport!" William Livingston wrote in his *Independent Reflector* in 1752, "while he surveys the despicable Slaves of *unlimited* Princes, to reflect, that his Person and Property are guarded by Laws, which the Sovereign himself cannot infringe." Livingston, a journalist and lawyer who became a delegate to the Constitutional Convention in 1787, provided a standard recitation of the joys of liberty and horrors of tyranny while heaping praise on England's king and constitution. A constitutional monarch could be a "Father" and "Benefactor," but absolute rulers were "more like imperial Wolves, or rather Beasts in human Shape, than rational and intelligent Beings." Intoxicated by power, the *Reflector* essay continued, despots waged war even on their own people, taking royal amusement in rapine and plunder and squandering lives and fortunes. "In *limited* Monarchies, the Pride and Ambition of Princes, and their natural Lust for Domination, are check'd and restrained," Livingston said. "If they violate their Oath, and sap the fundamental Constitution of the State, the People have a Right to resist them."[26]

Responding to ministerial policies adopted after the French and Indian War, the American colonists, so self-satisfied under the British constitution at mid-century, resisted what they regarded as royal encroachments on their civil liberties and as failures to recognize their rights of representation. Such constitutional violations should be opposed, the commonplace logic asserted, in order to avert the spread of tyranny. In the Stamp Act crisis and in the years that followed, Americans protested in great numbers, but tended to hold corruption in the ministry responsible for their grievances rather than launch direct attacks on George III himself. Yet, over time, the king's contempt for American petitions and his assent to the Intolerable Acts, the Port Bill, and other measures came to be interpreted as an abdication of his role as protector of the colonies. The balance of the constitution was shifting toward despotism, Americans believed, and they reluctantly concluded, after a decade of raising objections and receiving harsh responses, that their only other alternative was taking up arms. The king had, indeed, decided that only force would work.[27] In a letter typical of the sense of betrayal of affection that pervaded the colonies, "T. H." addressed the king in the *Pennsylvania Packet*, saying,

> [Y]ou have been pleased to call yourself the father of the people, you have acted with little love towards them, and have treated them not as children but as slaves; denying repeatedly their most submissive remonstrances, cherishing their enemies, and expelling from your confidence men who had your Majesty's welfare and the people's good at heart.[28]

With the help of journalists who played on themes of slavery if constitutional liberties were not respected,[29] George III was, in effect, placed in the same despised category as other monarchs, and the colonists interpreted his actions as a virtual declaration of war against them. Having regularly attributed the lack of peace in the world to the rapacious, callous conduct of kings and portrayed themselves as merely interested in legitimate self-defense,[30] many Americans were ready to discard ideas of dependence on the king and see separation as necessary, especially after the battles at Lexington and Concord in April 1775. Still, large numbers had enough remaining loyalty to the crown or fear of war or both to hesitate.

Thomas Paine addressed both concerns in *Common Sense*, published in January 1776. Reaching estimated sales of 120,000 copies within three months in a country with only a few million colonists, the pamphlet was the journalistic sensation of its time.[31] Paine began with an analysis of the "boasted" but "imperfect" English constitution and said that it was "farcical" to say that the three elements checked each other and that in reality the king was the "overbearing part." He then blasted the institution of monarchy and labeled George III "the Royal Brute," a man "that with the pretended title of FATHER OF HIS PEOPLE can unfeelingly hear of their slaughter, and composedly sleep with their blood upon his soul." Saying that "Europe is too thickly planted with Kingdoms, to be long at peace," Paine insisted that having a connection with England would involve America in future European wars and that the nation's true interest was to be a neutral trading partner with Europe rather than a large country subservient to a small island. "Everything that is right or reasonable pleads for separation," said *Common Sense*. "The blood of the slain, the weeping voice of nature cries, 'TIS TIME TO PART."[32]

Later in 1776, the Declaration of Independence contrasted the "inalienable rights" of life, liberty, and the pursuit of happiness and the necessity of self-rule with the status of the American colonists. That document, which consisted mostly of a list of hostile acts ascribed to George III, addressed the world with accusations that the king had "a history of repeated injuries and usurpations, all having, in direct object, the establishment of an absolute tyranny" and that he was at that moment sending "large armies of foreign mercenaries to complete the works of death, desolation, and tyranny, already begun, with circumstances of cruelty and perfidy scarcely paralleled in the most barbarous ages, and totally unworthy the head of a civilized nation." Having transformed their opinions of George III by concluding his reign was one of unconstitutional oppression rather than one concerned with approving what the Declaration called "laws the most wholesome and necessary for the public good," colonists of the patriot persuasion believed they had ample justification for fighting a rebellion—self-defense and a better, more peaceful future. Americans had to be resigned to the necessity of war, said a 1779 essay in *United States Magazine*, because tyranny had to be stopped by every people themselves and the conflict could be seen as "one of those beneficial operations of nature, designed by the Creator to remove present evil, and guard against its more fatal consequences."[33]

Americans self-consciously turned away from the direction the Declaration of Independence accused George III of taking, that of affecting "to render the military independent of, and superior to, the civil power." In the anxious months at the close of the war, General Washington, determined to play the role of the virtuous Cincinnatus rather than Caesar, made a point of deferring to democratic authority in a series of symbolic actions. In 1783, he used a moving appeal to public-spirited patriotism to stop a group of his officers, disgruntled at having their pay in arrears and no prospect for pensions from Congress, from resorting to force. Instead of reclaiming New York in triumph after the British evacuation, he rode into the city at the side of Governor George Clinton. Before and after speaking at an emotional ceremony for resigning his commission, one with carefully choreographed gestures of mutual respect, he bowed to the members of Congress, who removed hats but did not bow in return. The president of Congress, Thomas Mifflin, responded, acknowledging that Washington had conducted himself with "wisdom and fortitude invariably regarding the rights of civil power through all disasters and changes."[34]

In articulating their hopes for the nation's future at the end of the eighteenth century, American statesmen and journalists sketched out a picture of the United States as a peaceful republic, far from the costly warfare of Europe. The early numbers of the *Federalist*, a newspaper series by Alexander Hamilton, James Madison, and John Jay, said that the union being proposed would be strong enough to preserve peace within and between states as well as with foreign nations. Stressing the importance of "national security" and "self preservation," *Federalist* essays were optimistic about the ability of the nation to avoid what Hamilton called "the ambitious enterprizes and vainglorious pursuits of a Monarchy," but warned that the United States could still be drawn into wars by other countries that did not follow republican rules. Jay observed that kings had many motives that were not consistent with justice or the opinions and interests of their subjects. He wrote that "absolute monarchs will often make war when their nations are to get nothing by it, but for purposes and objects merely personal, such as, a thirst for military glory, revenge for personal affronts; ambition or private compacts to aggrandize or support their particular families, or partizans."[35]

Washington's farewell address, which was actually a newspaper essay rather than a speech, and Jefferson's first inaugural address, which expressed delight at being "separated by nature and a wide ocean from the exterminating havoc of one quarter of the globe," were among the statements by leaders that suggested that America, despite its relative weakness, was in a position to carry on peaceful pursuits without becoming embroiled in monarchical strife.[36] Eventually such sentiments helped to shape the Monroe Doctrine, which declared the Americas closed to further colonization and disavowed U. S. participation in wars of only European interest. A government created by the people for themselves, it seemed, could avoid war, at least if the country was far enough removed from what Washington's farewell called "the toils of European ambition, Rivalship, Interest, Humour or Caprice." National unity, Washington said, was the main security from external danger.[37] During his presidency, which he left hailed by many as the Cincinnatus, savior, and even "father" of the country, Washington attempted to pursue a course of republican restraint in matters of war and peace.[38]

Under Washington's leadership, the United States managed to avoid deep involvement in the war that spread across Europe in the 1790s as republican France fought a series of coalitions that each included England. Many Americans, at least initially, regarded the conflict as an expansion of the struggle against tyranny that their own revolution had begun, or, as journalists sometimes put it, "the cause of humanity" against "the cause of kings."[39] France, complained a Philadelphia newspaper correspondent, was "left to contend alone, unaided, unsupported, against the united efforts of imperial robbers and crowned villany, the sworn and eternal enemies of mankind."[40] Support declined, however, as news of the continuing internal violence and upheavals of the French Revolution reached America. Advocates of France became defensive, attempting to excuse the executions of the king and others by blaming the long history of monarchical oppression and the remaining threat of royalist influence. Americans, they argued in the press, had not faced such close and ruthless enemies in their own revolution.[41] Critics of France were able to argue—especially after the Directory assumed executive authority in 1795—that the country's new leaders had succumbed to what a newspaper essay by Alexander Hamilton called the "cravings of despotic rapacity."[42]

The sporadic continuation of the European war and the rise of Napoleon brought an end to visionary hopes of rapid republican triumph in the world. In 1797, an essay from a French newspaper reprinted in Philip Freneau's New York *Time Piece* expressed wonder at how, even in an "Age of Reason," Europe, the center of the world's information and sophistication, could fall prey to the horrors of war. "There cannot be a peculiar system of morality for the Governors of nations," the essay stated. "Every war that is not undertaken for the protection of the frontiers, or to defend allies unjustly attacked, is a crime against society and humanity." Reviewing the history of conquest, the writer noted that ambitious leaders like Caesar, Alexander, and Louis XIV could draw unthinking multitudes all too easily into war. People tended "to admire whatever is gigantic, and to deify the Colossus that overwhelms them," the essay concluded. "Wisdom alone is able to destroy these ancient prejudices, and to overturn these old idols."[43]

Americans may have avoided the carnage, but their disagreements over policies toward the belligerents did help spawn political parties—the Federalists, who tended to favor Britain, and the Jeffersonian Republicans, who were sympathetic to France. Debates ensued in the press over America's 1778 treaty obligations to France and whether Washington was going beyond his authority in declaring neutrality when, both sides agreed, Congress had been given sole power over matters of war. British interference with American shipping beginning in 1793 brought proposals from the Republicans for commercial sanctions and from the Federalists for increasing military expenditures. James Madison, the de facto leader of the Republicans, warned in his "Helvidius" newspaper essays that war involved the "strongest passions, and most dangerous weaknesses of the human breast" and was "the true nurse of executive aggrandizement." War, he wrote, gave the president forces to direct, funds to spend, and laurels to gain.[44] When Madison heard some of his opponents in Congress advocate allowing the president to declare war and raise armies while they were in recess, he responded forcefully in a pamphlet defending commercial reprisals as the safest solutions and linking America's fate to that of republican France. Lecturing his adversaries on the Constitution and the dangers of their policies, Madison wrote:

> Of all the enemies to public liberty war is, perhaps, the most to be dreaded, because it comprises and develops the germ of every other. War is the parent of armies; from these proceed debts and taxes; and armies, and debts, and taxes are the known instruments for bringing the many under the domination of the few. In war, too, the discretionary power of the Executive is extended; its influence in dealing out offices, honors, and emoluments is multiplied; and all the means of seducing the minds, are added to those of subduing the force, of the people.[45]

The goal of eighteenth-century republicanism was, as Thomas Paine depicted it in *The Rights of Man*, to change the "moral condition" of nations. "The inhabitants of every country, under the civilization of laws, easily associate together," he wrote, "but governments being yet in an uncivilized state, and almost continually at war, they pervert the abundance which civilized life produces to carry on the uncivilized part to a greater extent." Paine predicted that monarchy would be so discredited that it would be eliminated from "the enlightened countries" of Europe by the end of the century;[46] but Immanuel Kant, writing at the same time, observed that the world was still a long way from being morally mature and that improvements could not be expected "as long as states apply all their resources to their vain and violent schemes of expansion" rather than to educating the minds of their citizens. Kant hoped that in time democratic decision-making and international organizations would play a role in preserving peace, but he maintained that "practical moral reason" would triumph only when the mounting debts and distress of war weakened nations to the point that "sheer exhaustion must eventually perform what goodwill ought to have done."[47]

II.

America's second Constitution and its First Amendment were statements of an intent to establish a self-correcting governmental system, one that would keep the executive within certain bounds and would allow the press to continue its scrutiny of officials and their actions. In the first two hundred years of the Bill of Rights, however, the original modest conception of a chief executive informing Congress and carrying out its decisions was replaced by the reality of presidents taking unilateral, virtually unreviewable actions in the name of national security and employing rhetorical leadership of public opinion on a continuous basis to go over the heads of legislators and mobilize the nation.[48] Wartime presidents in particular have redefined the presidency by taking expansive views of their authority and making themselves appear to be the head of the whole government rather than just one branch. At the same time, presidents and their military bureaucracies have managed to exploit their expanding war powers to impose a variety of press restrictions, restrictions that were frequently aimed at stopping constitutionally protected statements of fact or criticism rather than preserving legitimate secrets. The exercise of such authority surely was not what was intended by those who established the presidency.

With its emphasis on limited government and the rule of law, the Constitution was a reflection of republican thought dating back to ancient Rome[49] and was a reaction to the long Anglo-American history of conflict over arbitrary power, a recurring problem that had been particularly acute after the accession of James I in 1603. A king who said he ruled by divine right, James did not claim absolute power, but he did assert an authority to surmount the laws in a series of clashes with the courts and Parliament. When Chief Justice Edward Coke argued at a Privy Council meeting that the king could not take cases out of courts to judge himself, James raised his fist, accused him of traitorous thinking, and said that laws were founded on reason and that he and others could reason as well as judges. Coke replied that His Majesty was not learned in the law and that legal issues were not decided by natural reason, but by artificial reason attained through long study and experience.[50] Coke was later dismissed by the king, but Parliament continued to question self-serving assertions of royal prerogative to the point of civil war in 1642 and the beheading of Charles I in 1649.

With the removal of James II in the Glorious Revolution of 1688, mainly for his feckless pursuit of arbitrary government, came the supremacy of Parliament and a Bill of Rights that said the king could not exercise the "pretended power" of suspending laws without the consent of Parliament. The Bill of Rights also made it illegal to jail or prosecute subjects for petitioning the king and did not allow anyone outside of Parliament to take legal action for statements made in its debates.[51] Licensing of the press ended in 1694 when the Regulation of Printing Act expired. Resolutions passed by the House of Commons in 1695 stated that the system of censorship prior to publication had lacked fixed standards and had allowed "great oppression."[52]

The freer political conditions after 1688 allowed John Locke to advocate the rule of law, the theory of social contract, and the idea of inalienable natural rights in his *Two Treatises of Government.* In an implicit criticism of the Stuart monarchs, Locke defined prerogative as the discretion left to the executive to take actions for the public good. Such actions, he said, could be taken where law did not exist or even where it did exist if they would benefit the community and would be accepted by the people. Examples of a proper use of prerogative, Locke observed, were pardoning some of-fenders, tearing down a house to prevent a fire from spreading to others, or making an emergency decision when a legislature is not in session or would be too slow to act. Locke maintained that prerogative was not legitimate when used against the public good or against "declared *limitations of Prerogative*" established by the people. Arbitrary prerogative could not exist, he said, where a power was "defined by positive Laws."[53] Locke thus endorsed the Enlightenment principle of *salus populi suprema lex*, the welfare of the people is the supreme law, but he recognized, like Coke, that a ruler's discretion could be restricted. For Locke, the sovereign people made the legislature the supreme organ of government, and executive power had to operate within the law unless an exception was made subject to general agreement. In no case, however, could a prerogative power be used if the authority had been specifically denied by the people.[54] In his *Commentaries on the Laws of England*, published on the eve of the American Revolution, Sir William Blackstone cited Locke and stated that lawful executive prerogative could be exerted "unless where the constitution hath expressly, or by evident consequence, laid down some exception or boundary."[55]

Clearly, the Americans who established the Constitution and Bill of Rights re-garded written constitutions and statutes as commands of the sovereign people[56] and did not intend to allow the use of any unauthorized prerogatives to interfere with basic liberties.[57] "The Constitution was adopted in a period of grave emergency," Chief Justice Charles Evans Hughes observed in a 1934 Supreme Court opinion. "Its grants of power to the Federal Government and its limitations of the power of the States were determined in the light of emergency and they are not altered by emer-gency."[58] The document drafted in 1787 was offered to an American public struggling politically and economically in the aftermath of the Revolutionary War. The accom-panying turmoil had included Shays's Rebellion in Massachusetts as well as mob threats to governments in other states. Even as the Convention was being called and then held in secret, an aggressive propaganda campaign was mounted to argue that a much stronger authority than the Articles of Confederation was desperately needed. The proponents of increased centralization warned that Americans would have to accept the wisdom of the delegates or suffer insurrection, disunion, invasion, and other calamities.[59] The *Federalist* papers argued that the new government was constructed to stand up to emergencies.[60]

Yet, to a considerable portion of the country's population, too many to ignore if the Constitution was to be ratified and successfully implemented, the framers' reorganization plan placed too much faith in the governors and gave too little protection to the governed. The framers and supporters of the unamended Constitution had, in fact, made forceful arguments for what they were establishing, but had not done enough to specify what they rejected, what would not be possible. At the Convention, Benjamin Franklin expressed a concern that "there is a natural Inclination in Mankind to kingly Government." His experience with European politics, especially in England, prompted him to advance the idea that salaries be denied to the executive branch so that offices would not combine honor and profit and thereby attract selfish, dangerous people. The struggles for such positions in the British government, he said, "are the true Source of all those Factions which are perpetually dividing the Nation, distracting its Councils, hurrying it sometimes into fruitless and mischievous Wars, and often compelling a Submission to dishonourable Terms of Peace." Franklin admitted, however, that his solution would be seen as "chimerical" and "Utopian."[61] He was, as he anticipated, politely ignored. The idea may have been impractical, but the fact that it was offered at all to a gathering of the political elite was some indication of the sentiment in favor of a more selfless and benign kind of leadership than most of the world experienced.

The opponents of ratification had criticisms of the courts and Congress under the Constitution, but were particularly worried that the president, in the words of one pseudonymous Antifederalist writer, "is in reality to be a KING."[62] Another like-minded essayist declared that the power and prestige of the presidency would attract "ambitious and designing men" and that such distant officers with an array of prerogatives "would soon become above the controul of the people, and abuse their power to the purpose of aggrandizing themselves, and oppressing them."[63] To the Antifederalists, the three branches that were each supposed to serve the public good in a particular way were instead one massive threat to liberty. They feared that the confederacy of republics was going to be swallowed up into a huge, unresponsive form of government that would, as an Antifederalist journalist put it, "sink first into monarchy, and then into despotism."[64] "We the people" were the ostensible authors of the document, but its detractors found in it too much leeway for the rulers and not enough guaranteed rights or respect for the ruled. Madison did, in fact, portray the proposed system as a cure for the "turbulence and contention" of too much democracy.[65]

Defending the work of the Convention delegates, Madison observed that they had faced the problem of "combining the requisite stability and energy in Government, with the inviolable attention due to liberty, and to the Republican form." Both Madison and Alexander Hamilton argued in the *Federalist* papers that the single executive being proposed would have the ability to act promptly and decisively to ensure the steady enforcement of laws and to protect the nation against external and internal threats. Hamilton recognized "the aversion of the people to monarchy" and the fears of the president "not merely as the embryo but as the full grown progeny of that detested parent." He complained, however, that Antifederalists drew on "the regions of fiction" to magnify presidential powers similar to those of a state governor "into more than royal prerogatives." In discussing the need of government to respond to insurrections and other emergencies with military force, Hamilton took pains to assure his readers that "the whole power of the proposed government is to be in the hands of the representatives of the people." He also argued that the president would be subject to "the restraints of public opinion" and to "being at all times liable to impeachment, trial, dismission from office, incapacity to serve in any other; and to the forfeiture of life and estate by subsequent prosecution in the common course of law."[66]

The president was, in short, empowered to act within the Constitution to protect the country, but not above the law. The head of the executive branch was given certain traditional prerogatives of kings such as vetoing legislation, issuing pardons, and carrying out war and diplomacy, but no power to conduct censorship as the Tudor and Stuart monarchs had done.[67] As the Tenth Amendment made clear, the government was to be one of delegated powers, and "powers not delegated to the United States by the Constitution, nor prohibited to it by the states, are reserved to the States respectively, or to the people."[68] Presidents acting without authority or against the law not only are in the vulnerable position of daring the courts to intervene, but also are risking removal from office "on impeachment for and conviction of, treason, bribery, or other high crimes and misdemeanors" (Article 2). Yet, presidents know it is difficult for anyone to stop them when they overstep their authority. If citizens, judges, and members of Congress approve of the ends, then ways can be found to ignore or justify the means, even if the behavior in question violates a provision of the Constitution as plain as the press clause. In this way, corrosive precedents are set and autocracy invades the Constitution. A document designed to preserve the rule of law becomes to some extent unable to do so because it relies on human will for enforcement.

The legitimacy of any presidential restraints on the press through the military presumably would have to rest on the authority of the document that the commander in chief must swear to "preserve, protect and defend" (Article 2). The Constitution was not written to permit a total executive authority in matters of war. The debates of the Constitutional Convention recognized a need for the president to repel sudden attacks without legislative deliberations, but not an executive power to initiate war.[69] Seeing the advantages of having one leader ultimately responsible for military decisions, the framers of the Constitution provided for an elected civilian commander in chief, but, fearing the president would misuse power as kings had done, they gave the authority to declare war, to raise and regulate the armed forces, and to "provide for the common defense" to the people's representatives in Congress. The grant of such "defense" powers to an elected body was a departure from English practice, in which Parliament was largely relegated to the role of appropriating funds.[70] Writing from Paris, Thomas Jefferson told James Madison that the Constitution had given "one effectual check to the Dog of war by transferring the power of letting him loose from the Executive to the Legislative body, from those who are to spend to those who are to pay."[71]

A consensus had been reached that war powers were mainly legislative; that the president, in the words of one of Alexander Hamilton's *Federalist* essays, would be merely the nation's "first General and Admiral."[72] The commander in chief was to be, as Hamilton put it during the Convention, simply the leader "of the land and naval forces and of the Militia of the United States—to have the direction of war, when authorised or began."[73] Hamilton was the foremost proponent of executive "energy" among the founders and regarded the president as "the bulwark of the national security" in "the conduct of war";[74] but he saw the commander in chief's responsibilities as the "executive details" of "the arrangement of the army and navy" and "the direction of the operations of war."[75] The commander in chief designation, he said, "would amount to nothing more than the supreme command and direction of the military and naval forces."[76] The president was not given authority over civilian journalists. When exercising their specified powers over the military, however, Congress and the president were given ample autonomy within the Constitution. "The authorities essential to the care of the common defence are these—to raise armies—to build and equip fleets—to prescribe rules for the government of both—to direct their operations—to provide for their support," Hamilton said. "These powers ought to exist without limitation: *Because it is impossible to foresee or define the extent and variety of national exigencies, or the corresponding extent & variety of the means which may be necessary to satisfy them*."[77] Congress was therefore given extensive discretion in its war powers, including the much-feared ability to maintain standing armies in times of peace, a highly unpopular practice in Anglo-American history from the time of Oliver Cromwell to the Boston Massacre.

The Constitution, however, also made certain restrictions such as a two-year limit on the term of military appropriations (Article 1) and a definition of treason as an "overt act" (Article 3), a provision that legal scholars have regarded as evidence of the early American intention to end seditious libel, the crime of criticizing government.[78] "It says, expressly, that treason against the United States shall consist only in levying war against them, or in adhering to their enemies, giving them aid and comfort," Richard Dobbs Spaight said during the North Carolina ratifying convention. "Complaining, therefore, or writing, cannot be treason."[79] Referring to the repeated failure of Britain to follow a medieval treason statute and make an actual deed necessary for the crime, James Madison observed in the *Federalist* that the Constitution's definition would prevent the "new-fangled and artificial treasons" with which factions "have usually wrecked their alternate malignity on each other."[80] (In 1945, the Supreme Court ruled that expression alone cannot be treason, but at other times courts and commentators have concluded that words could be treasonous.)[81] Some provisions of the Constitution and Bill of Rights were written to allow for wartime alterations in matters as specific as suspending the writ of *habeas corpus* (Article 1), giving consent for the quartering of troops in houses (Third Amendment), and making grand jury indictments (Fifth Amendment). Neither the Constitution of 1787 nor the Bill of Rights, however, made any allowances for suspending the First Amendment freedoms of religion, speech, press, assembly, and petition during a war.

A textual analysis, then, would suggest that in times of war the government is able to use its considerable defense powers to win on the battlefield, and the press is free to operate in the realm of public opinion within the bounds of the traditional legal actions individuals can take, such as libel suits.[82] The First Amendment's guarantee that "no law" will be made abridging freedom of the press does, of course, speak only of Congress. The specification of Congress and its lawmaking powers may have been a recognition of the principle of legislative supremacy and the idea that a law acquires legitimacy in the consent of the people through their representatives. On the other hand, the wording may have reflected the perception stated by Madison, among others, that Congress was the most dangerous branch because it had the most extensive and least defined powers. Madison believed that "it is against the enterprising ambition of this department, that the people ought to indulge all their jealousy and exhaust all their precautions."[83] Alexander Hamilton similarly wrote of the "tendency of the legislative authority to absorb every other."[84] In making his proposal for a bill of rights in 1789, Madison said, "In our government it is, perhaps, less necessary to guard against the abuse in the executive department than any other; because it is not the stronger branch of the system, but the weaker."[85]

Yet the prohibitions of the First Amendment can be applied to the courts and the president as well.[86] James Madison said that the Constitution secured rights against the ambitions of both the legislature and the executive;[87] however, a straightforward reading of the document would have suggested to those who wrote and ratified it that a limitation on the rather indefinite powers of Congress was all that was needed to protect press freedom in peace or war. The House and Senate were to pass laws and leave interpreting them to the judicial branch and carrying them out to the executive branch. The Constitution, after all, states that Congress has the authority to "make all laws which shall be necessary and proper" for carrying into execution its enumerated powers "and all other powers vested by this Constitution in the government of the United States, or in any department or officer thereof" (Article 1). If Congress was to "make all laws" and the First Amendment says "Congress shall make no law . . . abridging the freedom of speech, or of the press," then the words of the Constitution provide the so-called fourth branch of government with a complete exemption from having its liberty limited by any of the other three.

In the Constitution, Congress, not the commander in chief, is given the authority to "make rules for the government and regulation of the land and naval forces" (Article 1). Such rules apparently would only be for the military itself and could not be involuntary restraints on the news media if Congress is expressly forbidden to make laws abridging freedom of the press. In a 1957 Supreme Court opinion that found that the power of Congress to regulate military forces does not extend to civilians, even to carry out treaty obligations, Justice Hugo Black wrote, "The prohibitions of the Constitution were designed to apply to all branches of the National Government and they cannot be nullified by the Executive or by the Executive and the Senate combined." The case, which concerned military trials of civilian dependents accompanying armed forces abroad, gave Black an opportunity to discuss at length the "tradition of keeping the military subordinate to civilian authority" and how the "Founders envisioned the army as a necessary institution, but one dangerous to liberty if not confined within its essential bounds." Black's history lecture concluded with a warning that many nations lived under military rule and that even seemingly slight encroachments on the Bill of Rights "create new boundaries from which legions of power can seek new territory to capture."[88]

Nothing about presidential powers in the Constitution suggests any authority over reporting on military affairs, and, indeed, the Constitution would probably not have been ratified if the chief executive had been given authority expansive enough to reach the press. Federalists assured suspicious Americans that the Constitution had managed to provide sufficient executive powers while limiting presidential discretion. Charles Pinckney, one of the delegates who had met in Philadelphia, told the South Carolina ratifying convention that the Constitution combined a republic's advantages, including love of liberty and hatred of war, with a monarchy's good qualities, which were "unity of council, vigor, secrecy, and despatch." The president was subject to elections, he said, and the proposed plan of government "defined his powers, and bound them to such limits as will effectually prevent his usurping authorities dangerous to the general welfare."[89]

The president, the Constitution says, "shall take care that the laws be faithfully executed" (Article 2), a role of implementing and enforcing laws. The president was given a qualified veto and some specific tasks to perform, but statements of the leading delegates at the Constitutional Convention indicated that the presidency was to be, in Roger Sherman's words, "nothing more than an institution for carrying the will of the Legislature into effect." James Wilson said that the only powers "strictly Executive were those of executing the laws," and James Madison wanted the powers defined as executing the laws and any powers delegated by Congress.[90] "The essence of the legislative authority is to enact laws, or in other words to prescribe rules for the regulation of the society," Hamilton explained in a *Federalist* discussion of treaty-making powers. "While the execution of the laws and the employment of the common strength, either for this purpose or for the common defence, seem to comprise all the functions of the executive magistrate." Seeing the president and Senate as jointly responsible for formulating treaties with "decision, *secrecy* and dispatch," Hamilton regarded the president as "the most fit agent" for negotiations and the Senate, as a legislative body, most fit for "the vast importance of the trust" and for making treaties law. "The history of human conduct does not warrant that exalted opinion of human virtue," he wrote, "which would make it wise in a nation to commit interests of so delicate and momentous a kind as those which concern its intercourse with the rest of the world to the sole disposal of a magistrate, created and circumstanced, as would be a president of the United States."[91]

Accordingly, presidential discretion was extremely circumscribed by the Constitution. The course to take in a crisis was spelled out. Article 2 gives the president the responsibility to inform Congress on the state of the union "from time to time," to "recommend to their consideration such measures as he may judge necessary and expedient," and to convene one or both houses "on extraordinary occasions." The Constitution authorizes Congress not only to declare war but also to deal with the kind of haphazard hostilities that may fall short of full-scale war. In language that reflects the eighteenth-century practices of commissioning private ships and mobilizing temporary citizen-soldiers in an emergency, Article 1 gives Congress the power to "grant letters of marque and reprisal, and make rules concerning captures on land and water" as well as to "provide for calling forth the militia to execute the laws of the Union, suppress insurrections and repel invasions." The president takes an oath to preserve the Constitution, not the nation.[92]

The mention of "the executive power" at the beginning of Article 2 appeared to those who wrote it to mean the power to execute what others had decided in passing legislation and in ratifying the Constitution. "The natural province of the executive magistrate is to execute laws, as that of the legislature is to make laws," James Madison wrote in an analysis of war powers in 1793. "All his acts therefore, properly executive, must pre-suppose the existence of the laws to be executed."[93] Not even Hamilton, a champion of the vigorous executive, would have allowed the use of unspecified powers or the usurping of the role of Congress in determining matters of war and peace. When the nation faced a naval conflict with France in 1798, Hamilton privately told the secretary of war that "no doubtful authority ought to be exercised by the President" in formulating responses to provocations and that John Adams should place the matter under the review of Congress to demonstrate "an unwillingness to chicane the Constitution."[94] Adams and later presidents, however, were all too willing to resort to constitutional chicanery on matters of war.

III.

Except for what have wryly been called "rare genetic flaws in a handful of White House occupants,"[95] presidents have not hesitated to claim power without constitutional or legislative basis. The text of the Constitution is unequivocal in stating that Congress has the responsibility to "make all laws which shall be necessary and proper for carrying into execution" (Article 1) all the powers of the United States government and that the president "shall take care that the laws be faithfully executed" (Article 2). The notion that presidential-military power can be used to suspend the Constitution in an emergency was rejected by the Supreme Court in *Ex parte Milligan*, a decision involving the military arrest and trial of civilians in Indiana during the Civil War, and in the *Steel Seizure* case, in which the justices ruled that President Truman did not have inherent authority to take over private businesses during the Korean War.[96] Yet scholars and politicians sometimes have been impatient with the democratic process and have insisted that the president must have extraconstitutional powers to protect the country.[97] When taking military actions abroad without a declaration of war, presidents have claimed vast authority to safeguard lives and protect democracy as commanders in chief.[98] They have also claimed inherent executive authority to investigate violations of the law as they have sought to justify government spying on dissenters in politics and the press.[99] Proponents of broad presidential power have looked beyond the Constitution's "take care" clause to its "vesting" clause, which says the "executive power shall be vested in a President" (Article 2). The two words "executive power" have been taken to mean something resembling the arbitrary monarchical authority that eighteenth-century Americans abhorred. When the executive branch has imposed ostensible safety restrictions on journalists and other civilians, any objections from Congress and the courts have tended to be too little or too late.[100]

In 1940 the twentieth century's foremost scholar on the executive branch and the Constitution,[101] Professor Edward S. Corwin of Princeton University, published a book that discussed the extent to which presidencies were becoming "dangerously *personalized*" and liberties were being weakened by what he termed the presidency's "history of aggrandizement." Although he regarded Congress and public opinion as the ultimate voices, Corwin accepted "the great, the controlling, importance of presidential initiative" in times of crisis. Corwin recognized that American conceptions of executive power were extremely limited in the framers' era, but he asserted that the founders had from their common reading a picture of "a broadly discretionary, residual power which is available when other governmental powers fail." In support of this proposition, Corwin cited Locke's remarks on the beneficial uses of prerogative without including his adjacent statements on how prerogative could be limited by declared limitations in the law.[102] Corwin's observations were not surprising in view of his having advocated sweeping presidential power in World War I and the Depression;[103] but his misleading interpretation has had considerable influence on later scholars who have accepted the legitimacy of presidential prerogative in an emergency.[104]

Shortly after the publication of Corwin's book, a striking illustration of how illegitimate, ruthless, and expansive presidential-military power over civilians can be in wartime occurred with the internment of Japanese Americans following the attack on Pearl Harbor. Levels of public outrage and xenophobia were high, and people with Japanese ancestry were regarded automatically as security risks. Even before the war began, Franklin Roosevelt had warned the country about "Fifth Column" treachery. "Spies, saboteurs and traitors are the actors in this new strategy," he said in a fireside chat on national defense. "With all of these we must and will deal vigorously."[105] Incidents of anger being directed at anyone thought to be Japanese prompted *Life* magazine to publish facial photographs purporting to show "the anthropometric conformations that distinguish friendly Chinese from enemy alien Japs." The patrician-looking Chinese, the article said, have the "rational calm of tolerant realists" while the more "aboriginal" Japanese have the "humorless intensity of ruthless mystics."[106] Government propaganda and popular culture treatments of the enemy conveyed sinister and savage images. Editorial cartoons portrayed the Japanese as buck-toothed monkeys, and magazine illustrations depicted the Japanese as infesting insects that had to be annihilated.[107]

The president's reaction to anti-Japanese sentiment was one that displayed his deference to voter biases and his tactical deviousness. Two months after Pearl Harbor, as Americans were becoming increasingly outraged by a series of military disasters in the Pacific, Roosevelt responded to political pressures, prejudice, and hysteria.[108] He issued an executive order authorizing the secretary of war to designate "military areas" within the United States and to impose restrictions on anyone's right to be in those locations. Although they were not mentioned by name, the order was aimed primarily at West Coast residents of Japanese ancestry. Relying only on an assertion of the general powers of the president and commander in chief, Roosevelt's order explained that "the successful prosecution of the war requires every possible protection against espionage and against sabotage."[109] Military bureaucrats set up elaborate procedures to have enemy aliens photographed and fingerprinted and to have all people of Japanese ancestry excluded from a complex array of prohibited areas.[110] Recognizing the popularity of Roosevelt's action, a compliant Congress soon passed, with no opposing votes and little debate, Public Law 503, which provided penalties for disobeying regulations issued under the executive order.[111] Senator Robert Taft complained that the bill was "probably the 'sloppiest' criminal law" he had ever seen and asked that the legislation be redrafted, but the law, which was proposed by the War Department, gave support to the exercise of broad and vague military powers to combat saboteurs and spies within designated areas.[112]

No instance of sabotage or espionage by the affected population was ever documented, and thousands of Japanese American soldiers were able to give heroic and invaluable service in World War II;[113] but bureaucratic energy drove the security measures beyond the authority to establish restricted areas. The military imposed a curfew on people of Japanese ancestry in West Coast states and eventually wasted resources that could have gone into the war effort by interning 112,000 of them, 70,000 of whom were United States citizens, in inland detention centers where nearly every aspect of their lives was carefully supervised. In contrast to later investigations, an Army report said that the evacuation was "impelled by military necessity." The report was sent to the War Department by the central figure in the relocation process, Lieutenant General J. L. DeWitt, an excitable racist who treated rumors of fifth column activity as facts. DeWitt's cover memo said that it was "better to have had this protection and not to have needed it than to have needed it and not to have had it."[114] A *Harvard Law Review* article by Charles Fairman of Stanford University endorsed the military's position that a quick response was needed. Having individual hearings would take too long, Fairman wrote, and would be inconclusive because the Japanese were "inscrutable" to Americans. The article, which suggested that "the doctrine of the majority in Ex parte *Milligan* does not go far enough to meet the conditions of modern war," concluded that the courts would probably accept the emergency war power being used because they had "come to take a more understanding view of the relation of judicial control to administrative action."[115]

The country had few alternative viewpoints. Strong support for summary government action came from many otherwise rational opinion leaders, including columnist Walter Lippmann; California's attorney general, Earl Warren; and philosopher Alexander Meikeljohn.[116] An overwhelming majority of West Coast newspapers supported the evacuation and internment as a military necessity.[117] Periodicals published elsewhere either barely mentioned that civilians—most of whom were women, children, or elderly people—were being herded away or else reported on how well they were being treated. A *Life* magazine article on the Manzanar War Relocation Center, "Coast Japs Are Interned in Mountain Camp," described the scenic beauty of the surroundings as well as the kindness of the soldiers and the cooperation of the first internees.[118] Like the newspapers published by internees elsewhere, the *Manzanar Free Press* was subject to strict control and unable to criticize the internment policy.[119] The War Relocation Authority, the agency in charge of the camps, made documentary films ignoring racism and denying that the "evacuees" were prisoners.[120] Visiting photographers, who were forbidden to photograph guards, guard towers, or barbed wire, had difficulty conveying the realities of the internment. When Ansel Adams attempted to document life at Manzanar in ways that suggested innocent people were making a praiseworthy adjustment to a tragic decision, his book of photographs, *Born Free and Equal*, was publicly burned in some places, and many copies were destroyed by the publisher. Dorothea Lange photographed Manzanar for the War Relocation Authority, but she made a point of recording the residents' hardships and the army impounded much of her work. Few of Lange's Manzanar photographs were published during the war. A professional photographer from Los Angeles who was living at the camp, Toyo Miyatake, found himself forbidden, like other "Japanese," to have a camera, but he

Figure 1.1 *After Pearl Harbor, 112,000 people of Japanese ancestry, most of them U.S. citizens, were removed from the West Coast and placed in inland internment camps. The president and military claimed wartime authority for the action in an atmosphere of hysteria. The internees, one of whom (above) arrived at an assembly center in his World War I uniform, lost their constitutional rights. This photograph was impounded by the War Relocation Authority and apparently not released during the war. Photograph by Dorothea Lange (Arcadia, Cal., April 5, 1942). Courtesy of National Archives.*

was eventually allowed to send for his equipment and to use it, as long as a Caucasian tripped the shutter—a restriction that was later lifted by a lenient camp director.[121]

Apparently reading the Constitution by the flickering flames of public opinion despite their lifetime tenure, the justices of the Supreme Court of the United States accepted the notion that a supposed wartime necessity could justify allowing the military to single out citizens by national origin and strip them of their rights. In *Hirabayashi v. U.S.*, the Court unanimously upheld the conviction of a United States citizen of Japanese ancestry who had been found guilty of violating the military curfew. The opinion by Chief Justice Harlan F. Stone regarded the curfew as a public safety measure within the power of the president and Congress and as a reasonable response to an apparent threat of actions that would substantially affect the war effort. "If it was an appropriate exercise of the war power its validity is not impaired because it has restricted the citizen's liberty," the opinion said. "Like every military control of

the population of a dangerous zone in war time, it necessarily involves some infringement of individual liberty, just as does the police establishment of fire lines during a
fire, or the confinement of people to their houses during an air raid alarm—neither
of which could be thought to be an infringement of constitutional right."[122] The
Court thus equated brief traffic restrictions on anyone—which may or may not be
logical in particular circumstances—with a curfew for people of a certain demographic
description on the mere suspicion that their ancestry could incline them to have
political opinions that might lead them toward illegal acts.[123]

The Supreme Court supported group exclusion from West Coast military areas
without due process by a vote of six to three in *Korematsu v. U.S.*, a case in which
an American citizen of Japanese ancestry did not submit to exclusion and relocation.
Relying on the *Hirabayashi* reasoning on war powers, Justice Hugo Black's majority
opinion said that a loss of freedom due to ancestry had to be subjected to the "most
rigid scrutiny," but that the exclusion order could be constitutionally justified by the
"apprehension by the proper military authorities of the gravest imminent danger to
public safety."[124] Black, who was beginning to acquire his reputation as a civil libertarian, did not otherwise explain how freedoms could be simply sacrificed to fears or
how a constitution of limited powers could prove to be so unconfining.

Scorn for the *Korematsu* opinion and the constitutionally unrestricted military
authority it allowed over civilians began with the dissenters. Justice Robert Jackson
said he would not "distort the Constitution to approve all the military may deem
expedient," and Justice Frank Murphy thought that the exclusion order had gone over
the brink of constitutional power and "into the ugly abyss of racism."[125] James F.
Simon, a biographer of Black who called it his "worst judicial opinion," found *Korematsu* "devoid of meaningful analysis of the underpinnings of military policy," "de-
ceptive in its strained narrowing of the constitutional issues," and "a philosophically
incoherent defense of broad government power." Although he did not serve overseas,
Black had been an artillery captain during World War I and was ready to defer to
military authority with little serious reflection. One of the six-member majority, Justice
William O. Douglas (a man of both liberal and patriotic sympathies, who dodged a
vision test in order to get into the army during World War I) and others in decision-
making roles eventually expressed remorse, but not Black, who continued to maintain
that he had been right.[126] Fred Korematsu's 1942 conviction was vacated in 1984 on
the basis of archival evidence that the government had deliberately concealed official
reports contradicting the assertions of fact that General DeWitt had used to justify a
claim of military necessity. The federal district court judge who issued the ruling,
Marilyn Hall Patel, noted that the racial discrimination allowed by *Korematsu* had
been overruled in the court of history. The case, she wrote, stood as a caution that
government had to protect all citizens from fears and prejudice and that "in times of
distress the shield of military necessity and national security must not be used to
protect governmental actions from close scrutiny and accountability."[127]

The Supreme Court's *Korematsu* opinion, however, was issued on December 18,
1944, the same day as its decision in *Ex parte Endo*, a case in which the justices
unanimously ruled that a citizen of Japanese ancestry whose loyalty had been established had to be released. The opinion by Justice Douglas concluded that the War

Relocation Authority, which existed for the sole purpose of protection against espionage and sabotage, had "no authority" to detain a concededly loyal citizen who was
"by definition not a spy or a saboteur." Although relocation was intended, the opinion
said, neither the president nor Congress had explicitly authorized detention.[128] Acting
in concert with the administration, Chief Justice Stone delayed handing down the
Endo decision for more than a month so that it was not publicly known until the day
after the War Department announced the end of internment for all those deemed
loyal. Key officials in the military and cabinet had been arguing for a year or more
that the program was not necessary, and some anticipated the outcome of *Endo*, but
Roosevelt, not wanting to stir up opposition in California, waited until the presidential
election of 1944 was safely behind him and the policy change would not follow too
conspicuously on the heels of the voting. Having the military announcement come
first not only allowed the Court to escape blame for attacking wartime policy, but
also allowed the administration to appear to be acting on its own and sensitive to the
legal and moral issues. With significant battlefield gains being made by late 1944, the
decision against general internment had a subdued response, but the differing results
of *Korematsu* and *Endo* proved puzzling to many, especially editorial writers, who
wondered how the two cases could be reconciled.[129]

In none of the cases, however, did the Court deal directly with the constitutionality of the detention. In noting that the Court was not reaching the underlying
constitutional issues, the *Endo* opinion recognized the wide scope of legislative and
executive war powers. "At the same time, however," the Court said, "the Constitution
is as specific in its enumeration of many of the civil rights of the individual as it is
in its enumeration of the powers of his government." The opinion therefore advocated
the "greatest possible accommodation" between individual liberties and the exigencies
of war.[130] In 1980 Congress created a commission on the internment that found that
Roosevelt's executive order was not justified by military necessity and that the decisions
that followed were the result of racial prejudice, war hysteria, and a failure of leadership. Following commission recommendations despite much resistance, Congress
approved redress payments of twenty thousand dollars each to living victims, which,
after many delays, began arriving with a letter of apology from the president in 1990,
when more than half of the internees were dead and their heirs were not entitled to
anything. Francis Biddle, who was attorney general during World War II, wrote in
his memoirs that the relocation program violated constitutional rights, but that Roosevelt chose to defer to the War Department because the military was fighting the
war and he thought public opinion was on its side. Roosevelt "was never theoretical
about things," Biddle observed, adding that "the Constitution has never greatly bothered any wartime President."[131]

Like citizens of Japanese ancestry during World War II, American journalists have
been deprived of their constitutional rights by presidential-military power. Journalists
generally have been willing to accept reasonable self-censorship guidelines, but, in the
absence of a definitive Supreme Court ruling on battlefield restrictions for the press,
claims of military necessity have been used to impose prior restraint and to limit access
and information gathering. Not only has the right to report on defense topics been
diminished but also the principle of civilian control of the armed forces. When reporters pressed Franklin Roosevelt to explain his concept of defense secrecy, he said

that decisions on disclosure were made by the military, but added, "The test is what the Commander in Chief of the Army and Navy thinks it would be harmful to the defense of this country to give out."[132] When the news blackout was imposed on the Grenada invasion in 1983, Secretary of Defense Caspar Weinberger explained that the military did not want reporters along and that he "wouldn't ever dream of overriding a commander's decision."[133] The Grenada invasion, which was of highly doubtful legality and condemned in a United Nations Security Council resolution the United States was forced to veto, had many easily preventable errors that were concealed from the public until the stories were no longer news.[134] In the Gulf War, President George Bush left the decisions about press restrictions up to the Pentagon and field commanders.[135] Stories were delayed or distorted in a "security review" process that was used to prevent embarrassments rather than preserve lives. Navy officers, for instance, cut references to pilots watching pornographic films before missions. Journalists who wrote critical stories were refused access to sources.[136]

Letting the armed forces choose what can be known and said about war invites the kind of blunders and abuses the First Amendment was written to prevent. Battlefield censorship and access denial can be used to cover up military mistakes that are in need of attention. During World War II, for example, censorship concealed the names of officers who made foolish and even disastrous decisions.[137] Inasmuch as wartime provides excellent opportunities to advance in rank and military honor can be highly valued at any time,[138] officers and their aides tend to want flattering coverage and to characterize negative stories as inaccurate, sensational, or unpatriotic.[139] Trusting civilian officials to make decisions for the press is little better. Judges and legislators may have any number of political or personal motives for wanting to punish the press or to protect the image of the commander in chief and the armed forces. Censors in any branch of government have things to gain and lose by their decisions, but the military has the most at stake and often fails to investigate its own failings properly.[140] "No man is allowed to be a judge in his own case," James Madison pointed out in the *Federalist*, "because his interest would certainly bias his judgment, and, not improbably, corrupt his integrity."[141] Although the mass media also can gain or lose by their decisions, they are favored by the Constitution. For better or worse, the Bill of Rights left the ultimate decisions on war news and opinion to the independent press, but the country often has allowed the sword to be mightier than the pen.

The Purpose of the
Press Clause

Censorship in some form has occurred in every major war the
United States has fought. Yet the constitutional questions raised by government restraints on wartime reporting remain far from settled.[1] The absence of definitive Supreme Court decisions on battlefield press restrictions may be the result not only of
general discomfort and confusion in dealing with the clash of such important values
as safety and free expression, but also of the extent to which the press and the military
have cooperated in the past and of the fact that neither side could be sure of court
victory when the relevant precedents are so mixed. Scholarly analysis usually has been
critical of official restrictions, but has been preoccupied with making analogies to the
Supreme Court's access to information precedents, which could support different positions, and with applying the justices' equally equivocal set of rulings and dicta on
prior restraint.[2]

Meanwhile, the rights of journalists to see and relate the conduct of armed conflict
have not been established to an extent that would be consistent with the First Amendment. Perplexity over press freedom in wartime may not be an indication of a constitutional deadlock or breakdown so much as the result of a failure to refer back to
what Thomas Paine called "first principles."[3] Do government officials have, as some
have assumed, a general prerogative authority to overrule the Bill of Rights when they
think it necessary?[4] In particular, can presidential-military powers ever be used legally
to restrict journalists during a war? The Americans who demanded a guarantee of
press freedom did have in mind certain inflexible principles, principles that have been
violated ever since by government officials who have the sworn duty to uphold them.

I.

A refusal to allow any official restrictions on the press—in the military or any other
context—would have been easy to conceive when the First Amendment was added to
the Constitution. Although some scholars have doubted that the press clause was
intended to prevent government-initiated actions against journalists,[5] Anglo-American
libertarian thought had come to see an unobstructed press as vital to the operation of
any free political system.[6] The highly influential *Cato's Letters*, written for British
newspapers by John Trenchard and Thomas Gordon in the 1720s and cited many
times in the colonies over the following decades, made the explicit point that government existed to serve the people and that freedom of expression gave the people

the information they needed to evaluate the performance of their servants in official positions.[7] The two authors observed that honest leaders would want to have their actions subjected to such scrutiny and that only the guilty had anything to fear. Journalistic attacks might be denounced by officials as seditious and "inconsistent with the Safety of all Government," *Cato's Letters* said, but they "undoubtedly keep Great Men in Awe, and are some Check upon their Behaviour, by shewing them the Deformity of their Actions as well as warning other People to be on their Guard against Oppression."[8]

Public statements originating in the colonies also proclaimed the utility of having a press free to expose wrongdoing. At the seditious libel trial of New York printer John Peter Zenger in 1735, defense lawyer Andrew Hamilton made a successful and celebrated argument in favor of the fundamental right "of exposing and opposing arbitrary power." Far from being a danger to government, he told the jury, revealing the truth about official misdeeds was a duty citizens owed to each other if they were to avoid tyranny and resulting upheavals.[9] Concurring with Hamilton's position, James Alexander, a lawyer who had been the guiding force behind Zenger's newspaper, published a commentary that described free expression as "a *principal pillar* in a free government" and said that "the constitution is dissolved" without it. "Republics and limited monarchies derive their strength and vigor from a *popular examination* into the actions of the magistrates," he said. Alexander admitted that the freedom could be abused, but said that giving officials authority to punish words offered dangerous opportunities for suppression. "A magistrate who sincerely aims at the *good* of the society will always have the inclinations of a great majority on his side," he wrote, "and impartial posterity will not fail to render him justice."[10]

After countless journalistic and political repetitions of the theme of the press as a necessary check on government,[11] Congress in 1774 issued a statement listing the "invaluable rights" it was prepared to fight Britain to preserve. The fifth and final right listed was freedom of the press, "whereby oppressive officers are shamed or intimidated, into more honourable and just modes of conducting affairs."[12] Using terms such as "never" restrained and "inviolably preserved," nearly every new state constitution written after independence included an absolute prohibition on government interference with freedom of the press. Some of the guarantees referred to unfettered journalism as one of the "bulwarks of liberty" or as "essential to the security of freedom in a state."[13] Exerting the force of public opinion between elections or in place of impeachment, an independent "fourth branch" of government was seen as helping to enforce the formal and informal rules of just politics. A free press "subject only to liability for personal injuries," Thomas Jefferson said, brings public officials before the "tribunal of public opinion" and thereby "produces reform peaceably, which must otherwise be done by revolution."[14]

In the early years of nationhood, journalism was radically free. Although individuals retained an ill-defined right to sue for damage to their reputations, traditional government devices for muzzling the press—such as licensing, trials for seditious libel, and breach of legislative privilege cases—either had been long interred or had all but vanished with the separation from Britain.[15] Protections for press freedom were prominently featured in state constitutions and could be easily understood as preventing the government, particularly the branch that wrote the laws, from imposing any constraints. Commenting on a constitution for Kentucky, for instance, James Madison noted in 1785 that the power of a legislature seemed "in many respects to be indefinite" and needed to be limited by enumerating "the essential exceptions" that included restraining the representatives "from controuling the press."[16] When the federal Constitution was written in 1787, its advocates maintained that a press guarantee was not necessary because the new, constitutionally limited government was not being given any authority over the press. At the Convention, the only recorded statement on a motion to declare " 'that the liberty of the Press should be inviolably observed' " came from Roger Sherman, who insisted that it was not needed. "The power of the Congress does not extend to the Press," he said. An attempt to form a committee to prepare a bill of rights had been unanimously defeated two days earlier, but the motion to single out the occupation of journalism for an express protection failed by only one or two votes.[17]

The Constitution presented to the public, then, did not mention the press, but did contain what Madison called "inventions of prudence," distributions of power where "each may be a check on the other." Madison envisioned a puzzling arrangement in which the legislative, judicial, and executive branches would be "as little dependent as possible" on the others and would be able to "resist encroachments" on their authority. Such a system would allow government itself to protect "public rights," he maintained.[18] In the *Federalist*, he described how he thought Congress would "refine" public opinion and make it unlikely that "a majority of the whole will have a common motive to invade the rights of other citizens."[19]

Elaboration on the executive and judicial branches came from Alexander Hamilton, the delegate who had warned the Convention about "the amazing violence & turbulence of the democratic spirit" and who had advocated electing the executive and senators for life while praising the British government as "the best in the world." In the *Federalist*, Hamilton saw the president, a small number of conservative citizens in the Senate, and judges as the guardians of the public welfare. "Regard to reputation has a less active influence, when the infamy of a bad action is to be divided among a number, than when it is to fall singly upon one," he contended. "A spirit of faction which is apt to mingle its poison in the deliberations of all bodies of men, will often hurry the persons of whom they are composed into improprieties and excesses, for which they would blush in private capacity." A popular assembly with the people on its side could often overpower the other branches of government and upset the balance of the constitution, he maintained. When the people's inclinations were opposed to their own interests, he said, then the president in particular had to "withstand the temporary delusion, in order to give them time and opportunity for more cool and sedate reflection."[20]

Hamilton was therefore comfortable promoting the two branches he extolled, the ones he thought would solve the problems of popular government and, as such, would be the signal accomplishments of the Constitution. Like Madison, Hamilton believed that the courts had to be independent of the elected executive and Congress in order to perform their tasks properly and that lifetime tenure for judicial appointees would be necessary in order for the "weakest" and "least dangerous" branch to retain its autonomy and be "the citadel of the public justice and the public security." In a republic, Hamilton stated, an independent judiciary was an "excellent barrier to the encroachments and oppressions of the representative body" and would have a duty "to declare all acts contrary to the manifest tenor of the constitution void."[21]

The claim that government itself would protect the public from government was alarming to many Americans. Hard-won rights, skeptics charged, were to rest on little more than trust in officials operating in an elaborate, untested political mechanism. Specific concerns were voiced about the absence of language preserving a nongovernmental check: an independent press to inform the sovereign people about the performance of their servants in positions of power. At the Virginia ratifying convention, for instance, Patrick Henry stated that freedom of the press was left to depend on the "integrity" of members of Congress. "They should, from prudence, abstain from violating the rights of their constituents," he said. "They are not, however, expressly restrained. But whether they will intermeddle with that palladium of our liberties or not, I leave to you to determine." Henry left no question about where he stood, saying, "Reason, self-preservation, and every idea of propriety, powerfully urge us to secure the dearest rights of human nature."[22]

Henry was one of an array of early Americans who regarded a broad right to know as a matter of safety and who feared that the natural tendency of government was to encroach on basic liberties and to conceal its own improper actions.[23] Antifederalists regarded the secrecy of the Constitutional Convention itself as a suspicious precedent.[24] At Philadelphia, the delegates had struggled with the issue of how much secrecy to allow Congress. Only one state voted in favor of a motion to allow the two houses to exclude information on "treaties & military operations" from their published proceedings, a provision that had been in the Articles of Confederation.[25] "The people have a right to know what their Agents are doing or have done," James Wilson declared, "and it should not be at the option of the Legislature to conceal their proceedings." The possibility remained, however, that a majority could see a justifiable need to withhold information on some infrequent occasions that would be difficult to define in advance. Finally, by one vote, the Convention did approve language saying that each house of Congress could omit from their published journals such parts "as may in their judgment require secrecy" (Article 1).[26]

Allowing some secrecy in the federal government did not mean rejection of a right to know. At the Virginia ratifying convention, Henry agreed with George Mason's view that in "matters relative to military operations and foreign negotiations, secrecy was necessary sometimes," but, saying that he found the language of the Constitution too ambiguous, he insisted that the withholding of facts actually be for the "interests of the community" and that the practice continue only "till the end which required their secrecy should have been effected." Even as staunch a defender of liberty as Patrick Henry, then, did not deny the logic of official efforts to refuse to divulge a very narrow range of information, but he maintained a presumption in favor of openness and expected the press and public to know everything possible as soon as possible. "The liberties of a people never were, nor ever will be, secure," Henry observed, "when the transactions of their rulers may be concealed from them." The Constitution did, at least, require the government to publish not only the journals of both houses, but also "a regular statement and account of the receipts and expenditures of all public money" (Article 1).[27]

Allowing government to try to keep some secrets, of course, is not the same as allowing a prior restraint on information the press obtains. Prior censorship had not existed for most of the eighteenth century and was even rejected in all cases by a commentator as reactionary as Sir William Blackstone. Although he was no proponent of popular sovereignty or the right to criticize government, Blackstone stated flatly that "no *previous* restraints upon publications" were possible under English law. Moreover, if the cases of leaking that occurred are any indication, Americans of the late eighteenth century did not regard the unauthorized disclosure of government secrets as a crime. Confidential cabinet discussions, diplomatic correspondence, and secret documents were divulged without officials or publishers being held legally responsible for the exposures. Revealing "the truth" in such cases was not treated as an offense outside the protection of the Constitution.[28]

Clandestine activity was naturally suspect in Enlightenment theory. In an essay discussing the need to allow citizens to speak "freely and publicly" on matters of war and peace so that "light may be thrown on their affairs," Kant warned that "the possession of power inevitably corrupts the free judgement of reason." He argued, "All actions affecting the rights of other human beings are wrong if their maxim is not compatible with their being made public." Told that his diplomatic dealings in France were being watched by secret agents, Benjamin Franklin remarked that if his own valet were a spy, "as probably he is," he would not discharge him if he performed well in other respects. Franklin made it a rule, he said, not to do anything in his official functions that he would be ashamed to see made public. "When a Man's Actions are just and honourable," he wrote, "the more they are known, the more his Reputation is increas'd and establish'd."[29]

The opponents of the unamended Constitution worried about whether the more powerful government being proposed would be able to protect expression and to open its own activities to public scrutiny. During the Constitutional Convention's deliberations on Congressional secrecy, Roger Sherman remarked that "the Legislature might be trusted in this case if any." Federalists, however, had to reassure the critics and to warn them about the consequences of a failure to adopt the Constitution. At the Virginia ratifying convention, Madison asked Henry if the country was not "rapidly approaching to anarchy" that would lead to despotism. He told Henry that the new system with its separation of powers might be an "experiment," but that it "increases the security of liberty more than any government that ever was" and that there "never was any legislative assembly without a discretionary power of concealing important transactions, the publication of which might be detrimental to the community." Madison then added, "There can be no real danger as long as the government is constructed on such principles."[30]

Such explanations did not satisfy the likes of Patrick Henry, who objected to the absence of guaranteed rights and to the vagueness of the secrecy provision. A press completely protected from official interference would be needed as another counterweight in any new system, they reasoned. The checks and balances of the three branches of government were not enough to deal with the potential for wrongdoing, concealment, and suppression. Among those who believed that press freedom should not be restrained "in any matter whatever," who feared that government could use taxation and other "general powers" to control journalists, and who therefore spoke of the need for a written guarantee was "The Federal Farmer," the most prominent Antifederalist pamphleteer. "A free press is the channel of communication as to mercantile and public affairs; by means of it the people in large countries ascertain each others sentiments; are enabled to unite, and become formidable to those rulers who adopt improper measures," he wrote. "Newspapers may sometimes be the vehicles of abuse, and of many things not true; but these are but small inconveniences, in my mind, among many advantages."[31]

Responding to concerns about the limits of government power and about safeguards for the press, proponents of ratification argued, as Madison did in the *Federalist*, that the proposed government's "jurisdiction extends to certain enumerated objects only."[32] He said that understanding the Constitution required looking at its "clear and precise expressions" of enumerated powers rather than the "more doubtful and indefinite terms" used to describe a general authority such as providing for the nation's defense. "Nothing is more natural or common than first to use a general phrase," Madison observed, "and then to explain and qualify it by a recital of the particulars." Making the point that a seemingly expansive authority was not to prevail over fundamental liberties, he said that a general power such as taxation did not create a "power to destroy the freedom of the press." Alexander Hamilton reiterated the most salient objections to a bill of rights when he said in the *Federalist* that it would be difficult to list and define all rights in detail and that it would not be necessary because the people were sovereign and retained all their liberties. Hamilton contended that it would be absurd to protect against the abuse of an authority not given. "Why for instance," he asked, "should it be said, that the liberty of the press shall not be restrained, when no power is given by which restrictions may be imposed?"[33]

The idea that the Constitution delegated certain powers to government while fundamental liberties were "reserved" by the people found no more strenuous advocate than James Wilson, a respected legal scholar and Convention delegate from Pennsylvania. In a widely reprinted public speech defending the Constitution, Wilson maintained that "the proposed system possesses no influence whatever upon the press" and that making a formal declaration of a right was dangerous because it might be "construed to imply that some degree of power was given, since we undertook to define its extent." At the state ratifying convention, Wilson faced doubters who suggested several ways the wording of the Constitution could be stretched to allow restraints on the press. One brought up the possibility that the government simply would not be limited by the Constitution. "Tho it is not declared that Congress have a power to destroy liberty of the press; yet, in effect, they will have it," said Robert Whitehill, a delegate from Cumberland County. "For they will have the powers of self-preservation." With some exasperation, Wilson repeated the standard Federalist position that "there is given to the general government no power whatsoever concerning it; and no law in pursuance of the Constitution can possibly be enacted to destroy that liberty."[34]

Despite continued assurances to the same effect,[35] Antifederalist objections to the absence of a bill of rights in general and of a press guarantee in particular placed ratification in jeopardy.[36] The Constitution gave members of Congress an absolute freedom from outside legal action "for any speech or debate in either House" (Article 1), but the document written in Philadelphia did not mention a comparable privilege for journalists. Impassioned newspaper writings described liberty of the press as "the palladium of all civil, political and religious rights," "the scourge of tyrants," and the "alarm" that rouses citizens when their freedoms are in danger.[37] Fears were expressed that the failure to provide a bill of rights with a press guarantee was a conspiracy of the wealthy and powerful and that future journalists would be at the mercy of the federal government.[38] A more charitable assessment came from a member of Congress from North Carolina who remarked that "no express provision is made for the TRYAL BY JURY, and LIBERTY OF THE PRESS; things so interwoven with our political, or legal ideas, that I conceive the sacred immutablity of these rights to be such, as never to have occurred as questionable objects to the convention." The similarity of published complaints on the subject prompted a *Pennsylvania Gazette* correspondent to offer a satirical recipe for an Antifederalist essay. The list of ingredients included nineteen mentions of a statement by George Mason, who had drafted Virginia's seminal Declaration of Rights, that he would "sooner chop off his right hand than put it to the Constitution as it now stands." Mason, one of the three delegates who refused to sign the document at the conclusion of the Convention in Philadelphia, regarded the Constitution as fatally flawed without written protections for basic freedoms and immediately took a leading role in the campaign to add a bill of rights.[39]

The fight for a press guarantee intensified as each state in turn took up ratification. In South Carolina, the legislature heard objections about the "tyrant's scourge" not being protected and came within one vote of not calling a convention to consider the proposed Constitution. Charles Cotesworth Pinckney told the legislators that he and other delegates to the Constitutional Convention had debated the matter thoroughly and had concluded that nothing should be said about it. "The general government has no powers but what are expressly granted to it," he said, "it therefore has no power to take away the liberty of the press." Pinckney said that press freedom was secured in state constitutions and that "to have mentioned it in our general Constitution would perhaps furnish an argument, hereafter, that the general government had a right to exercise powers not expressly delegated to it."[40]

Toward the end of the ratification period the key struggles were in the populous states of Virginia and New York. In both cases the Constitution was narrowly ratified after Federalists agreed to seek written guarantees of what they said was silently protected. Along with North Carolina, which refused to ratify at all until Congress acted on a bill of rights, both Virginia and New York proposed amendments that included freedom of the press.[41] Virginia, the most crucial state in the whole process, ratified with a declaration that the people retained every power not granted, that no department or officer of the United States could deny a right unless authorized by the Constitution for that purpose, and that "among other essential rights, the liberty of conscience and of the press cannot be cancelled, abridged, restrained, or modified, by any authority of the United States." No part of the national government, Madison and the other delegates wanted it understood, had authority to do anything to restrict press freedom. When he later listed his reasons for proposing a bill of rights, he said that in many states the Constitution was adopted "under a tacit compact" that amendments would be made to protect basic rights and that in Virginia it "would have been *certainly* rejected, had no assurances been given by its advocates that such provisions would be pursued."[42]

Madison realized, however, that violations of the Constitution would occur. In 1788, while discussing with Jefferson the public demands for a bill of rights, Madison wondered if trying to protect liberties with written guarantees was not an exercise in futility. His chief concern was that "parchment barriers" would not be respected by "overbearing majorities." He complained that "experience proves the inefficacy of a bill of rights on those occasions when its control is most needed" and said that he was "inclined to think that *absolute* restrictions in cases that are doubtful, or where emergencies may overrule them, ought to be avoided" because "after repeated violations in extraordinary cases, they will lose even their ordinary efficacy." Madison encountered political pressures to agree to a bill of rights, but it seems to have been Jefferson's enthusiasm for the idea that finally convinced him of its value. Jefferson asked his ally to remember "the legal check which it puts into the hands of the judiciary"—a check that, if independent of politics, would be able to protect freedoms. He also argued that it was better to have a bill of rights than not to have one. "A brace the more will often keep up the building which would have fallen with that brace the less," he told Madison. Jefferson said that it was better to establish freedom of the press and other several other rights "in all cases" rather than not to do it in any.[43]

Answering charges from fellow Virginians that he did not want a federal bill of rights, Madison assured voters while running for a seat in the First Congress that he would seek to amend the Constitution with the "clearest and strongest provision" for freedom of the press and other "essential rights." He explained to one correspondent that producing a bill of rights was "a nauseous project," but one that "must be done" because of agreements with opponents of the Constitution and because "every Govt. power may oppress, and declarations on paper, tho' not an effectual restraint, are not without some influence." In offering his proposed bill of rights to Congress in 1789, Madison used the wording: "The people shall not be deprived or abridged of their right to speak, to write, or to publish their sentiments; and the freedom of the press, as one of the great bulwarks of liberty, shall be inviolable." Making it clear that he was conceiving of more protection than was afforded under English law, he said, "The freedom of the press and rights of conscience, those choicest privileges of the people, are unguarded in the British constitution." What the people wanted, he said, was to declare where "the government ought not to act, or to act only in a particular mode." Such declarations might be thought unnecessary, Madison said, but they would help "to establish public opinion in their favor" at times when they might be disregarded and would help assure that "independent tribunals of justice will consider themselves in a peculiar manner the guardians of those rights." Even if government kept within its limits, he said, it might abuse its discretionary powers under the "necessary and proper" clause in the absence of a bill of rights. During the House debate over the amendments, Madison explained that "the liberty of the press is expressly declared to be beyond the reach of government."[44]

The ratification of the First Amendment in 1791, however, created a constitutional provision that could be relied on, twisted, or ignored. A New Haven newspaper essayist had remarked that rights such as liberty of the press were "too important" to depend on paper protection. "For, guard such privileges by the strongest expressions, still if you leave the legislative and executive power in the hands of those who are or may be disposed to deprive you of them—you are but slaves."[45] Federalists had, in fact, cautioned that a protection for "freedom of the press" would not work. "Who can give it any definition which would not leave the utmost latitude for evasion?" Hamilton asked in the *Federalist*, saying that it "must altogether depend on public opinion, and on the general spirit of the people and of the government." In his public speech, James Wilson warned that "the very declaration might have been construed to imply some degree of power was given, since we undertook to define its extent." Wilson told the Pennsylvania ratifying convention that the freedom might be defined legally as merely the lack of prior restraint as it had been in England. On the other hand, the term "liberty of the press" could mean an "unlimited licence to publish *any thing and every thing* with impunity," as lexicographer and journalist Noah Webster said. "The Constitutions of several States *guarantee that very licence*," Webster complained, saying that he did not want to see protection "of any treatise, however obscene and blasphemous."[46]

Yet the desire to have a rigid, absolute press guarantee, one that could prevail over some potentially nebulous powers given to government, had proven overwhelming. One of the first newspaper essays to respond to James Wilson's views explained that under the strong new government "a thousand means may be devised to destroy effectually the liberty of the press" and that John Peter Zenger had demonstrated how displeasing a free press could be to those in power. "At any rate," the writer said, "I lay it down as a general rule, that wherever the powers of a government extend to the lives, the persons, and properties of the subject, all their rights ought to be clearly and expressly defined—otherwise they have but a poor security for their liberties."[47]

The wording of the Constitution and contemporary discussion left little doubt that the aim of both those who wanted a written guarantee and those who did not was to deny the legislative, executive, and judicial branches any power over the press. Officials might be justified in refusing to reveal some sensitive military or diplomatic information as long as the well-being of the nation required it, but, in order to perform its checking function, a separate, independent press needed to be absolutely free of prior restraints or subsequent penalties initiated by government. Both the government's ability to maintain any secrecy and the freedom of journalists to go about their work naturally involve some risks, but the concept of the "consent of the governed" required that the people be informed and that the government be accountable. Such understandings, however, have not necessarily been carried down through the successive periods of the nation's history.

II.

The logical mechanisms and limitations that James Madison helped to construct did not work as well as they should have in the two hundred years that followed the ratification of the Bill of Rights. The fears of the Antifederalists were realized, as each of the three branches failed to follow the constitutional design of limited government and unlimited press freedom. The framers had hoped that Congress would be able to deliberate calmly and not be frightened into violating individual liberties. To James Madison and like-minded civil libertarians, Congress not only could not pass laws abridging freedom of the press, but also would act improperly in even criticizing the use of the right. After President Washington denounced the Democratic-Republican organizations in the wake of the Whiskey Rebellion, an actual insurrection in 1794, Madison opposed a congressional resolution blaming the "self-created societies" for "deceiving and inflaming the ignorant and weak." He told the House, which did not pass the resolution, that the sovereign people should not be censured by their servants in government; that they had enough good sense and patriotism to reject unsound publications. "Opinions are not the objects of legislation," he said. "You animadvert on the abuse of reserved rights: how far will this go? It may extend to the liberty of speech, and of the press." The press, Madison said, "would not be able to shake the confidence of the people in the Government."[48]

The events of the 1790s, however, soon did produce the kind of stress fractures the constitutional system would suffer in later times. In particular, the seizing of American ships by England and then by France brought about reassessments of the nation's pacific hopes and political mechanisms. "At the close of our revolution war the phantom of perpetual peace danced before the eyes of every body," said a 1798 newspaper essay by Alexander Hamilton, an essay calling for a "limited and mitigated state of war" with France and increased defense spending. "We see at this early period with how much difficulty war has been parried and that with all our efforts to preserve peace we are now in a state of partial hostility." Citing problems with government secrecy that he had not acknowledged during the ratification process, Madison attributed the nation's war hysteria to John Adams' handling of the XYZ Affair dispatches that revealed French attempts to secure bribes from American peace envoys. The president, Madison thought, manipulated public ignorance and emotions by the way information on foreign relations was concealed "or disclosed in such parts & at such times as will best suit particular views."[49]

During the Washington and Adams administrations, Jeffersonian journalists and politicians denounced what they regarded as monarchical tendencies in the chief executive.[50] Although the concept of the monarch as protector and paterfamilias had been subjected to severe assault in the press, and a constitution had been written to give the national legislature responsibility in foreign policy and military affairs, the United States responded to the pressures of international politics in ways that raised questions about the authority of the executive in wartime and the rights of constitutionally protected journalists to discuss fighting between nations, questions that would arise again during subsequent armed conflicts. Replacing, in a sense, George III, George Washington had come to embody a new republican model of the president—rather than the king—as paternal protector. His proclamation of neutrality in 1793 was attacked in the press by Madison as encroaching on the authority of Congress to decide matters of peace and war and was defended by Hamilton, who advanced a more expansive view of the executive power than he had in the *Federalist*.[51] In stirring up fears about the domestic impact of the French Revolution, enlarging the military, and approving the Alien and Sedition Acts of 1798, John Adams and the Federalist party adopted an early version of the American national security state that pierced the Enlightenment republican vision of the United States as a land of tranquillity and freedom.[52]

Madison worried that Adams was taking steps toward war that violated the Constitution by usurping the role of Congress. The executive "is the branch of power most interested in war, & most prone to it," he wrote to Jefferson. The willingness of the Federalists to defer to presidential authority, Madison felt, was placing "the peace of the Country in that Department which the Constitution distrusts as most ready without cause to renounce it." When Federalists in Congress were about to pass the Sedition Act of 1798 in an effort to silence Republican critics of the nation's hostile relations with France, Madison told Thomas Jefferson, "Perhaps it is a universal truth that the loss of liberty at home is to be charged to provisions agst. danger real or pretended from abroad." Objecting to Adams' vehement public posturing against France and the accompanying war fever, Jefferson lamented, "There are many who think, that, not to support the Executive, is to abandon Government." Jefferson, Madison, and their fellow Republicans saw in the Adams administration not only exploitation of rhetorical leadership to arouse public opinion, but also an effort to expand the scope of the office. Jefferson complained that many Federalists wanted "the Executive to be the sole power in the government."[53]

Facing a war with France that was never declared, Congress passed the Sedition Act of 1798 to outlaw "false, scandalous and malicious writing" defaming itself, the president, or the federal government in general. Offenses could involve bringing those parts of the government (not the Republican vice president, Thomas Jefferson) "into contempt or disrepute" or inciting against any of them "the hatred of the good people of the United States."[54] The Federalists wrote the law to expire in 1801 on the last day of the term of President Adams. The statute, which was passed over Republican objections, was ostensibly a temporary defense measure necessary for protecting the nation from disloyal citizens who would aid and abet the enemy through writing and speaking.[55] In fact, the Sedition Act was the work of a party with brazen disregard for the Constitution and was used to prosecute the leading Jeffersonian Republican journalists. The transparently political aims of the Federalist majorities in both houses of Congress did not stop President Adams from signing the law or the courts from enforcing it. Proponents of the legislation may have maintained that they were protecting the country from invasion and insurrection, but each branch of the government was controlled by the Federalists, and each welcomed a chance to bully the opposition party.[56]

In response to the Republican charge that Congress was making a law abridging freedom of the press, one "striking at the root of free republican Government," Federalists introduced sophisms that would linger for many years in discussions of the First Amendment. Representative Harrison Gray Otis insisted that "every independent Government has a right to preserve and defend itself against injuries and outrages which endanger its existence" and from "the nature of things" was "invested with a power to protect itself" from expression that had a tendency to produce opposition to its measures and its officials. Relying on the assertion that the "necessary and proper" clause of the Constitution allowed Congress to pass laws to punish spoken or written interference with its functions, Representative Robert G. Harper asked if there could be so great an "absurdity" or "political monster" as "a Government which has no power to protect itself against sedition and libels?" Liberty of the press, he said, did not mean licentiousness and the freedom "to throw, with impunity, the most violent abuse upon the President and both Houses of Congress." For support of his proposition, Harper misrepresented and misquoted Benjamin Franklin's "The Court of the Press" essay, written in 1789 when Congress was drafting the Bill of Rights. Leaving out Franklin's definition of press freedom as a right for "discussing the Propriety of Public Measures and political opinions" subject only to liability for injury to individual reputation, Harper concocted a quotation that had Franklin saying that "Government" could be "affronted" by the press. Representative John Allen turned to Sir William Blackstone's reading of English common law on the eve of the Revolution and used his ingenious but incredible assertion that freedom of the press meant only freedom from prior restraint, not freedom from punishment for statements critical of the government, a fatuous logic that gave people the "freedom" to commit the crime of seditious libel and suffer the consequences.[57]

Republicans objected to the use of British precedents as inappropriate in the American context and said the law was bad policy because it would divide the country at a time of international crisis and make the people suspicious of a government that appeared to fear scrutiny of its actions. Representative Edward Livingston pointed out that citizens who objected to the passing of such an unconstitutional act could be prosecuted. "You may, by thus acting, establish error as soon as truth; you put them both on the same footing," Livingston said; "you crush them by the force of arms, and not by the force of reason." The legal issue, as Representative John Wilkes Kittera put it, amounted to one side arguing the bill was a violation of the Constitution and the other saying it was based on common law principles. "If the latter is true," said Kittera, a Federalist who supported the legislation, "then it may be wise and proper to pass this bill."[58] Choosing the British common law over the American Constitution, the Federalist majority in Congress passed the Sedition Act.

James Madison was at the forefront of the opposition to the Sedition Act, which he regarded as only one in a series of Federalist abuses of the "necessary and proper" clause to expand government power beyond the intent of the Constitution. In his Virginia Resolutions opposing the act, he said the law was taking an action "expressly and positively forbidden" by the press clause, which was "the only effectual guardian of every other right."[59] An address of Virginia's General Assembly to the public, which is usually attributed to Madison, stated that the legislation used the "pretext of necessity" to usurp power. "Exhortations to disregard domestic usurpation, until foreign danger shall have passed, is an artifice which may be forever used." The idea that every government has a right to "self-preservation" was nonsense "because the care expended in defining powers would otherwise have been superfluous."[60] In a lengthy report for the Virginia legislature, Madison said the press clause was "absolute" and that using the necessary and proper clause to justify restrictions on the press meant that Congress was seeking unlimited government control.[61] The naval conflict with France, however, was not the kind of full-scale fighting that would furnish pretexts for imposing prepublication censorship in later wars.

Laws and postal policies were used to suppress abolitionist opinion in the nineteenth century, but nothing as sweeping as the Sedition Act was passed again until the twentieth century.[62] Some states, reacting to the McKinley assassination and the growing numbers of political radicals, passed criminal anarchy laws making it a crime to advocate the overthrow of the government by force.[63] During World War I, Congress wrote the Espionage Act of 1917, a law that included provisions for punishing anyone intentionally making false reports that interfered with military operations, willfully obstructing the draft, or willfully causing, or attempting to cause, "insubordination, disloyalty, mutiny, or refusal of duty, in the military or naval forces of the United States." An amendment known as the Sedition Act, which was passed in 1918 and repealed in 1921, broadened the Espionage Act to include "any disloyal, profane, scurrilous, or abusive language" about the form of government of the United States, the Constitution, the flag, or the military, as well as "any language intended to incite, provoke, or encourage resistance to the United States, or to promote the cause of its enemies." Reacting to radical movements spawned in the Depression and to the outbreak of World War II, Congress passed the Smith Act of 1940, a statute that made it unlawful to publish "any written or printed matter advocating, advising, or teaching the duty, necessity, desirability, or propriety of overthrowing or destroying any government in the United States by force or violence."[64] The World War I laws were used to convict more than one thousand individuals out of nearly twenty-two hundred prosecuted; as many as one hundred people, most of them Communists prosecuted early in the Cold War, were convicted under the Smith Act.[65]

The rationales used for the World War I statute were similar to those used for the Sedition Act of 1798. Members of Congress cited the Blackstonian definition of press freedom[66] and answered objections based on the First Amendment and free press theory by saying, without citing any sources, that temporary safety needs were a higher law than the Constitution.[67] Contrary to James Madison, Representative Warren Gard, an Ohio Democrat, contended that the necessary and proper clause allowed Congress to restrict expression under its power to regulate the military, but added, "The authority to protect and defend the Government in time of war transcends all other authority." Gard's assumption was put even more concisely by Representative William W. Venable, a Mississippi Democrat, who said that "extraordinary occasions do away with ordinary rules."[68]

Both houses discussed the constitutionality and practicality of the Espionage Act at great length in 1917, when a statute for policing thought had not existed for well over a century, but the debate on the Smith Act was perfunctory, with only four members of the House voting against it. After the Hitler-Stalin pact and the German invasion of Poland, the mood in the United States was such that hundreds of Communists were being arrested on charges ranging from disorderly conduct to passport violations. A number of state and federal laws had been passed already to deny rights to Communists, and the military pressured Roosevelt to sign the Smith Act. Having lost the support of American Communists, which he would regain when the Soviet Union became an ally,[69] the president ignored the implications for First Amendment liberties when signing the law, but a week later, while sketching out his Four Freedoms for reporters, he listed "freedom to express one's self as long as you don't advocate the overthrow of Government" as he complained about "certain elements" in the country that were attracted to the "corporate state" models of Germany and Russia.[70]

In analyzing freedom of expression during the two world wars, key officials and a number of the nation's foremost intellectuals endorsed the position that democracy had to defend itself and that the federal government could be trusted to do a more professional job of controlling dangerous expression than state or local authorities, who were too likely to be influenced by the unthinking multitude.[71] Objecting to hysterical "pseudo patriotism" in the public, John Lord O'Brian, who was in charge of Justice Department enforcement of the World War I statutes, complained that he had received five thousand letters a day conveying suspicions and accusations that were almost always groundless. Although laws restricting expression were vague and could operate unjustly at times, he observed, carefully handled restraints were sometimes justified because of "the right of the nation in time of grave national danger to protect itself against utterances intended to weaken its power of self-defense."[72]

Just as Congress expanded its own authority by passing laws abridging freedom of the press, the limited power of the "commander in chief" was stretched into a general authority that included not only the ability to carry out military actions against other nations without the approval of Congress, but also a nearly dictatorial degree of control over the press in wartime. Presidential-military power was used in the nineteenth and twentieth centuries to conceal information, to deny journalists access to armed conflicts, and to impose censorship of press dispatches from war zones. Presidential power grew, as Hamilton thought it would, with perceived threats to the nation.[73] Hamilton believed that people faced with danger naturally sought security in "institutions, which have a tendency to destroy their civil and political rights," and thus accepted more autocracy and less democracy. He also remarked that it was "of the nature of war to increase the executive at the expence of the legislative authority."[74]

Reasons for the expansion of the president's power in international affairs are not difficult to find. Unlike Congress, the president has the institutional advantages of being always in session, of having ready access to intelligence, and of being able to act quickly and secretly. "When foreign affairs play a prominent part in the politics and policy of a nation," Woodrow Wilson wrote, "its Executive must of necessity be its guide: must utter every initial judgment, take every first step of action, supply the information upon which it is to act, suggest and in large measure control its conduct."[75] An enlarged role for the president, however, can mean escalating expectations, foreign policy misadventures, and "failed" presidencies. The collapse of Wilson's health while he was strenuously promoting the League of Nations is evidence for the view of some eighteenth-century critics of the Constitution that the American presidency, even as originally conceived, gives too much complex responsibility to a single person, a person who can become ill, misuse power, or be naive about some matters and rely on bad advice.[76]

Presidents, even ones who had been top generals, have had apprehensions about the growing impact of the armed forces. George Washington's farewell address warned of "overgrown military establishments, which under any form of Government are inauspicious to liberty." Washington wanted the country to avoid foreign involvements that would require military expenditures, but Dwight Eisenhower recognized that a vast, permanent defense establishment had arisen in the United States by the time of his administration. Eisenhower's farewell address admonished Americans to protect their freedoms by guarding against "the acquisition of unwarranted influence, whether sought or unsought, by the military-industrial complex."[77] In the half century that followed the end of World War II, as arms trading became the world's largest industry, followed by drug trafficking and oil production,[78] the United States solidified a policy of employing military predominance to contain the nationalistic ambitions of both allies and adversaries and to secure favorable economic conditions in the world, a policy that transcended the aim of subduing communism.[79] Given immense responsibilities, military leaders became more involved in politics and more willing to challenge civilian decisions. They fought defense cuts, flatly rejected presidential policies they disliked—such as President Bill Clinton's plan to allow acknowledged homosexuals in the services—and publicly resisted international interventions where they could not use overwhelming force. Somewhat paradoxically, the failure of American involvement in Indochina, which was blamed on feckless politicians, disloyal dissenters, and the liberal media, helped the armed forces to gain—particularly during the Reagan and Bush administrations—the autonomy and influence that Washington and Eisenhower had feared.[80]

A lack of confidence in elected officials, seemingly intractable domestic problems, and abuses of the democratic process had brought a considerable portion of the American public to a state of widespread cynicism by the bicentennial of the Bill of Rights in 1991.[81] By then the military was being asked to handle a broad range of civilian tasks ranging from education, health care, and infrastructure projects to environmental cleanups, counternarcotics missions, and disaster relief. The military hierarchy openly wondered whether taking responsibility for so many peripheral tasks identified as "national security" problems would undermine the armed forces' ability to fight an actual opponent.[82] An Air Force officer concerned about "the massive diversion of military forces to civilian uses, the monolithic unification of the armed forces, and the insularity of the military community" was the co-winner of the Chairman of the Joint Chiefs of Staff 1991–92 Strategy Essay Competition with a paper entitled "The Origins of the Military Coup of 2012," a dramatization of what could happen if current trends continued. "People need to understand that the armed forces exist to support and defend government," the essay's fictional protagonist says, "not to *be* the government."[83]

The other branches often did not provide the necessary checks on the growth of presidential-military power. Congress, to a large extent, allowed the erosion of its authority in the area of national security.[84] When difficult decisions were to be made, Congress could avoid the slow process of deliberation and escape blame for policy failures by letting the chief executive become the focus of events and the decision-maker. In 1972 a Senate committee found 470 statutes that could be invoked by the president to cope with a war or emergency. The 1976 National Emergencies Act ended states of emergency still in effect and required that future presidential emergency declarations be subject to congressional review. Although it left open ways to circumvent its provisions, the act regulated the use of national emergency authority.[85] However, in doing little to resist executive branch attacks on civil liberties during the first two hundred years of the Bill of Rights, Congress often failed to preserve the Constitution. Presidents, more than half of whom had significant military experience, seized the initiative.[86]

The issues raised by the empowerment of the executive and the exercise of military authority have been perplexing. Prerogative powers are difficult to define and analyze in a society that does not agree about how much freedom can be given up for the sake of security.[87] The president's authority to implement secrecy is essential to the conduct of foreign relations and defense, but can diminish the democratic process by putting more matters under executive control, and can obstruct citizens' First Amendment rights to debate controversial policy issues.[88] "The people who, under the war powers of the Constitution, surrender their liberties and give up their lives and their property have a right to know why our wars are unnecessarily prolonged," Brevet Major General Emory Upton, an erudite and proficient soldier, wrote after the Civil War. "They have a right to know whether disasters have been brought about through the neglect and ignorance of Congress, which is intrusted with the power to raise and support armies, or through military incompetency."[89] Courts have tolerated military decisions as arbitrary as closing an Air Force base to the press and public when the bodies of dead soldiers were returned from a war zone or banning the distribution of federal candidate campaign literature at a training post.[90]

The checks and balances in the Constitution were, of course, designed to preserve freedom and democracy by encouraging debate and counteracting certain human impulses. Among the impulses that Alexander Hamilton named in the *Federalist* papers were "the love of power," "a spirit of faction," and "impressions of the moment." The more often a measure was brought under consideration, he said, the less likely would be a misstep due to some passion or interest. Elsewhere in the *Federalist* papers, however, Madison pointed to a natural tendency that he believed governmental structure might not be able to control. Describing security from "foreign danger" as one of "the primitive objects of civil society," he acknowledged complaints that the Constitution did not limit the government's ability to create and provide for a military even in times of peace, but he did not think that "constitutional barriers to the impulse of self-preservation" would be possible as long as the Constitution could not set limits on what other nations could do to build up their armed forces. Madison's answer to critics who saw a standing army as costly to the treasury and dangerous to liberty was that it would not be prudent for the United States to "set bounds to the exertions for its own safety."[91]

Madison may not have thought the Constitution should restrict military expenditures, but he did see the document as guaranteeing rights for citizens and as establishing limits and checks on the discretion of public officials. "It may be a reflection on human nature, that such devices should be necessary to controul the abuses of government," he wrote in the *Federalist*. "But what is government itself but the greatest of all reflections on human nature? If men were angels, no government would be necessary." In introducing his proposed bill of rights to Congress in 1789, he explained that the purpose was to "fortify the rights of the people against the encroachments of the government." Express guarantees were necessary, he said, because "all power is subject to abuse," and even if the government is kept within the limits of its enumerated powers "it has certain discretionary powers with respect to the means, which may admit of abuse to a certain extent." As the amendments were being debated, Madison made it clear that the government had no authority over the press and that as long as the Constitution would exist, the people "must conform themselves to its dictates."[92]

Absolutist, textualist thinking such as Madison's has had few adherents among intellectuals and Supreme Court justices[93]—even if virtually anything is possible when government abandons a Constitution that has provisions for being amended, but not suspended.[94] Early in the twentieth century, Theodore Schroeder, the secretary of the

Free Speech League, complained that the country "stupidly went to sleep" after establishing constitutional guarantees for freedom of expression and allowed the rights to be disregarded by legislators and "judicially amended." The participants in America's revolution had made seditious statements, Schroeder observed, "and apparently for the very purpose of protecting future generations in the right to advocate sedition and revolution, did they put in the Constitution a guarantee for the freedom of speech and press, and omit the making of any exception."[95] The idea of extraconstitutional powers for suppression clashes with a written Constitution that declares itself "the supreme law of the land" (Article 6) and that guarantees certain rights while acknowledging that other unenumerated rights exist and are "retained by the people" (Ninth Amendment). Thus, finding rights in addition to those listed is possible, but no branch of government has authority to reject the unqualified protection of the press clause.

The issue of how to use the original intent of the Constitution, however, has created what one law professor has called "almost a cottage industry in the scholarly literature" and another has termed a "wildly uncontrolled and virtually impenetrable thicket of conflicting theories of constitutional interpretation."[96] Among the arguments deployed against the use of early American thought are that intent is often ambiguous at best, that the Constitution was a product of elite white males and neglected women and minorities, and that relying on past notions of rights would impede much social progress.[97] Originalists have countered that such views tend to ignore the fact that the Constitution does contain a considerable amount of definitive pronouncements (the ban on titles of nobility, for example, in Article 1), that the document was left open to amendment, and that, as the often-ignored Ninth Amendment says, the enumeration of certain constitutional rights does not deny that others exist and are retained by the people.[98] The Constitution was very precise about some matters of painful experience and yet kept open the prospect of expanding legal protections over time.

Reading the text of the Constitution and studying the values behind its provisions may not be the only valid method of interpretation, but they offer at least a starting point for understanding rights. The United States Constitution established a political system with certain limits rather than a perfectionist scheme that would employ every power thought necessary to solve every problem.[99] Inasmuch as the Constitution was made to control future governmental actions, those who accept its authority are obligated to heed whatever clear mandates it contains, whether such rules seem easy to comply with or not. The central figures in the founding of the republic believed that future generations should look back to the late eighteenth century for guidance in interpreting the document and that a constitution ratified by the people was binding until amended by the people.[100] When Madison took up the issue, for instance, his standard statement was that in interpreting the Constitution, the Supreme Court needed to remember "that the intention of the parties to it ought to be kept in view; and that as far as the language of the instrument will permit, this intention ought to be traced in the contemporaneous expositions."[101] There was, he said, "the duty of all to support it in its true meaning as understood *by the nation* at the time of its ratification."[102]

After long exposure to British misrule and increasingly chaotic conditions under the Articles of Confederation, the idea of having a functioning government with fixed understandings was appealing in 1787. One original, general purpose of the Constitution, James Madison wrote in the *Federalist*, was to manage the "particular moments in public affairs, when the people stimulated by some irregular passion, or some illicit advantage, or misled by the artful misrepresentations of interested men, may call for measures which they themselves will afterwards be the most ready to lament and condemn." Madison saw a need for a political system with components able to employ "reason, justice and truth" when citizens began violating their freedoms. "What bitter anguish would not the people of Athens have often escaped, if their government had contained so provident a safeguard against the tyranny of their own passions?" he asked. "Popular liberty might then have escaped the indelible reproach of decreeing to the same citizens, the hemlock on one day, and statues on the next."[103] In referring to the fate of Socrates, whose words were regarded as dangerous to Athenian society, Madison raised a question that continues to challenge democratic governments: How can the political system manage to avoid irrational, desperate measures against expression that make a travesty of guaranteed rights and therefore the rule of law?[104]

3

Suspending the Press Clause

Centuries of libertarian thought have produced a roll call of basic rationales for freedom of expression. The fundamental values or objectives said to be advanced by the right include attaining self-fulfillment, carrying out self-government, advancing knowledge, resolving conflict, and checking the misuse of power.[1] Such concepts reside at the core of democratic theory and can make powerful arguments in court cases, but ideas—however much they are revered—may be no match for instincts. Legal conflicts that pit survival, the most basic human instinct, against the ability to communicate, the most basic feature of a free society, are often resolved in favor of those asserting that military, civilian, or even governmental safety should outweigh the need for free speech and a free press.[2]

Although making survival the first priority may seem natural, too much emphasis on security claims can destroy the diversity of opinions and information that democracies need. Law often deals with conflicts by seeking to sustain and legitimate the status quo,[3] sometimes to the point of absurdity. The Supreme Court of the United States has made much-analyzed attempts to establish broad doctrines dealing with words that might pose a danger to life or "national security,"[4] but too often scholars have ignored the invalid assumptions that officials and courts have made when relying on the unwritten law of societal safety, the so-called higher law above the Constitution. More scrutiny would seem to be necessary in view of social science findings on the unrealistic perceptions and irrational fears that armed conflicts and perceived threats can induce.[5] Emotional thought involves sudden, vivid impressions, illogical connections, and categorical conclusions.[6] Public opinion polling has shown not only that presidential approval ratings can improve when military action is taken,[7] but also that support for the right to report on security matters may decline as war tensions rise.[8]

If First Amendment value commitments shift during a war and if courts should, as Vincent Blasi has contended, develop methodologies and doctrines "consciously designed to counteract the unusual social dynamics that characterize such periods," then attention should be given to the standards that are created and the quality of reasoning that is used in such cases.[9] The "Father of the Constitution," James Madison, had serious doubts about the ability of written guarantees of rights to withstand the pressures generated in times of crisis, but he came to believe that giving expression an absolute protection from government interference was the best solution. History has supported his concerns about hazardous emotions, but the courts have not always embraced his understanding of the First Amendment.

I.

Every nation has a constitution, a written or unwritten way of distributing sovereign power. Where the concept of constitutionalism has any meaning, it represents limited as opposed to arbitrary government. "The government of the United States has been emphatically termed a government of laws, and not of men," wrote Chief Justice John Marshall in *Marbury v. Madison.* "It will certainly cease to deserve this high appellation, if the laws furnish no remedy for the violation of a vested legal right."[10] The United States Constitution is not an ordinary law passed by a legislative majority but is rather the highest law, one that had to be ratified by a supermajority of the states.[11] Article 6 refers to the document as "the supreme law of the land," and Article 5 makes it difficult to amend. The preamble identifies "the people" as the ultimate source of power and says that two of the purposes for the Constitution being established were to "provide for the common defense" and to "secure the blessings of liberty to ourselves and our posterity."

If the common defense can cancel out First Amendment freedoms, then the blessings of liberty are not secured. As one writer has observed, "The philosophical difficulties in comparing the value of free speech versus the need for public safety are not entirely different in kind from the difficulties of comparing the intrinsic worth of wheat versus the intrinsic worth of shoes."[12] Both national security and civil liberties should be preserved if the constitutional mandate is to be respected. "The very purpose of a Bill of Rights," said Justice Robert Jackson in one of his Supreme Court opinions, "was to withdraw certain subjects from the vicissitudes of political controversy, to place them beyond the reach of majorities and officials and to establish them as legal principles to be applied by the courts." Enforcing those rights, he said, was to adhere "to individual freedom of mind in preference to officially disciplined uniformity for which history indicates a disappointing and disastrous end."[13]

Officially disciplined uniformity has been accepted for soldiers.[14] "There is nothing in the Constitution that disables a military commander from acting to avert what he perceives to be a clear danger to the loyalty, discipline, or morale of troops on the base under his command," Justice Potter Stewart wrote in a 1976 Supreme Court opinion.[15] Military restrictions have prevented members of the armed forces from speaking their minds to the news media and have limited what mass communication could reach them.[16] During World War II, for instance, the War Department authorized commanding officers to censor black newspapers in order to prevent racial unrest among soldiers.[17] During the Vietnam War, military censors did not allow the showing of the antiwar film *M*A*S*H* (1970) at army posts.[18] During the Gulf War, publications that offended Saudi beliefs were prohibited, and military personnel were given a list of "sensitive subjects" to be avoided.[19] Pool reporters usually were allowed to talk to soldiers only in the presence of a military public affairs officer.[20] A soldier who complained about unfair treatment and desert conditions in a series of letters to his hometown weekly in Michigan was ordered to submit future letters for approval by his base commander in Saudi Arabia. He did not obey the order. "Regardless of the interviews given, we are not all happy to be here, nor did we all expect to be here," Dick Runels wrote in one of his letters. "And we can't wait to get home."[21] In 1996 reporters were told that if they were "embedded" with U.S. troops in Bosnia for more than twenty-four hours, then they needed specific permission to quote the soldiers, and were to consider everything they heard and saw as being "on background." The rule was imposed after a *Wall Street Journal* reporter quoted an army colonel telling two African-American soldiers that Croatians were racists.[22]

The freedom of periodicals published by the armed forces themselves has depended largely on the tolerance levels of officers, but criticism of leaders has rarely been allowed in the military press.[23] Attempts to speak out almost anywhere could be regarded as a violation. During World War II, for example, Army Regulation 380-5, "Safeguarding Military Information," required authorization for disclosing information "which, although not endangering the national security, would be prejudicial to the interests of prestige of the nation, any governmental activity, or any individual or would cause administrative embarrassment or difficulty."[24] Soldiers leaving combat zones were warned to be silent for unlikely reasons. "They have been instructed not to talk about military operations at the time their leaves are granted but many of them do talk, nevertheless," complained an Office of Censorship official in 1943. "Frequently they tell many things that the enemy wants to know and that an espionage agent will learn if the interviews are printed just as they come from the lips of service men." The official, Frank C. Clough, who was on leave from the *Gazette* in Emporia, Kansas, insisted that enemy agents were prepared to obtain vital battlefield information "by the sedulous reading of newspapers" and noted that his agency's voluntary self-censorship code for journalists in the United States "asks that interviews with service men or civilians from zones of combat be submitted before publication to the Office of Censorship or the appropriate Army or Navy public relations officer."[25]

A more probable explanation for the cumbersome and unrealistic attempts to censor soldiers is fear that their experiences and opinions will anger and embarrass their superiors, but the news media themselves can be wary enough to use self-censorship. When a peacetime draft was instituted in 1940, for example, poorly operated camps began filling up with disgruntled soldiers who wanted to tell their stories but who had to be careful. *Life* magazine, one of the few news organizations to grapple with the issue, published an exposé that detailed serious shortcomings in leadership, training, and equipment. The magazine took the precaution of not naming the camp the reporter visited or the soldiers he quoted. "The papers are always talking about how good the morale is and how ready the Army is for battle," said one of the hundreds of privates interviewed. "The hell it is! Why don't they ask us?" The press had been reluctant to reveal the problems, *Life* observed, and "the soldiers feel their complaints are met by a conspiracy of silence."[26] A *New York Times* reporter wrote an account of the low Army morale, but his editors, finding the conclusions ominous, sent it to the War Department instead of publishing it.[27]

Soldiers who cooperated with military authorities could be shockingly mistreated. During World War II the United States produced tons of poison gas. The weapons were not used, but were tested on an estimated sixty thousand soldiers and sailors. Approximately four thousand of them were subjected to severe exposures and were sworn to secrecy. The men were thus forced to suffer in silence and did not receive proper monitoring and medical care.[28]

Journalists took into account the wishes of the military during "the good war," but their willingness to cooperate was abused. "Reports of Group editors show that some individual Army officers are feeling their oats and trying to suppress stories quite

Figure 3.1   *Office of Government Reports poster by Schlaikjer (1944). Courtesy of National Archives.*

without warrant so far as the public interest is concerned," said an item in the confidential newsletter for Gannett Newspapers employees early in 1941. "One case was the story of a soldier at an armory whose hand had been injured. The officer forbade its publication—but the newspaper published it just the same." The newsletter item then showed how soldiers could have trouble when their complaints reached the press. " 'From what I learn, commanding officers at various camps are taking it upon themselves to intimidate the boys against writing anything unfavorable,' " John Bowen, a Gannett journalist, was quoted as saying. Bowen cited the example of publishing a letter from the son of his "ad alley" foreman and then learning the young man had been threatened with punishment. " 'His father was much disturbed as the boy was in line for advancement,' " Bowen said. " 'I am waiting to see the outcome of the case.' "[29]

High-ranking soldiers themselves frequently have been disciplined for making logical assessments that conflicted with standard policy. The cases have included Colonel Billy Mitchell being suspended in 1925 for asserting that air power would be a major factor in future wars; General Douglas MacArthur being relieved of his command in Korea in 1951 after complaining to the press about the inability of United Nations forces to fight under the military constraints being imposed; and Vice Admiral Hyman G. Rickover twice being passed over for promotion because of his championing of the capabilities of nuclear-powered submarines.[30] In 1931 General Smedley D. Butler was arrested and ordered court-martialed by President Herbert Hoover for making a speech expressing doubt about the willingness of some "mad-dog" nations to follow disarmament agreements. Butler's specific offense was repeating a well-supported story that Italian Prime Minister Benito Mussolini had run over a child while speeding through the Italian countryside in his automobile and had not bothered to slow down. Secretary of State Henry Stimson made a formal apology to Mussolini, but public pressure forced a negotiated settlement in which Butler merely provided a letter of repentance and received a reprimand.[31] As the Gulf War was being planned in September 1990, Defense Secretary Dick Cheney fired the Air Force Chief of Staff, General Michael J. Dugan, after he spoke frankly to reporters about the option of a heavy bombing of Baghdad that would decapitate the Iraqi leadership. Dugan's arguments in favor of relying on air superiority had been rejected in private by officials who wanted more time for diplomacy and by General Colin Powell, the Chairman of the Joint Chiefs of Staff, an Army man who backed ground combat that would showcase his branch of the military services.[32]

Even trying to cooperate with the military and to denounce the wartime press can be risky for someone in the armed forces. In 1952, in accordance with Army rules requiring review of writings for deletion of classified material, Lieutenant Colonel Melvin B. Voorhees submitted a book manuscript on his experiences as the Eighth Army's chief censor in Korea. Military censors, working with vague and conflicting standards, delayed clearance by objecting to unclassified criticism, particularly of General Douglas MacArthur, who had been removed from his command a year earlier. The book, which mentioned some weaknesses of censors while portraying war reporters as ignorant and irresponsible, asserted that the general had broken a news blackout and possibly tipped off the enemy by issuing a communiqué announcing an imminent offensive and that a military censor had improperly passed it rather than oppose MacArthur. Unable to satisfy his own censors after protracted discussions, Voorhees told them he was going ahead with the publication. Although General Mathew Ridgway, who was commanding the Eighth Army in United Nations operations, had recognized the problem by asking MacArthur not to announce offensives, Voorhees was court-martialed, convicted of violating regulations, and sentenced to dismissal. The U.S. Court of Military Appeals affirmed the sentence, but on the "technical" basis of his having failed to obtain clearance before submitting two articles on the book to the New York *Journal-American*. The articles, which were mailed to censors the day before they were mailed to the paper with a note saying they had to be cleared, were not published and had no classified information.[33]

Such episodes deprive individuals of their ability to contribute to public debate and discourage the kind of critical thinking that a modern military requires;[34] however, the Supreme Court has regarded individuals subject to the Uniform Code of Military Justice as less protected than other citizens in expressing their opinions. In *Parker v. Levy*, for instance, the justices in 1974 upheld by a five-to-three vote the court-martial conviction of a doctor who told his patients that black soldiers should not serve in Vietnam and who described the Special Forces as murderers of women and children. "The fundamental necessity for obedience, and the consequent necessity for imposition of discipline, may render permissible within the military that which would be constitutionally impermissible outside it," said a majority opinion by Justice William H. Rehnquist that showed more interest in prerevolutionary British military antecedents than the United States Constitution.[35] In dissents that objected to the use of the code's "conduct unbecoming an officer and gentleman" language to punish the defendant, Justice Potter Stewart found the wording unconstitutionally vague, and Justice William O. Douglas observed that there were "no exempt classes" in First Amendment protection and that in a society "where diversities are supposed to flourish it never could be 'unbecoming' to express one's views, even on the most controversial public issue."[36]

The *Parker* opinion has been cited in later rulings as precedent for the doctrine that the military's need for uniformity outweighs First Amendment rights. In one case, the Supreme Court went as far as ruling against an orthodox Jew and rabbi who argued that his freedom to exercise his religious beliefs was infringed by being ordered not to wear a yarmulke while on duty as a commissioned officer in the Air Force.[37] In a case that demonstrated the gap between the rights of military personnel and civilians, the U.S. Army Court of Military Review in 1991 upheld the conviction of a private who was convicted of blowing his nose on the American flag while part of a flag-raising detail. The defendant's punishments included confinement for four months and a bad-conduct discharge. The court distinguished the case from Supreme Court precedent allowing such expressive conduct under the First Amendment by stating that military discipline is a compelling government interest.[38]

Court opinions otherwise have contributed to the confusion over when, if ever, personal safety or national security rationales may be used to overturn the Bill of Rights. Courts have sometimes found reasons not to become involved, sometimes allowed repression, and sometimes objected too late to make any difference.[39] Examples of the Supreme Court's gyrations with the issue were provided by two Depression-era cases. In a 1931 decision involving naturalization and conscientious objector status,

Justice George Sutherland, who was known for his bellicose approach to foreign policy, wrote that "the war power, when necessity calls for its exercise, tolerates no qualifications or limitations, unless found in the Constitution." Dicta later in the same paragraph, however, ignoring the limitations found in the First Amendment, stated that "freedom of speech may, by act of Congress, be curtailed or denied so that the morale of the people and the spirit of the army may not be broken by seditious utterances" and "freedom of the press curtailed to preserve our military plans and movements from the knowledge of the enemy." Such drastic powers, he said, were not acceptable during peace, but could be "exercised to meet the emergencies of war."[40] Three years later, in a case dealing with the contract clause and economic emergency, the high court issued an opinion saying that although the government could make a supreme effort to preserve the nation, emergencies do not create war powers. "But even the war power does not remove constitutional limitations safeguarding essential liberties," Chief Justice Charles Evans Hughes wrote. "When the provisions of the Constitution, in grant or restriction, are specific, so particularized as not to admit of construction, no question is presented."[41] Hughes thus denied that the Constitution could be altered in an emergency, but said that infringements of rights might be allowed if a right can be subjected to interpretation.

Hughes had displayed remarkable interpretive legerdemain in the 1931 *Near v. Minnesota* case, the Court's most important ruling supporting the proposition that in some cases government censorship does not violate the press clause of the First Amendment. Writing for the majority that a state law designed to suppress "nuisance" publications was an unconstitutional prior restraint, the chief justice said that the "chief purpose" of the press clause was to prevent censorship prior to publication and quoted William Blackstone's *Commentaries on the Laws of England* as saying that freedom of the press meant no prior restraint, but not freedom from punishment after publication. Hughes then quoted a sentence of James Madison as saying that the United States, in contrast to Britain, had a constitution that made freedom of the press " 'exempt' " from both executive and legislative restraint. Hughes, already in trouble because he was arguing that prior restraint was sometimes justified, conveniently left off the end of Madison's sentence, which said, "this exemption, to be effectual, must be an exemption, not only from the previous inspection of licensers, but from the subsequent penalty of laws." Unable to rely on the man he described as "the leading spirit in the preparation of the First Amendment," Hughes quickly shifted to a prudential approach to justify exceptions to the rule against prior restraint. The list of exceptions Hughes drew up began with safety and national security. "No one would question but that a government might prevent actual obstruction to its recruiting service or the publication of the sailing dates of transports or the number and location of troops," he wrote.[42]

The assumption that government should use prior restraint in such situations can, in fact, be questioned. As long as troop movements can be observed by many people or by technological means, censorship may not be as useful as making better preparations for attacks. The *Near* court did not choose to rely on the military's legitimate right to conceal plans and common sense to change them if they were, in fact, no longer secrets, as the possession of the information by journalists would indicate. When Major General Nelson A. Miles found that the plans for his expedition to

Figure 3.2 *In Near v. Minnesota (1931), the Supreme Court suggested that the government could impose prior restraints in some cases such as publication of the sailing times of troop ships or the number and location of soldiers. Office of Government Reports poster by Siebel (1942). Courtesy of National Archives.*

Puerto Rico in 1898 had been publicized, he decided to land at another point, since "it is always advisable not to do what your enemy expects you to do."[43] Nor, of course, did the *Near* court choose to rely on the patriotism and cooperation of the press, as the government's Committee on Public Information (CPI) had done during World War I. The CPI issued a list of "specific requests" that asked the press in the United States not to publish sensitive military information, including the number and location of troops and the location and sailing times of ships. The guidelines did not relieve the press of censorship at the front, but did test the ability of the press at home to avoid publications that could conceivably cost lives. In a report to the president at the end of the war, the chairman of the CPI, George Creel, expressed his satisfaction with a system that avoided laws and penalties, saying that some violations naturally occurred, "but as it was realized that the requests of Government were concerned with human lives and national hopes, as it was driven home that the passing satisfaction of a news item might endanger a transport or a troop train, the voluntary censorship grew in strength and certainty." Although some officials, including President Wilson, thought that a system of cooperation would fail, Creel, a former editor, recognized that domestic censorship would have too much potential for suppression and would be too costly, irritating, and difficult to enforce.[44]

The *Near* opinion thus said, contrary to even the most oligarchical of eighteenth-century English legal commentators, Sir William Blackstone, that prior restraint could sometimes be used by government. Blackstone, who accepted monarchy and a national religion, but not popular sovereignty or even truthful statements criticizing government, defined press freedom as only freedom from prior restraint and not freedom from subsequent punishment for "dangerous or offensive" writings at odds with "the preservation of peace and good order."[45] Blackstone's definition, which had evolved from centuries of British repression of opinion, was angrily rejected by the American libertarians who sought a Bill of Rights.[46] When Blackstonian logic on press freedom was used as a rationale for the Sedition Act of 1798, James Madison denounced the definition as a "mockery" that "can never be admitted to be the American idea of it: since a law inflicting penalties on printed publications, would have a similar effect with a law authorizing a previous restraint on them." Exempting the press from prior restraints and subsequent penalties may allow journalistic abuses, he observed, but the possible problems were not as important as maintaining the successful tradition of questioning authority that had helped rouse the nation to independence and a new Constitution. Blackstone's Britain, in contrast, had some limitations on royal prerogative, but had a Parliament "unlimited in its power" that could control journalists. Madison concluded:

> In the United States, the case is altogether different. The people, not the government, possess the absolute sovereignty. The legislature, no less than the executive, is under limitations of power. Encroachments are regarded as possible from the one, as well as from the other. Hence in the United States, the great and essential rights of the people are secured against legislative, as well as executive ambition. They are secured, not by laws paramount to prerogative; but by constitutions paramount to laws.[47]

Courts of later generations, however, did not always have ready access to eighteenth-century sources on intent. Not having any shortage of reasons to curtail the rights of expression, judges applied the readily available Blackstone in interpreting their state constitutions and said, as Blackstone did, that the "liberty" of the press was protected, but not its "licentiousness."[48] The New York Court of Appeals, for instance, had no difficulty upholding the conviction of the publisher of the weekly *Freiheit* for endangering the public peace by reprinting an anarchist essay advocating revolution and murder. The article, which happened to be printed on the same day President McKinley was shot by anarchist Leon Czolgosz, was, as the court noted, not directed to anyone in particular, did not urge the killing of any specific individual, and was not an actual breach of the peace. The court, however, used the Blackstonian formulation of press freedom and concluded that such publications "might naturally, as the history of the times shows, result in violence and murder." The guarantee of press freedom in the state's constitution, the court said, "does not deprive the state of the primary right of self-preservation."[49] In a 1907 case upholding a contempt judgment resulting from newspaper criticism of a Colorado court, the United States Supreme Court accepted the notion that the "main purpose" of state and federal press guarantees was to prevent prior restraints and not to eliminate subsequent punishments.[50] The assumption remained undisturbed in the *Near* opinion, which said that the press clause "has meant, principally although not exclusively, immunity from previous restraints" and that "punishment for the abuse of the liberty accorded to the press is essential to the protection of the public."[51]

The Supreme Court's acceptance of Blackstonian logic as the basis of the press clause in *Near* rested on little or no historical foundation and allowed not only subsequent punishment but also exceptions to the rule against prior restraint. The justices were either unfamiliar with the original absolutism of the press clause articulated by Madison and others or were unwilling to recognize it. The Court did not explain why prior restraint would have been the central fear of those demanding the press guarantee if censorship before publication had not existed or been an issue in the lifetimes of most Americans.[52] This point was made, oddly enough, by the Supreme Court itself in an opinion issued five years after the *Near* decision. "It is impossible to concede that by the words 'freedom of the press' the framers of the amendment intended to adopt merely the narrow view then reflected by the law of England that such freedom consisted only in immunity from previous censorship," wrote Justice George Sutherland, "for this abuse had then permanently disappeared from English practice."[53]

Despite the lack of historical authority for the *Near* conclusions, however, later courts and commentators have regularly referred back to the case to support the proposition that censorship can be employed to protect the nation as a whole, as well as the individuals in its armed forces and intelligence agencies.[54] The rule against prior restraint, in fact, has been struck so hard and so many times since *Near* that scholars have begun to wonder if the "no prior restraint" bedrock of First Amendment theory has broken down into shifting sand. If so, then an already diminished press clause can be subjected to newer and even narrower readings by courts and legal scholars.[55] The original understanding that rejected both prior restraints and subsequent penalties by government could be completely lost to the ravages of time and fear.

Of course, as demonstrated by the *Near* dictum that "[n]o one would question" a wartime exception to the rule against prior restraint, the perceived conflict between liberty and security does not have to be wrongly resolved solely by vacuous interpretations of the original meaning of the press clause and the vicissitudes that follow.[56] Supposed solutions can also be found by recognizing survival as a higher law than the Constitution. The press cannot "violate the legitimate rights of Americans to survive," Henry Mark Holzer has asserted. "In other words, there is no right to violate a right."[57] When courts see a need to balance survival against liberty, freedom of the press can seem pitifully abstract, unimportant, and perhaps even self-serving. Justice Jackson, for instance, warned his Supreme Court colleagues in 1949 that unless they tempered their logic on freedom of expression with "a little practical wisdom," they risked converting the Bill of Rights into "a suicide pact."[58] Such balancing can automatically give additional weight to freedom of expression as a "preferred" right or can be done on a case-by-case basis, a method that seems to rest on judges' somewhat unpredictable ideas of what is "prudent" in a given situation.[59] Philip Bobbitt has written:

> Prudential argument is constitutional argument which is actuated by the political and economic circumstances surrounding the decision. Thus prudentialists generally hold that in times of national emergency even the plainest of constitutional limitation can be ignored. Perhaps others share that belief; but the prudentialist makes it a legitimate, legal argument, fits it into opinions, and uses it as the purpose for doctrines, and it is this that makes him interesting to us.[60]

The Supreme Court's most trenchant critic of the prudential balancing approach, Justice Hugo Black, insisted that balancing had the effect of changing a government of limited powers into one that could do anything that it believed "reasonable." The framers, Black said, had already done all the balancing that was needed and had settled questions of conflicting values in ways that should not be changed without constitutional amendment. "They appreciated the risks involved and they decided that certain rights should be guaranteed regardless of these risks," he wrote. "Courts have neither the right nor the power to review this original decision of the Framers and to attempt to make a different evaluation of the importance of the rights granted in the Constitution." The prudential approach, he thought, was actually more perilous than an unqualified freedom of expression because "in times of emergency and stress it gives Government the power to do what it thinks necessary to protect itself, regardless of the rights of individuals." Black maintained that "the balancing approach to basic individual liberties assumes to legislators and judges more power than either the Framers or I myself believe should be entrusted, without limitation, to any man or any group of men."[61]

Black, perhaps more than any Supreme Court justice, based his views on reading the Constitution and studying eighteenth-century history. What he found when he read the writings and speeches of James Madison was a First Amendment absolutist who, in introducing and later defending the Bill of Rights, stated that the government would have no power or jurisdiction over the press.[62] Frustrated with the court's First Amendment rulings, Black turned to the law review format, where he used historical evidence to contend that the need for self-preservation did not cancel out the need for liberty. Indeed, as a First Amendment absolutist, he was fond of the textual argument that "no law" meant "no law."[63] The country should do "whatever is necessary" to preserve itself, he stated emphatically. "But," he added, "the question is:

preserve what? And how?" Black wanted the United States "preserved as the kind of Government it was intended to be" and not allowed to become a country "where my words could be censored by government." Government could respond to actions but could not regulate words, he believed, since there was not "*any* halfway ground if you enforce the protections of the First Amendment." Saying that Americans should answer rather than fear alien ideologies, he rejected the court's twentieth-century rationales for suppressing radical expression and stated that anyone had a right to talk.[64] Black steadfastly repudiated the view that there were no absolute prohibitions in the Constitution, that the guarantees in the Bill of Rights had to "compete" for survival against the general powers expressly granted to Congress, "and that all constitutional problems are questions of reasonableness, proximity, and degree."[65]

Basic freedoms are most likely to suffer in times of unresolved social and political tensions.[66] When the United States has been in turmoil, reasoning on rights has been strained past the limits of logic and historical accuracy. The First Amendment was not written to be rewritten by the fears or even common sense rationales of judges. "Among the many objects to which a wise and free people find it necessary to direct their attention, that of providing for their *safety* seems to be the first," wrote John Jay in the *Federalist*. "The *safety* of the people doubtless has relation to a great variety of circumstances and considerations, and consequently affords great latitude to those who wish to define it precisely and comprehensively." The long and inglorious history of defining away civil liberties in times of conflict is not surprising, but it has been unconstitutional, unjust, and unnecessary. In times of war or international crisis, each of the three branches of government has failed to protect the absolute freedom from government interference that the Constitution provided for the press. "Safety from external danger is the most powerful director of national conduct," Alexander Hamilton observed in the *Federalist*. "Even the ardent love of liberty will, after a time, give way to its dictates."[67]

II.

Rationales for suspending the Constitution can go well beyond assertions of necessity and reach the realm of fantasy. Americans have often succumbed to conspiracy theories asserting that the country is being threatened by the plots of powerful, ruthless enemies, a phenomenon that has been described as the "paranoid style" of American politics.[68] This mode of thinking requires not only a supporting cast of successive foreign and domestic archvillains, but also courts and legislatures that fall into a pattern of overreacting to fears and balancing away the rights of those whose statements of fact or opinion are regarded as beneath the protection of the Constitution. Explanations for, in effect, finding the Constitution unconstitutional have not been models of reasoned discourse. The process often begins with those who would restrict expression assuming strong "third-person" effects. They see "me" and "you" as largely immune from any pernicious influence of mass communication, but overestimate how "they" will respond.[69] Roscoe Pound, the eminent Harvard law professor, wrote in 1915 that free expression of political opinions was an instrument of social progress, but might have to be restricted where and when it could turn ignorant and economically deprived urban masses into dangerous mobs. Societal interests, he wrote in the *Harvard Law Review*, "may or may seem to require repression of forms of belief which threaten to overturn vital social institutions or to weaken the power of the state." In *Free Speech for Radicals*, published in 1916, Theodore Schroeder argued that expression should not "be penalized merely on the basis of a jury speculation about the prospective psychological tendency of the idea upon a hypothetical future reader."[70] Officials, however, may lack the necessary composure in the midst of a crisis and may be inclined to imagine the worst. During the debate on the Sedition Act of 1918, for instance, a senator spoke of America's immigrant communities as "the ripest soil that can be imagined for the dissemination of treasonable and semitreasonable utterances and propaganda."[71]

The justices of the Supreme Court allowed a frightened Congress to make laws suspending press freedom as they began deciding cases under the World War I statutes in 1919. In upholding the Espionage Act conviction of a Socialist party official for printing leaflets urging opposition to the draft, Justice Oliver Wendell Holmes Jr., wrote for a unanimous Court in *Schenck v. U.S.*: "When a nation is at war many things that might be said in time of peace are such a hindrance to its effort that their utterance will not be endured so long as men fight and that no Court could regard them as protected by any constitutional right." The question was one of "proximity and degree," Holmes said, and of "whether the words used are used in such circumstances and are of such a nature as to create a clear and present danger that they will bring about the substantive evils that Congress has a right to prevent." Making what would become a well-worn analogy in court decisions and public debate on press freedom, Holmes observed, "The most stringent protection of free speech would not protect a man in falsely shouting fire in a theatre and causing a panic."[72]

The theater analogy made little sense when applied to the Schenck leaflet, which presented opinions rather than false statements of fact and sought peaceful protest rather than mindless panic. The First Amendment protects freedom of speech and of the press, but not necessarily direct involvement in violence or coercion. False alarms, fraud, extortion, espionage, and many other traditional categories of wrongdoing may involve communication, but they are, in essence, distinct categories of illegal behavior and not simply the use of words to inform or to persuade the public.[73] A person who creates a panic with a false alarm could be sued by the victims or prosecuted by officials without freedom of expression being an issue. Freedom of expression was at issue in Schenck's publication of antiwar sentiments.

Nevertheless, seemingly sensible analogies to fire or similar dangers and the need to respond quickly and decisively without constitutional niceties soon became a staple of Supreme Court pronouncements on dissent. In another Espionage Act decision announced a week after *Schenck*, a unanimous court upheld the conviction of a pro-German publisher who opposed United States entry into World War I. Jacob Frohwerk had been fined and sentenced to ten years in prison for the "overt acts" of publishing twelve particular articles. The opinion Holmes wrote was similar to a number of later decisions by other justices in saying that the potential of a publication "to kindle a flame" was enough reason for government action.[74]

Later in 1919, however, Holmes and Justice Louis D. Brandeis began seriously questioning the court majority's bad tendency test for political heresy. After a number of libertarian scholars took him to task and he read books that condemned Civil War suppression and advocated absolute protection for opinion, Holmes began dissenting in the seditious libel cases that reached the Supreme Court.[75] In *Abrams et al. v. U.S.*, a Sedition Act case sustaining the conviction of a group of Russian-born radicals for the publication of an antiwar tirade, Holmes insisted that exceptions to the First Amendment were only for "the emergency that makes it immediately dangerous to leave the correction of evil counsels to time." Observing that "the surreptitious publishing of a silly leaflet by an unknown man" such as Abrams was not an immediate danger, Holmes said he wanted a test that would leave even "opinions that we loathe and believe to be fraught with death" to the marketplace of ideas "unless they so imminently threaten immediate interference with the lawful and pressing purposes of the law that an immediate check is required to save the country." Holmes denied the government's assertion that the First Amendment left the common law of seditious libel intact, but did not question the frequently repeated assertion of the Justice Department's brief that "every Government worthy of the name" has an inherent "power of self-preservation." Rejecting the fact that the First Amendment explicitly divested Congress of the authority to make laws abridging freedom of the press and ignoring the founders' conception of popular sovereignty, the government argued that "Congress is implicitly vested with power to enact legislation necessary in its judgment to preserve the form of government."[76]

The Supreme Court recognized something more than implicit power to violate the explicit commands of the Constitution in *Schaefer v. U.S.*, a 1920 Espionage Act case brought against Philadelphia journalists accused of publishing false and disloyal German-language articles. Justice Joseph McKenna wrote that the provisions of the statute were directed against the "conduct" of speech or writing that harmed military morale or obstructed recruitment. Relying on the court's recently crafted precedents, he had no difficulty concluding that the First Amendment simply did not hold up against the constitutional power of the government to declare and wage war. Arguing free speech rights, McKenna said, made a "curious spectacle" in which the Constitution was "invoked to justify the activities of anarchy or of the enemies of the United States, and by a strange perversion of its precepts it was adduced against itself." In a dissent joined by Holmes, Justice Brandeis said that the constitutional declaration protecting free expression was "to be the same in peace and in war" and could not be left to the mercy of "an intolerant majority, swayed by passion or by fear."[77]

The Espionage Act provided a reactionary legal system with an opportunity to strike at the specter of socialism. In 1912, the year Socialist candidate Eugene V. Debs received nearly nine hundred thousand of the fifteen million votes cast for president, American socialists had approximately twelve hundred elected officials and 323 publications. By the end of the war, socialism was in deep decline and split into several camps, many of its publications were out of business, and about a third of the Socialists' National Executive Committee was in jail.[78] Debs, who was sentenced to ten years for a speech saying that the working class was furnishing the corpses for a master class war, received 917,799 votes for president while behind bars in 1920. In a Supreme Court opinion written before his partial conversion on the First Amendment, Justice Holmes simply said Debs had been found to have had the requisite intent to state opinions with the "natural tendency and reasonably probable effect" of obstructing the war effort.[79] When the Supreme Court later upheld the conviction of several Socialists who distributed a four-page leaflet contending that the United States had economic motives for entering the war, Brandeis, in a dissent with Holmes, questioned the court majority's claims that the opinions expressed were false as a matter of common knowledge and that the defendants' "real purpose" was to hamper the military and not to gain converts to socialism as they had asserted.[80] Brandeis wrote that the government had not proven falsity, intent, or a clear and present danger and that a conclusion of President Wilson's own scholarly work was that capitalists and manufacturers controlled American politics.[81]

Holmes and Brandeis were, in effect, arguing that expression loses protection as it becomes more persuasive;[82] they were a relatively tolerant minority in the nation's legal community, where, in the heat of the nation's war fever and postwar nativism, strikingly loose interpretations of the Constitution predominated.[83] Claiming that "plenary power was given to Congress to wage war," Charles Evans Hughes told the American Bar Association, "Self-preservation is the first law of national life and the constitution itself provides the necessary powers in order to defend and preserve the United States." He said that Congress could pass "all laws which shall be necessary and proper" for carrying out its war power. "That power explicitly conferred and absolutely essential to the safety of the Nation," he said, "is not destroyed or impaired by any later provision of the constitution or by any one of the amendments." In a 1918 law review article, Henry J. Fletcher wrote that in providing for the suspension of the writ of *habeas corpus* the Constitution allowed for the temporary suspension of civil liberties. He thought that necessity demanded essentially absolute government power to subordinate individual rights to the safety of the state. "This is autocracy's supreme merit," Fletcher said, without a trace of irony.[84]

Attempts to identify a solid legal basis for wartime alterations in the First Amendment made ample use of sophistry, if not outright deception. The CPI, for instance, printed nearly two hundred thousand copies of its *War Cyclopedia* to inform the public on subjects ranging from potato production to presidential powers. Compiled by a group of scholars and distributed to schools and public speakers, the book used Lincoln quotations and out-of-context statements from the *Federalist* to convey the impression that the government could assume unlimited authority over individual rights when the country was fighting other nations.[85] The entry on freedom of the press began by noting that the First Amendment forbids Congress to make any law abridging press freedom, but then said that press freedom in wartime rested "largely with the discretion of Congress." The authority, the book explained matter-of-factly, came from the principle of majority rule and the power granted Congress to "pass all laws that are 'necessary and proper' to prosecute successfully a war which it has declared." Probably written by one of the book's three editors, Edward S. Corwin of Princeton University, the discussion of press freedom asserted that "of course, Congress may penalize publications which are calculated to stir up sedition, to obstruct the carrying out of the laws, or to 'give aid and comfort to the enemy' (which is treason)."[86]

In the fury of the war and the Red Scare that followed, Corwin and other scholars failed to make careful, dispassionate readings of some of the most critical protections in the Constitution.[87] The *War Cyclopedia* truncated the Constitution's definition of treason, which requires an "overt act" (Article 3). Other provisions were also treated in cavalier fashion. Congress can make "necessary and proper" laws for carrying out the powers listed in Section 8 of Article 1, but those powers do not include control of the press or any general authority to prosecute a war beyond the powers specified. Even as Chief Justice John Marshall declared in the Supreme Court's landmark *McCulloch v. Maryland* opinion that some powers could be implied from the necessary and proper clause, he stated that the actions had to follow the "letter and spirit of the constitution" and be ones "which are not prohibited."[88] Laws abridging press freedom are expressly prohibited by the First Amendment. In asserting that "of course" seditious publications were unprotected, the *War Cyclopedia* found an exception to the press clause that is not made in the Constitution.

Corwin did, however, soon publish a sketchy, eight-page *Yale Law Journal* article purporting to show that the First Amendment did not prohibit punishments for criticisms of the government and that, in any event, the complications and dangers of modern life required legislators to place the common welfare above individual rights. He said that "the cause of freedom of speech and press is largely in the custody of legislative majorities and of juries" and that Congress could make suppressive laws "necessary and proper" for protecting national interests.[89] Prior to the war, Corwin had begun propagating poorly conceived arguments to the effect that the Constitution had to mean different things at different times and answer to the purpose of the hour. Contrary to the position of Madison, Hamilton, Jefferson, and Marshall, as well as the most prominent nineteenth-century legal scholars, Corwin asserted that constitutional decisions should rely on judicial philosophies rather than the document's text and history. He promulgated muddled notions of "higher law" that he thought stood above a written Constitution.[90]

Corwin's opinions were nevertheless typical of the unsupported conclusions being reached in the legal community.[91] In his 1918 book *The Army and the Law*, Garrard Glenn maintained that the powers of the executive and of Congress grew in wartime while the rights of citizens shrank. The Espionage Act and other war measures passed by Congress, he wrote, rested on a principle "older than written constitutions," which was "that the rights of the individual must yield to those of the State in the time of the State's peril from the public enemy." Discussing the founders' intent regarding expression, W. R. Vance, dean of the University of Minnesota Law School, said it was "inconceivable that they intended to deprive the government of powers to preserve itself by making seditious utterances criminal offenses." He admitted that definitions of sedition were vague, but he thought that juries would reject prosecutions "violating the public sense of justice and freedom." Writing in the *Harvard Law Review* as a member of its editorial board, law student Day Kimball presented similar views about "the state's right of self-protection," about how "all lines are hard to draw," and about why "public opinion in this matter should rule" in the form of juries. Rather than rely on the "mere interpretation of the language employed" in the First Amendment, he said, it was necessary "for Congress to judge, in the light of existing conditions, whether of war or peace, as to the kind and amount of repression necessary."[92]

Relying on current opinion rather than the Constitution, however, can mean that liberty is subject to the emotions of the day in Congress and the courts. When the *Abrams v. U.S.* defendants were prosecuted under the Sedition Act, they not only were charged with violating a federal statute passed in a fit of wartime hysteria, but were also denied a fair trial. The judge, Henry D. Clayton Jr., wore a black armband in honor of his brother who had been killed by a German bomb in France. Clayton let the defendants know that he despised alien radicals like them and led the jury to a guilty verdict as if working for the prosecution. The effort may have been unnecessary, however. The United States attorney and the Bureau of Investigation screened jurors in Espionage Act and Sedition Act cases to eliminate any who might be sympathetic to the accused.[93] Before sentencing the defendants to as many as twenty years in a federal penitentiary, Clayton conducted a two-hour diatribe on Americanism and concluded that the congressional statute being used was justified by the "inherent right of self-defense."[94]

One of the more ironic cases of feelings being blurted from the bench came after copies of the film *The Spirit of '76* were seized by Los Angeles officials and the producer, Robert Goldstein, was arrested. Goldstein was charged with stirring up hatred of an ally in violation of Espionage Act provisions against arousing insubordination and refusal of duty. Scenes in the movie showed a British soldier holding up a baby on the point of his bayonet and others killing women and carrying off girls, a dramatization of past atrocities that was uncomfortably close to depictions of the enemy in the anti-German films of World War I. Ruling on a motion for the return of the reels, a district court judge, Benjamin F. Bledsoe, said he was "in no mood to weigh the financial losses" and "in no mood, either, particularly after having listened to the testimony of this man Goldstein, to consider the suggestion that the film be returned." The judge insisted that *The Spirit of '76* was sowing dissension and weakening confidence in an ally. "That which in ordinary times might be clearly permissible, or even commendable, in this hour of national emergency, effort, and peril, may be as clearly treasonable, and therefore properly subject to review and repression," Bledsoe said. "The constitutional guaranty of 'free speech' carries with it no right to subvert the purposes and destiny of the nation."[95] In a decision affirmed by the court of appeals, Goldstein was fined ten thousand dollars and sentenced to ten years in a federal penitentiary.[96] President Wilson commuted the sentence after the war, but Goldstein's production company went into bankruptcy.[97]

John H. Wigmore, a brilliant scholar on leave from Northwestern University to serve in the Judge Advocate General's Office in Washington during the war, took the idea of wartime transformations of the Constitution a step further. He wrote a visceral law journal article on the *Abrams* case, referring to the convicted antiwar pamphleteers as "Abrams and his band of alien parasites" and denouncing the dissent of his friend Oliver Wendell Holmes Jr. as blind to the dangers the country encountered during the war. The "moral right" of the majority to wage a war, Wigmore reasoned, was enough not only to justify federal legislation outlawing dissent, but also to justify physical violence against dissenters. If a "disaffected citizen" should try to convince troops on their way to the front that the cause was bad and they should not be in it, then "the state would have a moral right to step promptly up to that man and smite him on the mouth," he said. "So would any well-meaning citizen, for that matter." Wigmore believed that "all principles of normal internal order may be suspended" when a nation committed itself to a foreign war. "As property may be taken and corporal service may be conscripted, so liberty of speech may be limited or suppressed, so far as deemed needful for the successful conduct of the war," he wrote, contending that liberties "become subordinated to the national right in the struggle for national life."[98]

Only rarely were such assumptions challenged in intellectual circles. Perhaps the most emphatic effort came from Harold Laski, an English political scientist and socialist who was lecturing at Harvard during the war, whose 1919 book *Authority in the Modern State* seems to have had a role in making Justice Holmes a dissenter in suppression cases.[99] Laski argued that the idea of government prerogative had been inherited from a "medieval worship of unity." The vices of centralized authority, he contended, were despotic general rules and the loss of "the saving grace of experiment." Freedom of thought, Laski said, had to be "absolute" because, despite the difficulties created by dissent, a citizen's greatest contribution to a society is to "allow his mind freely to exercise itself upon its problems." Consent based on suppression was not real consent, he pointed out, and if people, who have a "natural political inertia," were protesting, then government actions deserved reexamination.[100] In 1920, shortly after his book was published, Laski left Harvard to join the staff of the London School of Economics.

Harvard was not necessarily a hospitable place for reexamining wartime issues. For questioning misconduct by officials in *Abrams* and other cases and for arguing that the people have a First Amendment right to criticize government policy, Zechariah Chafee Jr., a Harvard law professor, was subjected to a federal investigation and to an academic inquisition conducted by conservative alumni of the Harvard Law School. The alumni received help from the Justice Department, but Chafee managed to keep his job with the assistance of the president of Harvard, A. Lawrence Lowell, who wanted to preserve academic freedom.[101] Chafee's work, especially his article "Freedom of Speech in War Time" in the June 1919 issue of *Harvard Law Review*, influenced the conversion of Justice Holmes, who met him when Laski invited both men to tea in the summer of 1919. Chafee contended that the First Amendment was "intended to wipe out the common law of sedition, and make further prosecutions for criticism of the government, without any incitement to law-breaking, forever impossible in the United States of America."[102]

In his book *Freedom of Speech*, published in 1920, Chafee maintained that a nation at war needed critics to cross-examine the government "so that the fundamental issues of the struggle may be clearly defined, and the war may not be diverted to improper ends, or conducted with an undue sacrifice of life and liberty, or prolonged after its just purposes are accomplished." Yet, although he repudiated Blackstone's definition of press freedom and condemned punishing statements with a remote tendency toward hindering a war effort, Chafee did not think the First Amendment protected incitements to illegal acts and concluded that the "clear and present danger" test of Justice Holmes marked a proper limit that was in accord with the Constitution. Chafee believed that the First Amendment had to be balanced against the war clauses of the Constitution, but that freedom of expression "ought to weigh very heavily in the scale." Stressing the "social interest in national safety," he said that censorship or punishment could be justified when words were "clearly liable to cause direct and dangerous interference with the conduct of the war." Thus, even America's foremost scholar on freedom of expression accepted government authority over the press if it could be justified as protecting the nation, a position he repeated in his book *Free Speech in the United States*, published in 1942.[103]

In the decades following World War I, a majority of the Supreme Court, without even offering evidence, continued to see the American public not as oppressive in patriotic zeal but rather as a veritable tinderbox for dissenting propaganda. "A single revolutionary spark may kindle a fire that, smouldering for a time, may burst into a sweeping and destructive conflagration," the high court said in its *Gitlow v. New York* decision in 1925. "It cannot be said that the state is acting arbitrarily or unreasonably when in the exercise of its judgment as to the measures necessary to protect the public peace and safety, it seeks to extinguish the spark without waiting until it has enkindled the flame or blazed into conflagration." The Court upheld Benjamin Gitlow's conviction under New York's criminal anarchy statute for publishing a pamphlet advocating the violent overthrow of government, pointedly rejecting the defense brief's comparison of the case to prosecutions under the English common law and the Sedition Act of 1798 as casting "no helpful light upon the questions here."[104] In a dissent with Brandeis that said that Gitlow's words had no chance of starting a conflagration and therefore should not be punished, Holmes reiterated his interpretation of the "clear and present danger" doctrine he had wrought. Denying that the pamphlet was an "incitement," Holmes said every idea is an incitement and might be acted upon. The only difference between expressing an opinion and an incitement, he thought, "is the speaker's enthusiasm for the result."[105]

During World War II, the Supreme Court was unwilling to repeat some of the excesses of World War I. When a rare Espionage Act case reached the justices in 1944, they signaled their reluctance to accept a broad reading of the law by overturning the conviction of a man who no doubt would have been prosecuted successfully twenty-five years earlier, a fascist sympathizer who had written three anti-Semitic pamphlets advocating internal racial war, abandonment of the Allies, and the occupation of America by foreign troops. Although the defendant admitted that he wanted soldiers to think about whether or not to fight, and some of the pamphlets were sent anonymously to military officers and the United States Infantry Association, the Court ruled five to four in *Hartzel v. U.S.* that the evidence was insufficient to show that he had acted "willfully," as the law required, to cause insubordination or to obstruct recruiting. The opinion by Justice Frank Murphy, who was known as a strong civil libertarian, concluded that without such evidence "an American citizen has the right to discuss these matters either by temperate reasoning or by immoderate and vicious invective without running afoul of the Espionage Act of 1917." Although the ruling may have reflected the relative lack of unresolved political tensions in World War II, Murphy made a point of noting Elmer Hartzel's long family history in the United States, his military service in World War I, his education, his work for investment firms, his publications in "reputable business and financial periodicals," and his lack of association with "any foreign or subversive organization."[106]

An isolated fascist with some credentials might be tolerated by five justices in 1944 and the use of the Espionage Act against dissenters fall into disfavor, but the Cold War soon provided circumstances deemed too combustible for freedom of expression. In 1951, by a six-to-two vote, the Supreme Court upheld the Smith Act convictions of Eugene Dennis and ten other Communist party leaders. "Overthrow of the Government by force and violence is certainly a substantial enough interest for the Government to limit speech," said Chief Justice Frederick Vinson's plurality opinion, which referred to the existence of an international Communist conspiracy. "Indeed, this is the ultimate value of any society, for if a society cannot protect its very structure from armed internal attack, it must follow that no subordinate value can be protected." Government did not have to wait for subversive action to occur, Vinson wrote, and the relative strength of the Communist movement was not an issue. "If the ingredients of the reaction are present," he said, "we cannot bind the Government to wait until the catalyst is added." Justice Black, one of two dissenters in the decision, wrote that the nation would have to wait for calmer times for the First Amendment to be restored. "Undoubtedly, a government policy of unfettered communication of ideas does entail dangers," he said. "To the Founders of this nation, however, the benefits derived from free expression were worth the risk."[107]

In the years following the *Dennis* opinion, federal courts cited the precedent at length, as lower-ranking Communists were convicted of violating the Smith Act. In one such case, *Frankfeld v. U.S.*, the defense argued to no avail that the statute gave the government an unlimited power to burn books Nazi-style and would apply to writings of Jefferson and a significant portion of the world's cultural heritage. The Fourth Circuit Court of Appeals, however, found "nothing in the Constitution or in any sound political theory" to prevent the government from taking action against the danger of Communist conspiracies and their teachings. "They are pregnant with potential evil, which, while hidden from view in normal times, is likely to assert itself as an irresistible force when some national crisis presents an opportunity for a putsch or a coup d'état," the opinion said.[108] Ironically, such cases occurred while the government was mounting a postwar campaign for press freedom and democratic principles in other nations. The defense of the United States Constitution was left largely in the hands of Communists, as even the American Civil Liberties Union struggled to respond effectively and remain united in the face of suppression.[109]

The Supreme Court's hysteria was not limited to a fleeting red scare. Eight years after the *Dennis* decision, the justices sustained the contempt conviction of Lloyd Barenblatt, an educator who refused to answer House Un-American Activities Committee questions about Communist activities at the University of Michigan. The defense brief argued that First Amendment freedoms were being violated by the committee's inhibiting effect on the expression of political dissent, on the right of the general public to be exposed to nonconformist views, and on academic freedom in universities. With reasoning reminiscent of the Federalist justifications for using the Sedition Act of 1798 against the Jeffersonian Republicans, the government argued that the Communist party was not a "normal political association" and that it had "unlawful aims" and "unlawful ideas." A majority of the justices agreed in *Barenblatt* that the Communist Party was not "just an ordinary political party from the standpoint of national security." Citing "the right of self-preservation, 'the ultimate value of any society,' " the Court's opinion concluded "that the balance between the individual and governmental interests here at stake must be struck in favor of the latter, and that therefore the provisions of the First Amendment have not been offended."[110]

Justice Black wrote in dissent that the First Amendment was being read as saying that it guaranteed basic rights unless " 'on balance the interest of the Government in stifling these freedoms is greater that the interest of the people in having them exercised.' " Saying there was a right to err politically and that a belief in freedom was only strengthened by being tested, he dismissed the Court's "unarticulated premise that this Nation's security hangs upon its power to punish people because of what they think, speak or write about, or because of those with whom they associate for political purposes." The Constitution had been written to prevent the loss of liberties in times of "high emotional excitement," he insisted, and assumed "that the common sense of the people and their attachment to their country will enable them, after free discussion, to withstand ideas that are wrong." The First Amendment, he said, meant "that the only constitutional way our Government can preserve itself is to leave its people the fullest possible freedom to praise, criticize or discuss, as they see fit, all government policies and to suggest, if they desire, that even its most fundamental postulates are bad and should be changed."[111]

The Supreme Court's self-preservation rationale, which was basically a Blackstonian "bad tendency" test, did not serve the nation well in the cases brought under federal statutes. Although the radicals who were charged were never a serious threat to the nation, they did manage to shred a real and vital part of the Constitution with the help of the three branches of the federal government. In accepting justifications that assumed dissent would have powerful effects on the public, the Supreme Court not only ignored Madison's opposition to the concept of seditious libel, but also rejected the precepts of his and America's most famous political essay, "The Federalist No. 10." In its discussion of how to control a "faction" working against the rights and interests of other citizens or the community, Madison said that "destroying the liberty which is essential to its existence" was "worse than the disease." He argued that "factious leaders may kindle a flame" in one place, but would be "unable to spread a general conflagration" elsewhere because of representative democracy's ability to work toward the general good. Abolishing liberty because it nourished faction, Madison said, was as much a folly as "to wish the annihilation of air, which is essential to animal life, because it imparts to fire its destructive agency."[112]

With the collapse of the Soviet Union, fears of its influence abated, and the United States emerged from the Cold War as an unusually safe and strong nation. Relying on a political system that had exhibited both long-term stability and flexibility, the country continued to have the world's oldest written national constitution, but federal courts had torn up its press guarantee by recognizing what they regarded as the higher law of survival. Rulings such as the Supreme Court's 1971 *Pentagon Papers* decision, which allowed publication of a classified history of the Vietnam War leaked to news organizations, were rare.[113] More court precedents had accumulated on the side of a misguided national security mentality that recognized a power for Congress to make laws abridging freedom of the press. In the 1980s, for instance, the Supreme Court cited the legislation creating the Central Intelligence Agency (CIA), along with concerns about the personal safety of sources and agents, in allowing the agency to conceal information about its harm to American citizens and to review the writings of its employees prior to publication whether they contain classified material or not.

The high court also let stand a ruling that a government employee who provides the press with mundane classified information without authorization can be sentenced to jail under the Espionage Act.[114]

III.

Even when jurists appear to have serious, solid reasons for denying First Amendment freedoms, their prudential safety justifications often turn out to be based on dishonesty or self-delusion. Two examples of the willingness of courts to sacrifice law, justice, and the actual well-being of the public to a specious survivalist mentality involved Robert Warren, who was attorney general of Wisconsin from 1969 until 1974, when he was appointed a federal district court judge. The first case arose in 1970 after four inept antiwar protesters detonated explosives at Sterling Hall on the University of Wisconsin campus in Madison in an attempt to destroy the Army Mathematics Research Center. Responding to outrage at the death of a young physics researcher who was working in the building in the middle of the night and to the damage to campus buildings, Attorney General Warren and his assistants tried unsuccessfully to learn the identities of the bombers from the editor of an underground paper, Mark Knops, who had received and printed a communiqué from the four men that did not include their names. Asserting a constitutional privilege of journalists to protect news sources in order to maintain a free flow of information to the public, Knops refused to answer grand jury questions and spent four months in jail for contempt before a federal judge allowed him to be released on a one-thousand-dollar bond.[115]

The Supreme Court of Wisconsin upheld the contempt finding, although the Federal Bureau of Investigation (FBI) had named the four suspects and placed them on its "Most Wanted" list shortly after the bombing. The court recognized the privilege Knops claimed but said that the judicial system's need to know the identities outweighed the journalist's rights. Stating that members of the public could not walk into public buildings without fear for their lives, the opinion maintained that "in a disorderly society such as we are currently experiencing it may well be appropriate to curtail in a very minor way the free flow of information, if such curtailment will serve the purpose of restoring an atmosphere in which all of our fundamental freedoms can flourish." The court thus took judicial notice of the political atmosphere in Madison but did not provide any convincing reason why the editor's testimony was necessary. "The mere fact that the culprits are still at large is nearly conclusive proof that the state does not know who they are," the opinion said, overlooking the fact that four named suspects were being pursued by authorities. The question was not so much who they were, but where they were. Knops told a reporter after his sentencing that he had no information that would help to solve the case, but he was determined to take a stand against law enforcement officials and politicians who despised him and his newspaper.[116]

Three of the four fugitives eventually were arrested and received prison sentences for their roles in a painful event that was a key episode in the beginning of the end of the New Left. What the state attorney general saw, however, was continued danger. Claiming that a larger conspiracy existed, Warren said that radicals were "developing a domestic Ho Chi Minh trail." U.S. Deputy Attorney General Richard Kleindienst had already spoken of the need for action against what he saw as organized subversion so insidious that activists "should be rounded up and put in a detention camp."[117] What historians showed years later, however, was massive plotting on the part of the federal government to disrupt the antiwar movement and the underground press through infiltration, dirty tricks, harassment, and violence.[118] Some of the many bombings and attempted bombings that took place during the Vietnam War years, including the Sterling Hall explosion, may have been carried out with the knowledge or assistance of undercover provocateurs intent on discrediting the dissidents.[119]

Concepts of press freedom can seem idealistic and impractical when safety and self-preservation appear to be at stake, and authorities may want someone to punish even if it means violating rights and acting irrationally. Yet, as another case involving Robert Warren suggests, even seemingly unassailable national security logic on secrecy may not appear so strong under closer examination. In 1979, five years after his appointment to the federal bench, Warren heard a case in which government lawyers, citing the prior restraint provisions of the Atomic Energy Act of 1954, asked him to stop the publication in *Progressive* magazine of an article dealing with the physics of the hydrogen bomb.[120] The author, Howard Morland, wanted to demonstrate the realities of the nuclear menace and the impossibility of defense against attack in an article that would have technical credibility and make an argument for disarmament.[121] "The point of my article is that the myth of secrecy is used to create an atmosphere in which public debate is stifled and public criticism of the weapons-production system is suppressed," Morland said in an affidavit submitted to the district court. "I hope to dramatically illustrate that thesis by showing that what many people considered to be probably the ultimate secret is not really a secret at all."[122]

The magazine's case was severely hampered by galling secrecy requirements and assumptions. The government was able to place prior censorship on court filings and to require defense attorneys and expert witnesses to go through security clearances. The named defendants, who did not want to be burdened with additional classified information they could not publish, and some potential witnesses, who acted on principle, refused to submit to the lengthy clearance procedure. The defendants, who were denied access to portions of the briefs and court records as well as to closed sessions, found it difficult to participate in their own case.[123] Saying that he would like to think "a long hard time before I gave the hydrogen bomb to Idi Amin" and wanted to decide on "common sense grounds," Warren granted a temporary restraining order.[124] Later, in imposing a preliminary injunction, Warren relied on the *Near* dictum about troop movements while brushing aside evidence that the material in question was already widely available to the public and that building the weapon would require an enormous amount of money and a technological infrastructure that few countries would have. The story apparently was not a guide to making bombs, he admitted, but he thought that it might help some nations get the basic concepts faster. Faced with the stark choice, he said, most jurists would have no trouble choosing "the right to continued life" over freedom of the press.[125]

Judge Warren thus found a higher law than the Constitution, a "common sense" one that discarded the First Amendment in favor of the nebulous notion of safety. He did not consider the totalitarian potential of a ruling that placed security above liberty as suppressive regimes traditionally have done. Warren did not see that the real danger was not the information getting out, but rather lax security and export policies that raised fears that other less technologically advanced countries would obtain bomb materials and mechanisms they could not produce on their own.[126] Also not taken into account was the relative ease with which countries or individual terrorists can obtain other means of mass destruction, particularly chemical and biological weapons.[127] Industrialized nations spread less frightening but still lethal weaponry through conventional arms sales that helped account for the deaths of at least twenty million people, mostly unarmed civilians, in 120 armed conflicts during the Cold War.[128] Even if stopping the *Progressive* article had made sense, the information in it could be spoken by those who had read it or published elsewhere.[129] At any rate, evidence accumulated that the "secret" was not a secret, and other periodicals began printing versions of the physics of the hydrogen bomb. After facing tough questioning during oral arguments before the Seventh Circuit Court of Appeals, the government dropped the case and, after more than six months of prior restraint, the article was published with no apparent effect on nuclear proliferation.[130] Scientists concluded that the harm, if any, had been caused by the government advertising and confirming the information in question by prosecuting the magazine.[131]

The *Progressive* was right to suspect that the secrecy surrounding atomic energy was a fraud that prevented informed discussion and hid abuses in the nuclear industry.[132] Although successful spying allowed the Soviet Union to have the atomic bomb by 1949 and the information was published later in other countries, the United States maintained a massive security system to prevent disclosure of the "secret."[133] The actual secrets of the new atomic age included the careless handling of nuclear materials and government-sponsored radiation exposure experiments on thousands of unsuspecting adults, children, and newborns, experiments that took place from the 1940s through 1970s to study the effects nuclear war would have on human beings.[134] "It is desired that no document be released which refers to experiments with humans and might have adverse effect on public opinion or result in legal suits," said a classified government memo in 1947. "Documents covering such field work should be classified 'Secret.' "[135] As utopian planners sought to use atomic energy for electricity "too cheap to meter," and as extensive nuclear arms testing and development began, officials had worried that unfiltered information could interfere with the willingness of citizens to accept reactors and of military personnel to fight on nuclear battlefields. Open policy discussion on matters such as what weapons to develop and when to use them was discouraged by paternalistic leaders who regarded the public as too likely to respond with either panic or fatalism. Starting with Hiroshima, scientists and journalists who revealed the dangers of radiation were harassed and their reports denounced as Japanese or, later, Communist propaganda.[136]

Despite government efforts to suppress information, the kinds of fears that were evident in Judge Warren's ruling did arise in the relatively uncontrollable realm of popular culture. Films, television shows, books, and comics portrayed not only the horrors of nuclear holocaust but also the threat of atomic spies and saboteurs.[137] In the novel *Thunderball*, one example of the many fictional treatments of terrorists obtaining atomic bombs, James Bond fears that "soon every criminal scientist with a chemical set and some scrap iron" would be making the weapons and suspects that the *New York Times* knows about the case of nuclear extortion he is quietly handling.[138] So on edge was the Cold War public that when sirens sounded in Chicago in 1959 to celebrate the White Sox victory in the American League pennant race, thousands of hysterical people assumed a nuclear attack was under way. Ironically, Premier Nikita Khrushchev was visiting Iowa on the day of the panic and promoting a policy of peaceful coexistence.[139] By the time the *Progressive* was placed under a prior restraint twenty years later, the mystique of nuclear weapons was still clouding minds. "Many of the media, though not all, proved themselves pathetically eager to support the government's case," the magazine's editor, Erwin Knoll, recalled. "They argued that the First Amendment stopped where 'national security' began."[140] The fascination with the secrecy and the power of the bomb did not die out in the following decades. In 1995, fifty years after Hiroshima and Nagasaki, Speaker of the House Newt Gingrich coauthored a novel about Nazis trying to steal atomic secrets and sabotage nuclear weapons development during World War II.[141]

In their distrust of the Soviet Union and ignorance of concealed facts, few Americans of the Cold War era were prepared to question government policies on weapons production and use. Some civilian advisers, however, did condemn the secrecy of the arms race even as it began. In a December 1948 article in the *Atlantic Monthly*, industrialist Bradley Dewey, a member of the Joint Chiefs of Staff Evaluation Board for the atomic tests at Bikini, wrote that important information related to atomic policy was being withheld by the Truman administration. Upset at the suppression of a report by his board that had emphasized that the consequences of nuclear war went far beyond destroying military targets and had suggested that the president have authority for a first strike on another nation preparing an atomic attack on the United States, Dewey argued that the nation needed a "publicly known and endorsed atomic warfare policy" that would allow proper planning and alert adversaries to the circumstances that would provoke a use of nuclear weapons. He did not want the matter "decided with imprudent haste at times when situations are tense."[142]

In the same issue of the magazine David Bradley, a medical doctor who had observed the Bikini tests, concluded that secrecy was interfering with public recognition of the fact that there was no real defense against atomic weapons or effective means of decontaminating cities poisoned with radioactivity. The survival of humanity, he said, was "at stake in the indiscriminate use of atomic energy for political coercion." The people of Bikini had been evacuated in 1946 for what was thought to be a temporary move, but their atoll remained too radioactive for human habitation. In the following decades they experienced an odyssey of relocations and misery. One of the twenty-three Bikini tests from 1946 to 1958 was Bravo, the first deliverable hydrogen bomb. Equivalent in power to that of a freight train of TNT spanning North America, the 1954 surface detonation spread a "hot" shower over as much as fifty thousand square miles. Unwitting victims on other islands and on a Japanese fishing vessel were exposed to harmful amounts of Bravo's radioactive material. Atmospheric tests in Nevada from 1951 to 1962 exposed millions of Americans to hazardous levels of fallout.[143]

Successive administrations in Washington and quiescent news organizations perversely refused to fathom the finality of nuclear war. They asked the country to believe, contrary to overwhelming evidence, that fallout shelters were a means of preserving human life and civilization. Newspapers, including the *New York Times* and the *Chicago Tribune*, developed elaborate bomb shelter programs and plans for protecting their employees and their ability to publish in the event of an atomic attack.[144] Officials insisted on thinking that the amazingly powerful new weapons had to be usable somehow. Few Americans of the Cold War era realized the extent to which their own government made secret plans for winning a nuclear war or knew about the dozens of times presidents starting with Truman considered or threatened nuclear attacks.[145] In a top secret policy statement approved by President Eisenhower, the National Security Council said that the United States would "consider nuclear weapons to be as available for use as other munitions" in the event of any Soviet or Chinese aggression in the world.[146] Eisenhower did rule out a "preventative war," which key military officers wanted as a way to arrest the Communist threat, and acts of provocation, which nevertheless occurred in the form of secret reconnaissance flights over the Soviet Union.[147]

Shielded by secrecy, military and civilian leaders who regarded thermonuclear devices as a reasonable alternative to conventional warfare toyed recklessly with mass destruction. General Curtis LeMay, an Air Force officer who had overseen the killing of more than a million Japanese civilians in World War II firebombing and of what he estimated as 20 percent of the North Korean population in the Korean War, thought of "World War III" as the solution for the Cold War while serving as head of the Strategic Air Command and then as Air Force chief of staff. A proponent of a massive first strike if the Soviets ever appeared to be preparing for war, LeMay did not think a presidential order was always necessary before nuclear arms were used. During the Cuban missile crisis, LeMay, along with each of the joint chiefs, urged President Kennedy to bomb all military sites on the island. American forces did carry out a number of menacing maneuvers that could have provoked a Soviet attack, but Khrushchev capitulated, and LeMay regarded the episode as a lost opportunity. Richard Nixon gave serious thought to using nuclear weapons to break the stalemate in the Vietnam War and even to ward off Communist nation involvement in the India-Pakistan conflict of 1971. He also warned Moscow during the Sino-Soviet border dispute that any move to destroy the Chinese nuclear capability would not be tolerated, and he put U.S. forces on nuclear alert in 1973, at the time of the Watergate scandal's "Saturday Night Massacre," when he thought the Soviet Union might intervene in the war in the Middle East.[148]

The absence of a nuclear conflagration during the Cold War was remarkable in view of the deep tensions between the nations involved, but, in a sense, the doomsday weapons proved to be useless. Attacking another nuclear power could easily provoke massive retaliation, and using them against a nonnuclear nation, even one as despised and isolated as Japan was in 1945, would be condemned.[149] The weapons therefore may have been useful in impeding all-out war, even if the arms race itself was frightening and fiscally foolish. The existence of the bomb and reliable delivery systems could help to ward off apocalyptic attacks, as President Nixon recognized when he publicly renounced the use of biological warfare in 1970. "We'll never use the damn germs, so what good is biological warfare as a deterrent?" he told speechwriter William Safire. "If somebody uses germs on us, we'll nuke 'em."[150] Saddam Hussein made extensive preparations for germ warfare in the Gulf War, but was apparently cautious because of Bush administration messages with thinly veiled threats to obliterate Iraq if it used weapons of mass destruction. Bush had decided against any use of nuclear or chemical weapons, but, Secretary of State James Baker III later wrote, "There was obviously no reason to inform the Iraqis of this."[151] The American public, of course, also was not informed that such risky signals were being sent.

Finally, with mounting criticism and with changes in world affairs, the United States showed signs of awakening from its nuclear nightmare. A number of intellectuals who worried about the psychological health of the nation called for more openness and honesty as a remedy for rumors, misinformation, and ignorance.[152] Scientists argued that security restrictions were inhibiting the development of fusion technology for the generation of electricity. In 1990, as Cold War tensions lessened, the government at last responded by beginning the process of declassifying hydrogen bomb information. Six years later, trying to deal with one hundred million pages of material accumulated over half a century, the Department of Energy proposed dropping its "born classified" approach to documents on nuclear weapons and requiring that any new secrecy be justified. Existing procedures had covered up both useless facts and questionable activities, such as the Atoms for Peace program that shipped plutonium to thirty-nine other countries. In the 1990s the presidents of Russia and the United States agreed to eliminate two-thirds or more of their nuclear warheads.[153] The United States, the world's top arms supplier by far, remained the only nation ever to have used nuclear weapons in war and one of the few to have used chemical weapons.[154]

Little more than a decade after the *Progressive* case, then, unthinkable government actions—declassification and disarmament—became thinkable, and an individual was vindicated in his efforts to show how irrational nuclear war would be and yet how vulnerable the world actually was. Morland, an Air Force veteran who had conducted an extensive investigation of nuclear industry expedience as a citizen activist, had come to logical conclusions about the arms race and its fiscal and environmental impact on the United States. Nevertheless, he was censored by a court order as he attempted to show that atomic secrecy was a sham that hid abuses and abetted reckless thinking at odds with true security. Judge Warren, who was the real radical because he suspended the Constitution, was not qualified to deal with the facts of the case or likely to be sensitive to First Amendment claims. As a politician and then attorney general in Wisconsin, he had had many disagreeable personal experiences dealing with journalists, dissidents, and even the tragic use of a bomb. If Warren had heeded the press clause in the *Progressive* case instead of his frequently recognized progovernment, proprosecution instincts,[155] a small political magazine that had wanted to raise an important public policy issue would not have been faced with legal expenses of $240,000.[156] Mark Knops, who had no useful information on the fugitive bombers of Sterling Hall, would not have spent months in solitary confinement with only a Bible to read if Warren had simply read the First Amendment.[157]

The world may never be completely safe from violent conflicts, but "national security" also means the safety of rights and democratic processes. Justice Holmes, in an often-quoted statement, suggested that tools other than logic should be used when analyzing the development of law. "It is something to show that the consistency of a system requires a particular result, but it is not all," he wrote. "The life of the law has not been logic: it has been experience." Judging from experience, however, logic might have been a better guide to civil liberties than what Holmes called the "felt necessities of the time" and "prevalent moral and political theories."[158] Frightened speculation about the dangerous effects of words has shaped a modern First Amendment that, like the eighteenth-century British law the American Revolution rejected, places the wisdom of the rulers above that of the ruled. Self-preservation now, more than ever, depends on nations having informed citizens as well as mutual interests and mutual trust. Certainly the government has a right to try to conceal legitimate defense secrets, but it has no legal authority to restrict opinion or to control the dissemination of information that has become known to the press or that the public has a right to know. In any case, facts and ideas are difficult to contain, and secrecy can conceal much dangerous wrongdoing by governments. Restoring the press clause now will be a difficult task. The place to begin is where Hugo Black did—with the Madisonian legacy of free expression. Both Black and Madison understood what history has shown, that citizens have more to fear from their governments than their governments have to fear from them.

Part Two: "Higher Law" in Practice

The Federalists and the French Revolution

Wartime suppression of press freedom by the Congress and the president has been the result of a peculiar mixture of politics and paranoia. The first major test of the press clause of the First Amendment occurred in 1798, when the United States was contemplating a war with France that was never declared but that nevertheless proved costly in terms of military preparations and civil liberties. Taxes and borrowing were authorized and freedom of expression was suspended in an atmosphere of alarm promoted by Federalists like Alexander Hamilton, whose journalism warned that America could soon be surrendering its sovereignty to the French and making a new government "according to the fancy of the Directory."[1] Despite Enlightenment aspirations of concentrating on peaceful pursuits, isolated from the conflicts of other countries, many citizens were tormented by fears of foreign nations and reacting with near hysteria. The Sedition Act of 1798, which virtually outlawed criticism of government, demonstrated the willingness of some Americans to disregard the Bill of Rights and to attempt to silence those who expressed dissenting views.[2]

The political journalism of the 1790s, perhaps the most extreme and heated in American history, was mostly variations on the Jeffersonian Republican theme that the Federalists were war-mongering Anglophile monarchists and the Federalist charge that the Republicans were French-inspired radical democrats ready to revolt and cut off heads.[3] A contributor to a Federalist newspaper in Boston, for example, used the key terms in his party's propaganda lexicon to describe Republican leaders and writers in 1794. "There is no doubt that profligate men are employed, and there is little that they are *hired* to prepare the public for anarchy and war," he said. "One step towards both, is, to misrepresent and traduce the government, to render the advocates for peace and order suspected, and in this way to remove them from places of trust, where they may oppose this wicked conspiracy with success." Later the same year a Republican newspaper in Philadelphia published satirical entries from a spurious Federalist-style dictionary that included a definition of "Jacobin," the term for radical French democrats that was applied as an insult to the Jeffersonians. A "Jacobin" in Federalist parlance, according to the Republican paper, was "Any person who opposes the folly of the present war, or any of the measures of his majesty's ministers."[4]

Beyond the posturing was the constitutional issue of the wartime status of freedom of expression, an issue that has arisen repeatedly in American history without being adequately resolved. The American legal system has failed to clarify whether the sovereign will of the people is embodied in the absolutism of the First Amendment or

in the anxieties of the politicians the people choose to represent them. Popular government may be limited on paper, but it is subject to the minds of the individuals
who actually operate its mechanisms. The passage and enforcement of the Sedition
Act of 1798 merits particular attention because the crisis involved the generation that
wrote the press clause and revealed patterns that would be followed by later Americans,
particularly during the Cold War. The excesses of the Half-War with France, seven
years after ratification of the Bill of Rights, not only provided an example of the
natural tendency of leaders to overreact to foreign dangers, but also exposed the difficulty of maintaining democratic ideals in the face of domestic opposition. While
adherence to First Amendment principles was strong among libertarian-minded individuals like Thomas Jefferson who had insisted on constitutional protection for the
press, others of a more reactionary cast displayed their distaste for the new political
system that had been created and, despite their professed concerns about rationality
and order, embroiled the nation in a divisive and deluded attempt to punish journalistic affronts.

Personalities differ, and every individual has moods that will vary in response to
real or imagined states of affairs. Yet it may be possible to observe that at some critical
point the mere indignation someone may feel when being attacked in the press can
become a stronger, more hazardous feeling such as anger or even fear. Anger can be
described as a response to one's perception of having important interests thwarted. An
observation of psychology is that anger can build on anger until a person loses control.
The same may be true of fear, but fear looks toward real or imagined threats in the
future. A sense of uncertainty and of loss of control can induce a state of anxiety and
agitation even if the person realizes that the events foreseen are not very likely to
occur.[5] Together anger and fear make a powerful combination, one that can propel
even the most prominent members of society into what might be called a spiral of
spite, a situation in which the protagonists swirl lower and lower in a whirlpool of
malice.[6] The outcome can have less to do with how skillfully they handle the kind
of political communication Alexander Hamilton described as "manifestly designed to
induce the citizens to surrender their reason to the empire of their passions" than
with their ability to manage their own egocentric emotions while under attack.[7] The
Federalists and their successors in failed wartime repression followed their instincts
rather than what their intellects should have told them: that the suppression they
aimed at political enemies was likely to produce their own disgrace and perhaps self-
destruction.

I.

Both the second and third presidents of the United States regarded the collapse of the
Federalists in the election of 1800 as a revolution and saw the press as a major factor.
Thomas Jefferson, who had been quietly orchestrating press support for a decade,
called his election "the revolution of 1800" and said that it was as real a change in
principles of government as the one in 1776 had been in form.[8] He thought that one
newspaper in particular, the Philadelphia *Aurora*, which he supported in various ways,
had performed "incalculable services" and been "the rallying point" for his party in

its struggles with the Federalists.[9] A bitter John Adams blamed his party's being "over-thrown" on "liars" in the press and lamented the "revolutions in the moral, intellectual, and political world" that had forced his retirement.[10] The "doctrines of *sans-culotte*ism," he wrote to the Marquis de Lafayette a month after leaving office, were "productive of more plagues" than those of monarchism. The people, Adams said, are "never so ill used as when they take the government into their own hands."[11]

The late eighteenth century may have been the "age of the democratic revolution," but some of the principal figures of its political movements were not always prepared to see them become too democratic or too revolutionary.[12] Attitudes toward the lower strata of citizens and their participation in public life varied widely among political leaders. To Alexander Hamilton, for instance, the lower ranks represented a threat to social control during the American Revolution. Reacting to a mob attack in New York on the shop of loyalist printer James Rivington in 1775, he asked John Jay to use his influence in Congress to "procure a remedy for the evil" of such behavior. "In times of such commotion as the present, while the passions of men are worked up to an uncommon pitch there is great danger of fatal extremes," wrote Hamilton. "The same state of the passions which fits the multitude, who have not a sufficient stock of reason and knowledge to guide them, for opposition to tyranny and oppression, very naturally leads them to a contempt and disregard for all authority." On the other hand, James Madison observed earlier in the year that New Yorkers were failing to follow the example of Virginia in tarring and feathering. "I wish most heartily we had Rivington & his ministerial Gazetteers for 24. hours in this place," Madison remarked. "Execrable as their designs are, they would meet with adequate punishment."[13]

The political cultures of Hamilton's New York City and Madison's rural Virginia were quite different, of course, and respect for the rights of others to express their views can vary considerably with the immediate context, but a serious commitment to freedom of expression depends greatly on an individual's fundamental attitude toward participation in public affairs. Although Hamilton did object to the attack on Rivington's shop, the concerns he voiced were not about liberty of the press but were rather ones of anger and fear at the prospect of the lower ranks of society making political decisions of their own and carrying them out with violent means. He later objected to a constitutional guarantee for press freedom, and he did not oppose the Sedition Act of 1798.[14] As a young man participating in a revolution against monarchical authority, Madison may have approved of a symbolic and even violent assault on an editor he saw as opposing the country's liberties, but his later record as a journalist and politician, once a libertarian system was created, showed a basic acceptance of democratic decision-making and minority rights.[15] In a newspaper essay that appeared four days after the Virginia legislature completed the ratification of the Bill of Rights in 1791, Madison wrote: "Public opinion sets bounds to every government, and is the real sovereign in every free one." Hamilton, in contrast, reacted to press criticism of his zeal in putting down the Whiskey Rebellion by telling President Washington that he only hoped to have the esteem of the discerning people and that he had long before learned "to hold popular opinion of no value."[16]

Those Federalists of the 1790s who, like Adams and Hamilton, had unvarnished contempt for the populace and felt threatened by it had little problem placing their opponents and their opinions outside the boundaries of what they considered legitimate and acceptable in the political process, especially as the Jeffersonian Republicans supported revolutionary France in its wars and diplomatic maneuverings with Britain. As future generations of Americans would do with anarchists and communists, the Federalists projected frightening images of a sinister international conspiracy intent on the overthrow of virtually all established institutions from the government to religion and morality itself.[17] As was not the case in later scares, however, most citizens were, at least initially, enthusiastic about the foreign cause. France had been an ally in the War of Independence and by the 1790s had joined the United States in the ranks of republican nations. "What a happiness for America, that the sparks of her liberty kindled the flame in France," wrote "A Republican" in a Philadelphia newspaper, "for her example has reverberated, and the glow of our late revolution is again upon us."[18] For years, in fact, the brutality of the French Revolution was excused by Americans who were in sympathy with its assaults on monarchy and the religion of Rome. Republican journalists frequently argued that France was facing more powerful and determined enemies than Americans had in 1776 and that the French had been more oppressed. In calling for donations for revolutionary France, one newspaper writer commented:

> The crimes and excesses, inseparable from great commotions and popular fermentations, are undoubtedly greatly to be lamented, and though they may call forth the sigh and tear of pity, they ought not to be ascribed to the principle of the revolution, nor ought they to be considered as the necessary and unavoidable consequences attendant upon all revolutions. They originated in the licentious phrenzy of a mob, intoxicated with a draught to which they had been unaccustomed; or, it was the oppressed breaking their yokes on the necks of the oppressors. If we take a general retrospect of the general tenor and spirit of the conduct of the French nation, we shall see much to admire, and little to condemn.[19]

The ideological rift that formed the first national political parties was most apparent in their reactions to France and to the nation both the Americans and French had fought in order to preserve their revolutions, Britain. The Jeffersonian Republicans accused the Federalists of attempting to maintain British-style class structure and corrupt, deference politics. As early as the fiasco of Citizen Genêt's diplomatic mission in 1793, Republicans were describing what one Philadelphia correspondent regarded as "an *aristocratic* effort to give a death wound not only to the republican cause of France, but to republicanism itself in the United States."[20] Taking the Jeffersonian position that the controversial actions of the French Minister to the United States had been misrepresented by the Federalists, another writer remarked, "There seems to be a *combination* of some of the officers of Government against Mr. Genet, and for what reason, unless he is too *democratic* for them, I cannot divine."[21] The Federalists, as represented in the Republican press, were favoring monarchical Britain over republican France, were serving the wealthy with Hamiltonian fiscal policies, and were displaying contempt for the common citizen in their statements condemning the Democratic-Republican societies and the Whiskey Rebellion. They were, in short, depicted as counterrevolutionaries bent on turning back the tide of human progress toward equality and democracy.

Federalist writers regarded Republican rhetoric as evidence of dangerous French-inspired radicalism and responded with competing scare tactics and conspiracy theories. As the situation in France deteriorated, moderate Federalists joined their more reactionary cohorts in vigorously condemning what they regarded as the critical danger of too much rejection of the past. "It is an experiment to try whether *atheism* and *materialism*, as articles of national creed, will not render men more happy in society than a belief in a God, a Providence and the Immortality of the soul," Noah Webster observed in a 1794 pamphlet on the French Revolution. "The experiment is new; it is bold: it is astonishing." Deeply disturbed by what he saw as the moral degeneration of the world, the author of America's first dictionary was in the process of turning away from revolutionary utopianism to Federalism and, with the decline of the Federalists, to the belief of many conservatives that only patriarchal religion could save the country from social and moral chaos. Webster had little hope that the French people would improve their lives. "They are released, not only from the ordinary restraints of law, but from all their former habits of thinking," he wrote. "From the fetters of a debasing religious system, the people are let loose in the wide field of moral licentiousness; and as men naturally run from one extreme to another, the French will probably rush into the wildest vagaries of opinion both in their political and moral creeds."[22]

After the bitterly contested ratification of the Jay Treaty with Britain in 1795, an agreement that Republicans thought gave away trade advantages and insulted France, even the leading politicians descended into unrestrained portrayals of sinister influences at work. Thomas Jefferson and Alexander Hamilton, whose philosophical predilections had become evident in their feuding as members of Washington's cabinet, gave predictably different accounts of the forces behind American relations with the warring nations of Europe and of the willingness of the Federalists to accept the provisions of the Jay Treaty, which they themselves found hard to defend. In a letter to his friend Philip Mazzei that found its way into the press, Jefferson denounced the Federalists as "an Anglican monarchical, & aristocratical party" determined "to draw over us the substance, as they have already done the forms, of the British government." According to Jefferson, the Federalists consisted of "all the officers of the government, all who want to be officers, all timid men who prefer the calm of despotism to the boisterous sea of liberty, British merchants & Americans trading on British capitals, speculators & holders in the banks & public funds," and even men like Washington, "who were Samsons in the field & Solomons in the council, but who have had their heads shorn by the harlot England."[23]

Jefferson was keeping a safe distance from politics at the time, but Hamilton was quick to respond to the public protests of the treaty, which included mass meetings, burnings of Jay in effigy, and petitions to President Washington. Attempting to sway one angry crowd of protesters in July of 1795, Hamilton was hissed and pelted with stones. A few days later, after exchanging harsh words with a group of men on a street, he put up his fists and offered to fight every Republican there, an offer that was accepted by one man, whom Hamilton then snubbed.[24] In the midst of his public confrontations, Hamilton began "The Defence," a series of thirty-eight newspaper essays in support of the treaty. In the first he lamented the existence of the Republicans, "men irreconcilable to our present national constitution," who were exploiting public sympathy for France and enmity toward England as part of "a systematic effort against the national government and its administration." Blaming Jeffersonian "party spirit" and demagogic exploitation of "an enthusiasm for France and her revolution throughout all its wonderful vicissitudes" for the disruptions, Hamilton said he would address his pieces to "every man who is not an enemy to the national government, who is not a prejudiced partisan, who is capable of comprehending the argument, and passionate enough to attend to it with impartiality."[25]

More extreme francophobia and conspiracy theorizing was evident in the work of Philadelphia journalist William Cobbett, who wrote under the pen name Peter Porcupine. In a 1796 pamphlet, *History of the American Jacobins, Commonly Denominated Democrats*, Cobbett sketched the outlines of an international conspiracy that began when "the Jacobins of Paris sent forth their missionaries of insurrection and anarchy." French diplomats, he asserted, had attached themselves to "*Anti-federalists*" in the United States and already had inspired the Democratic-Republican societies and the Whiskey Rebellion. The American subversives, Cobbett said, were in general "men of bad moral characters" who were either in financial difficulty or the tools of those who were. "Men of this cast naturally feared the operation of a government endued with sufficient strength to make itself respected, and with sufficient wisdom to exclude the ignorant and wicked from a share in its administration," Cobbett said. The federal government had thereby received "at its birth, the seeds of a disease, which, unless its friends discover more zeal than they have hitherto done, will one day accomplish its destruction."[26]

II.

By the time of the Jay Treaty, then, the two parties had promulgated well-established themes in the battle for public opinion. Each side represented the other as the worst possible threat to the new and presumably vulnerable American system of government. With their outmoded hauteur and disdain for the reasoning abilities of the citizenry, the Federalists interpreted opposition party organizing and protests such as those that greeted the treaty as something inherently evil and misguided that could only have been stirred up by loathsome, manipulative incendiaries. Inasmuch as the Jeffersonian message was being conveyed by the press, the Federalists naturally regarded Republican journalists as part of the plot against the nation's well-being.

As he explained in a 1796 pamphlet entitled *The Bloody Buoy Thrown Out as a Warning to the Political Pilots of America*, William Cobbett thought that an overly sympathetic United States press had done too little to expose "the horrible effects of anarchy and infidelity" in the French Revolution. France, he charged, had embraced the "destructive doctrine of equality," "destroyed all ideas of private property," and effaced from the people's minds "every principle of the only religion capable of keeping mankind within the bounds of justice and humanity." As proof of the consequences Cobbett listed dozens of graphic examples of murder, mutilation, cannibalism, and sexual assault from French publications that he said were largely ignored. The doctrines and dangers of the French Revolution, he warned, were being spread to America by "troublers of society of every description" and were being applauded in the press and public assemblies. Cobbett predicted that unless Americans acted with zeal in the cause of their country they could expect to see their churches turned into stables, their waters tinged with blood, "and even the head of our admired and beloved President rolling on a scaffold." Cobbett insisted that the threat was not imaginary, that since ratification of the Constitution "disorganizing and infidel principles" had been advancing steadily "along with our silly admiration of the French Revolution." Liberty of the press, he wrote, had become "useless to us during this terrible convulsion of the civilized world" and "so perverted as to lead us into errors." Cobbett said that every French leader had been praised in the Jeffersonian journals while George Washington had been viciously maligned in terms "as bold, if not bolder than those which led to the downfall of the unfortunate French monarch."[27]

The Republicans meanwhile insisted that Jeffersonian journalists and politicians were performing the necessary and legitimate task of unmasking Federalist perfidy and that the fates of revolutionary France and America were linked. The Republican position, one that was repeated many times in many forms, was spelled out in a pamphlet written in 1795 by James Madison, who led the minority party's efforts in Congress and often contributed to the press at Jefferson's urging. Madison attributed the country's political turmoil to unsound and unconstitutional foreign policy decisions that were partial toward Britain despite that nation's interference with American shipping and other hostile acts. The Federalists' communication strategy, Madison observed, was "to invoke the name of Washington; to garnish their heretical doctrines with his virtues" and, with respect to France, "to be more struck with every circumstance that can be made a topic of reproach, or of chimerical apprehensions, than with all the splendid objects which are visible through the gloom of a revolution." Madison expressed confidence that the public would see through Federalist "misrepresentations" and that "truth, however, stifled or perverted for a time, will finally triumph in the detection of calumny, and in the contempt which awaits its authors." The true danger to the nation, Madison said, was that Britain and its allies would subdue republican France and then turn toward the American continent "to root out Liberty from the face of the earth."[28]

The Republicans needed no further justification for a vigorous journalistic assault on the administration, starting at the top. The most industrious of Washington's detractors was Benjamin Franklin Bache, a Philadelphia newspaper editor and the grandson of Benjamin Franklin. The grandfather had financed and directed Bache's education in Europe and America with a strong emphasis on inculcating republican principles. Bache, like most Jeffersonian Republican editors, championed the democratic ideals of the French Revolution and cheered France's military victories in the 1790s.[29] Saying citizens have "a RIGHT to know" and should not regard their government with "blind faith," Bache's paper spearheaded a successful campaign against the patrician Senate's denial of press and public access to its sessions, a policy finally abandoned when the members voted to stay open as a general rule in 1794.[30] The paper then opened fire on President Washington's efforts to conceal aspects of his troubled diplomacy with Britain and France. One of the essays complained that the administration wanted to keep the people ignorant while impressing them with the appearance "that the Executive and the Executive only, is the manager of every thing important to freemen."[31] When the administration negotiated the Jay Treaty and the

Senate debated it behind closed doors in 1795, Bache scored a journalistic coup by publishing a leaked copy of the confidential document and helping to raise the public outcry against its provisions. "Whenever a government abounds with secrets and mysteries," the paper editorialized, "you may be assured that something is rotten, or at least that private views and interests are preferred to the public good."[32]

Before Washington signed the Jay Treaty, Bache and his correspondents seemed almost as interested in criticizing the regal trappings of the president's social style as his personal reputation or politics.[33] After he signed the treaty, however, a cascade of letters and editorials in Bache's *Aurora* criticized Washington's military record, his intelligence, his drawing of salary before it was earned, his slaveholding, and his "secret hostility to the cause of France."[34] One correspondent urged Washington to retire immediately and another listed seventeen charges for impeachment that included forcing "the philosophic patriot" Jefferson to resign as secretary of state and establishing a foreign policy of ill will toward "the brave Republic, which has contended for the Rights of Man, against all the tyrants of the earth."[35] The writers defended themselves by saying that they were using liberty of the press against "the encroachments of power" and that the treaty and other antirepublican measures were only possible because the Federalists had exploited the public's idolatry of Washington.[36] "How long are the freemen of America to be the dupes of an administration and the sport of Great Britain!" demanded an *Aurora* editorial.[37]

Washington's private correspondence began reflecting anger about opposition journalism and fear of its influence as early as the Genêt controversy, when he wrote that Bache's publications were "outrages on common decency" that should alarm "dispassionate" people "because it is difficult to prescribe bounds to the effect." Other letters in the following years fumed at Bache's "impertinence" or "Impudence" and expressed concern that his "malignant industry, and persevering falsehoods" would "weaken, if not destroy, the confidence of the Public." Washington described Bache as "no more than the Agent or tool of those who are endeavoring to destroy the confidence of the people in the officers of Government" but thought that his attacks would gradually erode support "for drops of Water will Impress (in time) the hardest Marble."[38] Journalism such as Bache's did wear down Washington's patience, particularly when foreign policy was involved. During the public protests of the Jay Treaty, Washington wrote Hamilton to praise his newspaper series defending the document and commented:

> The difference of conduct between the friends, and foes of order, & good government, is in nothg. more striking than that, the latter are always working like bees, to distil their poison, whilst the former, depending, often times *too much*, and *too long* upon the sense, and good dispositions of the people to work conviction, neglect the means of effecting it.[39]

After a year of press attacks centering on relations with France, Washington could barely contain his fury. A section of his 1796 farewell address that was edited out before publication complained about his being subjected to "virulent abuse" in the press in order "to misrepresent my politics and affections; to wound my reputation and feelings; and to weaken, if not entirely destroy the confidence you have been pleased to repose in me." He concluded the section saying that he stood by the principles of his Neutrality Proclamation of 1793 "regardless of the complaints and attempts of *any of those* powers or their partisans to change them." In a letter to Hamilton he explained that one of the reasons he was quitting was "a disinclination to be longer buffited in the public prints by a set of infamous scribblers" and expressed the hope that the friends of the administration would defend it when he was attacked or other officials caused it embarrassment. Ten days later Washington told Thomas Jefferson about his frustration at being "accused of being the enemy of one Nation, and subject to the influence of another" and at being referred to "in such exaggerated and indecent terms as could scarcely be applied to a Nero; a notorious defaulter; or even to a common pickpocket." He quickly dropped the topic, however, saying, "But enough of this; I have already gone farther in the expression of my feelings, than I intended."[40]

Washington thus may have indulged in some self-pity privately, but he had enough control over himself to avoid taking any hasty or ill-advised steps to deal with his enemies in the press.[41] A leader who displayed relative equanimity about the French Revolution, he blamed Republican "ignorance of facts" and a Federalist failure to explain them for the controversy over relations with France.[42] In reaction to newspaper attacks, "indecent as they are void of truth and fairness," the president asked Secretary of State Timothy Pickering in 1796 to review all past diplomatic correspondence with revolutionary France in order to prepare for possible future explanations of administration conduct. "Under these circumstances, it were to be wished that the enlightened public could have a clear and comprehensive view of facts," Washington said.[43] On his last day in office, Washington deposited a letter in the Department of State to deny the authenticity of a spurious correspondence that Bache had republished to discredit him as a revolutionary hero. The forged letters, which were supposedly written by General Washington in 1776, conveyed uncertainty about the patriot cause. As pained as he was about the reappearance of the propaganda ploy, the retiring chief executive merely made what he called "a testimony of the truth to the present generation and to posterity."[44]

Instead of attempting to settle any scores with the press or political opponents, Washington used his farewell address to stress the highest republican ideals of peace, morality, and the belief that if "the structure of a government gives force to public opinion, it is essential that public opinion should be enlightened." Warning against "the spirit of party," he said, "A fire not to be quenched; it demands a uniform vigilance to prevent its bursting into a flame, lest instead of warming it should consume." He also cautioned against any "usurpation" of the Constitution, saying that "the precedent must always overbalance in permanent evil any partial or transient benefit which the use can at any time yield." Accordingly, Washington did not take any steps to suppress opinion and would later refuse to take a public stand in favor of the Sedition Act. His answer to words was more words and to remain devoted to ideals despite personal pain. Although the *Aurora* accused him of "the profession of republicanism, but the practice of monarchy and aristocracy; the profession of sympathy and interest for a great nation and an ally struggling for liberty, but a real devotion to the cause of the combined despots," Washington believed his motives were irreproachable and that the "arrows of malevolence, therefore, however barbed and well pointed, never can reach the most vulnerable part of me."[45] With such peace of mind, the first president was able to leave office with dignity and a public image that was still largely intact.

III.

An admirer of the British constitution who had little or no use for the concept of equality, President John Adams had less sympathy for the French Revolution than his predecessor and had, in fact, dismissed its prospects and ideals from the beginning.[46] "Reasoning has been all lost," Adams was able to say of France by 1796. "Passion, Prejudice, Interest, Necessity has governed and will govern; and a Century must roll away before any permanent and quiet System will be established."[47] Relations with France, which had been deteriorating since the Jay Treaty, were becoming increasingly ominous in 1797 when Adams took office. The French government had refused to accept the credentials of the new American minister, and Secretary of State Pickering reported that the French had seized more than three hundred American vessels on the high seas. As Adams oversaw a defense buildup and made defiant statements, Republicans accused him of wanting to plunge the country into war, but such a conflict would have been irrational for both sides and was only promoted by emotional nationalists and extreme Federalists.[48] Adams sensibly refused to go along with the powerful prowar faction of his party, steering the country instead toward a negotiated settlement, even after 1798 when the XYZ Affair revealed French attempts to get a bribe from American diplomats in Paris and the United States entered an undeclared naval war with France. Adams's cautious statesmanship may have averted a full-scale conflict with a stronger nation and led the country toward the Convention of 1800 that restored peace and diplomatic relations, but his political courage in dealing with fellow Federalists who wanted war split his party.[49]

The second president's reaction to Republican criticism, on the other hand, was less courageous than what might have been expected of a resolute statesman. Unlike Washington, Adams allowed pettiness and a sense of persecution to undermine his presidency. In his vanity, irritableness, and insecurity, John Adams was, as Benjamin Franklin put it, "sometimes, and in some things, absolutely out of his senses."[50] The political jabs and personal taunts he received in Bache's *Aurora*, which portrayed him as an antirepublican fool when he ran for president and as a senile, Anglophile warmonger during his administration, were attributed by Adams to mere prejudices Bache had acquired from his grandfather.[51] Franklin, Adams thought, had "conceived an irreconcilable hatred" of him when the two were diplomats in France and had passed on his feelings to Bache.[52] In reality, Franklin was simply bothered by Adams' smugness, and Adams was intensely jealous of Franklin's celebrity and popularity in Europe and America.[53]

So sensitive was Adams to personal slights that the mere mention of his dental problems in Bache's paper moved him to include in his autobiography a detailed explanation of how the teeth were weakened by "Mercurial Preparations" administered by his physicians. "I should not have mentioned this," Adams told his readers, "if I had not been reproached with this personal Defect, with so much politeness in the Aurora." His wife was even more incensed at what she described as the daring way "the vile incendiaries keep up in Baches paper the most wicked and base, voilent (*sic*) & caluminiating abuse."[54] In letter after letter in 1797 and 1798, Abigail Adams took offense at Bache's journalism, saying that he had "a tendency to corrupt the morrals of the common people," was trying to introduce "French manners in Religion and politicks," and conducted himself with "the malice & falshood of Satin."[55] The first lady concluded that the nation would come to civil war unless Bache and other Republican journalists were suppressed by a sedition law.[56]

America's Federalists had a model for such legislation. The British government had already passed a sedition act and other oppressive bills in an attempt to stem criticism of itself that was inspired by the French Revolution. The laws, which included measures for deporting aliens, were not used often, but trials for seditious libel were common. The judicial repression and effective counterpropaganda helped to destroy the movement for political reform.[57]

Voting along straight party lines, with Federalists supporting and Republicans opposing, Congress passed its own Alien and Sedition Acts in 1798.[58] Truth was a defense, but journalists were arrested for making statements of opinion, often insulting Adams, that were neither provably true nor false. One journalist, for example, was fined and sentenced to nine months in jail for a Jeffersonian election pamphlet that accused the president of being a "professed aristocrat" and "hoary headed incendiary" who wanted to embroil the country in war with France.[59] Realizing that it would not be used against them, Federalist journalists had called for the statute and urged its use against their "Gallic" competitors.[60]

One of the few doubters in the Federalist camp was John Marshall, who was soon to become chief justice of the United States. In a letter to a newspaper that was his only public statement in a campaign for Congress in 1798, Marshall said he opposed the Alien and Sedition Acts "because I think them useless; and because they are calculated to create, unnecessarily, discontents and jealousies at a time when our very existence, as a nation, may depend on our union." Privately, Marshall later said that "whatever doubts some of us may entertain" about the constitutionality of alien and sedition laws, the president and the courts took the position that they were legal.[61]

None of the Sedition Act cases reached the Supreme Court, but Federalist judges and juries packed by Federalist marshals made sure the statute was enforced even though war with France was only anticipated.[62] Fines and jail sentences were given to political opponents of the administration if they were Republicans, but not if they were extreme Federalists like Hamilton, who denounced Adams in print as thoroughly as anyone.[63] The prosecutions severely disrupted but did not entirely silence the Republican press. About two dozen people, including Bache and most of the other principal Republican journalists, faced either state or federal charges brought by Federalists during the Adams administration.[64] The resulting public outcry, along with defense taxes and political infighting over how aggressive to be with France, damaged the Federalist party beyond any hope of recovery. Adams later said of the alien and sedition laws in a letter to a newspaper:

> I knew there was need enough of both, and therefore I consented to them. But as they were then considered as war measures, and intended altogether against the advocates of the French and peace with France, I was apprehensive that a hurricane of

clamor would be raised against them, as in truth there was, even more fierce and violent than I had anticipated.[65]

Although he portrayed himself as taking a passive role, Adams contributed to the mood that produced the acts. In his responses to the patriotic addresses he received in the wake of the XYZ Affair, he took the opportunity to condemn what he called the "spirit of party, which scruples not to go all lengths of profligacy, falsehood, and malignity, in defaming our government." He repeatedly spoke in the most vivid terms of the French threat and said that "obloquy" was the nation's worst enemy because "it strives to destroy all distinction between right and wrong; it leads to divisions, sedition, civil war, and military despotism." Adams urged specific prosecutions through his secretary of state, Timothy Pickering, who was obsessed with what he called "our internal enemies." "Is there any thing evil in the regions of actuality or possibility, that the Aurora has not suggested of me?" Adams asked, in insisting on the prosecution of one old adversary.[66]

In his retirement years, Adams sought both to justify the Alien and Sedition Acts and to disassociate himself from them. He told Jefferson that the alien legislation was necessary because "French Spies then swarmed in our Cities and in the Country" and that some were "intollerably, turbulent, impudent and seditious." Responding to Jefferson's characterization of the Federalist actions against the Republicans as alarmist "terrorism," Adams accused his fellow former president of ignoring the "Terrorisms" of Shays's Rebellion, the Whiskey Rebellion, the Fries Rebellion, and the revolutionary potential of the mass public demonstrations against administration policies on France. He remarked that Jefferson was no doubt "fast asleep in philosophical Tranquility" when thousands of Philadelphians paraded one night in 1798 and Adams brought in arms to defend his residence against possible attack. Adams blamed Republican journalists and members of Congress for stirring up dissent during the decade, but admitted that both parties "excited artificial Terrors" and said they had the real fear that they would "loose the Elections and consequently the Loaves and Fishes."[67] As some of his supporters had done during the presidential election of 1800, Adams attempted to shift the blame for the laws passed in 1798, accusing Alexander Hamilton of using his influence to instigate the legislation and saying his "imagination was always haunted by that hideous monster or phantom, so often called a *crisis*, and which so often produces imprudent measures."[68]

Hamilton was, at the time of the Alien and Sedition Acts, resorting to the same kind of paranoid rhetoric he had used in response to the Jay Treaty protests. As Adams was preparing to take office, Hamilton began a series of six newspaper essays called "The Warning" that said France was seeking world domination and that "self preservation and self respect" required other nations to resist. "The specious pretence of enlightening mankind and reforming their civil institutions, is the varnish to the real design of subjugating them," he wrote. "The vast projects of a Louis XIV dwindle into insignificance compared with the more gigantic schemes of his Republican successors." In 1798 Hamilton produced a similar series, "The Stand," which asserted that Republican leaders were serving France's Directory and that their followers were "a contemptible few, prostituted to a foreign enemy," who were seemingly "willing that their country should become a province to France."[69]

Hamilton had many reasons to despise the opposition party, which had tried to block many of his programs, but he and other Federalists could do little to Republican politicians beyond claim that they were part of a French plot to enslave America. Jeffersonian journalists, who had subjected him to a number of embarrassments including the revelation of his affair with Maria Reynolds, were a more tempting target. In a letter written in 1799 to ask the attorney general of New York to prosecute a paper that had accused him of trying to buy the *Aurora* in order to suppress it, Hamilton referred again to a Republican conspiracy to overthrow the government and linked it to the press:

> One principal Engine for effecting the scheme is by audacious falsehoods to destroy the confidence of the people in all those who are in any degree conspicuous among the supporters of the Government: an Engine which has been employed in time past with too much success, and which unless counteracted in future is likely to be attended with very fatal consequences.[70]

At the same time, Hamilton was encouraging the Federalists to pass additional laws for use against the press. "To preserve confidence in the Officers of the General Government, by preserving their reputations from malicious and unfounded slanders, is essential to enable them to fulfil the ends of their appointment," he reasoned. "It is therefore both constitutional and politic to place their reputations under the guardianship of the Courts of the United States."[71]

In arguing for the Sedition Act, the Federalist members of Congress also used specious logic to circumvent the First Amendment's prohibition of laws abridging freedom of the press, but personal animosity and fears of revolutionary influences from abroad were clearly evident in the debates. The Federalists not only made assertions about the practical necessities of defense, but also claimed that their political opponents were part of an international conspiracy inspired by the French Revolution to deprive the wealthy of their lives and property. Representative John Allen, the Federalist spokesman for the measure in the House, said the press was inciting the poor and ignorant to insurrection and asked whether upright gentlemen should feel safe in their beds. "Who can doubt the existence of a combination against the real liberty, the real safety of the United States?" he asked. "I say, sir, a combination, a conspiracy against the Constitution, the Government, the peace and safety of this country, is formed, and is in full operation." Allen repeatedly quoted defiant opinions from Bache's *Aurora* as evidence that the "Jacobinic" paper was "the great engine of all these treasonable combinations" and was in league with Jefferson's party to destroy "the peace of our Zion." Representative Robert Goodloe Harper, a Federalist leader and co-author of the act, followed Allen's harangue with the statement that freedom of the press ought not to be allowed to those "who wish to overturn society, and trample everything not their own."[72]

Proponents of the bill voiced outrage at seeing themselves and their president ridiculed in the Republican press. Representative Allen, using quotations from the *Aurora*, noted Jefferson's relationship with Bache as evidence of "treasonable combinations" at work that would bring about "revolution and Jacobinic domination." Like France, Allen said, America would fall to "loud and enthusiastic advocates for liberty and equality" who used the press to incite "the poor, the ignorant, the passionate, and the vicious" against "the virtuous, the pacific, and the rich." Republicans not only fought the bill on constitutional grounds, but also questioned the existence of an emergency and maintained that the measure was not rational. Saying that government should not have to fear free discussion and that unfounded statements in one paper could be contradicted in another, Representative Nathaniel Macon warned the Federalists that they did not understand the American public and that the law would actually make the country less prepared for war because it would engender protests as well as suspicions that the government had something to hide. When war appeared so likely, he said, Congress should not endanger the country's unity by deciding "to pass a law which will produce more uneasiness, more irritation, than any act which ever passed the Legislature of the Union."[73]

Indeed, the Sedition Act made little sense. Adams had beaten Jefferson by only three electoral votes in 1796, and in the following years Federalists saw the Republican press as a threat to their candidates;[74] but the law gave the opposition party functionaries evidence for *their* conspiracy theory and a topic for their communications with voters for years to come.[75] When the act was passed, the Republicans were still reeling from XYZ Affair and President Adams was receiving hundreds of addresses from citizen groups of all kinds attesting to their loyalty and willingness to fight for their country. Adams had been extremely popular, and there was little doubt that the country would be unified against any nation that presented a threat.[76] The French miscalculation of American sentiment, especially references to France's being able to count on political and press support in the United States, played so well into the hands of the Federalists that Republican leaders were near despair, and even a paper as solidly pro-French as Bache's found little to say.

Soon, however, Jefferson could see the Alien and Sedition Acts acting "as powerful sedatives of the X. Y. Z. inflammation."[77] Republicans organized protests, signed petitions to Congress, and passed the Virginia and Kentucky Resolutions opposing the Sedition Act.[78] Moreover, the prosecutions were political trials that offered Republicans opportunities to ridicule and castigate the administration and become martyrs.[79] Federalists continued to berate their opponents as Jacobin incendiaries. "Behold France, that open Hell, still ringing with agonies and blasphemies, still smoking with sufferings and crimes, in which we see their state of torment, and perhaps our future state," admonished Fisher Ames in a newspaper essay published in 1799. Like other members of his party, Ames, who had been a Federalist stalwart in Congress, thought the sedition law was necessary to combat the Republicans and that liberty should be destroyed in order to save it. "The danger these men create must be repelled by arming our rulers with force enough, and appointing them to watch in our stead," he wrote. "Thus good citizens find that they must submit to laws of the more rigor, because the desperate licentiousness of the bad could not be otherwise restrained."[80]

French displeasure over the Jay Treaty had resulted in interference with the nation's shipping and in diplomatic insults, but the country was not in danger of invasion or an actual overthrow of the government and its Constitution. Several well-publicized Federalist attempts to expose treasonous Republican connections with France ended in ignominious failure.[81] George Washington agreed to lead American forces although he thought France would not invade;[82] however, he questioned the politics of the Sedition Act and took no public position on its constitutionality. He said that no arguments for it could change the behavior of the Republican leaders. "They have points to carry, from which no reasoning, no inconsistency of conduct, no absurdity, can divert them," Washington observed.[83] Adams also seemed to understand the futility of Federalist actions as he left office. "No party, that ever existed, knew itself so little, or so vainly overrated its own influence and popularity, as ours," he said in 1801. "None ever understood so ill the causes of its own power, or so wantonly destroyed them."[84]

Through their inability to rise above anger and fear, the Federalists lost much of the recognition they could have achieved for their role in establishing the nation. Although they may not have believed everything they said about a French conspiracy in the 1790s, they did have reason to resent their rivals and to be wary of their potential political power. In creating their shrill portrayals of the Jeffersonian Republicans as radical democrats, some Federalists may only have been exaggerating what they felt were the real tendencies of the opposition party. Perhaps for some the smear of disloyalty was a way of diverting attention from the administration's policy failures and unpopular ideology. In any case, in thinking that they could destroy a broadly based opposition and could uproot deeply held convictions about liberty, the Federalists overrated their political skills and misunderstood the American people as much as the French had in the XYZ Affair. In the election of 1800, the Federalists waged a hate-mongering campaign depicting Jefferson as a Jacobin atheist, but he was elected, and the Republicans took control of both houses of Congress.[85] The Sedition Act may have been the result of a brief pathological period in the nation's history and may have expired by its own terms in 1801, but if the First Amendment had been written by Congress in 1798 instead of 1789, the choice of words could have been very different.

The willingness of the Federalists to ignore the First Amendment and find a higher law in their own survival was based on an overweening fear both of the French and of political opponents, the Jeffersonian Republicans. The French, who were busy enough with European enemies, did not invade the United States, but the Jeffersonians found a rallying point in the Sedition Act and triumphed over their tormentors. At his inaugural in 1801, Thomas Jefferson issued an often-quoted call for national unity:

> We are all republicans—we are all federalists. If there be any among us who would wish to dissolve this Union or to change its republican form, let them stand undisturbed as monuments of the safety with which error of opinion may be tolerated where reason is left free to combat it. I know, indeed, that some honest men fear that a republican government cannot be strong; that this government is not strong enough. But would the honest patriot, in the full tide of successful experiment, abandon a government which has so far kept us free and firm, on the theoretic and visionary fear that this government, the world's best hope, may by possibility want energy to preserve itself? I trust not. I believe this, on the contrary, the strongest government on earth.[86]

Yet Jefferson was among the early presidents who, seeing weighty leadership responsibilities in their executive role, stretched their authority in defense and foreign relations.[87] Jefferson explained his illegal, or at least questionable, actions—which ranged from unauthorized spending for military supplies to the purchase of the Louisiana territory—by saying that the "unwritten laws of necessity, of self-preservation" could be a higher obligation than the written laws on some occasions when vital interests were at stake and time was a critical factor. He nevertheless readily admitted that he acted at his own peril when going outside the law and was still subject to "the justice of the controlling powers of the constitution." Presidents, he asserted, had a duty "to risk themselves" on important issues and then throw themselves on the mercy of the country with the rectitude of their motives.[88] Having pardoned journalists convicted under the Sedition Act of 1798, which he considered "a nullity as absolute and as palpable as if Congress had ordered us to fall down and worship a golden image," Jefferson evidently did not think that federal interference with the freedom of the press was the kind of action that could be justified.[89] Yet, despite all of his democratic proclivities, he helped to establish the pattern of presidents going beyond the boundaries of the law if they thought reason dictated and the action was defensible.[90]

The Rise of Presidential
Prerogatives

When pressured by paranoia or partisanship in a crisis, government leaders may simply weaken at some point and give in to their forebodings or frustrations about expression, even if their repressive actions are self-destructive and antidemocratic. Legislation comparable to the Sedition Act of 1798, however, was not passed again by Congress until 1917. In the meantime, wartime presidents and military officers with extravagant notions of their power managed to begin abridging freedom of the press on their own. In the Mexican War and the Civil War, haphazard and often arbitrary steps were taken to deny access, arrest journalists, censor dispatches, and suspend publications. Official obstructions for reporters were common by the time American soldiers were fighting in Cuba and the Philippines at the end of the nineteenth century. Although such denials of First Amendment freedoms were never without controversy or complications, presidential-military repression became a standard practice during wars. Presidents and their subordinates have contended that restrictions on journalism are necessary for security, but the constraints typically have had little to do with self-preservation and much to do with politics and public relations.

I.

If any president ever had an excuse for wartime restrictions on the press, it was James Madison during the War of 1812. Despite ample provocation in the form of malicious Federalist derision, British attacks that included the capture and burning of Washington, D.C., and the political dissent and disruptions that led to the secret deliberations of the Hartford Convention, Madison calmly avoided suppressive measures during the War of 1812. He felt surprised and pained at the opposition he encountered;[1] but his contemporaries commented frequently on his modesty, even temperament, and self-control, even in the most trying of circumstances. Some Republican officials urged that the Sedition Act be revived, but Madison recognized no governmental power over expression and was unwilling to seek a seditious libel law or to restrict the press through the military. In one case, Madison refused to send troops to defend a post office that a mob threatened to pull down because copies of a hated Federalist newspaper were inside. Madison said that intervention by the federal executive would not be proper.[2]

The only commander in chief to deal with a serious military invasion from outside North America, Madison reacted with a composure that allowed him to retire a popular president with a united country. In a Fourth of July oration delivered in Washington, D.C., in 1816, the speaker hailed Madison for overcoming powerful enemies abroad and at home "without one trial for treason, or even one prosecution for libel."[3] Even the crusty John Adams, whose pugnacious demeanor had helped to divide the nation in 1798, was able to tell Thomas Jefferson that Madison had "acquired more glory, and established more Union, than all his three Predecessors, Washington Adams and Jefferson, put together."[4] Madison's adherence to principle and his ultimate popularity stood in sharp contrast to the Federalists of 1798, who damaged their cause with repression when they merely thought a full-scale war with France could happen.

The War of 1812 did, however, give some indication of what was to come for the press in subsequent conflicts. Mob attacks were carried out against at least four Federalist editors.[5] General Andrew Jackson used martial law to impose military censorship for a brief period after his victory in the Battle of New Orleans. When a newspaper in the city published a letter protesting his denials of civil liberties and his failure to lift martial law after the signing of the Treaty of Ghent, Jackson had the writer, a Louisiana legislator named Louis Louaillier, arrested for mutiny and then sent a colonel and sixty men to arrest a judge who tried to free him with a writ of *habeas corpus*. The judge, Dominick Hall, was banished from the city on Jackson's orders until notice of the treaty's ratification was received and martial law was lifted. When Hall returned, he fined Jackson one thousand dollars for contempt of court. Although American law was not clear on whether the Articles of War applied to civilians and on who could impose martial law and under what conditions, Jackson did not appeal. He made a public statement acknowledging the need to submit to the law, but his actions needlessly tarnished his reputation at a moment of national euphoria and were later exploited by political opponents. Nearly thirty years after the Battle of New Orleans, Congress felt enough pity toward the frail and heavily indebted ex-president to refund the fine with interest, but did not exonerate him. The Senate Judiciary Committee proposed an amendment stating that the action was not meant as a censure of Judge Hall, but it was voted down, and the bill was passed after several Senators pointed out that Jackson himself had accepted the supremacy of the law and submitted to the judgment pronounced.[6]

In a written defense that Judge Hall ruled inadmissible, Jackson had maintained that he had to confront an uncertain military situation where "traitors within our own bosom" were able to spy for the enemy and he complained that "native Americans" like himself were being instructed on their privileges, as "Aliens & strangers became the most violent advocates of constitutional Rights." The general said, "Unlimited liberty of speech is incompatible with the discipline of a camp; & that of the press is the more dangerous when it is made the vehicle of conveying intelligence to the Enemy or exciting to mutiny among the soldiery." Not to have punished the writer, he said, would have been "a formal surrender of all discipline, all order, all personal dignity & public safety." Jackson explained that he "thought that in such a moment constitutional forms must be suspended for the permanent preservation of constitutional Rights, & that there could be no question whether it were better to depart, for a moment from the exercise of our dearest privileges, or have them *wrested* from us forever." He said that he did not regret using the powers that "the exigency of the times" had forced upon him because they had "saved the country."[7] In reality, the writer had done no more than comment on Jackson's policies, and the Battle of New Orleans had been fought without either side knowing that the Treaty of Ghent ending the war had been signed two weeks earlier.

Jackson's behavior did not escape the attention of an astonished President Madison, who wanted to record his disapproval. Through his acting secretary of war, Alexander J. Dallas, Madison asked the new national hero to provide a full explanation for reports that "liberty of the press has been suspended" in Louisiana. In answer to Jackson's defense of extreme military necessity while confronting enemies who could conquer the country and destroy the Constitution, Madison later instructed Dallas to write that he had confidence in the general and did not plan to challenge the evidence for his claims. Madison explained that he was not inclined to condemn measures taken where such a crisis existed, but he told the general that no one had authority to impose martial law beyond any authority granted by Congress and that he would have to suffer the consequences for violating the Constitution. The president took the position that when a military leader restrained liberty of the press, citizens' rights, and judicial authority, "he may be justified by the law of necessity, while he has the merit of saving his country, but he cannot resort to the established law of the land, for the means of vindication."[8] Madison, in other words, told Jackson his orders might have been justified at a primitive level, but that he had to answer for unconstitutional conduct.

Later presidents and administration officials were more willing to accept the argument of self-preservation and to allow repression in times of war and unrest. When he became president, Andrew Jackson sent a message to Congress denouncing the mailing of "inflammatory" antislavery publications to the South and called for severe penalties to stop them.[9] Congress considered legislation, but concerns about freedom of the press were expressed in the Senate and the House, and no bill was passed. Asserting that press freedom did not apply to abolitionist writings and that liberty would ruin the lives of slaves, Southern states did pass vaguely worded laws with death penalties for circulating antislavery journalism, but were unsuccessful in asking Northern legislatures to approve similar legislation. Southern postmasters thus found themselves required by federal law to deliver abolitionist mail and by state laws to stop it. When faced with this conflict, federal officials said they regarded the safety of society as their primary duty. Tacit approval was given to mobs that attacked abolitionist editors and to postmasters who would not deliver antislavery mail.[10] "We owe an obligation to the laws," explained Jackson's postmaster general, Amos Kendall, "but a higher one to the communities in which we live, and if the *former* be perverted to destroy the *latter*, it is patriotism to disregard them."[11]

The Mexican War provided a sharp contrast to the presidential integrity in the War of 1812. Madison had to lead a divided nation and incompetent military against an invader, but, with his devotion to republican principle and the Constitution, did not attempt to enlarge executive power. James K. Polk, more interested in conquest than in the Constitution, used ruthless means to whip up a divisive, expansionist war instead of relying on conventional diplomacy to obtain his objectives. He managed to provoke a border incident and rush Congress into war with Mexico in 1846, but public opinion was deeply divided over the conflict.[12] Critics of the administration's actions ranged from philosopher Henry David Thoreau to Ulysses S. Grant.[13] Grant served as a young officer in an army that had the highest death rate of any in American history and that had raped, murdered, and robbed its way through a neighboring country;[14] he later characterized the Mexican War as "one of the most unjust ever waged by a stronger against a weaker nation." He, like many others, thought the president was seeking to acquire territory like a European monarch and to increase the number of slave states.[15]

Among the Whigs who objected to the Democratic president's instigation of the war was a young Congressman from Illinois, Abraham Lincoln. In 1848, Lincoln joined a majority of House members who voted in favor of a resolution saying the war had been "unnecessarily and unconstitutionally begun by the President of the United States."[16] In a letter disagreeing with the position of his friend and law partner William H. Herndon, who thought that the president is the sole judge of when it was necessary to use force to repel another nation, Lincoln spelled out what he thought were the reasons for Congress having the war-making power. "Kings had always been involving and impoverishing their people in wars, pretending generally, if not always, that the good of the people was the object," Lincoln wrote. "This, our Convention understood, to be the most oppressive of all kingly oppressions; and they resolved to so frame the Constitution that *no one man* should hold the power of bringing this oppression upon us."[17]

With his popularity declining, the military situation tenuous, and additional funding for the war in doubt, Polk presented a strident annual message to Congress at the end of 1846. He defended his actions and complained about his critics' views being communicated not only to the nation, but also throughout Mexico and the world. "A more effectual means could not have been devised to encourage the enemy and protract the war than to advocate and adhere to their cause," he said, "and thus give them 'aid and comfort.' " Polk's opposition in Congress expressed resentment at having their views characterized as traitorous and accused the president of going beyond legitimate self-defense and the Constitution by establishing new governments in conquered territories on his own dictatorial authority. With repeated references to the safety of the army and of civilians, James A. Seddon, a Democratic member of the House, who was later Secretary of War for the Confederacy, spelled out a position that it was reasonable and necessary for commanders to establish provisional civil governments and to impose martial law when absolutely necessary for self-defense. The commander in chief, he argued, was in an unprecedented position to make decisions and would be subject to the review and legislation of Congress. But Polk could not count on all members of his own party for support. The spokesman for the other side of the issue was Representative Joseph A. Woodward, a South Carolina Democrat who insisted that the commander in chief was "a mere military officer" who was "wholly subordinate to Congress" in that capacity. As president, Woodward said, Polk was to execute laws and was not authorized to make laws or "to disturb vested rights, or any other rights."[18]

In the war zones and in occupied cities, United States Army officers used martial law and loose definitions of their orders to suppress at least five American newspapers and five Mexican newspapers whose opinions about American conduct angered the military authorities. Critical or annoying papers that were not shut down were sometimes subjected to censorship, economic pressures, or the threat of violence.[19] The publications that survived became semiofficial voices of the military, printing general orders and poetry submitted by soldiers.[20] Polk's Democratic party organ, the *Union*, published in Washington, D.C., declared that there could be no doubt that war zone newspapers critical of administration policies and actions were guilty of *"flagrant treason"* for giving "aid and comfort to the enemy" and were subject to "all the rigors of summary martial law." Attacks from Whig party newspapers within the United States, however, were not being punished. "No," a *Union* writer said, "give these *'moral traitors'* rope enough, and they will hang themselves." The *National Intelligencer* defended administration critics, saying that leaders "who respect the freedom of the press, and who can stand upon the strength of their own conscious rectitude" could bear invective in silence, as George Washington had done.[21]

As a practical matter, suppressing the newspapers of a well-established opposition party might have been more disastrous than the Sedition Act prosecutions had been. On the other hand, using summary military authority against a few isolated civilian journalists in a remote, contested region involved few risks. However, inasmuch as military justice exists to retain military discipline and martial law is not authorized by any specific provision of the Constitution, commanders did not have definite authority for their actions against civilians, even if they thought criticism was treason.[22] After consulting with the secretary of war and the attorney general, both of whom seemed to find martial law too sensitive politically, General Winfield Scott said he was "left in my own darkness on the subject" before departing for Mexico. The Polk administration did ask Congress to pass legislation allowing the imposition of martial law, but Congress did not comply. Generals like Scott, therefore, assumed the authority on their own responsibility.[23] The declaration of martial law Scott used in Mexican cities said that the action was based on an "unwritten code" that "all armies, in hostile countries, are forced to adopt—not only for their own safety, but for the protection of unoffending inhabitants and their property." Under Scott's formulation of what authority was to exist in addition to the military code written by Congress, Mexican police and courts were to continue their functions in most instances, but military commissions were to be established to deal with offenses by or against Americans that were illegal in the United States and that were, like murder, rape, and various other crimes, not "clearly cognizable by any court martial."[24]

If Polk had claimed power over civilians in his capacity as commander in chief, he surely would have invited political and legal trouble. In a case dealing with the status of an occupied Mexican port, the Supreme Court later stated that in a war the president's "duty and his power are purely military" and that his military authority was "placed by law at his command."[25] Officers in the Mexican War, therefore, may have violated civilians' constitutional rights as Andrew Jackson had in the War of 1812, but, with a Democrat serving as commander in chief and Whig generals Zachary Taylor and Winfield Scott in charge in the war zones, neither party had much incentive to fight for civil liberties, and a misbegotten precedent for military rule and censorship was created. In his memoirs, General Scott criticized the "cowardice of certain high functionaries" but expressed relief that his imposition of martial law had "worked like a charm" and had not resulted in legal action against him. He acknowledged that troops took the United States Constitution "with them beyond the limits of their own country," but did not explain how the military could violate the press clause by suppressing American and Mexican newspapers.[26]

President Polk did not let any concerns about the Constitution or the democratic principle of having an informed public interfere with his single-minded pursuit of the war. In addition to allowing his officers to crush dissenting views at the front, he attempted to stop embarrassing diplomatic leaks.[27] Another problem, however, came from the military itself. Soldiers' correspondence frequently included derogatory statements about the president and his policies and sometimes ended up in the press.[28] When war hero and Whig presidential prospect Zachary Taylor wrote to a fellow general to defend himself from Democratic criticism and to question the sense of expending so much "blood and treasure" in the war, the letter was passed along to a New York newspaper and was soon reprinted elsewhere.[29] Although nothing indicated that "Old Rough and Ready" had intended the letter to be published, Polk concluded that Taylor was "in the hands of political managers" and arranged for the *Union* to republish the letter and to allege, with little foundation and no specificity, that it contained "information which cannot fail to prove most injurious to us and advantageous to the enemy." Polk also had Secretary of War William Marcy write Taylor to say that the letter disclosed valuable information and would disincline the enemy to negotiate for peace because the letter suggested that the fruits of victory in Mexico would be of little value. The publication, therefore, was "most deeply to be regretted."[30] Taylor replied that he did not intend the letter for publication, but that he saw "nothing in it which, under the same circumstances I would not write again." The Mexicans had plenty of sources of information, he said, and many other soldiers and statesmen had expressed similar misgivings about the war.[31]

Marcy's letter, however, had referred Taylor to paragraph 650 of the Army regulations published in 1825. Paragraph 650 prohibited officers to allow a private letter or report about military operations to reach the press within a month of the termination of the campaign it described, a period that tended to eliminate the news value of a story and make it less likely to be published. Such reports, the regulation said, "are frequently mischievous in design, and always disgraceful to the army." The punishment for the offense was dismissal from the service. Marcy noted that the paragraph had been dropped from the compilation of Army regulations published in 1841, but said that "the President has directed it to be republished, and the observance of it strictly enjoined on all officers."[32] The appearance of the order in the *Union* prompted Whig reaction in the House of Representatives. Representative George Ashmun of Massachusetts complained that an "old rule, antiquated, obsolete, and almost forgotten, had been disinterred and paraded once more, with the odor of the grave still about it" in order "to serve a party purpose." Noting that uncritical letters from soldiers had been appearing in the *Union* without interference, Ashmun charged that the administration was maneuvering to keep discussion of issues one-sided in Congress and elsewhere until it was too late for opposing ideas to make any difference.[33]

Two weeks later, the Senate Whigs, joined by four disaffected Democrats known as the Balance of Power Party, decided to deny their chamber's floor and press gallery to the editors of the *Union*. The vote, of twenty-seven to twenty-one, was taken in response to an acerbic letter in the newspaper that said "the cause of Mexico is

THE ORGAN KICKED OUT.

Figure 5.1   In 1847 Washington Union *journalists were barred from the Senate floor and gallery after the newspaper, the "organ" of President James K. Polk, criticized congressional opposition to the administration's Mexican War policies. Senators Daniel Webster and John C. Calhoun (center) kick out the* Union *editor, Thomas Ritchie, who is shown as a court jester to Polk (far left). Lithograph by Edward Williams Clay (1847). Courtesy of the Library of Congress.*

maintained with zeal and ability" by Polk's detractors in the Senate. The main argument for the resolution came from Senator James Westcott of Florida, one of the Balance of Power Democrats, who denied that freedom of the press was being infringed. Press freedom, he explained, meant that individuals could take legal action for damage to their reputations, but that a government body did not have a character it could defend through the kind of prosecutions carried out under the discredited and unconstitutional Sedition Act of 1798. All the Senators were doing, he said, was withdrawing a privilege from editors who had wantonly accused them of treason. "I ask," Westcott said, "what right has the editor or reporter of any newspaper to such admission superior to that of any other citizen?" Without a trace of irony, Polk, who two weeks earlier had unilaterally imposed prior restraint on thousands of soldiers, wrote in his diary that the Senate's denial of special seating was a "foul deed" that "strikes a blow at the liberty of the press."[34]

To the further dismay of Polk, General Scott used Paragraph 650, the rule the president had revived, in bringing charges against one of the president's political cro-

SELF-INFLATING PILLOW.

Figure 5.2   *Using the pen name "Leonidas," General Gideon J. Pillow (kneeling) wrote a letter published in the September 10, 1847, issue of the New Orleans* Delta *to praise his own accomplishments in the Mexican War while belittling General Winfield Scott. Scott (right) had Pillow, a crony of President Polk, tried by a military court, but a paymaster, Major Archibald W. Burns (left), took the blame. Polk removed Scott, a political rival, from his command. Lithograph by Nathaniel Currier (1848). Courtesy of the Library of Congress.*

nies, General Gideon J. Pillow.[35] Scott, who was already at odds with the president in domestic politics and war policy,[36] accused Pillow of having written a newspaper story that excessively praised his own battle prowess at Scott's expense. Pillow, a vain, inept, and inexperienced soldier who owed his military rank to his friend in the White House, appeared to have an ambition to replace Scott and perhaps even to seek the presidency. Pillow was evidently responsible for the publication, but he defended himself ably, and his paymaster, who had edited the story for the press, took responsibility. A military court, which was packed with Democrats by Polk and Secretary Marcy, dropped the proceedings. Polk, who removed Scott from his command when he learned of the charge against Pillow, concurred with the result and promoted two of the three members of the court.[37] The president complained in his diary, "Gen'l Pillow is a gallant and highly meritorious officer, and has been greatly persecuted by Gen'l Scott, for no other reason than that he is a Democrat in his politics and was supposed to be my personal & political friend."[38] Yet Polk, like John Adams, was discovering how easy it is to be caught in one's own snares set for the suppression of political enemies.

II.

Like James Polk, President Abraham Lincoln did not have any legislation from Congress specifically authorizing restraints on journalists, but he let administration officials and military officers restrain press freedom during the Civil War. Lincoln and his War Department either ignored the First Amendment or attempted to override it by broadly construing powers given by Congress. With trite references to public safety needs, authorities issued jumbled, redundant, and often-ignored orders aimed at imposing strict military censorship of military news.[39] No matter what the official decrees were, however, many decisions on press restrictions were actually made by the commanders in the field. Journalists had their publications suspended in the exercise of military government and were tried by court-martial or summarily disciplined.[40] Reporters were therefore not inclined to criticize the officers they depended on and in some cases took bribes from for favorable coverage, but they did offend them.[41] Angry at coverage and claiming military necessity, Union generals arrested reporters, denied them access to camps, and sometimes closed down their newspapers.[42] Approximately ninety-two newspapers were either shut down or had employees jailed during the war, and at least III were attacked by mobs that often included Union soldiers.[43] More intent on achieving his ends than worrying about the means, the politician who was president preferred to avoid not only direct personal responsibility but also the formulation of a coherent policy.[44] Although journalists sometimes protested that their First Amendment rights were being violated, public officials dealt with the issue on an ad hoc and arbitrary basis.[45]

Autocratic telegraph censorship began shortly after the surrender of Fort Sumter when a mob of southern sympathizers in Baltimore stoned and shot at Union troops on their way to Washington. With the approval of Secretary of War Simon Cameron, soldiers took over the lines and stopped correspondents from transmitting stories on the incident. Secretary of State William Seward answered complaints by telling reporters that their stories "would only influence public sentiment, and be an obstacle in the path of reconciliation."[46] Before a major battle was even fought, Lincoln's top general imposed telegraph censorship on his own authority. On July 8, 1861, Winfield Scott issued a one-sentence order that said: "Henceforth the telegraph will convey no dispatches concerning the operations of the Army not permitted by the Commanding General." The order, which was put out nearly eight months before Lincoln was able to use an act of Congress to take military possession of the nation's telegraph lines, was approved by Secretary Cameron.[47]

Scott knew how the press had been subjected to dictatorial decisions during the Mexican War, but he had not explained how so many messages would be read or why only one means of conveying information was affected. Reporters held a protest meeting at the Capitol and convinced Scott to allow them to telegraph reports on the progress of battles as they were occurring. The correspondents agreed not to reveal or predict troop movements. American Telegraph Company officials were to decide when to censor material that could be helpful to the South.[48] The arrangement was discarded later in the month, however, when reports of the Union defeat at the first Battle of

Bull Run began to arrive in Washington. Favorable early accounts were sent without difficulty, but once the actual outcome was becoming apparent, near midnight, Scott ordered that transmissions be stopped. Newspapers that announced victory the next morning to rejoicing readers across the North later blamed the government for the public being misinformed.[49]

Telegraph censorship was aggravating. Reporters developed codes to convey information in innocuous-looking telegrams to their newspapers;[50] they complained bitterly about absurdity and incompetence in censorship.[51] Dispatches could be reduced to nonsense or excluded entirely if they contained a single objectionable fact. L. A. Gobright, a Washington correspondent for the Associated Press who had close relations with the administration and semiofficial status as a distributor of government announcements, was allowed to say that Union soldiers wounded at Fredericksburg were arriving in the city, but could not say where they had been because "the rule was, we must not let the enemy know what was taking place, as if the enemy did not already know he had fought a battle!"[52] News of the rout of a superior Union force was available in Washington, but the rest of the country was slow to realize the extent of the disaster due to censorship and the inaccurate reporting that resulted. News that flowed into Washington was printed by the local papers, but often the same stories could not be clipped and sent by telegraph to the rest of the country. The result was that the Washington newspaper accounts could pass through the long, porous front and reach Richmond faster than Boston.[53] Motives for wanting to delay or silence war coverage and commentary were abundant. Not only were Lincoln and his generals embarrassed by their battlefield blunders, but also the War Department was being disgraced by flagrant fraud and massive incompetence in purchasing that led to a lengthy Congressional investigation and finally to Cameron's resignation early in 1862.[54]

In reaction to military censorship of news and opinion sent by telegraph, the House of Representatives late in 1861 asked its Judiciary Committee to investigate whether telegraph censorship had been established; if so, what authority was being used; and "if such censorship has not been used to restrain wholesome political criticism." During the investigation Congress voted to allow the president to take military control of telegraph lines and railroads during the war "when in his judgment the public safety may require it." The statute authorized Lincoln to "prescribe rules and regulations" for the seized property, but appeared to be aimed at maintaining the telegraph and railroads for government uses and did not mention press censorship. When he took over all of the nation's telegraph facilities on February 26, 1862, the president gave his second secretary of war, Edwin M. Stanton, complete authority to censor stories sent by telegraph. The order, which simply noted the authority given for military possession of telegraph lines, stated that the War Department or a general would have to provide express approval for all telegraphic communications dealing with military operations. The order also included a provision that newspapers would not be allowed to receive information by telegraph or circulate papers by railroad if they published any "military news, however obtained" that was not authorized. The next day, after protests, the restriction was modified to say that newspapers "may publish past facts, leaving out all details of military force, and all statements from which the number, position, or strength of the military force of the United States can be inferred."[55]

After hearing testimony that opinions about the performance of the Army and administration often had not been permitted, the Judiciary Committee issued, on March 20, 1862, a report that was highly critical of the government's telegraph censorship as it had shifted from the Treasury Department, to the War Department, to the State Department and finally back to the War Department. Although the original purpose of censorship during the war had been to prevent the publication of military information useful to the Confederacy, the report said, dispatches "almost numberless, of a political, personal, and general character have been suppressed." The committee listed examples of embarrassing but "harmless" material that was stopped and cited State Department censorship instructions that assumed the power to handle both civil and military matters. The report stated that journalists who had testified did not object to "the suppression of despatches of a military character which could in any manner be tortured into disclosures of information to the enemy" and observed that the committee was "not aware of any interference on the part of the censor with any despatches except those of a military character" since the president had taken possession of the telegraph several weeks earlier.[56]

The committee, however, was faced with a situation Congress had fostered by granting a broad presidential power at a time of crisis. The imposition of a regime of press censorship almost certainly went beyond the legislative intent;[57] but the president was acting in the name of safety, and Congress evidently was not inclined to initiate a major confrontation over the issue. The committee report merely noted that censorship had been established and ended with a sentence recommending that the restraints "should not interfere with the free transmission of intelligence by telegraph when the same will not aid the public enemy in his military or naval operations." The committee thus chose to advise the executive branch on the practice of censorship rather than to question its legal foundation, but in the same concluding sentence appeared to distinguish between the use of authorized and unauthorized powers by adding that "it may become necessary for the government (under the authority of Congress) to assume exclusive use of the telegraph for its own legitimate purposes, or to assert the right of priority in the transmission of its own despatches."[58] Congress clearly had granted the president the power to use the telegraph in the war effort, but the administration had gone further and decided to control what reporters could report.

After the Post Office was placed under the War Department in 1862, commanding officers often had newspapers seized from the mails.[59] However, the Senate soon passed a resolution demanding to know what authority the officers were using. Postmaster Montgomery Blair answered that he presumed it was "the law of public safety" and explained that "military power" was being used.[60]

Secretary of War Stanton devoted a considerable amount of his relentless energy to stamping out civil liberties. "He was a man who never questioned his own authority, and who always did in war time what he wanted to do," General Grant later wrote. "He was an able constitutional lawyer and jurist; but the Constitution was not an impediment to him while the war lasted."[61] In his zeal to control information, Stanton used telegraph censorship to create a news void that he then filled with his own dispatches, which made their way to front pages across the North. He did not hesitate to restrict the movements of journalists by canceling their passes, to insist that Union casualty figures be lowered in stories about defeats, or to delay dispatches until they lost their news value.[62] He jailed reporters as he saw fit; for instance, he had Malcolm Ives of the New York *Herald* held by the military for four months without formal charges. Ives was taken into custody "as a spy," Stanton said in an official report, because he behaved "insolently" at the War Department in demanding news he was not authorized to print. Newspapers could provide "public facts as may be properly made known," the secretary of war stated, but "no matter how useful or powerful the press may be, like everything else, it is subordinate to the national safety."[63] In his memoirs, Grant did not dispute Stanton's position on civil liberties during the Civil War, but said that suppressing rebellion was an "inherent" right like self-defense. "The Constitution was therefore in abeyance for the time being, so far as it in any way affected the progress and termination of the war," Grant said.[64]

The idea that the press could be required to submit to officials making safety claims was less clear to others. In 1861 a federal grand jury in New York issued a presentment asking the court if four New York newspapers and the Brooklyn *Eagle* could be punished for "encouraging the rebels." If they were not committing a crime, the presentment said, "then there is a great defect in our laws, or they were not made for such an emergency." The court dropped the matter, but Postmaster General Blair ordered that the five papers presented as "dangerous for their disloyalty" be excluded from the mails. A month later, a grand jury in New Jersey issued a presentment against five newspapers that were denouncing Union leaders and "thwarting their efforts for self-preservation." Although the press was free to criticize public men and measures in peacetime, the grand jury said, the press "should uphold the existing Government, or be treated as its enemies" when the life of the nation and the lives of individuals were at stake. The presentment, however, did not seek a legal remedy. The newspapers were left "to the wholesome action of public opinion" by the grand jury, which thought that any who "do not hereafter give their unqualified support to the National Government" should be subjected to boycotts.[65]

When the House adopted a resolution asking its Judiciary Committee to investigate "by what authority of Constitution and law, if any" the postmaster general was excluding some newspapers from the mail, Blair claimed a temporary wartime power of the executive branch to deny the mails to publications that would instigate disloyalty. He quoted Justice Joseph Story's Blackstonian view that press freedom meant only freedom from prior restraint and not a right to attempt to subvert the government. Blair maintained that the Post Office was acting in the absence of any congressional assertion of its regulatory authority over the mails, and left "treasonable" newspapers free to publish what they pleased "but could not be called upon to give them circulation." Blair's bow to Congress and willingness to take sole responsibility met with the Judiciary Committee's approval, and its report backed his efforts as a wartime response to the dangers of dissent. The members noted that the Constitution allowed Congress to suppress rebellion, but they relied more on a "sense of common justice" argument that the machinery of government did not have to be open to those working against that very government. "Every government, unless by its constitution restricted, has the most ample power of self-preservation," their report asserted, "and it is by no means essential to that power that it should be enumerated among its expressly granted powers."[66] Thus recognizing constitutional restrictions on self-preservation, as well as sidestepping the "powers not delegated" language of the Tenth Amendment and the "no law" protection of the First Amendment, the committee was content to leave the problem in the hands of the Lincoln administration.

Congress, which had journalists in leadership and staff positions, did at least question the legitimacy of telegraph and mail censorship, but the rebellion was a grave crisis, and imposing limits on government power could be seen as creating an impediment to victory.[67] Yet devoting time and energy to defeating the press rather than enemy could impede victory as well. The administration and the armed forces claimed so much power, issued so many decrees aimed at the press, and acted so aggressively that critics and reporters were kept off balance, but such efforts distracted authorities and the public from more pertinent matters. One of the most effective Union officers was Ulysses S. Grant, who, when sober, concentrated on the task at hand. "Grant is very phlegmatic, and holds in great contempt newspaper criticism," noted General George Meade, "and thinks, as long as a man is sustained by his own conscience, his superiors, and the Government, that it is not worth his while to trouble himself about the newspapers."[68]

Although he often backed other generals when they did battle with the press, Grant was not too proud or too paranoid to bear carping in the press and was not inclined to see a news story as a breach of security.[69] On one occasion, however, he did order the arrest of Warren P. Isham of the *Chicago Times* for a fabricated story about the Confederacy having a fleet of ironclads at Pensacola.[70] Isham worked for Wilbur F. Storey, who once told one of his reporters, "Telegraph fully all news you can get and when there is no news send rumours."[71] One of the stories Isham had sent was about a Union general who had fled a bordello near Memphis without his clothes when a group of Confederate officers arrived.[72] Isham languished in the Alton military prison for several months before a reporter sent by Storey, Sylvanus Cadwallader, brought "scores of letters from influential men of the state of all shades of political opinion" asking for Isham's release and Grant relented, saying that he had been punished enough. Cadwallader then reported on illicit plundering and burning by Grant's troops and expected trouble himself. Grant, however, surprised the reporter by admitting the problem and saying that he would not stop correspondents from telling what they knew about Army operations already completed. Cadwallader, who later became chief correspondent for the New York *Herald*, developed a close relationship of mutual dependence with Grant and saved him from disgrace by covering up his bouts of drunkenness and keeping him away from the bottle as much as he could. Grant appreciated the reporter's integrity and gave him carte blanche to cross lines, take possession of transportation, and requisition supplies. Recalling how he carried orders and dispatches for the Army, Cadwallader said, "I was counted as a member of the staff."[73]

Other military leaders were not so accommodating. General Henry W. Halleck, for instance, refused to recognize passes given to reporters by the secretary of war and insisted on providing the news of one campaign himself, in what the New York *Tribune*'s correspondent called "a grave and weighty issue between the Military Power and the rights of the Press and the People." The passes allowed access to all military units, but, after being criticized in the press for his extremely slow progress toward Corinth, Mississippi, Halleck signed Special Field Order, No. 54, which said that "all *unauthorized hangers-on*" were to be denied access to his camps. Some reporters were officially authorized, but Halleck's order was aimed at journalists and not at many other civilians who accompanied his soldiers. Those who attempted to evade the order were to be forced into labor on military construction projects. After failing to reach a compromise with the general, twenty-one of the thirty reporters covering the campaign agreed to a protest stating that the public wanted information on the condition of the Army, the conduct of soldiers, and the management of the force of 125,000 men, but Halleck said that enemy spies were in the camps and that he would not respect any passes. Nearly all the reporters were forced to leave. Halleck did permit Associated Press (AP) dispatches prepared under his supervision. When Halleck reached Corinth, after traveling at a rate of only three quarters of a mile a day, he found that the Confederate army had managed to escape while making it appear that they were still in the city.[74]

Administration officials endorsed clamping down on the press. "You will have to protect yourself by rigid measures against the reporters in your army," Secretary of War Edwin M. Stanton told General Joseph Hooker, "and the Department will support you in any measure you are pleased to take on the subject." Stanton went as far as to disallow passes issued by Lincoln.[75]

Generals who had political ambitions could treat offending reporters as vermin. Major General Benjamin F. Butler, who had hopes of being a presidential nominee, told Cadwallader at one point he could have him "shot by drum-head court-martial in about fifteen minutes" but later offered him an appointment as a second lieutenant in an apparent attempt to win his favor.[76] Butler, a ruthless man who was eventually removed from his post by Grant, subjected journalists who portrayed his failings to dangerous physical ordeals without any legal process. Augustus Cazaran of the Boston *Traveller* was put to work digging trenches on the front lines for sixty days, but when he held up his ball and chain, Confederate soldiers stopped firing in his direction. Chaplain Henry Norman Hudson, a gray-haired Shakespeare scholar who criticized Butler's generalship in a letter published by the New York *Evening Post*, was brought before the general and subjected to a lengthy interrogation, but was not given any written charges or a trial. "You stabbed me in the dark, sir! You stabbed me in the dark!" Butler bellowed. "But I have caught you at last; I have you in my power now, sir, and I am going to punish you." The chaplain suffered fifty-three days of mistreatment, which included confinement in an ammunition tent and later in an uncleaned stable. After Hudson's release and resignation, he continued to criticize the general, and Butler attempted to have him tried by a court-martial for "calumnious, censorious, and defamatory criticism and censure of his superior officer." Hudson wrote a scathing pamphlet on the experience that haunted Butler in his later career as a member of Congress, governor of Massachusetts, and presidential candidate.[77]

Even the gentlemanly and efficient General Meade could let his pride and political ambitions affect his judgment. Angered by a *Philadelphia Inquirer* article that merely said he was more cautious than Grant in one engagement, Meade had reporter Edward Crapsey drummed out of camp riding backward on a horse with placards proclaiming

"Libeller of the Press" on his chest and back. Nearly universal action by reporters kept Meade's name out of the press after the incident and helped thwart his presidential aspirations. He became, Cadwallader said, as unknown in Army correspondence "as any dead hero of antiquity." Meade let Crapsey return in a few months, but the general later admitted to Cadwallader that even if the reporter had been inaccurate, the degrading punishment was one of the greatest mistakes of his life. Meade added that he himself had published an official account of the battle of Gettysburg using full reports from every command and yet discovered that he had committed many mistakes. The experience, the general said, made him willing to overlook the errors made by reporters while a battle was occurring. "His wonder," Cadwallader said, "was that more mistakes were not made under such circumstances."[78]

Some of the most serious violations of press freedom occurred as the result of the War Department order, of August 8, 1862, that cited broad, unspecified presidential authority in allowing military trial and imprisonment for acts, statements, or writings discouraging volunteer enlistments. The order was the basis for numerous arrests of journalists and others, particularly Democrats, who expressed doubts about the wisdom of the war and the Republican administration's methods of pursuing it.[79] The following month Lincoln issued his own sweeping national proclamation suspending the writ of *habeas corpus* and allowing military trials for "all persons discouraging volunteer enlistments, resisting militia drafts, or guilty of any disloyal practice."[80] One of those arrested was Dennis A. Mahony, the editor of the Dubuque *Herald* and the Democratic nominee for Congress in his Iowa district. Seized at his home in the middle of the night by a Republican marshal and jailed in Washington, D.C., for three months without formal charges, Mahony had opposed both abolition and secession. The experience prompted him to write *The Prisoner of State*, a book that documented many similar arrests and argued that the Bill of Rights was not suspended in wartime. He said that hundreds were having their First Amendment freedoms "ruthlessly violated by Executive power, assumed arbitrarily," and pointed out that the Sixth Amendment right to be informed of charges and given a speedy and fair trial applied to "ALL criminal prosecutions."[81]

Throughout the Civil War, people who gave orders to soldiers simply assumed they could give orders to the press, but some of the cases of arrogating power involved the pretense of enforcing military law. After the humiliating Union defeat in the first Battle of Bull Run, Secretary of War Cameron issued a statement approved by Lincoln that said that all communication of military operations or affairs "by writing, printing, or telegraphing" that was unauthorized by the commanding general would be "absolutely prohibited" and subject to punishment by a court-martial. For a legal justification Cameron cited the fifty-seventh article of war passed by Congress in 1806, which allowed punishments up to the death penalty for "holding correspondence with, or giving intelligence to, the enemy, either directly or indirectly." Thus enlarging a military regulation dealing with spies and traitors into censorship authority over journalists who were seeing and saying what many other civilians could, Cameron said, "Public safety requires strict enforcement of this article."[82]

Later analyses concluded that the articles of war did not provide any legal basis for the discipline of civilian correspondents;[83] however, the supposed authority to treat journalists as military spies was used for purposes of intimidating or excluding reporters. The editor of the *Sunday Chronicle* of Washington, D.C., for instance, was arrested in 1862 for publishing information on troop movements in violation of the fifty-seventh article. The editor was interrogated and then released after he issued an apology. After the Battle of Mobile Bay, the fifty-seventh article was cited as the basis for excluding two New York newspaper reporters from the command. They were accused of revealing information to the enemy and "engaging in a controversy calculated to disturb the harmony of the troops." In another incident, an assistant adjutant general advised a general who had complained of coverage by the *Philadelphia Inquirer* that the reporter in question could be tried by a military commission because "newspaper correspondents with the army are subject to military law" and could be "brought before such tribunals for any incorrect statement they may publish."[84]

In rare cases formal charges were filed. Private Newton B. Spencer appeared before a general court-martial for a letter he had written to an upstate New York newspaper, the *Pen Yan Democrat*, to complain about the Army's performance in the "Battle of the Crater" in Virginia. The letter described General Meade as an "unpopular nonentity" and a "military charlatan." The judges found Private Spencer guilty of violating military discipline and of showing contempt for Meade, but they refused to find him guilty of giving aid and comfort to the enemy or of violating the fifty-seventh article. Shocked at the verdict and at the lenient punishment that consisted of a reprimand and a forty-eight-dollar fine, superior officers insisted that the case be reconsidered, but the same court reached the same conclusion.[85] Writing critical comments for the press was thus seen as improper conduct for a soldier, but not as the equivalent of treason or communicating with the enemy.

Thomas Knox, a civilian reporter for the New York *Herald*, also had to face a court-martial under the fifty-seventh article.[86] William Tecumseh Sherman, an emotional general who had a particularly turbulent relationship with the press,[87] decided to prosecute Knox for mailing his paper a scornful account of a failed assault near Vicksburg, Mississippi, in 1862. Referring to Sherman's often-questioned leadership and state of mind, the story had concluded, "Insanity and inefficiency have brought their result." Angry that Sherman had issued an order expelling journalists from the expedition and that the military had confiscated his earlier correspondence on the battle, Knox also commented that Vicksburg would have been captured if the military had "acted as earnestly and persistently against the rebels as against the representatives of the press."[88] Sherman had the reporter brought to his quarters and confronted him with inaccuracies in the story. According to the general, Knox said that reporters were attacking him because " 'you are regarded the enemy of our set, and we must in self-defense write you down.' " Knox provided a written apology for the errors, but he attributed the mistakes to tight restrictions on journalists.[89]

Far from satisfied, Sherman took the time to write long, indignant letters to friends, relatives, and fellow officers. He told another general that Knox was a "spy and infamous dog" and that he could no longer tolerate the aspersions and misrepresentations of journalists. "I do know that the day will come when every officer will demand the execution of this class of spies," he said. Although the articles of war did not deal with civilians who published mistakes and insults, Sherman was determined to make an example of Knox. He told an admiral that he did not want the reporter

Figure 5.3 *Civil War reporters in the field with a New York* Herald *wagon. Mathew Brady collection. Courtesy of National Archives.*

shot, but that he did want "to establish the principle that such people cannot attend our armies, in violation of orders, and defy us, publishing their garbled statements and defaming officers who are doing their best." In another letter, which said that reporters were in fact spies because they gave intelligence to the enemy, Sherman declared that those who endangered an army "are by all belligerents punished summarily with the extremist penalties," regardless of their intent. The press had to be willing to surrender some of its rights to protect other freedoms, he added, or those who could be harmed "may in self-defense be compelled to take the law into our own hands for our safety."[90]

Sherman had good odds for his recourse to a more formal kind of law. As Knox described it, the court-martial consisted of stern-looking officers under Sherman's command "in full uniform, including sash and sword" and was "carefully watched by that distinguished military chieftan, throughout its whole sitting."[91] Yet, after two tedious weeks, most of the charges were rejected. The court could not bring itself to take seriously Sherman's claims that Knox had given information to the enemy indirectly through the newspaper and that he was a spy who had given aid and comfort to the enemy by making false charges against officers. The court also decided that Knox, who had a pass from General Ulysses S. Grant and an invitation from a prominent officer, was guilty with "no criminality" of accompanying the expedition against Sherman's order. The reporter was, however, found guilty of failing to submit his story to military censorship according to the policy announced by Secretary Cameron in

Figure 5.4 *A newspaper vending cart at General George Meade's camp in Virginia. Photograph by Alexander Gardner (1863). Courtesy of the Library of Congress.*

1861 and then promulgated as General Orders No. 67. He was therefore sentenced "to be sent without the lines of the army, and not to return under penalty of imprisonment."[92]

Both the defendant and the accuser were appalled. Knox said in his memoirs that telegraph dispatches were routinely censored but that neither he nor other reporters had ever heard of any order requiring a commander's permission to send a story by mail. "Correspondents everywhere had done the same thing," he said, "and continued to do it till the end of the war."[93] During the trial, the defense had argued that General George McClellan had modified General Orders No. 67 to allow reporters to send descriptions of battles when they were over, but the prosecution contended that McClellan's modification did not apply to western armies.[94] Sherman, who had been on the stand for two days arguing that Northern newspapers provided valuable intelligence to the South, failed on most of his accusations, but continued to maintain

Figure 5.5 *Regarding Civil War journalists as spies who damaged public morale, General William Tecumseh Sherman restricted what they could write and had a New York* Herald *reporter tried by a court-martial. Mathew Brady collection (ca. 1864–65). Courtesy of the National Archives.*

that reporting hindered military operations and that commanding officers needed to be able to decide who would accompany them. "In this point I may be in error, but, for the time being, I am the best judge," he insisted, adding that journalists stirred up dissension in the military and elsewhere and that "they shall not insult me with impunity in my own camp."[95]

Both Sherman and a group of prominent correspondents supporting Knox wanted Lincoln to make a decision on the matter. The journalists, who had gathered signatures on a petition and even arranged for two high-ranking generals to make a plea for Knox, formed a delegation with a congressional representative from the territory of Colorado that went to the White House to confront the president.[96] Needing good relations with both his generals and the press, Lincoln sought to extricate himself with a letter written to "Whom it may concern." Noting that the president of the court-martial and "many other respectable persons" believed that the "offense was technical, rather than willfully wrong, and that the sentence should be revoked," Lincoln decided that the "sentence is hereby so far revoked as to allow Mr. Knox to return to Gen. Grant's Head-Quarters, and to remain, if Gen. Grant shall give his express assent."[97]

Lincoln thus appeared to be helping the reporter, but affirmed that a punishable "offense" had taken place and that the matter could be left with the military. Rather than aggravate Sherman, a soldier he depended on, Grant turned the matter over to him with a written scolding of Knox that should have vindicated the general and preserved his honor. Sherman, however, was not to be assuaged by the diplomatic gestures of his superiors. He informed Knox that he did not consider disobedience and defamation "as mere technical offenses," even if the president and other officers had reached that conclusion. Knox would be welcomed back if he took up a sword or musket, Sherman said, but never as a representative of the press. After depriving Knox of his reporting assignment, Sherman told Grant that Lincoln had feared the enmity of the *Herald* and should decide whether the paper would rule him or he would rule the paper. He said that a demoralized press was driving the country to anarchy and that the people were beginning to "look to our armies as the anchor of safety." Sherman evidently thought his victory over the press was worth the time and effort in the middle of a war. "I still threaten the newspaper men with instant death as spies and they give me a wide berth," he later wrote proudly.[98] As a result, Sherman's success in slicing across the South was inadequately reported.[99]

An indication of how much power a commanding officer could have under Lincoln's habit of deference to the military was a letter General Sherman wrote to the editors of the *Memphis Bulletin* in 1863, a letter that was similar to those issued to newspapers by other generals.[100] Expressing his "mortification" at the "nauseating accounts" of military actions being offered to the public, Sherman accused the paper of printing inaccurate stories and gave instructions on avoiding controversy. Saying his "first duty is to maintain 'order and harmony,' " he told the editors to "print nothing that prejudices government or excites envy, hatred, and malice in a community." Explaining that he had authority over the paper and that it had to heed his "advice," Sherman remarked, "Freedom of speech and freedom of the press, precious relics of former history, must not be construed too largely." When asked to be more precise, the general wrote again to admit that it was "difficult to define clearly my wishes" but said that "the executive of a nation by his army and navy must control all the physique and morals of the nation" when restoring order and that the press needed to "allay rather than arouse the passions of men" by publishing only what was true, necessary for the public good, and not defamatory. Sherman was better able to summarize his expectations in a letter to a fellow general: "No anonymous letters, no praise or censure of officers, no discussion of the policy or measures of Government without the article is reviewed by the commanding officer at Memphis, and editor responsible for the general tenor of extracts from other papers."[101] Working under such restrictions, journalists had little to say about graft, desertion, draft resistance, illness, incompetence, low morale, and the mistreatment of prisoners in the Civil War.[102]

III.

Lincoln may have objected to the Mexican War when he was a Whig member of Congress, but he could be intolerant of dissent when he became president, and he needed all of his homespun, lawyerly inventiveness to explain his exercise of wide-ranging, extraconstitutional rule.[103] In the eleven weeks between the surrender of Fort Sumter and the convening of a special session of Congress on July 4, 1861, Lincoln had assumed authority that one historian of the presidency has described as "a reversion to primitive conceptions of executive power."[104] His actions included suspending the writ of *habeas corpus* in certain places, increasing the size of the Army and Navy, spending unappropriated funds, allowing the military detention of civilians, restricting "treasonous" correspondence, and blockading Southern ports. In his explanation to Congress, Lincoln claimed a general "war power" combination of commander in chief and law enforcement responsibilities that far exceeded the limited role of military leadership assigned to the president in the Constitution. The president said that he had made difficult choices necessary for public safety and the preservation of the nation, but had clearly overstepped his authority and was slow to call Congress into session. Even after Congress met, Lincoln continued to issue proclamations without legislative approval. Contending that he had the authority to issue the Emancipation Proclamation as a war measure, he said, "I think the constitution invests its commander-in-chief, with the law of war, in time of war."[105]

At times, Lincoln seemed to reject the Constitution altogether and seek legitimacy for his policies in the broad principles of the Declaration of Independence or in his election by the people.[106] In his first inaugural address, given as the nation was breaking apart, he affirmed his intention to preserve the union "unless my rightful masters, the American people, shall withhold the requisite means, or, in some authoritative manner, direct the contrary." He condemned the secession of states as the "essence of anarchy" because they would not acquiesce to majority rule, and he argued that "if the policy of the government, upon vital questions, affecting the whole people, is to be irrevocably fixed by decisions of the Supreme Court," then "the people will have ceased, to be their own rulers." Lincoln said, in effect, he would be responsible to what he called "the judgment of this great tribunal, the American people" and that he would do what he thought necessary and suffer any consequences. "While the people retain their virtue, and vigilance, no administration, by any extreme of wickedness or folly, can very seriously injure the government, in the short space of four years," he said. His inaugural address spoke of minority rights being guaranteed by the Constitution and of a Lockean-Jeffersonian right of revolution if they were denied.[107] But Lincoln and his generals did not always allow the "vigilance" that his critics offered in speeches and the press. The courts and Congress did little to deter the trampling of basic liberties. If the crisis was serious and the president was taking responsibility for bringing the nation through, then the other branches were willing to allow his judgment to reign supreme despite the mechanisms and guarantees of the Constitution.

Although even a defender of the Lincoln record on civil liberties has described the system created under his assumption of authority as one of "secret police, paid informers, agents provocateurs, midnight arrests, and dank prisons," Lincoln did not aspire to be an absolute ruler, at least not permanently.[108] He contended that his internal security efforts were preventative rather than punitive and that the nation had ways to stop him if he abused his power.[109] His prerogative, he admitted, had some limits. Believing that elections were "a necessity" in a free government, Lincoln noted that he did not suspend the presidential race of 1864. Having rested much of his wartime authority on the principle of majority rule, he was willing to submit his presidential record to the voters. "It has long been a grave question whether any government, not *too* strong for the liberties of its people, can be strong *enough* to maintain its own existence, in great emergencies," he told a group of citizens shortly after he was reelected. Having disclaimed despotic intentions, he was prepared to give up his extraordinary authority at the end of the crisis. "The Executive power itself would be greatly diminished by the cessation of actual war," Lincoln said in his last annual message to Congress.[110]

Using an expansive view of specified presidential powers and of his general authority as "the Executive,"[111] Abraham Lincoln thus became what has been termed a constitutional dictator, an elected official who suspends civil liberties and commits other unconstitutional acts in order to preserve the Constitution and the public safety.[112] In a speech delivered in 1838, "The Perpetuation of Our Political Institutions," Lincoln had reacted to the antiabolitionist violence of the time by advocating respect for the Constitution and the rule of law and by urging united resistance to any Caesar or Napolean who might arise. Faced with the Civil War a quarter century later, Lincoln saw his authoritarian actions as the answer to upheaval. In 1864, he told a newspaper editor that often a limb had to be amputated to save a life and that he had to preserve the nation and government that had the Constitution as organic law. "I felt that measures, otherwise unconstitutional, might become lawful, by becoming indispensable to the preservation of the constitution, through the preservation of the nation," he said. Two weeks later he told a charity fund-raising gathering that people did not mean the same thing when they talked about liberty. "The shepherd drives the wolf from the sheep's throat, for which the sheep thanks the shepherd as a *liberator*," he said, "while the wolf denounces him for the same act as the destroyer of liberty, especially as the sheep was a black one."[113]

Lincoln's sleight of hand in turning unconstitutional actions into constitutional ones may have been made possible by his fatalistic personal philosophy. A man who had to deal with serious mental depression during his life, Lincoln tended to deny the prospects for human progress and propriety.[114] While running for Congress in 1846 he responded to attacks on his lack of a religious affiliation by explaining that early in life he had embraced "what I understand is called the 'Doctrine of Necessity'— that is, that the human mind is impelled to action, or held in rest by some power, over which the mind itself has no control." In a speech delivered in 1854, Lincoln gave a lesson in how to dispense with the nation's fundamental law. "Jefferson saw the necessity of our government possessing the whole valley of the Mississippi," he told the audience, "and though he acknowledged that our Constitution made no provision for the purchasing of territory, yet he thought that the exigency of the case would justify the measure, and the purchase was made." In the third year of the Civil War he told a small group of visiting dignitaries that "God alone" was responsible for the outcome of the conflict. "I claim not to have controlled events, but confess plainly that events have controlled me," he remarked. The Bill of Rights proved to be no match for such necessitarian logic in the president's mind.[115]

Lincoln, whose preparation for a legal career did not extend much beyond reading Blackstone, had an ability to twist and temporize on freedom of expression that was demonstrated in two cases initiated by General Ambrose E. Burnside.[116] When Burnside took command of the Military Department of the Ohio in 1863, the general declared his outrage at "treasonable expressions" in newspapers and in public meetings denouncing the efforts to extinguish the rebellion. Burnside, a particularly incompetent Union general whose hapless decisions had cost thousands of lives and earned him a transfer to a place where he would presumably do less harm, soon issued General Orders No. 38 mandating expulsion to the South for anyone sympathizing with the enemy. "It must be distinctly understood that treason, expressed or implied, will not be tolerated in this department," the order said. Burnside believed that martial law existed ipso facto in the emergency of the Civil War and that as long as the people did not vote his superiors out of office, he had the power to stamp out criticism that might demoralize the Army or interfere with recruitment. Any dissent, he believed, amounted to treason. "The simple names 'Patriot' and 'Traitor' are comprehensive enough," he said.[117]

As reckless with civil liberties as he was with soldiers' lives, Burnside used General Orders No. 38 to arrest former Ohio congressman and antiwar Democrat Clement L. Vallandigham for "declaring disloyal sentiments and opinions" in a public speech. The charge specified statements that the country was fighting "a wicked, cruel and unnecessary war," that it was a "war for the purpose of crushing out liberty and erecting a despotism," and that Burnside's policy of equating dissent with treason was "a base usurpation of arbitrary authority." Vallandigham's arrest, which occurred after troops broke down the door of his house in Dayton in the middle of the night, prompted local rioters to burn the office of the *Daily Dayton Journal*, a Republican newspaper that had been critical of him. Responding to Republican requests, Burnside not only declared martial law but also arrested a Democratic editor who had denounced the general's action and suspended his newspaper, the *Daily Dayton Empire*. Evidently realizing that a jury might not convict a politician who was then seeking the Democratic nomination for governor of Ohio, Burnside had Vallandigham tried by a military commission, a quasi-judicial tribunal without clear jurisdiction over civilians. The civilian defendant insisted that a military commission had no authority to hear his case when civil courts were available and established that his speech opposed

Figure 5.6   *General Ambrose E. Burnside thought dissent was treason and acted accordingly during the Civil War. His arbitrary actions to suppress expressions of opinion prompted public protests. Mathew Brady collection (ca. 1861). Courtesy of the National Archives.*

disunion and advocated no resistance except through the ballot box. Nevertheless, Vallandigham was convicted and, by Lincoln's order, banished to the confederacy.[118] His angry remark that he did not want to belong to the United States inspired Edward Everett Hale to write "The Man without a Country."[119]

Vallandigham's martyrdom to the Copperhead cause resulted in protests across the North and forced Lincoln to publicly confront the issue of the right to express opinions. Insisting that the purpose was to prevent problems with enlistment and desertion and that the case was not political, the Republican president explained his position in a letter to a group of New York Democrats who had met to express their objections. Despite the disturbances that had occurred in Dayton, Lincoln defended Burnside's action by making repeated references to temporary "public Safety" needs that he said the framers of the Constitution recognized when they allowed the writ of *habeas corpus* to be suspended during a rebellion or invasion. The "life of the nation," he said, depended on the military that Vallandigham was "warring upon" and that therefore had "constitutional jurisdiction to lay hands upon him." Lincoln also maintained that the case was like General Andrew Jackson's arrests in New Orleans, arrests by which the "permanent" freedom of the press "suffered no detriment whatever." He claimed, without providing any evidence, that Congress had approved of Jackson's conduct by remitting his fine and he did not mention that President Madison thought Jackson had violated the Constitution.[120]

Lincoln thus relied mainly on his interpretation of a sentence in Article 1 that deals with legislative powers: "The privilege of the writ of *habeas corpus* shall not be suspended, unless when in cases of rebellion or invasion the public safety may require it." In his explanation of the legal grounds for Vallandigham's arrest, he took the position that actions denying liberties such as freedom of expression and trial by jury "are constitutional when, in cases of rebellion or Invasion, the public Safety requires them."[121] Lincoln evidently believed legislative approval was not necessary for the arrest and confinement of thousands of dissenters and others he regarded as hindering the war effort. He overlooked the fact that the chief justice of the United States had ruled in 1861 that Congress had the exclusive power to suspend the writ of *habeas corpus*, something Lincoln nevertheless did again on his own authority in 1862 for the entire nation.[122] Congress passed its Habeas Corpus Act two months before Vallandigham was arrested in 1863, but it left open the question of whether prior suspensions by the president had been legal.[123] The First Amendment, which says Congress shall make "no law" abridging press freedom, presumably rules out any congressional suspension of *habeas corpus* affecting journalism. Moreover, a claim by any branch of government to such authority does not apply to all wars, only to "rebellion or invasion," circumstances that did not exist in later armed conflicts when officials who relied on Lincoln administration precedent placed restrictions on journalists.[124]

Not satisfied with the trouble he had caused by arresting a politician, Burnside again used the authority he had created to suspend publication of the *Chicago Times*. The *Times* was a racist, Democratic paper that lampooned Lincoln and called the prosecution of Vallandigham an attempt by the administration to "put away the written law, by which itself has an existence, and set up the rule of military despotism!" Burnside charged the paper with "the repeated expression of disloyal and incendiary statements."[125] Although a federal judge issued a restraining order to stop military action against the *Times*, soldiers occupied the newspaper's office. As the court took up further proceedings, Judge Thomas Drummond observed that citizens had a right to comment on public matters and that the government was one of laws "and not a Government of mere physical force." When word reached Springfield, the Illinois House of Representatives passed, by a vote of forty-seven to thirteen, a resolution denouncing Burnside's action as a violation of the state and federal constitutions.[126] Lincoln was warned by Chicago officials that the suppression order had the city on the verge of mob violence;[127] he asked Burnside to revoke the order, saying that he approved of his motives, but wanted to be consulted before civilians were arrested or newspapers closed. The problems caused by shutting down the paper, he noted, were likely to do more harm than the publication would do.[128]

Lincoln's political instincts were correct. The incident provoked fifteen New York newspaper editors to meet and pass a resolution maintaining "the right of the press to criticize firmly and fearlessly the acts of those charged with the administration of the Government." Approximately twenty thousand Democrats held a mass protest meeting in Chicago and passed resolutions saying that Burnside was acting outside the law, that a person who violated the constitutional right of publishing opinions was a "traitor to law and liberty," that military power was subordinate to civil power, and that they were willing to "sacrifice life and fortune and all but liberty" to preserve the Union.[129] Illinois Republicans took a stand supporting the suppression and began criticizing those in their ranks who, fearing violence, had asked the President to rescind Burnside's edict. Evidently discovering that many of his Republican allies in Illinois wanted the *Times* silenced, Lincoln sent another message to Burnside instructing him to withhold the revocation of the suppression order if it was not too late to do so. The second message apparently arrived too late, because the *Times* was given permission to publish again. By taking one position and then the other, Lincoln managed to anger both sides in the controversy. A year later he wrote that he was "far from certain to-day that the revocation was not right," that he could "only say I was embarrassed with the question between what was due the Military service on the one hand, and the Liberty of the Press on the other," and that it was the fear of public backlash conveyed to him "that turned the scale in favor of my revoking the order."[130]

The Knox, Vallandigham, and *Chicago Times* cases, all of which occurred in the first six months of 1863, seem to have shown Lincoln the hazards of allowing generals to take action against civilians who expressed upsetting opinions. On the same day that Burnside issued his order to restrain the *Chicago Times*, Lincoln had written to Burnside to recommend that he remove Brigadier General Milo S. Hascall from his post as the head of the District of Indiana. If Burnside had received the letter before he took action against the *Times*, he might have had second thoughts. Hascall had angered the antiadministration press and Indiana politicians, including the governor, with threats to use Burnside's General Orders No. 38 against newspapers. Editors responded with ridicule and pledges to defy the general.[131] The situation became so heated and so ridiculous that Lincoln had to intervene. Secretary Stanton, writing for the president, told Burnside that Hascall was interfering unnecessarily with the "political condition" of the state and talked about "the necessity for a good understanding" with the governors of Indiana, Ohio, and Illinois. Burnside was told that it would be "expedient" to consult with state authorities before taking any coercive actions against civilians not involved in actual hostilities. "No one can understand better than yourself what harm may be done by an indiscreet or foolish military officer," Stanton wrote, "who is constantly issuing military proclamations and engaging in newspaper controversies upon questions that agitate the public mind." Hascall was quickly relieved of his command. His last act was to revoke his General Orders No. 9 which had started the whole controversy by threatening to use Burnside's General Orders No. 38 against the press.[132]

Lincoln was an astute politician who knew how to cultivate favorable press coverage through patronage and personal contacts;[133] he was starting to see that censorship of opinion could be a rallying point for his critics and that his generals needed to be reined in. A postscript to Stanton's letter to Burnside noted that after it was written, Lincoln had been informed about the suppression of the *Chicago Times*, that the president wanted the order revoked, and that he normally wished to be consulted before civilians were arrested or newspapers were shut down. Six weeks later Lincoln chided General John M. Schofield for arresting a Democratic editor in Missouri who had published a letter from Lincoln to Schofield without permission. The letter had discussed how the president wanted the general to take a middle position between the state's Union factions, but Lincoln told Schofield that he cared very little about the publication of any letter he had written. He did, however, care about the political effects of arresting editors. "Please spare me the trouble this is likely to bring," Lincoln wrote. After the editor went free, Lincoln advised Schofield to exercise his discretion with "great caution, calmness, and forbearance." Newspapers should only be suppressed and individuals arrested, he said, "when they may be working *palpable* injury to the Military in your charge; and, in no other case will you interfere with the expression of opinion in any form, or allow it to be interfered with violently by others."[134]

Opinion was not the issue in 1864 when two New York City newspapers, the *World* and the *Journal of Commerce*, fell for a cleverly executed hoax that brought down Lincoln's wrath. The two papers unwittingly published a forged presidential proclamation calling for a new draft of four hundred thousand men. The story was aimed at pushing up the price of gold and making a profit for the perpetrator, Joseph Howard, Jr., of the *Brooklyn Daily Eagle*, who had bought gold the day before. On the day the hoax appeared it was immediately denied, and the journalists explained satisfactorily how they had been fooled, but Lincoln signed an order drafted by Secretary Stanton that called the publication "treasonable" and ordered that the editors and publishers be arrested for trial before a military commission and that the two newspapers, both of which were administration critics, be seized by military force. The administration lifted the suspension within a few days and the duped journalists were free to publish again.[135] Howard, who in 1861 had concocted a story that Lincoln had arrived in Washington for his inauguration disguised in a Scotch plaid cap and long coat, spent three months in jail before the president responded to a plea from a prominent supporter, Henry Ward Beecher, and released him.[136]

The incident offered another opportunity to Lincoln's critics. Governor Horatio Seymour of New York, who was using the denial of civil liberties as a campaign issue in 1864 and who was to be the Democratic candidate for president in 1868, maintained that the seizure of the newspaper offices was executed "without due legal process, and without the sanction of State or national laws." He asked the district attorney to prosecute, but the grand jury reported that it would be "inexpedient to examine into the subject." At the governor's urging, the district attorney then brought the case to a city court, and warrants were issued for the arrest of Major General John A. Dix, commander of the Department of the East, and other officers who had carried out Lincoln's orders. The charges included forcible entry and kidnapping. Lincoln ordered Dix not to be deprived of his liberty, but the general said that he would bow to the supremacy of the law if he had violated any state laws. The defense argued that the president's authority for the actions was his broad war powers and that he could be impeached if he were acting like a dictator as the prosecution argued. The district attorney contended that the newspapers were punished before investigation or a trial and that Lincoln was "not the military commander of citizens of the United States, but of its soldiers." The state's attorney general insisted that Lincoln violated the First Amendment and could not rely on martial law, because the Constitution did not recognize it and it could only be proclaimed when a particular place was invaded and the courts were suspended.[137]

The central issue in the case, however, was the constitutionality of the Habeas Corpus Act of 1863, which allowed those making seizures and arrests under the president's orders during the rebellion to have immunity from any resulting legal actions.[138] In passing the statute Congress had dealt with the complaint that the president alone could not suspend the privilege by giving him the power, but Democrats argued that his suspension of one remedy, the ability of a judge to issue a writ of *habeas corpus* for delivery of a person to the court for a determination of the legality of a detention or other loss of personal liberty, did not necessarily mean that those whose rights were denied had no legal recourse. Citizens and prosecutors might still be able to take a case to court when freedoms were being violated.[139] In the New York case, the prosecution stated that the president could not be placed " 'higher' than the fundamental law" of the Constitution with unlimited authority to make laws and to define offenses after they had been committed. Judge A. D. Russell agreed that the Habeas Corpus Act was based on the "very novel and startling doctrine" that the president could be made "an absolute monarch" who is "incapable of doing any wrong." He concluded that General Dix and his officers were "subject to the action of the grand jury," but no further action was taken.[140]

As long as he wielded unconstitutional power, Lincoln gave his enemies an issue they could exploit. Political prisoners were honored in mass rallies, and some were nominated for political office in absentia. The arrests became a campaign issue in the elections of 1862 and helped the Democratics achieve an upsurge at the polls. "Our newspaper's, by vilifying and disparaging the administration, furnished them all the weapons to do it with," Lincoln lamented.[141] In his inaugural address in 1862, Jefferson Davis remarked that the "malignity and barbarity" of the Union's handling of civil liberties "proclaimed the incapacity of our late associates to administer a Government as free, liberal, and humane as that established for our common use." Davis said that "through all the necessities of an unequal struggle there has been no act on our part to impair personal liberty or the freedom of speech, of thought, or of the press."[142] Confederate officials and officers did sometimes impose press restrictions as the war progressed, but were proud of being more tolerant than their Northern counterparts.[143]

When General Robert E. Lee complained that a paragraph in the *Richmond Daily Dispatch* had violated voluntary restrictions on reporting troop strengths and movements, Secretary of War George W. Randolph reminded Richmond editors that they were expected to censor themselves on military matters. "It is the ardent wish of the Department that this revolution may be successfully closed without the suppression of one single newspaper in the Confederate States," he said, "and that our experience may be able to challenge comparison with our enemy."[144] The South, in fact, did less damage to civil liberties in what could be considered a fair comparison. The North may have had more trouble with dissent, but most of the battles were fought in the South.[145] Southern editors made frequent use of their freedom to berate Davis and his administration, and then had their papers seized or suspended when they offended occupying Union forces.[146]

Legal scholars reached opposing conclusions about Lincoln's actions. A pamphlet backing the president, one that went through many editions during the conflict, was *The War Powers of the President*, by William Whiting. Noting that a free press could reveal military plans to the enemy, the author maintained that constitutional rights could be suspended to protect the government during a war. Authorities could act in self-defense, he thought, so that one part of the Constitution would not nullify the rest. "It has been said that '*amidst arms* the *laws are silent*,'" Whiting wrote. "It would be more just to say, that while war rages, the *rights*, which in peace are sacred, must and do give way to the higher right—the right of *public safety*—the right which the COUNTRY, *the whole country, claims* to be protected from its enemies, domestic and foreign—from spies, from conspirators, and from traitors." Charles F. Blake responded to Whiting's work with *Prerogative Rights and Public Law*, a pamphlet describing English battles against arbitrary rule and discussing the American conception of limited government. Invoking public safety to override the rights of the people, Blake thought, was not only inappropriate in the United States, but dangerous. "The reign of Charles I., and the rule of Robespierre, Danton and Marat," he said, "are alike rich in precedents to guide a government which desires to enter upon that path." Pointing out that the Constitution did not have provisions for suspending press freedom and other liberties, Blake asked where such war powers came from and how they were limited, if at all.[147]

Lincoln's perceived integrity, ultimate success, and tragic death helped to transform his decisions into "historically forgiven illegalities," unconstitutional maneuvers that often have been seen as passing, in effect, the Lockean-Jeffersonian test of justifiable prerogative that the people could judge.[148] In a book published in 1862, Sidney George Fisher, a Philadelphia lawyer and prolific writer on legal topics, observed that the president could be replaced at the next election if the people were dissatisfied. Analyzing how "freedom of the press was suspended" and "over the whole country was stretched the arm of a discretionary power, paramount to the Constitution," he said Lincoln's actions were meant to save the nation and dismissed the "untrue" notion of the government having only limited powers. Fisher argued "that a Government must have power sufficient to protect public safety, and that, should the limits of its authority be found too narrow for that purpose, those limits will be broken, for necessity supersedes all law."[149] Later scholars tended to ignore or downplay Lincoln's attacks on the Constitution.[150] The 1992 Pulitzer Prize for history was awarded to a study of civil liberties in the Civil War that not only minimized the political dimension of the actions taken but also concluded that Lincoln's behavior offers "no clear lesson" for the future and that his "ability to balance short-term practicality and long-term ideals is perhaps the essence of statesmanship."[151]

During the war, the Supreme Court avoided interfering with Lincoln. In the *Prize Cases*, which arose from the presidentially proclaimed blockade of the Confederacy, the Supreme Court reached a five-to-four decision upholding the seizure of ships before Congress retroactively ratified Lincoln's initial military moves. Regarding the conflict as an insurrection with attributes of a war between nations, the majority was satisfied that Lincoln had responded to the fact of war and had received subsequent congressional approval. The administration had maintained that Lincoln did not need congressional authorization to "repel war with war" while protecting the nation and that there were "overwhelming reasons of necessity" that justified the capture of ships.[152] James M. Carlisle had argued for the claimants whose vessels had been seized that the powers being exercised were "not Constitutional, but revolutionary" in their very nature. "The principle of self-defense is asserted; and all power is claimed for the President," he told the justices. "This is to assert that the Constitution contemplated and tacitly provided that the President should be a dictator, and all Constitutional Government be at an end, whenever he should think that 'the life of the nation' is in danger."[153] The four dissenters were troubled by the ex post facto nature of the legislative action and insisted that a president had no authority to initiate a blockade.[154] The narrow decision, however, was enough to suggest that Lincoln could act on his own, at least if he was later supported by Congress. Artfully contending that it lacked jurisdiction to review military commission rulings, the Supreme Court refused to accept an appeal from Vallandigham.[155]

Shortly after the war, however, the high court overcame its reluctance and ruled in *Ex parte Milligan* that military commissions did not have jurisdiction to try civilians where the civil courts were functioning. Admitting that the issue could not have been "discussed and decided without passion" during the war, the Supreme Court was ready to recognize limits to the practice of conducting trials without an impartial jury and denying other constitutional guarantees.[156] Another factor may have been the public outcry arising from the controversial use of a military commission to convict the conspirators in the Lincoln assassination. In the *Milligan* case the Army had arrested a small group of anti-Lincoln Democrats in Indiana during the war and charged them with participation in a conspiracy to take federal munitions and to free Confederate prisoners. The alleged traitors included Joseph J. Bingham, a newspaper editor who was the party's state chairman, and Lambdin P. Milligan, a Democratic lawyer who had just lost a primary race for governor. The case was concocted and then sensationalized for political gain by Republicans immediately before the elections of 1864. Instead of being tried in Indiana courts, where a conviction was not assured, the defendants were turned over to a military commission that could act more quickly and surely. Judge Advocate Major Henry L. Burnett insisted that martial law was "one of the prerogatives of the Executive" and his subordinates and that the right of self-preservation made things lawful in times of war that were not lawful in times of peace. The whole country had come under military rule, he said, and the "civil rights of the citizen became dead for the time being, if necessary to preserve the life of the nation." Sentenced to hang, Milligan maintained he had a right to a jury trial.[157]

The Supreme Court's ruling proved to be a strong repudiation of emergency authority in time of war. The government told the justices that once a war begins, the president has powers "without limit" and is "the sole judge of the exigencies, necessities, and duties of the occasion, their extent and duration." Rejecting the sweeping claim of executive prerogative and noting that the nation "has no right to expect that it will always have wise and humane rulers," the Supreme Court observed that the president was "controlled by law," that he "is to execute, not to make, the laws," and that a military commission was not "a court ordained and established by Congress" as required by the Constitution. The opinion by Justice David Davis emphatically denied that commanders in a foreign or domestic war could "on the plea of necessity, with the approval of the Executive" deny rights at their will. "Civil liberty and this kind of martial law cannot endure together; the antagonism is irreconcilable," the opinion said, "and, in the conflict, one or the other must perish." Davis wrote that the framers of the Constitution intended that only the writ of *habeas corpus* could be suspended in times of crisis and that all other rights in the Constitution would remain inviolable. "The Constitution of the United States is a law for rulers and people, equally in war and in peace, and covers with the shield of its protection all classes of men, at all times, and under all circumstances," the opinion stated. "No doctrine, involving more pernicious consequences, was ever invented by the wit of man than that any of its provisions can be suspended during any of the great exigencies of government."[158]

IV.

Despite the embarrassments and recklessness of the repression in the Civil War and the unanimous ruling in *Ex parte Milligan*, Lincoln's willingness to tamper with the Constitution become a model for the assumption of executive branch power over the press.[159] As the United States stumbled into war with Spain in 1898, press issues were again handled by presidential-military initiative. Congress did little more than refuse to pass a bill to prohibit making public "any information" about fortifications and batteries in the United States. Passage was urged by War Department officials and by representatives who regarded the measure as a matter of common sense, but House members observed, in a lengthy debate, that the information in question was readily available and that the law was so broad that it could interfere with such routine activities as proposing defense legislation and providing engineering education. Members pointed out that the bill would violate the First Amendment and could be used against journalists by their enemies. "We do not want to convert ourselves into slaves in order to free somebody else," remarked Representative Richard Bland, a Democrat from Missouri. Bland said that the country depended on free speech and a free press and had to "take these rights with the disabilities necessarily attending them."[160]

Yet neither Congress nor the courts moved to stop the imposition of strict military censorship on the telegraph and the mails as the war began, and a confused public was left with rumors and little unfettered reporting. The government took over cable offices in Florida and New York City, and Admiral William T. Sampson cut the connection from Key West to Havana at the order of the Navy Department. Secretary of the Navy John Long ordered naval personnel not to speak with reporters and Secretary of War Russell Alger, who resigned a year later, after the airing of complaints about censorship and investigations into military incompetence and inefficiency, denied access to his clerks and records. Correspondents were notified that they would have their credentials revoked for censorship violations, and press boats were not allowed to accompany the troop transports as they departed for the invasion of Cuba on June 14, 1898. Journalists were kept away from much of the fighting by the unfit commanding officer, General William Shafter, whom they privately blamed for many unnecessary hardships they and the soldiers suffered.[161]

Facing the prospect of losing credentials and of upsetting readers at home, few reporters had the nerve to reveal how poorly trained, equipped, and organized the troops were. Writing to his brother about the miserable situation, the famed war correspondent Richard Harding Davis said he did not bring up the War Department's failings in his newspaper writing "because, if I started to tell the truth at all, it would do no good, and it would open up a hell of an outcry from all the families of the boys who have volunteered."[162] When fellow correspondent Poultney Bigelow exposed some of the terrible conditions and then lost his credentials, Davis wrote articles condemning him as disloyal.[163] Public opinion finally turned against officials when returning soldiers disclosed the War Department's blunders and the prevalence of disease.[164] Of the 5,462 deaths in the conflict, only 379 came in battle.[165]

The serious fighting did not begin until after the war, when the United States spent several years and more than four thousand lives to crush an insurrection in the Philippines, which had been taken from Spain.[166] As many as six hundred thousand Filipinos died on Luzon Island alone.[167] A large number of the dead were the victims of atrocities committed or condoned by American soldiers. With military censorship limiting what could be reported, information on such brutality emerged slowly, as soldiers returned home and the perpetrators faced legal action as well as inquiries by journalists and members of Congress. Not until the spring of 1902 was much public outrage apparent, as Americans heard reliable stories of reprisals, summary executions, civilian concentration camps, and the "water cure," a torture in which water was repeatedly poured down the throat of the victim and then beaten out to give the sensation of drowning.[168] Among those officers who were punished for atrocities, often very lightly, was "Hell Roaring" Jake Smith, a brigadier general who responded to a guerrilla attack on Samar Island by conducting a campaign of widespread terror and devastation. According to the charges in Smith's court-martial, he told a major, who later had eleven Filipino guides executed for failing to inform hungry soldiers about edible plants, not to take any prisoners and to kill everyone over the age of ten who could bear arms. "I wish you to kill and burn," Smith allegedly said. "The more you kill and burn, the better you will please me."[169]

American officials and jingoists were not eager for the horrors of war to come to light. Filipinos were subjected to martial law, press suppression, and a sedition law that made it illegal to advocate independence. An American editor in the Philippines was arrested for republishing the Declaration of Independence.[170] Ripples of opposition appeared in the United States, largely from the literary and academic communities. Mark Twain wrote that the United States flag be adapted to fly in the Philippines "with the white stripes painted black and the stars replaced by the skull and cross-bones." Noting in a speech that he had been called a traitor who should be "dangling from a lamp-post somewhere" for his opposition to the Philippine-American War, Twain remarked that citizens should stand together "if the country's life was in danger," but that when it is "only some little war away off, then it may be that on the question of politics the nation is divided, half-patriots and half-traitors, and no man can tell which from which."[171] Other dissenters included the members of the Anti-Imperialist League, who disseminated accounts of disease, destruction, and torture in the fighting. When one of the founders of the organization, Edward Atkinson, tried to send protest pamphlets to the top brass in the Philippines, Attorney General John W. Griggs condemned the writings as seditious, and Postmaster General Charles E. Smith had them seized. Secretary of War Alger ordered that any of Atkinson's pamphlets reaching the Philippines should be taken from the mail and destroyed. Atkinson did not take the matter to court, but the publicity increased demand for the publications, and over 130,000 pamphlets were distributed around the country.[172]

Correspondents in Manila were subjected to the press restrictions of Elwell S. Otis, the governor general and commander of military forces in the Philippines. Otis was authorized to censor by Secretary Alger and by President William McKinley, who simply left the matter to his "discretion and judgment."[173] General Otis instructed his censor " 'to let nothing go that can hurt the Administration' " and frankly admitted that the suppression was aimed at keeping the American public uninformed rather than preventing information from reaching the insurgents. When reporters complained to the general in the summer of 1899 that he was making the entire press his personal propaganda organ, Otis accused them of conspiring against the government and threatened them with a general court-martial. In a joint protest, cabled from Hong Kong to evade censorship and printed in major American newspapers, eleven correspondents reacted with a statement that the public was only getting an "ultra optimistic view that is not shared by the general officers in the field." Censorship, they said, was stopping stories about failed operations and about the crimes and ill health of soldiers. In a more detailed explanation written a few weeks later, Robert M. Collins, the chief AP correspondent in the Philippines, told about reporters being forbidden to send accurate casualty figures or stories about soldiers looting, mutilating, blackmailing, getting drunk, and being on the verge of mutiny. As the situation grew worse, Collins said, "we were sending rose-colored pictures of successful war and inhabitants flocking to the American standard." He quoted a censor as saying, " 'Of course we all know that we are in a terrible mess out there, but we do not want the people to get excited about it.' "[174]

Despite revelations of wrongdoing, criticism of censorship, and the contention that the Philippine-American War was fought without congressional consent, expansive notions of executive authority continued in the wake of the conflict. Theodore Roosevelt, whose exuberant military service in Cuba propelled him into political prominence, praised the "Jackson-Lincoln theory of the Presidency" in advancing a "steward of the people" notion of executive power. Roosevelt advocated acting "for the common well-being of all our people, whenever and in whatever manner was neces-

Figure 5.7 *The military governor of the Philippines from 1898 to 1900, Elwell S. Otis (left), suppressed insurrection and did not allow reporters to send dispatches that might cause trouble for the administration of President William McKinley (small picture on wall next to the larger picture of Republican Party boss Mark Hanna). Cartoon by George B. Luks on the cover of* The Verdict, *August 21, 1899.*

sary, unless prevented by direct constitutional or legislative prohibition." Like Locke, he took the position that the executive had to accept express restrictions, but was otherwise free to act if compelled to do so for the general good. Contrasting his use of power with the "Buchanan-Taft" school in his autobiography, Roosevelt said, "I declined to adopt the view that what was imperatively necessary for the Nation could not be done by the President unless he could find some specific authorization to do it."[175]

Buchanan had actually approved of the "lesser evil" of Lincoln usurping authority to deal with an emergency if Congress was not in session;[176] but William Howard Taft replied, in *Our Chief Magistrate and His Powers*, that he found Roosevelt's "higher law" thinking "a little startling in a constitutional republic." Such opinions, he said, made the president "play the part of a Universal Providence and set all things right" using "undefined" powers dangerous to personal liberties. "The grants of Executive power are necessarily in general terms in order not to embarrass the Executive within the field of action plainly marked for him," Taft explained, "but his jurisdiction must be justified and vindicated by affirmative constitutional or statutory provision, or it does not exist." Admitting that executive discretion could be difficult to contain in an emergency, Taft concluded, as Jackson, Lincoln, and Roosevelt had, that in the end the only effective control was public opinion.[177] He did not, however, have an answer to the problem of public support for civil liberties being at low ebb in times of war or national hysteria. When Congress created the Sedition Act in 1918, former president Roosevelt said he approved of "any legislation, no matter how extreme, that will reach the men who vilify and defame America."[178]

Jackson, Lincoln, and Roosevelt, in effect, presented themselves as Americanized versions of Viscount Bolingbroke's "patriot king," an active, courageous executive who would attract followers and achieve greatness by purporting to do what was necessary for the people.[179] Bolingbroke did not conceive of a constitution as anything more than a mutable assemblage of ordinary laws and government practices;[180] similarly, such presidents have not seen the Constitution as superior to their will. Like James I, they held the natural reason of expediency above artificial legal reasoning based on long experience. To such elected autocrats, the Constitution is a rough description of government, not a rigid prescription of rules to be obeyed. Lincoln's eloquence and humanity made him, according to polls of both scholars and the public, the most respected person in American history.[181] "Throughout the Civil War," wrote an admiring essayist, "Lincoln mobilized every national resource but hatred."[182] The same cannot be said of some later wartime presidents, but Lincoln did teach his successors how power could be seized in troubled circumstances. With the shackles of the Constitution removed, the president may be regarded as a dynamic, even heroic figure, but the people will be less free.

6

The Bureaucratization of
Wartime Censorship

Approximately 110 million people were killed in about 250 wars during the twentieth century. Few civilians were killed in nineteenth-century combat, but they were roughly half of war-related casualties from 1900 to 1950 and three fourths of casualties by the 1980s.[1] As the nations of the world completed the conversion of armed conflict into an industrial operation with mass civilian involvement, governments abandoned haphazard wartime suppression for more bureaucratic approaches. In World Wars I and II, the totalitarian regimes of Germany and Russia operated in predictably heavy-handed ways to control the press, but even the more democratically minded nations of Europe developed elaborate systems of censorship.[2] In commenting on the "power instinct" behind fanatical, unjustifiable secrecy, Max Weber observed, "Bureaucratic administration always tends to exclude the public, to hide its knowledge and action from criticism as well as it can."[3] The secrecy bureaucracies that developed in the twentieth century not only seemed to provide self-protection and a sense of superiority for the insiders, but also tended to expand the categories of what could be deemed relevant to national security and of who should be considered the enemy.[4]

In the United States the more methodical approach was compatible with Progressive Era and New Deal assumptions about the benefits of increasing state and federal power while emphasizing the needs of the social order—as determined by officials and experts—over individual rights. Priority often was given to the reputed rationalizing of human behavior rather than to heeding restrictions from the eighteenth century.[5] Byron Price, director of the Office of Censorship from 1941 to 1945, contended that the Constitution had survived because courts had viewed its provisions as "fluid and elastic, to be applied for the greatest good of the greatest number according to the circumstances and requirements of our recurring national crises." In such times, he asked, "can not even lawyers admit that there is a force higher and more potent and more significant than any force of law?"[6]

Maintaining American unity and cultural nationalism in the face of crisis and change also at times appeared to be more important than preserving civil liberties.[7] In the "Americanism" plank of its 1916 platform, Woodrow Wilson's Democratic Party called for the country to be "welded" together in patriotism and said that anyone who "creates discord and strife among our people so as to obstruct the wholesome process of unification, is faithless to the trust which the privileges of citizenship repose in him and is disloyal to his country."[8] In an eight-to-one decision reached in 1940, the Supreme Court held that a Jehovah's Witness who refused to salute the flag for religious reasons could be expelled from school because a free society required cohesive sentiment. "National unity is the basis of national security," wrote Justice Felix Frankfurter.[9] The opinion, which was handed down as the last troops evacuated Dunkirk, was met with approval by President Franklin Roosevelt and, apparently, by mobs across the country, which soon attacked other Jehovah's Witnesses for refusing to salute the flag.[10] In overruling its decision three years later, the Court noted that the enforcement of unity produced strife and that compulsory patriotism made "an unflattering estimate of the appeal of our institutions to free minds." The 1943 opinion said that First Amendment guarantees were based on eighteenth-century philosophies of official noninterference with individual rights, but that such principles had withered in the twentieth century as "social advancements are increasingly sought through closer integration of society and through expanded and strengthened government controls." Infringement of First Amendment rights, the court said, was allowable "only to prevent grave and immediate danger to interests which the state may lawfully protect."[11]

The imperative of conformity to asserted societal needs required a rethinking of the nation's most basic understandings in the first half of the twentieth century. The United States did not have the kind of sweeping defense emergency laws that existed in Britain and France;[12] however, constitutional provisions were, conveniently, being regarded increasingly as "organic living institutions" evolving over time, as Justice Holmes wrote in a 1914 Supreme Court opinion.[13] Holmes, a modernist in jurisprudence, saw the law as a social instrument and cared little about abstract principles and the dignity of the individual. Having been wounded several times in the Civil War, Holmes was skeptical about causes and saw life as a struggle for survival. Although he thought armed conflict should be avoided, he condemned "armchair pacifists" in a 1928 letter because he saw war as "inevitable and rational" in the current state of human development. "But I don't pass moral judgments, least of all on nations," he wrote. "I see the inevitable everywhere."[14]

With the idea of a "living" constitution came a paternalistic government of unenumerated powers and of centralized controls reaching even the most basic rights of expression. Political opinions, wrote Harvard legal scholar Roscoe Pound in 1915, "may so affect the activities of the state necessary to its preservation as to outweigh the individual interest or even the social interest in free belief and free speech."[15] Although the First Amendment forbids Congress to abridge freedom of speech and freedom of the press, federal legislation—especially the Espionage Act, the Sedition Act, and the Smith Act—erected a broad new authority over opinion that was upheld by the Supreme Court. In addition, news reporting during both world wars was routinely subjected to formal military censorship at the front, and the press at home was under pressure to follow government guidelines. Despite the founders' vision of a free and critical press, military control and official management of information became entrenched and seemingly essential.

I.

The presidents in office during World Wars I and II greatly admired Lincoln and, as he did, enlarged the authority of the office they held. At a 1916 ceremony honoring Lincoln, Woodrow Wilson, noting that he had read many biographies of the sixteenth president, spoke of his cabin birthplace as "an altar upon which we may forever keep alive the vestal fire of democracy." Yet, at the same time, Wilson said Lincoln was a "natural ruler of men" and a brooding, isolated soul who had to discern the nation's destiny. "And the hopes of mankind cannot be kept alive by words merely, by constitutions and doctrines of right and codes of liberty," Wilson said in praise of Lincoln's autocratic approach to governing. "The object of democracy is to transmute these into the life and action of society, the self-denial and self-sacrifice of heroic men and women willing to make their lives an embodiment of right and service and enlightened purpose." Leaders, he concluded, should be "real democrats and servants of mankind."[16] Thus, in Wilson's formulation, benevolent rulers knew what was best.

As a person who evaluated issues on the basis of his own religious beliefs and who made a point of saying that his being elected president and the outcome of World War I were determined by divine providence, Wilson recognized higher laws than the ones he swore to obey in his oath of office.[17] Divine providence, he said in 1917, was a mysterious force that "the wise heart never questions" and that had made the United States "an instrument in the hands of God to see that liberty is made secure for mankind."[18] Feeling he was on a mission from God, Wilson did not find zones of moral neutrality or reasons for tolerance. Believing there was "more of a nation's politics to be gotten out of its poetry than out of all its systematic writers upon public affairs and constitutions," he was not predisposed to be bound by the words of the Bill of Rights.[19] As a political scientist, Wilson saw opportunities in the emergence of stronger presidential leadership, and he adopted the rhetoric of contemporary reformers who said that the Constitution should be a flexible, living organism rather than a static, antiquated piece of machinery.[20] In a speech he made four days after paying homage to Lincoln, Wilson contrasted the moral and spiritual dimensions of American life with the "merely" legal, disparaging what he regarded as the "Newtonian" conceptions of the founders. "If you pick up *The Federalist*, some parts of it read like a treatise on astronomy instead of a treatise on government," he remarked. "They speak of the centrifugal and the centripetal forces, and locate the President somewhere in a rotating system." The whole thing, he complained, "is a calculation of power and an adjustment of parts."[21]

With such contempt for the spirit of the Constitution, Wilson saw no need to be restrained by the press clause. Immediately after declaring neutrality when the war broke out in Europe in 1914, he issued an executive order forbidding radio stations to transmit any "unneutral" messages and authorized the Secretary of the Navy to enforce the order with any action he thought necessary.[22] Amid suspicions that foreign-controlled broadcast facilities were being used to convey coded orders to ships at sea, the Navy placed censors at German and British long-distance stations on the Atlantic coast and soon began taking over their operations. The Marconi Company protested the actions against the British stations, contending that the government was acting without any legal authority.[23] Attorney General Thomas W. Gregory backed the administration's moves with an opinion saying that the president's "powers are broad" in the "preservation of the safety and integrity of the United States." Presidents had exercised emergency powers before, the opinion noted, and were responsible to the American people. Gregory was able to cite the "additional authority" of the Radio

Act of 1912 that allowed the president to close or exercise control over radio stations in time of war, public peril, or disaster[24] (a provision that was later included in the Radio Act of 1927[25] and the Communications Act of 1934[26]). Marconi took its case to a federal district court that concluded that it lacked jurisdiction.[27]

As soon as the United States entered the war, Wilson cited "public safety" needs in issuing an executive order imposing Navy censorship of submarine cables and War Department censorship of telegraph and telephone lines.[28] Under the wartime authority given to the president by the Radio Act of 1912, almost all of the nation's civilian broadcast facilities were either shut down or turned over to the Navy.[29] Officials vied for permanent control of the medium, as Navy supervision brought about technological improvements in radio and allowed the administration to broadcast its ideology to other nations through the high-power stations.[30] At a cabinet meeting on March 27, 1917, Josephus Daniels, a newspaper editor who was serving as secretary of the Navy, suggested that the Navy buy all the country's radio stations and "make wireless a government monopoly." Postmaster General Albert S. Burleson immediately served notice that radio must be under his department's control when the peace came. "Is that a threat or a prophecy?" Wilson asked. "It is a bluff or boast," Daniels responded.[31] The Navy secretary soon asked Congress for the authority to purchase the stations, but the bill died in committee after members pointed out that the Navy already controlled them. Daniels then angered Congress by using general Navy funds to buy the Marconi shore stations. After the armistice he proposed purchasing the rest of the nation's radio facilities, and the Navy advocated government operation of telephone, telegraph, and cable services as well, but by then the Republicans had gained control of both houses, and the public had been fed up with federal direction of private industry during the war. The government had taken over the telephone system and the railroads with lamentable results, and plans for nationalizing industries had inadequate support. After Marconi officials warned that the legislation would lead to government censorship of press and business messages, the bill was tabled in committee.[32]

A number of social reformers had hoped the war could be used to promote not only public ownership, but also progressive principles in general.[33] Wilson, however, expected the war to curtail civil liberties. He, like Lincoln, believed mortals could do little to prevent what God had ordained and thought that the discarding of freedoms at a time of crisis was both necessary and inevitable. The night before he asked Congress for a declaration of war against Germany, Wilson summoned *New York World* editor Frank Cobb to the White House for a soul-searching conversation that began in the early morning hours. The president told his friend and foremost advocate in journalism that Germany had forced him to act, but that he knew people would " 'go war-mad, quit thinking and devote their energies to destruction.' " Maintaining that he had only a choice of evils, Wilson stated that free speech would disappear as the country put all its strength into the war. He would try to preserve democratic ideals, he said, but circumstances would require " 'illiberalism at home to reinforce the men at the front.' " Wilson remarked that conformity would be " 'the only virtue.' "[34]

Wilson thus tried to portray himself as reluctant to censor when talking to one of the country's premier editorial writers; but instead of being a check on suppressive legislation during World War I, the president and his cabinet encouraged it.[35] Unlike Lincoln, Wilson and the members of his administration worked with Congress to truncate freedom of expression.[36] Elaborate bureaucratic schemes for licensing and regulating war correspondents were discussed in military circles prior to World War I.[37] After the war broke out in Europe in 1914 the Army prepared a report entitled "The Proper Relationship between the Army and the Press in War," that described the restrictions being used by other countries and made recommendations for the United States. Based on a study ordered by the chief of staff, the document said the needs of the armed forces become "paramount" in war and the press "by adverse criticism, may tend to destroy the efficiency of these agencies." The report presented a draft bill for giving the president complete authority to impose censorship of military news "whenever in his judgment the defense of the country requires such action." In the absence of legislation at a time of national peril, the report said, the president should require censorship and, if necessary, declare "martial law to an extent necessary to effect arbitrary suppression of publication or communication of matter that might prove detrimental to national defense or useful to a possible enemy."[38]

Immediately after Congress declared war in 1917, bills were drafted to provide the president with general authority to issue rules forbidding the publication of information useful to the enemy.[39] Wilson gave his assurance that the power would not be used to punish criticism of the administration, and there was language in the proposed legislation to that effect.[40] However, political opponents in Congress feared that presidential censorship could be used against them and that mistakes would be covered up.[41] Representative Fiorello La Guardia of New York reminded the House of the scandals of 1898 and said that the press could help expose the "domestic enemy who is willing to turn American blood into gold and sell rotten cornbeef, wormy beans, paper shoes, defective arms for our American boys." He said that it was the responsibility of the military not to reveal secret information in the first place and that the restrictions being proposed would be a "flagrant and daring violation" of the spirit of the First Amendment.[42] Representative Henry A. Cooper of Wisconsin observed that Congress could make "no law" abridging press freedom and could not give authority over the press to an executive branch that was "not to make laws but only to execute them." The First Amendment, he said, "is clear, explicit, and what is equally important, it is mandatory."[43]

Newspaper journalists were quick to express their apprehensions in meetings with cabinet members;[44] and on their editorial pages the proposed authority was characterized as more appropriate for the Kaiser or the Czar.[45] Sensing that support was being squandered at a critical time, White House adviser Joseph Tumulty informed the president that even the administration's strongest backers in the press were upset. "The experience of the Administration of President Adams in fostering the Alien and Sedition laws bids us beware of this whole business," Tumulty warned.[46] Members of Congress echoed the charge that Wilson was seeking autocratic power.[47]

Congress was willing to expand many areas of executive authority in 1917, but, in spite of strenuous administration lobbying, did not cater to Wilson's desire for presidential power over the press. During the debates, Secretary of State Robert Lansing caused a furor by ordering the lower-ranking officials in his department not to give the press any information at all. Attorney General Gregory angered the press further by giving members of Congress a Justice Department memo purporting to reveal enemy influence in the nation's journalism. House Republicans agreed in caucus to resist newspaper censorship in any form, and many Democrats failed to support the president in a series of votes.[48] Hoping to find a compromise, presidential confidant Frank Cobb told Wilson that the "censorship controversy has been so unfortunate that I know you will be eager to consider any proposal that gives promise." With his characteristic obstinacy, Wilson refused to yield and told the chairman of the House Judiciary Committee that prepublication newspaper censorship was "absolutely necessary to the public safety";[49] but Congress, after many hours of debate, refused to give him the authority.

Laws were soon passed, however, to punish the expression of virtually any dissenting views. Under the Espionage Act of 1917, individuals were sentenced to as many as twenty years in prison for expressing opinions regarded as disloyal or obstructive to the war effort, and critical publications could be declared unmailable. Thus, mailing privileges were denied to all of the National Civil Liberties Bureau pamphlets, including *Freedom of Speech and of the Press*, which a postal inspector thought had an inappropriate topic for debate in wartime.[50] The Sedition Act of 1918 amended the Espionage Act to include a greater number of thoughts that could not be expressed (including contempt for the government, the Constitution, the armed forces, the flag, and military uniforms) and to allow the postmaster general to refuse to deliver mail to anyone he thought was violating the statute.[51] Thus, publications that did not conform to an official's sense of patriotism could be denied subscription renewals and other business letters without even a hearing. The Trading with the Enemy Act passed in 1917 required foreign-language publications to submit English translations of any writings dealing with the government or the war to a postmaster on or before the date of mailing, a burdensome requirement that could be waived by the president for publications deemed not detrimental to the war effort. The statute also authorized the president to censor mail and all other communications between the United States and other countries whenever he thought "public safety" required it. A Censorship Board set up by executive order oversaw a coordinated and comprehensive effort of government agencies to control the flow of information and ideas into and out of the United States. Materials with radical opinions were not allowed to enter the country, and those that might be embarrassing, such as publications of the Free Press Defense League of Aurora, Missouri, could be prevented from leaving.[52]

The scope of postal authority over the press was construed broadly.[53] Postmaster General Burleson stated that publications would not be allowed to "impugn the motives of the Government" or "say that the Government is controlled by Wall Street or munition manufacturers." Burleson said, "We will not permit the publication or circulation of anything hampering the war's prosecution or attacking improperly our allies."[54] The postmaster general's power was upheld by the Supreme Court in a case brought by the *Milwaukee Leader*, a socialist paper that had its second-class mail privilege revoked. In an opinion that cited articles condemning allies and arguing that the government was plutocratic and the president was autocratic, Justice John H. Clarke, a Wilsonian progressive, wrote that the First Amendment did not protect words the court regarded as false and deliberately intended to encourage illegal acts, disloyalty, and the giving of aid and comfort to enemies. "The Constitution was adopted to preserve our Government," the opinion said, "not to serve as a protecting screen for those who while claiming its privileges seek to destroy it." Clarke insisted that second-class rates were "special favors" that the government bestowed to the press and could deny to its "insidious foes."[55] Dissents by Justices Brandeis and Holmes decried the ease with which postal officials could withhold a vital service to periodicals and denied that the law provided authority to interfere with future circulation on the basis of what they were likely to publish.[56]

The plainly arbitrary enforcement of the various statutes severely hampered or silenced many publications;[57] but the repression was also damaging to Wilson and his party. A number of the president's supporters already felt betrayed after backing him in 1916, when his campaign slogan had been that he "kept the country out of war," but Wilson received a spate of warnings on his efforts to crush dissent. One of the most blunt letters came from Allen W. Ricker, publisher of *Pearson's Magazine*, who, after complaining about Post Office interference with his mail, said, "A political grave-yard is being prepared in the public mind for a long list of men holding office in Washington." Herbert Croly, the Wilsonian editor of the *New Republic*, told the president that intelligent, moderate men "who have constituted the best element in your following in the past" were abandoning him because they considered the suppression of publications "an issue of importance scarcely inferior to that of the war itself."[58] There were many more such alerts.[59] In response, Wilson told Postmaster General Burleson that he wanted the "utmost caution and liberality in all our censorship";[60] but he meekly accepted Burleson's replies that he was only enforcing laws passed by Congress in accordance with court decisions.[61] Wilson, who had to work with Congress, relied on the skills of the postmaster general in political patronage.[62] Not surprisingly, he defended Burleson, who threatened to resign if he could not have his way;[63] Wilson said he was misunderstood and was trying to be judicious in the exercise of his powers.[64] By placing himself squarely in the middle of the issue, Wilson pleased neither side.

Wilson not only had to spend a considerable amount of presidential time explaining his administration's actions against dissent and dealing with responses to particular cases, but also suffered a loss of reputation with fellow writers and intellectuals who found repression foolish. Saying that "suppression convinces nobody" and weakens patriotic enthusiasm, Upton Sinclair asked the president, "What good does it do us to fight for freedom abroad if, in the mean time, we are losing it at home?" Sinclair, who had cut his ties to socialism to support American entry into the war, said that he did not think expression should be unrestricted when the nation had to protect itself but that Wilson's subordinates were using methods that were too autocratic and divisive. Walter Lippmann advised the administration that the actions were reducing liberal and radical support and said that the government "ought to suppress only military secrets and advice to break the law or evade it." Calling for a more tolerant and imaginative approach to censorship, Lippmann alluded to "the long record of folly which is the history of suppression." Colonel House, Wilson's close friend and adviser, gave Lippmann's letter to the president, saying that more harm than good could easily be done by suppression and that he should deal with the issue himself because Burleson "could never have a proper understanding of it."[65]

Wilson had been narrowly reelected in 1916 by a left-wing coalition that included socialists and radicals, but the administration's attacks on civil liberties played a significant role in the crumbling of his base of support.[66] With many of his former allies disillusioned and the public in general annoyed by various domestic actions, Wilson struggled for political survival. The Republicans gained majorities in the House and Senate in 1918, despite Wilson's call for a Democratic Congress to back his vision of the postwar future.[67] A few days after the election, George Creel, chairman of the CPI, which spread the Wilsonian gospel of progressive democracy around the world during the war, told the dejected president that the blame could be assigned to the repressive activities of the Justice Department and the Post Office. "All the radical, or liberal friends of your anti-imperialist war policy were either silenced or intimidated," Creel said, adding that if Wilson wanted to sell his program for peace, then the "liberal, radical, progressive, labor and socialist press will have to be rallied to the President's support."[68] John Palmer Gavit, editor of the *New York Evening Post*, told Wilson he was "not having now the liberal backing that is your right" because of civil liberties concerns, and he urged the president to "uplift and electrify the liberal forces in this and other countries" by freeing everyone convicted for expression of opinion.[69]

Wilson was unyielding when pressed to give a general amnesty for political prisoners. He provided encouragement to those who made the pleas, but put off a decision;[70] he preferred to follow the advice of Attorney General Gregory and commute a number of sentences.[71] When Clarence Darrow petitioned the president for the release of the Socialist leader and journalist Eugene V. Debs, the famed lawyer said he knew "that self-preservation is the first law of nations" but that once a war was over it was possible to consider a person's motives, and that Debs had sincerely felt it was his duty to oppose the war. The president, however, went along with a new attorney general, A. Mitchell Palmer, who opposed the release because he thought the action would be exploited by opponents of the Versailles Treaty. Wilson did send Burleson a two-sentence message saying that he did not believe "that it would be wise to do any more suppressing" and that it would be necessary to "meet these poisons in some other way," but at the bottom of the note Burleson wrote: "Continued to suppress and Courts sustained me every time." Wilson appeared to be on the verge of declaring an amnesty when, in September 1919, he had a debilitating stroke while touring the country in his unsuccessful campaign for ratification of the peace treaty and the League of Nations by the Republican Senate.[72] A year later the Republicans won the presidential election in a landslide and increased their majorities in Congress, ushering in a period of "normalcy" marked by the upsurge of the Ku Klux Klan and other illiberal movements.

Ironically, one person who appeared to favor free expression more than the idealistic Wilson was his Republican successor in office, Warren G. Harding. A party regular whose pleasant personality and atrocious speaking style made him a sharp contrast to Wilson, Harding had no delusions about his own greatness, but he was an Ohio newspaper publisher who evidently saw the press as less of a threat. As a senator Harding participated in the successful fight against presidential censorship that portrayed the plan as repugnant to American principles and as a dangerous extension of executive power. After he became president in 1921, second-class mailing permits were granted to the radical publications that had been hounded by the Wilson administration. When journalist Lincoln Steffens approached him about a general amnesty for wartime dissenters and labor activists, Harding said he would go along with the idea if Steffens could get two particular members of his cabinet to agree. When

Steffens got an emphatic refusal from Herbert Hoover and another cabinet secretary, Harding, who apparently had expected the result, had a "loud and sardonic" laugh and then showed him a pardon for Debs that his attorney general had prepared. Steffens remarked that he would not pardon anyone who would subscribe to the kind of "dirt-eating promise" the document required, and Debs was pardoned without any conditions. "The war psychology, which in America was also an anti-labor, anti-radical mass psychology, was still too strong in Harding's day for any pacific gesture," Steffens recalled in his autobiography, "and my general amnesty scheme was too sweeping."[73]

The suppression of the World War I period not only backfired for a party and its president, but also distracted a nation fighting a war and disrupted the democratic force of public opinion. Wilson's ill-fated interest in legislation was apparent as early as his 1915 state of the union address in which he urged the enactment of federal laws to use against immigrants "who have poured the poison of disloyalty into the very arteries of our national life." Showing the strain of a year of U-boat attacks and of some notable incidents of espionage and political violence in the United States, Wilson said bitterly that "the gravest threats against our national peace and safety have been uttered within our own borders." Making no distinction between preaching and practicing, he lumped dissenters in with saboteurs and spies. "Such creatures of passion, disloyalty, and anarchy must be crushed out," he told Congress. "They are not many, but they are infinitely malignant, and the hand of our power should close over them at once."[74] Attorney General Gregory twice asked Congress to pass laws to punish espionage and restrict freedom of expression before war was declared, but no bill was passed.[75]

The rhetoric intensified as the country entered the war, and officials proclaimed the existence of a threat they needed to control within the nation. In seeking the presidential prior restraint powers he did not receive in 1917, Wilson said that he needed such authority because "some persons," presumably the German-language and socialist press in particular, could be "highly dangerous to the nation in the midst of a war." A few weeks later, in a Flag Day address delivered to about five million homes by the Boy Scouts and widely distributed to schools, the president stated that the "military masters of Germany" had "filled our unsuspecting communities with vicious spies and conspirators and sought to corrupt the opinion of our people in their own behalf." He claimed that the "sinister intrigue" was also employing labor leaders and socialists.[76] Actual conspirators were in short supply, however. Almost everyone considered dangerous had been taken into custody immediately after war was declared. Still, at least half a dozen federal agencies—including the Bureau of Investigation, the Secret Service, and Military Intelligence—strove for preeminence in combating subversion. The resulting bureaucratic boom helped to launch the career of a counter-radical specialist in the Department of Justice, J. Edgar Hoover, who would later achieve infamy for spying on Americans as director of the FBI.[77]

Paranoid bombast such as Wilson's and suspicions whipped up in government propaganda and Hollywood movies also helped to incite thousands of episodes of harassment and mob violence during the war.[78] In what was, to a large extent, an expression of nativist loathing of the foreign-born and irrational fear of radical groups, suspect individuals were subjected to vandalism, beatings, tarring and feathering, shootings, lynchings, and various forms of public humiliation. Few successful prosecutions of the perpetrators were possible at a time when the courts and the legal profession were dominated by reactionary, xenophobic values.[79] The Justice Department itself had an auxiliary of hundreds of thousands of citizen-spies known as the American Protective League (APL). Spurred by conspiracy theories, the APL conducted warrantless searches, opened mail, infiltrated radical and labor groups, and roughed up and illegally arrested supposed subversives and "slackers."[80] State and local defense or "public safety" councils interrogated individuals suspected of disloyalty, pressured people to buy Liberty Bonds, and worked to remove German literature from library shelves and eliminate German language instruction from schools. Some councils had formal statutory authority and some were simply appointed by governors, but, in either case, they did not let concerns about civil liberties impede their efforts.[81]

A state with a relatively high concentration of German-Americans could have an acute case of anxiety about dissent. As the United States entered the war, the *Literary Digest* suggested where problems lurked by publishing a map of the United States "SHOWING WHERE THE TEUTONIC STRAIN IS THE GREATEST." One such state was Wisconsin, where more than a hundred federal indictments were brought and at least eighty-one state or local legal actions were taken for "disloyal" comments. In extralegal actions, people were shot, tarred and feathered, and forced to buy war bonds.[82] The *Capital Times*, a prolabor, Progressive-inspired daily in Madison, invited trouble through its connections to Robert M. La Follette, the Wisconsin senator who had opposed the declaration of war on Germany. At the request of competing newspapers, the Association of Commerce, and the Wisconsin Council of Defense, the newspaper was investigated by the Department of Justice on the suspicion that it was receiving money from pro-German people around the state. A young paper with shaky finances, the *Capital Times* was cleared, but was boycotted and burned in effigy.[83]

Many newspapers in Wisconsin not only condemned La Follette as a traitor but also incited or excused vigilante violence against German-Americans, labor activists, and socialists.[84] The *Milwaukee Sentinel* explained that constitutional rights of expression did not apply in wartime and, in any case, "are established, not to gratify the citizen, but to conserve the interests of the public and the stability and welfare of orderly government." The paper said that only opponents of the war had trouble and that "no loyal American is clamoring for free speech." Another Wisconsin paper, the *Janesville Gazette*, tried to strike a moderate pose with humor, saying that tar was needed for sidewalks and feathers for beds and joking that "stripping German spies and painting them green" was a needless affront to Irish citizens. In an issue reporting on "strong arm" squads intimidating people who had not made war bond payments, the Janesville paper editorialized that the law would take its course with those who painted others yellow for their reluctance to buy bonds, but that it should not be surprising when "something snaps" if some people refused to do their share while others sacrificed their lives. "It may not be according to the law of the land," the *Gazette* said of the violence, "but it is according to the law of mankind."[85] Sometimes newspapers themselves became the target. Even in small, isolated communities the tension was such that when a weekly editor in Waupun, Wisconsin, took down a flag in his shop window, a mob did not accept his explanation that he was going to wash the glass and forced him to kiss the Stars and Stripes.[86]

Various methods of intimidation were used against dissenters who questioned war on moral grounds. Oswald Garrison Villard, the pacifist editor of the New York *Evening Post* and the *Nation*, despised the government's anti-German propaganda, questioned Wilson's depiction of the war as a noble crusade for lasting peace and democracy, and "revolted against the whole idea that good could come out of the slaughter of millions." Soon he was ostracized for seeking "a peace of justice." Rumors said he would not defend his wife or daughter from raping Huns and that he was in daily communication with the kaiser. After being snubbed at clubs, asked to resign from the presidency of the Philharmonic Society board, and afflicted by the harassment of his young children and family dog, Garrison found out who his "real friends" were. "I soon discovered that half of mine were afraid that I would land in prison and that the other half was afraid that I would not," he said. Regarding his one-time friend Woodrow Wilson as a dictator with "greater power by far than had ever been Abraham Lincoln's," Villard defended civil liberties but was forced to sell his paper in 1918 and had to ward off postal censorship of the *Nation* by asking for help from the president. Villard realized that he was too prominent and well-connected for harsher government action, and that serious suppression was aimed at "terrifying helpless fry who could not strike back."[87]

One target of the more severe kind of suppression was the black press, which was subjected to government warnings, surveillance, and legal actions. Determined to extinguish racial tensions exacerbated by black migration to the North and mobilization for the war, officials attributed increasingly strident wartime complaints about segregation, disfranchisement, and lynching in black periodicals to the work of thousands of enemy provocateurs. In fact, the criticism merely pointed out the inconsistency between Wilson's moral rhetoric on democratic leadership in the world and the racial realities of America. Minority journalists were exposing injustices, but they did not advise readers to undermine the war effort. A special conference of black editors held in 1918 passed resolutions stating that the war against Germany was paramount and that they would make every effort to promote self-sacrificing participation.[88] Few mainstream journalists worried that the reputed foreign intrigue would incite blacks. The *Literary Digest*, for instance, found the nation's editors agreed that "the German effort to set the country ablaze with a negro insurrection" would fail, but the magazine noted that with the war "negro journals take advantage of the occasion to protest against the treatment they receive."[89]

Such protests were portrayed as unpatriotic in bureaucrats' reports and provided the pretext for interfering with valid, lawful complaints. One of the nation's most influential black newspapers, the *Chicago Defender*, received particularly close attention because of its national circulation and its piercing commentary that included comparing "Hun" war atrocities to racist violence in the United States. Editor Robert S. Abbott, who was said to be conveying German propaganda and fostering racial strife, was interrogated by the Bureau of Investigation and was warned to be cautious by Military Intelligence and by the Post Office, which monitored the paper for illegal content. The *Defender* continued to advocate minority rights, but Abbott promised the authorities that he would be careful and publicly demonstrated his allegiance with support of loan drives and participation in the government's speakers bureau.[90] Similar bullying tactics were used against other black journalists, including W. E. B. Du Bois, the editor of the NAACP's *Crisis*, who urged his readers to close ranks with whites and forget their grievances until the end of the war.[91]

President Wilson's indifference to the liberties of nonconformist periodicals was displayed in a letter to Max Eastman, the Socialist publisher of *The Masses*, who had written to the president to protest that soldiers had broken up a meeting he was addressing and had threatened to lynch him and that his magazine had lost its mailing privileges for allegedly promoting resistance to the draft. Wilson blandly replied, "I think that a time of war must be regarded as wholly exceptional and that it is legitimate to regard things which would in ordinary circumstances be innocent as very dangerous to the public welfare." Observing that it was difficult to say what should and should not be permitted, he said that "a line must be drawn," even if "clumsily."[92] Wilson thus maintained, without citing any authority, that a wartime exception existed to the guarantee of a free press and that the government could make restrictions on expression when they were deemed necessary. Yet, by the end of 1917, he apparently was regretting the havoc created by the suppression. In his state of the union address he said that dissenters were merely "noisily thoughtless and troublesome" and that "men here and there fling themselves in impotent disloyalty against the calm, indomitable power of the nation." Such people, he advised, "may be safely left to strut their uneasy hour and be forgotten."[93]

The difficulties created by some publications were officially tolerated. While weak, radical, or foreign-language publications took a battering, the more powerful, more mainstream press remained relatively safe, even when angering the authorities and the public. One of the most frequent offenders was the *Washington Post*, which Wilson blamed for causing embarrassment in diplomatic relations with allies and which had a tendency to reveal military movements and developments in weaponry.[94] Another problem was newspaper chain owner William Randolph Hearst, who wanted the country to stay out of the war. Although he had been a sensational, saber-rattling publisher in 1898, Hearst was Anglophobic and was averse to having American casualties on the other side of the Atlantic.[95] Press and public opposition to involvement abroad was widespread when Wilson campaigned for reelection in 1916, but was not acceptable after the president asked Congress for a declaration of war on April 2, 1917. According to one magazine's analysis of newspaper editorials, Wilson's speech asking for a declaration of war "worked a miracle of crystallization and unification in American sentiment" and even caused the Hearst papers to back the president's stand. The newspapers in Hearst's chain, however, were accused of being pro-German and lost revenue. Hearst himself was publicly denounced and burned in effigy. The administration kept the press lord under surveillance, and a federal agent was placed as butler in his home, but the Democratic president refused to allow legal action against the erstwhile Democratic politician, saying that nothing proved "that Mr. Hearst had overstepped the bounds of law, outrageous as he has been."[96]

Wilson, the former Princeton president, regarded journalism with disdain. Reserved and stubborn, he failed to charm members of the White House press corps as Theodore Roosevelt had. Wilson was more private, and his relationship with reporters was one of mutual distrust. Early in his first term he tried to use press conferences to educate the public and guide journalists, but he provided little newsworthy information and typically did not allow his remarks to be quoted. Wilson professed the ideal of open, democratic government, but he did not like the reality of having to answer questions and sometimes gave answers that were misleading. With few exceptions, he stopped giving news conferences in 1915. Wilson cited the sensitive international situation, but he was frustrated by dealing with reporters who wanted to know what they wanted to know rather than what he wanted them to know.[97] After the United States entered the war and he failed to get censorship powers, the president thought the administration's information policies had serious "embarrassments of lack of coordination and single management" and that there were problems with the press that "nobody can control" and that had to be left to "take care of themselves" in the long run. "Unfortunately, personally," Wilson said to an assistant secretary of state, "I believe the proper cooperation of the newspapers to be impossible because of the small but powerful lawless elements among them who observe no rules, regard no understandings as binding, and act always as they please."[98]

Following the advice of cabinet members and journalists who thought that the emphasis should be on rallying Americans to the cause rather than implementing severe censorship like that in force in France and Britain, Wilson signed Executive Order 2594 to create the CPI, which consisted of the secretaries of state, war, and the Navy as well as a civilian chairman, George Creel. Creel was a zealous reformer, a strong advocate of American democratic principles, and an experienced journalist who had produced campaign literature for Wilson's reelection in 1916.[99] Creel was appointed after he gave Wilson a memorandum saying that censorship is "offensive to Americans" and that the role of the new agency should be to gain the cooperation of the press in protecting the small amount of material "properly secret" and in publicizing the war effort. The government should not attempt to approve everything written for publication, Creel said, but could pass judgment on questionable stories voluntarily submitted and punish breaches of security. Wilson expressed satisfaction with the memo, and Creel's organization soon began a massive campaign promoting nationalism and patriotism in every available medium.[100]

The CPI issued to the press a set of self-censorship guidelines that were edited by Wilson himself.[101] The guidelines created three categories of war journalism within the United States: dangerous matter that was not to be mentioned, questionable matter that was to be submitted to the committee for review prior to publication, and matter that did not affect the war effort and was therefore "governed only by peacetime laws of libel, defamation of character, etc." Dangerous material included news on military operations in progress "except that officially given out." The questionable news categories were narrative accounts of military operations, including life in training camps, information on defense technologies, and rumors. Questionable stories that were submitted and regarded as safe could be marked "Passed by the Committee on Public Information."[102] A voluntary agreement also called for all still photographs and motion pictures dealing with the war to be submitted to the CPI for approval.[103] Creel publicly insisted that the CPI's emphasis was "ever on expression, not suppression" and that, in contrast to the news censorship in European countries, "no law stood behind these requests, compliance resting entirely upon honor and patriotism."[104] The guidelines were concerned with "human lives and national hopes," he said, and the enforcement was left to the press itself.[105]

The cooperation of the news and entertainment industries with the CPI was promoted as entirely voluntary;[106] but Creel was in a position to seek action against those who did not comply. He was a member of the Censorship Board, which censored publications being exported or imported, and he had close connections to the Department of Justice, the military, and the Post Office, as well as to the War Trade Board, which could cut off newsprint supplies and stop film exports.[107] The CPI worked out film export guidelines with the motion picture industry that admonished producers not to disparage the United States or its allies and not to give comfort to the enemy. The guidelines effectively controlled the domestic film market because foreign distribution was critical to making a profit.[108] Believing there "is a difference between free speech and seditious speech" and that people "have no right to kick against a law after Congress passes it," Creel denied that he was a censor but regularly urged repression in his dealings with other bureaucrats and at times confronted editors directly. On one occasion, for example, an enraged Creel wired Hearst and demanded his sources for a story on troopship defenses and told him that publishing the information was prohibited by law.[109] The CPI guidelines on news urged journalists to report violators "promptly and confidentially" and noted that those who did not clear questionable matter with the committee did so at their own risk and were "subject to any penalties that may be provided by law." Editors who rejected dangerous material were asked to report the incident in order to assist the Secret Service in detecting enemy agents. Victory rested on "unity and confidence," the guidelines said, and "the term traitor is not too harsh" for journalists who neglected their responsibilities. Some publications turned to the public for assistance. *Literary Digest*, for instance, noted what it regarded as "pro-German propaganda" in some newspapers and asked readers "to clip and send us any editorial utterances they encounter which seem to them seditious or treasonable." Local vigilante organizations also placed the press under surveillance.[110]

Press censorship was clearly not voluntary at the front, where reporters were told to wear uniforms, herded around, and made to submit all their copy for approval. On September 12, 1917, the commander in chief of the American Expeditionary Force in Europe, John J. Pershing, issued General Orders No. 36, which required war correspondents to sign agreements to submit their dispatches to a press officer for censorship deletions that the journalists would be allowed to see before the stories were sent to their news organizations. Reporters were forbidden to give the names or locations of Army units and to reveal defenses or future plans "either known or fictitious." Their movements were to be governed by a press officer and they were to "avoid any personal or professional conduct which might injure the morale or discipline of our soldiers." Breaches of the regulations could be punished by loss of accreditation, detention while an operation was in progress, and dismissal from the war zone with a public reprimand. Later regulations gave unprecedented bureaucratic attention to details such as the color of envelopes for personal letters to be censored and the numbering and registering of censors' stamps.[111] Of particular importance was a mimeographed list of regulations released by the military on April 2, 1918, as large numbers of American soldiers were arriving in France. In a statement of four censorship principles the document said that stories must be accurate, must not supply military information to the enemy, must not injure morale, and "must not embarrass the United States." Officers were not to be quoted without permission, only approved casualty figures were to be used, and plans, ship movements, and troop numbers were not to be discussed.[112] In practice, the rules meant that a story could be stopped if Americans killed a German who surrendered or if they accepted cases of wine from the French, a fact the censors thought could offend temperance advocates in the United States. The noted Kansas editor William Allen White wrote an editorial comparing the four censorship principles to the thinking behind the booster role played by small town newspapers.[113]

During the war at least four prominent reporters lost their accreditation, a punishment that resulted in the forfeiture of the good behavior bonds they had been required to post.[114] Reginald Wright Kauffman, a Philadelphia journalist, surrendered his credentials as a protest against the praetorian censorship he encountered, but the Army, which had been urged by Secretary of State Lansing to stop his critical reporting, announced that he was being expelled and took possession of his bond.[115] Wythe Williams of the *New York Times* was suspended after sending *Collier's Weekly* an uncensored article blaming French politicians for the failure of an offensive. Williams contended that the article, which was based on confidential information from the French statesman Georges Clemenceau, did not have to be censored because it was not about American forces, but Pershing and his staff decided that it was a diplomatic embarrassment that disclosed military policy.[116] Heywood Broun of the *New York Tribune* created a controversy by revealing that American soldiers were not as wholesome, well-trained, and well-equipped as Pershing claimed they were and by suggesting that censorship was keeping Americans unaware of the problems their troops faced. Fearing a public relations backlash, the Army did not revoke his credentials and seize his bond until he wrote a story with faulty source material that questioned the wisdom of sending thirteen major generals to Europe on the same ship.[117] Westbrook Pegler, a United Press correspondent, was disaccredited after censors read a letter he wrote to a colleague that detailed the military's efforts to mislead journalists and the officers' indifference to soldiers' hardships, including frequent deaths from pneumonia.[118]

The military not only used harsh measures against reporters, but also discouraged its personnel from talking about their problems. Soldiers in the United States and Europe were ordered to avoid public discussion of military matters in general.[119] Everyone in the armed forces in the United States who wrote for publication was required to submit to security censorship and was to understand "the fact that criticism of superiors and the spreading of false reports which would tend to injure the military service constitute breaches of military discipline." Journalists who visited training camps had to "rigidly adhere" to CPI guidelines on secrecy or "be deprived of the privileges of the camp."[120] Mail from troops sailing to Europe was censored for military details as well as "extraordinary incidents";[121] letters from troops in Europe were not to contain criticism of "operations, superior officers, non-commissioned officers, conditions of life, subsistence, etc." or of "the appearance, equipment, or conduct" of Allied soldiers.[122] The result, as one Wisconsin newspaper editorial pointed out, could be suspiciously bland, inane letters. "Of course the fact that they are well is a great satisfaction, but one would think that it would not 'give aid to the enemy' to tell something more and it would be far more satisfying to the recipients," the editorial said. "Of course orders are orders and must be obeyed, but 'what's doing' that there is so much secrecy about it all?"[123]

Censorship covered up incompetence leaders did not want to acknowledge. Responding to published denials by the secretaries of war and the Navy that deplorable conditions existed in training camps, Theodore Roosevelt used letters he received to expose failures to deal with contagious diseases and to provide warm clothing. Officers were working on the difficulties, he said, but "they would have been corrected far more quickly if there had been outspoken criticism of them."[124] American tanks and aircraft were not manufactured and shipped in time to be of any use in the war zone before the armistice.[125] Soldiers received lawn mowers, floor wax, and other superfluous items in abundance but lacked adequate food, clothing, and military equipment. A noted surgeon brought from Johns Hopkins to organize base hospitals in Europe threatened to quit if medical supplies were not loaded on the next ships from the United States, and gas masks that did arrive malfunctioned. With urgent requests producing no results and reporters trying to write about logistics blunders, Pershing asked the War Department to allow censors to pass their supply stories, but was denied permission by the secretary of war, Newton D. Baker. Republican congressmen toured France and brought back evidence of the troubles soldiers were facing, but reporters were reduced to devising ways to evade censorship to get their stories out. Figuring that French postal officials would not stop a letter addressed to a former president, Reginald Wright Kauffman sent reports to Theodore Roosevelt, who forwarded them to the *Philadelphia North American*.[126] Heywood Broun went back to New York, where he wrote a blistering series exposing the supply scandal and condemning censorship as a means of protecting reputations rather than lives.[127]

II.

By World War II, the president had ample precedents for restricting press freedom, but suppression had been foolish for Wilson and did not fit the democratic ethos Franklin Roosevelt tried to project. On the eve of the war, Roosevelt made a point of declaring his devotion to First Amendment values. He derided the Sedition Act of 1798, said free speech was essential to democracy, and insisted that anyone is "constitutionally entitled to criticize and call to account the highest and the lowest in the land."[128] Roosevelt's rhetoric on free government and free expression continued in the war years, but began to ring hollow. His fireside chat on Germany's invasion of Poland in 1939 spoke proudly of Americans being "the most enlightened and the best informed people in all the world" but also spoke vaguely of "certain ideas and certain ideals of national safety." As the crisis deepened in 1940, Roosevelt spoke of "the compass of the world" pointing to the single fact of armed aggression and of obligations to the institutions of freedom outweighing the right of personal choice. His State of the Union Message in 1941 listed freedom of expression as the first of "four essential human freedoms" in the world, but also spoke of the nation's strength being in its unity and of anything in the way of defense preparations having to yield to national needs. "No one can tell the exact character of the emergency situations that we may be called upon to meet," he said. "The Nation's hands must not be tied when the Nation's life is in danger." He contended that if "the few slackers or trouble makers in our midst" could not be shamed by patriotic example, then the best thing to do would be "to use the sovereignty of government to save government." In a radio address on the 150th anniversary of the ratification of the Bill of Rights, eight days after Pearl Harbor, Roosevelt described the war as a contest between dictatorship and democracy. "We will not, under any threat, or in the face of any danger," he said, "surrender the guarantees of liberty our forefathers framed for us in our Bill of Rights." Early in 1942 Roosevelt told a fireside chat audience to have "complete confidence that your Government is keeping nothing from you except information that will help the enemy in his attempt to destroy us." Yet the president's actions did not necessarily match his words. "If anything, he thought that rights should yield to the necessities of war," Attorney General Francis Biddle later observed. "Rights came after victory, not before."[129]

Roosevelt was comfortable with an approach to democracy that did not always respect civil liberties and the rule of law. He believed the nation's fundamental law was flexible enough to be bent and twisted without being broken. The Constitution, he said in his first inaugural address, "is so simple and practical that it is possible always to meet extraordinary needs by changes in emphasis and arrangement without loss of essential form." What was essential form to Roosevelt, as he explained in his Jackson Day Dinner speech in 1938, was what he called the "morals of democracy," which he defined as the good, tolerant instincts of the common citizen, and a faith in majority rule. In explaining his court-packing plan to the public in 1937, he said he agreed with the remark of Chief Justice Hughes that " 'the Constitution is what the Judges say it is.' " Finding nothing sacred about an eighteenth-century document or its interpretation by unelected justices, Roosevelt made it clear that he wanted a Supreme Court that would provide " 'a system of living law' " and would "save our national Constitution from hardening of the judicial arteries." He felt that the court's interference with New Deal legislation failed to recognize the broad powers of Congress to secure the "general welfare," but when Congress balked at part of his efforts to curb wartime inflation in 1942, Roosevelt threatened to assume broad executive powers to ensure the safety of the nation, powers that would "automatically revert to the people" after the war. Congress complied and thus did not give the president an opportunity to carry out his threat.[130]

Like Lincoln and Wilson, Roosevelt seemed to justify assaults on the constitution on the basis of his being elected by a majority and then having to act for the common good. Some Americans, of course, were willing to contemplate the possibility of an even stronger leader than Roosevelt was. In the movie *Gabriel over the White House* (1933), a president guided by God and by Lincoln's example takes emergency control of the government and uses the prerogatives of a benevolent dictator to solve the nation's problems. In his 1940 Jackson Day Dinner speech Roosevelt said he concluded from his reading of history that the greatest men in public life were those who had a disinterested devotion to serving the country and who "did the big job that their times demanded be done." Such people, he said, included Hamilton, who fought financial chaos; Jefferson, who helped establish "real democracy"; Jackson, who sought "economic democracy"; and Lincoln, who "did the big job which then had to be done—to preserve the Union." Laying out his formula for presidential success, he said, "If leaders have good motives and good manners and, at the same time intimate knowledge of the different parts of the country and plenty of experience, you can be fairly safe in assuming that they won't wreck your Government." In other words, Roosevelt thought the country should have more faith in politicians than the founders did. While campaigning for reelection in 1940, Roosevelt repeated Lincoln's story about the wolf and the sheep disagreeing about the definition of liberty and said that it was up to Americans to decide what the word "liberty" meant. In his 1941 Jackson Day address he quoted Lincoln's question to Congress in 1861: " 'Must a government, of necessity, be too strong for the liberties of its own people, or too weak to maintain its own existence?' " "Lincoln answered that question as Jackson had answered it—not by words, but by deeds," Roosevelt said. "And America still marches on."[131]

More interested in issuing marching orders than complying with existing law, Roosevelt got Congress to grant him vague emergency powers to deal with national crises. Congress had not proven itself very adept at managing the economy or dealing with foreign affairs after World War I, but Roosevelt was prepared to take strong actions he deemed politically acceptable. When, for example, he wanted to provide military assistance to beleaguered Britain in 1940, Roosevelt devised his own unilateral exchange of American destroyers for British bases, a decision of doubtful legality that was simply announced as a *fait accompli* without public discussion. After referring to Roosevelt's extramarital romance with Lucy Mercer, the White House ban on photographs of the president in a wheelchair, and the "hubris" of his court-packing scheme, the author of a history of the destroyer deal concluded that there were "two hallmarks of FDR's character: his obsession with secrecy and his bent for artifice." As Roosevelt moved toward his later lend-lease arrangements, which were approved by Congress, he used a fire analogy as the Supreme Court often had done in First Amendment cases. The president told a news conference that if a neighbor's house were burning, he would lend a hose without expecting anything more than replacement if it were to be damaged. What he was actually doing, of course, was aligning a neutral nation against Germany, but Roosevelt had the ability to make complex political and constitutional problems appear to have easy, common-sense solutions. According to Attorney General Biddle, he was "a great man," but his faults were "his passion for manipulation, his lack of frankness, his streak of vindictiveness, his often amateur approach to the problems of government."[132]

One of Roosevelt's amateur solutions was to incarcerate about sixteen thousand Japanese, Germans, and Italians prior to the mass internment of people of Japanese ancestry on the West Coast. Immediately after war was declared, Roosevelt signed proclamations allowing the instant arrest of "alien enemies" who had been classified as suspicious by the Justice Department before Pearl Harbor. When Attorney General Biddle brought the proclamation for arresting Germans and Italians to the president, Roosevelt asked how many Germans were in the country. Biddle told him there were about six hundred thousand, and Roosevelt made what Biddle later described as the "impulsive and absurdly impractical suggestion" that they should all be interned. " 'I don't care so much about the Italians,' " Roosevelt said. " 'They are lot of opera singers, but the Germans are different, they may be dangerous.' " Biddle explained that "not quite all" of the Germans were going to be arrested. "The prospect of action always made him feel better," Biddle said of Roosevelt, who was being treated for a sinus attack by a physician during their conversation. Hearings were not required, but citizen boards were set up to examine those arrested and to recommend internment, parole, or unconditional release. The aliens were not allowed to have lawyers represent them, a decision that the attorney general later noted "put the procedure on a prompt and common-sense basis."[133]

In an article in *Collier's*, Biddle contended that administration policy was "not to suppress expressions of opinion, however critical of the government" and that officials were treating the enemy aliens fairly and only holding those "dangerous to our safety." His examples of those worthy of parole included an old German woman who said Hitler "could lick anyone—even America—and would if he had to." The attorney general said being held on Ellis Island "hasn't hurt her" and that with some advice "she may think it wiser to hold her tongue for a while, for war's on now and such talk isn't popular." Another example was parole being given to an Italian barber who "expressed the opinion that Mussolini was a great man and that this country had better not dare fight against him." Having to report to a probation officer for one's thoughts was acceptable, Biddle believed, but prosecutions were another matter. "Men should never, under our law," he said, "be prosecuted for their opinions, however they may disturb the beliefs we cherish or oppose the moral assumptions that most of us share." Biddle remarked that "it will be possible for us to avoid the stupid whispering and cruel witch-hunting of the last war." Still, the attorney general said that "the executive officers of the government have very broad discretion" in wartime and that the country should "*take absolutely no chances.*" While downplaying the threat and saying that few aliens were actually disloyal, Biddle endorsed the position of Justice Holmes, whose biography he had just written, that opinions could be tolerated " 'unless they so imminently threaten immediate interference with the lawful and pressing purposes of the law that an immediate check is required to save the country.' "[134]

The president, on the other hand, was not particularly interested in legal doctrines. Freedom of the press, he told the American Society of Newspaper Editors in 1941, was not "a mere form of words, a constitutional abstraction," but rather had a "living meaning" in press practices that government could not control except for "vital military information." He said, "It would be a shameful abuse of patriotism to suggest that opinion should be stifled in its service."[135] Despite his pronouncements on freedom of expression and his public affability with reporters, Roosevelt was a politician who could be angered by critics.[136] In a fireside chat on national defense in 1940, he blasted isolationist dissent as "undiluted poison" that "must not be allowed to spread." Names of people who wrote him to complain about American policies after the outbreak of the war were turned over to the Justice Department. Attempts were made to monitor the purveyors of "subversive" ideas and to reveal their funding. Regarding statements in conservative, isolationist periodicals as suspiciously similar to foreign propaganda broadcasts, Roosevelt thought they might be subject to legal action and publicly denounced them as fascist-inspired. A number of publications during the war suggested that conservatives and isolationists were in league with fifth columnists and contended that "defeatist propaganda" should be banned.[137]

Before the war, the threat of government regulation induced the movie and radio industries to promote administration perspectives.[138] Many of the nation's press lords, however, had bitterly attacked Roosevelt's foreign and domestic policies, and some tolerated or even admired fascism. Robert McCormick's *Chicago Tribune*, for instance, had criticized Hitler but found him no worse than Roosevelt and had thought the United States could coexist with Nazi Germany.[139] William Randolph Hearst, who despised Roosevelt, had signed a four-hundred-thousand-dollar-a-year deal to supply American news to the Third Reich press and praised Hitler and Mussolini.[140] Such opponents backed the United States when the war came, but continued to find fault with the administration. McCormick's cousin, Joseph Medill Patterson, publisher of the *New York Daily News*, went to the White House after Pearl Harbor to make amends and volunteer for service, but Roosevelt berated his editorials and sent him away in tears. In 1942 one of Patterson's correspondents, John O'Donnell, wrote some biting remarks about censorship and was sarcastically awarded Germany's Iron Cross at a presidential press conference. The Justice Department conducted content analyses of the newspapers published by McCormick, Hearst, and Patterson to compare them to Axis broadcasts, but found no relationship and took no action.[141] Another means of countering antiadministration sentiment materialized with the creation of a new agency. The Office of War Information (OWI), established by executive order in 1942, analyzed American public opinion on the war and attempted to coordinate the dissemination of government information. The OWI undertook marketing efforts for the allied cause, but stirred up controversy with its emphasis on Roosevelt's leadership.[142]

Roosevelt used the FBI to spy on critics, ranging from the well-financed, isolationist America First Committee to George Seldes, the iconoclastic, left-wing publisher of *In Fact*.[143] Among the many minority publications the FBI scrutinized was the Oklahoma City *Black Dispatch*, which an agent found "sprinkled with such well-known Communist phrases as 'Civil Liberties,' 'Inalienable Rights,' and 'Freedom of Speech and of the Press.' "[144] The investigations, which often involved questionable methods, revealed little of note except for the sexual relationship that *Washington Times-Herald* gossip columnist Inga Arvad had in 1942 with a future president, John F. Kennedy, whose isolationist father recently had been ambassador to Britain. Arvad worked for an anti-Roosevelt newspaper and had been on friendly terms with Hitler and other Nazi leaders while living in Europe. Her phone was tapped, and her apartment was broken into in order to make copies of her personal papers. Roosevelt thought that her publisher, Joseph Patterson's sister, Eleanor Patterson, had a subversive mind and was assured by Biddle that she too was under surveillance.[145]

Fears of foreign agents and an American fifth column were rampant early in the war. The FBI recruited tens of thousands of American Legion members to be confidential informants. In 1940 Harrison Salisbury, who was then working for United Press, had his house broken into and searched on the suspicion that he was a code expert employed by Germany. Apparently a neighbor with an active imagination had told police that the home was full of espionage equipment, but they found no evidence. The incident was reported to the FBI, however, and Salisbury was placed on a list of security risks to be detained in the event of a declaration of war against Germany. Salisbury was "cleared," but for the rest of his distinguished career the information remained in government files and may have caused his difficulties in getting security clearances.[146]

Sources of hysterical ideas were widely available. Sinister-looking OWI posters used slogans such as "Loose Talk Causes Loss of Life" and "A Careless Word—A Needless Loss." Although enemy-directed sabotage and espionage were very rare occurrences in the United States during the war, they were common fare in Hollywood films. In 1942, a year in which 60 percent of 122 war features focused on espionage, the OWI's Bureau of Motion Pictures issued a report complaining that the studios were exaggerating the menace, and the number of films dealing with enemy intrigue dropped substantially in 1943 and 1944.[147]

In the tense early months of the war, Roosevelt pressured Biddle and Postmaster General Frank Walker to take action against publications he regarded as subversive. The Post Office revoked at least six second-class mailing permits for political opinions, but ran into resistance from the Justice Department and restored two. Postal authorities, as well as the FBI, conducted extensive monitoring of periodicals, but the Justice Department, following the pronouncements of Justice Holmes and Zechariah Chafee on the Espionage Act, stymied suppression.[148] At weekly cabinet meetings the president needled the attorney general with demands for action. "He was not much interested in the theory of sedition, or in the constitutional right to criticize the government in wartime," Biddle recalled.[149] Perhaps as a way of defusing some of the tension that arose between the two men on the subject of dissent, Roosevelt decided to tease his attorney general by telling him to draft a proclamation "abrogating so far as possible all freedom of discussion and information during the war." Biddle, who had just arrived in the Cabinet Room where the people present had been let in on the joke, paced the floor speaking vehemently against the idea for five minutes before Roosevelt and the others burst out laughing. Biddle took the joke well, but he stayed on for the rest of the afternoon as the State of the Union Message was being prepared. "Maybe he thought there might be a germ of truth in it after all," a presidential aide observed.[150]

World War II proved to be less controversial than other major wars, and the government brought comparatively few cases against the press.[151] In what he later said was an attempt to have the Supreme Court overturn the Smith Act's prohibitions on advocating the violent overthrow of government, Biddle did authorize the prosecution of a group of Minneapolis Trotskyites under the statute in 1941. The defendants, who were rivals of local labor union backers of the president, used the trial as an opportunity to promulgate their revolutionary program, which included urging soldiers to regard the government as imperialist and warmongering. Eighteen of the twenty-nine radicals who had been indicted were convicted, after an extensive review of their statements and publications. Concluding that action could be taken against utterances that had a tendency to cause military insubordination and the overthrow of the government, the appeals court affirmed the judgment. The Supreme Court, however, refused to take the case. Biddle later wrote that he regretted allowing the prosecution because there had been "no substantial overt act outside of talk and threats" and no " 'clear and present danger' to the government." He admitted he "may have been motivated by the instinct to display firmness on appropriate occasions" and said he "doubted whether any speech or writing should be made criminal."[152] As attorney general, he received assurances from several Supreme Court justices that convictions of the administration's more severe critics would be upheld in cases with a sound legal basis and proper attention to due process. He and other government officials agreed early in 1942 that a limited number of actions should be taken and that the nation's newspapers would not support publications making extreme challenges to the country's foreign policies.[153]

Worried about repeating the "extravagant abuse" of the World War I sedition laws, Biddle released people arrested for "palpably innocuous" utterances and directed that any federal sedition prosecutions receive his personal written approval. "I announced that freedom of speech should be curtailed only when public safety was directly imperiled," he said. The attorney general was more specific about his guidelines in responding to constant demands from Roosevelt to take action against domestic fascists who attacked his leadership. Biddle told the president that he would act only where they interfered with recruitment or some connection with propaganda centers in Germany could be established. In some instances his standards were met. Twenty-six fascists were indicted in 1942 under the Espionage Act of 1917 and the Smith Act of 1940, but the obstruction tactics of the nearly forty lawyers involved made the lengthy trial, in Biddle's words, a "bedlam" and "a dreary farce." The case was dropped after the death of the exhausted judge, Edward C. Eicher. "The trial had killed him," Biddle said.[154]

The attorney general did not risk having a prolonged legal offensive when he decided in the spring of 1942 to take action against Father Charles Coughlin, a conspicuous hatemonger who habitually denounced Roosevelt. "One could count on its being dragged out for at least two or three years—the very years when national unity was essential to our success," Biddle said later. Church and government officials conferred on how to deal with the priest, who had close contacts with Axis agents and who appeared to be receiving financial support through them. Among those who insisted that the administration act was Justice Frank Murphy, who told a Roosevelt subordinate that Coughlin was giving aid and comfort to the enemy and supplied examples from the priest's pro-Nazi and anti-Semitic *Social Justice*. Roosevelt forwarded the writings to Biddle and met with him and J. Edgar Hoover on the subject. The attorney general soon engineered the loss of second-class mailing privileges for *Social Justice*, and a full-scale federal investigation of the priest's activities was undertaken. Facing the possibility of indictment under the Espionage Act and a prison term, Coughlin agreed not to be involved in any future publication without explicit permission from his archbishop. "F.D.R. was delighted with the outcome," Biddle noted. "That was the end of Father Coughlin."[155]

Another longtime Roosevelt antagonist, the *Chicago Tribune*, was the target of an abortive prosecution after publishing a front-page story on the Battle of Midway on June 7, 1942. The story indicated that the United States had advance knowledge of how Japanese forces were arrayed, a statement the Navy regarded as a disclosure that the enemy's code had been broken. Roosevelt's first thoughts were to have the Marines occupy the Tribune Tower and to have McCormick charged with treason, but legal obstacles were in the way. Finally, acting on orders from the president, Navy Secretary Frank Knox demanded an Espionage Act prosecution, but Biddle told him that "the essence of the case was the harm done to the national safety" and that witnesses would have to testify that the newspaper had revealed that the code had been broken. Knox reluctantly agreed to cooperate, and a grand jury in Chicago began an investigation of the *Tribune* and the story's reporter, Stanley Johnston. Knox, who was the publisher of the rival Chicago *Daily News*, soon had his motives questioned in Congress and the press and decided that the case should be dropped. He told the attorney general that the Navy, which had little indication that any damage had been caused by the publication, would not provide evidence because the information could be helpful to the enemy. The grand jury refused to indict. "I felt like a fool," Biddle recalled.[156]

Routine civilian censorship of the nation's print publications and radio stations was handled by an ad hoc government agency responsible for both mandatory and voluntary controls.[157] In the First War Powers Act, Congress gave Roosevelt the authority to censor all communications with other countries whenever, during the war, "the President shall deem that the public safety demands it." The statute, which was approved on December 18, 1941, set penalties for evading censorship that included a fine of up to ten thousand dollars and imprisonment for up to ten years. The next day Roosevelt signed an executive order to establish the Office of Censorship and to give its director "absolute discretion" over communications entering and leaving the United States. "All Americans abhor censorship, just as they abhor war," Roosevelt said in a prepared statement. "But the experience of this and of all other Nations has demonstrated that some degree of censorship is essential in wartime, and we are at war." He said that military information of use to the enemy had to be not only prevented from leaving the country, but also "scrupulously withheld at the source." In addition, he noted, the press was being called upon "to abstain voluntarily from the dissemination of detailed information of certain kinds, such as reports of the movements of vessels and troops." The president selected Byron Price, the executive news editor of the AP, to be the director of censorship and soon gave him the additional task of coordinating voluntary censorship.[158] The office quickly grew into an operation of 14,462 civil service and military employees and was integrated with censorship bureaucracies in allied countries.[159]

Treating the First Amendment as irrelevant at the border, Congress barely bothered to notice the censorship provisions of the hastily passed War Powers Act. The members apparently saw no need to raise constitutional issues as long as censorship within the United States was to remain voluntary. "This is an attempt only to control international communications," said Representative Emanuel Celler of New York, as the legislation was being considered. Price insisted that freedom of the press stopped at the water's edge and did not mean allowing communications that could aid enemy propaganda and foster distrust among the Allies. Plans for border censorship had been in preparation since at least 1935 and were rapidly implemented, but the voluntary domestic code was not written until war was declared and intense discussions were held with the military. The military influence on the domestic functions of the Office of Censorship was strong at the beginning and remained significant. "The Code provisions did not emanate from the brainwaves of a handful of newspaper men temporarily in government service at Washington," Price noted at a meeting of editors during the war, adding that "assistance is given the Office of Censorship hourly by Army and Navy officers." Thus, although Price claimed that his office operated "in complete independence of the War and Navy Departments," self-censorship had a patina of Pentagon approval.[160]

Figure 6.1   *Three central figures in civil liberties issues during World War II were (left to right) FBI Director J. Edgar Hoover, Director of Censorship Byron Price, and Attorney General Francis Biddle. Photograph (1942). Courtesy of the State Historical Society of Wisconsin. Negative WHi (✕3) 50998.*

Roosevelt, who had been an assistant secretary of the Navy when Woodrow Wilson became embroiled in controversy over domestic censorship powers, rejected the pleas of high-ranking officials who wanted a government takeover of the radio industry and a statute imposing prior restraint within the United States. As he performed his work, Price cautioned journalists that a failure to abide by voluntary rules would invite passage of censorship legislation, a warning they took seriously. The confidential newsletter circulated among Gannett Newspapers employees, for instance, often repeated the conventional wisdom that government guidelines on news could "seem silly," but "they are the rules and their observance has protected American newspapers in voluntary rather than enforced censorship."[161] Violations could also mean bad publicity and, possibly, government punishments, ranging from a loss of press credentials to export restrictions and espionage prosecutions. The director of censorship, however, preferred to see the arrangement in a more positive light. "The declaration of the President for a voluntary system of censorship was hailed generally by the press, which came forward with a universal pledge of coöperation," Price noted in 1943. "There had been no prelude of controversy in Congress as in the case of World War I."[162]

Controversy did develop once copies of the guidelines were distributed to the nation's mass media, from the largest daily newspapers to church and lodge bulletins. Early in 1942 the Office of Censorship issued its first *Code of Wartime Practices for the American Press*, which listed the self-restraints newspapers and magazines were expected to observe. Editors were asked to "follow the dictates of common sense" and to refuse to publish information on troop movements and other details of military operations. They were to wait until news on such subjects was made available "by appropriate authority," since "the Government unquestionably is in the best position to decide when disclosure is timely." A separate code for broadcasters had additional provisions that included avoiding "dramatic programs which attempt to portray the horrors of combat," as well as musical requests, public service announcements, and various forms of audience participation that could allow an enemy agent to convey information. Even letters to Santa Claus could not be read on the air unless they were edited or rewritten. "Free speech will not suffer during this emergency period beyond the absolute precautions which are necessary to the protection of a culture which makes our radio the freest in the world," the code declared.[163] Later editions of the guidelines included refinements and additions such as a section asking that interviews dealing with combat zones be submitted for approval and that letters from those areas conform to the voluntary code even if they had passed through military censorship.[164]

The initial media reaction to the voluntary codes was generally positive, but complaints naturally arose.[165] *Time* magazine protested that the restrictions were written in "blanket terms" and that the public would be kept in the dark about the progress of war production and other important matters. "In short, the publication of virtually any news about the U.S. war effort is now forbidden unless specifically sanctioned by the Government," the magazine said when the code appeared. "Since all information is of value to the enemy in one degree or another, Censor Price's code could be literally stretched to a ridiculous extent."[166] Henry Luce, the publisher of *Time*, *Life*, and *Fortune*, was not inclined to accept guidelines that could constrain his brisk feigning of omniscience on public affairs.[167] "Among all of the men in control of the publishing empires of the period," the director of censorship recalled, "he alone

never came forward in our support." In fact, Price observed, Luce's employees indulged in "constant harassment" of the Office of Censorship. Nothing serious occurred, however, until Luce's *March of Time* newsreel outfit insisted on showing the
sinking of a tanker in a documentary despite the Navy's objections. "It was a time of
great peril on the sea," Price explained, "publication of such material would tend to
discourage enlistment in the tanker fleet which was essential to the conduct of the
war." Secretary Knox told his public relations officers to "do their utmost to secure
press cooperation in toning down the gruesome details of sinkings, particularly the
news regarding tankers." The director of censorship decided to use the powers of his
office to deny the film an export license, an action that meant it would not make a
profit. The objectionable material was removed, and Price was assured that relations
with his office would improve. The resistance from Luce's organization faded away.[168]

Price and his staff often stated and usually followed the principal that voluntary
censorship was not aimed at restricting opinion;[169] but they did play the tedious and
usually futile charade of trying to hide facts that were already revealed or not particularly important. The Office of Censorship insisted that radar was a secret weapon
and did not want even disclosed information about it discussed in the press, but enemy
forces used the device, and allied officials frequently leaked details of its features.
(Broken radar facilities were difficult to fix because the Army decided that printing
repair manuals would be a security risk.) When the office stopped references to Americans using napalm and being attacked by kamikaze pilots it was keeping information
not from the other side so much as from citizens who might have raised disturbing
questions. Fears of attacks on the United States produced stringent self-censorship on
weather news that reached even annual almanacs and the annual Groundhog Day
predictions on February 2. The Office of Censorship sent Eleanor Roosevelt a stern
letter for mentioning the weather in her "My Day" column. Broadcasters were asked
not to provide any information or forecasts unless warnings were necessary. Thus
sportscasters were not supposed to explain why games were being delayed or how
conditions were affecting the contest.[170]

The most controversial of all voluntary censorship provisions may have been the
one restricting news of presidential travel.[171] In the early morning hours of September
18, 1942, Roosevelt slipped out of Washington in his armor-plated, 142-ton train car,
the *Ferdinand Magellan*,[172] for a two-week, 8,754-mile inspection tour of the nation's
defense plants. Nothing about the trip was supposed to be reported until he returned
to the White House, and only three wire service reporters were allowed to accompany
him. Thousands saw him, and news organizations were flooded with calls demanding
to know why the trip was not receiving any coverage. Indulging in his infatuation
with intrigue, Roosevelt apparently was hoping for a burst of favorable publicity at
the end of the trip when congressional campaigns would be at a critical stage. Instead
he received criticism from members of Congress, a frosty reception at the first news
conference after his return, and a signed protest from thirty-three Washington correspondents. The journalists argued that although precautions had to be taken for the
president's safety, a long delay in coverage meant "doubts are inevitably raised as to
the completeness and authenticity of other news emanating from the government."
"Arthur Krock of the *New York Times* wrote of a coming disclosure in phrases so
mysterious," Byron Price noted in his memoirs, "that some people in Wall Street

were disturbed and rumors circulated that news of a national disaster was being suppressed by Censorship."[173]

Price and Attorney General Biddle found that the president had a "blind spot" about voluntary censorship and that he thought the Office of Censorship could simply order the news media not to cover a sensitive topic such as official travel. "On that score he gave us many anxious moments," Price remembered. "Not only did he overestimate the government's power over the press in wartime, but he took unexpected advantage of the immunities afforded him by the Code provisions which were designed to protect his personal safety." Saying that he had wanted to concentrate on his work instead of politics and publicity, Roosevelt told a radio audience that he planned to make other trips in the same way he made his defense plant tour.[174] Reporters made little progress as they continued feuding with Roosevelt on the issue, and they were not allowed to disclose the fact that his train stopped at the New Jersey estate of Lucy Mercer Rutherford, a woman his wife Eleanor did not want him to see again, after his earlier relationship with her had nearly ended their marriage.[175] Commenting on the absurdity of not publishing the location of the president when many would know it, an *Editor & Publisher* magazine editorial agreed that his itinerary might be withheld, but added that he could not travel "incognito" and that the safety precautions were "a dead give away." "The Code survived all of this," Price concluded. "I never thought that FDR really wanted to wreck it, as nearly as he came to doing so. I think he was only having fun according to the complicated pattern of his congenital inconsistency."[176]

The censorship of periodicals, mail, and other communications crossing the border did help uncover some minor spying, security breaches, and illegal activities;[177] but it also created an enormous amount of drudgery, inconvenience, and resentment. Occasionally concerns were expressed about careless or inconsistent work. Early in the war, for instance, the *Los Angeles Times* found that stories were being removed by laying copies of the paper on a table and using a razor blade to slice through not only the part in question but also the pages underneath. A subscriber in Mexico noted that the *Times* was arriving with holes while a Texas paper was arriving untouched, suggesting that different standards existed in different parts of the country. Raymond Clapper, a political commentator for the Scripps-Howard newspapers, said journalists had few problems publishing within the United States, but that the Office of Censorship insisted on screening political commentaries and embarrassing news on racial and labor incidents that were going abroad where they could be exploited in enemy propaganda. "Actually," Clapper said, "anything that is published in the United States quickly reaches the Axis by way of neutral routes out of the Western Hemisphere."[178] Letters were often censored if they aired complaints or took a gloomy view of the conflict, though the censors were supposed to be looking for information that conceivably could be of military use. References to the eruption of Mauna Loa a few weeks after Pearl Harbor, for example, were deleted on the fear that the Japanese could use the glow for a night attack. So zealous were the censors that a frequent complaint was that mail from loved ones arrived looking like spaghetti or Venetian blinds. Censors even cut out the Xs that stood for kisses on the theory that they might be code. Determined letter-writers risked fines with such ruses as inventing codes, writing behind the stamp, or having the envelope carried by hand to the destination.

In one case a censor demanded to know the identity of a person in London who had sent a cablegram signed only "George." The answer said: "FULL NAME IS GEORGE REX; ADDRESS, BUCKINGHAM PALACE."[179]

Office of Censorship restrictions were especially galling for British journalists in the United States prior to D-Day as they were trying to convey American news and opinion to their anxious readers. The correspondents were upset about having American criticism of British policies and actions deleted from their dispatches. They complained that suppression of opinion from the United States not only violated principles of free discussion and suggested that England could not take criticism, but also encouraged rumors and made it difficult for the British to understand American concerns and to reply. The journalists scoffed at the censors' explanation that they wanted to avoid feeding the enemy propaganda machine. "The argument that nothing may be said that might provide a little verbal ammunition for the Axis seems tantamount to surrendering the freedom of the press to the whim of Dr. Goebbels," said British United Press correspondent Harold Hutchinson. "If we are not capable of withstanding the blows of Axis shortwave radios we must be very fragile indeed." In an interview with the *New York Times*, Byron Price insisted that his office's censorship had to go beyond national security information because other countries were taking sides in the war and journalists sometimes distorted public opinion. "I think there is a point in being a little careful about letting too pessimistic news go out of the country," he explained, "because it serves no purpose and it might do damage."[180]

In a *Harper's* article published in 1943, Alex Faulkner of the *Daily Telegraph* listed examples of dispatches he had not been permitted to send to England. They included stories on Justice Owen Roberts condemning complacency in the United States, Wendell Willkie deploring racial discrimination in the Navy, and Donald W. Douglas appealing to his aircraft workers for less absenteeism. Since weather stories were regarded as potentially useful to the enemy, he could not relate the conditions on election day in 1942, and, after two attempts to give a vague description were rejected by the censors, he was able to write: "As far as the outside world is concerned, the question of whether 'Republican' or 'Democratic' weather prevailed to-day must for some time remain a closely guarded secret." Criticizing censorship, however, was not safe. Faulkner could not send a portion of a Chicago *Sun* editorial demanding to know why censors were suppressing stories on race, poverty, and other matters that might reflect badly on the United States. The word "tremendously" was removed from a sentence he wrote saying that some Americans were tremendously indignant about Roosevelt's threat to act without Congress if it did not pass legislation to deal with inflation. Faulkner was not allowed to describe consumer product shortages in an article he thought would help his readers understand American sacrifices for the war effort, and he was forbidden to summarize the "secret route" Willkie had taken from China to the United States fifteen days before Willkie himself recounted it in a radio broadcast.[181]

Office of Censorship officials publicly defended their actions. Byron Price maintained that his agency "in no way and to no degree seeks to influence editorial opinion" in the domestic press and described censorship as "a necessary evil" and as a vital weapon of war. "Both experience and common sense testify convincingly to the dangers which might result to a nation struggling for its life if the public prints were left untrammeled and unguided by considerations of security," he said. The press clause did not appear to be an impediment. First Amendment rights were "by no means absolute rights," Price insisted, and "cannot be reasonably stretched to include a guarantee of freedom to be criminally careless with information in war time."[182] Immersed in the drama and intrigue of the war as they were, citizens who could even read an advertisement for a " 'Black-out safety luminous gardenia' " could be sympathetic to pleas for precautions.[183] Theodore Koop, who held several high positions in the Office of Censorship during the war, said in a book on his agency's work, *Weapon of Silence*, that it received some letters with complaints, "but virtually all insisted that Censorship go to any length necessary to protect the nation and its fighting men." Koop then quoted Justice Holmes: " 'When a nation is at war, many things that might be said in time of peace are such a hindrance to its effort that their utterance will not be endured as long as men fight.' "[184]

Silence, however, could be dangerous. When balloon-transported bombs launched in Japan began reaching the United States late in 1944, the Office of Censorship asked American news organizations not to report on their existence so that the enemy would be deprived of information on their effectiveness. The resulting lack of knowledge may have played a minor role in Japan's decision to suspend the balloon attacks less than six months after they began, but the program was relatively expensive, and American bombing had made essential components difficult to obtain. Only a small fraction of the more than nine thousand balloon bombs survived the ocean crossing, and few caused any significant damage, but public ignorance of the weapons seems to have been responsible for the only incident of civilian casualties on the mainland during World War II. A woman and five Sunday-school students in Oregon came across a balloon bomb during an outing and were killed by an explosion when they examined the device. After the deaths the government dropped its policy and publicized the hazards, but only after the bombs were no longer being launched.[185] In 1944 the Japanese had considered a plan to use balloons for biological warfare against North America, but Hideki Tojo, the politician and military leader who was later hanged for war crimes, rejected the idea as too likely to bring germ or chemical retaliation from the United States. Japanese biological warfare researchers, who performed horrifying experiments on prisoners of war, were later granted war crimes immunity by the United States Army in exchange for their data, and an American cover-up allowed a number of them to become leading figures in postwar Japan.[186]

Over time the Office of Censorship became frustrated in its attempts to work with the armed forces. A persistent problem was the military acting on its own to instruct the press on how to cover specific stories despite the voluntary approach. Incidents included Army officers telling journalists not to identify a B-29 that had flown over eighty thousand people at a University of Michigan football game, not to report on a military plane crashing into the Empire State Building, not to have a headline wider than one column on a story about an Army officer being arrested for maligning the president, not to provide news already distributed by others, not to publish anything about tides, not to say anything about four soldiers being killed in an automobile accident in Arizona, not to print a photograph showing an untidy War Department office building site, not to release information outside of certain regions, and not to mention anything about Alaska, which was thought to be threatened by the Japanese. Journalists could call on the Office of Censorship to help resolve such isolated cases, but they were also concerned about more prevalent problems. Although Byron Price was long an advocate of voluntary measures and praised the press for its compliance with the code, he was insisting by the final year of the war that the military conduct "a comprehensive review" of its special requests for secrecy. In a confidential letter to the Joint Chiefs of Staff, Price noted that journalists were in a state of "incipient rebellion" because they were being asked to suppress information "already in the hands of the enemy" and "having nothing to do with security, but relating only to policy matters." Price asked the military to re-examine its thinking on a long list of topics from atrocity stories to the presence of a U.S. base in the Azores. Journalists were constantly withholding stories of high news value, he argued, but if they were finding the requests were made without just cause "they would consider it their responsibility, from the overall viewpoint of national interest, to make their own decisions as to what should be published and broadcast."[187]

Participants in the 1944 annual convention of the American Society of Newspaper Editors labored over a series of resolutions to express their concerns. One stated a determination to "condemn the practice in any government of regarding the press as an instrument of government," and another said each member "hereby pledges himself or herself to remain keenly alert in defense of the freedom of the press." Pointed complaints were made about official obstructions of the flow of public information and "a pernicious system of departmental and bureaucratic propaganda disseminated by a veritable horde of press agents." After recognizing "the tremendous achievements of American armed forces in all parts of the world," a resolution maintained that military authorities harmed public morale by withholding facts with no bearing on security that the press had a right to know promptly. "Such policies serve to deprive the people of information which could only create better public understanding of the scope and nature of this terrible war and aid in a more expeditious victory," the resolution said. Voluntary censorship did continue until the end of the war, when it reached what Price had earlier predicted would be "its unlamented end."[188]

Despite their complaints, journalists were consistent cheerleaders for the war effort. Press support took many forms, including the donation of an estimated $1 billion in public service advertising related to the war. The news media were so inclined to give a favorable picture of the war that words and images were fabricated at times. One example was the famous "Send us more Japs!" quote supposedly uttered by a Marine officer at Wake Island. When he returned to a hero's welcome in the United States after nearly four years as a prisoner of war, James Devereux denied making the statement. "None of us was that much of a damn fool," he said. "We already had more Japs than we could handle." Joe Rosenthal's Pulitzer prize-winning AP photograph of the flag-raising on Iwo Jima for AP was actually not a candid shot of a heroic feat on Mount Suribachi but rather a picture of men replacing the original flag with a larger one. The press and the public, however, liked the Rosenthal image and treated it as a representation of the actual event, which had been photographed by Lou Lowery for *Leatherneck*.[189]

Battlefield censorship regulations were published in a field manual issued by the secretary of war and the Army chief of staff six weeks after Pearl Harbor. The manual followed patterns set in World War I but flatly asserted that reporters "although not in the military service, are subject to military law." They could not only lose credentials for intentionally violating their signed censorship agreements, but also be "placed in arrest to await deportation or trial by court martial" in "extreme cases of offense." The manual said that the general censorship principles were "truthfully disclosing" the facts about Army operations and "refraining from disclosing those things which, though true, would be disastrous to us if known to the enemy." Yet deletions could be made in stories said to "injure the morale of our forces, the people at home, or our allies" or to "embarrass the United States, its allies or neutral countries." Reporters were allowed to talk to troops when granted permission by the officer present, but could only quote officers with the specific authorization of the theater commander. The work of censors in the European theater was recorded in excruciating detail (including the exact number of words and images submitted) and guided by a two-hundred-page mimeographed document that was supplemented by daily directives and other materials.[190]

What was said on paper, however, was subject to what military officers would do in practice. Correspondents complained about news blackouts, about delays and inconsistencies in censorship, and about refusals to release stories for political reasons or because they contained the "horrifics" of war. The censorship was upsetting, and reporters were ejected for such actions as unapproved reporting on the liberation of Paris and the German surrender;[191] however, cumbersome requirements on interviewing and access to the front could be ignored.[192] General Dwight D. Eisenhower ordered his unit commanders to give correspondents all reasonable assistance and to allow them to talk freely with officers and enlisted men and to see the machinery of war in operation so that the public would be aware of the conditions soldiers faced. In an off-the-record session with reporters before D-Day, he said that the public should know if the leadership was at fault and that he would not impose censorship of criticism because he did not think that officers in high positions should use their extraordinary powers to protect themselves. As his forces advanced into Germany, Eisenhower issued memoranda on the need for policies that would get "to the American people more vivid accounts of the accomplishments of American soldiers." Too much censorship, he said, damaged the morale of troops, since they appreciated recognition. "The freest possible flow of news is not only in keeping with our traditions; it is the best way to keep the public accurately informed and working in support of the war effort," Eisenhower wrote. "The saving of lives and military success are normally the only sound reasons for interference."[193]

Eisenhower realized that the military needed scrutiny. While in England preparing for the cross-Channel invasion, he found dangerous and sometimes deadly frictions between white and black soldiers being covered up. Instead of pretending the problem did not exist, Eisenhower ordered a study of soldiers' censored mail to analyze the causes and took steps to reduce the conflicts that included keeping the troops hard at work, training together, and living together. In a circular letter he told his senior officers to spread the message that derogatory statements about any group must be promptly punished as a breach of discipline.[194] He revoked a ban on reporting about the racial conflicts despite the protests of some journalists who thought that reporting on the incidents would cause dissension back in the United States. Eisenhower said in his book *Crusade in Europe* that he "never failed to regret" the rare occasions when he imposed censorship for reasons other than withholding information from the enemy.[195] In his book *My War*, journalist Andy Rooney, who was then a staff writer for the *Stars and Stripes*, mentioned Eisenhower's noninterference policy several times and noted that he "made it possible to publish an honest newspaper in the military." Notions of false security remained, however. Rooney related the story of a reporter for the *Stars and Stripes* who was threatened with a court-martial for writing about the new P-47 fighter, even though the information came only from published sources and two of the planes already had been forced down in good condition behind enemy lines.[196]

Eisenhower's temperament was a contrast to the bluster and bearing of General Douglas MacArthur in the Pacific. "When you start to tear down, to destroy public confidence in the leaders of a military movement, you practically destroy an army," MacArthur told a gathering of fifty correspondents in 1942. "As far as I personally am concerned, I am always glad to give you my full knowledge and full opinion on any subject, but you must regard it as background entirely." The general insisted that journalists could criticize, but his subordinates made sure that unflattering references to him were censored. MacArthur sought to create a dashing image of himself and made constant efforts to manage the news. Although he said any of his conversations with the press would be open to all reporters, those who praised him got exclusive interviews and inside information. Japanese journalists, who had to answer to him once the American occupation began, were forced to avoid offending MacArthur and the military. MacArthur, who was preening himself as a possible presidential contender, decreed that reporters who conducted interviews without permission would be banned from the combat zone and that the offending soldiers would be court-martialed.[197]

Protests against MacArthur's policies were heard from time to time. At a luncheon in Chicago in 1943, for instance, Robert McCormick, publisher of the *Chicago Tribune*, denounced "dangerous and dishonest censorship" while introducing one of his correspondents, Clay Gowran, who had returned from the South Pacific. McCormick charged that shortcomings in the war effort were being concealed from the public and said that news organizations should organize to demand the truth. "Furthermore," he said, "it has become a complete political censorship to control public opinion." Not all the criticism of MacArthur's dishonesty came from the press. Many soldiers complained that he and his superiors were wrong to give false hope for the relief of forces fighting in the Philippines in 1942. Meanwhile, MacArthur's press office burnished his image as an intrepid, ingenious leader who inflicted devastating harm on the enemy while experiencing only light losses. He insisted on having personal credit for successes and on excluding others from the limelight. As soon as MacArthur lifted military censorship in 1945, reporters at his headquarters in Tokyo inundated news organizations with dispatches describing his "dictatorial" and "unreasonable" methods.[198]

The problems in the Pacific began with Pearl Harbor, an attack that proved to be more humiliating than debilitating for the armed forces. Although 2,403 Americans were killed and only a fourth of approximately four hundred military aircraft were left airworthy, much of the damage to ships was repairable and merely delayed offensive action. Some ships were ready for the sea within weeks, and all but three were put back into service eventually. All the Japanese vessels that participated in the attack were later sunk.[199] Yet the initial reaction was to cover up the facts. Military newsreel footage and photographs of the destruction were released a year later when they could be distributed with upbeat information on the repairs.[200] Photographs and newsreels showing deaths were delayed for almost two years.[201] Officials issued misleading statements minimizing the losses and justified their refusal to provide details as a matter of military security, even though successive waves of enemy pilots had observed the battle and the Japanese news media began carrying more accurate accounts than the ones available in the United States.[202] When columnist Drew Pearson attempted to publish leaked details on the losses and the lack of proper preparation, Roosevelt had his temporary censorship director, J. Edgar Hoover, tell Pearson that the statements were inaccurate and unpatriotic. Threatened with loss of his press privileges and perhaps even jail, Pearson said that he had not violated any law, but he agreed to changes in the column. Observing that Japan could have "immediate factual reports through any one of a number of different easy channels—most plausibly through 'neutral' consular officials," a correspondent who was at Pearl Harbor remarked that the Navy was "terrified to let anything out, partly because too many naval reputations were at stake."[203]

The events of December 7, 1941, were acutely embarrassing. In addition to its lopsided losses at the naval base, the military caused a number of civilian deaths and approximately forty explosions in nearby Honolulu with errant antiaircraft fire. On the day of the attack, the military prohibited photographs of Pearl Harbor, cut off nonofficial communication to the mainland, and, with a proclamation from the territorial governor, put Hawaii under martial law. Three days later the military governor issued General Orders No. 14, which with later amendments, imposed licensing and censorship on the Hawaiian print and broadcast media. The news organizations were cooperative, even before being placed under military authority. Honolulu's *Star-Bulletin*, which was selling the first of three "extra" editions at the gates of the naval base before the Japanese attack ended, decided not to reveal the extent of the damage to ships. In the following months, news stories that might perturb the armed services, including ones on prostitution, were suppressed. Hawaii's two Japanese-language dailies, which were ordered to close for a month following the attack, were not allowed to say anything critical or even analytical. Formal military controls remained in force until March 1943, when they were replaced by a combination of military demands and Office of Censorship restrictions.[204]

The use of martial law in Hawaii ended in October 1944 without any legal challenges from journalists, but a case heard by the Supreme Court exactly four years after the Pearl Harbor attack did dissolve the statutory foundation of the press controls. In *Duncan v. Kahanamoku*, a decision on the appeal of two civilians tried by military courts, the justices ruled that the territory's Organic Act authorized presidentially approved martial law for public safety purposes but did not allow the military to replace civilian courts with its own tribunals. The Supreme Court interpreted the law to mean that the armed forces could assist a functioning civilian government but not supplant it. Noting that the military "did, by simply promulgating orders, govern the day to day activities of civilians," Justice Hugo Black's majority opinion said that civilians in Hawaii were entitled to the same constitutional protections as those living elsewhere in the country. Pointing out that the Constitution did not refer to "martial law" and that Congress had not defined the term in the statute, Black expounded on the history of civilian supremacy over the military and said that the founders "were opposed to governments that placed in the hands of one man the power to make, interpret and enforce the laws."[205]

Navy news was a continuing problem for journalists. Even before Pearl Harbor, Secretary Knox asked the press not to report on the arrivals and departures of British ships using American ports, movements that were apparent to anyone nearby. President Roosevelt said the self-censorship was hindering German espionage, but he may have been more concerned about the politics of having British ships arriving to be outfitted or repaired under the Lend-Lease agreement.[206] When the United States entered the war, reporters could not get clearance for stories on submarine attacks off the American coast that were common knowledge.[207] The Navy was very slow to provide information when its ships were in a battle or sunk, and often the first news the public had was reports of what enemy sources were claiming.[208] For some weeks, for example, Japanese radio reporting was the only source for news on the daring air raid on Tokyo led by Jimmy Doolittle in 1942. A year passed before censors would allow the news media to say that the raid had been launched from a carrier, a fact that many reporters knew and anyone could guess. President Roosevelt joked that the planes, B-25s that were normally land-based, had taken off from the fictional land of Shangri-La. The War Department asked the Office of Censorship to stop press speculation on the place of departure, but Byron Price refused the request as too likely to antagonize journalists and their readers.[209] In a candid, classified report to the president in 1945, Elmer Davis, a journalist who was head of the OWI, said that the Navy may have wanted to be silent for security reasons in many cases, but that the reticence encouraged rumors and increased the public distrust of official sources that began with unconvincing and later-revised statements about Pearl Harbor. Davis wrote that "naval estimates of how much the enemy knew and did not know were not always very plausible, and the effect on public opinion was bad, no matter how good the intention."[210]

Davis and Price fought bureaucratic battles with the Navy for the release of war news. A particularly tense confrontation occurred in October 1942 after a *New York Times* reporter, Hanson Baldwin, told them about unacknowledged sinkings of American ships in the South Pacific and said that a large percentage of naval personnel believed the losses were being covered up to protect the careers of inefficient commanders. Arthur Hays Sulzberger, publisher of the *Times*, added that his paper would defy officials and publish what it knew if secrecy was too extensive, but agreed to consult with Price first. The *Times* did not have to act on its threat. Davis, who had not been informed of the losses by the Navy as he was supposed to be, set up a meeting with Price and Admiral Ernest J. King, chief of naval operations. Before the meeting, King consulted with President Roosevelt who, being an astute politician, told him to give out more information and to balance reports of ship losses with statements on replacements whenever possible. The Navy soon announced some of the sinkings, which had happened more than two months earlier, and, following Roosevelt's advice, mentioned new ships becoming available. King then met with Davis and Price and agreed to keep the OWI informed with a daily digest of dispatches marked to show what needed to be withheld for security reasons. Davis said his office would reserve

Figure 6.2 *"If he is asleep it isn't altogether his fault," a commentary on Navy Secretary Frank Knox's attempts to keep the bad news on ship sinkings from the American public during World War II. Ding Darling cartoon for the* Des Moines Register *(February 7, 1943). Reproduction permission granted by the J. N. Ding Darling Foundation.*

the right to discuss any suppression of information and agreed that the Navy would use its expertise to write the public communiqués on naval affairs.[211]

The agreement, however, did not solve the basic problem of the Navy controlling the flow of information. Admiral King, who even failed to keep Navy Secretary Knox informed, distrusted journalists, and a story circulated in Washington that he wanted only one piece of news published about the war, the one that said the Allies had won. The Navy was called the "silent service," and its own officers grumbled about the lack of attention given to their exploits in the press. Reacting to the frequent losses in the first year of the war, Representative Melvin J. Moss, a Marine Reserve officer who arranged to take a four-month tour of duty in the Pacific, said in a CBS radio network broadcast that official optimism and concealment had given Americans a false sense of security and had caused the public to lose confidence in the government as the truth emerged. "They frankly refuse to believe any good news," Moss said. In his first press conference after Pearl Harbor, the president had said that the public could have any information that was accurate and not "aid and comfort to the enemy." Decisions on what constituted "aid and comfort," he said, would be left to the secretary of war and the secretary of the Navy. On September 1, 1943, however, Roosevelt directed the two secretaries to allow Davis to make the decisions about what news would be released and told them to bring any irreconcilable disagreements on security issues to himself. The president, Davis said in his 1945 report, should make the final decisions as the civilian and military head of the government. No appeals were brought to Roosevelt, but Davis did experience what he called "bureaucratic resistance" in the form of delays. He noted that the military's attitude toward releasing news "greatly improved" as the Allies turned the tide of the war and had little to report but victories.[212]

Restrictions on still pictures and newsreels also were loosened as the war progressed. Photographers, like journalists, avoided depicting the most gruesome details of harm to soldiers, but initially official censorship went to great lengths to retouch the horrors of war or eliminate them altogether. As in World War I, visual images were rejected if they showed Americans killed, badly injured, or emotionally distressed. As the war wore on and the Allies were more successful, however, President Roosevelt became less concerned with civilians being demoralized and more worried about complacency in the war effort. With the public becoming more skeptical about the sanitized coverage and the press more restive about the lack of explicit treatments, the president and his subordinates implemented a policy of allowing and even promoting more frankness in photographs. Officials concluded that stronger doses of the facts were useful in war bond drives and could help inspire the public for the final push to victory, but still made sure that the pictured bodies were not identifiable or too shocking. The administration realized that reality, or at least what the news media themselves found fit to print, could be an important motivational tool for rallying the country.[213] Germany, on the other hand, used documentary photographs for ideological indoctrination and did not show its dead combatants in either still or moving pictures.[214] Both sides in the Pacific theater, however, suggested the nauseating results of war by depicting their enemies as beasts and indulging in kill-or-be-killed propaganda.[215] The Roosevelt administration timed the release of news about Japanese atrocities to political purposes.[216] Complaining about "sinister" news management, General

MacArthur thought that information on the Bataan Death March was withheld for nine months because "the Administration, which was committed to a Europe-first effort, feared American public opinion would demand a greater reaction against Japan."²¹⁷

Atrocities, looting, and other offenses committed by American soldiers were usually rejected either by the censors or the journalists themselves. "While censorship was seldom onerous we all understood that pessimistic reports, reports of great losses, or negative stories about our own men were seldom passed," recalled Andy Rooney. Rooney noted that *Stars and Stripes* did publish accounts of civilians being killed by German bombs. "The stories were true if sometimes exaggerated," he said, "and they carried with them the implication that our bombers never hit a hospital, a church, or a school and did not kill women, children, or the sick." Accounts of wrongdoing emerged gradually once the fighting was over. In his memoirs, entitled *Not So Wild a Dream*, published in 1946, CBS correspondent Eric Sevareid described prisoners of war being shot for little reason and commented, "I could never again bring myself to write or speak with indignation of the Germans' violations of the 'rules of warfare.'" Edgar L. Jones, a veteran of the war who was also a correspondent present at the assaults on Iwo Jima and Okinawa, wrote in a 1946 *Atlantic Monthly* article that Americans should not consider themselves morally superior as they prosecuted war criminals and made far-reaching decisions in the postwar world. Jones said, "We shot prisoners in cold blood, wiped out hospitals, strafed lifeboats, killed or mistreated enemy civilians, finished off enemy wounded, tossed the dying into a hole with the dead, and in the Pacific boiled the flesh off enemy skulls to make table ornaments for sweethearts, or carved their bones into letter openers."²¹⁸

Decades later, stories were still coming out. In Studs Terkel's oral history of World War II, published in 1984, a combat photographer, Walter Rosenblum, told about taking movie footage of captured SS troops being lined up and shot. "I sent it back to the army and got back my regular critique: This film could not be screened due to laboratory difficulties." In 1993 *Harper's* published a declassified report from 1944 that indicated that George Bush, the former president, may have strafed a lifeboat when he was a Navy pilot. In the final weeks of the 1992 presidential campaign, several major news organizations had copies of the report and were investigating the incident it described. Candidate Bush, who was contrasting his service in World War II with opponent Bill Clinton's avoidance of the draft during the Vietnam War, was not asked for an explanation of the possible war crime before the election, and the document was not published. A year later, the *Harper's* article reported that after many calls, Bush's Houston office gave a response: "no comment." Recalling his experiences as a correspondent during the war, the novelist John Steinbeck remarked that the truth about cowardice, cruelty, and ignorance was automatically bad and secret "largely because there was a huge and gassy thing called the War Effort."²¹⁹

Trying to convey some of the more poignant aspects of soldiers' lives could be a trying experience. Ernie Pyle, who became the war's top newspaper correspondent by telling the stories of ordinary GIs, detested the slaughter he witnessed, but he was expected to play the part of a morale-building celebrity journalist. "Ernie Pyle was so popular and so depended on by readers at home that in importance he much outranked most general officers," Steinbeck said. "The strain of almost constant combat since the African landings is beginning to tell on him," a *Yank* magazine profile observed in October 1944. "He's had a bellyful." Pyle, who was about to leave France for a respite in the United States, denied a *Time* magazine assertion that he had premonitions of death. "I figured if I didn't get out pretty soon I'd be a psycho case or something," Pyle told *Yank*. Six months later, during the Okinawa campaign, he was killed by a Japanese sniper. Soldiers erected a crude marker that said: "AT THIS SPOT/THE 77Th INFANTRY DIVISION/LOST A BUDDY/ERNIE PYLE/18 APRIL 1945."[220]

Another favorite of the GIs was the ironic, irreverent Bill Mauldin, whose cartoons lampooned military life with depictions of two unshaven infantrymen named Willie and Joe. The drawings aired the gripes of enlisted men in a humorous way, but officers sometimes took offense. When General George S. Patton Jr. threatened to ban *Stars and Stripes* from the Third Army because of the cartoons, General Eisenhower had an aide call Patton to arrange a meeting with the cartoonist. "If that little son of a bitch sets foot in Third Army I'll throw his ass in jail," Patton bellowed. The meeting did take place at Patton's office in Luxembourg's royal palace, but the general spent most of the time lecturing Sergeant Mauldin on the necessity of military discipline. When *Time* magazine published an account of the confrontation that quoted Mauldin as saying that Patton had not persuaded him to change his mind, the general blew up and again threatened to throw him in jail if he ever appeared again in the Third Army.[221]

Censorship for political reasons was particularly evident in 1945 as the Allies were deciding how to present themselves as victors. The military would not allow correspondents to report that American forces, who were encountering little opposition, were halting their advance on Berlin so that the Red Army, which was facing stiff resistance, could capture the city. Secret pro-Soviet policies adopted by Franklin D. Roosevelt and Harry S. Truman were creating the conditions for the subsequent Cold War disposition of Europe. Kent Cooper, the general manager of the AP at the time, speculated that open discussion by an enlightened American public might have prevented the later problems. "The fact that they needlessly conducted all political matters in secret and kept them so under protection of war censorship should be the basis of remonstrance from a democratic people," he wrote.[222] At the end of Hitler's regime, Cooper again saw political manipulation at work when Truman agreed to postpone the announcement of the German surrender at General Eisenhower's headquarters in France until Kremlin leaders could stage a surrender in Berlin that would glorify the Soviet Union. An AP correspondent who witnessed the surrender at Reims, Edward Kennedy, broke the news embargo and reported the story, an action that set off celebrations around the world a day before the official announcement was to occur.[223]

Kennedy's V-E Day story illustrated classic problems with military censorship. First, prior restraint was imposed originally for security reasons and later was used to subvert the democratic process. Americans were not informed enough to discuss what Kennedy called a policy of "appeasement and concession toward Moscow," in an *Atlantic Monthly* article on the incident titled "I'd Do It Again." Second, the American public was being denied information the enemy already had. Kennedy said that he was not after a "scoop," but felt he had a duty to report the news, and that if any personal feeling was involved, it was "the accumulated vexation over the dishonesties of censorship under which I had worked during five years of war." Third, the facts were not being contained by the military authorities themselves. Before Kennedy decided to phone in his story, the surrender was announced to troops and the Supreme Command ordered the German foreign minister to inform the German public on radio, a broadcast that was reported by the BBC after being monitored and distributed by the British Ministry of Information. "The absurdity of attempting to bottle up news of such magnitude was too apparent," Kennedy remarked. "I knew from experience that one might as well try to censor the rising of the sun." Fourth, the military created arbitrary and artificial restrictions that angered journalists. Correspondents who were not selected to witness the surrender showed up at the Reims headquarters and were told they would not be admitted because of space limitations. Although WAC and Red Cross girlfriends of the officers were slipped into the room, the reporters outside were chased away by MPs with threats of arrest. After Kennedy's story was sent out by AP, other correspondents were allowed to quote it but were still forbidden to send their own dispatches until the official release time. "The autocratic power which the American people confer on the heads of their armed forces in wartime was in this instance assumed to continue after the enemy's surrender ended the war," Kent Cooper later noted.[224]

The V-E Day news fiasco also showed the difficulties the military can have in punishing censorship violations and journalists can have in supporting each other. Kennedy's action had substantial public and press support, but, after telling the chief American censor that he felt the news was out, he had broken the pledge not to evade censorship signed by war correspondents. Brigadier General Frank A. Allen, head of the Supreme Command's Public Relations Division, immediately suspended AP operations in the European theater, an order that was reversed eight hours later by Secretary of War Henry L. Stimson after Cooper complained to him and General Eisenhower that the whole organization should not suffer for the action of one man. Furious at AP for having benefited from the story while they remained silent, a group of fifty-four correspondents at Supreme Headquarters in Paris signed a letter protesting the lifting of the ban on AP, but Eisenhower simply stated that the whole organization could not be punished. "Here was an episode in the long struggle for the freedom of the press never likely to be set on canvas," Kennedy later wrote, "an elite battalion of knights of the press waging a fight to deny part of the press the right to report news, with a five-star graduate of West Point as the champion of their prey." Although AP members published Kennedy's dispatch and many thought he had done nothing wrong, the president of the wire service issued an apology for breaking the embargo, and the general manager, finding Kennedy unrepentant for disregarding a pledge, placed him officially "on vacation" and eventually took him off the payroll. He received severance pay, but not an explanation. The Supreme Headquarters disaccredited Kennedy, but a year later, at the prodding of two senators, Eisenhower announced, without changing the earlier decision, that Kennedy could be a military correspondent in the future.[225]

Journalists also had problems with what they could report at the end of the war in the Pacific. Although both the military and the news media were responsible for a number of unintentional leaks, the press cooperated so well with the Office of Censorship in concealing the atomic bomb project that even Vice President Truman did not learn about the nature of the program until he became president.[226] When the secret new weapon was first tested in the New Mexico desert, officials released phony information that an ammunition dump had exploded accidentally with no deaths and little damage to property.[227] The subsequent atomic bombings of Hiroshima and Nagasaki, which came as a surprise to the public, might have been avoided with more thought and open discussion. Although they had little sympathy for the nations they were fighting, Americans and their leaders might not have allowed some of the indiscriminate bombing that occurred late in the war if they had been better informed. When the Royal Air Force, which killed five hundred thousand German civilians in a three-year campaign against cities, dropped incendiary bombs on Dresden in a February 1945 raid coordinated with American attacks, an AP story suggested that the Allies were using terror tactics. Fearing bad publicity, Secretary Stimson and the military investigated the incident. The blame fell on the British, who had fought with more of a total war approach since the Luftwaffe's Blitz, and the matter was quickly dropped, but the Dresden inferno took at least thirty thousand lives in a city of cultural treasures and was exploited in enemy propaganda and remembered with revulsion long past the end of the war. The firestorm in Dresden and an accidental bombing of Swiss territory soon prompted an American policy statement on restricting air raids to military targets and limiting attacks in populated areas. President Truman's announcement of the first atomic bombing described Hiroshima as "an important Japanese Army base."[228]

Few understood very well how American forces, known for a devotion to the ideal of precision bombing, had been sliding toward incinerating large numbers of civilians in Japan.[229] Truman and Stimson avoided facing the issue of mass civilian deaths.[230] Chafing over the shortcomings of previous methods and neglecting to inform his superiors about his plans, Major General Curtis LeMay began extensive incendiary bombings of Japanese cities early in 1945. A raid on Tokyo in March accounted for as many as one hundred thousand deaths and left over a million people homeless. LeMay was untroubled by ethical considerations and was, like other military leaders, anxious to end the war quickly. Secretary Stimson, who seemed to learn about the attacks from press accounts that were as short on information on deaths as the military's own reports, worried about Americans being considered as evil as their enemies and, paradoxically, about suitable targets being left for demonstrating the atomic bomb. He was assured that harm to noncombatants was being kept to a minimum, and mission reports insisted that the objectives were industrial and strategic, but crews on the low-level night raids were being sickened by the stench of burning flesh carried into the sky by superheated updrafts. By the time the atomic bombs were used in August, air, land, and sea attacks had almost completely eliminated Japan's ability to wage war.[231] A detailed War Department study published in 1946 concluded that in the final months of 1945 "Japan would have surrendered even if the atomic bombs had not been dropped, even if Russia had not entered the war, and even if no invasion had been planned or contemplated." General Eisenhower, General MacArthur, Admiral William D. Leahy, and other top military leaders objected to the use of nuclear weapons on Hiroshima and Nagasaki as brutal and unnecessary. Available evidence suggests that officials wanted a demonstration of the bomb's power in order to justify the $2 billion spent on its development and to make the Soviet Union more malleable in the postwar world. American leaders actually may have prolonged the war by waiting for the bomb to be ready while at the same time refusing to give Japan assurances on the fate of the emperor after a surrender.[232]

Not surprisingly, the federal government discouraged debate on the new weapon and its use.[233] On the day voluntary censorship ended in 1945, the War Department announced that it did not want uncontrolled discussion of the atomic bomb. "It is the duty of every citizen, in the interest of national safety," the statement said, "to keep all discussion of this subject within the limits of information disclosed in official releases." President Truman sent a confidential note to editors and broadcasters asking them, for reasons of "the highest national security," not to deal with a wide range of bomb-related matters without first consulting with the War Department. Apparently for political rather than security reasons, film shot by Japanese crews in Hiroshima and Nagasaki was confiscated by United States occupation forces, classified as secret, and kept from the public for more than twenty years.[234] Foreign correspondents who tried to report from the two cities had limits placed on what they could see and say. The victors were concerned about their image and about possible unrest among the vanquished, but radiation sickness was a particularly sensitive topic. Accounts of the effects of exposure were censored or downplayed when they did appear. Government officials insisted that fears of radiation were wildly exaggerated.[235] General Leslie R. Groves, director of the bomb project, told a Senate hearing that doctors thought radiation poisoning was "a very pleasant way to die."[236] American authorities imposed blanket censorship that prevented the Japanese themselves from addressing the issues raised by the atomic devastation.[237] "There shall be no destructive criticism of the Allied Forces of Occupation and nothing which might invite mistrust or resentment of those troops," said the "Press Code for Japan."[238] The restrictions extended beyond the press to books, mail, and motion pictures. By the summer of 1946, 8,734 people worked for the Civil Censorship Detachment. Although allied occupation policies were designed to introduce democracy to the defeated nation, the suppression was so rigorous that even the mention of censorship itself was forbidden. The authorities thus found it awkward to announce the end of Civil Censorship on October 31, 1949.[239]

In the absence of adequate information and debate, Americans showed little concern about the area fire attacks carried out prior to Hiroshima;[240] they insisted on believing Truman's assertion that the country faced a choice between the bomb and hundreds of thousands of casualties in an invasion of Japan.[241] A Roper survey in late 1945 showed that only 4.5 percent of the public thought no atomic bombs should have been used, while 22.7 percent thought many more of them should have been dropped before Japan had a chance to surrender. A majority thought that the two bombs were used just as they should have been.[242] Secretary Stimson published an article in *Harper's* stating that a million American casualties had been avoided.[243] In the following decades similar views were conveyed in textbooks, popular histories, and politicians' statements.[244] Other perspectives gained strength when all of the editorial space in the *New Yorker* issue of August 31, 1946, was devoted to John Hersey's reporting on the human suffering in Hiroshima and the account became a best-selling book, but such views were confined mainly to elite audiences.[245] Scholarship indicating that leaders did not have to use nuclear weapons had little impact.[246] Fifty years after the atomic bombs were dropped, the Smithsonian Institution's National Air and Space Museum made use of the historical research for a planned exhibit on the subject, but encountered fierce opposition from veterans groups and members of Congress who charged that the revisionist view of Japan being defeated before Hiroshima was anti-American. The museum's director resigned, and the exhibit was delayed, pared down, and altered so as to be more palatable to the public.[247] Apparently the belief that the bomb saved lives was preferable to the fact that better options existed.[248] Secrecy and news management at the end of World War II had created a myth that would not die.

In the aftermath of the most deadly and costly war in human history, technology and the military stood triumphant, terrifyingly powerful, and trusted to an astonishing degree by the public, while the Constitution and its values seemed of little consequence. Over the course of World War II, the burgeoning military-industrial complex moved well beyond the check of democratic deliberation and might have gone further. In his book *Weapon of Silence*, published in 1946, former Office of Censorship official Theodore Koop wrote that he doubted the military would have given voluntary censorship a chance to continue if the United States had been invaded by the Germans or Japanese. "One of the first acts of martial law unquestionably would have placed the printing press and the microphone under Army control," he said. In the atomic age a conflict could bring sudden devastation and the need for everyone to follow military orders, he continued. "It is logical to assume that the Army would insist on stringent control of all avenues of communication, domestic as well as international."[249]

Presidents and their military bureaucracies did make plans for nuclear attack that included martial law.[250] In 1945 Koop's boss, Byron Price, advised President Truman to make confidential preparations for administering censorship in any future war. With little public knowledge, efforts were undertaken to have available a system not unlike the one used during World War II.[251] Koop, who became head of CBS News in Washington, was secretly appointed the standby director of the United States Office of Censorship, a shadowy agency reporting to the president that was given the more euphemistic name of the Wartime Information Security Program during the Nixon administration. Koop and other would-be censors were part of the National Defense Executive Reserve, a group of prominent citizens who would fill important posts in the event of a national emergency. Activating censorship was essentially left to the president, who could act under a draft executive order or ask Congress to pass standby legislation. The executive order appeared to be for a nuclear attack, but the wording of the draft legislation allowed complete, mandatory control of communications into and out of the country whenever the president decided the public safety required it. A standby code for voluntary domestic censorship by the news media covered a broad range of information that included war plans, troop movements, weather forecasts, travel by high-ranking officials, and enemy attacks. The code stated that the press should not inform the enemy or promote panic by disclosing what attacks on the United States had accomplished, but would be free to report on individual "feats of heroism."[252]

The Long, Cold War

The Cold War and the fear of nuclear annihilation brought more tests of freedom and more autocratic lawlessness. With its clandestine actions abroad and interference with domestic political processes, the struggle against communism provided new occasions for assertions that a president could violate the law for reasons of national security or act without authority in dealing with a crisis. "The integrity of our system will not be jeopardized by any measures, covert or overt, violent or non-violent, which serve the purposes of frustrating the Kremlin design," said a top secret government report in 1950, "nor does the necessity for conducting ourselves so as to affirm our values in actions as well as words forbid such measures, provided only they are appropriately calculated to that end and are not so excessive or misdirected as to make us enemies of the people instead of the evil men who have enslaved them." The report, which was adopted by the NSC with President Harry S. Truman presiding, was the harbinger of a sudden tripling of the defense budget.[1] Truman and most of his Cold War successors fit the pattern of chief executives who said they were preserving freedom but who accomplished more actual subversion of democracy than any internal dissenters or foreign adversaries. A swelling presidential-military protectorate used domestic spying, massive secrecy, and subtle methods of suppression to circumvent public discussion and place the United States under what amounted to a new form of government.[2]

I.

At the outbreak of the Korean War in 1950, General Douglas MacArthur's headquarters announced that he considered censorship "abhorrent" and that he preferred "that the press establish a voluntary code that will ensure the security of operations and the safety of personnel." Secretary of Defense Louis Johnson gave his approval to the voluntary approach and, as his spokesman explained, "pointed out that there is no statutory provision for military censorship of news and, therefore, that security control in connection with the issuance of information must function from military sources." Johnson distributed a memorandum on July 13 directing the military services not to release information on troop and ship movements, the strength of forces, and the status of equipment. Observing that no two military censors would agree on the details of security review of stories, MacArthur followed up with a statement that fixed rules were "unrealistic" and "ineffective." The general, who had been severely criticized for his suppression of news in World War II, said any censorship "must be of the spirit and applied only by those themselves who print the news." MacArthur added, however, that the press should avoid not only information of military value to the enemy, but also "such as may contribute through undue emphasis or emotional stress psychologically to his cause by raising the morale of his forces while depressing that of ours."[3]

MacArthur's caveat was an apparent reference to reporters being free to convey the harsh realities of the disorganized retreats in the early battles. "We felt it our responsibility to report the disasters as we saw them," said Marguerite Higgins of the New York *Herald Tribune*. "And we knew how passionately the guys who were doing the fighting wanted 'the folks back home' to know what they were up against."[4] Inexperienced, badly outnumbered, and ill-equipped, American soldiers fought desperately and complained to correspondents, who, like Higgins, earned the enmity of the brass for telling the world what was happening. Lieutenant General Walton H. Walker, the commander of the ground forces, ordered Higgins flown to Tokyo under the escort of a public information officer, ostensibly because he thought women did not belong at the front, and two male correspondents who had reported on demoralized troops, Tom Lambert of the AP and Peter Kalischer of United Press, were banned from the war zone by the Army Command on the grounds that they were "giving aid and comfort to the enemy." Although the three journalists were quickly reinstated by MacArthur, some correspondents, angered by the banishments and by the security breaches that occurred with vague guidelines and the military's poor coordination of information, called for formal censorship.[5] Supporters of self-censorship included the *New York Times*, which said "any effort to pretty this war up" was an insult to the soldiers. "The American service man is unromantic about war," a *Times* editorial said. "A correspondent who represented him as glorying in being outnumbered and out-gunned would be telling a lie that no one—not even a North Korean—would believe."[6]

MacArthur continued to resist mandatory rules, but he was urged by officials in Washington to impose censorship. "President Truman has been described as deeply concerned about published and broadcast information coming from the Far East," the *New York Times* reported. Saying that they did not blame the correspondents and admitting that the military itself had released information of value to the enemy, Pentagon officials suggested that the Far East Command set up a definitive censorship code.[7] The situation in Korea deteriorated in late November and early December as China staged a huge counteroffensive and United Nations troops retreated. At MacArthur's request, the newly appointed secretary of defense, George C. Marshall, held a meeting with a dozen news media representatives on December 18, 1950. They sent a message to MacArthur in Tokyo that said that the military had the sole responsibility for the security of information in a combat area and that "if the military feels some further action is necessary," then the action should be "consistent with a minimum interference" with the flow of news. Press executives who were present at the meeting later denied that they were calling for compulsory controls, but MacArthur said the participants "made it unequivocally clear that military censorship should be imposed."[8]

With MacArthur removing his objections, officers of the Eighth Army in Korea, many of whom were angry about the press coverage, placed journalists under censorship in late December. Before checking with higher-level officials who were apparently hoping to avoid responsibility by having the rules made in the combat area, the Eighth Army issued a censorship code.[9] An *Editor & Publisher* editorial said the code "is not only unnecessarily stringent but is ridiculous in some extremes and implies a distrust of the correspondents which is unjustified."[10] The code was nearly identical to the regulations issued during World War II. All news copy originating in Korea had to follow a precise format and be cleared by censors. Stories could be censored if they were inaccurate, supplied military information to the enemy, injured troop morale, or embarrassed the United States, its allies, or neutral countries. Quotations from officers had to be specifically authorized, and casualty figures were not to be reported before they were announced officially. Although they were not in military service, journalists were to be under the control of army commanders and subject to military law and disciplinary actions that included court-martial in extreme cases. Facing a furious reaction from the press, MacArthur and Pentagon officials tried to distance themselves from the Eighth Army's rules, but they were enforced.[11]

The censorship code was justified as a means of preserving lives and liberties. "Inherent in wartime censorship is this vital factor: what is at stake in a war zone combat crisis is the freedom or very life of a man, a platoon, a battalion, a division, an army, or even an entire nation," said Melvin Voorhees, the Eighth Army's chief censor. "Finality is at hand for you and yours, or for the enemy and his."[12] In reality, of course, news was suppressed that had little or nothing to do with military security. Censors refused to allow the publication of stories about official corruption in South Korea, dissent in North Korea, and incompetence in American units.[13] They stopped reports of inmate disturbances in United Nations prisoner of war camps;[14] and they told returning American POWs they could not talk about their experiences, which included a surprising amount of collaboration with the enemy.[15] The Pentagon did not release documents indicating that North Korea failed to free more than nine hundred American soldiers who were alive at the end of the war.[16]

Censorship made manipulation of the news easier. Official communiqués gave absurdly high figures on enemy casualties and bombing effectiveness. In one case a widely published Air Force photograph of a bridge said to have been hit by "pin point bombing" turned out to be an image of a structure blown up by Army engineers during a retreat. "Many of us who sent the stories knew they were false," said United Press correspondent Robert C. Miller, "but we had to write them for they were official releases from responsible military headquarters, and were released for publication even though the people responsible knew they were untrue."[17]

Encountering not only public consternation over the Korean War, but also discord within official circles, Truman took additional steps to limit debate and restrict information. On December 5, 1950, he issued a memorandum telling executive branch officials to have all public statements on foreign policy cleared by the Department of State and all public statements on military policy cleared by the Department of Defense. Advance copies of speeches and press releases on foreign or military policy were to be submitted to the White House. "The purpose of this memorandum is not to curtail the flow of information to the American people," he said, "but rather to insure that the information made public is accurate and fully in accord with the policies of the United States Government." In a separate memo, Truman told the secretaries of state and defense to order military commanders and diplomats "to exercise extreme caution in public statements, to clear all but routine statements with their departments, and to refrain from direct communication on military or foreign policy with newspapers, magazines, or other publicity media in the United States."[18]

The December 5 memoranda were the result of Truman's exasperation with statements made to the press by General MacArthur. The comments, which the president regarded as insubordinate, were frank assessments of the difficulties the general had in trying to fight under the limitations placed on him by Truman and the Allies. In the following months, MacArthur, who wanted a victory rather than the negotiated settlement the administration decided to seek, continued to be outspoken in ways that soon prompted Truman to remind him of the December 5 directives. On April 5, 1951, Republican leader Joseph W. Martin read to the House of Representatives a letter he had received from MacArthur that called for more forceful measures in Korea and that concluded, "There is no substitute for victory." Truman decided to relieve the general of his command on the ground that he had not obeyed the rules on discussing policy.[19]

The Democratic president had long harbored suspicions about MacArthur, who had been a Republican candidate for president in 1948 until he made poor showings in the early primaries. In his memoirs, Truman compared him to General George B. McClellan, who frustrated Lincoln and ran against him in 1864. Truman compared himself to the "mistreated" Andrew Johnson, who was attacked "unmercifully" in the press. "I could sympathize with him," Truman wrote, "because I received a good measure of the same kind of opposition." Truman decided to deal with a general in a way he could not deal with the press and later explained that he saw MacArthur's willingness to speak his mind as a threat to civilian control of the military. "He had been openly critical," Truman complained. Truman said that it was natural for "every second lieutenant" to think his superiors were blind when they didn't see things his way. "But General MacArthur—and rightly, too—would have court-martialed any second lieutenant who gave press interviews to express his disagreement," Truman wrote.[20]

Fighting dissent and disarray as he was at the end of 1950, Truman was in no mood to stand the heat.[21] In late November, MacArthur had launched a United Nations offensive he hoped would have the soldiers home by Christmas, an effort that collapsed under Chinese assault and led to renewed partisan debate over the course of the war. At a November 30 press conference Truman was petulant with reporters who were pressing for clarifications of administration policies and charged that "attacks and speculations and lies" in the press were undermining his efforts to resolve the conflict. "I am getting tired of all this foolishness," he said, "and I'm going to 'bust loose' on you one of these days." At the press conference Truman sounded as if he were ready to bust loose elsewhere by stating that the use of atomic bombs was under consideration and that MacArthur would be in charge of the weapons.[22]

The president was speaking more dangerously than either MacArthur or the press. Before administration backtracking could begin, reports on the possibility of nuclear war were spread around the world.[23] Among the most shocked was Prime Minister Clement Attlee of Britain, whose Labour government had already been shaken by the Korean situation. Attlee asked Truman for an immediate visit to Washington, a visit that was in progress when the December 5 memoranda were issued. On December 5 Truman's press secretary and high school classmate, Charles Ross, died of a coronary occlusion while preparing to go before television cameras with a briefing on the day's events.[24] The president nevertheless attended a concert given that evening in Washington by his daughter Margaret, a soprano; she drew applause from a friendly audience but an unfavorable review from the *Washington Post*. The next morning, Truman read the paper and wrote the reviewer a furious letter saying that if he met him, he would "need a new nose, a lot of beefsteak for black eyes, and perhaps a supporter below."[25] Ten days later, when he issued a declaration of national emergency in order to expedite military procurement and impose economic controls, the president said Americans were fighting the war to preserve liberties such as "the right of free speech including the right to criticize their Government."[26]

Truman's conception of that liberty clearly had its limits. He exercised his own freedom of expression but tended to think others in government or in the military had to give up theirs. Truman could no doubt direct the military as commander in chief, but MacArthur and others were subjected to a system of prior restraint on opinions. Truman's directives denied a commanding general's First Amendment rights to provide the public with his appraisal of the crisis the nation was facing. Rather than reason on the issues, Truman turned to repression in an atmosphere of partisan bickering and accused MacArthur of not obeying directives.

In stating a preference for a policy, MacArthur was not necessarily insubordinate. The traditional limits on military expression began with regulations Congress passed in 1776. A section that dealt with mutiny and disobedience of lawful commands said that commissioned officers could be dismissed and others in the army punished for "traiterous (*sic*) or disrespectful words against the authority" of Congress or the state legislatures. An additional article declared that anyone in the military could be subject to the judgment of a court-martial for words tending to the "hurt or dishonor" of "the general, or other commander-in-chief of the forces of the United States." In 1804 the House of Representatives rejected a proposal to include the president in the provision against "traitorous or disrespectful words" after hearing a Jeffersonian Republican member say that the regulation would be another Sedition Act and that the concept of traitorous words had no meaning or constitutional validity.[27] When the revised Articles of War were passed in 1806, the word "traitorous" was removed, and no Jeffersonians objected to language that allowed punishment for "contemptuous or disrespectful words" against the president, vice president, or Congress.[28] Specific military regulations forbidding contemptuous language about the president were used to court-martial about a hundred officers and enlisted men through the time of the Vietnam War.[29]

MacArthur, however, neither questioned authority nor defamed a president. Whether right or wrong in his assertions, he was seen as a political adversary and was fired for stating views that the president's critics in Washington also held. "MacArthur did not consider stalemate a meaningful objective," Henry Kissinger later wrote in arguing that Truman had an unrealistic fear of the conflict escalating into World War

III and that his vague and shifting approaches prolonged the war and the casualties. The practice of censoring the opinions of officers continued, but was controversial enough to be the subject of Senate hearings in 1962. In a statement prepared for the hearings, Dwight Eisenhower, who had just been replaced by a president from another party, said that he had reassessed the issue and come to the conclusion that reviewing utterances for anything besides security violations was "smothering the concept of personal responsibility under a practice of heavy-handed and unjustified staff supervision."[30] Later administrations nevertheless carried on efforts to review statements by officials for adherence to policy.[31]

Truman's attempts to control opinion went beyond anything that could be justified under the Constitution. His prior restraint memoranda, issued on his own authority, were clearly overbroad and were aimed at silencing opinions other than his own. He did oppose some of the more extreme anticommunist measures adopted by Congress while he was in office, including the Internal Security Act of 1950 and the McCarran-Walter Act of 1952;[32] but his vetoes were easily overriden by lawmakers in the grips of McCarthyism.[33] In vetoing the Internal Security Act, which included provisions for the detention of radicals in an emergency and for obstructing communist association and expression, Truman spoke at length about how such legislation would delight the nation's adversaries because it would destroy the liberties Americans sought to preserve. "In a free country, we punish men for the crimes they commit," he said, "but never for the opinions they have." In his memoirs Truman depicted the Cold War as yet another period of mass hysteria when the Bill of Rights was violated by unprincipled demagogues. Yet, seeing himself as the president whose administration had "saved Western civilization from Communist control," he was chagrined about Republican charges in the 1952 election that Democrats were soft on communism. Referring to the *Dennis* case, he said, "It was the Democratic administration that prosecuted the known Communist conspirators in this country and convicted them without throwing away the Bill of Rights by resorting to totalitarian methods."[34] Truman did not explain how prosecuting citizens for their opinions squared with the Bill of Rights.

In dealing with Communists, as in dealing with MacArthur, Truman's commitment to reason and First Amendment liberties was subject to political considerations. Caught between liberals who denounced redbaiting and conservatives who were beginning to sense the opportunities domestic anticommunism offered as a popular campaign issue, he made statements on both sides of the topic and satisfied neither camp as he made domestic security decisions that seemed too much for some and too little for others. In 1946 Truman named a commission on federal employee loyalty three weeks after Republicans took control of both houses of Congress. Four months later, shortly after announcing his "Truman Doctrine" for communist containment abroad, the president issued an executive order establishing an extensive federal employee loyalty program that led to investigations of beliefs, associations, reading habits, and personal behavior.[35] Two years later, when Truman was running for election, the administration tried to time the *Dennis* prosecution of Communist Party leaders for maximum political advantage. His vetoes of the Internal Security Act and the McCarran-Walter Act came after his surprise victory of 1948, his last campaign for public office.[36]

Truman was frustrated by what he regarded as security breaches during his final years in the White House. He thought that the news media should not publish aerial photographs of cities and the locations of "atomic installations" because the information—which would be all but impossible to conceal in any case—could be used for an attack. He also complained about leaking by military leaders and bureaucrats who thought coverage who help them win recognition and bigger budgets.[37] Although the president's authority to classify information may have been implied by the granting of constitutional responsibilities in defense and foreign affairs, Congress had a long history of passing legislation on the custody and availability of federal government records.[38] A military classification system based on British and French practice was used in World War I and recognized by Franklin Roosevelt's Executive Order 8381 on March 22, 1940. Finding that civilian agencies also possessed documents dealing with national security, Truman in 1951 issued an executive order extending to them the authority to classify materials as top secret, secret, confidential, and restricted. Later chief executives made modifications in the handling of secrets, but Truman solidified the practice of presidents assuming prerogative power over classification.[39] His executive order did not alter the right to publish information, but did attempt to impose censorship at the source. Asked to explain his action, Truman told reporters that his record on civil liberties demonstrated that he had no desire to deny freedom of expression, but that "the safety and welfare of the United States of America comes first with me." Journalists protested that the standards and procedures were nebulous and that the public's right to know was to be determined by the government agencies themselves.[40]

Truman did not think that his powers were limited to the executive branch of government. He thought that they extended to private industry and the press as well. When Truman seized the steel mills without statutory authority in 1952, he said that he could not allow labor-management disputes to "immediately endanger the safety of our fighting forces abroad and weaken the whole structure of our national security." The Justice Department took the position that the president is the "sole organ" of foreign relations and had authority resting on "a combination of provisions" in Article 2 to act in emergencies and protect troops. The government lawyers relied on their reading of the Supreme Court's 1936 opinion in *U.S. v. Curtiss-Wright Export Corp.* that referred to "the very delicate, plenary and exclusive power of the President as the sole organ of the federal government in the field of international relations." The *Curtiss-Wright* "sole organ" dictum merely recognized the president's exclusive authority to carry out diplomatic communication and negotiation. The "sole organ" sentence of the opinion ends by saying that the power "like every other governmental power, must be exercised in subordination to the applicable provisions of the Constitution."[41] Nevertheless, the dictum has often been misconstrued by government attorneys and even some members of the Supreme Court as support for expansive conceptions of executive power.[42]

Truman said he regarded himself as "a very close student of the Presidency."[43] After he issued the steel seizure order, he told a press conference that uses of emergency power had "made the Republic better" and listed examples starting with Jefferson. "Mr. Lincoln exercised the powers of the President to meet the emergencies with which he was faced," Truman said. "So did President Roosevelt." Reporter May Craig then asked Truman if he did not dread a departure into inherent powers. "Well, of course I do, May," Truman answered. "But then when you meet an emergency in an emergency, you have to meet it." Under questioning, Truman was evasive about the limits of such power and about an offhand statement he had made a week earlier suggesting that he could seize the print and broadcast media just as he had seized the steel mills. He did not intend to seize news organizations, he said, but the president "has very great inherent powers to meet great national emergencies" and until the emergencies arise "cannot say specifically what he would do or would not do." What was at stake, he said, was "the welfare of the country."[44] In a letter on this point written a month later, Truman observed that in an emergency Lincoln "took over several newspapers when they published treasonable articles . . . but his objective was always the same—that was to save the union and keep this a free republic from the Atlantic to the Pacific."[45] The "close student of the presidency" failed to note that Congress had rejected the idea of giving Woodrow Wilson authority over the nation's press during World War I and had said even in the Internal Security Act of 1950 that nothing in the legislation "shall be construed to authorize, require, or establish military or civilian censorship."[46]

Truman's position on emergency presidential power was tested in the *Steel Seizure* case. Assistant Attorney General Holmes Baldridge stated in district court that the president was relying on "whatever inherent, implied or residual powers may flow" from Article 2 of the Constitution and that the president's power to act in an emergency was limited only by the ballot box or impeachment.[47] Baldridge's assertion that the Constitution did not limit the powers of the executive set off a storm of controversy that prompted Truman to state publicly that the president was limited by constitutional provisions, "particularly those that protect the rights of individuals," but that he "felt sure that the Constitution does not require me to endanger our national safety by letting all the steel mills shut down at this critical time."[48] As the case quickly moved to a Supreme Court consisting of five Roosevelt and four Truman appointees, few expected a ruling against the president. By a vote of six to three, however, the high court sustained an injunction granted by the district court. Justice Black's majority opinion stated that the seizure order amounted to legislation Congress had refused to pass and that only Congress had lawmaking power "in both good and bad times."[49]

The apotheosis of the executive received a blunt repudiation in the *Steel Seizure* decision. The concurring opinion of Justice Robert Jackson was particularly telling in its denial of what he called "unmentioned powers" and in its criticism of the solicitor general's reliance on Article 2 to justify the seizure. Noting the government's brief had claimed the vesting clause " 'constitutes a grant of all the executive powers of which the Government is capable,' " Jackson asked, "If that be true, it is difficult to see why the forefathers bothered to add several specific items, including some trifling ones." The commander in chief clause, Roberts said, should not be interpreted, as the government apparently argued, to mean "that a President whose conduct of foreign affairs is so largely uncontrolled, and often even is unknown, can vastly enlarge his mastery over the internal affairs of the country by his own commitment of the Nation's armed forces to some foreign venture." Before reciting a number of domestic "war powers" assigned to Congress, Roberts observed that the title "Commander in Chief *of the Army and Navy*" did not also mean "Commander in Chief of the country, its industries and its inhabitants."[50]

Truman remained unbowed. He promptly returned the steel mills to their owners, but he argued in his memoirs that the ruling was a mistake. Citing his oath and the vesting clause, he said the office had "immense power" and that the president, in the interest of the people, "must use whatever power the Constitution does not expressly deny him." Amazed that the Court had ignored administration affidavits attesting to the harm that would be caused, Truman said that economic issues could not be separated from national security and that it was "fortunate that nothing more serious happened in Korea" than some shortages of ammunition. He accused the press of "inflaming public opinion" on the case and said, without directly addressing the points raised by the majority, that he hoped that the support he had received from the three dissenters would someday be recognized as the correct position. Referring to the fact that each of the six justices in the majority had written an opinion, he concluded, "Whatever the six justices of the Supreme Court meant by their differing opinions about the constitutional powers of the President, he must always act in a national emergency."[51]

II.

Truman's raw assertions of presidential power and his open confrontation with communism in Korea were hazardous, high-profile ventures. Taking a more furtive approach to national security, later presidents made use of the secrecy mechanisms and intelligence and covert action capabilities that were constructed during the Truman administration.[52] The face of war changed, with shrouded attempts abroad to overthrow governments, assassinate leaders, and strike deals with dictators.[53] The Constitution and proper democratic processes were, to a large extent, discarded. In 1954, while the CIA was conducting propaganda, paramilitary, and internal disruption campaigns in at least forty-eight countries, a commission on government organization provided President Dwight Eisenhower with a top secret report on intelligence agencies that concluded that the United States faced an "implacable enemy" seeking world domination. "There are no rules in such a game," the report said. "Hitherto acceptable norms of human conduct do not apply." Eisenhower told his secretary of defense in 1954 that throughout the country's history the president had withheld information whenever its disclosure would "jeopardize the safety of the Nation." A secret legal memorandum prepared for the CIA's general counsel in 1962 after the failure of the Bay of Pigs invasion claimed "broad powers" for the president to preserve the safety and integrity of the nation. The document based its argument on the misconstrued *Curtiss-Wright* "sole organ" dictum.[54]

President Eisenhower's penchant for counterinsurgency and the overthrow of hostile governments was hardly noticed at the time by journalists, who routinely reported official pronouncements and condemned communists and nationalists. As secret interventions occurred with little public or congressional scrutiny in Guatemala, Iran, and other countries, the press did little to question the role of the United States. At Time, Inc., Henry Luce had been heralding the "American Century," and many others, including his friend Dwight Eisenhower, agreed that the United States, with its apparent generosity and integrity, seemed ideally suited for a predominant role in the affairs of the postwar world. Under Eisenhower's leadership the nation sought an enduring peace, but attacked the growth of movements that threatened American political and economic interests. The country did undertake education and development programs to counteract the appeal of antagonistic ideologies, but it also implemented policies designed to extend the nation's military and propaganda presence around the world. Eisenhower detested war, but hated communism.[55] On the trip for Winston Churchill's funeral in 1965, the former president told Chief Justice Earl Warren, one of his appointees, that he was disappointed that the Supreme Court had made convictions of Communists under the Smith Act more difficult. When Warren asked what he would do with Communists, Eisenhower replied, "I would kill the S.O.B.s."[56]

Journalists and politicians invited trouble when they appeared to deviate from the rigid pro-American, anticommunist orthodoxy. News organizations, at least at first, gave Senator Joseph McCarthy the publicity he craved in his redbaiting, and Eisenhower avoided direct confrontation with his fellow Republican. Although he was irritated by McCarthy, the president was cautious about preserving his own popularity and maintaining his consensus-building efforts in Washington. Less interested in headlines and less bombastic in his anticommunism, Eisenhower used bureaucratic measures for internal security at home and inconspicuous but often heedless actions abroad.[57] In the absence of strong opposition to McCarthyism, members of Congress used rough tactics against supposed subversives and their First Amendment rights. Among the casualties of a Senate subcommittee investigation of Communist Party influence on the press in 1955 and 1956 were three *New York Times* employees who were fired for refusing to answer questions the paper asked them about their politics.[58] Reporters at *Time* and CBS who ventured to inform the public about China were silenced by their superiors, and Eisenhower himself rebuked CBS for broadcasting an interview with Nikita Khrushchev in 1957.[59]

One of Eisenhower's last covert operations was CIA preparation of Cuban refugees for the Bay of Pigs invasion in 1961. The invasion fiasco, which occurred less than three months after John F. Kennedy took office, involved a web of government falsehoods that included phony accounts of rebellion on the island, official denials of U.S. participation in the attack, and prefabricated news bulletins from the CIA-organized Cuban Revolutionary Council. Cuban and Soviet leaders meanwhile made accurate charges about United States support and training.[60] A week before the invasion, as American and Soviet journalists were predicting the attack, Arthur M. Schlesinger Jr., a special assistant to Kennedy, had written a "Protection of the President" memo. "When lies must be told, they should be told by subordinate officials," he said. "At no point should the President be asked to lend himself to the cover operation."[61] At a press conference four days after the failed landing, Kennedy said he would not take questions on Cuba, but he took blame as "the responsible officer of the Government" when pressed by a reporter for "the real facts" behind the "propaganda lambasting" the nation was taking around the world. In an editorial entitled "The Right Not to be Lied To," the *New York Times* said that a democracy required informed public opinion and that officials were, in effect, "re-elected day by day by popular understanding and support."[62]

Kennedy thought that the dangers of the Cold War required American journalists to be more discreet and supportive in stories about secret activities;[63] he responded to press criticism by calling for more voluntary "self-discipline" at an American Newspaper Publishers Association meeting ten days after the invasion. "In time of 'clear and present danger,' " he remarked, "the courts have held that even the privileged rights of the First Amendment must yield to the public's need for national security." No war had been declared, Kennedy observed, but the nation's way of life was under attack and was being "opposed around the world by a monolithic and ruthless conspiracy that relies primarily on covert means for expanding its sphere of influence."[64] The timing of the speech, in the aftermath of the Bay of Pigs, ensured a hostile reaction from the press. Kennedy soon met with a group of news executives who told him they would not accept new restrictions of any kind in the absence of a declaration of national emergency. The president told them the Cold War was a continuing emergency and made a futile attempt to interest them in the idea of having the press appoint a representative to work with officials and advise the nation's news media on whether or not to run particular stories on security matters. Richard Nixon, Kennedy's 1960 election opponent who would later accuse the press of revealing too much when he occupied the White House, reacted with a statement that pleas for secrecy in peacetime demonstrated a "profound misunderstanding of the role of a free press" and could create a "cloak for errors, misjudgments and other failings of government."[65]

Kennedy did find other ways to manipulate coverage. He charmed the press and public in his live news conferences and maintained close relationships with leading journalists. Friendly reporters were taken into his confidence and given extraordinary access in ways that seemed to dull their critical faculties. Those who offended him could be quickly ostracized. The administration also opened itself up to charges of news management by establishing an information-coordinating committee, by clamping down on leakers, and by exercising control over statements made by top military officers. Further tightening occurred in the midst of the Cuban missile crisis in 1962. The White House asked journalists to refrain from reporting on twelve sweeping categories of military information and to seek guidance from the Defense Department when in doubt. Pentagon personnel were required to report on contacts with journalists, and the press was denied access to the ships responsible for the quarantine of Cuba and, ostensibly for safety reasons, to the American base on the island. The president and the Defense Department made a number of false or misleading statements about developments during the crisis.[66] Pentagon spokesman Arthur Sylvester publicly argued that the government had a right "to lie to save itself." In his press conference of February 21, 1963, however, Kennedy wryly noted that his administration "had very limited success in managing the news, if that's what we have been trying to do."[67]

Kennedy, a smooth but reckless playboy politician, had to lie about or conceal many of the facts about his public and private lives.[68] His press secretary, Pierre Salinger, provided an extended justification for Cold War deceit and secrecy in his book *With Kennedy*. Salinger maintained that the people's right to know was "at best, a tricky doctrine" that, if taken too far, "would effectively deprive the government of one of its key weapons in the battle to protect itself—the 'right of the enemy *not to know*.'" Raising the question of whether the press or the president was better equipped to draw the line on national security, Salinger said that covert actions against the nation's enemies were necessary. "JFK took the entirely realistic position that the cold war was never more than a moment away from flaring into a hot war," he wrote. "This being true—and what editor or publisher could dispute it?—our very survival could depend on our ability to maneuver secretly." The Bay of Pigs demonstrated the difficulty of mounting covert operations in a democracy, Salinger said, and the missile crisis showed "how the ability of the government to shroud its activities in secrecy for a limited amount of time can have a devastating effect on the enemy and result in a major victory for this country."[69]

The Kennedy administration's misadventures in covert actions, however, could have had devastating effects. Perhaps the most irrational and inept ones were the dozens of CIA schemes to topple the Soviet-backed regime in Cuba, schemes that included paramilitary raids, counterfeiting, contamination of sugar crops, and a series of plots to kill Castro with the help of organized crime figures. The Cuban intrigues, apparently covered up by a willing press, were, by many accounts, a major factor in the Soviet Union's decision to place nuclear weapons in Cuba. Kennedy had domestic political reasons to be dangerously belligerent, but others could be even more heedless. During the missile crisis many of his military and national security advisers wanted an air strike on Cuba after an American U-2 plane was shot down over the island and Castro asked Khrushchev for a nuclear attack on the United States in the event of aggression against his country. Some American military leaders and many Cubans, including Castro, were furious at the negotiated solution to the crisis.[70] The immediate public and journalistic reactions were praise for Kennedy's apparent adroitness in managing the situation, but few understood how he had provoked the problems in the first place with hostile rhetoric and covert actions against Cuba.[71]

With much to hide, the administration was nervous about the press. Like earlier and later presidents, Kennedy used government agencies to spy on and sometimes harass journalists who managed to uncover sensitive or embarrassing information.[72] In an effort to find the sources of leaks, the FBI wiretapped the residences of two of the most prominent military correspondents, Lloyd Norman of *Newsweek* and Hanson Baldwin of the *New York Times*. In a 1963 *Atlantic Monthly* article on the administration's press policies, Baldwin quoted James Madison's observation that freedom was more likely to be lost "'by gradual and silent encroachments of those in power than by violent and sudden usurpation.'" Baldwin complained about reporters being questioned at their homes about sources, being shadowed in the corridors of the Pentagon, and having their phones tapped. Journalists who wrote unfavorable stories received angry protests from the president and White House officials, he wrote, and government officials and military officers were interrogated on their contacts with the press. Baldwin contended that the press had to weigh its decisions about what to publish on a case-by-case basis, but owed its "ultimate loyalty" to the "ultimate power," the people, and had to foster "that great diversity of judgment which is the salvation of democracy."[73]

Official dishonesty, news management, and pressure on reporters were some of the methods used to try to shape coverage of the undeclared war in Vietnam. The government in Saigon put reporters under surveillance and imposed censorship restrictions. Some journalists were expelled and others were beaten up by plain-clothes police.[74] The American military and the Kennedy and Johnson administrations kept critical facts about United States involvement from the public, gave misleading assessments of progress, and steered the press away from problems.[75] Officials and reporters clashed often, particularly over casualty figures and other information dispensed at the daily military briefings in Saigon, which were nicknamed the Five O'Clock Follies.[76] The horrors of war were treated with cold-blooded terms such as "search and destroy missions" or euphemisms such as "neutralized targets." Public repugnance was the natural result of modern mass media vividly exposing the realities of war while officials tried to conceal them, observed Colonel Harry G. Summers Jr. in a widely read book on Vietnam. "Censorship is not the answer," he said, concluding that Americans needed to have a clear understanding of the objectives and the costs of a war.[77]

Many of the small number of journalists who were covering the early years of the war resisted the optimism conveyed in briefings and VIP tours. "Why don't you get on the team?" Admiral Harry Felt asked Malcolm Browne of the AP at a Saigon press conference in 1962. In 1963 David Halberstam of the *New York Times* experienced the wrath of top administration officials for reporting that the military situation was deteriorating in the vital Mekong Delta. When his publisher, Arthur Ochs Sulzberger, later visited the White House, Kennedy questioned the reporter's professionalism and asked if the newspaper had been thinking about transferring Halberstam to another place. Sulzberger replied the newspaper was satisfied with his work and his present assignment, but the *Times* immediately canceled a vacation Halberstam was scheduled to take in order to avoid the appearance of acquiescing to presidential intimidation.[78] Lyndon Johnson, who quickly became obsessed with critical coverage, ordered the FBI to dig up dirt on AP correspondent Peter Arnett, who was reporting on the army's brutality, faulty equipment, and experimentation with gas warfare. Johnson invited AP's personnel chief, Keith Fuller, to lunch and asked him if Arnett had not been in Vietnam too long. Arnett continued to report on the war, but his bosses often cautioned him to avoid reporting that could be criticized as biased or inflammatory. One of Arnett's controversial stories, one which made an angry President Johnson send senior officers scurrying to find the source, quoted a major as saying, " 'It became necessary to destroy the town to save it.' "[79]

American forces did not subject reporters to a system of prior restraint in Indochina. At first officials tried to conceal the fact that the military was engaged in combat at all, and later they feared that censorship would be not only unpopular but also unenforceable. Formal procedures would have been difficult to administer where widespread guerrilla warfare was being waged without obvious battle lines, and, in any event, United States forces were not relying on secrecy so much as immense firepower.[80] Reporters were given a considerable amount of access and amenities, but those who were accredited agreed not to do unauthorized reporting on categories of information that included troop movements, details on search and rescue missions in progress, and casualty figures before they were announced in Saigon. Credentials were rarely lifted for violating the ground rules.[81] However, the penalty could be imposed for petty reasons. John Steinbeck Jr., son of the novelist and a part-time CBS technician, lost his accreditation for joining a peace crusade led by Palm Tree Prophet, a Buddhist monk who gained press attention by meditating while perched in trees.[82]

In some cases, attempts to cooperate with the military could be frustrated for political reasons. When the work of Dickey Chapelle, a magazine writer and photographer, was voluntarily submitted to the Department of Defense, she experienced delays and dubious objections. Her journalism, which was staunchly anticommunist, documented greater military involvement in the war than the Kennedy administration wanted to admit to.[83] In one case, *National Geographic* was asked to omit a photograph showing a Marine holding his weapon in a combat-ready position. The picture, which showed Americans were going beyond a training role in 1962, ran in the magazine after Chapelle protested that the enemy knew what was happening but that soldiers' morale was suffering because the American public did not realize what they were enduring.[84] In another case, hundreds of her negatives showing Special Forces operations in Laos were "lost" in the security review process. One of the "missing" photographs, she noticed, appeared in *Army Digest* with credit to the Army.[85] Army censors also had "lost" forty-eight frames of her photographs taken in Panama during World War II. They were, she said at the time, "Pearl Harborized."[86]

Following journalistic norms and practices, the press avoided graphic pictures of combat in Vietnam and coverage of American atrocities that could be regarded as harmful to the war effort.[87] In 1965 CBS executives wondered if they should broadcast a report by Morley Safer showing a Marine unit casually burning the huts in the small village of Cam Ne. They worried about the reactions of viewers who would be eating dinner, about what the competition would have about the incident, and, finally, about how they could defend *not* showing the realities of the war.[88] After the network put the story on the air, the Marines said that the film was faked, and the Defense Department demanded that CBS remove Safer from Vietnam. Safer feared being killed by angry soldiers, and Lyndon Johnson gave expletive-laced tongue-lashings to CBS President Frank Stanton, accusing him of being a disloyal friend and his network of being unpatriotic. Pretending that investigations had shown that Safer had communist ties, the president threatened to go public with the information unless the correspondent was fired and CBS coverage improved. Safer was spared, but Secretary of State Dean Rusk, who believed the story was staged, continued to think the reporter had connections to Soviet spies.[89] Four months after the Cam Ne broadcast, AP's Peter Arnett prepared an account of American soldiers decapitating an attacker, passing the head around, and being promised a case of whiskey by their commander as a reward, but the wire service rejected the story and photographs. The president's press secretary, Bill Moyers, and other administration officials concluded that Arnett, a New Zealander, and Safer, a Canadian, did not have basic American interests at heart. Arnett, whom army and CIA investigators tried to link to the Vietcong, observed that it would have been "professional suicide" for him to suggest that enemy forces were as superbly trained and highly motivated as they were.[90]

Challenging war policies was hazardous. In December 1966 Harrison Salisbury of the *New York Times* visited North Vietnam and wrote a series of stories that undermined impressions created by the president and the Defense Department that the

Figure 7.1 *Journalists argued in 1962 that the Kennedy Administration was making futile attempts to cover up the extent of U.S. involvement in Vietnam. Jack Knox cartoon for the* Nashville Banner *(February 17, 1962).Reproduced by permission of Edith Knox (Mrs. Jack Knox). Reproduced courtesy of Cartoon Research Library, The Ohio State University Library.*

United States was carrying out only precise bombing of military targets. Salisbury also suggested publicly what intelligence analysts and Defense Secretary Robert McNamara were concluding in secret, that massive air attacks were not very effective. Salisbury's editors backed his reporting, but the FBI investigated him, and officials denounced his work as communist propaganda.[91] The series, however, had a powerful impact on the public. "While additional loss of faith in the word of the government was the dominant part of that reaction," recalled Phil Goulding, a Pentagon spokesman at the time, "another part was deeper disenchantment with the war itself." The "credibility disaster" could have been avoided, Goulding said, if the government had been more willing to admit that "of course we were killing civilians" despite the care being taken.[92] Salisbury's reporting from North Vietnam was chosen by the jury for the Pulitzer Prize in international reporting, but the judges and trustees overturned the decision on close votes that appeared to reflect individual positions on the war.[93]

American journalism became less deferential as the shallow support for the war slowly evaporated and the cause appeared more hopeless and morally flawed.[94] Seymour Hersh, a free-lance writer, did win the Pulitzer Prize in 1970 for his reporting on the massacre of civilians at My Lai by American soldiers in 1968. The military, which had initially announced that 128 Vietcong had been killed in combat, had been keeping the deadly rampage quiet, and major news organizations did not show interest in the story at first, but the mass murder became a serious scandal, and other atrocity reports emerged once Hersh's account was distributed by an obscure news service.[95] In 1970, Tom Harkin, a congressional staff member who was later elected to the Senate from Iowa, went to South Vietnam on a fact-finding trip and photographed the mistreatment of political prisoners. When the official report whitewashed the use of "tiger cages," Harkin sold his pictures to *Life*, but he lost his staff job.[96]

The lengthy and often shameful involvement in the war displayed presidential arrogance at its fullest. Johnson did convince Congress to pass, with only two dissenting votes in the Senate and none in the House, the Tonkin Gulf Resolution, which supported the president's use of "all necessary measures to repel any armed attack against the forces of the United States and to prevent further aggression." The resolution said the country was "prepared, as the President determines, to take all necessary steps" to assist the nations of Indochina in defending their freedom. Johnson's ideas of presidential prerogative were so elastic, however, that he did not think legislative approval was needed for him to act abroad. Fearing a leftist victory in the Dominican Republic's civil war in 1965, for example, he sent more than twenty thousand soldiers there without congressional consent on the pretext of saving Americans. Johnson did not have a sudden emergency in Vietnam or U.N. resolutions, as Truman had had in the Korean War, but he did have political reasons for wanting to consult with his former colleagues in Congress as the country stepped up involvement. "We stated then, and we repeat now, we did not think the resolution was necessary to do what we did and what we are doing," Johnson said in 1967. "But we thought it was desirable."[97]

The Tonkin Gulf Resolution was revoked after Richard Nixon took office, but the powers of the presidency had inflated to the point that even such small nods to Congress were not regarded as obligatory. When asked in 1970 what legal basis he would have for continuing an undeclared war, Nixon replied that as commander in chief he had constitutional powers "to protect American forces when they are engaged in military actions" and that he believed "the majority of the American people will support me." William H. Rehnquist, an assistant attorney general who would later be appointed to the Supreme Court by Nixon, had given the president a legal memorandum stating he had the authority to send Americans into areas of low-intensity fighting, including Cambodia. "Although the authority to declare war is vested in the Congress," Rehnquist wrote, "the President as Commander-in-Chief and sole organ of foreign affairs has constitutional authority to engage U.S. forces in limited conflict."[98]

By the time of Nixon's "imperial presidency," Arthur M. Schlesinger Jr. wrote, "the title Commander in Chief had acquired almost a sacramental aura, translating its holder from worldly matters into an ineffable realm of higher duty."[99] The Constitution had become so flexible in practice on matters of "national security" that the head of the executive branch could feel little or no restraint except from the public. In fact, many citizens were seeking to be heard on the subject of the Vietnam War. Two tense weeks of antiwar demonstrations in Washington, D.C., in the spring of 1971 included a rally of two hundred thousand protesters.[100] With memories of the 1968 Democratic Convention and the 1970 shootings at Kent State University still fresh, the quasi-revolutionary throbbings of a counterculture continued to shake the nation. In his memoirs, Nixon said the first months of 1971 were the "lowest point of my first term" and that Henry Kissinger had found the situation "revolutionary." The antiwar demonstrators in Washington, Nixon said, were "led by hard-core agitators who had been openly encouraged by the North Vietnamese."[101] On the evening of May 8, the president attended the annual White House Correspondents' Association Dinner. In a memo to H. R. Haldeman dictated the next day, Nixon described "sitting through three hours of pure boredom and insults" and complained that the journalists being honored were "way out left-wingers" and that each was "receiving an award for a vicious attack on the Administration." He told his chief of staff that he was facing a re-election campaign that would be "a fight to the death," that 95 percent of the Washington press corps was unalterably opposed to him, and that in the future he wanted only friendly reporters invited to White House functions. "I'm not a bit thin-skinned," he told Haldeman, "but I do have the responsibility and everybody on my staff has the responsibility to protect the office of the Presidency from such insulting incidents." Administration staff members did not understand, Nixon said, that journalists were "just waiting for the chance to stick the knife in deep and twist it."[102]

Nixon did receive consolation from Chief Justice Warren Burger, who, like the president, had been a redbaiter early in his career and was not known as a friend to the press.[103] The chief justice sent Nixon a fulsome letter expressing his "unbounded admiration" for the presidential forbearance in the face of "gross rudeness" from the assembled journalists. "Having been reading closely some of the events from 1789 to 1800, fairness to the present day press corps compels acknowledgment that they are now slightly less savage, less sadistic and less cruel than 150 to 200 years ago," Burger wrote. "So viewed, this is progress of sorts." Writing in response, Nixon agreed with his appointee's reading of history as "certainly true," observing that the press of President Washington's era was "more vitriolic" but adding that modern presidents had to cope with the "sensationalism" of television and had to know how to use it to survive politically.[104] Other than television, Nixon had few overt weapons to use against his detractors in the press and elsewhere. The Federalists had passed the Sedition Act in 1798 to bludgeon the opponents of their foreign policy, but in 1971 such measures would not have survived the scrutiny of the Supreme Court or met with adequate acceptance in Congress or in public opinion.[105] Like the Federalists of the 1790s, however, members of the Nixon administration in the 1970s helped bring about their own spectacular fall from power by embarking on irrational, self-defeating attempts to suppress or at least take revenge on its outspoken opponents.

The most dramatic legal confrontation occurred in 1971, when the *New York Times* began publishing the Pentagon Papers, a classified history of American mistakes and duplicity in Vietnam that was commissioned by Defense Secretary Robert McNamara in 1967 when he had become disillusioned with the war. At first Nixon had no intention to obstruct the *Times* because the leaked study was only embarrassing to previous presidents, but his national security adviser, Henry Kissinger, insisted that not retaliating against such a large disclosure of secrets would appear weak and make future diplomacy more difficult. Few other officials showed much concern, but, prodded by Kissinger and frustrated by leaks in his administration, Nixon considered his options. Asked to provide a quick legal analysis, William Rehnquist relied on *Near v. Minnesota* to suggest that prior restraints could be granted in exceptional cases and that the current fighting of a war would improve the administration's chances. The president and his appointees began playing up the possibility that publication could violate espionage laws and damage the position of the United States on Vietnam and other foreign policy issues. "I was outraged," Nixon said in his memoirs. "I did not consider that rights conveyed by the First Amendment for the publication of these documents superior to the right of an American soldier to stay alive in wartime." With little advice and a longstanding grudge against the news media, Nixon decided to take legal action, and within two weeks, after initial legal skirmishing stopped publication, the expedited case reached Supreme Court.[106]

The arguments in the *Pentagon Papers* case had to confront the issue of presidential powers. Citing the *Near v. Minnesota* dictum on troop ships, the government brief asked for an injunction against further publication and, citing *Curtiss-Wright*, said that diplomacy required secrecy that the president was better equipped to decide about than the courts. As commander in chief, the brief stated, the president has "the duty to preserve military secrets whose disclosure might threaten the safety of troops engaged in combat." The First Amendment, the government said, did not prevent enjoining publication of material that could pose " 'grave and immediate danger' " to the nation's security.[107] Noting that the government lacked a statute authorizing injunctive relief, the *Times* brief cited the *Steel Seizure* case in denying that the president had any inherent power to make substantive law in an emergency. The newspaper did not deny that the president had an inherent authority to classify government documents, but said that if authority could be found for prior restraint, then the facts of the case at hand would not meet a test that the publication would "lead directly and almost unavoidably to a disastrous event for the country."[108] Although the government wrote a secret portion of its brief providing eleven examples of information in the papers that involved "a serious risk of immediate and irreparable harm to the United

States and its security," the solicitor general, Erwin Griswold, could not make a particularly strong case that disclosure would have serious consequences.[109]

The Supreme Court voted six to three to refuse a permanent injunction but did not deny that prior restraints could be imposed under some circumstances. In a short *per curiam* decision issued only four days after the oral arguments, the majority explained simply that the government had not met the " 'heavy burden' " against prepublication censorship.[110] Little guidance for future cases was provided. Each of the nine members of the court wrote a separate opinion. Four of the concurring justices attempted to describe circumstances in which prior restraints or subsequent penalties could be justified.[111] Two justices, Hugo Black and William Douglas, took absolutist positions. Black did not want the courts to "make" a law abridging press freedom in the name of inherent presidential power or vague national security. "The guarding of military and diplomatic secrets at the expense of informed representative government provides no real security for our Republic," he wrote.[112] The three dissenters, who included Chief Justice Burger, complained mainly about the haste of the decision and, citing *Curtiss-Wright*, expressed a willingness to defer to the president.[113] "The First Amendment, after all, is only one part of an entire Constitution," said Justice Harry Blackmun, who relied on *Schenck* and *Near*. "Article II of the great document vests in the Executive Branch primary power over the conduct of foreign affairs and places in that branch the responsibility for the Nation's safety."[114]

Publication of the Pentagon Papers resumed without significant repercussions for national security, but the documents did foster legislative and public debate on America's Vietnam policies. During the first six months of 1971, twenty-two votes were taken in the House or Senate to curtail presidential war power or to set a date for withdrawal. All the attempts failed until the Pentagon Papers litigation. Four days before the case was argued in the Supreme Court, the Senate, by a vote of fifty-seven to forty-two, passed a nonbinding resolution calling on the president to withdraw military forces from Vietnam as soon as possible.[115] By 1971 the war itself had become a danger to national security by tearing the country apart internally.[116] Years later, even Erwin Griswold, who had argued the government's case, wrote that he knew of "no harm" caused by the disclosures and had realized "that there was probably not adequate ground for an injunction."[117]

The courts were not the only place Nixon could seek help. The White House used agencies such as the FBI and the Internal Revenue Service to intimidate the press, protesters, and political opponents and, after the Pentagon Papers began appearing, set up its own secret "Plumbers" unit to investigate leaks to the news media.[118] Even public broadcasting was not immune, as Nixon attempted to use budget cuts and appointments to the Corporation for Public Broadcasting to punish what he regarded as liberal bias in its programming. At one point, recalled broadcaster Robert MacNeil, "The conversion of public broadcasting into the feared domestic Voice of America seemed at hand."[119] Nixon displayed, even in public, a visceral rancor for the news media;[120] he complained to his aides that journalists were intellectually arrogant and that the mass media were dominated by Jews.[121] More than fifty prominent journalists were on his "enemies lists";[122] some, such as Daniel Schorr of CBS, were subjected to background investigations.[123] In addition to having his State Department office ransacked twice, CBS diplomatic correspondent Marvin Kalb was placed on the enemies list, smeared as a "Rumanian agent," audited frequently by the Internal Revenue Service, and wiretapped.[124] Wiretaps of dubious legality were placed on the phones of a number of reporters and officials in order to discover the sources of leaked information on the administration's hidden machinations on Vietnam.[125]

The government's claim of inherent power vested in the president to use warrantless wiretaps for ongoing surveillance of "subversive forces" to protect the government was rejected in 1972 by a unanimous Supreme Court that included Chief Justice Burger and other Nixon appointees. The president has a constitutional duty to protect domestic security, the Court admitted, but the government was using a vague concept of national security and was risking infringement of privacy and lawful dissent in the absence of a warrant procedure that would provide a check on executive discretion. "Although some added burden will be imposed upon the Attorney General," the court said, "this inconvenience is justified in a free society to protect constitutional values."[126] Two days before the Court announced its opinion, a team of Nixon's "plumbers" was arrested during a break-in at the Democratic National Committee offices at the Watergate building in Washington, D.C.[127] Nixon's extensive program of domestic spying and political skullduggery was sparked largely by the Pentagon Papers leak and his fears about the 1972 election;[128] his irrational schemes ultimately brought about his resignation after the Supreme Court rejected grandiose claims of general presidential immunity in the Watergate tapes case. Nixon's lawyers had argued that he was subject to criminal laws "only after he has been impeached and convicted, and thus stripped of his critical constitutional functions."[129]

In the wake of his scandals and resignation, Nixon was far from contrite. Comparing his difficulties during the Vietnam War to Lincoln's during the Civil War, he said his illegal actions against critics were not actual violations of the law. "When the president does it," he said in a televised interview four years after leaving office, "that means that it is not illegal." Nixon quoted Lincoln as saying that unconstitutional actions could become legal if taken to preserve the nation. Although Nixon recognized that there was "nothing specific that the Constitution contemplates in that respect," he insisted that "in wartime, a president does have certain extraordinary powers."[130] Nixon thought he could do no wrong, even if he had taken an oath to preserve the Constitution. While serving Nixon as secretary of state, Henry Kissinger admitted to an interviewer that "when you have power in your hands and have held it for a long period of time, you end up thinking of it as something that's due you." He said he himself "always acted alone," a trait that Americans liked "immensely" in the movie cowboy. The cowboy character, who could "show others that he rides into town and does everything by himself," suited him "precisely," Kissinger said.[131]

III.

The denial of press access to the Grenada invasion in 1983 and the "security review" of pool stories in the Gulf War of 1991 demonstrated the ability of more recent presidents and the Department of Defense to take a forceful approach in the name of military secrecy and personal safety.[132] Courts avoided the First Amendment claims made as the result of those fleeting episodes, saying that actions challenging the prohibitions were moot because the restrictions had been lifted and that declaratory relief would be difficult to grant without knowing the specific circumstances and regulations of a future war.[133] With judges evidently only willing to examine the issue on an ad hoc balancing basis while restraints are in effect, the news media and the military were left to air mutual suspicions while attempting to negotiate solutions.[134] The result was an uneasy stalemate between journalists who wanted First Amendment protection in distant nations and administrations that asserted authority to make war and control the coverage at their discretion.[135]

Civilian and military officials attempted to justify excluding the press until the third day of the Grenada invasion by citing a need for surprise and for the safety of journalists. News media in Grenada and throughout the Caribbean, however, had been predicting the attack. When questioned about it by reporters, White House spokesman Larry Speakes said, "Preposterous!" repeating a lie he had been told by an NSC official, John Poindexter. Twelve hours later the invasion of Grenada began. When Speakes asked President Ronald Reagan why reporters were kept out, Reagan told him, " 'It was a commando raid, it had to be a surprise, lives were at stake, and the media might have jeopardized the success of the invasion.' " The press, which had a long history of accompanying troops into battle, was anxious to describe the events to a public that was receiving little or no information from official sources. Vice Admiral Joseph Metcalf III, commander of the task force, established an exclusion zone around Grenada. On the second day he ordered a fighter plane to fire warning shots at a charter boat carrying reporters headed for Grenada. When the boat stayed on course, Metcalf told the pilot to fire another burst and to sink the vessel if it did not turn around. The boat turned around after the second set of shots. Metcalf, who was left to make decisions about press coverage on his own, said that the safety of reporters and military personnel was his "primary consideration" and that "the arguments about 'First Amendment Rights' was unknown to me at the time."[136] By a nearly three-to-one margin, the Senate called for an end to press restrictions that did not jeopardize the forces;[137] but the whole matter of the invasion died down in Congress once the operation appeared to have won the approval of a majority of Americans.[138]

Still, administration actions were hard to defend. British Prime Minister Margaret Thatcher adamantly opposed invading part of the British Commonwealth as the Grenada operation was being planned and more than one hundred countries in the United Nations General Assembly voted to condemn the action after it occurred. The Reagan administration claimed that a palace coup had placed more than two hundred American medical students on the island in danger and that the Soviets and Cubans, who had been providing technical assistance to the overthrown leftist government, had plotted with more radical hardliners who took power to extend Communist influence in the region. Cuban President Fidel Castro, however, condemned the killing of Prime Minister Maurice Bishop, and both Cuban and Grenadian officials provided repeated assurances that the students were in no danger and could leave if they wished. Shortly before the invasion Secretary of State George Shultz notified the new leaders that their promises were rejected because their government had questionable legitimacy. In fact, the students, who easily could have been harmed or taken hostage if they were imperiled, were not evacuated until the invasion was nearly over. Contrary to administration statements, intelligence sources said there was no clear evidence of a threat to the students, and no evidence surfaced to indicate that Cubans were planning to take over the island or that it was being prepared for terrorist training. The Grenada airport, which the Cubans were helping to build and the American government was portraying as a likely Soviet-bloc base, was the result of three decades of studies and of World Bank support aimed at increasing tourism. Harming the students would have endangered vital tourist and medical school income.[139]

As earlier presidents had done, Ronald Reagan relied on Lincoln's unilateral actions as precedent for virtually unrestricted presidential power over matters of war and foreign policy. As he carried out a number of overt and covert operations abroad without legislative approval, Reagan stood ready to confront Congress with a position he found articulated in an essay by conservative scholar Walter Berns.[140] By quoting the *Federalist* and Locke out of context[141] and giving the broadest possible reading to the vesting clause, Berns concluded that the president is an "independent" representative of the supreme people and was therefore not limited by the law. Executive power came from the people, he reasoned, and could be used, as Lincoln had, in prerogative fashion because "under our written Constitution, law is not supreme." Berns judged Lincoln to be "the greatest of American presidents" and regarded his willingness to take action against dissenters as justified by his adherence to the cause of free government. "Words precede deeds," Berns observed, quoting Lincoln as saying that it was " 'not only constitutional, but a great mercy,' " to silence the " 'wily agitator' " who induces a " 'simple-minded soldier boy' " to desert and be sentenced to the firing squad.[142] In using this "bad tendency" logic, neither Berns nor Lincoln explained why authorities could not rely on their own ample opportunities for persuasion or what would protect legitimate complaints about matters such as incompetent military leadership.

Oliver North, a member of Reagan's NSC staff who ran rogue operations to send supplies to Nicaraguan Contra rebels and arms to Iran, testified that he relied on the *Curtiss-Wright* precedent for taking secret action abroad.[143] In news reports Colonel North was also linked to government contingency plans for the repression of domestic dissent. From 1982 to 1984 North was the NSC's liaison to the Federal Emergency Management Agency, where he reportedly worked on a secret martial law scheme for suspending the Constitution and imposing censorship in the event of a national emergency such as nuclear war or mass antiwar protests. Although the initial story in the *Miami Herald* cited leaked government documents, North told Congress that he did not plan or advocate measures for suspending the Constitution. "This story was not only wrong, but offensive," North said in an autobiographical book. "The whole point of The Project was to protect our constitutional system even under the worst imaginable conditions." He wrote that he prepared "several directives which President Reagan signed, authorizing further steps to be taken to ensure that our government could not be rendered impotent by enemy action or an extraordinary disaster." Whatever was drawn up remained secret, as did most of the nearly three hundred National Security Decision Directives Reagan signed, but in his book North made no secret of his anger at the press coverage he received, using descriptions such as "bombastic and outrageous" and "set me off like a rocket."[144]

The news media and the Pentagon did reach some agreement on access to war zones after the Grenada debacle. Major news organizations signed up for a newly created Department of Defense Media Pool to be dispatched to trouble spots, but few details of its operation were established. When the scheme had its first significant test in the 1989 invasion of Panama, an operation condemned by the United Nations General Assembly and the Organization of American States, journalists did not see much of what amounted to little more than a one-day war. Official excuses and acknowledgments of error were provided. Secretary of Defense Richard Cheney, acting with what he said was a need to protect lives and what a Pentagon report later described as an excessive concern for secrecy, delayed the activation of the pool and obstructed Army efforts to create a pool of reporters who were already in Panama. Reporters eventually began arriving in Panama City, but they were kept away from the fighting by military escorts or confined to a military base. Officers of the Southern Command blamed logistics problems and said that they were worried about the safety of journalists. Pete Williams, the chief Pentagon spokesman, who explained that he and the Southern Command had been guilty of "incompetence," prohibited pool photographs of wounded Americans, a decision that was justified as a means of preventing relatives from being notified by the media. A colonel, who later said he may have acted in the heat of the moment, ordered that no pictures be taken of caskets. The government, claiming security concerns, refused to release its videotapes of the invasion.[145]

An almost unseen, quickly concluded war was one that could make few lasting impressions and be promptly forgotten. Although the sudden use of military force against another nation should raise legal and moral questions, little opposition developed within the American public and mainstream news organizations.[146] The media generally followed the administration's propaganda script that the invasion was in support of democracy, but, in fact, the country's corrupt leader had long been a tool of the CIA and had become uncooperative in implementing policies on Cuba, Nicaragua, and El Salvador.[147] The attack, which was planned in advance and which apparently only awaited the pretext of a provocation, was hardly a surprise. Numerous security leaks occurred, and scores of transport planes were landing on a military air strip in the canal zone at five-minute intervals the day before the invasion.[148]

President George Bush assured Americans that "the dictator of Panama, General Manuel Noriega, an indicted drug trafficker," had become an "imminent danger" to the thirty-five thousand United States citizens in Panama. "As President, I have no higher obligation than to safeguard the lives of American citizens," he said. "And that is why I directed our Armed Forces to protect the lives of American citizens in Panama and to bring General Noriega to justice in the United States." Bush's primary evidence of danger was that an American soldier had been shot and killed by Panamanian forces.[149] After the invasion, reports indicated that the soldier was running a Panamanian roadblock in a restricted military area when he was killed.[150] (American soldiers shot a Panamanian woman in labor and her husband when they sped past a checkpoint on their way to the hospital three days after the invasion.[151]) The ostensible goal of protecting lives was undercut by the fact that twenty-six Americans died in the invasion and 312 were injured, in addition to a death toll of hundreds and perhaps thousands of Panamanians. The number of Panamanian deaths was the subject of debate, but 34 percent of the U.S. casualties were due to "friendly fire" or accidents.[152] Approximately $1 billion in damage was done to an impoverished country, and drug traffic continued at preinvasion levels.[153]

When Bush said in 1990 that he would take action to drive Iraqi invaders out of Kuwait whether given Congressional authorization or not, critics of his stand had to contend with historical evidence showing that Congress explicitly declared war only five times in the first two hundred years of the republic, while presidents, relying on legislative acquiescence or appropriation of funds, sent troops abroad more than two hundred times. As he maneuvered the country toward war by putting hundreds of thousands of military personnel in the Persian Gulf over a period of five months, Bush insisted that he could wage war on his own authority as commander in chief. Congress did not invoke and no president had ever recognized as constitutional the 1973 War Powers Resolution requiring a president to consult with Congress whenever possible before deploying troops, to report a deployment within forty-eight hours when hostilities appear imminent, and to remove troops within sixty days in the absence of legislative approval, unless the president requests a thirty-day extension for the safety of soldiers. Without a Supreme Court decision on the resolution and with the lower courts seeing the issue as one to be settled by the "political" branches, Congress, with a margin of only five votes in the Senate, passed a last-minute resolution authorizing the use of force under United Nations resolutions and the War Powers Resolution.[154] The decision was apparently influenced by a Kuwaiti-funded $11.5 million public relations campaign that orchestrated exaggerated congressional testimony on Iraqi atrocities. One of the key witnesses, a girl known as Nayirah, related a tale of Iraqi soldiers removing babies from hospital incubators. She was later identified as the daughter of Kuwait's ambassador to the United States.[155]

As President Bush claimed an unrestricted power to initiate war, his subordinates announced and revised lists of ground rules and guidelines for press coverage.[156] As the forces and equipment arrived in the Middle East, journalists were told very little and were asked not to identify military personnel in Saudi Arabia because of the possibility of terrorist reprisals against their relatives at home. The prohibition, which did not apply to commanders and which suggested that perpetrators would need the media for the information, was unpopular with troops and was dropped after protests from reporters.[157] Other restrictions were eased following more complaints;[158] but the military said that combat coverage would be limited to pool reporting and would be reviewed by a public affairs escort officer before release. The security review was to be limited to a list of twelve ground rules that prohibited the publication or broadcast of facts about military plans, capabilities, operations, or vulnerabilities. Disputes on security review were to be resolved by the military's Joint Information Bureau in Saudi Arabia and could be appealed to the Pentagon's public affairs office. The process would delay the story, but criticism and embarrassing facts were to be allowed, and the news organization was to make the ultimate decision on what to say.[159]

The restrictions were said to be necessary to protect the lives of troops and journalists but were difficult to implement. The Defense Department warned that reporters who broke free of escorted pools would lose their credentials. Public affairs officers interfered with interviews, and soldiers—as well as their families—quickly learned that they were not supposed to question the wisdom of their superiors or the

Figure 7.2   *Arthur Kent, an NBC correspondent, preparing a script in the back of a Bradley Fighting Vehicle during the Gulf War. Stories from the war zone were subject to military delays. Kent, the famed "SCUD Stud" of the war, later fought the network over professional standards in international reporting and was suspended, but took legal action and won an impressive settlement package. Photo by Tom Baer. Reproduced by permission of Fast Forward Films Limited.*

Bush administration. Critical reporters were denied access to the top brass, and stories were delayed and lost as they went through military review. With more than fourteen hundred journalists in the gulf region, the pool system, which was allowing less than two hundred reporters, photographers, and technicians to cover over half a million Americans in the armed forces, created strong resentments and quickly collapsed under combat conditions. At least two dozen reporters and photographers were detained by the United States or Saudi military for trying to cover the war outside of pools. Some lost their credentials temporarily. Many others managed to evade the military police or to find sympathetic units that would allow them to work without supervision. In some cases reporters wore military clothing to avoid detection. Unauthorized reporting did provide opportunities for verifying or questioning official versions of the fighting, but reporters and soldiers who cooperated with the press were subjected to threats and intimidation.[160]

The words of the Constitution and their interpretation by courts have not always been barriers to government officials who have wanted to use powers they have not been granted. In wartime, press freedom and other rights have been diminished by the kind of human failings that the ratifiers of the First Amendment did not hope to correct, but did hope to control. The Bill of Rights lasted and was the object of much veneration during its first two hundred years, but citizens were not adequately informed about its provisions, and politicians frequently ignored its limitations on their actions.[161] If the words of the Constitution had been respected in practice rather than merely revered in rhetoric, then guaranteed freedoms would not have been denied, and the powers of government would not have swollen to unconstitutional proportions. The responsibility for reporting would have remained with the press, and official actions in times of war would have rested on the rule of law, not on the rule of autocrats.

Part Three: The Risks of Repression

The Mass Media:
Scapegoats and Sycophants

Even if wartime press controls have not been authorized by the Constitution and have not been used well in American history, are they necessary at times? Arguments have been made that journalists are a menace to military operations and the safety of soldiers.[1] Some legal scholars have maintained that some government-imposed restraints are reasonable and should be allowed because they make sense.[2] Although journalists might be an additional hazard and burden for the armed forces, their presence is only one of many challenges and their coverage serves vital functions. The Marines did a relatively good job of working with the press in the Gulf War because they adopted the attitude that coping with the media is necessary. "We didn't view the news media as a group of people we were supposed to schmooze," said Chief Warrant Officer Eric Carlson. "We regarded them as an environmental feature of the battlefield, kind of like the rain. If it rains, you operate wet."[3] The military can use its skills in logistics to accommodate reporters in a combat zone, and reporters should be able to take the risk of being harmed in battle, as they have done in all the nation's wars, if they choose to do so.

Of particular concern to those who insist on worrying about the press is the existence of rapid and realistic mass communication that apparently annihilates the ability of the military to carry out operations with adequate secrecy and public support. How can combat be conducted and media audiences retain their composure when intense, instantaneous images of the battlefield are being beamed around the world? Any evaluation of such questions requires an examination of how officials and jour-nalists shape perceptions of war. Political and military leaders can, of course, be ex-pected to deceive the enemy, the public, and often themselves. Not as well understood, however, is the role of the mass communication. Although sometimes accused of aiding the enemy or becoming advocates, media professionals actually assist authorities in a variety of ways, including keeping them informed and conveying their propaganda and disinformation. The mass media can be an ally in making war and, sadly, can even make armed conflict appear entertaining.[4] When officials attempt involuntary suppression and the doctoring of information, they alienate journalists and undermine the credibility of all concerned. Such actions violate democratic principles and can be seen as avoidable if the realities of war are taken into account.

I.

Twentieth-century developments in communication helped to destabilize a number of oppressive regimes around the world;[5] but technological advancements were also of concern to more democratic governments.[6] By World War I, news media existed that could allow large audiences to experience combat with an immediacy and realism never before possible. Officials responded with repression. When the *New York Herald* radio station issued a bulletin about a German U-boat sinking ships near Nantucket in 1916, for instance, the Navy regarded the story as unneutral because it could help the British find the submarine and therefore sent censors to the station.[7] Before the United States entered World War II, tens of millions of Americans listened to the CBS radio reports of Edward R. Murrow who, with a censor at his side, described devastating air attacks on London from the roof of the BBC building.[8] Newsreel coverage of the two world wars was limited to what the military considered safe for public morale and what theater managers thought would not upset squeamish customers. Civilian newsreel companies were denied access to the front in World War I and therefore faked battle scenes or relied on censored footage furnished by the Signal Corps. Projection facilities were set up for members of Congress to see unedited views of actual conditions, while the government was making propaganda films such as *All the Comforts of Home* about services provided for soldiers and *There Shall Be No Cripples* about the efforts of the surgeon general's office. In World War II the newsreel companies pooled their coverage and submitted their work for military censorship. The result could be long delays and dull stories.[9] The field manual for the press noted that censors were to consider the "time element" of how quickly stories might reach the enemy and to give "the closest supervision" to communication by cable, telegraph, and radio.[10]

Television was in nearly all American homes by the time American soldiers began pouring into Vietnam and often has been seen as a crucial factor in the war. In a 1968 status report that took note of the unprecedented television coverage of the conflict, General William Westmoreland, the commander of U.S. forces in Vietnam, spoke of the "major role" that reporting had in shaping public opinion and asserted that "the accuracy and balance of the news coverage has attained an importance almost equal to the actual combat operations." In his memoirs Westmoreland complained that television news had to be "compressed and visually dramatic" and that what Americans saw of the war was "almost exclusively violent, miserable, or controversial."[11] One former correspondent, Robert Elegant, wrote, "For the first time in modern history, the outcome of a war was determined not on the battlefield, but on the printed page and, above all, on the television screen."[12] Although social scientists may have many unanswered questions about the possible "effects" of the mass media on individuals, the effects on institutions may be considerable, as sociologist Herbert J. Gans has recognized. "The Pentagon ran so scared after the news coverage of Vietnam that it virtually took over the news coverage of the Grenada, Panama, and Gulf wars— an impressive, if unappreciated, compliment to the effects it ascribed to uncensored television news," he said.[13]

Those who promoted the conventional wisdom that the media were to blame for the outcome of the Vietnam War included a number of military officers and public officials.[14] Henry Kissinger, who helped to formulate American policy in the region as national security adviser and secretary of state, asserted that television dramatized the war with visual images that provided "a running editorial commentary" not balanced adequately by reporting of enemy atrocities in areas they controlled. "The news

Figure 8.1 *At first, only the Army Signal Corps was authorized to photograph American soldiers fighting in Europe during World War I. Eventually correspondents and civilian photographers were allowed to take pictures that they submitted to military censorship. Censors did not approve photographs they felt would be useful to the enemy or harmful to morale. Photograph of Second Lt. George E. Stone, Signal Corps, by Sgt. Charles E. Mace (Cochem, Germany, January 9, 1919). Courtesy of the National Archives.*

anchor turned into a political figure," he said, "in the sense that only a president could have reached as many people—and certainly not with such regularity." After the enemy's massive Tet Offensive of 1968 that brought attacks even to the American embassy in Saigon, Kissinger said, television anchorman Walter Cronkite "sent shock waves through the White House by predicting failure" in Vietnam. Kissinger, who won the 1973 Nobel Peace Prize for his negotiations with North Vietnam, expressed regret that Lyndon Johnson soon "buckled" under the barrage of criticism from the press and politicians. Instead of offering negotiations that Hanoi was not serious about and announcing that he would not run for reelection, Johnson could have "really gone for broke" militarily, Kissinger insisted, because "the Viet Cong guerrillas ceased being an effective fighting force" after Tet, and the North Vietnamese army's regular units did almost all of the remaining fighting.[15]

Although the Tet offensive may not have been a military loss for the United States, the fighting alarmed American television viewers because they had been given confident assessments of progress in Vietnam and because no level of attrition seemed intolerable to the other side.[16] In his book *No More Vietnams* Richard Nixon, who owed his presidency in large part to Lyndon Johnson's troubles in Indochina, offered a rendition of the reporting on Tet that was almost identical to Kissinger's. The press, Nixon said, interpreted a military disaster for North Vietnam as evidence that the United States was losing the war. "Reporters, most of whom knew nothing about military affairs, missed the big picture," the former commander in chief charged. "Instead, they focused on isolated, dramatic incidents, often getting their stories dramatically wrong." The Saigon bureau chief for the *Washington Post* later wrote that the Tet fighting was seen as a debacle for the United States because television used shocking pictures and created a first impression that officials, who were slow to provide facts and interpretation, were unable to overcome. When ABC correspondent John Scali persisted in asking Secretary of State Dean Rusk why the Tet offensive should be considered an American victory, Rusk blurted out, "Whose side are you on, anyway?"[17]

Yet the pictures, which were some of the most vivid of the war because the combat was in the open and in daylight, did not exactly create what both Kissinger and Nixon, echoing many others, called a major "psychological victory" for Hanoi.[18] Polls published after Tet showed an increasingly realistic outlook, with 13 percent fewer Americans thinking the war would be over in two years or less and those believing progress was being made sinking from 51 to 32 percent, but the numbers also revealed an apparent "rally round the flag" effect. Compared to three months earlier, the number of self-described "hawks" increased from 56 to 61 percent, and Americans favoring a withdrawal dropped from 44 to 24 percent. The loser was Lyndon Johnson, whose approval rating fell to 26 percent just before he announced he would not run again. Johnson suffered both from a "credibility gap" on Vietnam and from the opinion of many that he was not aggressive enough. Eugene McCarthy, a Democrat running as a peace candidate, nearly matched the number of votes the incumbent president received in an organized write-in campaign in the New Hampshire primary soon after Tet, but later research showed that McCarthy voters who thought Johnson was not tough enough on the war outnumbered those who favored withdrawal by nearly three to two. After two years of decline, public support for the war picked up in the aftermath of Tet but then resumed a downward trend. Surveys conducted in 1980 found that 65 percent of the public and 82 percent of Vietnam combat veterans thought the United States had simply failed to do what was needed to win.[19]

The news media, then, may have fostered inaccurate impressions of Tet, but at the same time they gave the public a better sense of the tenacity of the opponent and of the problems with the administration response. The American involvement did not seem successful, and critics increasingly felt justified in speaking out. The nation grew tired of the longest war in its history, but the pattern of decline of support in the polls was strikingly similar to that of the Korean War, which had strict censorship and a negligible amount of television coverage. Support for the Vietnam War did not drop below the level for the Korean War until the war had gone on longer and had higher casualties.[20] In a book published by the U.S. Army's Center of Military History, William M. Hammond took issue with the military's assumption that the press—television in particular—had turned the public against the war and instead attributed the consternation to the mounting casualties, the administration's limited war strategy, and the perception of officials' dissembling. For all its faults, Hammond said, the reporting was "still often more accurate than the public statements of the administration in portraying the situation in Vietnam."[21] Perhaps the most substantial failing of the press was its constant focus on combat activity at the expense of social and political coverage. In his book *Living-Room War*, Michael J. Arlen described the networks' combat stories as having an "almost unvarying implicit deference to the importance of purely military solutions" and "an excessively simple, emotional, and military-oriented view of what is, at best, a mighty unsimple situation."[22]

Military victory would have required unreasonable costs, and Vietnam was ultimately irrelevant to the outcome of the Cold War, but leaders who did not want to be perceived as losing ground to Communism let the killing drag on until three million Vietnamese and fifty-eight thousand Americans were dead.[23] Robert S. McNamara, who was secretary of defense during the Johnson administration's escalation of the war, publicly admitted three decades later that presidential-military decisions had been wrong, a conclusion he had reached privately by 1967 but chose not to reveal. The United States had good intentions, he wrote in a book published in 1995, but poor judgment about the region and about the options available.[24] Another *mea culpa* book, published four years earlier by McNamara's replacement as defense secretary, Clark Clifford, placed the blame on South Vietnamese allies who were "corrupt, inefficient, and poorly motivated" and on the "false premises and false promises" of American policy. Clifford said that "the bulk of the reporting from the war zone reflected the official position" and that "reporters and the anti-war movement did not defeat America in Vietnam" but that the administration failed to investigate "the growing gap between the optimistic reports of progress that were coming in through the official chain of command, and the increasingly skeptical reporting by some of the journalists covering the war."[25]

Some journalists were raising doubts about the war, but, at least in the early years, the concerns were more about the lack of results than about policies. Many others were simply cheerleaders for much of the Vietnam period. *Time* magazine, for instance, rewrote or discarded the pessimistic reports of its own correspondents and instead relied on the administration's more favorable accounts.[26] Studies of the coverage of the antiwar movement and of the fighting in Vietnam refute the enduring notion that the news media in general were in the forefront of the opposition.[27] Summarizing his research and the work of others, Daniel C. Hallin wrote that "day-to-day coverage was closely tied to official information and dominant assumptions about the war, and critical coverage didn't become widespread until consensus broke down among political elites and the wider society."[28] Content analyses of television stories on Vietnam have found that the public saw little combat and that only about 3 percent of the reports showed casualties.[29] The public did, however, see antimilitarist movies at the time. Film producers, for instance, released *The Activist, Catch 22, Ice, M*A*S*H, Little Big Man, Patton, RPM, Soldier Blue,* and *The Strawberry Statement* in 1970 and *Johnny Got His Gun, Homer, Punishment Park, Summertree,* and *No Drums, No Bugles* in 1971.[30]

American ground rules for journalists discouraged close-ups of the dead and wounded;[31] but the mass media were becoming increasingly visual, and some still images of the war were particularly haunting in their brutal hyperreality: a Buddhist monk setting himself on fire as a protest against the government, the head of a summarily executed Vietcong prisoner jerked by a bullet on a Saigon street during Tet, a naked, screaming, burned girl running from a napalm attack. "The transformation of mass calamity into individual people and incidents arrests the viewers," said Susan D. Moeller in a study of wartime photojournalism. "Through photography, war becomes personal and comprehensible—more than just grand patriotic schemes and unintelligible statistics."[32]

Photographs thus suggested that the struggle for the "hearts and minds" of the Vietnamese was taking a horrific toll on their bodies in ways that were difficult to explain away. Officials did, however, try. The Diem regime claimed that an AP photographer had bribed Buddhist monks to set the monk on fire.[33] In a 1986 speech dealing with distortions in international news coverage, General Westmoreland tried to rewrite history by stating that an investigation had determined that the burned girl, one of five fleeing children in the photograph, had actually been injured in an accident with a hibachi, an open grill. Neither Westmoreland nor the Army, however, could cite any source for the assertion;[34] and the photographer, Nick Ut, had recorded the sequence of events beginning with the napalm being dropped.[35] In a 1989 interview, the woman who had been the girl in the picture and who had survived through fourteen months in a hospital and years of excruciating pain, was not bitter about the attack. "The past is past," said Phan Thi Kim Phuc. "I would ask those pilots what they can do to bring us all together."[36]

Shortly before the Grenada invasion in 1983, a candid article on how to avoid a graphically reported war appeared in the *Naval War College Review.* The author, Arthur A. Humphries, a Navy public affairs specialist, contended that the public had not been able to cope with the "repeated doses of blood and guts" from Vietnam. Reviewing the disinformation and government controls used in the brief war between Argentina and Great Britain in 1982, Humphries concluded that the answer was to "control access to the fighting, invoke censorship, and rally aid in the form of patriotism at home and in the battle zone." The access control turned out to be so extreme in Grenada that little else was necessary. Administration officials and the task force commander, Vice Admiral Joseph Metcalf III, simply prevented reporters from going to the island. Metcalf later wrote that the operation could be seen a "watershed" in "information warfare." The Grenada experience, he thought, would help establish an "equilibrium" between the media, the military, and the government after the ill will that arose over the coverage of Vietnam. In a book on being President Reagan's chief imagemaker, Mike Deaver said he was pleased that the administration "got away with" keeping the press out of Grenada because Americans did not like seeing killing in their living rooms. "I firmly believe that television has absolutely changed our military strategy," he wrote, and "that we will never again fight a major ground war."[37]

The last days of the Gulf War provided evidence for the observation that live, "real-time" coverage pressures leaders to make decisions quickly if public opinion is being aroused by bloodshed or other concerns.[38] In the final hours of the ground fighting, the public could see the devastation of fleeing Iraqi convoys on the "Highway of Death." A controversy soon erupted in the United States and other nations over what appeared to be mass slaughter. General Schwarzkopf received phone calls saying the White House was concerned about the reaction. "I felt irritated," he recalled, "Washington was ready to overreact, as usual, to the slightest ripple in public opinion." Schwarzkopf would "have been happy to keep on destroying the Iraqi military for the next six months" but reassessed his position and decided that the mission of driving the invaders from Kuwait was accomplished and that he should not continue to risk the lives of his soldiers. Another phone call told him that President Bush would announce the end of offensive operations after one hundred hours. "I had to hand it to them," Schwarzkopf thought; "they really knew how to package an historic event."[39]

Packaging the war for media audience consumption was believed to be necessary.[40] The military took extraordinary steps to minimize civilian deaths and fended off Iraqi charges that a "bomb shelter" and a "baby milk plant" had been hit, but lost credibility by concealing carnage.[41] The Pentagon released videotapes showing unerring "smart bombs" blowing up targets but not going astray or killing people. When officers did allow reporters to see a squad of terrified young Iraqis being ripped apart by rounds from an Apache helicopter, the video was quickly removed from circulation.[42] A senior Pentagon official, who was asked for an explanation, said: "If we let people see that kind of thing, there would never again be any war."[43] A guideline for pool photographers said that pictures of recognizable casualties should not be used until the next of kin were notified.[44] Few gruesome pictures became available under the pool restrictions on access.[45] Only 38 of the 1,104 Operation Desert Storm photographs in America's three major newsmagazines showed actual combat activity, while 249 were noncombat, catalogue-style pictures that included images from the Defense Department and arms manufacturers of the Allied military hardware.[46]

In a speech to the National Newspaper Association shortly after the Gulf War ended, General Colin L. Powell, chairman of the Joint Chiefs of Staff, said the military was "as truthful as possible within the necessary and reasonable constraints of security." He pointed out that he and other briefers were aware that what they said "was also being heard by the enemy at the same moment that we said it" and insisted that any restrictions were temporary measures only to protect the lives of soldiers. "In this new environment of thousands of vivid impressions portrayed at warp speed to a world audience," Powell remarked, "we will have to seek new ways to satisfy our dual obligations of informing the people and protecting their legitimate secrets."[47]

The acceleration and democratizing of information allows leaders to convey messages rapidly to each other and to the public, but they may feel pressured to act too swiftly and to create a sound bite for the evening news instead of taking the time to deal with the complexities of an issue.[48] Immediate communication, however, has existed at least since the introduction of the telegraph;[49] and many factors are involved in actual decisions. According to a study of the phenomenon, a media impact seems to be most likely when policies are weakly held, poorly communicated, already in the process of being changed, or lacking in public support.[50] General John M. Shalikashvili, who became chairman of the Joint Chiefs of Staff after the Gulf War, acknowledged a "CNN effect" on leaders but said that they should still be able to make choices and that the decisions would not be as difficult as some imagined. "Governments and publics will become more sophisticated," he asserted, saying that he thought constant exposure to pictures of suffering would only dull the senses.[51] Shalikashvili, however, expressed relief when Americans experienced so few casualties in the occupation of Haiti in 1994. Leaders acting with limited public support have reason to appear as if they do not fear the effects of television, because admitting their vulnerability to public opinion might invite more aggressive resistance from opposing forces.[52] On the other hand, seeing the results of the fighting could make viewers "rally round the flag" if they back a war or could induce a losing enemy to surrender sooner. The scant research that is available has found that seeing realistic pictures of war either has no effect on support or makes viewers more hawkish.[53] At any rate, in the years following the Gulf War, concerns about the sensitivities of electronic media audiences contributed to the development of a new array of nonlethal weapons that are designed to stop but not kill an opponent.[54]

Complaints were also made during and after the Gulf War that live reporting can reveal valuable military information;[55] but such concerns often do not take into account the realities of modern warfare. Commercial satellites can be used by nearly anyone for reconnaissance purposes.[56] Facts are freely dispensed to some opponents. Americans induced fear by giving civilians general warnings about future bombing during World War II;[57] but so weak were Iraqi defenses after continuous air attacks that the Fourth Psychological Operations Group from Fort Bragg set up a radio station, Voice of the Gulf, that announced the precise targets of daily bombing runs in a successful effort to encourage desertions.[58] Before the United States intervened in Haiti three years later, the military gave the press detailed information on the invasion plans in an apparent attempt to intimidate the other side and to speed up negotiations with Haitian authorities. A retired Army officer hired by CNN for commentary advised Haitians not to fight. An agreement was reached, the invasion was called off, and, when the first poorly informed troops of the U.S. "military mission" arrived by helicopter at the Port-au-Prince airport, belly-down and ready to fire their rifles in case of armed resistance, they were relieved to find themselves greeted by reporters. "Emotions were running high," said a soldier interviewed live on CNN. "Then, when we landed over here, I saw a bunch of press, which was good. I assumed that if the press was here, then the enemy probably wasn't."[59]

In more evenly matched armed conflicts, both sides can have many sources of information[60]—often more than they can absorb if they have technologically advanced intelligence-gathering capabilities.[61] The availability of massive amounts of intelligence calls for the use of swiftness and deception. In the Gulf War, coalition soldiers used multiple, high-speed flanking movements based on the fundamental American military doctrine that had been dubbed AirLand Battle and described in a manual sold by the Government Printing Office. Even if his command and control links had not been cut or jammed as they were in the ground war, Saddam Hussein would not have been able to make much sense of what was happening and could hardly have adjusted his orders fast enough, because the American-led forces, unlike his own, had field commanders with considerable discretion to act in quickly changing conditions. "Airland Battle emphasizes the use of American advantages in fast armor and aerial logistics to disorient the enemy with rapidly shifting attacks that are not what they seem; and especially to make sudden flanking movements," explained journalist Gregg Easterbrook.[62]

So many factors of resources, training, tactics, strategy, and moral energy contribute to a victory or loss that it would be difficult to say when the availability of any particular set of rudimentary televised sounds and images would make a difference, especially if enemy troops are already present.[63] A simple television picture of fighting in progress is not usually detailed or comprehensive and is highly unlikely to provide much useful information. In the fast-moving confusion of battle, enemy forces will use their own eyes and equipment. In any event, reporters can now arrive in a combat zone equipped with so many electronic communication devices that censorship can be extremely difficult.[64] At the same time, technological developments in warfare are making actual military operations harder for the news media to see. Overhead reconnaissance and long-distance, precision strike weapons make combat activity less a matter of secret troop movements and more a matter of spending for "smart" or "brilliant" munitions.[65]

The information that is available through the news media can add to the opponent's confusion. Coalition forces and the news media sent so many mixed signals before the ground war that Iraq had little idea what to anticipate. At one point, *Newsweek* published a map showing the possibility of a flanking attack in an empty part of southern Iraq that Schwarzkopf was actually planning to use as a surprise. He was angry, but General Powell told him not to overreact. "Other magazines are full of maps showing other battle plans," Powell said. "They're all just speculating." The *Newsweek* map did not prompt any change in Iraq's deployment of forces.[66] Schwarzkopf, meanwhile, kept the press expecting an amphibious assault on Kuwait City, a feint that fooled both Iraq, which kept ten divisions looking the wrong way, and the news media, which kept twenty-two of the fifty-three Marine pool reporters waiting offshore for an attack that never occurred. Reporters were not watching movements to the west, where soldiers and supplies were being taken for the flanking maneuver. The "Hail Mary" advance into Iraq was a success, and the Marines avoided having to storm the beaches, an extremely dangerous kind of attack. Later analysis concluded that although Schwarzkopf had worried about the ability of CNN to beam information into Saddam's bunker in Baghdad, the general had used the electronic media to make the enemy think what he wanted them to think.[67]

II.

Wartime journalism may help inform the public and assign blame for problems but, like most attempts to recount reality, can be subject to lies and manipulation. As long as commanders have the ability to feign actions and make last-minute changes, the press can be a poor guide to whatever strategies and tactics will actually be used. In fact, military censorship can be difficult to justify at all because so much disinformation is used in armed conflict that an enemy is foolish to rely on the mass media for intelligence gathering. American military leaders have fed falsehoods to their opponents since George Washington, but the press was frequently involved by the Civil War.[68] At one point, for instance, General Ulysses S. Grant's headquarters in Cairo, Illinois, gave reporters a detailed statement about its plans for a large and imminent expedition into Kentucky. Although the story was a ruse and should have been suspicious because of censorship and the need for security, it was widely published, to the anger of reporters who later realized they were duped.[69] At the request of General Robert E. Lee, two Richmond newspapers, the *Whig* and the *Enquirer*, published inaccurate information to deceive General George B. McClellan. So many rumors and distorted stories were printed in the South that a familiar headline was "Important—If True." In 1898 the United States planted fabrications about ship movements in newspapers to keep Spain distracted.[70]

The use of the press to spread lies became a more expected practice in the twentieth century. During World War I dispatches were faked to mislead the other side or to supply some "news" when military restrictions prevented access to the battlefield. By World War II, disinformation and deception were common. In order to delude the enemy the Office of Strategic Services (OSS) conveyed fictitious news stories to neutral countries, spread rumors, and distributed phony publications, but the falsehoods often found their way into the American press and into the intelligence files of the OSS itself.[71] Preparations for battles, especially for D-Day in 1944, made systematic use of deception techniques that included phony radio traffic.[72] Members of Congress and reporters were fooled into believing that the invasion would be led by a nonexistent force headed by General George S. Patton Jr. According to one journalist, "Patton was the perfect military man to attract attention to himself and to the Army that wasn't."[73] The code name for the overall deception plan was Bodyguard, a name possibly inspired by an observation of Winston Churchill: "In wartime, truth is so precious that she should always be attended by a bodyguard of lies."[74] The mass media often were used for disinformation in the Cold War and the Gulf War.[75]

President Eisenhower mastered a method of avoiding the realities of the world. His well-known meanderings at news conferences were later understood to be the deliberate blurring of sensitive issues. A seasoned tactician who was thoroughly briefed, he decided in advance what should be said and what should be circled around. He exercised extraordinary self-control over his public statements while appearing to be a bumbling speaker. During the Quemoy-Matsu crisis, for example, his press secretary, James Hagerty, advised him to give a no-comment answer to reporters, but Eisenhower replied that he would just confuse them if the subject came up. Responding to citizen complaints about fallout from Nevada test sites, Eisenhower told the Atomic Energy

Commission to keep the public "confused" about the nature of the explosions that were killing livestock while officials declared in secret that nothing would be allowed to delay arms development.[76]

The Eisenhower administration, however, saw how costly misleading statements could be when an American U-2 spy plane crashed in the Soviet Union in 1960. A CIA cover story issued by NASA said that a weather observation plane had been lost, and the State Department, apparently assuming that the pilot would have followed instructions by blowing up the U-2 and killing himself if necessary, told reporters that no deliberate attempt had been made to violate Soviet airspace. The Soviets then announced they had captured the pilot, Francis Gary Powers, and that he had confessed to spying. The wrecked plane was put on public display along with an array of damning evidence. The State Department had to admit to the peacetime espionage, but said the flight was unauthorized. Having authorized all U-2 flights himself while denying such secret activities were occurring abroad, Eisenhower was in a position where a leak could destroy what remained of his credibility. Nikita Khrushchev ridiculed the idea the government was not in charge of its forces and said that his country did not send planes over American territory. The president, who was grumbling that he felt like resigning, decided to take general responsibility for asking for intelligence on a Cold War adversary, but not to admit to his knowledge of the missions. At a press conference where he would only speak about the need for his "broad directives," Eisenhower said no one wanted another Pearl Harbor and that the "safety of the whole free world" required intelligence-gathering activities carried out by "their own rules." Less than a week later a summit meeting in Paris collapsed when Khruschev demanded an apology from Eisenhower.[77] In his book *Six Crises*, Richard Nixon pointed to the U-2 affair and an economic slump as major reasons for John F. Kennedy's narrow victory over him in the 1960 presidential election.[78]

The escalation of the Vietnam War occurred under the leadership of a man without a strict devotion to the truth. Before and during his presidency, Lyndon Johnson liked to give reporters wildly exaggerated accounts of his having been on a "suicide mission" during his brief, politically advantageous service in World War II.[79] In 1964, as he faced decisions as commander in chief, key advisers were concluding that the situation in Vietnam was deteriorating and that he should have a congressional resolution for increased intervention. The Tonkin Gulf Resolution was quickly approved after reports indicated that Navy ships had been attacked twice by North Vietnamese patrol boats. The first incident, which amounted to very little, was in apparent retaliation for covert South Vietnamese raids against North Vietnam that were supported by American forces. The second episode probably never occurred. Yet official falsehoods and obfuscations roused the public to accept a new level of commitment. Journalists, conditioned to concur with Cold War certainties, agreed with Johnson that the United States had to respond to aggression and gave little thought to why small patrol boats would confront destroyers.[80]

Every four years voters have an opportunity to be a check on presidential distortions in security matters, but during the twentieth century a prostrate press aided successful candidates in conveying what turned out to be misleading impressions about national defense. Less than a month after being inaugurated for a second term in 1917, Woodrow Wilson, who had campaigned as the man who kept the country out of war, asked Congress to declare war on Germany. Throughout 1940, the year he was elected to a third term, Franklin Roosevelt insisted that the government had no intention of sending troops abroad;[81] but in the following year he sought to involve the United States in World War II with a Europe-first policy. He lied to a reluctant Congress and public about German provocations and may have prompted Adolf Hitler's December 11, 1941, declaration of war on the United States with the help of a press leak three days before Pearl Harbor that detailed a confidential plan for an American expeditionary force in Europe.[82] In 1960 the press accepted the bogus claim of John F. Kennedy that the United States had a "missile gap" with the Soviet Union and was falling behind its Cold War adversary in defense. In 1964 Lyndon Johnson said he was not ready to have "American boys" take over the fighting in Vietnam, but involvement was being covertly expanded, and a troop buildup began shortly after his inauguration in 1965. In 1968 Richard Nixon said he had a "secret plan" for a quick end to the conflict, but he widened the war stealthily once in office. Two weeks before the 1972 election, Nixon's national security adviser, Henry Kissinger, announced that peace was at hand, but instead the war continued until the surrender of the Saigon government in 1975.[83] In 1984 Ronald Reagan was touting his Strategic Defense Initiative antiballistic missile system while his administration was misrepresenting or suppressing classified government reports that made an overwhelming case against the project.[84]

The difficulty journalists have in investigating a presidential candidate's knowledge of secret security issues was illustrated in the long-frustrated attempts to question George Bush's claim that he, as vice president, had been "out of the loop" in the Reagan administration's Iran-Contra arms-for-hostages scandal.[85] For years government officials had been guiding and misleading the press on their covert activities in Central America. In 1988 reporters could not get clear and accurate answers to their questions on Bush's role in the scandal, and his campaign staff stonewalled, charging that the inquiries were partisan.[86] By 1992 the accusations of his involvement were well documented;[87] before agreeing to news program interviews, he insisted that he not be questioned on the subject even though it was becoming a major issue in the presidential race. Four days before the election, former Defense Secretary Caspar Weinberger was charged with making false statements to Congress by saying he had not taken notes relevant to the Iran-Contra affair. The indictment cited notes he had written that contradicted Bush's denials. Before leaving office, Bush, who thought that the disclosure destroyed a comeback surge in the polls and ruined his chances of re-election, may have avoided further revelations by pardoning Weinberger and five others who were connected with the scandal. "President Bush's pardon of Caspar Weinberger and other Iran-Contra defendants undermines the principle that no man is above the law," independent counsel Lawrence E. Walsh said, reacting to the Christmas Eve pardon. "It demonstrates that powerful people with powerful allies can commit serious crimes in high office—deliberately abusing the public trust—without consequence."[88] The combination of presidential secrecy and presidential pardons before a trial allows government officials to cover up wrongdoing and to escape punishment if detected, as Richard Nixon did in receiving a pardon from Gerald Ford.[89]

Richard Nixon was one of the great masters of dangerous self-delusion and phony national security pretexts. As his administration attempted to conceal the American bombing of neutral Cambodia from Congress, the public, and even top military and State Department officials, the White House ordered the FBI to wiretap reporters and government officials in order to detect leaks to the press. The folly of unilaterally waging war in another country, the falsification of bombing records by military personnel who were obeying thousands of irregular orders, and the spying on journalists, who actually did less than they might have with the story, helped to propel Nixon toward impeachment proceedings and resignation. Twenty years after Nixon left office, Henry Kissinger wrote that the mistakes of Vietnam were the lack of clear, realistic objectives and the folly of conducting a war by executive fiat. Kissinger observed that it was the "crucial function" of the media and Congress to expose "intentional misrepresentation by the Executive Branch," but that the leaders "had above all deceived themselves."[90]

Not long after leaving the government, however, Kissinger had harbored few regrets about the attempts to hide the bombing in Cambodia. Although those who were the targets of the air raids clearly knew what was happening, he defended the wiretaps by saying that the electronic eavesdropping was necessary when military decisions were being made. "The motive, which I strongly shared," Kissinger wrote in his 1979 memoirs, "was to prevent the jeopardizing of American and South Vietnamese lives by individuals (never discovered) who disclosed military information entrusted to them in order to undermine policies decided upon prayerful consideration and in our view justified in law and in the national interest."[91] The reasons for the wiretaps, which were made without court orders and which were therefore illegal, according to a later Supreme Court ruling, may have extended beyond dubious arguments for protecting mission security.[92] The White House, journalist Seymour Hersh speculated, may have been concerned about other stories coming to light, including ones that Nixon was drinking heavily when North Korea accidentally shot down an American spy plane over international waters in 1969 and was considering a range of options, including nuclear retaliation.[93]

Norman Schwarzkopf was one of the few high-ranking officers who acknowledged that body counts were fabricated in the Vietnam War. Having been pressured to participate in a "bureaucratic sham" while in combat and convinced that the Army was in "bad shape" morally in those years, he vowed to tell the truth while leading forces in the Gulf War. According to his autobiography, he told himself: " 'Think back to what caused the disenchantment of the American people with Vietnam: they felt that they were constantly being misled with false body counts and optimistic talk about the light at the end of the tunnel.' " His memoirs also noted many failures he had observed in the Grenada invasion, but said he was relieved that the deficiencies were acknowledged in the military's own reports. "We were through trying to paper over problems as we had in Vietnam," he said, "for me, this was the best evidence that the military had changed."[94]

The news blackout in Grenada had concealed a multitude of military blunders, such as the bombing of a mental hospital, the drowning of a SEAL commando team that was not fired upon, the downing of sophisticated helicopters by World War II surplus guns, and serious logistical and intelligence-gathering problems. Declassified documents later revealed poor planning and equipment failures. Because the Navy and ground troops had incompatible radios, for instance, an Army officer had to use his personal credit card to phone his office in North Carolina to arrange air support.[95] Congress, recognizing that interservice rivalries had contributed to the Grenada fiascoes, did pass a bill in 1987 to reorganize chains of command, and the Pentagon, embarrassed by human errors and the failures of high-tech machinery, adopted a more realistic approach to training and a more serious attitude about the need for reliable weapons. The changes helped the armed forces look better in Desert Storm, but, despite administration attempts to make the enemy appear formidable, the American military was outspending Iraq's by as much as forty-to-one, and the Baghdad regime had primitive intelligence capabilities, incompetent officers, and miserable, unmotivated, and poorly trained soldiers who were anxious to surrender. The result could hardly have been anything but a rout. Fewer than 150 Americans died in combat, while roughly one hundred thousand Iraqi soldiers were killed and three hundred thousand were wounded.[96]

Despite Schwarzkopf's professed devotion to honesty, the truth could be a scarce commodity in the Gulf War. As in the Grenada episode, journalists were denied timely access to people and places, and the main sources of information were officials who would have motives to claim credit and avoid blame.[97] Skillful, upbeat briefings kept the press and public sufficiently satisfied with the results of the military operations. The Pentagon's daily briefer, Lieutenant General Thomas Kelly, was given a warm reception on NBC's *Tonight Show*, and Schwarzkopf's press briefing declaring victory was sold as a video.[98] Kelly signed up to earn several million dollars in speaking fees, and Schwarzkopf made a $5 million book deal.[99] The war offered the media an opportunity to achieve better ratings and circulation figures.[100] Journalists who considered Iraqi viewpoints, questioned administration policies, or scoffed at public patriotism could find themselves in trouble and even out of a job.[101]

News stories on the Gulf War usually followed official explanations and marveled at the technical prowess of the armed forces.[102] Survey results showed soaring job approval ratings for the president, as well as overwhelming majorities backing restrictions on press coverage and believing the military was not hiding bad news.[103] As attention shifted to other matters after Desert Storm, however, news stories exposed misleading assessments of weapons performance, gross overestimates of the size of enemy forces, incompatible armed forces computer systems, the statistic that nearly a fourth of American combat deaths were from friendly fire, the evacuation of twelve hundred pregnant women who were on duty in the Gulf, and the Pentagon's failure to inform soldiers about their possible exposure to Iraqi nerve gas.[104] Trickling out as they did in the years following the fighting, such accounts slowly deflated the first euphoric impressions of presidential-military performance.

III.

Proponents of press restrictions often fail to note the extent to which the mass media have worked hand in hand with the government, as they did through the CPI during World War I, the Office of Censorship during World War II, and the CIA during the Cold War. The cooperation could begin at the highest levels of a news organization. CBS Chairman William S. Paley brought Edward R. Murrow to the brink of resignation in 1950 by taking seriously the Army's ban on criticism and refusing to let Murrow, who was about to return from Korea, air a bleak assessment of American prospects and performance in the war.[105] During the 1950s Paley screened employees for communist sympathies;[106] and he allowed the CIA to use CBS press credentials, to gather information from the network's foreign correspondents, to transfer funds through his foundation, and even to allow lip readers to use a CBS booth at the United Nations to figure out what was being said in consultations among members of the Soviet delegation.[107] In 1960 President Eisenhower was angered by an NBC documentary that dared to question the policies behind the crash of the American U-2 spy plane in the Soviet Union earlier in the year. He contacted the head of NBC's corporate parent, RCA's David Sarnoff, a superpatriotic Russian immigrant who replied that he would do all that he could to correct any unpleasantness. Sarnoff, who had been Eisenhower's special assistant for communications in World War II and who had used the network in 1955 to mount a successful military reserve recruitment drive at the president's request, soon ordered a televised tribute to Eisenhower as he left office.[108]

The Cold War press objected to some of the hubristic excesses of secret government;[109] but it often played along with "plausible deniability" for the president, with planted stories, and with other stratagems.[110] From the earliest days of the republic, journalists had supplied confidential information to officials and had even carried out clandestine assignments;[111] but the connections were especially cozy in the Cold War. During the Cuban missile crisis, for instance, ABC's State Department correspondent, John Scali, secretly acted as a contact and negotiator between the two sides.[112] Richard Nixon later appointed him a special consultant for foreign affairs and communications and then United States representative to the United Nations, where he served before returning to ABC News in 1975.[113] Such revolving door experiences were not uncommon. Journalists took jobs in government, and government officials and military officers took jobs in journalism.[114] The phenomenon was particularly striking when it occurred between the news media and the CIA.[115] The more prominent examples include William F. Buckley Jr. having a stint with the agency before becoming a media pundit and Richard Helms, a former wire service reporter who had interviewed Hitler, becoming director of the CIA in 1966.[116] The CIA jeopardized journalists by allowing its agents to pose as employees of news organizations and to use American reporters as paid sources, practices that were discontinued for the most part after many postwar spy agency abuses were revealed in the 1970s.[117]

Often the teamwork with the government has involved editors and reporters withholding highly sensitive information. Believing that mutual trust was possible, Dwight Eisenhower experimented with revealing detailed battle plans to reporters during World War II so that they would have "a feeling of the same responsibility that I and my associates bore" and would not speculate on future troop movements.[118] Back in the United States, journalists honored voluntary restrictions on describing the development of the atomic bomb. William Laurence, a *New York Times* science reporter, was given full access to the project's top secret sites and allowed to ask any questions he had. He was able to witness the first test explosion in the New Mexico desert and the bombing of Nagasaki. Although he knew he could not publish his personal accounts of the events until after the war, Laurence did prepare the government information released by the White House and the War Department when the atomic bomb was dropped on Hiroshima.[119]

Relying on reporters not to reveal the follies and misdeeds they know about, however, makes little sense. During the Sicilian campaign in World War II, one of Eisenhower's most troublesome and yet valued generals, George S. Patton Jr., slapped two sick, hospitalized soldiers and accused them of trying to avoid the battlefront. Cursing in both cases, he kicked one, who had dysentery and malaria, out of the receiving tent and a week later threatened the other, who had symptoms of dehydration and exhaustion, with execution by firing squad. To make his point to the second soldier, the general reached for his pistol and said he ought to shoot the patient himself. Reporters met and agreed to discuss the matter with Eisenhower, who severely reprimanded Patton and told him he would be removed from his command unless he apologized to those who had been present during both episodes and to each of his divisions. Eisenhower told correspondents they were free to report the story but that he believed it could be used as enemy propaganda and might undermine Patton's effectiveness. Although Patton gave vague apologies that attempted to justify his conduct before thousands of soldiers, and the senior AP correspondent, Edward Kennedy, assured Eisenhower that the information would find its way into the press, the journalists did not report the story until several months later, when it drifted back to the United States and was revealed by gossip columnist and broadcaster Drew Pearson. Even Pearson checked first with the domestic branch of the Office of Censorship, which, lacking a provision in its code for objecting, approved the story over the War Department's protests that it would harm morale.[120]

Journalists of the Cold War era often consulted with officials before deciding to publish sensitive stories;[121] and in some cases they concealed facts already known to adversaries.[122] Years before the crash of the U-2 spy plane in 1960, journalists at the *New York Times* and other newspapers had realized that the United States was making secret flights over the Soviet Union, but had voluntarily remained silent, even though they knew the other side was apparently aware of the practice.[123] The American people, however, were ignorant of a long history of frequent, highly provocative espionage flights over the Soviet Union and China. More than 250 airmen went down in hostile territory between 1950 and 1970 while conducting espionage or support missions. At least twenty-four died and ninety survived, but many were simply unaccounted for and may have become prisoners. Families were given false or incomplete information.[124] Despite the U-2 lesson in 1960, journalists suppressed or toned down stories on the preparations for the ill-fated Bay of Pigs invasion in 1961, but enough information came out by various other means for the plan to be common knowledge in Havana and Moscow. President Kennedy later lamented that if more had been published, the United States might have been spared a colossal mistake.[125] In 1962 the *New York Times* agreed to delay the story of nuclear missiles being in Cuba until Kennedy announced their presence.[126]

Journalists can keep leaders informed during an armed conflict and help them communicate with each other. During the Mexican War newspapers could convey war information to Washington more quickly, completely, and accurately than the government's own couriers. During the Civil War, members of Congress relied on journalists for the latest information and called them to testify before committees.[127] President Lincoln often received early news on battles from wire stories;[128] and reporters gave him eyewitness accounts.[129] The first news to reach Washington during the Wilderness campaign, for instance, came from Henry E. Wing, a New York *Tribune* reporter who risked his life in a frantic rush to reach a telegraph. Wing asked for permission to send a hundred words to his newspaper on a government line before telling the War Department all that he knew. Secretary Stanton, however, replied that he wanted to be informed first and threatened the reporter with arrest as a spy if he did not cooperate. Lincoln broke up the resulting standoff by overruling Stanton and allowing the story to go through and to be transferred to the AP. Wing was brought to Washington on a special train and was interviewed by Lincoln and his cabinet when he reached the White House at 2 A.M. Delivering a personal message after the others had left, Wing told Lincoln: " 'General Grant told me to tell you, from him, that, whatever happens, there is to be no turning back.' " Lincoln, who wanted a general willing to fight, gave the reporter an exuberant kiss on the forehead.[130]

Journalists could also be the bearers of bad but important news. During World War II General Eisenhower wanted a reporter to be able "to go wherever he wanted, whenever he wanted" so that suspicions would not arise that "error and stupidity" were being covered up. "These, when discovered," he said, "could be promptly aired and therefore did not grow into the festering sores that would have resulted from any attempt at concealment." Eisenhower regarded reporters as "quasi staff officers" whose mission was to inform the public. "Civilian effort produces the fighting formations and the equipment necessary to achieve victory," he observed. "Civilians are entitled to know everything about the war that need not remain secret through the overriding requirement of military security."[131] General Westmoreland had many frustrations with journalists in Vietnam, but he recognized the contributions of their vigilance. "In the constant search for the negative," he wrote in his memoirs, "the press served as a kind of adjunct to my Inspector General and informed me of many matters that I otherwise might have missed." Westmoreland cited the example of an investigation that was initiated after a reporter showed him a photograph of Americans dragging the body of an enemy soldier behind an armored personnel carrier. "There can be no question that a free and independent press is an essential component of the American form of democracy," Westmoreland said. "So vital an institution is it, so basic, such a staunch bulwark of the American system, that it is well to tolerate some mistakes and derelictions, to make every effort to assure that total freedom and independence continue to exist."[132] Official suppression of the dismal realities of Vietnam meant that the president himself could be inadequately informed.[133]

CNN's reports from Baghdad during the Gulf War were labeled "Cleared by Iraqi Censors";[134] but accusations were made that the network conveyed enemy propaganda.[135] Senator Alan K. Simpson, a Wyoming Republican, called CNN's Peter Arnett an Iraqi "sympathizer" and made the erroneous charge that Arnett's Vietnamese wife had a brother who had been "active in the Vietcong."[136] (One of a group of senators who met with Saddam Hussein in Iraq on April 12, 1990, Simpson told the Iraqi dictator that his problem was with the spoiled Western news media and not with the U.S. government.)[137] Even some competitors suggested that CNN was too cozy with the Iraqis.[138] The network's coverage, however, gave the people of Kuwait hope that the invaders would be driven out, and when CNN crews arrived in Kuwait City they received heroes' welcomes.[139]

CNN served as an immediate messenger service between governments around the world.[140] King Fahd of Saudi Arabia stayed tuned to CNN on sets throughout his palace;[141] and broadcasts from the Middle East regularly provided American officials with useful information. U.S. intelligence agencies studied the video coverage closely for clues about the state of mind of the leaders in Baghdad.[142] President Bush remarked that he learned more from CNN than from the CIA;[143] and General Powell gave CNN credit for telling him and the country what was happening as the war began.[144] "You know, some people are mad at CNN," said Lieutenant General Charles Horner, the Gulf War coalition's supreme air commander. "I used it. Did the attack go on time? Did it hit the target? Things like that."[145] Members of Congress relied on the news media for material not being supplied by the military, but took no action on the problems of access and censorship after getting mired in the apparent conflict between the public's right to know and the safety of soldiers.[146]

General Schwarzkopf worried about the possibility of American journalists revealing valuable military facts, but the most serious incident might have been CNN showing female dancers doing bumps and grinds for United States troops, coverage that upset Saudi religious activists who complained to King Fahd. The story alerted the general to the fact that his orders to respect the host country's sensibilities were not being followed. He canceled later performances by the dancers, who, he discovered, were American employees of a Saudi-owned oil company and their family members. Broadcasts from the enemy's side could also be useful. Halfway through the ground campaign Schwarzkopf learned from a Baghdad radio station report that Iraqi troops were pulling out of Kuwait. He could, of course, use the news media himself. In a case of a general wanting "troop movements" known, Schwarzkopf made sure that television crews had ample opportunities to show the first arrivals of soldiers and equipment in Saudi Arabia to make it appear that they were already there in large numbers. He found the broadcast news conference a good way to convey to Iraq what he called his "message" about the consequences of challenging the coalition, since he assumed "Saddam and his bully boys were watching me on CNN in their headquarters."[147]

The military has also made use of the media to send its messages to more friendly audiences. The more simplistic methods have included posters and animated cartoons.[148] A more subtle approach has been "information subsidies" to journalists. Robert C. Miller, a United Press correspondent during the Korean War, complained about how helpful public information officers were in providing press releases and making sure reporters could get food, liquor, and accommodations. "You can cuss out a censor and the PIO officer will be right there helping you find the right adjective," Miller said, admitting that he and other reporters were spoiled by the assistance and, as a result, were hindered in trying to report critically.[149] When CBS made "The Selling of the Pentagon," a 1971 documentary evidently inspired by Senator J. W. Fulbright's book *The Pentagon Propaganda Machine*, the network successfully fought an attempt by a House of Representatives subcommittee to subpoena the film outtakes. The subcommittee was investigating alleged distortion in the documentary, but the House refused to find CBS and its president, Frank Stanton, in contempt.[150] During the Reagan administration, the Pentagon's public relations activities involved a staff of more than three thousand and an annual budget of $100 million.[151] With the help of military sources and demonstrations, an insurance agent named Tom Clancy became a wealthy, best-selling author of high-tech warfare novels in the 1980s. An advocate of the Strategic Defense Initiative and advanced weapons systems, Clancy helped build support for costly defense programs with his books and the movies based on them.[152]

The motion picture is perhaps the most important means of influencing public perceptions of the armed forces. Understanding the potential impact of films, the military has made its expensive hardware available for movies that convey ideas and images it considers acceptable.[153] The practice of providing equipment existed as early as 1914, when D. W. Griffith filmed the Civil War scenes of his racist epic *The Birth of a Nation* with Army cannons and live ammunition. Before the United States entered World War I, Hollywood produced a number of films decrying war, including *Civilization*, (1916), which relied on Navy assistance to recreate the sinking of the *Lusitania*. The pacifist themes made the film a box office success and helped to boost Wilson's campaign for a second term, but after war was declared the industry immediately began turning out anti-German movies with titles such as *The Claws of the Hun* (1918) and *The Kaiser—Beast of Berlin* (1918). Griffith, who had preached against hate in the three-hour-long *Intolerance* (1916), vilified German soldiers in *Hearts of the World* (1918), with the encouragement and underwriting of the British War Office.[154]

In the following decades the American military became increasingly involved in the movie business. A sequence in *The Big Parade*, a 1925 film directed by King Vidor, used three thousand soldiers, two hundred trucks, and one hundred airplanes.[155] In 1926 the War Department agreed to provide whatever assistance was needed for *Wings*, a story of the thrills and camaraderie experienced by World War I flying aces. The climax of the film used thirty-five hundred troops and sixty planes. When the general in command of the troops was not cooperative enough, the director, William Wellman, "gently reminded him that whether he liked it or not he was working for Paramount Pictures."[156] Such studio control could cause conflicts. Shortly before the release of *Hell Divers*, a 1932 film that presented Clark Gable in his first feature role, the Navy insisted for security reasons that MGM black out portions of shots showing how the landing hook mechanism worked on the aircraft carrier *Saratoga*. The movie was such impressive propaganda for military spending that it was required viewing in the schools of Nazi Germany.[157] By 1986, when Tom Cruise starred in a film about Navy pilots, *Top Gun*, the military clearly had gained the upper hand. The Navy received script approval rights in exchange for the filmmaker's use of Miramar Naval Air Station, two aircraft carriers, and a small fleet of F-14 jets. The only charge was for the fuel the $37 million planes used, at the rate of thousands of dollars an hour. The Navy did not need to make many changes in the movie, which, according to the *New York Times*, drew "explosive cheers from youthful audiences stirred by its Ramboesque triumph over the forces of Communism."[158] *Top Gun* was a Hollywood recruiting poster that helped the Navy score points in its interservice rivalry with the Air Force, but a fatal accident in the film is suggestive of the actual safety problems that caused 170 of the military's 675 F-14s to crash between 1972 and 1996.[159]

The granting or withholding of assistance was particularly important during World War II, when many war movies were made;[160] but other forms of control also existed. Before Pearl Harbor, the movie industry's own self-regulatory apparatus, the Hays Office, discouraged treatments of the crisis in Europe.[161] The office's production code told Hollywood to avoid explicit cruelty or violence and topics that would incite hatred between nations. Charlie Chaplin was able to make *The Great Dictator*, a burlesque of Hitler released in 1940, but as it was being produced the Hays office threatened to create censorship difficulties and forwarded protests to Chaplin, including one from Germany's chief consul.[162] Between the invasion of Poland and Pearl Harbor, however, the industry, which was losing its European markets, stopped ignoring the tragic events and began stressing the need for preparedness and increased involvement. Producers, who were facing antitrust action at the time, offered their services to the White House and set up committees for cooperation with the government on national defense.[163] During the war the Hays Office prevented the use of profanity in portrayals of military life and the showing of the more gruesome results of battle.[164] The Hays Office continued to request the elimination of gore in war movies, such as *The Longest Day* (1962), until its replacement by a movie rating system in 1968.[165] Civilian and soldier audiences sometimes disliked the results.[166] "After the war, I went with another ex-Marine to see John Wayne in *The Sands of Iwo Jima*," recalled veteran and historian William Manchester. "The manager had to ask us to leave the theater because we couldn't stop laughing. It was so bogus. When someone was shot and killed, it looked as though he went to sleep. He just laid down, intact." On Okinawa in 1945, Manchester had been injured by an exploding shell that splattered him with his best friend's body parts. Nearly fifty years later, doctors studying an X-ray of Manchester's heart discovered a bullet in the right ventricle.[167]

The OWI exploited the government's control of movie export licenses to force filmmakers to follow its own guidelines, which emphasized the idea of a "people's war" against fascism. As a result, social and racial problems in the United States were downplayed or eliminated, and, in contrast to Hollywood films of the following decades, the Soviet Union, an American ally, was portrayed favorably. President Roosevelt himself took a strong personal interest in the production of *Mission to Moscow*, a 1943 film that depicted him as an oracular statesman and the Russian people as living happily under a benign government. Detecting a liberal bias in the agency's work, Congress slashed the budget of the OWI's domestic branch in 1943, but the movie liaison work was merely shifted to the overseas branch. Until the end of the war, OWI officials scrutinized scripts to make sure that movies would conform to propaganda standards. An OWI evaluation of *Casablanca* (1943), for instance, complained that Humphrey Bogart's character, Rick, was too cynical for too long, but the film met the agency's criteria (which included lauding popular resistance and distinguishing between good and bad Germans) and became a classic. The OWI, concerned about America's tangled relationships with Vichy and the Free French, did, however, prevent shipment of the movie to North Africa.[168]

After World War II the Pentagon developed explicit regulations for assisting films that promoted military views and denying help to those that did not. An Air Force directive written in 1947, for example, stated that no cooperation would be given when the movie expressed "opinions contrary to Air Force policies."[169] The result was government-approved films such as *Fighter Squadron* (1948), the movie that introduced Rock Hudson to movie audiences. *Fighter Squadron* made such effective use of stock color footage from the Air Force that the movie was used for instructional purposes.[170] Some tightening of military assistance policies occurred after a number of controversies arose over the filming of *The Longest Day* and a soldier was killed while preparing explosives for another movie in 1962. Earlier that year President Kennedy authorized the use of Navy ships for the filming of *PT-109*, a movie that, to the disgust of his political opponents, glorified his service in World War II.[171] The Army supplied technical advisers, equipment, extras, and a military base for *The Green Berets* (1968), a John Wayne movie in which a dovish reporter played by David Janssen is converted to the Pentagon's viewpoint on Vietnam. Francis Ford Coppola tried for several years to get Defense Department assistance in the making of his anti–Vietnam War film *Apocalypse Now* (1979) but was unsuccessful and had to settle for military surplus equipment.[172] In 1991 the Defense Department cooperated with the production of an ABC movie, *The Heroes of Desert Storm*, which used a script approved by the White House. President Bush provided an introduction in which, said a *New York Times* critic, "his war against an outmatched enemy that scarcely fought back was elevated to the invasion of Nazi-controlled Europe."[173] In following years the Pentagon gave help to action hero films such as *Clear and Present Danger*, *True Lies*, *Apollo 13*, *Goldeneye*, and *Air Force One* while refusing to assist movies such as *Major Payne*, *Forrest Gump*, *Crimson Tide*, *Sgt. Bilko*, and *Courage under Fire*, which conveyed unfavorable impressions of the military.[174]

Despite help from Hollywood, government efforts to produce its own films to indoctrinate and inspire have often run into trouble.[175] The CPI shaped much of the crude movie propaganda of World War I;[176] the ignominious results helped engender the widespread distrust of attempts to manipulate the public mind in the following decades.[177] World War II information campaigns began when America's first peacetime draft was instituted in 1940 and soldiers stationed in miserable camps were nearly mutinous.[178] Troops were skeptical and bored at the canned lectures they heard, and officers and politicians disliked what appeared to be propaganda. Thinking that young draftees had only hazy ideas about the reasons for the war, the chief of staff, General George C. Marshall, recruited a popular and idealistic Hollywood director, Frank Capra, to replace the lectures with the acclaimed *Why We Fight* films. Capra's struggle against red tape and a lack of resources could have been the subject for one of his triumph-of-the-little-guy films such as *Mr. Smith Goes to Washington* (1939). His bureaucratic infighting was aggressive enough for him to be threatened with a court-martial in a battle over possession of enemy propaganda films he was incorporating into his work. The seven-part *Why We Fight* series received praise from Allied leaders, and the first one, *Prelude to War* (1942), won an Academy Award for best documentary and had been seen by nine million soldiers by 1945.[179] However, according to surveys conducted by social scientists for the Army's Information and Education Division, the films had no effects on the soldiers' motivations.[180] The Army used every available medium to motivate, explain, and reassure;[181] but studies found the communication efforts to be ineffective and even harmful to morale. American soldiers appeared to be too cynical about authority and too unconvinced that the country was actually in danger.[182] Polls conducted in 1942 found that as much as 35 percent of the public did not have a clear idea of what the nation was fighting for.[183]

A film that did have a strong emotional impact was John Ford's *The Battle of Midway* (1942). Ford, the famed director of westerns, had formed a documentary unit in the OSS that was to make uncensored reports for top officials. Wounded while recklessly filming some of the Midway battle himself, Ford smuggled the exposed footage past Navy censors and had the editing done in secret. The result was shown at the White House, where President Roosevelt was so moved by the scenes of heroic sacrifice that he declared, "I want every mother in America to see this picture." Movie audiences, accustomed to the blandness of films that were heavily censored, were deeply impressed by the reality of war, and people shouted and wept through showings. *The Battle of Midway* shared the Oscar for best documentary with *Prelude to War*, but Ford's next major documentary, *December 7th* (1943), was his downfall as a director of films for the government. The OSS asked Ford to have a crew make a factual documentary on the bombing of Pearl Harbor, but the film, made by cinematographer Gregg Toland, whose credits included *Citizen Kane* (1941), was a semi-documentary with recreated battle scenes and fictional characters who spouted confusing and politically sensitive propaganda. The film upset OWI officials, as well as Admiral Harold Stark, the chief of naval operations when Pearl Harbor was attacked. Stark assailed the film for implying that the Navy had failed to be prepared. Roosevelt ordered that *December 7th* be banned from all showings and that Ford's unit submit all of its productions to censorship by the OWI's Bureau of Motion Pictures. Ford's best subsequent work for the government was sanitized, impounded, or lost, but he did have the eighty-three minutes of *December 7th* chopped down to a much shorter version that was acceptable. The edited version, which avoided controversy and featured an upbeat ending with workers repairing the fleet, won an Oscar for best short documentary.[184]

Another legendary director, John Huston, was clearly at odds with the military mindset in his work for the Signal Corps during World War II. Huston, who had been a boxer and journalist before turning to movie acting and screenplays, had made his directorial debut with *The Maltese Falcon* in 1941. A cynical realist who was adept at film noir, he portrayed the gore, destruction, and futility of war in *The Battle of San Pietro*. Twice during the filming he was nearly killed after Army intelligence told him it was safe to enter the small Italian town and he had to escape bullets and shelling. The high-ranking officers present at the first showing walked out in disgust, and a War Department official told Huston that the film was "anti-war." "I pompously replied that if I ever made a picture that was pro-war, I hoped someone would take me out and shoot me," Huston said in his memoirs. *The Battle of San Pietro* was regarded as bad for morale and classified secret until General Marshall decided that soldiers in training should see the film to be prepared for the shock of combat. Marshall thought the film would be too strong for the public, but he watched it with Ben Hibbs, the editor of the *Saturday Evening Post*, who convinced him that it would awaken America's fighting spirit. "The sheep fell into line," Huston recalled. "Everyone praised the picture. I was decorated and promoted to major." Marshall did want some of the dismemberments and body bags eliminated, but the edited version that was released in 1945 did contain enough of the horrors of war to have a powerful impact. The War Department, however, refused to release Huston's last documentary for the Army, *Let There Be Light*, which depicted the psychiatric treatment of returning soldiers. The War Department contended that the film invaded the privacy of the patients, said that their signed releases had mysteriously disappeared, and refused to seek any new permissions. The Army's public relations office did agree to a showing at the Museum of Modern Art, but two military police officers confiscated the print shortly before it was to go on the screen. In 1970 the Archives of American Films, a government agency in Washington, D.C., was refused a print to show in a series of Huston's documentaries. Huston concluded the military "wanted to maintain the 'warrior' myth, which said that our American soldiers went to war and came back all the stronger for the experience."[185]

Generally more subdued than their predecessors, the government propaganda movies of the Vietnam era had to compete with more critical press coverage and an increasingly strong antiwar movement. Defense Department films, which were not released theatrically, were mainly for influencing soldiers who had to fight a war that was much more controversial and difficult to understand than World War II. Like the *Why We Fight* series, *Why Vietnam?* (1965) explained official American thinking and blamed enemy aggression for the conflict. *The Unique War* (1966) and *Vietnamese Village Reborn* (1967) adopted an ethnographic appearance to depict paternalistic American benevolence toward a people in need. *Know Your Enemy—the Viet Cong* (1968) instructed soldiers on the methods used by the enemy, and *Your Tour in Vietnam* (1970) stressed the rewards of male bonding, using technologically sophisticated equipment, and defending freedom.[186] The soldiers, of course, had their own firsthand experiences with the war and could simply reject the indoctrination.

The task of winning civilian hearts and minds was complicated by already existing viewpoints. Propaganda aimed at the South Vietnamese, which relied on perceptions and psychological warfare techniques developed in the United States, publicized the advantages of liberal democracy, but the leaders in Saigon showed few signs of willingness to share power, and their American backers had difficulty overcoming the appearance of being the latest in a series of foreign invaders. Many of the people caught between the opposing forces remained uncommitted until the conflict was resolved militarily.[187] In 1971 the United States Information Agency released *Vietnam! Vietnam!* in a vain effort to drum up enthusiasm for the war in other countries. Although the film was an impressive effort, with Charlton Heston as the narrator and John Ford as the nominal producer, an overwhelming majority of foreign outposts, apparently fearing local reaction to faltering policies, refused to show it. Not merely another blast of good-versus-evil propaganda, the film did acknowledge dissent by including comments from critics of the war. The dissenters, however, were immediately answered by war veterans and refugees from communist countries, and demonstrations against the war were condemned as encouraging to the other side. *Vietnam! Vietnam!* could not be very convincing as long as viewers were aware of American wrongdoing in the war and of crime, racism, and other social ills in the United States.[188]

If individuals are sophisticated enough to doubt censored stories and to see through government propaganda, then the role of the more or less independent news media in supplying perceptions of a war can be particularly important. A press that is supposed to be free, skeptical, and objective can be regarded as a credible source of information and ideas, but news organizations are vulnerable to outside and self-imposed pressures.[189] Officials who cannot stop the flow of mass communication can find ways to delay stories until they are no longer news and to divert attention with easily gathered, government-processed information. People in power can manage facts and manipulate images to blunt the sharper edges of coverage and commentary, but journalists themselves can be less than honest and informative. "We edited ourselves much more than we were edited," John Steinbeck said of World War II journalism. "We felt responsible to what was called the home front."[190] CBS received thousands of telephone calls, most of them hostile, after broadcasting Morley Safer's story on Marines burning Cam Ne in 1965.[191] Recalling the angry letters he received, veteran war correspondent Malcolm Browne said in his memoirs that candid reporting is the last thing most people want when the subject is armed conflict. "War is thundering good theater," he said, "in which cheering the home team is half the fun."[192]

Reporters who do dare to challenge authority and conventional thinking can encounter stiff resistance. The correspondents who were revealing American deceit in the early years of the Vietnam War, for instance, found themselves under fire not only from the government, but also from news organizations that included their own. Their stories were revised or killed, and they suffered other indignities.[193] David Halberstam, Vietnam correspondent for the *New York Times*, lost a substantial portion of his $195 weekly paycheck because the paper deducted $12 a day from the salaries of overseas reporters since they were on expense accounts and were therefore saving money they would have spent at home. Neil Sheehan of United Press International was told to take time to sign up new clients in Vietnam for his wire service and to collect from the ones who owed money.[194] The American press pays little attention to the situations in most other countries until a crisis erupts and then often fails to understand what is happening.[195] Media companies violate a momentous trust by not resisting government deceit and controls, by not investing in the quality of their products, and by not risking the displeasure of a public that has a right but sometimes not a strong desire to know.

Conclusion

The tattered history of the First Amendment shows how freedom of expression deteriorates not only because of the inherent difficulty of appreciating abstract ideals, but also because of shortsighted impulses. The practice of silencing dissenters on defense issues seems to suggest that all truth has been established and that other viewpoints could not be useful.[1] On the other hand, constraints on mere words may imply that one's position cannot stand up to questioning or that discord is so debilitating for a weak-minded public that nonconformity must be bludgeoned. Although war is an excruciating experience, healthy disagreement exists on other painful topics without society grinding to a halt. Americans have been cohesive and courageous enough to fight for causes.[2] The liberties guaranteed in the First Amendment need not and may not be suspended, but politicians and the armed forces have assumed the power to violate its prohibition of government abridgment of freedom of the press. Officials could be stopped by legal actions if courts were willing to accept the plain meaning of the Bill of Rights or at least were able to reject the illusory arguments that have supported restraints on reporting and commentary.

The press clause has been discarded at times that are said to be too perilous for the founders' faith in freedom of expression. Yet suppression itself is dangerous. After the Sedition Act of 1798 proved damaging to the Federalists, no serious consideration was given to passing such legislation again until World War I, when enforcement of the Espionage Act and Sedition Act was politically costly to the Democrats. Over the same span of time, however, presidents and military officers began claiming an extraconstitutional authority to act for the safety of soldiers and the nation. With predictable results, they stretched their authority to include control of the press and sought personal advantages in repression. The pitfalls should have been obvious after Andrew Jackson's ill-fated attempt to use martial law in the War of 1812 and the embarrassments caused by the erratic, crude prior restraints employed in the remaining wars of the nineteenth century. Censorship techniques, both voluntary and mandatory, became more bureaucratic in the two world wars but were still highly controversial. At various times in later conflicts the military chose to emphasize secrecy, news management, and access denial, methods that can prevent the press from having information in the first place. Whatever methods are used, the government can jeopardize its own efficiency with the confusion and cumbersome procedures of concealment. Excessive secrecy, for instance, complicated the Carter administration's attempt to rescue hostages in Iran in 1980. Security precautions were so tight that preparations were made without sufficient advice and without adequate information for the forces involved.[3] The failure of the mission contributed to Carter's defeat in the 1980 election.

Wartime restraints and lies may occasionally offer short-term benefits for a politician, but they give ammunition to opponents and corrode the ethos of a democracy. In contrast to presidents who have understood the problems with press restraints, such as George Washington and James Madison, those who have violated the press clause, such as John Adams, Abraham Lincoln, and Woodrow Wilson, or who failed to be frank and forthcoming with journalists, such as Lyndon Johnson and Ronald Reagan, invited the harm that was done to their political support and historical reputations. Presidents, for the most part, have been left to make their own choices. When Bill Clinton was asked about policies on coverage of military actions in 1994, he said he did not know enough to make a decision and had not made up his mind. "I'm not rebuffing you," he told the questioner at a meeting of the American Society of Newspaper Editors, "I'm just telling you I have not thought it through, and I don't know what my options are." Clinton did go on to say that the nation's founders had set up "untrammeled" journalistic freedom "because nobody could think of any practical way to limit the press."[4]

Even if the Constitution did provide a presidential-military power to restrict press freedom, the authority would not be beneficial in most cases. Early and careful media analysis of troubles not being addressed can help the military avoid costly mistakes. Unrestricted news coverage helps to assure that the armed conflict conforms to international law[5]—and to the political and psychological dimensions of national defense. As military public affairs analyst Harry F. Noyes III has pointed out, nations do not just fight in wars, they also "must take sound diplomatic, economic, social and cultural measures and communicate them well." He has argued that the military and the media need each other, and that press accounts are as much a part of war as the weapons, because winning in the battle of public opinion requires that combat be "*credibly* communicated to the world." The forces of a free nation, Noyes contended, should show faith in free institutions and should realize that having negative stories enhances believability. "Sometimes in the Gulf we seemed to be stacking the deck for 100 percent positive coverage," Noyes said. "That hurt us more than it helped."[6]

If, as Thucydides concluded, the origins of wars can be traced primarily to highly emotional perceptions of danger, honor, and interest, then citizens need to see through the smoke of propaganda and censorship.[7] If they do not, then their leaders may have unchecked power. When the various branches of government fail to limit groundless prerogative, public opinion may be the last resort.[8] Therefore, although the president and military may have to control territory on a map, they should not have the power to subdue the realm of thought. Journalists who rely too much on official sources and underproduce vital information have to share the blame for the nation's blunders. Research shows that people are highly resistant to elite persuasion when adequately informed, but that they are more likely to be deceived when government officials monopolize knowledge—as they tend to do with military and foreign policy matters— and authoritative opposition voices are not being heard. American public opinion is remarkably stable and predominantly rational in the sense that it reflects prevalent values and is responsive to new facts and circumstances. Ignorance—often combined with the manipulation of popular, patriotic symbols—gives leaders leeway to take unpopular and irresponsible actions.[9] "In the land of the blind," says the ancient adage, "the one-eyed man is king."

Candor and informed debate may appear to be dangerous luxuries in wartime, but fostering cynicism by distorting reality or limiting consideration of alternatives can be an even greater risk. Preferring democratic discussion, rectitude, and legitimacy is a less romantic notion than the idea that any leadership will be so rational and honest that public examination and deliberation will be unnecessary. The American political system rests on its ability to protect the future from the past and present. Under a liberal constitution that adheres to the principle of limited government, laws and leaders are only legitimate as long as they can be changed, and change must rest upon the opinions of an enlightened citizenry. Public controversy can be seen as a positive, creative force.[10]

Accepting suppression as a solution leads to unintended consequences. Policies built on lies, dogma, and forced assent tend to ring hollow, cover up failures, and collapse ignominiously. Striving for as much common sense and bona fide consensus as it can when under stress is one indication of a nation's mental and moral health. Being honest enough to admit mistakes and accept responsibility readily, however, is an uncommon trait. The press has to be involved in tweezing out the thorns that infect national defense. The military, for instance, long resisted journalistic investigations of its careless handling of many kinds of toxic materials. By the final decade of the twentieth century, thousands of dangerously polluted sites were scattered across the United States. The Pentagon's inspector general estimated that the cleanup costs could be as much as $120 billion.[11]

Having to follow senseless notions of security can be disheartening and ultimately foolish. Frederick Palmer, a distinguished war correspondent who served as General Pershing's chief censor in World War I, wrote in his memoirs that he had played "the part of a public liar to keep up the spirit of the armies and the peoples of our side" but thus had worn a "hair shirt which had cut through my flesh to the ribs to my very soul." Arguing against censorship laws, George Creel, the chief American propagandist in World War I and a person who had difficulty admitting that he participated in repression, remarked after the war that it is the tendency of such legislation "to operate solely against the weak and powerless" and to slip "over into the field of opinion, for arbitrary power grows by what it feeds on." Byron Price, director of the Office of Censorship during World War II, expressed his frustration by complaining in his memoirs about "the belief among men in uniform in wartime that, regardless of the ground rules, a Divine Right to censor had been bestowed upon the Military." Elmer Davis, head of the OWI from 1942 to 1945, had similar experiences with military officers who, he said, had difficulty understanding that "a democracy fighting a total war will fight it more enthusiastically and effectively if it knows what is going on" and feels that all the facts that should be available are available. Pierre Salinger, President Kennedy's press secretary, concluded in 1966 that a lesson to be learned from the "improvisation" of media relations in Vietnam was "that despite all the motivations which exist to the contrary the government can never expect success for a press policy which does not rely on total candor."[12]

Leaders often delude themselves by leaping to conclusions, by failing to define realistic objectives, and by ignoring history and culture.[13] Because they lack complete wisdom and knowledge, the question of how they come to see their errors is of critical importance. Candid accounts by an independent, unfettered press can reveal problems rapidly to decision makers who otherwise would have to rely to a great extent on the slowly filtered versions of their government bureaucracies. Attaining peace in a world that has suffered countless wars requires active efforts to avoid miscalculations and misunderstandings. Having accurate knowledge of another nation's intentions, strength, and strategies can deter hostilities in some cases by showing that a war is unnecessary or would be too costly to fight.[14] When information is kept from the other side, unsafe suspicions about plans and capabilities can arise. "Ignorance breeds prejudice and distrust," CBS correspondent Eric Sevareid wrote, in an essay on the censorship problems he experienced during World War II. "From distrust comes fear, and from fear, in the modern world, nothing can come save war."[15]

In any event, thought and communication are difficult to restrain, especially in an age of electronic interaction that does not stop at national borders.[16] In applying a "futility principle" to First Amendment jurisprudence, courts could conserve resources and preserve respect for the law by recognizing that suppressing speech is usually a highly difficult or impossible task.[17] Controls on fact and opinion often fail to work. Even Germans living under Hitler listened to broadcasts from Allied countries, despite penalties that included death for repeating what they heard. People could be executed for resistance as meager as joking about the Nazi regime, but in some cases public dissent did obtain reversals of repressive policies.[18] Yet, while many thousands of German citizens actively participated in the horrors of the Holocaust, most simply acquiesced or, as Primo Levi has written, "didn't know because they did not want to know."[19] The perpetrators made efforts to hide their crimes and treated the details as a state secret, but the scale of the operations made them all but impossible to ignore.[20] With many Germans feeling guilt and choosing to distance themselves from the genocide, Nazi propaganda insisted that annihilation of the Jews was necessary for German survival and warned that they would take terrible revenge if the war were lost.[21] Ultimately, however, people have an undeniable responsibility for the actions of their governments and cannot excuse themselves by saying they were ignorant, afraid, or deceived.

If the United States government asks citizens to give up their resources and risk their lives for a war, then they deserve to have the pertinent information on the conflict so that they can discuss the options free of constraints. Individuals who are well informed are unlikely to fight for inconsequential reasons or to tolerate egregious errors in the armed forces. Even in the depths of the Cold War, the *Army Almanac* recognized that the people "have the right to know, in whatever detail they desire" how the military is spending its money and treating its soldiers. Yet military personnel are not disinterested parties, and they avoid providing the public with significant information about their failures. In his report to the president on the OWI, Elmer Davis complained that high-ranking officers got little or no training in press relations and realized that a serious mistake could ruin their careers. "Naturally this encourages a tendency to play safe," Davis wrote, "or what seems to be safe."[22]

The government has gone to great extremes for supposed safety. Policies on openness frequently have been ignored where they could lead to embarrassment or some form of retribution. Five years after the end of the Cold War, the Pentagon was still spending about $5 billion a year on what a member of the House Permanent Select Committee on Intelligence described as "a document classification system stuck on autopilot."[23] The government was still keeping secrets from before World War I;[24] more than thirty-two thousand employees were managing classified documents in the mid-1990s.[25] More than two million federal officials and a million people in private industry were authorized to keep information secret.[26] At the same time, more than $25 billion was being spent annually on spy satellites and other means of collecting information abroad.[27] Although the Constitution requires that "a regular statement and account of the receipts and expenditures of all public money shall be published from time to time" (Article 1), tens of billions of dollars a year were being hidden in false accounts for secret weapons programs and intelligence activities.[28] The lack of public accountability allowed numerous follies. Not until 1995, for example, did the CIA determine, after spending tens of millions of dollars, that a Cold War program of hiring psychics to "spy" on other countries was a waste of money.[29] By then, after years of overrating the Soviet threat and being fooled by a series of moles and double agents, the CIA had acquired what one senator called an "aura of incompetence."[30]

Many of the day-to-day activities of the government are more detrimental than anything the press is capable of perpetrating. The most serious security breaches of the 1980s and 1990s, for instance, involved not journalists publishing information but rather poorly supervised intelligence community insiders who sold enormous quantities of highly sensitive information in order to buy conspicuous luxury items.[31] One of them, Aldrich Ames, a CIA counterintelligence officer, revealed more than a hundred covert operations and the identities of more than thirty spies, at least ten of whom disappeared or were executed.[32] In a statement made as he was sentenced to life in prison in 1994, Ames said he felt "shame for this betrayal of trust, done for the basest of motives" but explained that he had come to see the espionage business as a "self-serving sham" involving "scare-mongering by bureaucrats who know better."[33]

Secret government activities are so common that Americans frequently accept conspiracy theories.[34] Some spend enormous amounts of time investigating claims ranging from government involvement in the assassination of John F. Kennedy to military contact with alien spacecraft. Such speculations are fed by actual lies, secrecy, and revelations of wrongdoing. The Kennedy killing, which occurred against the backdrop of Cold War plots and of politicians' connections to organized crime, has been difficult to study because many thousands of pages of documents remained unavailable, even after Congress passed a law in 1992 to open them.[35] Seemingly the only theory that is not advanced in the hundreds of books on the Kennedy assassination is that he killed himself.[36] Much of the conjecture about contact with UFOs has centered on a Nevada air base so secret the government has refused to admit that it exists, a facility where workers have complained of injuries from toxic materials and immense "black budget" sums have been spent on highly questionable projects.[37] In some cases, such as the POW/MIA issue, suspicions have been promoted by candidates seeking support and movie producers trying to fill theater seats.[38]

The military and spy agencies should have realistic insecurities about their levels of performance and should be as open to scrutiny as possible. The United States may have more freedom for public outcry than many countries, but official actions in the Cold War, particularly in Vietnam, demonstrated the dangers of public ignorance.

Reporters who specialize in defense matters are few in number;[39] and official sources dominate national security stories.[40] Members of Congress tend to see excessive military spending as a jobs program and, ultimately, a source of votes and campaign contributions.[41] Close inspection should be given to the military programs of a country that had nearly four trillion dollars in costs for nuclear weapons in the fifty years following Hiroshima and Nagasaki[42]—a country of social decay where black males can be murdered at double the death rate of American soldiers in World War II and where, in contrast to the fifty-eight thousand Americans who died in the ten years of the Vietnam War, two hundred thousand people can be killed and many more wounded by their fellow citizens in a decade.[43] With cuts in superfluous and scandalously expensive defense programs, tens of billions of dollars a year could be redirected toward the environment, housing, education, and infrastructure improvements that would provide jobs and reduce the nation's domestic warfare.[44]

The military's habit of hampering coverage of foreign wars can mean that impressive feats and moving episodes of battle are not recorded for posterity.[45] Reporters had access to much of the fighting in World War II and were able to produce some of the most poignant and powerful journalism ever written about soldiers.[46] "Certainly the presence of journalists gave them some slight lifting of the heart in the knowledge that they and their work were not obscure and unnoticed, that if they became victims, somebody somewhere would know why and how it happened," Eric Sevareid said. "Nothing is quite so awful as anonymity."[47] In contrast, during the Gulf War, the press was unable to witness the *Missouri*, the dreadnought on which the Japanese surrender had been signed in 1945, providing naval gunfire support for the first time since World War II because the captain refused to have reporters aboard the ship.[48] General John M. Shalikashvili, chairman of the Joint Chiefs of Staff during a number of military operations in the 1990s, said that his experience showed that more access for reporters meant better-informed stories and therefore a better-informed and more supportive public. "In fact, I submit that the press should be free to go and do its job with restrictions only in the narrowest sense for safety and operational security," he said, adding that any restrictions should be quickly lifted.[49]

Unless they can control all means of transportation to a war and all means of communication from the battlefields, military authorities must be prepared to work with the news media. Journalists should be able to accept self-imposed limits if they are mutually agreed upon and truly intended to protect themselves and soldiers.[50] A year after the end of the Gulf War, media representatives and Pentagon officials met and established nine principles for open and independent combat coverage. The two sides agreed that pools should not be the standard method, but could be used to provide early access to an area and then be disbanded as soon as possible. Journalists could expect access to all major units, transportation when feasible, and the ability to transmit stories with or without military help. The statement said military public affairs officers were not to interfere with reporting, but that journalists who did not follow clear military security ground rules for the protection of forces and their operations could lose their credentials and be excluded from the combat zone.[51] A separate Defense Department "Principles of Information" policy maintained that information would not be withheld "to protect the government from criticism or embarrassment" but could be withheld "only when disclosure would adversely affect national security or threaten the safety or privacy of the men and women of the Armed Forces."[52] The military had wanted security review of stories for troop and operational safety with the final decisions being made by the news organization involved, but the media representatives said the process would be unwarranted and unnecessary, since journalists could be expected to follow proper ground rules.[53] The military did not insist subsequently on security review while enforcing the "air-exclusion zone" in Iraq and the troop deployment in Bosnia.[54]

The Constitution leaves the final determination of what to publish and broadcast to the news media, but the military may not be required to give total cooperation to reporters who jeopardize their lives and missions. In any case, reasons for suppression often evaporate on close examination. In criticizing the Gulf War restrictions on the press, Walter Cronkite, the venerable CBS anchor, recalled winning arguments with censors by pointing out that the enemy already had the information in question. "Once in England the censors held up my report that the Eighth Air Force had bombed Germany through a solid cloud cover," he wrote. "This was politically sensitive; our air staff maintained we were practicing only precision bombing on military targets. But the censors released my story when I pointed out the obvious—Germans on the ground and the Luftwaffe attacking bombers knew the clouds were there. The truth was not being withheld from Germans but Americans."[55]

Will journalists who are free to report what they know violate principles fixed firmly in public opinion and place lives in jeopardy? The resulting outrage would be a formidable deterrent, and reporters can exercise self-control even when they have an exciting story. When Iranians took hostages at the American embassy in Teheran in 1979, for instance, a number of journalists knew but did not disclose that some American diplomats had escaped and gone into hiding at the Canadian embassy.[56] If opponents acquire information while it is still apparently useful, how can they rely on what might be disinformation? If the military insists on keeping legitimate secrets from the press—such as the fact a pilot is awaiting rescue behind enemy lines[57]— then the concealment should be done with the kind of professionalism and self-discipline the armed forces should possess. If the press nevertheless obtains important military information without authorization, such as plans for troop movements, are the plans really secret, and should they not be changed? In a brief he filed in the *Pentagon Papers* case and in later testimony before a Senate subcommittee, Thomas I. Emerson argued colloquially that a cat in the bag cannot be treated the same way as a cat outside the bag: that information that escapes from government possession becomes part of the public domain.[58] In the first two hundred years of the Bill of Rights, many presidential-military mistakes and misdeeds were covered up in the name of safety. Achieving international peace and battlefield proficiency is difficult, because politicians and soldiers operating out of public view are unlikely to do an adequate job of policing themselves.[59] In theory press freedom can cost lives, but in reality the incompetence and unsound policies journalists should be exposing are the most serious hazards in the domain of national security.

The cultures of the military and the news media do not have to clash on coverage of defense issues. Mutual mistrust can be overcome with better communication and with confidence-building efforts to find solutions. "On one hand was the press, impatient of reticence and suspicious of concealments, and on the other hand were generals and admirals reared in a school of iron silence," George Creel said of his CPI experiences during World War I. "Both, however, grew in understanding. The press finally realized our honesty of purpose, and the military experts came to have an increasing faith in the power of absolute frankness."[60] Despite his complaints about working with the Army and Navy during World War II, Elmer Davis expressed satisfaction with "the day-to-day collaboration which was in the main harmonious and productive."[61] Agreements should be possible when military leaders understand that fears do not simply cancel fundamental freedoms and when reporters are able to admit that they are responsible for more than beating the competition and holding the attention of news consumers. As ethics codes for journalists have recognized, the press needs to respect both the importance of truth and the necessity of minimizing harm.[62] The military must comprehend the nature of news work and grasp the fact that a democratic nation demands information. Even General William T. Sherman, as he blasted war correspondents in his memoirs, realized that, as a practical matter, the public was so hungry for news that obstructing coverage was hazardous for a commander. "Time and moderation must bring a just solution to this modern difficulty," he wrote.[63]

Freedom of the press, like any liberty, naturally involves some uncertainty, but the dangers associated with First Amendment rights are frequently exaggerated, and so-called secrets often are not secret at all. Yet officials can insist on so much concealment that the press has difficulty finding out and publishing adequate amounts of defense information in a timely way. "The appeal to public emotions, the temptations to exploit national security claims for illegitimate purposes, the absence of normal political safeguards due to secrecy factors, and the inherent vagueness of the national security concept," Thomas I. Emerson observed, "all make the supervisory and checking powers of the courts especially relevant in national security cases." What the courts should recognize in making their rulings is that the Constitution's prohibition of laws abridging press freedom means what it says. "Precisely because the survival argument is so seductive, it should be taboo in American constitutional discourse and in the public discourse of all open societies," Rodney A. Smolla has contended. "Let governments cry that the sky is falling and that Constitutions must yield, and let the people have the courage to ignore them." Allowing the president and the military a prerogative power to curtail rights as important as the press clause is more risky than relying on news organizations to do their tasks properly. "Those who would give up essential Liberty, to purchase a little temporary Safety," wrote Benjamin Franklin, "deserve neither Liberty nor Safety."[64]

Notes

Works frequently cited in the notes have been indentified with the following abbreviations:

CJR *Columbia Journalism Review*
E&P *Editor & Publisher*
FED Hamilton, Alexander, James Madison and John Jay. *The Federalist*. Edited by Jacob E. Cooke. Middletown, Conn.: Wesleyan University Press, 1961.
NYT *New York Times*
OR *The War of the Rebellion: A Compilation of the Official Records of the Union and Confederate Armies*. Washington: Government Printing Office, 1880–1902.
PAH *The Papers of Alexander Hamilton*. Edited by Harold C. Syrett et al. New York: Columbia University Press, 1961–1987.
PJM *The Papers of James Madison*. Edited by William T. Hutchinson et al. Chicago and Charlottesville: University of Chicago Press and University Press of Virginia, 1977–.
PWW *The Papers of Woodrow Wilson*. Edited by Arthur S. Link. Princeton: Princeton University Press, 1966–1994.
WAL *The Collected Works of Abraham Lincoln*. Edited by Roy P. Basler. New Brunswick, N.J.: Rutgers University Press, 1953.
WGW *The Writings of George Washington*. Edited by John C. Fitzpatrick. Washington: Government Printing Office, 1931–1944.

Preface

1. Benjamin Franklin to Sir Joseph Banks, July 27, 1783, in *The Writings of Benjamin Franklin*, ed. Albert H. Smyth (New York: Macmillan, 1905–1907), 9: 74.

2. At a Grand Army of the Republic convention in 1880, Sherman said, "There is many a boy here today who looks on war as all glory, but boys, it is all hell. You can bear this warning voice to generations yet to come." In repetitions by others, the observation was shortened to the more pithy and famous comment, "war is hell." Paul F. Boller Jr. and John George, *They Never Said It: A Book of Fake Quotes, Misquotes, and Misleading Attributions* (New York: Oxford University Press, 1989), 119.

Farewell Radio and Television Address to the American People, January 17, 1961, in *Public Papers of the Presidents of the United States, Dwight D. Eisenhower, 1960–61* (Washington, D.C.: Government Printing Office, 1961), 1038.

Chapter 1

1. Madison, "The Federalist No. 10," in *FED*, 59.

2. *The Rights of Man*, pt. 2, chap. 5, in *The Complete Writings of Thomas Paine*, ed. Philip S. Foner (New York: Citadel Press, 1945), 1: 400.

3. "On the Common Saying: 'This May Be True in Theory, but It Does Not Apply in Practice,' " in *Kant: Political Writings*, 2nd ed., ed. Hans Reiss, trans. H. B. Nisbet (Cambridge: Cambridge University Press, 1991), 92. For several examples, see M. C. Jacob, ed., *Peace Projects of the Eighteenth Century* (New York: Garland, 1974). One of the efforts was printed, with doubts about its chances for success, by Benjamin Franklin at his press near Paris in 1782. See Pierre-André Gargaz, *A Project for Universal and Perpetual Peace* (New York: George Simpson Eddy, 1922). For an American attempt, see Sidney Kaplan, ed., "A Plan of a Peace Office for the United States by Benjamin Rush," *Massachusetts Review* 25 (Summer 1984): 269–84.

4. Peter Gay, *The Enlightenment: An Interpretation* (New York: W. W. Norton, 1966, 1969), 2: 401; on the views of Voltaire, Kant, and others, see 401–7.

5. Montesquieu, *The Spirit of Laws*, trans. and ed. Anne M. Cohler, Basia Carolyn Miller, and Harold Samuel Stone (Cambridge: Cambridge University Press, 1989), 132, 139.

6. "Perpetual Peace: A Philosophical Sketch," in Reiss, *Kant*, 100.

7. *National Gazette*, January 31, 1792, in *PJM*, 14: 206–9.

8. On the notion of the king as benevolent unifier, see Jerrilyn Greene Marston, *King and Congress: The Transfer of Political Legitimacy, 1774–1776* (Princeton: Princeton University Press, 1987), 20–34.

9. [Philadelphia] *General Advertiser*, October 16, 1790.

10. *Rights of Man*, pt. 2, chap. 3, in Foner, *Writings of Thomas Paine*, 1: 361–63.

11. Jeffery A. Smith, "The Enticements of Change and America's Enlightenment Journalism," in *Media and Revolution: Comparative Perspectives*, ed. Jeremy D. Popkin (Lexington: University Press of Kentucky, 1995), 74–89.

12. On the rural market for print, see David Jaffee, "The Village Enlightenment in New England, 1760–1820," *William and Mary Quarterly*, 3rd ser., 47 (July 1990): 327–46.

13. [Boston] *Columbian Centinel*, November 23, 1793.

14. The only issue of *Publick Occurrences* was dated September 25, 1690. For background, see William David Sloan, "Chaos, Polemics, and America's First Newspaper," *Journalism Quarterly* 70 (Autumn 1993): 666–81; Clyde A. Duniway, *The Development of Freedom of the Press in Massachusetts* (New York: Longmans, Green, 1906), 68–69.

15. Adam Smith, *An Inquiry into the Nature and Causes of the Wealth of Nations*, ed. Edwin Cannan (New York: Modern Library, 1937), 872.

16. Jeffery A. Smith, "A Reappraisal of Legislative Privilege and American Colonial Journalism," *Journalism Quarterly* 61 (Spring 1984): 97–103, 141.

17. *A Narrative of the Late Massacres*, 1764, in *The Papers of Benjamin Franklin*, ed. Leonard W. Labaree et al. (New Haven: Yale University Press, 1959–), 11: 55, 65.

18. *Poor Richard*, 1737, 1745, 1746, and 1752, in Labaree, *Papers of Benjamin Franklin*, 2: 166; 3: 5, 66; 4: 247.

19. *The American Magazine and Historical Chronicle* 3 (September 1746): 394.

20. [Williamsburg] *Virginia Gazette*, January 10 and 17, 1771. For a similar treatment of monarchs going to war over trifles, see *New York Weekly Magazine* 1 (November 25, 1795): 161.

21. [Charleston] *South-Carolina Gazette*, December 15, 1746. See also the *Gazette* issues of April 13 and 20, 1747.

22. *New-York Gazette: or, The Weekly Post-Boy*, November 1, 1756.

23. William C. Stinchcombe, *The American Revolution and the French Alliance* (Syracuse, N.Y.: Syracuse University Press, 1969), 104–32. For examples of loyalist writings, see [New York] *Royal Gazette*, October 17 and 31, 1778; January 6, 1779.

24. See Alan Rogers, *Empire and Liberty: American Resistance to British Authority, 1755–1763* (Berkeley: University of California Press, 1974). For an example of a reader complaining that published criticisms were divisive and an editor's response, see *New-York Gazette: or, the Weekly Post-Boy*, November 8, 1756.

25. *New-York Gazette: or, the Weekly Post-Boy*, November 1, 1756. For the attack on the Virginia regiment, see *Virginia Gazette*, September 3, 1756; Worthington C. Ford, ed., "Washington and 'Centinel X,'" *Pennsylvania Magazine of History and Biography* 22 (1898): 436–51.

26. "The Different Effects of an Absolute and a Limited Monarchy," December 21, 1752, in William Livingston et al., *The Independent Reflector*, ed. Milton M. Klein (Cambridge: Harvard University Press, 1963), 76–81. For another example of colonial self-satisfaction under limited monarchy, see [New Haven] *Connecticut Gazette*, April 12, 1755.

27. See Pauline Maier, *From Resistance to Revolution: Colonial Radicals and the Development of American Opposition to Britain, 1765–1776* (New York: Knopf, 1972); Barbara W. Tuchman, *The March of Folly: From Troy to Vietnam* (New York: Knopf, 1984), 128–231; Marston, *King and Congress*, 35–99.

28. [Philadelphia] *Pennsylvania Packet*, September 12, 1774.

29. See Bernard Bailyn, *The Ideological Origins of the American Revolution* (Cambridge: Harvard University Press, 1967).

30. See Reginald C. Stuart, *War and American Thought: From the Revolution to the Monroe Doctrine* (Kent, Ohio: Kent State University Press, 1982).

31. Richard Gimbel, *Thomas Paine: A Bibliographical Check List of Common Sense with an Account of Its Publication* (New Haven: Yale University Press, 1956), 57.

32. [Thomas Paine], *Common Sense*, 2nd ed. (Philadelphia: R. Bell, 1776), 6, 8, 10, 37–38, 47, 57.

33. *United States Magazine* 1 (November 1779): 472.

34. Robert Middlekauff, *The Glorious Cause: The American Revolution, 1763–1789* (New York: Oxford University Press, 1982), 582–84; Garry Wills, *Cincinnatus: George Washington and the Enlightenment* (Garden City, N.Y.: Doubleday, 1984), 3–16; Report of a Committee on Arrangements for the Public Audience, December 22, 1783, "Washington's Address to Congress Resigning his Commission," December 23, 1783, and Report of a Committee on the Response by the President of Congress, December 22, 1783, in *The Papers of Thomas Jefferson*, ed. Julian P. Boyd et al. (Princeton: Princeton University Press, 1950–), 6: 409, 411–13.

35. Hamilton, "The Federalist No. 29," in *FED*, 182, 187; Hamilton, "The Federalist No. 34," in *FED*, 213; Jay, "The Federalist No. 4," in *FED*, 19.

36. Thomas Jefferson, "First Inaugural Address," March 4, 1801, in *The American Enlightenment: The Shaping of the American Experiment and a Free Society*, ed. Adrienne Koch (New York: George Braziller, 1965), 405.

37. *Washington's Farewell Address*, ed. Victor H. Paltsits (New York: New York Public Library, 1935), 144, 156.

38. Samples of the generally rapturous press assessments of Washington's career can be found in Paltsits, *Washington's Farewell Address*, 55–74.

39. See, e. g., [Philadelphia] *General Advertiser*, July 17, August 18, October 26, 1792; March 15, 1793.

40. [Philadelphia] *General Advertiser*, March 15, 1793.

41. See, e. g., [Philadelphia] *General Advertiser*, September 5, 1791; November 11, December 12, 1792; January 25, March 15, 22, 26, 1793.

42. "The Stand No. VI," April 19, 1798, in *PAH*, 21: 437.

43. *The Time Piece, and Literary Companion*, March 15, 1797.

44. "Pacifus No. 1," June 29, 1793, in *PAH*, 15: 33–43; " 'Helvidius' Number 1," August 24, 1793, in *PJM*, 15: 66–74, 108.

45. *Political Observations*, April 20, 1795, in *PJM*, 15: 518.

46. *Rights of Man*, pt. 2, chap. 5, in Foner, *Writings of Thomas Paine*, 1: 399, 400; *Rights of Man*, preface to pt. 2, 1: 352.

47. "Idea for a Universal History with a Cosmopolitan Purpose," in Reiss, *Kant*, 49; "On the Common Saying: 'This May Be True in Theory, but It Does Not Apply in Practice,' " in Reiss, *Kant*, 90, 92.

48. For an introduction to the topic, see Louis Fisher, *Presidential War Power* (Lawrence: University Press of Kansas, 1995).

See Karlyn Kohrs Campbell and Kathleen Hall Jamieson, *Deeds Done in Words: Presidential Rhetoric and the Genres of Governance* (Chicago: University of Chicago Press, 1990).

49. M. N. S. Sellers, *American Republicanism: Roman Ideology in the United States Constitution* (New York: New York University Press, 1994).

50. Catherine Drinker Bowen, *The Lion and the Throne: The Life and Times of Sir Edward Coke* (Boston: Little, Brown, 1956), 302–6.

51. Bill of Rights, 1689, in *Sources of English Constitutional History: A Selection of Documents from 600 A.D. to the Present*, ed. and trans. Carl Stephenson and Frederick George Marcham (New York: Harper, 1937), 601.

52. Commons' Resolutions on the Licensing Bill, 1695, in Stephenson and Marcham, *Sources of English Constitutional History*, 620; for the act itself, see 548–51.

53. John Locke, *Two Treatises of Government*, 2nd ed. (Cambridge: Cambridge University Press, 1967), 392–98. For a sketch of Locke's views as they relate to the U. S. Constitution, see Larry Arnhart, " 'The God-Like Prince': John Locke, Executive Prerogative, and the American Presidency," *Presidential Studies Quarterly* 9 (Spring 1979): 121–30.

54. For Locke's views on sovereignty, see F. H. Hinsley, *Sovereignty*, 2nd ed. (Cambridge: Cambridge University Press, 1986), 146.

55. William Blackstone, *Commentaries on the Laws of England: A Facsimile of the First Edition of 1765–1769* (Chicago: University of Chicago Press, 1979), 1: 243, 244.

56. Morton J. Horwitz, *The Transformation of American Law, 1780–1860* (Cambridge: Harvard University Press, 1977), 17.

57. Robert Louis Berg, "Presidential Power and the Royal Prerogative" (Ph.D. diss., University of Minnesota, 1958); Arnhart, " 'The God-Like Prince,' " 125–30.

58. Home Building & Loan Association v. Blaisdell, 290 U.S. 398, 425 (1934).

59. John K. Alexander, *The Selling of the Constitutional Convention: A History of News Coverage* (Madison, Wis.: Madison House, 1990).

60. See, in particular, Hamilton, "The Federalist No. 23" and "The Federalist No. 28," in *FED*, 146–51, 176–80.

61. "Speech on Salaries," June 2, 1787, in *The Writings of Benjamin Franklin*, ed. Albert H. Smyth (New York: Macmillan, 1905–1907), 9: 591–93.

62. "An Old Whig V," [Philadelphia] *Independent Gazetteer*, November 1, 1787, in *Federalists and Antifederalists: The Debate over the Ratification of the Constitution*, ed. John P. Kaminski and Richard Leffler (Madison, Wis.: Madison House, 1989), 86.

63. "Brutus I," *New York Journal*, October 18, 1787, in Kaminski and Leffler, *Federalists and Antifederalists*, 13.

64. "An Old Whig IV," [Philadelphia] *Independent Gazetteer*, October 27, 1787, in Kaminski and Leffler, *Federalists and Antifederalists*, 18.

65. Madison, "The Federalist No. 10," in *FED*, 61.

66. Madison, "The Federalist No. 37," in *FED*, 233–34; Hamilton, "The Federalist No. 70," in *FED*, 477; Hamilton, "The Federalist No. 67," in *FED*, 452; Hamilton, "The Federalist No. 28," in *FED*, 178; Hamilton, "The Federalist No. 70," in *FED*, 471–80; Hamilton, "The Federalist No. 77," in *FED*, 520–21.

67. For a detailed history of British press law, see Fredrick S. Siebert, *Freedom of the Press in England, 1476–1776, The Rise and Fall of Government Control* (Urbana: University of Illinois Press, 1952).

68. See Robert Scigliano, "The President's 'Prerogative Power,' " in *Inventing the American Presidency*, ed. Thomas E. Cronin (Lawrence: University Press of Kansas, 1989), 236–56.

69. Fisher, *Presidential War Power*, 1–12; military security treaties and the U.N. Charter have been used to expand presidential powers (xi–xiii, 12). For the view that the "Constitution does grant the President the power to decide unilaterally whether national security requires the use of military force under exigent circumstances," see David L. Hall, *The Reagan Wars: A Constitutional Perspective on War Powers and the Presidency* (Boulder, Colo.: Westview Press, 1991), 272. Even Hall, however, says that the "Constitution does not permit the President to use the military to abridge the Bill of Rights" (271).

70. Forrest McDonald, *Novus Ordo Seclorum: The Intellectual Origins of the Constitution* (Lawrence: University Press of Kansas, 1985), 247–48; Marston, *King and Congress*, 27–28; W. Taylor Reveley III, "Constitutional Allocation of the War Powers between the President and Congress: 1787–1788," *Virginia Journal of International Law* 15 (Fall 1974): 73–147; Charles A. Lofgren, "War-Making under the Constitution: The Original Understanding," *Yale Law Journal* 81 (March 1972): 672–702; Bernard Donahue and Marshall Smelser, "The Congressional Power To Raise Armies: The Constitutional and Ratifying Conventions, 1787–1788," *Review of Politics* 33 (April 1971): 202–11.

71. Thomas Jefferson to James Madison, September 6, 1789, in Boyd, *Papers of Thomas Jefferson*, 15: 397. For an account of the development of war powers since 1787, see Francis D. Wormuth and Edwin B. Firmage, *To Chain the Dog of War: The War Power of Congress in History and Law*, 2nd ed. (Urbana: University of Illinois Press, 1989).

72. Hamilton, "The Federalist No. 69," in *FED*, 465.

73. Plan of Government, June 18, 1787, in *PAH*, 4: 208.

74. Hamilton, "The Federalist No. 70," in *FED*, 476.

75. Hamilton, "The Federalist No. 72," in *FED*, 486, 487. See also Hamilton, "The Federalist No. 74," in *FED*, 500.

76. Hamilton, "The Federalist No. 69," in *FED*, 465.

77. Hamilton, "The Federalist No. 23," in *FED*, 147, 148. For a similar statement by Madison, see "The Federalist No. 41," in *FED*, 270.

78. See, in particular, William T. Mayton, "From a Legacy of Suppression to the 'Metaphor of the Fourth Estate,' " *Stanford Law Review* 39 (November 1986): 154–57.

79. *The Debates in the Several State Conventions on the Adoption of the Federal Constitution*, ed. Jonathan Elliot (Philadelphia: J. B. Lippincott, 1881), 4: 209.

80. Madison, "The Federalist No. 43," in *FED*, 290.

81. Cramer v. United States, 325 U.S. 1, 27, 28, 61 (1945). Lower courts have held that making propaganda broadcasts for the enemy turns words into acts and can be treason. See, e.g., Gillars v. United States, 182 F.2d 962, 971 (D.C. Cir. 1950); Chandler v. United States, 171 F.2d 921, 940 (1st Cir. 1949). For commentators, see, for example, Charles Warren, "What Is Giving Aid and Comfort to the Enemy?" *Yale Law Journal* 27 (January 1918): 338, 340, 343.

82. For the view that the press clause guarantees an absolute freedom to discuss government policies but does not eliminate any individual's right to reputation, see Jeffery A. Smith, *Printers and Press Freedom: The Ideology of Early American Journalism* (New York: Oxford University Press, 1988).

83. Madison, "The Federalist No. 48," in *FED*, 334.

84. Hamilton, "The Federalist No. 71," in *FED*, 483.

85. Amendments to the Constitution, [June 8, 1789], in *PJM*, 12: 204.

86. Mark P. Denbeaux, "The First Word of the First Amendment," *Northwestern University Law Review* 80 (Spring 1986): 1156–1220.

87. "The Report of 1800," in *PJM*, 17: 336–38.

88. Reid v. Covert, 354 U.S. 1, 17, 23–24, 39, 40 (1957). Black's support for civilian supremacy was also evident in an opinion limiting the martial law authority imposed on Hawaii after Pearl Harbor. Duncan v. Kahanamoku, 327 U.S. 304 (1946).

89. Elliot, *Debates in the State Conventions*, 4: 329.

90. June 1, 1787, in James Madison, *Notes of Debates in the Federal Convention of 1787* (Athens, Ohio: Ohio University Press, 1966), 46–47.

91. Hamilton, "The Federalist No. 75," in *FED*, 504, 505–6, 507.

92. This point is made in Arnhart, " 'The God-Like Prince,' " 128.

93. " 'Helvidius' Number 1," August 24, 1793, in *PJM*, 15: 69.

94. Alexander Hamilton to James McHenry, May 17, 1798, in *PAH*, 21: 462.

95. Larry Berman, "The President: Executive Energy and Republican Safety," in *Constitutional Principle and Institutional Government*, ed. Sarah Thomas (New York: University Press of America, 1988), 127.

96. *Ex parte* Milligan, 71 U.S. (4 Wall.) 2 (1866); Youngstown Co. v. Sawyer, 343 U.S. 579 (1952).

97. For a variety of viewpoints from a panel of scholars and current or past public officials assembled to address the issue, see Charles J. Cooper, Orrin Hatch, Eugene V. Rostow, and Michael Tigar, "What the Constitution Means by Executive Power," *University of Miami Law Review* 43 (September 1988): 165–210.

98. See, for example, Address to the Nation Announcing United States Military Action in Panama, December 20, 1989, in *Public Papers of the Presidents of the United States, George Bush, 1989* (Washington, D.C.: Government Printing Office, 1990), 2: 1722–23; A Conversation with the President about Foreign Policy, July 1, 1970, in *Public Papers of the Presidents of the United States, Richard Nixon . . . 1970* (Washington, D.C.: Government Printing Office, 1971), 546–47, 552–53.

99. Athan Theoharis, *Spying on Americans: Political Surveillance from Hoover to the Huston Plan* (Philadelphia: Temple University Press, 1978). William Rehnquist was among those in the Nixon administration who advocated executive authority for wiretapping and surveillance without a court order. As an assistant attorney general, he told a Senate subcommittee in 1971 that the president had inherent powers to take care that the laws be executed and an implicit duty to investigate and prevent violations of federal law. Rehnquist became an associate justice of the Supreme Court a year later and chief justice in 1986 (65).

100. See, for example, Pete Williams, "The Press and the Persian Gulf War," *Parameters* 21 (Autumn 1991): 2–9.

101. For this assessment, see Kermit L. Hall, "Corwin, Edward Samuel," in *The Oxford Companion to the Supreme Court*, ed. Kermit L. Hall (New York: Oxford University Press, 1992), 200.

102. Edward S. Corwin, *The President: Office and Powers, History and Analysis of Practice and Opinion* (New York: New York University Press, 1940), 10, 126–27, 165, 299–300, 307–8, 310, 315, 316. Corwin's quotations of Locke, 6–8, can be compared with Locke, *Two Treatises*, 392–96.

103. Stephen L. Vaughn, *Holding Fast the Inner Lines: Democracy, Nationalism, and the Committee on Public Information* (Chapel Hill: University of North Carolina Press, 1980), 54–55.

104. On Corwin's influence and his often slippery scholarship, see Scigliano, "President's 'Prerogative Power,' " 236–48.

105. Fireside Chat on National Defense, May 26, 1940, in *Nothing to Fear: The Selected Addresses of Franklin Delano Roosevelt, 1932–1945*, ed. B. D. Zevin (Cambridge, Mass.: Houghton Mifflin, 1946), 211.

106. "How To Tell Japs from the Chinese," *Life*, December 22, 1941, 81.

107. On American attitudes in the mass media and elsewhere, see John W. Dower, *War without Mercy: Race and Power in the Pacific War* (New York: Pantheon Books, 1986); Edmund P. Russell III, " 'Speaking of Annihilation': Mobilizing for War against Human and Insect Enemies, 1914–1945," *Journal of American History* 82 (March 1996): 1505–7; Nancy Brcak and John R. Pavia, "Racism in Japanese and U.S. Wartime Propaganda," *Historian* 56 (Summer 1994): 671–84; Richard W. Steele, " 'The Greatest Gangster Movie Ever Filmed': *Prelude to War*," *Prologue* 11 (Winter 1979): 221–35.

108. Peter Irons, *Justice at War* (New York: Oxford University Press, 1983).

109. Exec. Order No. 9066, 7 Fed. Reg. 1407 (1942). Some sabotage had occurred in the United States before World War I, but, according to one Justice Department official, the activity died down once the country entered the war, and during the last fifteen months "not a single instance of damage to property was traceable to enemy activity." John Lord O'Brian, "Restraints upon Individual Freedom in Times of National Emergency," *Cornell Law Quarterly* 26 (June 1941): 527.

110. Roger Daniels, *Prisoners without Trial: Japanese Americans in World War II* (New York: Hill and Wang, 1993), 33–34; Charles Fairman, "The Law of Martial Rule and the National Emergency," *Harvard Law Review* 55 (June 1942): 1299–1301.

111. Ch. 191, 56 Stat. 173 (1942).

112. Congress, Senate, 77th Cong., 2nd sess., *Congressional Record* (March 19, 1942), vol. 88, pt. 2, 2722–26.

113. John Armor and Peter Wright, *Manzanar* (New York: Times Books, 1988), 18–25, 35, 44, 147–53; Ronald Smothers, "Japanese-Americans Recall War Service," *NYT*, June 19, 1995, A6 (national edition).

114. *Final Report: Japanese Evacuation from the West Coast, 1942* (Washington, D.C.: Government Printing Office, 1943), vii. See also Irons, *Justice at War*, 3–74, 279–87, 305–7; Donna K. Nagata, "The Japanese-American Internment: Perceptions of Moral Community, Fairness, and Redress," *Journal of Social Issues* 46 (1990): 133–46. For a thoughtful analysis of the legal issues, as well as a comparison to the *Ex parte Milligan* case of 1866, see Jacobus tenBroek, Edward N. Barnhart, and Floyd W. Matson, *Prejudice, War and the Constitution* (Berkeley: University of California Press, 1968), 225–49; the curfew was for Japanese, German, and Italian aliens and citizens of Japanese ancestry (225). The evacuation and internment program applied almost exclusively to persons of Japanese ancestry, but also briefly included Italian Americans. Stephen Fox, *The Unknown Internment: An Oral History of the Relocation of Italian Americans during World War II* (Boston: Twayne, 1990). Among the Americans who were interned in Japan were reporters who were mistreated and subjected to pressure to write Japanese propaganda. Robert Bellaire, "Torment in Japan," *Collier's*, January 2, 1943, 13, 46.

115. Fairman, "Law of Martial Rule," 1254, 1301, 1302.

116. Samuel Walker, *In Defense of American Liberties: A History of the ACLU* (New York: Oxford University Press, 1990), 139; Armor and Wright, *Manzanar*, 38–50; Irons, *Justice at War*, 41, 60–61; Francis Biddle, *In Brief Authority* (Garden City, N.Y.: Doubleday, 1962), 216–18.

117. Lloyd Chiasson, "Japanese-American Relocation during World War II: A Study of California Editorial Reactions," *Journalism Quarterly* 68 (Spring–Summer 1991): 263–68; Lloyd Chiasson, "The Japanese-American Encampment: An Editorial Analysis of 27 West Coast Newspapers," *Newspaper Research Journal* 12 (Spring 1991): 92–107.

118. Walt Stromer, "Why I Went Along: 1942 and the Invisible Evacuees," *CJR* (January–February 1993); 15–17; "Coast Japs Are Interned in Mountain Camp," *Life*, April 6, 1942, 15.

119. Lauren Kessler, "Fettered Freedoms: The Journalism of World War II Japanese Internment Camps," *Journalism History* 15 (Summer–Autumn 1988): 70–79; *Final Report*, 213–14; Armor and Wright, *Manzanar*, 133–34.

120. Greg Garrett, "It's Everybody's War: Racism and the World War Two Documentary," *Journal of Popular Film and Television* 22 (Summer 1994): 75–76.

121. Armor and Wright, *Manzanar*, xvii–xx; Karin Becker Ohrn, "What You See Is What You Get: Dorothea Lange and Ansel Adams at Manzanar," *Journalism History* 4 (Spring 1977): 14–22, 32.

122. Hirabayashi v. U.S., 320 U.S. 81, 92, 95, 99, 101 (1943).

123. For an analysis that concludes the government's policies were based on suspicions about political opinions when "punishment only for individual behavior is basic to all systems of civilized law," see Eugene V. Rostow, "The Japanese American Cases—A Disaster," *Yale Law Journal* 54 (June 1945): 532.

124. Korematsu v. U.S., 323 U.S. 214, 216, 217–18 (1944).

125. Korematsu v. U.S., 323 U.S. at 244 (Roberts, J., dissenting); Korematsu v. U.S., 323 U.S. at 233 (Murphy, J., dissenting).

126. James F. Simon, *The Antagonists: Hugo Black, Felix Frankfurter and Civil Liberties in Modern America* (New York: Simon and Schuster, 1989), 146–56; William O. Douglas, *Go East, Young Man: The Early Years* (New York: Random House, 1974), 92–93; Leonard Baker, *Brandeis and Frankfurter* (New York: Harper and Row, 1984), 397–98.

127. Korematsu v. U.S., 584 F. Supp. 1406, 1420 (N.D. Cal. 1984).

128. *Ex parte* Endo, 323 U.S. 283, 297, 300–302 (1944).

129. Irons, *Justice at War*, 268–77, 341, 344–46.

130. *Ex parte* Endo, 323 U.S. at 298–302.

131. *Personal Justice Denied: Report of the Commission on Wartime Relocation and Internment of Civilians* (Washington, D.C.: Government Printing Office, 1982); Daniels, *Prisoners without Trial*, 90–105; Biddle, *In Brief Authority*, 212, 213, 219.

132. Press Conference No. 720, February 21, 1941, in *Complete Presidential Press Conferences of Franklin D. Roosevelt* (New York: Da Capo Press, 1972), 17: 140–48.

133. Congress, Senate, 98th Cong., 1st sess., *Congressional Record*, vol. 129, no. 145, daily ed. (October 29, 1983), S14965. For testimony on how decisions were being made, see Congress, House, Committee on Armed Services, *Full Committee Hearing on the Lessons Learned as a Result of the U.S. Military Operations in Grenada*, 98th Cong., 2nd sess., 1984.

134. Ingrid Detter De Lupis, *The Law of War* (New York: Cambridge University Press, 1987), 79; Stuart Taylor Jr., "Legality of Grenada Attack Disputed," *NYT*, October 26, 1983, A19 (late edition).

Richard Bernstein, "U.S. Vetoes U. N. Resolution 'Deploring' Grenada Invasion," *NYT*, October 29, 1983, A1 (late edition).

One retired officer, voicing military complaints that the public is weak and short-sighted and that journalists are sensational and superficial, wrote of the Grenada operation that "we may believe that nothing, literally nothing, was concealed that the First Amendment was framed to uncover." Wayne P. Hughes, "Guarding the First Amendment—For and From the Press," *Naval War College Review* 37 (1984): 31–32. A more dispassionate assessment, however, would indicate that the news blackout concealed evidence of military mistakes and ineptitude. See Robert J. Beck, *The Grenada Invasion: Politics, Law, and Foreign Policy Decisionmaking* (Boulder, Colo.: Westview Press, 1993); Reynold A. Burrowes, *Revolution and Rescue in Grenada: An Account of the U.S.-Caribbean Invasion* (New York: Greenwood Press, 1988); Gilbert S. Harper, "Logistics in Grenada: Supporting No-Plan Wars," *Parameters* 20 (June 1990): 50–63; William

Schaap, "Remembering Grenada," *Lies of Our Times*, June 1994, 16–17; Stuart Taylor Jr., "In the Wake of Invasion, Much Official Misinformation by U.S. Comes to Light," *NYT*, November 6, 1983, 20 (late edition).

135. Jason DeParle, "Long Series of Military Decisions Led to Gulf War News Censorship," *NYT*, May 5, 1991, 1 (national edition); Frank Aukofer and William P. Lawrence, *America's Team; The Odd Couple—A Report on the Relationship between the Media and the Military* (Nashville, Tenn.: Freedom Forum First Amendment Center, 1995), 102, 108, 155. In Bosnia a decision to require reporters to get permission for quotations from soldiers they were with for more than twenty-four hours was made by the assistant secretary of defense/public affairs and a colonel in Tusla. Debra Gersh Hernandez, " 'Embedding' Leads to Restrictions," *E&P*, May 25, 1996, 10.

136. John E. Smith, "From the Front Lines to the Front Page: Media Access to War in the Persian Gulf and Beyond," *Columbia Journal of Law and Social Problems* 26 (Winter 1993): 291–339; Jason DeParle, "Keeping the News in Step: Are the Pentagon's Gulf Rules Here To Stay?" *NYT*, May 6, 1991, A5 (national edition).

137. Fletcher Pratt, "How the Censors Rigged the News," *Harper's*, February 1946, 98.

138. A dramatic example occurred in 1996 when the Navy's top admiral, Jeremy M. Boorda, committed suicide when faced with news media disclosure that he was wearing decorations he may not have earned. For background on Boorda's troubles, see Gregory L. Vistica, *Fall From Glory: The Men Who Sank the U.S. Navy* (New York: Simon and Schuster, 1995), 316; Peter J. Boyer, "Admiral Boorda's War," *New Yorker*, September 16, 1996, 68–75, 77–86.

139. Bernard E. Trainor, "The Military and the Media: A Troubled Embrace," in *Newsmen & National Defense: Is Conflict Inevitable?* ed. Lloyd Matthews (Washington, D.C.: Brassey's [US], 1991), 128; William A. Wilcox Jr., "Media Coverage of Military Operations: OPLAW Meets the First Amendment," *Army Lawyer* (May 1995): 42–53; Steven S. Neff, "The United States Military vs. the Media: Constitutional Friction," *Mercer Law Review* 46 (1995): 1007–8, 1013.

140. For Air Force examples, see Mark Thompson, "Placing Blame at Any Cost," *Time*, December 2, 1996, 43–44; Mark Thompson, "So, Who's to Blame?" *Time*, July 3, 1995, 27; Mark Thompson, "Way, Way Off in the Wild Blue Yonder," *Time*, May 29, 1995, 32–33; Tim Weiner, "Military is Accused of Lying on Arms for Decade," *NYT*, June 28, 1993, A8 (national edition); Michael R. Gordon, "New Report Says General Knew Stealth Failed," *NYT*, July 2, 1990, A1 (national edition). The Army began making serious efforts to learn from its mistakes after Vietnam. Thomas E. Ricks, "Army Devises System To Decide What Does, and Does Not, Work," *Wall Street Journal*, May 23, 1997, A1.

141. Madison, "The Federalist No. 10," in *FED*, 59.

Chapter 2

1. On the somewhat surprising lack of case law, see Mark C. Rahdert, "The First Amendment and Media Rights during Wartime: Some Thoughts after Operation Desert Storm," *Villanova Law Review* 36 (November 1991): 1513–58.

2. See Michael D. Steger, "Slicing the Gordian Knot: A Proposal to Reform Military Regulation of Media Coverage of Combat Operations," *University of San Francisco Law Review* 28 (Summer 1994): 957–1007; John E. Smith, "From the Front Line to the Front Page: Media Access to War in the Persian Gulf and Beyond," *Columbia Journal of Law and Social Problems* 26 (Winter 1993): 291–339; John W. Spelich, "In the Crossfire: A Reporter's Right of Access to the Battlefield in Time of War," *Detroit College of Law Review* 1992 (Winter 1992): 1055–99; Kevin P. Kenealey, "The Persian Gulf War and the Press: Is There a Constitutional Right of Access to Military Operations?" *Northwestern University Law Review* 87 (Fall 1992): 287–325;

Heather A. Rogalski, "The Pentagon v. The Press: Is the Pool System a Solution to the Conflict?" *Bridgeport Law Review* 13 (Fall 1992): 107–54; Michelle Tulane Mensore, "The First Amendment Fights Back: A Proposal for the Media to Reclaim the Battlefield after the Persian Gulf War," *Washington and Lee Law Review* 49 (Summer 1992): 1145–82; Karl Tage Olson, "The Constitutionality of Department of Defense Press Restrictions of Wartime Correspondents Covering the Persian Gulf War," *Drake Law Review* 41 (1992): 511–44; Michelle D. Boydston, "Press Censorship and Access Restrictions During the Persian Gulf War: A First Amendment Analysis," *Loyola of Los Angeles Law Review* 25 (April 1992): 1073–1106; Matthew J. Jacobs, "Assessing the Constitutionality of Press Restrictions in the Persian Gulf War," *Stanford Law Review* 44 (February 1992): 675–726; David A. Frenznick, "The First Amendment on the Battlefield: A Constitutional Analysis of Press Access to Military Operations in Grenada, Panama and the Persian Gulf," *Pacific Law Journal* 23 (January 1992): 315–59; Gara LaMarche, "Managed News, Stifled Views: Free Expression as a Casualty of the Persian Gulf War," *Journal of Human Rights* 9 (Fall 1991): 45–83; Roger W. Pincus, "Press Access to Military Operations: Grenada and the Need for a New Analytical Framework," *University of Pennsylvania Law Review* 135 (March 1987): 813–50; John B. Engber, "The Press and the Invasion of Grenada: Does the First Amendment Guarantee the Press a Right of Access to Wartime News?" *Temple Law Quarterly* 58 (Winter 1985): 873–901.

3. Thomas Paine, *Dissertation on First Principles of Government* (Philadelphia: Conrad, 1795).

4. See, for example, Morris D. Forkosch, "Speech and Press in National Emergencies," *Gonzaga Law Review* 18 (1982–1983): 1–52; June D. W. Kalijarvi and Don Wallace Jr., "Executive Authority to Impose Prior Restraint upon Publication of Information Concerning National Security Affairs: A Constitutional Power," *California Western Law Review* 9 (Spring 1973): 468–96. In one survey, 23 percent of Americans said that a president could suspend the Bill of Rights during wartime. "Harper's Index," *Harper's*, July 1992, 9.

5. See, in particular, Leonard W. Levy, *Emergence of a Free Press* (New York: Oxford University Press, 1985). For a brief summary of the long-running debate on this topic, see Gaspare J. Saladino, "The Bill of Rights: A Bibliographic Essay," in Stephen L. Schechter and Richard B. Bernstein, *Contexts of the Bill of Rights* (Albany: New York State Commission on the Bicentennial of the United States Constitution, 1990), 84–87.

6. See, in particular, Jeffery A. Smith, *Printers and Press Freedom: The Ideology of Early American Journalism* (New York: Oxford University Press, 1988); David A. Anderson, "The Origins of the Press Clause," *UCLA Law Review* 30 (February 1983): 455–541.

7. Bernard Bailyn, *The Ideological Origins of the American Revolution* (Cambridge: Harvard University Press, 1967), 36.

8. *London Journal*, February 4, 1720/1; *British Journal*, October 20, 1722.

9. James Alexander, *A Brief Narrative of the Case and Trial of John Peter Zenger*, ed. Stanley N. Katz, 2nd ed. (Cambridge: Harvard University Press, 1972), 80–81, 84, 88, 89–90, 99.

10. *Pennsylvania Gazette*, November 17, 1737, in Alexander, *Brief Narrative*, 181.

11. For examples from the revolutionary period, see Smith, *Printers and Press Freedom*, 144–150.

12. "To the Inhabitants of the Province of Quebec," *Journals of the Continental Congress, 1774–1789*, ed. Worthington C. Ford (Washington, D.C.: U.S. Government Printing Office, 1904–1937), 1: 108.

13. *The Bill of Rights: A Documentary History*, ed. Bernard Schwartz (New York: Chelsea House, 1971), 1: 235, 266, 278, 284, 287, 300, 335, 342, 378. The state press guarantees are listed and discussed in Anderson, "Origins of the Press Clause," 464–66, 538–39.

14. Thomas Jefferson to Adamantios Coray, October 31, 1823, in *The Writings of Thomas Jefferson*, ed. Andrew A. Lipscomb and Albert E. Bergh (Washington, D.C.: Thomas Jefferson Memorial Association, 1904–1905), 15: 489.

15. Smith, *Printers and Press Freedom*, 7–11, 83–84; Jeffery A. Smith, "A Reappraisal of Legislative Privilege and American Colonial Journalism," *Journalism Quarterly* 61 (Spring 1984): 97–103, 141.

16. James Madison to Caleb Wallace, August 23, 1785, in *PJM*, 8: 351.

17. *Commentaries on the Constitution: Public and Private*, ed. John P. Kaminski and Gaspare J. Saladino, vol. 13 of *The Documentary History of the Ratification of the Constitution* (Madison: State Historical Society of Wisconsin: 1981), 1: 197–98.

18. Madison, "The Federalist No. 51," in *FED*, 348, 349.

19. Madison, "The Federalist No. 10," in *FED*, 62, 64.

20. Speech of June 16, 1787, in James Madison, *Notes of Debates in the Federal Convention of 1787* (Athens: Ohio University Press, 1966), 135; Hamilton, "The Federalist No. 15," in *FED*, 96; Hamilton, "The Federalist No. 71," in *FED*, 482–83.

21. Madison, "The Federalist No. 51," in *FED*, 348; Hamilton, "The Federalist No. 78," in *FED*, 522, 523, 524.

22. *The Debates in the Several State Conventions on the Adoption of the Federal Constitution*, ed. Jonathan Elliot (Philadelphia: J. B. Lippincott, 1881), 3: 449; Elliot, *Debates in the State Conventions*, 315.

23. See David M. O'Brien, *The Public's Right To Know: The Supreme Court and the First Amendment* (New York: Praeger, 1981), 28–54.

24. See, for example, "Centinel II," [Philadelphia] *Freeman's Journal*, October 24, 1787, in Kaminski and Saladino, *Commentaries on the Constitution*, 1: 457–58.

25. August 11, 1787, in Madison, *Notes of Debates in the Federal Convention of 1787*, 433; Articles of Confederation, article 9.

26. Madison, *Notes of Debates in the Federal Convention of 1787*, 434.

27. June 17, 1788, in *The Papers of George Mason*, ed. Robert A. Rutland (Chapel Hill: University of North Carolina Press, 1970), 3: 1087; Elliot, *Debates in the State Conventions*, 3: 170, 315.

28. William Blackstone, *Commentaries on the Laws of England* (Philadelphia: Robert Bell, 1772), 4: 151; Daniel F. Hoffman, "Contempt of the United States: The Political Crime That Wasn't," *American Journal of Legal History* 25 (October 1981): 343–60. See also Everette E. Dennis, "Stolen Peace Treaties and the Press: Two Case Studies," *Journalism History* 2 (Spring 1975): 6–14.

29. "Perpetual Peace: A Philosophical Sketch," in *Kant: Political Writings*, 2nd ed., ed. Hans Reiss, trans. H. B. Nisbet (Cambridge: Cambridge University Press, 1991), 115, 126; Benjamin Franklin to [Juliana Ritchie], January 19, 1777, in *The Papers of Benjamin Franklin*, ed. Leonard W. Labaree et al. (New Haven: Yale University Press, 1959–), 23: 211.

30. Madison, *Notes and Debates in the Federal Convention of 1787*, 434; Elliot, *Debates in the State Conventions*, 3: 399, 409.

31. *Letters from the Federal Farmer to the Republican*, ed. Walter H. Bennett (University, Ala.: University of Alabama Press, 1978), 111–12.

32. Madison, "The Federalist No. 39," in *FED*, 256.

33. Madison, "The Federalist No. 41," in *FED*, 277, 278; Hamilton, "The Federalist No. 84," in *FED*, 578–79.

34. James Wilson, Speech at a Public Meeting in Philadelphia, October 6, 1787, in Kaminski and Saladino, eds., *Commentaries on the Constitution*, 1: 340; *Ratification of the Constitution by the States: Pennsylvania*, ed. Merrill Jensen, vol. 2 of *Documentary History of the Ratification of the Constitution* (1976), 454, 455.

35. Similar statements by prominent Americans include [Roger Sherman], "Observations on the New Federal Constitution," [Hartford] *Connecticut Courant*, January 7, 1788, in Kaminski and Saladino, *Commentaries on the Constitution*, 3: 282; [James Iredell], *Answers to Mr. Mason's Objections to the New Constitution*, in *Pamphlets on the Constitution of the United States*,

Published During Its Discussion by the People, 1787–1788, ed. Paul L. Ford (Brooklyn, N.Y.: Privately Printed, 1888), 360–61.

36. James Madison to Edmund Randolph, October 21, 1787, in Kaminski and Saladino, *Commentaries on the Constitution*, 1: 429; Robert A. Rutland, *The Birth of the Bill of Rights, 1776–1791* (Chapel Hill: Published for the Institute of Early American History and Culture by the University of North Carolina Press, 1955), 119–25.

37. "Philadelphiensis VIII," [Philadelphia] *Freeman's Journal*, January 23, 1788, in Kaminski and Saladino, *Commentaries on the Constitution*, 3: 458, 459; for similar statements, see 1: 336; 2: 255; 3: 25, 107, 360, 548.

38. For examples, see Kaminski and Saladino, *Commentaries on the Constitution*, 1: 239, 335–36, 345, 378, 388, 457, 531–33, 535, 541; 2: 11–12, 47, 125, 151, 165, 271, 351, 368; 3: 107, 231–33.

39. James White to Governor Richard Caswell, November 13, 1787, in Kaminski and Saladino, *Commentaries on the Constitution*, 2: 96; *Pennsylvania Gazette*, November 14, 1787, in Kaminski and Saladino, *Commentaries on the Constitution*, 2: 103; Rutland, *Birth of the Bill of Rights*, 30–40, 115–125, 162–70.

40. Elliot, *Debates in the State Conventions*, 4: 314–17.

41. Rutland, *Birth of the Bill of Rights*, 159–89, 215–16; Anderson, "Origins of the Press Clause," 467–75.

42. Elliot, *Debates in the State Conventions*, 3: 656; James Madison to Richard Peters, August 19, 1789, in *PJM*, 12: 347.

43. James Madison to Thomas Jefferson, October 17, 1788, in *PJM*, 11: 297–99; Thomas Jefferson to James Madison, March 15, 1789, in *PJM*, 12: 13, 14; Thomas Jefferson to James Madison, July 31, 1788, in *PJM*, 11: 212.

44. James Madison to Thomas Mann Randolph, January 13, 1789, in *PJM*, 11: 416; James Madison to Richard Peters, August 19, 1789, in *PJM*, 12: 346–47; Amendments to the Constitution, [June 8, 1789], in *PJM*, 12: 201, 203, 204, 205, 207; Amendments to the Constitution, [August 15, 1789], in *PJM*, 12: 340. For Madison's evolving views on a national bill of rights, see Stuart Leibiger, "James Madison and Amendments to the Constitution, 1787–1789: 'Parchment Barriers,'" *Journal of Southern History* 59 (August 1993): 441–68; Jack N. Rakove, "James Madison and the Bill of Rights: A Broader Context," *Presidential Studies Quarterly* 22 (Fall 1992): 667–77.

45. "A Countryman II," *New Haven Gazette*, November 22, 1787, in Kaminski and Saladino, *Commentaries on the Constitution*, 2: 173. For a similar comment, see "Uncus," *Maryland Journal*, November 9, 1787, in Kaminski and Saladino, *Commentaries on the Constitution*, 2: 81.

46. Hamilton, "The Federalist No. 84," in *FED*, 580; Wilson, Speech at a Public Meeting in Philadelphia, October 6, 1787, in Kaminski and Saladino, *Commentaries on the Constitution*, 1: 340; Jensen, *Ratification of the Constitution*, 2: 455; *New York Daily Advertiser*, December 31, 1787, in Kaminski and Saladino, *Commentaries on the Constitution*, 3: 196.

47. "A Democratic Federalist," *Pennsylvania Herald*, October 17, 1787, in Kaminski and Saladino, *Commentaries on the Constitution*, 1: 388.

48. *Annals of Congress*, 3rd Cong., 2nd sess., 899, 934–35.

49. "The Stand No. VI," April 19, 1798, in *PAH*, 21: 436, 438; James Madison to Thomas Jefferson, May 13, 1798, in *PJM*, 17: 130.

50. For the criticisms of Washington and Adams, see Jeffery A. Smith, *Franklin and Bache: Envisioning the Enlightened Republic* (New York: Oxford University Press, 1990), 111–63.

51. On the Pacifus-Helvidius exchange of Hamilton and Madison, see John C. Koritansky, "Alexander Hamilton and the Presidency," in *Inventing the American Presidency*, ed. Thomas C. Cronin (Lawrence: University Press of Kansas: 1989), 282–303.

52. See Manning J. Dauer, *The Adams Federalists* (Baltimore: Johns Hopkins Press, 1953).

53. James Madison to Thomas Jefferson, February 1798, in *The Writings of James Madison*, ed. Gaillard Hunt (New York: Putnam, 1900–1910), 6: 312; James Madison to Thomas Jefferson, May 13, 1798, in *PJM*, 17: 130; Thomas Jefferson to Colonel Bell, May 18, 1797, in *The Writings of Thomas Jefferson*, ed. Albert E. Bergh (Washington, D.C.: Thomas Jefferson Memorial Association, 1907), 9: 386; Thomas Jefferson to Thomas Mann Randolph, May 10, 1797, as quoted in Adrienne Koch, *Madison and Jefferson: The Great Collaboration* (New York: Oxford University Press, 1964), 173.

54. Ch. 74, § 2, 1 Stat. 596, 596–97 (1798).

55. See, in particular, the version of the statute proposed by Representative Robert G. Harper on July 6, 1798. *Annals of Congress*, 5th Cong., 2nd sess., 2115–16.

56. For a detailed history of the 1798 statutes, see James M. Smith, *Freedom's Fetters: The Alien and Sedition Laws and American Civil Liberties* (Ithaca, N.Y.: Cornell University Press, 1956).

57. *Annals of Congress*, 5th Cong., 2nd sess., 2102, 2104, 2146, 2167, 2169. For Franklin's essay, which discussed and dismissed actions that might be taken when the *public* was affronted (not when the "Government" was affronted, as Harper said), see "An Account of the Supremest Court of Judicature in Pennsylvania, viz. The Court of the Press," in *The Writings of Benjamin Franklin*, ed. Albert H. Smyth (New York: Macmillan, 1905–1907), 10: 36–40.

58. *Annals of Congress*, 5th Cong., 2nd sess., 2104, 2105, 2106, 2113, 2154.

59. Virginia Resolutions, December 21, 1798, in *PJM*, 17: 185, 189, 190.

60. "Address of the General Assembly to the People of the Commonwealth of Virginia," January 10, 1799, in Hunt, *Writings of James Madison*, 6: 332, 333, 335. The editors of the latest edition of Madison's papers have doubts about Madison's authorship; editorial note, in *PJM*, 17: 199–206.

61. "The Report of 1800," January 7, 1800, in *PJM*, 17: 334–35, 340.

62. See Michael Kent Curtis, "The Curious History of Attempts to Suppress Antislavery Speech, Press, and Petition in 1835–37," *Northwestern University Law Review* 89 (Spring 1995): 785–870; *Freedom of the Press from Hamilton to the Warren Court*, ed. Harold L. Nelson (Indianapolis: Bobbs-Merrill, 1967), 167–220.

63. Linda Cobb-Reiley, "Aliens and Alien Ideas: The Suppression of Anarchists and the Anarchist Press in America, 1901–1914," *Journalism History* 15 (Summer/Autumn 1988): 50–59. For background, see William Preston Jr., *Aliens and Dissenters: Federal Suppression of Radicals, 1903–1933* (New York: Harper and Row, 1966). Most of the eight "conspirators" convicted following the Haymarket Square bombing in 1886 were outspoken individuals with connections to anarchist newspapers. Paul Avrich, *The Haymarket Tragedy* (Princeton: Princeton University Press, 1984), 215–39. The judge's instructions to the jury said the defendants could be found guilty as accessories for encouraging murder even though the bombthrower was not identified or apprehended (276–78).

64. Espionage Act, ch. 30, tit. I, § 3, 40 Stat. 217, 219 (1917); Sedition Act, ch. 75, 40 Stat. 553, 553 (1918); Alien Registration Act, ch. 439, § 2(a), 54 Stat. 670, 671 (1940).

65. John D. Stevens, *Shaping the First Amendment: The Development of Free Expression* (Beverly Hills, Calif.: Sage Publications, 1982), 47; Stephen L. Vaughn, *Holding Fast the Inner Lines: Democracy, Nationalism, and the Committee on Public Information* (Chapel Hill: University of North Carolina Press, 1980), 216; Don R. Pember, "The Smith Act as a Restraint on the Press," *Journalism Monographs*, no. 10, May 1969, 2.

66. See, for example, *Congressional Record*, vol. 55, pt. 2, 1711, 1809, 2004, 2005.

67. See, for example, *Congressional Record*, vol. 55, pt. 2, 1695, 1697, 1714, 1750, 1770, 1809, 1810, 1813; for examples of the First Amendment being invoked, see 1697, 1704, 1705, 1706, 1751, 1764, 1778.

68. *Congressional Record* (May 2, 1917), vol. 55, pt. 2, 1721; 1701.

69. For background, see Margaret A. Blanchard, *Revolutionary Sparks: Freedom of Expression in Modern America* (New York: Oxford University Press, 1992), 149–88; Michal R. Belknap, *Cold War Political Justice: The Smith Act, the Communist Party, and American Civil Liberties* (Westport, Conn.: Greenwood Press, 1977), 24–27; Richard Polenberg, *War and Society: The United States, 1941–1945* (Philadelphia: Lippincott, 1972), 37–41.

70. Statement by the President on Signing the Alien Registration Act, June 29, 1940, in *The Public Papers and Addresses of Franklin D. Roosevelt* (New York: Macmillan, 1941), 1940: 274–75; The Six Hundred and Fifty-eighth Press Conference, July 5, 1940, in *Public Papers of Roosevelt,* 1940: 282–85.

71. Richard W. Steele, "Fear of the Mob and Faith in Government in Free Speech Discourse, 1919–1941," *American Journal of Legal History* 38 (January 1994), 55–83. See also David M. Rabban, "Free Speech and Progressive Social Thought," *Texas Law Review* 74 (April 1996): 951–1038.

72. John Lord O'Brian, "Restraints upon Individual Freedom in Times of National Emergency," *Cornell Law Quarterly* 26 (June 1941): 525, 526, 529, 534. For O'Brian's similar viewpoint during World War I, see Richard Polenberg, *Fighting Faiths: The Abrams Case, the Supreme Court, and Free Speech* (New York: Penguin Books, 1989), 29–31.

73. For commentary and a collection of documents on this topic, see William M. Goldsmith, *The Growth of Presidential Power: A Documented History,* 3 vols. (New York: Chelsea House, 1974).

74. Hamilton, "The Federalist No. 8," in *FED,* 45, 46.

75. Woodrow Wilson, *Congressional Government: A Study in American Politics* (Boston: Houghton Mifflin, 1925), xix–xx.

76. See, in particular, *Remarks Occasioned by the Late Conduct of Mr. Washington as President of the United States* (Philadelphia: Printed for Benjamin Franklin Bache, 1797).

77. *Washington's Farewell Address,* ed. Victor H. Paltsits (New York: New York Public Library, 1935), 144; Farewell Radio and Television Address to the American People, January 17, 1961, in *Public Papers of the Presidents of the United States, Dwight D. Eisenhower, 1960–61* (Washington, D.C.: Government Printing Office, 1961), 1038.

78. "Harper's Index," *Harper's,* December 1996, 13.

79. See Benjamin Schwarz, "Why America Thinks It Has To Run the World," *Atlantic Monthly,* June 1996, 92–96, 98, 100–102.

80. See Robert Buzzanco, *Masters of War: Military Dissent and Politics in the Vietnam Era* (New York: Cambridge University Press, 1996), 1–23.

81. See E. J. Dionne Jr., *Why Americans Hate Politics* (New York: Simon and Schuster, 1991).

82. Don M. Snider and Miranda A. Carlton-Carew, eds., *U.S. Civil-Military Relations: In Crisis or Transition?* (Washington, D.C.: Center for Strategic and International Studies, 1995); Mike O'Connor, "Does Keeping the Peace Spoil G.I.'s for War?" *NYT,* December 13, 1996, A3 (national edition); Robert D. Kaplan, "Fort Leavenworth and the Eclipse of Nationhood," *Atlantic Monthly,* September 1996, 86, 88; Thomas E. Ricks, "Colonel Dunlap's Coup," *Atlantic Monthly,* January 1993, 23–25.

83. Charles J. Dunlap Jr., "The Origins of the American Military Coup of 2012," *Parameters* 22 (Winter 1992–93): 2, 3.

84. Joan M. Jensen, *Army Surveillance in America, 1775–1980* (New Haven: Yale University Press, 1991); Nelson W. Polsby, "Congress, National Security, and the Rise of the 'Presidential Branch,'" in *The Constitution and National Security: A Bicentennial View,* ed. Howard E. Shuman and Walter R. Thomas (Washington, D.C.: National Defense University Press, 1990), 201–10.

85. Michael A. Genovese, "Democratic Theory and the Emergency Powers of the President," *Presidential Studies Quarterly* 9 (Summer 1979): 286–87; Harold C. Relyea, "Reconsidering the National Emergencies Act: Its Evolution, Implementation, and Deficiencies," in *The Presidency and National Security Policy*, ed. R. Gordon Hoxie (New York: Center for the Study of the Presidency, 1984), 274–323.

86. Some presidents served in the military, but were not in combat. Twenty-one of the presidents from George Washington to George Bush saw battle. Sixteen are listed in Richard Brookhiser, "A Man on Horseback," *Atlantic Monthly*, January 1996, 55. According to a letter to the editor about Brookhiser's article, five more (James Madison, James Buchanan, Abraham Lincoln, Lyndon Johnson, and Gerald Ford) were also under enemy fire. William E. Rooney, "Man on Horseback," *Atlantic Monthly*, May 1996, 14.

87. Daniel P. Franklin, *Extraordinary Measures: The Exercise of Prerogative Powers in the United States* (Pittsburgh: University of Pittsburgh Press, 1991), 13. See also Thomas S. Langston, *With Reverence and Contempt: How Americans Think About Their President* (Baltimore: Johns Hopkins University Press, 1995), 92–115.

88. Harold Edgar and Benno C. Schmidt Jr., "*Curtiss-Wright* Comes Home: Executive Power and National Security Secrecy," *Harvard Civil Rights-Civil Liberties Law Review* 21 (Summer 1986): 352–3, 354.

89. Emory Upton, *The Military Policy of the United States* (Washington, D.C.: Government Printing Office, 1917), xi–xii; for a description of Upton and his accomplishments, see the preface to Upton's far-seeing and long-neglected work by Secretary of War Elihu Root (iii–v).

90. JB Pictures Inc. v. Department of Defense, 24 Med. L. Rptr. 2017 (D.C. Cir. 1996); Greer v. Spock, 424 U.S. 828 (1976).

91. Hamilton, "The Federalist No. 73," in *FED*, 495; Madison, "The Federalist No. 41," in *FED*, 269, 270.

92. Madison, "The Federalist No. 51," in *FED*, 349; Amendments to the Constitution, [June 8, 1789], in *PJM*, 12: 199, 205, 209; Amendments to the Constitution, [August 15, 1789], in *PJM*, 12: 340–41.

93. In the early years of the twentieth century, the Free Speech League, which was later eclipsed by the less libertarian ACLU, took the position that the expression of all viewpoints should be protected. David M. Rabban, "The Free Speech League, the ACLU, and Changing Conceptions of Free Speech in American History," *Stanford Law Review* 45 (November 1992): 47–114.

On the absolutism of two justices, see Howard Ball and Phillip J. Cooper, *Of Power and Right: Hugo Black, William O. Douglas, and America's Constitutional Revolution* (New York: Oxford University Press, 1992).

94. On this point, see [Charles F. Blake], *Prerogative Rights and Public Law* (Boston: William Guild, 1863), 8–10.

95. Theodore Schroeder, *Free Speech for Radicals*, enl. ed. (New York: Free Speech League, 1916; repr., New York: Burt Franklin, 1969), 1–2, 33.

96. Ronald D. Rotunda, "Original Intent, the View of the Framers, and the Role of the Ratifiers," *Vanderbilt Law Review* 41 (April 1988): 509; L. Kinvin Wroth, "The Constitution and the Common Law: The Original Intent about the Original Intent," *Suffolk University Law Review* 22 (Fall 1988): 553.

97. For criticisms of reliance on original intent, see, e. g., Charles McC. Mathias Jr., "Ordered Liberty: The Original Intent of the Constitution," *Maryland Law Review* 47 (Fall 1987): 174–88; Larry G. Simon, "The Authority of the Framers of the Constitution: Can Originalist Interpretation Be Justified?" *Virginia Law Review* 73 (July 1985): 1482–1539; Mark Tush-

net, "Following the Rules Laid Down: A Critique of Interpretivism and Neutral Principles," *Harvard Law Review* 96 (February 1983): 781–827; Paul Brest, "The Misconceived Quest for the Original Understanding," *Boston University Law Review* 60 (March 1980): 204–38; John Hart Ely, "Constitutional Interpretivism: Its Allure and Impossibility," *Indiana Law Journal* 53 (1978): 399–448.

98. For a variety of perspectives on the Ninth Amendment, see Randy E. Barnett, ed., *The Rights Retained by the People: The History and Meaning of the Ninth Amendment* (Fairfax, Va.: George Mason University Press, 1989).

99. Henry P. Monaghan, "Our Perfect Constitution," *New York University Law Review* 56 (May–June 1981): 353–96.

100. Charles A. Lofgren, "The Original Understanding of the Original Intent?" *Constitutional Commentary* 5 (Winter 1988): 77–113; Raoul Berger, " 'Original Intention' in Historical Perspective," *The George Washington Law Review* 54 (January and March 1986): 296–337. Both Lofgren and Berger take issue with the historical accuracy of H. Jefferson Powell, "The Original Understanding of Original Intent," *Harvard Law Review* 98 (March 1985): 885–948.

101. James Madison to Spencer Roane, May 6, 1821, in Hunt, *Writings of James Madison*, 9: 59. For a discussion of Madison's position in the context of his political theory, see Drew McCoy, *The Last of the Fathers: James Madison and the Republican Legacy* (Cambridge: Cambridge University Press, 1989), 78–79.

102. James Madison to John G. Jackson, December 27, 1821, in Hunt, *Writings of James Madison*, 9: 74. For a similar observation by Jefferson, see Thomas Jefferson to Judge Johnson, June 12, 1823, in *The Writings of Thomas Jefferson*, ed. H. A. Washington (Washington, D.C.: Taylor and Maury, 1853–54), 7: 296.

103. Madison, "The Federalist No. 63," in *FED*, 425.

104. See I. F. Stone, *The Trial of Socrates* (Boston: Little, Brown, 1988). Despite complaints, war-related topics could be discussed with an extraordinary amount of freedom of expression in Athens. Eli Sagan, *The Honey and the Hemlock: Democracy and Paranoia in Ancient Athens and Modern America* (New York: Basic Books, 1991; Princeton: Princeton University Press, 1994), 82–86.

Anglo-American history had given Madison reason for both concern and hope on the issue of popular support for freedom of expression. See Jeffery A. Smith, "Public Opinion and the Press," in *Media Voices: An Historical Perspective*, ed. Jean Folkerts (New York: Macmillan, 1992), 105–20.

Chapter 3

1. Vincent Blasi, "The Checking Value in First Amendment Theory," *American Bar Foundation Research Journal* 1977 (Summer 1977): 523–28; Thomas I. Emerson, "Colonial Intentions and Current Realities of the First Amendment," *University of Pennsylvania Law Review* 125 (April 1977): 737–60.

2. See Daniel P. Franklin, *Extraordinary Measures: The Exercise of Prerogative Powers in the United States* (Pittsburgh: University of Pittsburgh Press, 1991).

3. See Mark Tushnet, "Critical Legal Studies: A Political History," *Yale Law Journal* 100 (March 1991): 1524, 1526.

4. See Harold Hongju Koh, *The National Security Constitution: Sharing Power after the Iran-Contra Affair* (New Haven: Yale University Press, 1990).

5. See, for example, Thomas J. Scheff, *Bloody Revenge: Emotions, Nationalism, and War* (Boulder, Colo.: Westview Press, 1994); Karla Schweitzer, Dolf Zillmann, James B. Weaver, and Elizabeth Luttrell, "Perception of Threatening Events in the Emotional Aftermath of a Televised College Football Game," *Journal of Broadcasting & Electronic Media* 36 (Winter 1992): 75–82.

6. Daniel Goleman, *Emotional Intelligence* (New York: Bantam Books, 1995), 291–96.

7. "Harper's Index," *Harper's*, February 1996, 11; "When Bombs Fall, Polls Rise," *Time*, July 12, 1993, 11.

8. See Robert O. Wyatt, *Free Expression and the American Public: A Survey Commemorating the 200th Anniversary of the First Amendment* (Murfreesboro: Middle Tennessee State University, 1991), 28, 31.

9. Vincent Blasi, "The Pathological Perspective and the First Amendment," *Columbia Law Review* 85 (April 1985): 513.

10. Marbury v. Madison, 1 Cranch (5 U.S.) 137, 163 (1803).

11. For background, see Sung Hui Kim, " 'We (the Supermajority of) the People': The Development of a Rationale for Written Higher Law in North American Constitutions," *Proceedings of the American Philosophical Society* 137 (September 1993): 364–89.

12. Peter J. Hammer, "Free Speech and the 'Acid Bath': An Evaluation and Critique of Judge Richard Posner's Economic Interpretation of the First Amendment," *Michigan Law Review* 87 (November 1988): 513.

13. West Virginia State Board of Education v. Barnette, 319 U.S. 624, 637, 638 (1943).

14. C. Thomas Dienes, "When the First Amendment Is Not Preferred: The Military and Other 'Special Contexts,' " *University of Cincinnati Law Review* 56 (1988): 779–843.

15. Greer v. Spock, 424 U.S. 828, 840 (1976).

16. On repression of people in the military, see, for example, William V. Kennedy, *The Military and the Media: Why the Press Cannot Be Trusted To Cover a War* (Westport, Conn.: Praeger, 1993), 31, 135–36; Richard Moe, *The Last Full Measure: The Life and Death of the First Minnesota Volunteers* (New York: Holt, 1993), 69–72; James R. Mock, *Censorship 1917* (Princeton: Princeton University Press, 1941); "The Court-Martial of Private Spencer: From the Records of the U.S. Army," *Civil War Times Illustrated* 27 (February 1989): 35–40. In some cases the military has attempted to interfere with press access to the civilian survivors of personnel who have died while on duty. See, for example, Delbert Willis, "The Press vs. the General," *Neiman Reports*, July 1951, 17–18. On limitation of access to mass media, see, for example, Nancy K. Bristow, *Making Men Moral: Social Engineering during the Great War* (New York: New York University Press, 1996), 44; Paul Blanshard, *The Right to Read: The Battle Against Censorship* (Boston: Beacon Press, 1955), 113–21; William M. Leary Jr., "Books, Soldiers and Censorship during the Second World War," *American Quarterly* 20 (Summer 1968): 237–45.

17. Patrick S. Washburn, *A Question of Sedition: The Federal Government's Investigation of the Black Press during World War II* (New York: Oxford University Press, 1986), 153.

18. Frank J. Wetta and Stephen J. Curley, *Celluloid Wars: A Guide to Film and the American Experience of War* (New York: Greenwood Press, 1992), 6–7.

19. "Touchy Topics in the Gulf," *Harper's*, November 1990, 18, 20; Eric Schmitt, "The News from Home (but Nothing Offensive)," *NYT*, September 6, 1990, A6 (national edition).

20. John R. MacArthur, *Second Front: Censorship and Propaganda in the Gulf War* (New York: Hill and Wang, 1992), 165–91; John E. Smith, "From the Front Lines to the Front Page: Media Access to War in the Persian Gulf and Beyond," *Columbia Journal of Law and Social Problems* 26 (Winter 1993): 328–29.

21. Dick Runels, "Desert Shield: A Reservist's Chronicle," *Harper's*, February 1991, 26–28.

22. Debra Gersh Hernandez, " 'Embedding' Leads to Restrictions," *E&P*, May 25, 1996, 10–11.

23. Alfred E. Cornebise, *Ranks and Columns: Armed Forces Newspapers in American Wars* (Westport, Conn.: Greenwood Press, 1993); Ken Zumwalt, *The Stars and Stripes: World War II and the Early Years* (Austin, Tex.: Eakin Press, 1989); General Accounting Office, *Stars and Stripes: Inherent Conflicts Lead to Allegations of Military Censorship* (Washington, D.C.: General

Accounting Office, 1988); Alfred E. Cornebise, "American Armed Forces Newspapers in World War II," *American Journalism* 12 (Summer 1995): 213–24; William S. Lind, "Reading, Writing, and Policy Review: The Air Force's Unilateral Disarmament in the War of Ideas," *Air University Review* 36 (November–December 1984): 66–70; Alan L. Gropman, "On Nonconformity," *Air University Review* 37 (September–October 1986): 100–101.

24. " 'Gag Rule' Still Operative in War Dept.," *E&P*, November 15, 1947, 12.

25. Frank C. Clough, "Operations of the Press Division of the Office of Censorship," *Journalism Quarterly* 20 (September 1943): 224.

26. "This Is What the Soldiers Complain About," *Life*, August 18, 1941, 17–19.

27. Laurence W. Mazzeno, "Getting the Word to Willie and Joe," *Military Review* 67 (August 1987): 70; *The Army Almanac: A Book of Facts Concerning the United States Army*, 2nd ed. (Harrisburg, Penn.: Stackpole, 1959), 352.

28. Warren E. Leary, "U.S. To Compensate 4,000 Injured by Poison Gases," *NYT*, January 7, 1993, A11 (national edition). In 1996 the U.S. Army began a seven-year, $12 billion program for destroying tens of thousands of tons of mustard and nerve gas. "Army Commences the Burning of a Vast Chemical Arsenal," *NYT*, August 23, 1996, A12 (national edition).

29. "Varied Views on Possible Censorship," *Bulletin*, February 13, 1941. Copies of the *Bulletin* are available in the Gannett Archives, Freedom Forum World Center, Arlington, Virginia.

30. See Cathy Packer, *Freedom of Expression in the American Military: A Communication Modeling Analysis* (New York: Praeger, 1989), 195–98.

31. Hans Schmidt, *Maverick Marine: General Smedley D. Butler and the Contradictions of American Military History* (Lexington: University Press of Kentucky, 1987), 208–11.

32. Richard Halloran, "Soldiers and Scribblers Revisited: Working with the Media," *Parameters* 21 (Spring 1991): 13; John Barry, "A Second Look at an Air War," *Newsweek*, January 7, 1991, 18; Bruce van Voorst, "Ready, Aim, Fired," *Time*, October 1, 1990, 55; Debra Gersh, "General Fired for Talking to the Press," *E&P*, September 22, 1990, 22; Eric Schmitt, "Air Force Chief Is Dismissed for Remarks on Gulf Plan; Cheney Cites Bad Judgment," *NYT*, September 18, 1990, A1 (national edition).

33. U.S. v. Voorhees, 4 C.M.A. 509 (1954); Melvin B. Voorhees, *Korean Tales* (New York: Simon and Schuster, 1952); Billy C. Mossman, *Ebb and Flow: November 1950–July 1951* (Washington, D.C.: Center of Military History, United States Army, 1990), 305, 319.

34. See Dienes, "When the First Amendment Is Not Preferred," 816–17; Lind, "Reading, Writing, and Policy Review," 70. The issue may also be extremist political views, as in the case of Major General Edwin A. Walker, a member of the John Birch Society who was relieved of his command in West Germany. "Milestones," *Time*, November 15, 1993, 35.

35. Parker v. Levy, 417 U.S. 733, 758 (1974).

36. Parker v. Levy, 417 U.S. 733, 774; Parker v. Levy, 417 U.S. 733, 768, 769.

37. Goldman v. Weinberger, 475 U.S. 503 (1986).

38. U.S. v. Wilson, 33 M.J. 797, 799 (A.C.M.R. 1991).

39. Clinton Rossiter, *The Supreme Court and the Commander in Chief*, expanded ed. (Ithaca, N.Y.: Cornell University Press, 1976), 128–29. One reason used for refusing to become involved in foreign policy issues is that courts should leave such matters to the "political branches." For the position that the "political question" doctrine "is all too often a judicial code word for avoiding a judicial duty to protect litigants from unlawful exercises of executive power," see Michael Tigar, "What the Constitution Means by Executive Power," *University of Miami Law Review* 43 (September 1988): 177–88.

40. U.S. v. Macintosh, 283 U.S. 605, 622 (1931). See Joel F. Paschal, *Mr. Justice Sutherland: A Man against the State* (Princeton: Princeton University Press, 1951; repr., New York: Greenwood Press, 1969).

41. Home Building & Loan Association v. Blaisdell, 290 U.S. 398, 426 (1934).

42. Near v. Minnesota, 283 U.S. 697, 713, 714, 716, 717 (1931); "The Report of 1800," in *PJM*, 17: 337. As early as 1912 the Supreme Court had heard the argument that the press clause was intended to prevent both prior restraint and subsequent punishment. The argument was made for an unsuccessful appellant in a case involving the postal classification of publications. "The history, which preceded the First Amendment," the attorney argued, "clearly shows that it was made to prevent a censorship of the press either by anticipation through a licensing system or retrospectively by obstruction or punishment." Lewis Publishing v. Morgan, 229 U.S. 288, 292 (1913).

43. Nelson A. Miles to Francis J. Higginson, July 22, 1898, in *Nelson A. Miles: A Documentary Biography of His Military Career, 1861–1903*, ed. Brian C. Pohanka (Glendale, Cal.: Clark, 1985), 282.

44. *Complete Report of the Chairman of the Committee on Public Information* (Washington, D.C.: Government Printing Office, 1920), 10–13; Stephen Vaughn, *Holding Fast the Inner Lines: Democracy, Nationalism, and the Committee on Public Information* (Chapel Hill: University of North Carolina Press, 1980), 218–21. The issue of the legality of suppressing information on troop movements is an old one in America. Colonial officials operating under British law during the French and Indian War sometimes thought they had the power to control press accounts of military operations as intelligence useful to the enemy and sometimes wondered what authority, if any, they could exercise. For two contrasting cases, see *Journals of the House of Representatives of Massachusetts, 1755* (Boston: Massachusetts Historical Society, 1957), 32, pt. 1: 155; *Minutes of the Provincial Council of Pennsylvania* (Harrisburg: Theo. Fenn, 1851), 7: 339, 447. The motivation for attempts to restrict the press, however, may have had more to do with the desire to stop critical accounts of military expeditions than with security. See Clyde A. Duniway, *The Development of Freedom of the Press in Massachusetts* (New York: Longmans, Green, 1906), 121–22.

45. William Blackstone, *Commentaries on the Laws of England* (Philadelphia: Robert Bell, 1772), 4: 151–53. See Daniel J. Boorstin, *The Mysterious Science of the Law: An Essay on Blackstone's Commentaries* (Cambridge: Harvard University Press, 1941).

46. Jeffery A. Smith, *Printers and Press Freedom: The Ideology of Early American Journalism* (New York: Oxford University Press, 1988); Stephen A. Smith, "The Origins of the Free Speech Clause," *Free Speech Yearbook* 29 (1991): 48–82; David A. Anderson, "The Origins of the Press Clause," *UCLA Law Review* 30 (February 1983): 455–541. For the much-criticized view that the founders relied on Blackstone and did not intend to wipe out the crime of seditious libel, see Leonard W. Levy, *Emergence of a Free Press* (New York: Oxford University Press, 1985). For some of the failures of Levy's scholarship, see Smith, *Printers and Press Freedom*, 4–11; David A. Anderson, "Levy vs. Levy," *Michigan Law Review* 84 (February–April 1986): 777–86; David M. Rabban, "The Ahistorical Historian: Leonard Levy on Freedom of Expression in Early American History," *Stanford Law Review* 37 (February 1985): 795–56. Levy himself has admitted that he distorted history to spite scholars who had rejected his interpretation. Levy, *Emergence of a Free Press*, vii–ix.

47. "The Report of 1800," in *PJM*, 17: 336–38.

48. See Margaret A. Blanchard, "Filling in the Void: Speech and Press in State Courts prior to *Gitlow*," in *The First Amendment Reconsidered: New Perspectives on the Meaning of Freedom of Speech and Press*, ed. Bill F. Chamberlin and Charlene Brown (New York: Longman, 1982), 14–43.

49. People v. Most, 171 N.Y. 423, 429–32 (1902). Prior to the McKinley assassination and World War I, authorities tended to avoid the use of statutes and court cases to suppress disquieting views. They may have recalled the consequences of the Sedition Act of 1798 and wished to avoid the kind of accusations that formal violations of press freedom could bring. See Paul

L. Murphy, "*Near v. Minnesota* in the Context of Historical Developments," *Minnesota Law Review* 66 (November 1981): 129.

50. Patterson v. Colorado, 205 U.S. 454, 462 (1907).

51. 283 U.S. 697, 715, 716.

52. This point is made in Anderson, "Origins of the Press Clause," 534.

53. Grosjean v. American Press Co., 297 U.S. 233, 248 (1936). For background on the switch in Supreme Court thinking, see Richard C. Cortner, *The Kingfish and the Constitution: Huey Long, the First Amendment, and the Emergence of Modern Press Freedom in America* (Westport, Conn.: Greenwood Press, 1996).

54. For examples of the *Near* dictum being used to justify suppression, see Haig v. Agee, 453 U.S. 280, 308 (1981); United States v. Progressive, 467 F.Supp. 990, 992 (1979); New York Times v. U.S., 403 U.S. 713, 749 (1971) (Burger, C.J., dissenting). For commentators, see, for example, Henry Mark Holzer, "The First Amendment and National Security," *University of Miami Law Review* 43 (September 1988): 64, 66; Marshall Silverberg, "Constitutional Concerns in Denying the Press Access to Military Operations," in *Defense Beat: The Dilemma of Defense Coverage*, ed. Loren B. Thompson (New York: Lexington Books, 1991), 166–69.

A federal law, the Intelligence Identities Protection Act of 1982, prohibits anyone, including reporters, to make an unauthorized disclosure of information identifying covert United States intelligence officers and their informants. Pub. L. No. 97–200, 96 Stat. 122 (1982).

55. On problems with prior restraint doctrine, see Steven Helle, "Prior Restraint by the Backdoor: Conditional Rights," *Villanova Law Review* 39 (1994): 817–77; Jeffery A. Smith, "Prior Restraint: Original Intentions and Modern Interpretations," *William and Mary Law Review* 28 (Spring 1987): 439–72.

56. 283 U.S. 697, 716.

57. Holzer, "First Amendment and National Security," 65.

58. Terminiello v. Chicago, 337 U.S. 1, 37 (1949) (Jackson, J., dissenting).

59. See William T. Mayton, "Seditious Libel and the Lost Guarantee of a Freedom of Expression," *Columbia Law Review* 84 (January 1984): 141.

60. Philip Bobbitt, *Constitutional Fate, Theory of the Constitution* (New York: Oxford University Press, 1982), 61.

61. Hugo L. Black, "The Bill of Rights," *New York University Law Review* 35 (April 1960): 878, 879. See, in the same issue, an attack on balancing by a Madison biographer: Irving Brant, "The Madison Heritage," 882–902.

62. Black, "Bill of Rights," 865, 874.

63. See, e. g., "Justice Black and First Amendment 'Absolutes': A Public Interview," *New York University Law Review* 37 (June 1962): 554.

64. "Justice Black and First Amendment 'Absolutes,' " 554, 555, 558, 559, 563.

65. Black, "Bill of Rights," 866.

66. Jeffery A. Smith, "Further Steps toward a Theory of Press Control," *Journalism History* 8 (Autumn-Winter 1981): 93–95.

67. Jay, "The Federalist No. 3," in *FED*, 13–14; Hamilton, "The Federalist No. 8," in *FED*, 45.

68. Richard Hofstadter, *The Paranoid Style in American Politics and Other Essays* (New York: Knopf, 1965).

69. See James L. Baughman, " 'The World Is Ruled by Those Who Holler the Loudest': The Third-Person Effect in American Journalism History," *Journalism History* 16 (Spring–Summer 1989): 12–19; W. Phillips Davison, "The Third-Person Effect in Communication," *Public Opinion Quarterly* 47 (Spring 1983): 1–15.

70. Roscoe Pound, "Interests of Personality [pt. 2]," *Harvard Law Review* 28 (March 1915): 453, 454, 455; Theodore Schroeder, *Free Speech for Radicals*, enl. ed. (New York: Free Speech League, 1916; repr., New York: Burt Franklin, 1969), 93.

71. Congress, Senate, 65th Cong., 2nd sess., *Congressional Record* (May 4, 1917), vol. 56, pt. 6, 6038.

72. Schenck v. U.S., 249 U.S. 47, 52 (1919).

73. For a critique of the fire analogy that makes similar and additional points, see Alan Dershowitz, "Shouting 'Fire!'" *Atlantic Monthly*, January 1989, 72–74. On the difficult issues involved in crime and communication, see Kent Greenawalt, *Speech, Crime, and the Uses of Language* (New York: Oxford University Press, 1989); C. Edwin Baker, *Human Liberty and Freedom of Speech* (New York: Oxford University Press, 1989), 47–91.

74. Frohwerk v. U.S., 249 U.S. 204, 205, 209 (1919).

75. See Richard Polenberg, *Fighting Faiths: The Abrams Case, the Supreme Court, and Free Speech* (New York: Penguin Books, 1989), 218–28; Edward J. Bloustein, "Criminal Attempts and the 'Clear and Present Danger' Theory of the First Amendment," *Cornell Law Review* 74 (September 1989): 1118–50; David M. Rabban, "The Emergence of Modern First Amendment Doctrine," *University of Chicago Law Review* 50 (Fall 1983): 1205–1355; David S. Bogen, "The Free Speech Metamorphosis of Mr. Justice Holmes," *Hofstra Law Review* 11 (Fall 1982): 97–189; Robert M. Cover, "The Left, the Right and the First Amendment, 1918–1928," *Maryland Law Review* (1981): 349–88; Donald L. Smith, "Zechariah Chafee Jr. and the Positive View of Press Freedom," *Journalism History* 5 (Autumn 1978): 86–92; Fred D. Ragan, "Justice Oliver Wendell Holmes, Jr., Zechariah Chafee, Jr., and the Clear and Present Danger Test for Free Speech: The First Year, 1919," *Journal of American History* 58 (June 1971): 24–45.

76. Abrams et al. v. U.S., 250 U.S. 616, 628, 630–31 (1919) (Holmes, J., dissenting); Brief on Behalf of the United States, Abrams et al. v. U.S., in *Landmark Briefs and Arguments of the Supreme Court of the United States: Constitutional Law*, ed. Philip B. Kurland and Gerhard Casper (Arlington, Va.: University Publications of America, 1975–), 19: 842, 846–57.

77. Schaefer v. U.S., 251 U.S. 466, 477, 495 (1920).

78. Lauren Kessler, *The Dissident Press: Alternative Journalism in American History* (Beverly Hills, Calif.: Sage Publications, 1984), 128–29; Kenneth E. Hendrickson, "Urban Socialism," in *Historical Dictionary of the Progressive Era, 1890–1920*, ed. John D. Buenker and Edward R. Kantowicz (New York: Greenwood Press, 1988), 442; Frederick C. Giffin, "Socialist Party of America," in Buenker and Kantowicz, *Historical Dictionary of the Progressive Era*, 443–44.

79. Debs v. U.S., 249 U.S. 211, 213, 216 (1919).

80. Pierce v. U.S., 252 U.S. 239, 250–52 (1920).

81. Pierce v. U.S., 252 U.S. at 270–71 (Brandeis, J., dissenting).

82. This point about the "clear and present danger" test is made in Richard W. Steele, "Fear of the Mob and Faith in Government in Free Speech Discourse, 1919–1941," *American Journal of Legal History* 38 (January 1994), 64.

83. See Paul L. Murphy, "Sources and Nature of Intolerance in the 1920s," *Journal of American History*," 51 (June 1964): 60–76.

84. Charles E. Hughes, "War Powers under the Constitution," *Marquette Law Review* (1917–1918): 3, 10, 18; Henry J. Fletcher, "The Civilian and the War Power," *Minnesota Law Review* 2 (January 1918): 130–31.

85. *War Cyclopedia: A Handbook for Ready Reference on the Great War*, ed. Frederic L. Paxson, Edward S. Corwin, and Samuel B. Harding (Washington, D.C.: Government Printing Office, 1918), 218, 295–96. The *Federalist* spoke of unlimited authority to commit resources to war and to direct the military, but not, as the *War Cyclopedia* implied, to curtail liberties. See, for example, Hamilton, "The Federalist No. 23," in *FED*, 147, 148.

For a description of the book project in the context of similar efforts involving scholars, see George T. Blakey, *Historians on the Homefront: American Propagandists for the Great War* (Lexington: University Press of Kentucky, 1970), 34–56.

86. Paxson, Corwin, and Harding, *War Cyclopedia*, 101; Vaughn, *Holding Fast the Inner Lines*, 229.

87. On the labor strife and irrational fears that followed World War I, see Robert K. Murray, *Red Scare: A Study in National Hysteria, 1919–1920* (Minneapolis: University of Minnesota Press, 1955; New York: McGraw-Hill 1964); Stanley A. Coben, *A. Mitchell Palmer: Politician* (New York: Columbia University Press, 1963).

88. McCulloch v. Maryland, 17 U.S. (4 Wheat.) 316, 421 (1819).

89. Edward S. Corwin, "Freedom of Speech and Press under the First Amendment: A Résumé," *Yale Law Journal* 30 (November 1920): 54–55.

90. For a critique of Corwin's claims that provides a contrast to earlier constitutional theory and points out historical inaccuracies, see Gary L. McDowell, "Coke, Corwin, and the Constitution: The 'Higher Law Background' Reconsidered," *Review of Politics* 55 (Summer 1993): 393–420.

91. See Christopher N. May, *In the Name of War: Judicial Review and the War Powers since 1918* (Cambridge: Harvard University Press, 1989), 19–21; Thomas A. Lawrence, "Eclipse of Liberty: Civil Liberties in the United States during the First World War," *Wayne Law Review* 21 (November 1974): 33–112.

92. Garrard Glenn, *The Army and the Law* (New York: Columbia University Press, 1918), 143–44; W. R. Vance, "Freedom of Speech and of the Press," *Minnesota Law Review* 2 (March 1918): 258–59, 260; Day Kimball, "The Espionage Act and the Limits of Legal Toleration," *Harvard Law Review* 33 (January 1920): 446, 447, 448. For an article that uses eighteenth-century sources to reach the unusual conclusion that the First Amendment is absolute, but which nevertheless justifies the Espionage Act and Sedition Act by arguing that defendants were advising others to disobey the law, see Fred. B. Hart, "Power of Government Over Speech and Press," *Yale Law Journal* 29 (February 1920): 410–28.

93. Polenberg, *Fighting Faiths,* 101, 103; Zechariah Chafee Jr., *Freedom of Speech* (New York: Harcourt, Brace and Howe, 1920), 125–48.

94. Abrams trial transcript, as quoted in Polenberg, *Fighting Faiths,* 142.

95. U.S. v. Motion Picture Film "The Spirit of '76," 252 F. 946, 947, 948 (S. D. Cal., S. D., 1919).

96. Goldstein v. U.S., 258 F. 908 (9th Cir. 1919).

97. For background, see Larry W. Ward, *The Motion Picture Goes to War: The U.S. Government Film Effort During World War I* (Ann Arbor, Mich.: UMI Research Press, 1985), 118–19; Edward de Grazia and Roger K. Newman, *Banned Films: Movies, Censors and the First Amendment* (New York: R. R. Bowker, 1982), 20; James R. Mock and Cedric Larson, *Words That Won the War: The Story of the Committee on Public Information* (Princeton: Princeton University Press, 1939), 147–48.

98. John H. Wigmore, "*Abrams v. U.S.*: Freedom of Speech and Freedom of Thuggery in War-time and Peace-time," *Illinois Law Review* 14 (March 1920): 549, 552–53, 554. For an article that attempted to make legal sense of the federal legislation, see Thomas F. Carroll, "Freedom of Speech and of the Press in War Time: The Espionage Act," *Michigan Law Review* 17 (June 1919): 621–65.

99. Polenberg, *Fighting Faiths,* 223–28.

100. Harold J. Laski, *Authority in the Modern State* (New Haven: Yale University Press, 1919), 23, 56, 57, 78.

101. Peter H. Irons, " 'Fighting Fair': Zechariah Chafee, Jr., the Department of Justice, and the 'Trial at the Harvard Club,' " *Harvard Law Review* 94 (April 1981): 1205–36; Zechariah Chafee Jr., "Freedom of Speech in War Time," *Harvard Law Review* 32 (June 1919): 947.

102. Polenberg, *Fighting Faiths,* 222–24.

103. Chafee, *Freedom of Speech,* 8–11, 25, 32–34, 36, 37, 38, 88–89, 155–60; Zechariah Chafee Jr., *Free Speech in the United States* (Cambridge: Harvard University Press, 1942). Chafee continued to oppose First Amendment absolutism and to promote the "clear and present danger"

test into the period of the Smith Act prosecutions. See his review of Alexander Meiklejohn's *Free Speech: And Its Relation to Self-Government* in *Harvard Law Review* 62 (March 1949): 891–901. For a detailed discussion of Chafee's views, see Donald L. Smith, *Zechariah Chafee, Jr.: Defender of Liberty and Law* (Cambridge: Harvard University Press, 1986).

104. Gitlow v. People of New York, 268 U.S. 652, 669, 672 (1925).

105. Gitlow v. People of New York, 268 U.S. at 672–73 (Holmes, J., dissenting).

106. Hartzel v. U.S., 322 U.S. 680, 682–83, 684–87, 689 (1944).

107. Dennis v. U.S., 341 U.S. 494, 509, 511, 580, 581 (1951).

108. Brief for Appellants, at 121, 125, 126, Frankfeld v. U.S., 198 F.2d 679 (4th Cir. 1952) (No. 6437), Records and Briefs, Vol. 1009, National Archives, Mid-Atlantic Region, Philadelphia, Pennsylvania; Frankfeld v. U.S., 198 F.2d 679, 682 (4th Cir. 1952).

109. Margaret A. Blanchard, *Exporting the First Amendment: The Press-Government Crusade of 1945–1952* (New York: Longman, 1986); Samuel Walker, *In Defense of American Liberties: A History of the ACLU* (New York: Oxford University Press, 1990), 173–96, 244.

110. Brief for the Petitioner, Barenblatt v. U.S., in Kurland and Casper, *Landmark Briefs*, 54: 828–30; Brief for the United States, Barenblatt v. U. S., in Kurland and Casper, *Landmark Briefs*, 54: 916, 917, 919; Barenblatt v. U.S., 360 U.S. 109, 128–29, 134 (1959).

111. Barenblatt v. U. S., 360 U.S. at 143, 144, 145–146, 151 (1959) (Black, J., dissenting). For an article agreeing with Black and arguing that political freedom is the ultimate value, see Alexander Meiklejohn, "The Balancing of Self-Preservation against Political Freedom," *California Law Review* 49 (March 1961): 4–14.

112. Madison, "The Federalist No. 10," in *FED*, 58, 64.

113. New York Times v. U.S., 403 U.S. 713 (1971).

114. CIA v. Sims, 471 U.S. 159, 172 (1985); Snepp v. U.S., 444 U.S. 507, 512 (1980); U.S. v. Morison, 844 F.2d 1057 (4th Cir. 1988), *cert. denied*, 486 U.S. 330 (1988).

115. For a detailed account of the Sterling Hall incident, see Tom Bates, *Rads: The 1970 Bombing of the Army Math Research Center at the University of Wisconsin and Its Aftermath* (New York: HarperCollins, 1992).

116. State v. Knops, 49 Wis. 2d 647, 657–59 (1971); Carolyn Stewart Dyer, "Today *Kaleidoscope*; Tomorrow the *New York Times*," paper presented to the Association for Education in Journalism convention, Madison, Wisconsin, August 24, 1977.

117. Warren, as quoted in Bates, *Rads*, 396; Kleindienst, as quoted in Ward Churchill and Jim Vander Wall, *The Cointelpro Papers: Documents from the FBI's Secret Wars against Domestic Dissent* (Boston: South End Press, 1990), 165.

118. Angus MacKenzie, *Secrets: The CIA's War at Home* (Berkeley: University of California Press, 1997); M. Wesley Swearingen, *FBI Secrets: An Agent's Exposé* (Boston: South End Press, 1995), 105–27; James Kirkpatrick Davis, *Spying on America: The FBI's Domestic Counterintelligence Program* (New York: Praeger, 1992), 153–55; Churchill and Vander Wall, *Cointelpro Papers*, 165–230; Abe Peck, *Uncovering the Sixties: The Life and Times of the Underground Press* (New York: Pantheon Books, 1985); Kessler, *Dissident Press*, 148–53; Geoffrey Rips, *The Campaign against the Underground Press* (San Francisco: City Lights Books, 1981).

119. Churchill and Vander Wall, *Cointelpro Papers*, 226. For the theory that the Sterling Hall bombing suspect who was not arrested was a government informant, see Bates, *Rads*, 399, 434.

120. 42 U.S.C. § 2280 (1988).

121. Howard Morland, *The Secret That Exploded* (New York: Random House, 1981), 152–53.

122. These excerpts from the affidavit are quoted in Howard Morland, " 'The Ultimate Secret Is Not Really a Secret,' " *Washington Post*, March 28, 1979, A23.

123. Erwin Knoll, "The H-Bomb and the First Amendment," *William & Mary Bill of Rights Journal* 3 (Winter 1994): 708–9.

124. Judge Robert Warren's temporary restraining order, as quoted in Morland, *The Secret That Exploded*, 156.

125. U.S. v. Progressive, Inc., 467 F.Supp. 990, 992, 993, 995 (1979). On the great difficulties involved in making an explosive device from plutonium or uranium, see Michael D. Lemonick, "Can a Free-Lancer Build a Bomb?" *Time*, August 29, 1994, 48–49.

126. John Barry, "Reality Check," *Newsweek*, October 6, 1997, 42–43; Bruce W. Nelan, "Formula for Terror," *Time*, August 29, 1994, 46–51.

127. Bruce W. Nelan, "America the Vulnerable," *Time*, November 24, 1997, 50–51.

128. Richard J. Barnet, "Still Putting Arms First," *Harper's*, February 1993, 62.

129. On the difficulty of containing information in such cases, see Eric B. Easton, "Closing the Barn Door after the Genie Is Out of the Bag: Recognizing a 'Futility Principle' in First Amendment Jurisprudence," *DePaul Law Review* 45 (Fall 1995): 1–64.

130. Morland, *The Secret That Exploded*, 158–228. Along with Morland and a number of other observers, the editor of the *Progressive*, Erwin Knoll, believed that the government dropped the case because it feared losing and thereby endangering the broad provisions of the Atomic Energy Act. Erwin Knoll to Jeffery A. Smith, April 3, 1986, letter in possession of the author.

131. A. DeVolpi, G. E. Marsh, T. A. Postol, and G. S. Stanford, *Born Secret: The H-Bomb, the Progressive Case and National Security* (New York: Pergamon Press, 1981), 97, 108–9. For a detailed account of the case, see Bill Lueders, *An Enemy of the State: The Life of Erwin Knoll* (Monroe, Maine: Common Courage Press, 1996), 151–200.

132. Erwin Knoll, " 'Born Secret': The Story behind the H-Bomb Article We're Not Allowed to Print," *Progressive*, May 1979, 12–22; Howard Morland, "The H-Bomb Secret: To Know How Is To Ask Why," *Progressive*, November 1979, 14–23.

133. Tim Weiner, "U.S. Discloses How It Discovered That Soviets Sought Atomic Bomb," *NYT*, July 12, 1995, A1 (national edition). One of the more absurd actions was to bar reporters from test explosions that were witnessed by thousands of soldiers. "Reporters Can't See What Soldiers Will," *E&P*, October 20, 1951, 7.

134. Philip J. Hilts, "Secret Radioactive Experiments To Bring Compensation by U.S.," *NYT*, November 20, 1996, A1 (national edition); Michael D. Lemonick, "Rocky Horror Show," *Time*, November 27, 1995, 69–70; Philip J. Hilts, "Fallout Risk Near Atom Tests Was Known, Documents Show," *NYT*, March 15, 1995, A13 (national edition); Philip J. Hilts, "Panel Finds Wide Debate in 40's on the Ethics of Radiation Tests," *NYT*, October 12, 1994, A1 (national edition); Keith Schneider, "Signatures in Experiment Called Forgeries," *NYT*, April 12, 1994, A11 (national edition); Debra D. Durocher, "Radiation Redux," *American Journalism Review*, March 1994, 34–37. Biological weapon experiments were also conducted on human subjects. Leonard A. Cole, "The Worry: Germ Warfare. The Target: Us," *NYT*, January 25, 1994, A15 (national edition).

135. Colonel O. G. Haywood Jr. to "Dr. Fidler," April 17, 1947, as quoted in Robert Jay Lifton and Greg Mitchell, *Hiroshima in America: Fifty Years of Denial* (New York: Putnam, 1995), 64.

136. Lifton and Mitchell, 23–92; Allan M. Winkler, *Life under a Cloud: American Anxiety about the Atom* (New York: Oxford University Press, 1993); James G. Hershberg, *James B. Conant: Harvard to Hiroshima and the Making of the Nuclear Age* (New York: Knopf, 1993), 349–90; Brian Balogh, *Chain Reaction: Expert Debate and Public Participation in American Commercial Nuclear Power, 1945–1975* (Cambridge: Cambridge University Press, 1991); Paul Boyer, *By the Bomb's Early Light: American Thought and Culture at the Dawn of the Nuclear Age* (New York: Pantheon Books, 1985).

137. James F. Farrell, "American Atomic Culture," *American Quarterly* 43 (March 1991): 157–64; William W. Savage Jr., *Comic Books and America, 1945–54* (Norman: University of Oklahoma Press, 1990), 14–23; David Dowling, *Fictions of Nuclear Disaster* (Iowa City: University of Iowa Press, 1987).

138. Ian Fleming, *Thunderball* (New York: Viking Press, 1961), 75, 122.

139. "White Sox Win Pennant!" *Chicago Tribune,* September 23, 1959, 1 (final edition); "Use of Sirens to Hail Sox Angers Many," *Chicago Tribune,* September 24, 1959, 1; "Nikita Urges Regular Talks, Visits Iowans," *Chicago Tribune,* September 23, 1959, 1; "Lusty Talks at End of Lusty Journey," *Life,* October 5, 1959, 35–43.

140. Knoll, "The H-Bomb and the First Amendment," 706, 712.

141. Newt Gingrich and William R. Forstchen, *1945* (Riverdale, N.Y.: Baen, 1995).

142. Bradley Dewey, "High Policy and the Atomic Bomb," *Atlantic Monthly,* December 1948, 37–39.

143. David Bradley, "No Place to Hide," *Atlantic Monthly,* December 1948, 70; William S. Ellis, "A Way of Life Lost: Bikini," *National Geographic* 169 (June 1986): 810–34; Matthew L. Wald, "U.S. Atomic Tests in 50's Exposed Millions to Risk," *NYT,* July 29, 1997, A8 (national edition).

144. David M. Rubin and Constance Cummings, "Nuclear War and Its Consequences on Television News," *Journal of Communication* 39 (Winter 1989): 39–58; Winkler, *Life under a Cloud,* 109–35; "Newspapers Plan Defense Programs, Bomb Shelters," *E&P,* January 20, 1951, 9.

145. Michio Kaku and Daniel Axelrod, *To Win a Nuclear War: The Pentagon's Secret War Plans* (Boston: South End Press, 1987). See also, Marc Trachtenberg, "A 'Wasting Asset': American Strategy and the Shifting Nuclear Balance, 1949–1954," *International Security* 13 (Winter 1988–1989): 5–49; Roger Dingman, "Atomic Diplomacy during the Korean War," *International Security* 13 (Winter 1988–1989): 50–91; Rubin and Cummings, "Nuclear War and Its Consequences on Television News," 44–45.

146. NSC 162/2, October 30, 1953, paragraph 39.b., *Foreign Relations of the United States, 1952–1954,* vol. 2, *National Security Affairs* (Washington, D.C.: Government Printing Office, 1984), 593.

147. Richard Rhodes, "The General and World War III," *New Yorker,* June 19, 1995, 47–48, 53–59.

148. Richard Rhodes, *Dark Sun: The Making of the Hydrogen Bomb* (New York: Simon and Schuster, 1995), 438–42, 566–67, 574–76; Rhodes, "The General and World War III," 47–48, 53–59; "Nixon Says He Considered Using Atomic Weapons on Four Occasions," *NYT,* July 22, 1985, A12 (late edition).

149. These points are made in Hendrik Hertzberg, "The Nuclear Jubilee," *New Yorker,* July 31, 1995, 6–7.

150. Nixon discussion with Safire, as quoted in William Safire, "Iraq's Ton of Germs," *NYT,* April 13, 1995, A15 (national edition).

151. Christopher Dickey, "Plagues in the Making," *Newsweek,* October 9, 1995, 50–51; Christopher Dickey, "His Secret Weapon," *Newsweek,* September 4, 1995, 34; Douglas Waller, "Saddam Spills Secrets," *Time,* September 4, 1995, 41; James A. Baker III, "The Politics of Diplomacy," *Newsweek,* October 2, 1995, 57.

152. For the views of one early critic, James B. Conant, who was president of Harvard and a government adviser on nuclear policy, see Hershberg, *James B. Conant,* 348–54.

153. William J. Broad, "U.S. Is Starting To Declassify H-Bomb Fusion Technology," *NYT,* September 28, 1992, A1 (national edition); Matthew L. Wald, "Burden of Too Many Secrets Weighs Down Energy Agency," *NYT,* February 7, 1996, A12 (national edition); William J. Broad, "U.S., in First Atomic Accounting, Says It Shipped a Ton of Plutonium to Thirty-nine Countries," *NYT,* February 6, 1996, A6 (national edition); Steven L. Meyers, "U.S. 'Updates' All-Out Atom War Guidelines," *NYT,* December 8, 1997, A3 (national edition).

154. In the years following the collapse of the Soviet Union, Russian arms sales dropped sharply, while U.S. arms sales accounted for as much as 70 percent of the world market. Mark Thompson, "Going Up, Up in Arms," *Time,* December 12, 1994, 47; Steven Erlanger, "Russia

Sells War Machines To Pay for High Costs of Peace," *NYT*, February 3, 1993, A1 (national edition).

During the Vietnam War, the United States military used massive amounts of deadly napalm and the dioxin-tainted defoliant Agent Orange. Jonathan Feldman, *Universities in the Business of Repression: The Academic-Military-Industrial Complex and Central America* (Boston: South End Press, 1989), 39–46; Jay Peterzell, "Agent Orange Redux," *Time*, August 9, 1993, 51. By 1996 the Department of Veterans Affairs was providing benefits for nine ailments linked to Agent Orange. Todd S. Purdum, "Clinton Orders Expanded Agent Orange Benefits," *NYT*, May 29, 1996, A1 (national edition). A story that was later retracted suggested that nerve gas may have been used in some high-risk operations. April Oliver and Peter Arnett, "Did the U.S. Drop Nerve Gas?" *Time*, June 15, 1998, 37–39.

155. *Almanac of the Federal Judiciary: Profiles and Evaluations of All Judges of the United States District Courts*, ed. Christine Housen and Stacey Levy (Englewood Cliffs, N.J.: Prentice Hall, 1992), 1: 54 (Seventh Circuit).

156. John Soloski and Carolyn Dyer, "The Cost of Prior Restraint: *U.S. v. The Progressive*," *Communications and the Law* 6 (April 1984): 11.

157. On Knops and his confinement, see Bates, *Rads*, 27–28, 35, 50.

158. Oliver Wendell Holmes Jr., *The Common Law* (Boston: Little, Brown, 1923), 1.

Chapter 4

1. "The Stand No. VI," April 19, 1798, in *PAH*, 21: 435.

2. James Morton Smith, *Freedom's Fetters: The Alien and Sedition Laws and American Civil Liberties* (Ithaca, N.Y.: Cornell University Press, 1956). General histories of the period include Stanley Elkins and Eric McKitrick, *The Age of Federalism* (New York: Oxford University Press, 1993); James Roger Sharp, *American Politics in the Early Republic: The New Nation in Crisis* (New Haven: Yale University Press, 1993).

3. See Donald H. Stewart, *The Opposition Press of the Federalist Period* (Albany: State University of New York Press, 1969).

4. [Boston] *Columbian Centinel*, March 5, 1794; [Philadelphia] *General Advertiser*, September 27, 1794.

5. See Robert M. Gordon, *The Structure of Emotions: Investigations in Cognitive Philosophy* (Cambridge: Cambridge University Press, 1987); James Chowning Davies, ed., *When Men Revolt—and Why: A Reader in Political Violence and Revolution* (New York: Free Press, 1971).

6. The idea of a spiral of spite might be considered an alternative to the "spiral of silence" theory and its assertion that people may stop speaking out as their side appears to be losing ground in public opinion. See Elisabeth Noelle-Neumann, *The Spiral of Silence: Public Opinion—Our Second Skin* (Chicago: University of Chicago Press, 1984).

7. "The Defence No. 1," July 22, 1795, in *PAH*, 18: 485.

8. Thomas Jefferson to Spencer Roane, September 6, 1819, in *The Works of Thomas Jefferson*, ed. Paul L. Ford (New York: Putnam, 1904–1905), 12: 136.

On the mobilization and content of the Republican press, see Lance Banning, *The Jeffersonian Persuasion: Evolution of a Party Ideology* (Ithaca, N.Y.: Cornell University Press, 1978); Noble E. Cunningham Jr., *The Jeffersonian Republicans: The Formation of a Party Organization* (Chapel Hill: Published for the Institute of Early American History and Culture by the University of North Carolina Press 1957); Adrienne Koch, *Jefferson and Madison: The Great Collaboration* (New York: Knopf, 1950); William David Sloan, " 'Purse and Pen': Party-Press Relationships, 1789–1816," *American Journalism* 6 (1989): 103–27.

9. Thomas Jefferson to William Wirt, March 30, 1811, in *The Writings of Thomas Jefferson*, ed. Paul L. Ford (New York: Putnam, 1892–1899), 9: 316–17. On Jefferson's relationship with

the *Aurora*, which was originally called the *General Advertiser*, see Jeffery A. Smith, *Franklin and Bache: Envisioning the Enlightened Republic* (New York: Oxford University Press, 1990), 106, 107–8, 148, 151–52, 165.

10. John Adams to Benjamin Stoddert, March 31, 1801, in *The Works of John Adams*, ed. Charles Francis Adams (Boston: Little, Brown, 1856), 9: 582.

11. John Adams to the Marquis de Lafayette, April 6, 1801, in Adams, *Works of John Adams*, 9: 583.

12. See R. R. Palmer, *The Age of Democratic Revolution: A Political History of Europe and America, 1760–1800* (Princeton: Princeton University Press, 1959).

13. Alexander Hamilton to John Jay, November 26, 1775, in *PAH*, 1: 176, 177; James Madison to William Bradford, [early March 1775], in *PJM*, 1:141. On the attacks on Rivington, see Dwight L. Teeter, " 'King' Sears, the Mob and Freedom of the Press in New York, 1765–76," *Journalism Quarterly* 41 (Autumn 1964): 539–44.

14. Hamilton, "The Federalist No. 84," in *FED*, 580–81; James Morton Smith, "Alexander Hamilton, the Alien Law, and Seditious Libels," *Review of Politics* 16 (July 1954): 305–33.

15. On Madison's views and popular support for press freedom in the eighteenth century, see Jeffery A. Smith, "Public Opinion and the Press," in *Media Voices: An Historical Perspective*, ed. Jean Folkerts (New York: Macmillan, 1992), 105–20.

16. [Philadelphia] *National Gazette*, December 19, 1791; Alexander Hamilton to George Washington, November 11, 1794, in *PAH*, 15: 172–73.

17. One of the few studies of the representation of anarchists is Nathaniel Hong, "Constructing the Anarchist Beast in American Periodical Literature, 1880–1903," *Critical Studies in Mass Communication* 9 (March 1992): 110–30.

18. [Philadelphia] *General Advertiser*, February 9, 1793.

19. [Philadelphia] *General Advertiser*, March 15, 1793; see November 1, December 12, 1792, January 25, March 15, 22, 26, May 13, 1793, July 15, 1794 for other examples.

20. [Philadelphia] *General Advertiser*, December 23, 1793. See Harry Ammon, "The Genet Mission and the Development of American Political Parties," *Journal of American History* 52 (March 1966): 725–41.

21. [Philadelphia] *General Advertiser*, December 27, 1793.

22. [Noah Webster], *The Revolution in France, Considered in Respect to its Progress and Effects* (New York: George Bunce, 1794), 32–33.

23. Thomas Jefferson to Philip Mazzei, April 24, 1796, in Ford, *Writings of Thomas Jefferson*, 7: 75, 76.

24. See Jerald A. Combs, *The Jay Treaty: Political Battleground of the Founding Fathers* (Berkeley: University of California Press, 1970), 162–63. See also the notes accompanying "The Defence No. 1," in *PAH*, 18: 475–89.

25. "The Defence No. 1," in *PAH*, 18: 480, 481, 482, 483, 486–87.

26. Peter Porcupine [William Cobbett], *History of the American Jacobins, Commonly Called Democrats* (Philadelphia: Printed for William Cobbett, 1796), 7, 8, 9.

27. Peter Porcupine [William Cobbett], *The Bloody Buoy Thrown Out as a Warning to the Political Pilots of America; or a Faithful Relation of a Multitude of Acts and Horrid Barbarity Such as the Eye Never Witnessed, the Tongue Never Expressed, or the Imagination Conceived, Until the Commencement of the French Revolution* (Philadelphia: Benjamin Davies, 1796), ix, x, 226–27, 232, 237, 239, 240.

28. *Political Observations*, April 20, 1795, in *PJM*, 15: 517, 522, 523, 533.

29. See Smith, *Franklin and Bache*, 45–106.

30. [Philadelphia] *General Advertiser*, December 28, 1793; see November 16, 17, 20, 28, December 19, 1792; February 7, 28, December 13, 28, 30, 31, 1793; February 24, 1794 for examples of the sentiments on Senate secrecy expressed in Bache's paper.

Reporters gained access to the House of Representatives as the members took up their first agenda items in 1789. For background and a description of the efforts of another Jeffersonian editor, see Gerald L. Grotta, "Philip Freneau's Crusade for Open Sessions of the U.S. Senate," *Journalism Quarterly* 48 (Winter 1971): 667–71.

31. [Philadelphia] *General Advertiser*, March 5, 1794.

32. [Philadelphia] *Aurora*, July 10, 1795 (Bache changed the name of his paper to *Aurora* in November 1794); see April 30, June 16, 18, 22, 1795 for examples of protests against the Jay Treaty secrecy. For background, see James Tagg, *Benjamin Franklin Bache and the Philadelphia Aurora* (Philadelphia: University of Pennsylvania Press, 1991), 239–63.

33. See, for example, [Philadelphia] *General Advertiser*, March 4, April 23, 1791; February 5, 18, 1793; May 9, 1794.

34. [Philadelphia] *Aurora*, September 24, October 3, 21, 23, December 10, 29, 1795; January 1, April 4, 12, 16, December 23, 1796; January 23, March 3, 1797; April 14, 1798.

35. [Philadelphia] *Aurora*, October 16, November 20, 1795.

36. [Philadelphia] *Aurora*, June 25, 1794; August 1, September 21, October 12, 1795; March 9, April 7, 1796.

37. [Philadelphia] *Aurora*, April 7, 1796. For examples of pamphlet attacks, see Thomas Paine, *Letters to George Washington* (Philadelphia: Benjamin Franklin Bache, 1796); *Remarks Occasioned by the Late Conduct of Mr. Washington as President of the United States* (Philadelphia: Printed for Benjamin Franklin Bache, 1797).

38. George Washington to Henry Lee, July 21, 1793, in *WGW*, 33: 24; George Washington to the Secretary of State, October 16, 1794, in *WGW*, 34: 3; George Washington to Jeremiah Wadsworth, March 6, 1797, in *WGW*, 35: 421; George Washington to Benjamin Walker, January 12, 1797, in *WGW*, 35: 364; George Washington to William Gordon, October 15, 1797, in *WGW*, 36: 50; George Washington to the Secretary of the Treasury, July 6, 1796, in *WGW*, 35: 126.

39. George Washington to Alexander Hamilton, July 29, 1795, in *PAH*, 18: 525.

40. Farewell Address, [First Draft], [May 15, 1796], in *WGW*, 35: 59; George Washington to Alexander Hamilton, June 26, 1796, in *WGW*, 35: 102, 103; George Washington to Thomas Jefferson, July 6, 1796, in *WGW*, 35: 120.

41. Washington had to practice patience while dealing with critics in the press and politics during the revolution. Robert Leckie, *George Washington's War: The Saga of the American Revolution* (New York: HarperCollins, 1992), 445–51. For an essay that analyzes Washington's ability to exercise control over his temper, see Richard Brookhiser, "A Man on Horseback," *Atlantic Monthly*, January 1996, 50– 64.

42. Farewell Address, [First Draft], [May 15, 1796], in *WGW*, 35: 59. On Washington's equanimity, see Louis Martin Sears, *George Washington and the French Revolution* (Detroit: Wayne State University Press, 1960).

43. George Washington to the Secretary of State, July 18, 1796, *WGW*, 35: 144–45.

44. *Letters from General Washington to Several of His Friends, In June and July, 1776* (Philadelphia: Federal Press [Benjamin Franklin Bache], 1795); George Washington to the Secretary of State, March 3, 1797, in *WGW*, 35: 414–16.

45. Farewell Address, September 19, 1796, in *WGW*, 35: 228, 229, 230; [Philadelphia] *Aurora*, December 17, 1796; George Washington to Henry Lee, July 21, 1793, in *WGW*, 33: 23.

46. See, for example, John Adams to Richard Price, April 19, 1790, in *The American Enlightenment: The Shaping of the American Experiment and a Free Society*, ed. Adrienne Koch (New York: George Braziller, 1965), 199–200. For a sketch of Adams's political theory and its unpopularity, see Banning, *Jeffersonian Persuasion*, 93–98. For a contrasting view of Adams and his influence, see M. N. S. Sellers, *American Republicanism: Roman Ideology in the United States Constitution* (New York: New York University Press, 1994).

47. John Adams to Thomas Jefferson, January 31, 1796, in *The Adams-Jefferson Letters: The Complete Correspondence between Thomas Jefferson and Abigail and John Adams*, ed. Lester C.

Cappon (Chapel Hill: Published for the Institute of Early American History and Culture by the University of North Carolina Press, 1959), 1: 259.

48. See Lawrence S. Kaplan, *Colonies into Nation: American Diplomacy, 1763–1801* (New York: Macmillan, 1972), 216–96; Alexander DeConde, *The Quasi-War: The Politics and Diplomacy of the Undeclared War with France, 1797–1801* (New York: Scribner's, 1966).

49. William Stinchcombe, *The XYZ Affair* (Westport, Conn.: Greenwood Press, 1980); Manning J. Dauer, *The Adams Federalists* (Baltimore: Johns Hopkins Press, 1953).

50. Benjamin Franklin to Robert Livingston, July 22, 1783, in *The Writings of Benjamin Franklin*, ed. Albert H. Smyth (New York: Macmillan, 1905–1907), 9: 62.

51. For examples of attacks on Adams, see [Philadelphia] *Aurora*, October 21, 25, November 1, 2, 4, 1796; May 19, June 8, July 20, November 28, 1797; March 21, July 3, 1798.

52. John Adams to Benjamin Rush, April 12, 1809, in Adams, *Works of John Adams*, 9: 619.

53. William B. Evans, "John Adams' Opinion of Benjamin Franklin," *Pennsylvania Magazine of History and Biography* 92 (April 1968): 220–38.

54. *Diary and Autobiography of John Adams*, ed. L. H. Butterfield (Cambridge: Harvard University Press, 1961–1962), 3: 280; Abigail Adams to Mary Cranch, April 26, 1798, in *New Letters of Abigail Adams, 1788–1801*, ed. Stewart Mitchell (Boston: Houghton Mifflin, 1947), 165.

55. Abigail Adams to Mary Cranch, December 12, 26, 1797; April 21, 1798, in Mitchell, *New Letters of Abigail Adams*, 117, 120, 159.

56. Abigail Adams to Mary Cranch, April 26, May 10, 1798, in Mitchell, *New Letters of Abigail Adams*, 165, 172.

57. See H. T. Dickinson, *British Radicalism and the French Revolution* (New York: Blackwell, 1985). On the connection between the British and American suppression, see Dauer, *Adams Federalists*, 157–59.

58. John D. Stevens, "Congressional History of the 1798 Sedition Law," *Journalism Quarterly* 43 (Summer 1966): 247–56.

59. Trial of James Thomson Callender, in *State Trials of the United States during the Administrations of Washington and Adams*, ed. Francis Wharton (Philadelphia: Casey and Hart, 1849), 688–89.

60. See John Lofton, *The Press as Guardian of the First Amendment* (Columbia: University of South Carolina Press, 1980), 20–47; Smith, *Freedom's Fetters*, 176–81.

61. "To a Freeholder," September 20, 1798, in *The Papers of John Marshall*, ed. Herbert A. Johnson et al. (Chapel Hill: Published for the Institute of Early American History and Culture by the University of North Carolina Press, 1974–), 3: 505; John Marshall to St. George Tucker, November 18, 1800, in Johnson, *Papers of John Marshall*, 6: 14–15.

62. On the patterns and partiality of the Federalists' enforcement, see Smith, *Freedom's Fetters*, 176–87, 420–24.

63. This point was made by the Virginia jurist St. George Tucker in seeking John Marshall's assistance in obtaining a pardon of James Thomson Callender, a journalist convicted under the Sedition Act. St. George Tucker to John Marshall, November 6, 1800, in Johnson *Papers of John Marshall*, 6: 4–5. Marshall thought that Adams would not consider the request. John Marshall to St. George Tucker, November 18, 1800, in Johnson, *Papers of John Marshall*, 6: 14–15. For an example of Hamilton attacking Adams in print, see *Letter from Alexander Hamilton, Concerning the Public Conduct and Character of John Adams, Esq. President of the United States* (New York: Printed for John Lang by George F. Hopkins, 1800).

64. Bache died of yellow fever before he could be brought to trial. A few cases were dropped for practical or political reasons. Most of the other journalists were either sentenced to jail or forced out of business. Smith, *Franklin and Bache*, 162–63, 167; Smith, *Freedom's Fetters*.

65. "To the Printers of the Boston Patriot," 1809, in Adams, *Works of John Adams*, 9: 291.

66. To the Mayor, Alderman, and other Citizens of the City of Philadelphia, April 1798, in Adams, *Works of John Adams,* 9: 182; To the Young Men of Boston, Massachusetts, May 22, 1798, in Adams, *Works of John Adams,* 9: 194–95; Timothy Pickering to Alexander Hamilton, April 9, 1798, in *PAH,* 21: 409; John Adams to Timothy Pickering, August 1, 1799, in Adams, *Works of John Adams,* 9: 5. See also John Adams to Timothy Pickering, August 13, 1799, in Adams, *Works of John Adams,* 9: 13– 14.

67. John Adams to Thomas Jefferson, June 14, 1813, in Cappon, *Adams-Jefferson Letters,* 2: 329; Thomas Jefferson to John Adams, June 15, 1813, in Cappon, *Adams-Jefferson Letters,* 2: 331; John Adams to Thomas Jefferson, June 30, 1813, in Cappon, *Adams-Jefferson Letters,* 2: 346– 47. On the situation in Philadelphia and Adams' role in fostering Republican anger, see Charles Ellis Dickson, "Jeremiads in the New American Republic: The Case of National Fasts in the John Adams Administration," *New England Quarterly* 60 (June 1987): 187–207.

68. "To the Printers of the Boston Patriot," 1809, in Adams, *Works of John Adams,* 9: 289–91; Richard Buel Jr., *Securing the Revolution: Ideology in American Politics, 1789–1815* (Ithaca, N.Y.: Cornell University Press, 1972), 213.

69. "The Warning No. 1," January 27, 1797, in *PAH,* 20: 494; "The Stand No. 1," March 30, 1798, in *PAH,* 21: 384.

70. Alexander Hamilton to Josiah Ogden Hoffman, November 6, 1799, in *PAH,* 24: 6. The printer, David Frothingham of the New York *Argus,* was sentenced to four months in jail and fined one hundred dollars. Smith, *Freedom's Fetters,* 398–417.

71. Alexander Hamilton to Jonathan Dayton, [October–November, 1799], in *PAH,* 23: 604.

72. *Annals of Congress,* 5th Cong., 2nd sess., 2096–97, 2098, 2100, 2102.

73. *Annals of Congress,* 5th Cong., 2nd sess., 2096–2107.

74. See, for example, David Ford to Alexander Hamilton, April 11, 1798, in *PAH,* 21: 410– 11; "Laocoon No. 1," April 1799, in *Works of Fisher Ames,* ed. Seth Ames (Boston: Little, Brown, 1854), 2: 116.

75. For examples, see *Circular Letters of Congressmen to Their Constituents, 1789–1829,* ed. Noble E. Cunningham Jr. (Chapel Hill: Published for the Institute of Early American History and Culture by the University of North Carolina Press, 1978), 1: 177–78, 212–13, 304, 344–45.

76. Thomas M. Ray, " 'Not One Cent for Tribute': The Public Addresses and American Popular Reaction to the XYZ Affair, 1798–1799," *Journal of the Early Republic* 3 (Winter 1983): 389–412.

77. Thomas Jefferson to Elbridge Gerry, January 26, 1799, in Ford, *Writings of Thomas Jefferson,* 7: 33.

78. See James Morton Smith, "The Grass Roots Origins of the Kentucky Resolutions," *William and Mary Quarterly,* 3rd ser., 27 (April 1970): 221–45; Adrienne Koch and Harry Ammon, "The Virginia and Kentucky Resolutions: An Episode in Jefferson's and Madison's Defense of Civil Liberties," *William and Mary Quarterly,* 3rd ser., 5 (April 1948): 145–76.

79. For example, Representative Matthew Lyon, who was convicted under the Sedition Act for his writings, won an election from his jail cell. See Aleine Austin, *Matthew Lyon: "New Man" of the Democratic Revolution, 1749–1822* (University Park: Pennsylvania State University Press, 1981), 108–30.

80. "Laocoon No. 1," April 1799, in Ames, *Works of Fisher Ames,* 2: 111, 112.

81. These include the suspicion that Bache was in communication with French officials, including Talleyrand; the "Tub-Plot," which also involved dispatches from France; and, of course, the notion of an Illuminati conspiracy in America. See Buel, *Securing the Revolution,* 225–27.

82. George Washington to Alexander Hamilton, May 27, 1798, in *WGW,* 36: 272.

83. George Washington to Bushrod Washington, December 31, 1798, in *WGW,* 37: 81. Some historians have assumed, mistakenly, I would argue, that Washington supported the

Sedition Act prosecutions because in 1799 he was anxious to know "whether the Officers of Government intended to be acquiescent under the direct charge of bribery" in the *Aurora*. Washington, as he did when president, said the problem was "silence" on the part of the administration. George Washington to the Secretary of State, August 4, 1799, in *WGW*, 37: 323. For the poorly supported conclusion that Washington "explicitly approved and actively defended" the Sedition Act after it was passed, see Marshall Smelser, "George Washington and the Alien and Sedition Acts," *American Historical Review* 59 (January 1954): 334. In some cases historians see his acceptance of the alien laws as approval of the Sedition Act. In other cases, support has been inferred from his opposition to what he perceived as the potential dangers in Madison's Virginia Resolutions of 1798, which suggested that states could decide to resist the Sedition Act as unconstitutional.

84. John Adams to Benjamin Stoddert, March 31, 1801, in Adams, *Works of John Adams*, 9: 582.

85. Charles O. Lerche Jr., "Jefferson and the Election of 1800: A Case Study in the Political Smear," *William and Mary Quarterly*, 3rd ser., 5 (October 1948): 467–91.

86. First Inaugural Address, March 4, 1801, in Koch, *American Enlightenment*, 405.

87. See Arthur M. Schlesinger Jr., *The Imperial Presidency* (Boston: Houghton Mifflin, 1973), 13–25; David Gray Adler, "The President's War-Making Power," in *Inventing the American Presidency*, ed. Thomas E. Cronin (Lawrence: University Press of Kansas, 1989), 132–34; Robert Scigliano, "The President's 'Prerogative Power,'" in Cronin, *Inventing the American Presidency*, 249–51.

88. Thomas Jefferson to John B. Colvin, September 20, 1810, in Ford, *Writings of Thomas Jefferson*, 9: 279–82.

89. Thomas Jefferson to Abigail Adams, July 22, 1804, in Cappon, *Adams-Jefferson Letters*, 1: 275. For Jefferson's views, which have been carelessly disparaged at times, see Jeffery A. Smith, *Printers and Press Freedom: The Ideology of Early American Journalism* (New York: Oxford University Press, 1988), 11–12, 40–41, 59, 69, 88–90.

90. Robert M. Johnstone Jr., *Jefferson and the Presidency: Leadership in the Young Republic* (Ithaca, N.Y.: Cornell University Press, 1978), 52–75.

Chapter 5

1. James Madison to S. Spring, September 6, 1812, in *The Writings of James Madison*, ed. Gaillard Hunt (New York: Putnam, 1900–1910), 8: 214–15; James Madison to Jonas Galusha, November 30, 1812, in Hunt, *The Writings of James Madison*, 8: 231.

2. See Donald R. Hickey, "The Baltimore Riots," *Constitution* 3 (Fall 1991): 35–41. For background, see Paul A. Gilje, "The Baltimore Riots of 1812 and the Breakdown of the Anglo-American Mob Tradition," *Journal of Social History* 13 (Summer 1980): 547–64.

3. Benjamin Lincoln Lear, as quoted in Irving Brant, *James Madison, Commander in Chief, 1812–1836* (Indianapolis: Bobbs-Merrill, 1961), 407. For a similar address praising Madison for conducting the war "without infringing a political, civil, or a religious right," see James Blake to James Madison, March 4, 1817, Madison Papers, Library of Congress microfilm.

4. John Adams to Thomas Jefferson, February 2, 1817, in *The Adams-Jefferson Letters: The Complete Correspondence between Thomas Jefferson and Abigail and John Adams*, ed. Lester J. Cappon (Chapel Hill: Published for the Institute of Early American History and Culture by the University of North Carolina Press, 1959), 2: 508. On Madison's reputation and behavior during and after the War of 1812, see Drew R. McCoy, *The Last of the Fathers: James Madison and the Republican Legacy* (Cambridge: Cambridge University Press, 1989), 9–35.

5. Donna Lee Dickerson, *The Course of Tolerance: Freedom of the Press in Nineteenth-Century America* (New York: Greenwood Press, 1990), 39–46.

6. Jonathan Lurie, *Arming Military Justice*, vol. 1, *The Origins of the United States Court of Military Appeals, 1775–1950* (Princeton: Princeton University Press, 1992), 11–20; Dickerson, *Course of Tolerance*, 46–52; *Congressional Globe*, 28th Cong., 1st sess., February 13, 1844, 267–69; February 14, 1844, 274.

7. Andrew Jackson to the United States District Court, Louisiana [March 27, 1815], in *The Papers of Andrew Jackson*, ed. Samuel B. Smith et al. (Knoxville: University of Tennessee Press, 1980–), 3: 329, 332, 333, 334.

8. Alexander James Dallas to Andrew Jackson, April 12, 1815, in ibid., 3: 345; Alexander James Dallas to Andrew Jackson, July 1, 1815, in ibid., 375–77.

9. Andrew Jackson, Seventh Annual Message to Congress, December 7, 1835, in *Freedom of the Press from Hamilton to the Warren Court*, ed. Harold L. Nelson (Indianapolis: Bobbs-Merrill, 1967), 216–17.

10. Russell B. Nye, *Fettered Freedom: Civil Liberties and the Slavery Controversy, 1830–1860* (East Lansing: Michigan State University, 1963), 117–73; Dorothy G. Fowler, *Unmailable: Congress and the Post Office* (Athens: University of Georgia Press, 1977), 26–41; Clement Eaton, "Censorship of the Southern Mails," *American Historical Review* 48 (October 1942): 266–80. For the unofficial opposition to abolitionist publications, see John Nerone, *Violence against the Press: Policing the Public Sphere in U. S. History* (New York: Oxford University Press, 1994), 84–110; Leonard L. Richards, *"Gentlemen of Property and Standing": Anti-Abolition Mobs in Jacksonian America* (London: Oxford University Press, 1970).

11. Amos Kendall to Postmaster Huger, August 4, 1835, in Nelson, *Freedom of the Press*, 213.

12. William M. Goldsmith, *The Growth of Presidential Power: A Documented History* (New York: Chelsea House, 1974), 2: 779–877; Louis Fisher, *Presidential War Power* (Lawrence: University Press of Kansas, 1995), 29–34.

13. On the Mexican War controversy, see Samuel Eliot Morison, Frederick Merk, and Frank Freidel, *Dissent in Three American Wars* (Cambridge: Harvard University Press, 1970), 35–63.

14. See James M. McCaffrey, *Army of Manifest Destiny: The American Soldier in the Mexican War, 1846–1848* (New York: New York University Press, 1992); John S. D. Eisenhower, *So Far from God: The U.S. War with Mexico* (New York: Random House, 1989); Justin H. Smith, *The War with Mexico* (New York: Macmillan, 1919), 2: 210–32.

15. Ulysses S. Grant, *Memoirs and Selected Letters* (New York: Library of America, 1990), 41, 42.

16. *Congressional Globe*, 30th Cong., 1st sess., January 3, 1848, 95.

17. Abraham Lincoln to William H. Herndon, February 15, 1848, in *WAL*, 1: 451–2.

18. *Congressional Globe*, 29th Cong., 2nd sess., December 8, 1846, 4; December 10, 1846, 20–28. For the context of the message, see John H. Schroeder, *Mr. Polk's War: American Opposition and Dissent, 1846–1848* (Madison: University of Wisconsin Press, 1973), 62–88.

19. Tom Reilly, "Newspaper Suppression during the Mexican War, 1846–48," *Journalism Quarterly* 54 (Summer 1977): 262–70.

20. McCaffrey, *Army of Manifest Destiny*, 197–99; Tom Reilly, " 'Run Up the Flag Boldly': American Occupation Newspapers in Mexico City, 1847–48," paper presented at the Symposium on the Antebellum Press, the Civil War and Free Expression, University of Tennessee at Chattanooga, November 3, 1995.

21. [Washington, D.C.] *Union*, May 27, 1847; [Washington, D.C.] *Daily National Intelligencer*, May 25, 1847.

22. See Jonathan Lurie, "Military Justice" and "Military Trials and Martial Law," in *The Oxford Companion to the Supreme Court of the United States*, ed. Kermit Hall (New York: Oxford University Press, 1992), 545–47.

23. Ralph H. Gabriel, "American Experience with Military Government," *American Historical Review* 44 (July 1944): 631–35; Robert Selph Henry, *The Story of the Mexican War* (Indianapolis: Bobbs-Merrill, 1950), 202–3; William L. Marcy to Winfield Scott, February 15, 1847, in 30th Cong., 1st sess., House Executive Documents, vol. 7, no. 60, 873–74; Winfield Scott, *Memoirs of Lieut.-General Scott, LL.D.* (New York: Sheldon, 1864), 2: 392–96.

24. Scott, *Memoirs*, 2: 540–46. For a discussion of how the "military laws of the time did not anticipate an American force fighting in a foreign country," see Joseph E. Chance, *Jefferson Davis's Mexican War Regiment* (Jackson: University Press of Mississippi, 1991), 116–17.

25. Fleming v. Page, 9 How. (50 U.S.) 603, 615 (1850).

26. Scott, *Memoirs*, 2: 393, 395–96.

27. Anna Kasten Nelson, "Secret Agents and Security Leaks: President Polk and the Mexican War," *Journalism Quarterly* 52 (Spring 1975): 9–14, 98; Everette E. Dennis, "Stolen Peace Treaties and the Press: Two Case Studies," *Journalism History* 2 (Spring 1975): 9–14.

28. Margaret A. Blanchard, "Free Expression and Wartime: Lessons from the Past, Hopes for the Future," *Journalism Quarterly* 69 (Spring 1992): 8. On the problems soldiers faced, see Chance, *Jefferson Davis's Mexican War Regiment*, 115–18.

29. On the letter and its repercussions, see Edward J. Nichols, *Zach Taylor's Little Army* (Garden City, N.Y.: Doubleday, 1963), 197–200; Brainerd Dyer, *Zachary Taylor* (Baton Rouge: Louisiana State University Press, 1946), 242–44. For the letter itself, see [Washington, D.C.] *Union*, January 26, 1847.

30. James K. Polk, *The Diary of James K. Polk during His Presidency, 1845 to 1849*, ed. Milo Milton Quaife (Chicago: A. C. McClurg, 1910), 2: 353–57; [Washington, D.C.] *Union*, January 26, 1847; William L. Marcy to Zachary Taylor, January 27, 1847, in 29th Cong., 2nd sess., House Executive Documents, vol. 4, no. 119, 109–10.

31. Zachary Taylor to William L. Marcy, March 3, 1847, in 30th Cong., 1st sess., House Executive Documents, vol. 7, no. 60, 809–10.

32. William L. Marcy to Zachary Taylor, January 27, 1847, in 29th Cong., 2nd sess., House Executive Documents, vol. 4, no. 119, 110.

33. *Congressional Globe*, 29th Cong., 2nd sess., January 30, 1847, 296–97.

34. *Congressional Globe*, 29th Cong., 2nd sess., February 13, 1847, 406–17; [Washington, D.C.] *Union*, February 9, 1847; Polk, *Diary*, 2: 375–78.

35. *Message from the President of the United States, Communicating, in Compliance with a Resolution of the Senate, the Proceedings of the Two Courts of Inquiry in the Case of Major General Pillow*, August 2, 1848, 30th Cong., 1st sess., Senate Executive Documents, vol. 8, no. 65, 454–55.

36. On the politics of being an Army officer during the Polk administration, see Charles Sellers, *James K. Polk: Continentalist, 1843–1846* (Princeton: Princeton University Press, 1966), 433–44; Eisenhower, *So Far from God*, xxv.

37. Eisenhower, *So Far from God*, 351–55, 364; K. Jack Bauer, *The Mexican War, 1846–1848* (New York: Macmillan, 1974), 371–74; Smith, *War with Mexico*, 376–77, 435–37; Nathaniel C. Hughes Jr. and Roy P. Stonesifer Jr., *The Life and Wars of Gideon J. Pillow* (Chapel Hill: The University of North Carolina Press, 1993), 105–20.

38. Polk, *Diary*, 3: 507; 4: 7–8, 17.

39. See, for example, *OR*, ser. 3, 1: 390, 879, 899. Several of the orders are compiled in *The American Annual Cyclopædia and Register of Important Events of the Year 1862* (New York: Appleton, 1867), 2: 480.

40. For a treatise that cites a number of actions against newspaper correspondents during the Civil War, see William Winthrop, *Military Law and Precedents*, 2nd ed. (Washington, D.C.: Government Printing Office, 1920; repr., New York: Arno Press, 1979), 97–102, 815–17.

41. See John F. Marszalek, *Sherman's Other War: The General and the Civil War Press* (Memphis: Memphis State University Press, 1981), 14; Phillip Knightley, *The First Casualty:*

From Crimea to Vietnam: The War Correspondent as Hero, Propagandist, and Myth Maker (New York: Harcourt Brace Jovanovich, 1975), 23–24; Adolph O. Goldsmith, "Reporting the Civil War: Union Army Press Relations," *Journalism Quarterly* 33 (Fall 1956): 478–87; Benjamin Perley Poore, *Perley's Reminiscences of Sixty Years in the National Metropolis* (Philadelphia: Hubbard, 1886), 2: 126. On the practice of praising for profit, see Sylvanus Cadwallader, *Three Years with Grant*, ed. Benjamin P. Thomas (New York: Knopf, 1956), 11. On the South's spending for favorable coverage in Britain, see Knightley, *First Casualty*, 34.

42. Dickerson, *Course of Tolerance*, 147–86; Emmet Crozier, *Yankee Reporters, 1861–65* (New York: Oxford University Press, 1956); J. Cutler Andrews, *The North Reports the Civil War* (Pittsburgh: University of Pittsburgh Press, 1955); Louis M. Starr, *Bohemian Brigade: Civil War Newsmen in Action* (New York: Knopf, 1954); Robert S. Harper, *Lincoln and the Press* (New York: McGraw-Hill, 1951).

43. Marszalek, *Sherman's Other War*, 13; Nerone, *Violence against the Press*, 117, 118, 119, 226–30. A study of actions taken against Democratic newspapers in Indiana during the Civil War found eight instances of threats, fifteen episodes of violence, and six arrests. The military was involved in at least twenty-one of the twenty-nine incidents. Jon Paul Dilts, "Testing Siebert's Proposition in Civil War Indiana," *Journalism Quarterly* 63 (Summer 1986): 365–68. For the frequent actions taken against editors in Maryland, where Southern sympathies were particularly strong, see Harper, *Lincoln and the Press*, 154–64.

44. For the view that Lincoln discouraged generals from taking journalists into custody and "maintained a consistent attitude toward such arrests throughout the war," and for a partial list of journalists who were state prisoners, see Mark E. Neely Jr., *The Fate of Liberty: Abraham Lincoln and Civil Liberties* (New York: Oxford University Press, 1991), 28.

45. See, for example, Reed W. Smith, *Samuel Medary & the Crisis: Testing the Limits of Press Freedom* (Columbus: Ohio State University Press, 1995).

46. Poore, *Perley's Reminiscences*, 2: 74–79.

47. *OR*, ser. 3, 1: 324.

48. Starr, *Bohemian Brigade*, 42; Andrews, *North Reports the Civil War*, 95.

49. L. A. Gobright, *Recollections of Men and Things at Washington During the Third of a Century*, 2nd ed. (Philadelphia: Claxton, Remses, and Haffelfinger, 1869), 315–18; Andrews, *North Reports the Civil War*, 88–99; Menahem Blondheim, *News over the Wires: The Telegraph and the Flow of Public Information in America, 1844–1897* (Cambridge: Harvard University Press, 1994), 132–33.

50. Edwin C. Fishel, *The Secret War for the Union: The Untold Story of Military Intelligence in the Civil War* (Boston: Houghton Mifflin, 1996), 325.

51. See, for example, Gobright, *Recollections*, 319–24; Poore, *Perley's Reminiscences*, 2: 127.

52. Gobright, *Recollections*, 318; see also 323. On Gobright's status within the Lincoln administration, see Richard A. Schwarzlose, *The Nation's Newsbrokers* (Evanston, Ill.: Northwestern University Press, 1989), 1: 243–47.

53. Andrews, *North Reports the Civil War*, 326–36; Poore, *Perley's Reminiscences*, 2: 127.

54. *Government Contracts*, 1862, 37th Cong., 2nd sess., House Reports, vol. 2, no. 2, pt. 2; Stephen B. Oates, *With Malice toward None: The Life of Abraham Lincoln* (New York: Harper and Row: 1977), 276–77; Neely, *Fate of Liberty*, 105–7.

55. March 20, 1862, 37th Cong., 2nd sess., House Reports, vol. 3, no. 64, 1; An Act to Authorize the President of the United States in Certain Cases to take Possession of Railroad and Telegraph Lines, and for Other Purposes, ch. 15, 12 Stat. 334, 334, 335 (1862); February 25, 1862, in *OR*, ser. 3, 1: 899; E. S. Sanford to J. M. Wightman, February 26, 1862, in March 20, 1862, 37th Cong., 2nd sess., House Reports, vol. 3, no. 64, 13.

56. March 20, 1862, 37th Cong., 2nd sess., House Reports, vol. 3, no. 64, 1–8, 13.

57. Congress did not appear to have had censorship in mind when the railroad and tele-graph law was passed. The resolution to have the House Judiciary Committee investigate was quickly passed by unanimous consent. *Congressional Globe*, 37th Cong., 2nd sess., December 5, 1861, 19.

58. March 20, 1862, 37th Cong., 2nd sess., House Reports, vol. 3, no. 64, 13, 14.

59. Dickerson, *Course of Tolerance*, 171–72; Robert J. Chandler, "Fighting Words: Cen-soring Civil War California Journalism," *Californians* 8 (May–June 1990): 46–57.

60. *Congressional Globe*, 37th Cong., 3rd sess., January 16, 1863, 349–50; Letter of the Postmaster General, January 19, 1863, in 37th Cong., 3rd sess., Senate Executive Documents, no. 19, 1–2.

61. Ulysses S. Grant, *Personal Memoirs of U. S. Grant* (New York: Charles L. Webster, 1885), 2: 506.

62. David T. Z. Mindich, "Edwin M. Stanton, the Inverted Pyramid, and Information Control," *Journalism Monographs*, no. 140, August 1993; Cadwallader, *Three Years with Grant*, 218–24; Knightley, *First Casualty*, 27.

63. *The American Annual Cyclopædia and Register of Important Events of the Year 1862*, 2: 509.

64. Grant, *Personal Memoirs*, 506, 507.

65. *The American Annual Cyclopædia and Register of Important Events of the Year 1861* (New York: Appleton, 1867), 1: 329–30.

66. *Postmaster General's Authority over Mailable Matter*, January 20, 1863, 37th Cong., 3rd sess., House Miscellaneous Documents, no. 16, 1, 2–3, 8, 9, 10, 11, 12, 14, 15. On Story's views, which he offered in his *Commentaries on the Constitution of the United States*, see Timothy W. Gleason, *The Watchdog Concept: The Press and the Courts in Nineteenth-Century America* (Ames: Iowa State University Press, 1990), 45–47.

67. On journalists having positions in Congress, see Donald A. Ritchie, *Press Gallery: Congress and the Washington Correspondents* (Cambridge: Harvard University Press, 1991), 67–68.

68. George G. Meade to Mrs. George F. Meade, October 31, 1864, in George Meade, *The Life and Letters of George Gordon Meade*, ed. George Gordon Meade (New York: Scribner's, 1913), 2: 238.

69. See Starr, *Bohemian Brigade*, 275–86.

70. Cadwallader, *Three Years with Grant*, 3–4.

71. *Chicago Daily Journal*, April 22, 1924, as quoted in Knightley, *First Casualty*, 23.

72. Starr, *Bohemian Brigade*, 279; Crozier, *Yankee Reporters*, 319–20.

73. Cadwallader, *Three Years with Grant*, 5, 14, 19–22, 103–13, 270–71.

74. New York *Tribune*, May 26, 1862; Andrews, *North Reports the Civil War*, 182–88.

75. Edwin M. Stanton to Joseph Hooker, April 30, 1863, in *OR*, ser. 1, 25 pt. 2: 300–301; Cadwallader, *Three Years with Grant*, 111, 221–22.

76. Cadwallader, *Three Years with Grant*, 275–77.

77. Henry Norman Hudson, *A Chaplain's Campaign with Gen. Butler* (New York: Printed for the Author, 1865), 4–7, 12, 16–35; Benjamin F. Butler to James A. Woodward, March 21, 1866, in *Private and Official Correspondence of Gen. Benjamin F. Butler during the Period of the Civil War* (Norwood, Mass.: Plimpton Press, 1917), 5: 702; Benjamin F. Butler to Reverend Thomas M. Clarke, July 12, 1865, in *Correspondence of Benjamin Bulter*, 5: 492–95; Benjamin F. Butler to Ulysses S. Grant, January 14, 1865, in *Correspondence of Benjamin Bulter*, 5: 486; Benjamin F. Butler to Joseph Holt, January 14, 1865, in *Correspondence of Benjamin Bulter*, 5: 487–90; Robert Werlich, *"Beast" Butler: The Incredible Career of Major General Benjamin Frank-lin Butler* (Washington, D.C.: Quaker Press, 1962), 108–11; Starr, *Bohemian Brigade*, 277–78.

78. George Gordon Meade to Mrs. George Gordon Meade, June 9, 1864, in Meade, *Life and Letters of George Gordon Meade*, 2: 202–3; George Gordon Meade to Mrs. George Gordon Meade, September 16, 1864, in Meade, *Life and Letters of George Gordon Meade*, 2: 228; Cadwallader, *Three Years with Grant*, 206–10, 255–58; Crozier, *Yankee Reporters*, 392–94; C. A. Dana to Edwin M. Stanton, June 8, 1864, in *OR*, ser. 1, 36 pt. 1: 92–93.

79. *OR*, ser. 3, 2: 321; Neely, *Fate of Liberty*, 51–74.

80. Proclamation Suspending the Writ of Habeas Corpus, September 24, 1862, in *WAL*, 5: 436–37.

81. D. A. Mahony, *The Prisoner of State* (New York: Carleton, 1863), 1–28. For background, see Harper, *Lincoln and the Press*, 148–51; Frank L. Klement, *The Copperheads in the Middle West* (Chicago: University of Chicago Press, 1960). A similar work, which went through dozens of editions, was John A. Marshall, *American Bastile: A History of the Illegal Arrests and Imprisonment of American Citizens during the Late Civil War*, 18th ed. (Philadelphia: Thomas W. Hartley, 1875).

82. August 7, 1861, in *OR*, ser. 3, 1: 390; Ch. 20, art. 57, 2 Stat. 359, 366 (1806).

83. Frank Geere, "The Government of War Correspondents," *Journal of the Military Service* 44 (May-June 1909): 411.

84. *The American Annual Cyclopædia and Register of Important Events of the Year 1862*, 2: 480; General Orders, No. 39, August 20, 1864, in *OR*, ser. 1, 41 pt. 2: 778–89; S. Williams to W. S. Hancock, November 25, 1864, in *OR*, ser. 1, 42 pt. 3: 706.

85. "The Court-Martial of Private Spencer: From the Records of the U.S. Army," *Civil War Times Illustrated* 27 (February 1989): 35–40.

86. By some accounts, the Knox case was a unique occurrence for a civilian journalist. Michael Fellman, *Citizen Sherman: A Life of William Tecumseh Sherman* (New York: Random House, 1995), 128; John F. Marszalek, *Sherman: A Soldier's Passion for Order* (New York: Free Press, 1993), 213; Marszalek, *Sherman's Other War*, 13; Maury M. Breecher, "Meet Only Reporter Court-Martialed in U.S. History," *Media History Digest* 13 (Spring–Summer 1993): 48–58.

87. See, generally, Marszalek, *Sherman's Other War*. For a summary of Sherman's reactions to the press in the context of his tendencies toward military dictatorship, see Fellman, *Citizen Sherman*, 124–34.

88. "The Battle of Chickasaw Bayou," New York *Herald*, January 18, 1863. On Sherman's depression and the origins of newspaper stories discussing his sanity, see Joseph H. Ewing, "The New Sherman Letters," in *Newsmen and National Defense*, ed. Lloyd J. Matthews (Washington, D.C.: Brassey's [US], Inc., 1991), 21–22; Marszalek, *Sherman*, 162–67.

89. W. T. Sherman to Mr. Halsted, April 8, 1863, in *OR*, ser. 1, 17 pt. 2: 896; Thomas W. Knox to W. T. Sherman, February 1, 1863, in *OR*, ser. 1, 17 pt. 2: 580–81. Reporters sometimes answered complaints about inaccuracies by saying the military made it difficult to obtain accurate information. See, for example, New York *Tribune*, May 26, 1862.

90. W. T. Sherman to F. P. Blair, February 2, 1863, in *OR*, ser. 1, 17 pt. 2: 587, 588; W. T. Sherman to David D. Porter, February 4, 1863, in *OR*, ser. 1, 17 pt. 2: 889; W. T. Sherman to Thomas Ewing, February 17, 1863, in Ewing, "New Sherman Letters," 24, 25, 26.

91. Thomas W. Knox, *Camp-fire and Cotton-field: Southern Adventure in Time of War* (New York: Blelock, 1865), 256, 257.

92. *Ibid.*, 253–57; General Orders, No. 13, February 19, 1863, in *OR*, ser. 1, 17 pt. 2: 889–92.

93. Knox, *Camp-fire and Cotton-field*, 255–56.

94. For a summary of the proceedings based on the original records in the National Archives in Washington, D.C., see Marszalek, *Sherman's Other War*, 131–38.

95. W. T. Sherman to Mr. Halsted, April 8, 1863, in *OR*, ser. 1, 17 pt. 2: 895–97.

96. W. T. Sherman to John A. Rawlins, February 23, 1863, in *OR*, ser. 1, 17 pt. 2: 892–93; Crozier, *Yankee Reporters*, 303.

97. Abraham Lincoln to "Whom It May Concern," March 20, 1863, in *WAL*, 6: 142–43.

98. U. S. Grant to Thomas W. Knox, April 6, 1863, in *OR*, ser. 1, 17 pt. 2: 894; W. T. Sherman to Thomas Knox, April 7, 1863, in *OR*, ser. 1, 17 pt. 2: 895; W. T. Sherman to U. S. Grant, April 8, 1863, in *OR*, ser. 1, 17 pt. 2: 895; W. T. Sherman to Philemon B. Ewing, as quoted in Ewing, "New Sherman Letters," 28.

99. Knightley, *First Casualty*, 28.

100. See, for example, a notice issued in Cincinnati that threatened newspapers with suppression and arrests if they published military information or "articles of a seditious and treasonable character." The notice concluded, "The press is also requested to exercise great caution in the publication of any articles calculated unnecessarily to disturb the public mind." Circular, September 13, 1862, in *OR*, ser. 1, 16 pt. 2: 514.

101. W. T. Sherman to Editors of the *Memphis Bulletin*, October 27, 1863, in *OR*, ser. 1, 31 pt. 1: 765; W. T. Sherman to J. B. Bingham, November 9, 1863, in *OR*, ser. 1, 31 pt. 3: 97–98; W. T. Sherman to S. A. Hurlbut, October 26, 1863, in *OR*, ser. 1, 31 pt. 1: 747–48.

102. Knightley, *First Casualty*, 29–31.

103. When a group of Ohio Democrats pointed out that Lincoln had dissented in the Mexican War yet was intolerant of critics in the Civil War, he denied that they could find "evidence to prove your assumption that I 'opposed, in discussions before the people, the policy of the Mexican war.'" Lincoln may not have regarded his complaints in Congress as "discussions before the people," but he could not deny the basic thrust of the group's observation. Abraham Lincoln to Matthew Birchard and others, June 29, 1863, in *WAL*, 6: 302.

104. Edward S. Corwin, *Total War and the Constitution* (New York: Knopf, 1947), 19.

105. Message to Congress in Special Session, July 4, 1861, in *WAL*, 4: 421–41; Abraham Lincoln to James C. Conkling, August 26, 1863, in *WAL*, 6: 408. On the legal issues Lincoln's actions created during the Civil War, see Edward S. Corwin, *The President: Office and Powers, History and Analysis of Practice and Opinion* (New York: New York University Press, 1940), 155–66; James G. Randall, *Constitutional Problems under Lincoln* (New York: Appleton, 1926); Larry Arnhart, "'The God-Like Prince': John Locke, Executive Prerogative, and the American Presidency," *Presidential Studies Quarterly* 9 (Spring 1979): 126–30.

106. Garry Wills, *Lincoln at Gettysburg: The Words that Remade America* (New York: Simon and Schuster, 1992), 132–33; Neely, *Fate of Liberty*, xiv, 216–17; Thomas E. Cronin, "The President's Executive Power," in *Inventing the American Presidency*, ed. Thomas E. Cronin (Lawrence: University Press of Kansas, 1989), 204.

107. First Inaugural Address—Final Text, March 4, 1861, in *WAL*, 4: 262–71.

108. Don E. Fehrenbacher, *Lincoln in Text and Context: Collected Essays* (Stanford: Stanford University Press, 1987), 135.

109. Abraham Lincoln to Matthew Birchard and others, June 29, 1863, in *WAL*, 6: 303.

110. Response to a Serenade, November 10, 1864, in *WAL*, 8: 100–101; Annual Message to Congress, December 6, 1864, in *WAL*, 8: 152.

111. Message to Congress in Special Session, July 4, 1861, in *WAL*, 4: 421–41; Abraham Lincoln to Erastus Corning and others, [June 12], 1863, in *WAL*, 6: 260–69; Abraham Lincoln to Matthew Birchard and others, June 29, 1863, in *WAL*, 6: 300–306.

112. Clinton Rossiter, *Constitutional Dictatorship: Crisis Government in Modern Democracies* (New York: Harcourt, Brace and World, 1963).

113. Address before the Young Men's Lyceum of Springfield, Illinois, January 27, 1838, in *WAL*, 1: 114–15; Abraham Lincoln to Albert G. Hodges, April 4, 1864, in *WAL*, 7: 281; Address at the Sanitary Fair, Baltimore, Maryland, April 18, 1864, in *WAL*, 7: 301, 302.

114. David Herbert Donald, *Lincoln* (New York: Simon and Schuster, 1995), 27, 57, 102, 163–64, 371, 514–15, 517. For a collection of essays dealing with Lincoln's mind and personal philosophies, see Gabor S. Boritt, ed., *The Historian's Lincoln: Pseudohistory, Psychohistory, and*

History (Urbana: University of Illinois Press, 1988). On Lincoln's emotional reactions to press attacks, see Michael Burlingame, *The Inner World of Abraham Lincoln* (Urbana: University of Illinois Press, 1994), 193–95.

115. Handbill Replying to Charges of Infidelity, June 31, 1846, in *WAL*, 1: 382; Speech at Bloomington, Illinois, September 12, 1854, in *WAL*, 2: 231; Abraham Lincoln to Albert G. Hodges, April 4, 1864, in *WAL*, 7: 282. On Lincoln's doctrine of necessity, see Donald, *Lincoln*, 14–15, 49, 114, 514, 566.

116. Donald, *Lincoln*, 53–55, 102.

117. Report of Major General Ambrose E. Burnside, November 13, 1865, in *OR*, ser. 1, 23 pt. 1: 12; General Orders, No. 38, April 13, 1863, in *OR*, ser. 1, 23 pt. 2: 237; *Chicago Times*, May 14, 1863.

118. *OR*, ser. 2, 5: 633–46; 656–58; Frank L. Klement, *The Limits of Dissent: Clement L. Vallandigham and the Civil War* (Lexington: University Press of Kentucky, 1970), 156–72.

119. Edward Everett Hale, "The Man without a Country," *Atlantic Monthly*, December 1863, 665–79.

120. Abraham Lincoln to Erastus Corning and Others, [June 12], 1863, in *WAL*, 6: 260–69.

121. Abraham Lincoln to Erastus Corning and Others, [June 12], 1863, in *WAL*, 6: 262, 264, 267. For other examples, see Message to Congress in Special Session, July 4, 1861, in *WAL*, 4: 430; Abraham Lincoln to Matthew Birchard and Others, June 29, 1863, in *WAL*, 6: 302–3.

122. *Ex parte* Merryman, 17 Fed. Cas. 144 (1861); Proclamation Suspending the Writ of Habeas Corpus, September 24, 1862, in *WAL*, 5: 436–37.

123. See Neely, *Fate of Liberty*, 68.

124. This point is made in Fehrenbacher, *Lincoln in Text and Context*, 139–40.

125. *Chicago Times*, May 22, 1863; General Orders, No. 84, June 1, 1863, in *OR*, ser. 1, 23 pt. 2: 381.

126. *The American Annual Cyclopædia and Register of Important Events of the Year 1863*, 3: 423–24.

127. Lyman Trumbull and Isaac N. Arnold to Abraham Lincoln, June 3, 1863, in *OR*, ser. 1, 23 pt. 2: 385; Theodore J. Karamanski, *Rally 'Round the Flag: Chicago and the Civil War* (Chicago: Nelson-Hall, 1993), 188–97.

128. Lincoln's thoughts were conveyed in Edwin M. Stanton to A. E. Burnside, June 1, 1863, in *OR*, ser. 2, 5: 724.

129. *The American Annual Cyclopædia and Register of Important Events of the Year 1863*, 3: 424–25; *Chicago Times*, June 5, 1863.

130. General Orders, No. 91, June 4, 1863, in *OR*, ser. 1, 23 pt. 2: 386; Abraham Lincoln to Isaac N. Arnold, May 25, 1864, in *WAL*, 7: 361. See Craig D. Tenney, "To Suppress or Not To Suppress: Abraham Lincoln and the Chicago *Times*," *Civil War History* 27 (September 1981): 248–59.

131. For examples, see *OR*, ser. 2, 5: 725–26.

132. Edwin M. Stanton to A. E. Burnside, June 1, 1863, in *OR*, ser. 2, 5: 724. For a description of the Hascall episode, see Harper, *Lincoln and the Press*, 251–54.

133. Ritchie, *Press Gallery*, 68; Culver H. Smith, *The Press, Politics, and Patronage: The American Government's Use of Newspapers, 1789–1875* (Athens: University of Georgia Press, 1977), 161–81, 212. 233–36.

134. Edwin M. Stanton to A. E. Burnside, June 1, 1863, in *OR*, ser. 2, 5: 724; Abraham Lincoln to John M. Schofield, [July 13], 1863, in *WAL*, 6: 326; Abraham Lincoln to John M. Schofield, October 1, 1863, in *WAL*, 6: 492.

135. Abraham Lincoln to John A. Dix, May 18, 1864, in *WAL*, 7: 347–48; Harper, *Lincoln and the Press*, 289–303.

136. Abraham Lincoln to Edwin M. Stanton, August 22, 1864, in *WAL*, 7: 512. For an account of the disguise story, see Harper, *Lincoln and the Press*, 89–90.

137. *The American Annual Cyclopædia and Register of Important Events of the Year 1864* (New York: Appleton, 1867), 4: 389–93.

138. An Act Relating to Habeas Corpus, and Regulating Judicial Proceedings in Certain Cases, ch. 81, 12 Stat. 755, 756 (1863).

139. For Democratic arguments to this effect, see Neely, *Fate of Liberty*, 196–99.

140. *The American Annual Cyclopædia and Register of Important Events of the Year 1864*, 4: 392, 393.

141. Abraham Lincoln to Carl Schurz, November 10, 1862, in *WAL*, 5: 494. See Klement, *Copperheads in the Middle West*, 17–23; Chandler, "Fighting Words," 50.

142. Inaugural Address, February 22, 1862, in *The Messages and Papers of Jefferson Davis and the Confederacy, Including Diplomatic Correspondence, 1861–1865*, ed. and comp. James D. Richardson (New York: Chelsea House-Robert Hector, 1966), 1: 184–85.

143. See J. Cutler Andrews, *The South Reports the Civil War* (Princeton: Princeton University Press, 1970); Hodding Carter, *Their Words Were Bullets: The Southern Press in War, Reconstruction, and Peace* (Athens: University of Georgia Press, 1969), 27–30; Stephen A. Smith, "Freedom of Expression in the Confederate States of America," in *Free Speech Yearbook: 1978*, ed. Gregg Phifer (Falls Church, Va.: Speech Communication Association, 1978), 17–37.

144. R. E. Lee to George W. Randolph, July 7, 1862, in *OR*, ser. 1, 11 pt. 3: 635–36; Indorsement, July 9, 1862, in *OR*, ser. 1, 11 pt. 3: 136.

145. James F. Rhodes, *History of the Civil War, 1861–1865*, ed. E. B. Long (New York: Frederick Ungar, 1961), 392–95.

146. Carl R. Osthaus, *Partisans of the Southern Press: Editorial Spokesmen of the Nineteenth Century* (Lexington: University Press of Kentucky, 1994), 95–117; Carter, *Their Words Were Bullets*, 24–26, 29–30. For examples of press criticism of Robert E. Lee, see Gary W. Gallagher, "Another Look at the Generalship of R. E. Lee," in *Lee: The Soldier*, ed. Gary W. Gallagher (Lincoln: University of Nebraska Press, 1996), 283–84; Carol Reardon, "From 'King of Spades' to 'First Captain of the Confederacy': R. E. Lee's First Six Weeks with the Army of Northern Virginia," in Gallagher, *Lee: The Soldier*, 313–14.

147. William Whiting, *The War Powers of the President, and the Legislative Powers of Congress in Relation to Rebellion, Treason and Slavery*, 7th ed. (Boston: John L. Shorey, 1863), 59–61; [Charles F. Blake], *Prerogative Rights and Public Law* (Boston: William Guild, 1863), 8–10.

148. Alexander J. Groth, "Lincoln and the Standards of Presidential Conduct," *Presidential Studies Quarterly* 22 (Fall 1992): 765–77.

149. Sidney George Fisher, *The Trial of the Constitution* (Philadelphia: Lippincott, 1862), 60–63; see also 54–55, 196–201.

150. For a discussion of the scholarly work on Lincoln and civil liberties, see Neely, *Fate of Liberty* 224–32.

151. Ibid., 222, 233–34, 235.

152. The Prize Cases, 2 Black (67 U.S.) 635, 659–60, 666–71 (1863).

153. The Prize Cases, 2 Black 635, 648.

154. The Prize Cases, 2 Black 635, 697–99.

155. *Ex parte* Vallandigham, 68 U.S. (1 Wall.) 243 (1863).

156. *Ex parte* Milligan, 71 U.S. (4 Wall.) 2, 109 (1866).

157. *The Trials for Treason at Indianapolis: Disclosing the Plans for Establishing a North-Western Confederacy*, ed. Benn Pitman (Cincinnati: Moore, Wilstach, and Baldwin, 1865), 68–69; for a list of the charges, see 74–77. For background and analysis, see Lurie, *The Origins of the United States Court of Military Appeals*, 35–42; Jacobus tenBroek, Edward N. Barnhart, and Floyd W. Matson, *Prejudice, War and the Constitution* (Berkeley: University of California Press,

1968), 227–31; Lewis J. Wertheim, "The Indianapolis Treason Trials, the Elections of 1864, and the Power of the Partisan Press," *Indiana Magazine of History* 85 (September 1989): 236–60; Kenneth M. Stampp, "The Milligan Case and the Election of 1864 in Indiana," *Mississippi Valley Historical Review* 31 (June 1944): 41–58.

158. *Ex parte* Milligan, 71 U.S. (4 Wall.) at 18, 94–96, 120–21, 124–26. Milligan subsequently sued the members of the military court for damages and was awarded the symbolic sum of five dollars. William D. Foulke, *Life of Oliver P. Morton* (Indianapolis: Bowen-Merrill Co., 1899), 1: 431–32.

159. Justice Davis wrote the opinion of the Court, but four justices joined in a concurring opinion that reached the same conclusion about military commissions on other grounds.

160. Congress, House, 55th Cong., 2nd sess., *Congressional Record* (May 18, 1898), vol. 31, pt. 5, 5012–17.

161. Mary S. Mander, "Pen and Sword: Problems of Reporting the Spanish-American War," *Journalism History* 9 (Spring 1982): 2–9, 28; Charles H. Brown, "Press Censorship in the Spanish-American War," *Journalism Quarterly* 42 (Autumn 1965): 581–90. For background on the cable cutting and censorship, see Daniel R. Headrick, *The Invisible Weapon: Telecommunications and International Politics, 1851–1945* (New York: Oxford University Press, 1991), 82–84.

162. Richard Harding Davis to Charles B. Davis, May 29, 1898, in *Adventures and Letters of Richard Harding Davis*, ed. Charles B. Davis (New York: Scribner's, 1917), 243–44.

163. On the public bickering between Davis and Bigelow, see Arthur Lubow, *The Reporter Who Would Be King: A Biography of Richard Harding Davis* (New York: Scribner's, 1992), 163–66.

164. Brown, "Press Censorship in the Spanish-American War," 589.

165. *The Almanac of American History*, ed. Arthur M. Schlesinger Jr., (New York: Putnam, 1983), 392.

166. Richard E. Welch Jr., *Response to Imperialism: The United States and the Philippine-American War, 1899–1901* (Chapel Hill: University of North Carolina Press, 1979), xiii.

167. For this statistic and a brief description of the war that includes a photograph of American soldiers standing on a large heap of Filipino bones, see Roger Butterfield, *The American Past: A History of the United States from Concord to the Great Society* (New York: Simon and Schuster, 1976), 285.

168. Welch, *Response to Imperialism*, 133–40.

169. *Trials of Courts-Martial in the Philippine Islands in Consequence of Certain Insurrections*, March 3, 1903, 57th Cong., 2nd sess., Senate Documents, vol. 15, no. 213, 1–6; Welch, *Response to Imperialism*, 41.

170. Alfred E. Cornebise, *Ranks and Columns: Armed Forces Newspapers in American Wars* (Westport, Conn.: Greenwood Press, 1993), 59; Welch, *Response to Imperialism*, 41; Theodore Schroeder, *Free Speech for Radicals*, enl. ed. (New York: Free Speech League, 1916; repr., New York: Burt Franklin, 1969), 23–24.

171. Welch, *Response to Imperialism*, 132; Morison, Merk, and Freidel, *Dissent in Three American Wars*, 67–95; Mark Twain, "To the Person Sitting in Darkness," *North American Review* 172 (February 1901): 176; Mark Twain, March 23, 1901, in *Speeches at the Lotos Club* (New York: Printed for the Lotos Club, 1911), 14–15.

172. E. Berkeley Tompkins, *Anti-Imperialism in the United States: The Great Debate, 1890–1920* (Philadelphia: University of Pennsylvania Press, 1970), 206–9; Robert L. Beisner, *Twelve against Empire: The Anti-Imperialists, 1898–1900* (New York: McGraw-Hill, 1968), 98–100; Russell Alger to Elwell S. Otis, April 25, 1899, in *Correspondence Relating to the War with Spain* (Washington, D.C.: Government Printing Office, 1902), 2: 973.

173. The authorizations for censorship are conveyed in H. C. Corbin to Elwell S. Otis, January 13, 1899, in *Correspondence Relating to the War with Spain*, 2: 878; H. C. Corbin to Elwell S. Otis, July 27, 1899, in *Correspondence Relating to the War with Spain*, 2: 1041.

174. Congress, Senate, 56th Cong., 1st sess., *Congressional Record* (June 4, 1900), vol. 33, pt. 7, 6527–29. Censorship became less onerous after the correspondents' complaints were made public, but did continue in the Philippines, at least on a sporadic basis. See Eugene W. Sharp, "Cracking the Manila Censorship in 1899 and 1900," *Journalism Quarterly* 20 (December 1943): 280–85. General John J. Pershing imposed harsh censorship during the Moro insurgencies and in Mexico during his pursuit of Pancho Villa. Frank E. Vandiver, *Black Jack: The Life and Times of John J. Pershing* (College Station: Texas A & M University Press, 1977), 1: 557–58, 2: 618, 630–37; "Military vs. Press: Troubled History," *NYT*, October 29, 1983, 7.

175. Theodore Roosevelt, *An Autobiography* (New York: Macmillan, 1914), 372, 379, 380.

176. *Mr. Buchanan's Administration on the Eve of Rebellion*, in *The Works of James Buchanan*, ed. John B. Moore (Philadelphia: Lippincott, 1908–1911), 12: 141.

177. William Howard Taft, *Our Chief Magistrate and His Powers* (New York: Columbia University Press, 1916) 140, 144, 146, 156–57. For statements by Jackson and Roosevelt recognizing ultimate accountability to the people, see Arthur M. Schlesinger Jr., *The Imperial Presidency* (Boston: Houghton Mifflin, 1973), 410.

178. Theodore Roosevelt, as quoted in Richard Polenberg, *Fighting Faiths: The Abrams Case, the Supreme Court, and Free Speech* (New York: Penguin Books, 1989), 32.

179. For the influence of the patriot king model on earlier presidents, see Ralph Ketcham, *Presidents above Party: The First American Presidency, 1789–1829* (Chapel Hill: Published for the Institute of Early American History and Culture by the University of North Carolina Press, 1984).

180. Gordon S. Wood, *The Creation of the American Republic, 1776–1787* (Chapel Hill: Published for the Institute of Early American History and Culture by the University of North Carolina Press, 1969), 260–61.

181. David Thelen, "The Practice of American History," *Journal of American History* 81 (December 1994): 952. On the image of the Great Emancipator, see Merrill D. Peterson, *Lincoln in American Memory* (New York: Oxford University Press, 1994).

182. Sidney Blumenthal, "Reinventing Lincoln," *New Yorker*, November 14, 1994, 106.

Chapter 6

1. Scott Anderson, "Prisoners of War: The Lure of Enemy Gunfire and the Enemy Within," *Harper's*, January 1997, 37.

2. Painstaking bureaucratic procedures were clearly in force during the two world wars. See Phillip Knightley, *The First Casualty: From Crimea to Vietnam: The War Correspondent as Hero, Propagandist, and Myth Maker* (New York: Harcourt Brace Jovanovich, 1975), 80–81, 85–86, 90–101, 139–40, 244–333; Ross F. Collins, "The Development of Censorship in World War I France," *Journalism Monographs*, no. 131, February 1992; Ralph O. Nafziger, "World War Correspondents and Censorship of the Belligerents," *Journalism Quarterly* 14 (September 1937): 226–43.

3. Max Weber, *Economy and Society: An Outline of Interpretive Sociology*, ed. Guenther Roth and Claus Wittich (New York: Bedminster Press, 1968), 992.

4. See Sissela Bok, *Secrets: On the Ethics of Concealment and Revelation* (New York: Pantheon Books, 1982), 177, 198.

5. For background, see David Steigerwald, *Wilsonian Idealism in America* (Ithaca, N.Y.: Cornell University Press, 1994); Ellis W. Hawley, *The Great War and the Search for a Modern Order: A History of the American People and Their Institutions, 1917–1933* (New York: St. Martin's Press, 1979); David M. Rabban, "Free Speech and Progressive Social Thought," *Texas Law Review* 74 (April 1996): 951–1038; David M. Rabban, "The Free Speech League, the ACLU,

and Changing Conceptions of Free Speech in American History," *Stanford Law Review* 45 (November 1992): 52–55.

6. Byron Price, "Censorship and Free Speech," *Indiana Law Journal* 18 (October 1942): 17, 21.

7. William E. Leuchtenburg, *The Supreme Court Reborn: The Constitutional Revolution in the Age of Roosevelt* (New York: Oxford University Press, 1995); Lucas A. Powe Jr., *The Fourth Estate and the Constitution: Freedom of the Press in America* (Berkeley: University of California Press, 1991), 69–70; Mark A. Graber, *Transforming Free Speech: The Ambiguous Legacy of Civil Libertarianism* (Berkeley: University of California Press, 1991), 50–121; Paul L. Murphy, *World War I and the Origin of Civil Liberties in the United States* (New York: Norton, 1979); Richard Polenberg, "The Good War? A Reappraisal of How World War II Affected American Society," *Virginia Magazine of History and Biography* 100 (July 1992): 295–322.

8. Donald B. Johnson and Kirk H. Porter, comps., *National Party Platforms, 1840–1972* (Urbana: University of Illinois Press, 1973), 195.

9. Minersville School District v. Gobitis, 310 U.S. 586, 595 (1940).

10. On the case, Roosevelt's reaction, and some of the mob actions, see Leonard Baker, *Brandeis and Frankfurter: A Dual Biography* (New York: Harper and Row, 1984), 399–409.

11. West Virginia State Board of Education v. Barnette, 319 U.S. 624, 639, 640, 641 (1943).

12. See Rosamund M. Thomas, *Espionage and Secrecy: The Official Secrets Acts 1911–1989 of the United Kingdom* (London: Routledge, 1991); Evan J. Wallach, "Executive Powers of Prior Restraint over Publication of National Security Information: The UK and the USA Compared," *International and Comparative Law Quarterly* 32 (April 1983): 424–51; Charles Fairman, "The Law of Martial Rule and the National Emergency," *Harvard Law Review* 55 (June 1942): 1254–56.

13. Gompers v. U.S., 233 U.S. 604, 610 (1914).

14. Oliver Wendell Holmes Jr. to Sir Frederick Pollock and Lady Pollock, September 20, 1928, in *Holmes-Pollock Letters: The Correspondence of Mr. Justice Holmes and Sir Frederick Pollock, 1874–1932*, ed. Mark DeWolfe Howe (Cambridge: Harvard University Press, 1941), 2: 230. For an essay describing the debt Holmes owed to Darwin and utilitarianism, see Thomas C. Grey, "Bad Man from Olympus," *The New York Review*, July 13, 1995, 4–7.

15. Roscoe Pound, "Interests of Personality [pt. 2]," *Harvard Law Review* 28 (March 1915): 456.

16. An Address on Abraham Lincoln, [September 4, 1916], in *PWW*, 38: 142, 144, 145.

17. Arthur S. Link, *The Higher Realism of Woodrow Wilson and Other Essays* (Nashville: Vanderbilt University Press, 1971), 129; William F. McCombs, *Making Woodrow Wilson President* (New York: Fairview, 1921), 180–81, 207–8; Edith Bolling Wilson, *My Memoir* (Indianapolis: Bobbs-Merrill, 1939), 355–56.

18. Remarks to Confederate Veterans in Washington, June 5, 1917, in *PWW*, 42: 452.

19. Woodrow Wilson, " 'Mere Literature,' " *Atlantic Monthly*, December 1893, 823.

20. Woodrow Wilson, *Congressional Government: A Study in American Politics* (Boston: Houghton Mifflin, 1925), xiii, xix–xxi; Michael Kammen, *A Machine That Would Go of Itself: The Constitution in American Culture* (New York: Knopf, 1986), 18–20, 169–70, 399.

21. An Address in Atlantic City to the National American Woman Suffrage Association, September 8, 1916, in *PWW*, 38: 162, 163.

22. To Enforce Neutrality of Wireless Stations, August 5, 1914, in *A Compilation of the Messages and Papers of the Presidents* (New York: Bureau of National Literature, n.d.), 18: 7962.

23. "Marconi Co. Denies Censoring is Legal,"*NYT*, August 23, 1914, 7; "Marconi Company Must Obey or Quit," *NYT*, September 20, 1914, 8. For background and analysis, see Daniel R. Headrick, *The Invisible Weapon: Telecommunications and International Politics, 1851–1945* (New York: Oxford University Press, 1991), 144; Susan J. Douglas, *Inventing American Broadcasting: 1899–1922* (Baltimore: Johns Hopkins University Press, 1987), 268–74.

24. 30 Op. Att'y Gen. 291, 292–93 (1914). For the relevant portion of the Radio Act of 1912, see ch. 287, 37 Stat. 302, 303.

25. Ch. 169, 44 Stat. 1162, 1165.

26. Ch. 652, 48 Stat. 1064, 1104–5.

27. "Marconi Suit Thrown Out," *NYT*, October 9, 1914, 5.

28. Exec. Order No. 2604 (1917).

29. Headrick, *Invisible Weapon*, 144; Erik Barnouw, *A History of Broadcasting in the United States*, vol. 1, *A Tower in Babel* (New York: Oxford University Press, 1966), 37.

30. Headrick, *Invisible Weapon*, 144–45; Douglas, *Inventing American Broadcasting*, 276–80. See also James Schwoch, *The American Radio Industry and Its Latin American Activities, 1900–1939* (Urbana: University of Illinois Press, 1990), 31–55.

31. From the diary of Josephus Daniels, March 27, 1917, in *PWW*, 41: 484.

32. Erik Barnouw, *Tube of Plenty: The Evolution of American Television*, 2nd rev. ed. (New York: Oxford University Press, 1990), 18–21; Douglas, *Inventing American Broadcasting*, 279–85; "Mexican Wireless Depicted as Peril," *NYT*, December 18, 1918, 17; "Wants Radios Returned," *NYT*, January 18, 1919, 18.

33. David M. Kennedy, *Over Here: The First World War and American Society* (New York: Oxford University Press, 1980), 40.

34. John L. Heaton, *Cobb of "The World"* (New York: Dutton, 1924), 267–70. Doubts are sometimes expressed about the accuracy of this account, but I see no reason to question it.

35. Wilson was less interested in broad, European-style censorship than some members of his cabinet. Diary entry, April 6, 1917, in *The Cabinet Diaries of Josephus Daniels, 1913–1921*, ed. E. David Cronon (Lincoln: University of Nebraska Press, 1963), 130; From the diary of Josephus Daniels, April 17, 1917, in *PWW*, 42: 90–91.

36. See Margaret A. Blanchard, *Revolutionary Sparks: Freedom of Expression in Modern America* (New York: Oxford University Press, 1992), 71–109. For comparisons of actions taken by Lincoln and Wilson to restrict expression, see Clinton Rossiter, *Constitutional Dictatorship: Crisis Government in Modern Democracies* (New York: Harcourt, Brace, and World, 1963), 241–45; J. G. Randall, "Lincoln's Task and Wilson's," *South Atlantic Quarterly* 29 (October 1930): 349–68; Betty Houchin Winfield, "Two Commanders-in-Chief: Free Expression's Most Severe Tests," Research Paper R-7, Joan Shorenstein Barone Center, John F. Kennedy School of Government, Harvard University, August 1992.

37. See, for example, Frank Geere, "The Government of War Correspondents," *Journal of the Military Service* 44 (May–June 1909): 401–18.

38. U.S. War College Division, General Staff Corps, *The Proper Relationship Between the Army and the Press in War* (Washington, D.C.: Government Printing Office, 1916), 5, 12. For background, see Nafziger, "World War Correspondents," 243.

39. For a convenient compilation of the legislative history, see the notes accompanying Josephus Daniels to Woodrow Wilson, April 11, 1917, in *PWW*, 42: 39; Woodrow Wilson to Josephus Daniels, April 12, 1917, in *PWW*, 42: 43; Joseph Patrick Tumulty to Woodrow Wilson, April 20, 1917, in *PWW*, 42: 106–7; Joseph Patrick Tumulty to Woodrow Wilson, May 8, 1917, in *PWW*, 42: 244–47; Woodrow Wilson to Edwin Yates Webb, May 22, 1917, in *PWW*, 42: 369–70.

40. For Wilson's statement to an influential Hearst editor that he would not permit the law to be used as a shield against criticism, see Woodrow Wilson to Arthur Brisbane, April 25, 1917, in *PWW*, 42: 129.

41. See, for example, *Congressional Record*, vol. 55, pt. 2, 1751–52, 1753, 1777, 1778; some Democrats also saw the dangers in censorship: see, for example, 2004, 2008. For the view that Congress was more concerned with preserving partisan criticism than with the ideal of a free press when it rejected Wilson's request, see Kennedy, *Over Here*, 25–26.

42. Congress, House, 65th Cong., 1st sess., *Congressional Record* (May 2, 1917), vol. 55, pt. 2, 1700, 1701; for other references to 1898, see 1716, 1753, 1764–65, 1772.

43. Congress, House, 65th Cong., 1st sess., *Congressional Record* (May 3, 1917), vol. 55, pt. 2, 1778.

44. Diary entry, April 2, 1917, in Cronon, *Cabinet Diaries of Josephus Daniels*, 127.

45. For samples of the press reaction, see George Juergens, *News From the White House: The Presidential-Press Relationship in the Progressive Era* (Chicago: University of Chicago Press, 1981), 190–91; John Lofton, *The Press as Guardian of the First Amendment* (Columbia: University of South Carolina Press, 1980), 172–73.

46. Joseph P. Tumulty to Woodrow Wilson, May 8, 1917, in *PWW*, 42: 245–46.

47. For examples of the charge that Wilson wanted autocratic power, see *Congressional Record*, vol. 55, pt. 2, 1715, 1752, 1771, 1777, 2004.

48. "Lansing Closes Sources of News of America's Foreign Relationships," *NYT*, May 8, 1917, 1; Seward W. Livermore, *Politics Is Adjourned: Woodrow Wilson and the War Congress, 1916–1918* (Middletown, Conn.: Wesleyan University Press, 1966), 32–37.

49. Frank Irving Cobb to Woodrow Wilson, May 22, 1917, in *PWW*, 42: 371; Woodrow Wilson to Edwin Yates Webb, May 22, 1917, in *PWW*, 369–70.

50. Ch. 30, 40 Stat. 217, 219, 230; Murphy, *World War I*, 168.

51. Ch. 75, 40 Stat. 553, 554.

52. Ch. 106, 40 Stat. 411, 413, 425–26; Exec. Order No. 2729–A (1917); Stephen L. Vaughn, *Holding Fast the Inner Lines: Democracy, Nationalism, and the Committee on Public Information* (Chapel Hill: University of North Carolina Press, 1980), 221–22, 224–25.

53. Dorothy G. Fowler, *Unmailable: Congress and the Post Office* (Athens: University of Georgia Press, 1977), 109–25; Jon Bekken, " 'These Great and Dangerous Powers': Postal Censorship of the Press," *Journal of Communication Inquiry* 15 (Winter 1991): 55–71; Donald Johnson, "Wilson, Burleson, and Censorship in the First World War," *Journal of Southern History* 28 (February 1962): 46–58.

54. *War Cyclopedia: A Handbook for Ready Reference on the Great War*, ed. Frederic L. Paxson, Edward S. Corwin, and Samuel B. Harding (Washington, D.C.: Government Printing Office, 1918), 163.

55. Milwaukee Social Democratic Publishing Co. v. Burleson, 255 U.S. 407, 410, 413–14, 416 (1921).

56. Milwaukee Social Democratic Publishing Co. v. Burleson, 255 U.S. at 436 (Brandeis, J., dissenting); Milwaukee Social Democratic Publishing Co. v. Burleson, 255 U.S. at 437–38 (Holmes, J., dissenting).

57. Kennedy, *Over Here*, 76–77, 83; Murphy, *World War I*, 116–17. Approximately sixty socialist publications lost their second-class mailing privileges. Fowler, *Unmailable*, 115. Case studies include Mick Mulcrone, " 'Those Miserable Little Hounds': World War I Postal Censorship of the *Irish World*," *Journalism History* 20 (Spring 1994): 15–24.

58. Allen W. Ricker to Woodrow Wilson, August 3, 1917, in *PWW*, 43: 382; Herbert David Croly to Woodrow Wilson, October 19, 1917, in *PWW*, 44: 408.

59. Other cautionary letters included Lillian D. Wald and others to Woodrow Wilson, April 16, 1917, in *PWW*, 42: 118–19; Max Eastman and others to Woodrow Wilson, July 12, 1917, in *PWW*, 43: 165; W. I. Irvine and Paul Hanna to Woodrow Wilson, August 4, 1917, in *PWW*, 43: 383; Oswald Garrison Villard to Joseph Patrick Tumulty, September 26, 1917, in *PWW*, 44: 271–73; Daniel W. Hoan to Woodrow Wilson, October 4, 1917, in *PWW*, 44: 339–40; Grenville Stanley Macfarland to Woodrow Wilson, October 12, 1917, in *PWW*, 44: 366; John Spargo to Woodrow Wilson, November 1, 1917, in *PWW*, 44: 491–92; John Nevin Sayre to Woodrow Wilson, September 19, 1918, in *PWW*, 51: 77.

60. Woodrow Wilson to Albert Sidney Burleson, October 11, 1917, in *PWW*, 44: 358. See also Woodrow Wilson to Albert Sidney Burleson, October 18, 1917, in *PWW*, 44: 397–98; Woodrow Wilson to Albert Sidney Burleson, October 30, 1917, in *PWW*, 44: 472–73; Woodrow Wilson to Albert Sidney Burleson, September 16, 1918, in *PWW*, 51: 12.

61. See, for example, Albert Sidney Burleson to Woodrow Wilson, July 16, 1917, in *PWW*, 43: 187–88; Albert Sidney Burleson to Woodrow Wilson, October 16, 1917, in *PWW*, 44: 389–90.

62. Burleson demoted and dismissed black postal employees in the South to open opportunities for loyal white Democrats. Murphy, *World War I*, 97.

63. Ray Stannard Baker, *Woodrow Wilson: Life and Letters* (New York: Doubleday, Doran, 1939), 7: 165.

64. See, for example, Woodrow Wilson to Grenville Stanley Macfarland, October 18, 1917, in *PWW*, 44: 397; Woodrow Wilson to Herbert David Croly, October 22, 1917, in *PWW*, 44: 420.

65. Upton Beall Sinclair to Woodrow Wilson, October 22, 1917, in *PWW*, 44: 467–72; Walter Lippmann to Edward Mandell House, October 17 [1917], in *PWW*, 44: 393–94; Edward Mandell House to Woodrow Wilson, October 17, 1917, in *PWW*, 44: 392–93.

66. This point is made in Thomas J. Knock, *To End All Wars: Woodrow Wilson and the Quest for a New World Order* (New York: Oxford University Press, 1992), viii–x.

67. Livermore, *Politics Is Adjourned*, 245–47.

68. George Creel to Woodrow Wilson, November 8, 1918, in *PWW*, 51: 645. For similar sentiments, see Oswald Garrison Villard to Joseph Patrick Tumulty, November 8, 1918, in *PWW*, 51: 646.

69. John Palmer Gavit to Woodrow Wilson, February 24, 1919, in *PWW*, 55: 255. For a similar plea that warned Wilson that he needed the support of radical groups for the League of Nations, see Dudley Field Malone to Woodrow Wilson, February 28, 1919, in *PWW*, 55: 337–38.

70. Knock, *To End All Wars*, 237–38, 255–56; Lincoln Steffens, *The Autobiography of Lincoln Steffens* (New York: Harcourt, Brace, 1931), 843.

71. The attorney general denied that anyone had been convicted for merely expressing opinion, but urged executive clemency in some cases. Thomas Watt Gregory to Woodrow Wilson, March 1, 1919, in *PWW*, 55: 345–47. By July 1919 the sentences of more than one hundred people convicted under the Espionage Act had been commuted. Alexander Mitchell Palmer to Woodrow Wilson, July 30, 1919, in *PWW*, 62: 58.

72. Clarence Seward Darrow to Woodrow Wilson, July 29, 1919, in *PWW*, 62: 58–59; Alexander Mitchell Palmer to Woodrow Wilson, July 30, 1919, in *PWW*, 62: 58; Woodrow Wilson to Albert Sidney Burleson, February 28, 1919, in *PWW*, 55: 327; Woodrow Wilson to Alexander Mitchell Palmer, August 29, 1919, in *PWW*, 62: 555; Woodrow Wilson to John Spargo, August 29, 1919, in *PWW*, 62: 559.

73. Livermore, *Politics Is Adjourned*, 35; Juergens, *News from the White House*, 204; Steffens, *Autobiography of Lincoln Steffens*, 843–44.

74. An Annual Message on the State of the Union, December 7, 1915, in *PWW*, 35: 306, 307.

75. Kennedy, *Over Here*, 24–25; Murphy, *World War I*, 54–55.

76. Woodrow Wilson to Edwin Yates Webb, May 22, 1917, in *PWW*, 42: 369–70; A Flag Day Address, June 14, 1917, in *PWW*, 42: 499, 503. On the publication of the address by the government's Committee on Public Information and the distribution, see Juergens, *News from the White House*, 182.

77. Curt Gentry, *J. Edgar Hoover: The Man and the Secrets* (New York: Norton, 1991), 68–74.

78. Walton Rawls, *Wake Up, America: World War I and the American Poster* (New York: Abbeville Press, 1988); Earl E. Sperry, *German Plots and Intrigues in the United States during the Period of our Neutrality* (Washington, D.C.: Committee on Public Information, 1918); David M. White and Richard Averson, *The Celluloid Weapon: Social Comment in the American Film* (Boston: Beacon Press, 1972), 13–16.

79. John D. Stevens, *Shaping the First Amendment: The Development of Free Expression* (Beverly Hills, Calif.: Sage Publications, 1982), 44–54; Murphy, *World War I*, 127–32; "Mob Violence in World War I," in *Freedom of the Press from Hamilton to the Warren Court*, ed. Harold L. Nelson (Indianapolis: Bobbs-Merrill, 1967), 307–20; Thomas A. Lawrence, "Eclipse of Liberty: Civil Liberties in the United States during the First World War," *Wayne Law Review* 21 (November 1974): 33–39, 58–59, 111–12.

80. Joan M. Jensen, *The Price of Vigilance* (Chicago: Rand McNally, 1968); Emerson Hough, *The Web* (Chicago: Reilly and Lee, 1919).

81. Carl H. Chrislock, *Watchdog of Loyalty: The Minnesota Commission on Public Safety during World War I* (St. Paul: Minnesota Historical Society Press, 1991); Wayne A. Wiegand, *"An Active Instrument for Propaganda": The American Public Library during World War I* (New York: Greenwood Press, 1989); Murphy, *World War I*, 116–18.

82. *Literary Digest*, April 14, 1917, 1044; John D. Stevens, "Press and Community Toleration: Wisconsin in World War I," *Journalism Quarterly* 46 (Summer 1969): 257; "Mob Violence in World War I," in Nelson, *Freedom of the Press*, 309, 311, 312, 316.

83. William T. Evjue, *A Fighting Editor* (Madison, Wis.: Wells, 1968), 274–345.

84. Stevens, "Press and Community Toleration," 255–59. On the hostility La Follette experienced, see Bernard A. Weisberger, *The La Follettes of Wisconsin: Love and Politics in Progressive America* (Madison: University of Wisconsin Press, 1994), 179–224.

85. "Free Speech," *Milwaukee Sentinel*, October 15, 1917, 6; *Janesville Gazette*, April 25, 1918, 4; *Janesville Gazette*, May 3, 1918, 4; "Payments to County War Chest Are Due," *Janesville Gazette*, May 20, 1918, 2; "Yellow," *Janesville Gazette*, May 20, 1918, 4.

86. Stevens, "Press and Community Toleration," 257. For other examples, see John Nerone, *Violence against the Press: Policing the Public Sphere in U.S. History* (New York: Oxford University Press, 1994), 160–63.

87. Oswald Garrison Villard, *Fighting Years: Memoirs of a Liberal Editor* (New York: Harcourt, Brace, 1939), 326–31; Juergens, *News from the White House*, 200–202.

88. Patrick S. Washburn, *A Question of Sedition: The Federal Government's Investigation of the Black Press during World War II* (New York: Oxford University Press, 1986), 14–22; Lee Finkle, *Forum for Protest: The Black Press during World War II* (Cranbury, N. J.: Associated University Presses, 1975), 39–50.

89. "German Plots among Negroes," *Literary Digest*, April 21, 1917, 1153.

90. Theodore Kornweibel Jr., " 'The Most Dangerous of All Negro Journals': Federal Efforts to Suppress the *Chicago Defender* during World War I," *American Journalism* 11 (Spring 1994): 154–68.

91. "Close Ranks," *The Crisis*, July 1918, 1; William Jordan, " 'The Damnable Dilemma': African-American Accommodation and Protest during World War I," *Journal of American History* 81 (March 1995): 1562–83.

92. Max Eastman to Woodrow Wilson, September 8, 1917, in *PWW*, 44: 169–172; Woodrow Wilson to Max Eastman, September 18, 1917, in *PWW*, 44: 210–11. Wilson had earlier tried to intercede on behalf of *The Masses* but was rebuffed by Postmaster General Burleson, who told him that the actions taken by the Post Office were proper under the Espionage Act and that the publication had brought suit in federal district court. Woodrow Wilson to Albert Sidney Burleson, with Enclosure, July 13, 1917, in *PWW*, 43: 164–65; Albert Sidney Burleson to Woodrow Wilson, July 16, 1917, in *PWW*, 43: 187–89. Saying that press freedom meant only freedom

from prior restraint, a federal court of appeals ruled the use of the Espionage Act of 1917 against *The Masses* was not a violation of the First Amendment. Masses Pub. Co. v. Patten, 246 F. 24 (2d. Cir. 1917).

93. An Annual Message on the State of the Union, December 4, 1917, in *PWW*, 45: 195.

94. Woodrow Wilson to Edward Beale McLean, July 12, 1917, in *PWW*, 43: 154; Woodrow Wilson to Breckinridge Long, November 20, 1917, in *PWW*, 45: 86–87; Juergens, *News from the White House*, 187–88.

95. Ian Mugridge, *The View from Xanadu: William Randolph Hearst and United States Foreign Policy* (Montreal: McGill-Queen's University Press, 1995), 7–18, 32–38, 108–16.

96. "War for Democracy," *Literary Digest*, April 14, 1917, 1043–44; W. A. Swanberg, *Citizen Hearst: A Biography of William Randolph Hearst* (New York: Scribner's, 1961), 306, 312–13; Woodrow Wilson to Albert Sidney Burleson, October 4, 1917, in *PWW*, 44: 302.

97. Bok, *Secrets*, 171–72; Juergens, *News from the White House*, 126–66; introduction to *PWW*, 50: xii–xiv; Elmer E. Cornwell Jr., "The Press Conferences of Woodrow Wilson," *Journalism Quarterly* 39 (Summer 1962): 292–300.

98. Woodrow Wilson to Breckinridge Long, November 20, 1917, in *PWW*, 45: 86, 87.

99. On Creel and his committee, see Vaughn, *Holding Fast the Inner Lines*; Robert Jackall and Janice M. Hirota, "American's First Propaganda Ministry: The Committee on Public Information during the Great War," in *Propaganda*, ed. Robert Jackall (New York: New York University Press, 1995): 137–73.

100. A Memorandum by George Creel, an enclosure with Josephus Daniels to Woodrow Wilson, April 11, 1917, in *PWW*, 42: 39–41; Woodrow Wilson to Josephus Daniels, April 12, 1917, in *PWW*, 42: 43; James R. Mock and Cedric Larson, *Words That Won the War: The Story of the Committee on Public Information* (Princeton: Princeton University Press, 1939). See also Juergens, *News from the White House*, 167–204.

101. Woodrow Wilson to George Creel, May 17, 1917, in *PWW*, 42: 304–13. The version Wilson approved differs in some ways from the one published in the *Official Bulletin* on June 2, 1917.

102. "Statement to the Press of the United States," *Official Bulletin*, June 2, 1917, 12–15. For a revision of the guidelines, see "Requests for Censorship by Press of Certain War News, as Revised and Urged upon All American Publishers, Are Given Out by the Committee on Public Information," in *PWW*, December 31, 1917, 10, 16.

103. *Complete Report of the Chairman of the Committee on Public Information* (Washington, D.C.: Government Printing Office, 1920), 4; Vaughn, *Holding Fast the Inner Lines*, 211.

104. *Complete Report of the Chairman of the Committee on Public Information*, 1, 10, 12. On the contrast with European censorship, see also "Statement to the Press of the United States," 12; George Creel, *How We Advertised America* (New York: Harper, 1920), 16–27.

105. "Scope and Activities of Committee on Public Information Shown, in Report by Chairman Creel Made to the President," *Official Bulletin*, February 4, 1918, 10.

106. *National Service Handbook* (Washington, D.C.: Government Printing Office, 1917), 18; "Requests for Censorship by Press of Certain War News," 10.

107. Juergens, *News from the White House*, 193–95; Vaughn, *Holding Fast the Inner Lines*, 218, 221, 224–25, 234; Mock and Larson, *Words That Won the War*, 20, 44, 46, 84, 142.

108. Larry W. Ward, *The Motion Picture Goes to War: The U.S. Government Film Effort during World War I* (Ann Arbor, Mich.: UMI Research Press, 1985), 123.

109. "Creel Answers Some Pointed Queries," *E&P*, May 18, 1918, 32; Vaughn, *Holding Fast the Inner Lines*, 222–28; Mock and Larson, *Words That Won the War*, 86.

110. "Statement to the Press of the United States," 13, 14; "Treason's Twilight Zone," *Literary Digest*, June 9, 1917, 1763, 1765; Juergens, *News from the White House*, 189–90; Mock and Larson, *Words That Won the War*, 83.

111. John Hohenberg, *Foreign Correspondence: The Great Reporters and Their Times* (New York: Columbia University Press, 1964), 234–39; General Orders, No. 36, September 12, 1917, in *United States Army in the World War, 1917–1919* (Washington, D.C.: Historical Division, Department of the Army, 1948), 16: 73–74; General Orders, No. 146, September 1, 1918, in *United States Army in the World War,* 435, 436.

112. The April 2, 1918, regulations are quoted in full in Cedric Larson, "Censorship of Army News during the World War, 1917–1918," *Journalism Quarterly* 17 (December 1940), 317–19.

113. Frederick Palmer, *With My Own Eyes: A Personal Story of Battle Years* (Indianapolis: Bobbs-Merrill, 1933), 364; Knightley, *First Casualty,* 130; Sally Foreman Griffith, *Home Town News: William Allen White and the* Emporia Gazette (New York: Oxford University Press, 1989), 207.

114. Accounts of the amount of the bonds vary. According to one version, the standard amount was ten thousand dollars. Knightley, *First Casualty,* 124.

115. Emmet Crozier, *American Reporters on the Western Front, 1914–1918* (New York: Oxford University Press, 1959), 192.

116. Hohenberg, *Foreign Correspondence,* 238; Crozier, *American Reporters,* 192–93.

117. Richard Kluger, *The Paper: The Life and Death of the* New York Herald Tribune (New York: Knopf, 1986), 197–98; Richard O'Connor, *Heywood Broun: A Biography* (New York: Putnam, 1975), 53–65; Crozier, *American Reporters,* 191–92.

118. Finis Farr, *Fair Enough: The Life of Westbrook Pegler* (New Rochelle, N.Y.: Arlington, 1975), 63–67; Oliver Pilat, *Pegler: Angry Man of the Press* (Boston: Beacon Press, 1963), 75–80; Knightley, *First Casualty,* 130.

119. General Orders, No. 21, March 1, 1918, in *Extracts from General Orders and Bulletins, War Department, March, 1918* (Washington, D.C.: Government Printing Office, 1918), 7.

120. General Orders, No. 1, January 2, 1918, in *Extracts from General Orders and Bulletins, War Department, January, 1918* (Washington, D.C.: Government Printing Office, 1918), 7–8.

121. General Orders, No. 41, April 24, 1918, in *Extracts from General Orders and Bulletins, War Department, April, 1918* (Washington, D.C.: Government Printing Office, 1918), 14.

122. General Orders, No. 146, September 1, 1918, in *United States Army in the World War,* 16: 438.

123. *Janesville Gazette,* April 26, 1918, 4. See James R. Mock, *Censorship 1917* (Princeton: Princeton University Press, 1941).

124. Theodore Roosevelt, *National Strength and International Duty* (Princeton: Princeton University Press, 1917), 23–29.

125. Knightley, *First Casualty,* 129.

126. Crozier, *American Reporters,* 178–83.

127. Knightley, *First Casualty,* 130; O'Connor, *Heywood Broun,* 61–63; Crozier, *American Reporters,* 183.

128. Address at the Jackson Day Dinner, January 8, 1938, in *Nothing to Fear: The Selected Addresses of Franklin Delano Roosevelt, 1932–1945,* ed. B. D. Zevin (Cambridge, Mass.: Houghton Mifflin Co., 1946), 127; Fireside Chat on Party Primaries, June 24, 1938, in Zevin, *Nothing to Fear,* 152; Address to Congress on the One Hundred and Fiftieth Anniversary of Congress, March 4, 1939, in Zevin, *Nothing to Fear,* 178.

129. Fireside Chat on the European War, September 3, 1939, in Zevin, *Nothing to Fear,* 180, 182; Radio Address to the Democratic National Convention Accepting the Third Term Nomination, July 19, 1940, in Zevin, *Nothing to Fear,* 217; "Four Freedoms" Speech, January 6, 1941, in Zevin, *Nothing to Fear,* 259, 264–65, 266, 267; Radio Address Commemorating the 150th Anniversary of the Ratification of the Bill of Rights, December 15, 1941, in *The Public Papers and Addresses of Franklin D. Roosevelt,* comp. Samuel I. Rosenman (New York: Harper,

1950), 1941: 556; Fireside Chat on the Progress of the War, February 23, 1942, in Zevin, *Nothing to Fear,* 318; Francis Biddle, *In Brief Authority* (Garden City, N.Y.: Doubleday, 1962), 226.

130. First Inaugural Address, March 4, 1933, in Zevin, *Nothing to Fear,* 16; Address at the Jackson Day Dinner, January 8, 1938, in Zevin, *Nothing to Fear,* 126; Fireside Chat on the Plan for the Reorganization of the Judiciary, March 9, 1937, in Zevin, *Nothing to Fear,* 96, 97, 99, 102; Fireside Chat on Inflation, September 7, 1942, in Zevin, *Nothing to Fear,* 337–38; Arthur M. Schlesinger Jr., *The Imperial Presidency* (Boston: Houghton Mifflin, 1973), 115–16.

131. White and Averson, *Celluloid Weapon,* 50–51; Address at the Jackson Day Dinner, January 8, 1940, in Zevin, *Nothing to Fear,* 195, 197–98, 202; Rear-platform Remarks on "Liberty," October 23, 1940, in *The Public Papers and Addresses of Franklin D. Roosevelt* (New York: Macmillan, 1941), 1940: 483–85; Radio Address from the U.S.S. *Potomac* to Jackson Day Dinners, March 29, 1941, in Rosenman, *Public Papers of Franklin Roosevelt,* 1941: 87.

132. Schlesinger, *Imperial Presidency,* 100–126; Robert Shogan, *Hard Bargain: How FDR Twisted Chruchill's Arm, Evaded the Law, and Changed the Role of the American Presidency* (New York: Scribner, 1995), 28–29, 234–39, 267–71; The Seven Hundred and Second Press Conference, December 17, 1940, in *The Public Papers and Addresses of Franklin D. Roosevelt,* 1940: 604–8; Biddle, *In Brief Authority,* 364.

133. Biddle, *In Brief Authority,* 205–11. The processing of enemy aliens is described in Eugene V. Rostow, "The Japanese American Cases—A Disaster," *Yale Law Journal* 54 (June 1945): 492–93.

134. Francis Biddle, "Taking No Chances," *Collier's,* March 21, 1942, 21, 40–41.

135. A Letter to the American Society of Newspaper Editors on Free Speech and Free Press, April 16, 1941, in Rosenman, *Public Papers of Franklin Roosevelt,* 1941: 120, 121.

136. Betty Houchin Winfield, *FDR and the News Media* (Urbana: University of Illinois Press, 1990; New York: Columbia University Press, 1994), 27–77.

137. Fireside Chat on National Defense, May 26, 1940, in Zevin, *Nothing to Fear,* 212; Richard Polenberg, *War and Society: The United States, 1941–1945* (Philadelphia: Lippincott, 1972), 43, 45; Richard W. Steele, "Franklin D. Roosevelt and His Foreign Policy Critics," *Political Science Quarterly* 94 (Spring 1979): 19–21, 29–31. For background, see Francis MacDonnell, *Insidious Foes: The Axis Fifth Column and the American Home Front* (New York: Oxford University Press, 1995). For a book that attempted to show that the news media received information with an enemy slant, see Matthew Gordon, *News Is a Weapon* (New York: Knopf, 1942).

138. Richard W. Steele, "The Great Debate: Roosevelt, the Media, and the Coming of the War, 1940–1941," *Journal of American History* 71 (June 1984): 69–92.

139. Winfield, *FDR and the News Media,* 127–53; Marion T. Marzolf, *Civilizing Voices: American Press Criticism, 1880–1950* (New York: Longman, 1991), 149–62; George Seldes, *Witness to a Century: Encounters With the Noted, the Notorious, and the Three SOBs* (New York: Ballantine Books, 1987), 327; Jerome E. Edwards, *The Foreign Policy of Col. McCormick's Tribune* (Reno: University of Nevada Press, 1971), 64–66, 91–96, 110, 116–17, 131–37, 171–73.

140. Mugridge, *View from Xanadu,* 39–41, 81–87, 119–24, 153–54; Seldes, *Witness to a Century,* 307, 474; Piers Brendon, *The Life and Death of the Press Barons* (London: Secker and Warburg, 1982), 145.

141. Winfield, *FDR and the News Media,* 67–68, 179; Steele, "Franklin D. Roosevelt and His Foreign Policy Critics," 28–30; "FDR Gives Iron Cross to Correspondent," *E&P,* December 26, 1942, 8.

142. Exec. Order No. 9182, 7 Fed. Reg. 4468 (1942); Allan M. Winkler, *The Politics of Propaganda: The Office of War Information, 1942–1945* (New Haven: Yale University Press, 1978); David Lloyd Jones, "Marketing the Allies to America," *Midwest Quarterly* 29 (Spring 1988): 366–83; Sydney Weinberg, "What To Tell America: The Writers' Quarrel in the Office of War

Information," *Journal of American History* 55 (June 1968): 73–89; Hillier Krieghbaum, "The Office of War Information and Government News Policy," *Journalism Quarterly* 19 (September 1942): 241–50.

143. Steele, "Franklin D. Roosevelt and His Foreign Policy Critics," 17, 23.

144. W. G. Banister to Director, Federal Bureau of Investigation, November 23, 1942, as quoted in Patrick S. Washburn, "The Black Press: Homefront Clout Hits a Peak in World War II," *American Journalism* 12 (Summer 1995): 362.

145. Michael R. Beschloss, *The Crisis Years: Kennedy and Khrushchev, 1960–1963* (New York: HarperCollins, 1991), 613–14; Athan Theoharis, "The FBI, the Roosevelt Administration, and the 'Subversive' Press," *Journalism History* 19 (Spring 1993): 3–10.

146. Athan Theoharis, "The FBI and the American Legion Contact Program, 1940–1966," *Political Science Quarterly* 100 (Summer 1985): 271–86; Harrison E. Salisbury, *A Journey for Our Times: A Memoir* (New York: Harper and Row, 1983), 156–62.

147. MacDonnell, *Insidious Foes*, 71, 152–53; Bernard F. Dick, *The Star-Spangled Screen: The American World War II Film* (Lexington: University Press of Kentucky, 1985), 101–23, 236–39.

148. Washburn, *A Question of Sedition*, 118–208. Postmaster General Frank Walker was more active in denying second class permits to publications dealing with sex and birth control than with politics. Samuel Walker, *In Defense of American Liberties: A History of the ACLU* (New York: Oxford University Press, 1990), 158–59. On efforts to stop the delivery of publications deemed foreign propaganda, see Fowler, *Unmailable*, 144–47.

149. Biddle, *In Brief Authority*, 237–38.

150. Samuel I. Rosenman, *Working with Roosevelt* (New York: Harper, 1952), 321–22.

151. Walker, *In Defense of American Liberties*, 135–69; Polenberg, *War and Society*, 47; Zechariah Chafee Jr., *Government and Mass Communications* (Chicago: University of Chicago Press, 1947), 1: 450.

152. Biddle, *In Brief Authority*, 151, 152; Thomas L. Pahl, "G-String Conspiracy, Political Reprisal or Armed Revolt?: The Minneapolis Trotskyite Trial," *Labor History* 8 (Winter 1967): 30–51; Dunne et al. v. U.S., 138 F.2d 137 (8th Cir. 1943); Dunne et al. v. U.S., 320 U.S. 790 (1943).

153. Byron Price, Notebooks, Byron Price Papers, State Historical Society of Wisconsin, Madison, 2: 111–12. For one example of the prosecutions that followed the decision to pursue a limited number of cases, see U.S. v. Pelley, 132 F.2d 170 (7th Cir. 1942).

154. Biddle, *In Brief Authority*, 233–43.

155. Donald Warren, *Radio Priest: Charles Coughlin, the Father of Hate Radio* (New York: Free Press, 1996), 229–68; Biddle, *In Brief Authority*, 243–48.

156. Richard N. Smith, *The Colonel: The Life and Legend of Robert R. McCormick, 1880–1955* (Boston: Houghton Mifflin, 1997), 429–41; Biddle, *In Brief Authority*, 248–51; Larry J. Frank, "The United States Navy v. the Chicago Tribune," *Historian* (February 1980): 284–303; Price, Notebooks, 2: 120–38, 161–62. On the lack of impact from the *Tribune* story, see John Prados, *Combined Fleet Decoded: The Secret History of American Intelligence and the Japanese Navy in World War II* (New York: Random House, 1995), 341–43, 346; Edward J. Drea, *MacArthur's ULTRA Codebreaking and the War against Japan, 1942–1945* (Lawrence: University Press of Kansas, 1992), 43; Ronald Lewin, *The American Magic: Codes, Ciphers and the Defeat of Japan* (New York: Farrar Straus Giroux, 1982), 116–17; Dina Goren, "Communication Intelligence and the Freedom of the Press: The *Chicago Tribune*'s Battle of Midway Dispatch and the Breaking of the Japanese Naval Code," *Journal of Contemporary History* 16 (October 1981): 668–69.

157. *A Report on the Office of Censorship* (Washington, D.C.: Government Printing Office, 1945); Elmer Davis and Byron Price, *War Information and Censorship* (Washington, D.C.: Amer-

ican Council on Public Affairs, 1943); Edward N. Doan, "Organization and Operation of the Office of Censorship," *Journalism Quarterly* 21 (September 1944): 200–216.

158. Ch. 593, 55 Stat. 838, 840–41; Exec. Order No. 8985, 6 Fed. Reg. 6625 (1941); The President Issues a Statement and Establishes the Office of Censorship, Executive Order 8985, December 19, 1941, in Rosenman, *Public Papers of Franklin Roosevelt,* 1941: 574; Franklin D. Roosevelt to Byron Price, January 27, 1942, in Rosenman, *Public Papers of Franklin Roosevelt,* 1941: 577.

159. Theodore F. Koop, *Weapon of Silence* (Chicago: University of Chicago Press, 1946), 5, 10, 26–30, 47–58; Byron Price, "Governmental Censorship in War-Time," *American Political Science Review* 36 (October 1942): 842.

160. Congress, House, 77th Cong., 1st sess., *Congressional Record* (December 16, 1941), vol. 87, pt. 9, 9863; Koop, *Weapon of Silence,* 22–24, 248–49; *Report on the Office of Censorship,* 3–4; Byron Price, "Nation's Press Has Complied with Censorship Code," *Journalism Quarterly* 20 (December 1943): 318–19; Price, "Governmental Censorship in War-Time," 842.

161. Koop, *Weapon of Silence,* 176–78; Byron Price, "The American Way," in *Journalism in Wartime,* ed. Frank L. Mott (Washington, D.C.: Council of Public Affairs, 1943), 32; Price, Notebooks, 2: 114–19; "Avoid Censorship Problems," *Bulletin,* July 20, 1944, 2.

162. Chafee, *Government and Mass Communications,* 1: 459–60; Price, "The American Way," 29.

163. Frank C. Clough, "Operations of the Press Division of the Office of Censorship," *Journalism Quarterly* 20 (September 1943): 222; *Code of Wartime Practices for the American Press* [January 15, 1942] (Washington, D.C.: Government Printing Office, 1942), 1, 2; *Code of Wartime Practices for American Broadcasters* [January 15, 1942] (Washington, D.C.: Government Printing Office, 1942), 1–7. On Christmas lists and similar applications of the code, see Koop, *Weapon of Silence,* 176–88. "It is well known that enemy agents could, if permitted, use the microphone to transmit information by means of a prearranged code," the director of censorship said. Price, "Governmental Censorship in War-Time," 847.

164. *Code of Wartime Practices for the American Press and Radio* [May 15, 1945] (Washington, D.C.: Government Printing Office, 1945), 4.

165. Richard W. Steele, "News of the 'Good War': World War II News Management," *Journalism Quarterly* 62 (Winter 1985): 713–16, 783.

166. "Censorship Ground Rules," *Time,* January 26, 1942, 56, 58.

167. For an analysis of Luce and his philosophies, see James L. Baughman, *Henry R. Luce and the Rise of the American News Media* (Boston: Twayne, 1987).

168. Byron Price, Memoir, Byron Price Papers, State Historical Society of Wisconsin, Madison, 3 (sec. 2): 307–12; Frank Knox, to Harry Hopkins, March 26, 1942, as quoted in Steele, "News of the 'Good War,' " 710.

169. *Report on the Office of Censorship,* 42; Davis and Price, *War Information and Censorship,* 79; Clough, "Operations of the Press Division," 222; Price, "Governmental Censorship in War-Time," 848, 849.

170. Koop, *Weapon of Silence,* 206–9, 245, 265–67; Fletcher Pratt, "How the Censors Rigged the News," *Harper's,* February 1946, 100, 101–2.

171. *Code of Wartime Practices for the American Press* [January 15, 1942], 4; *Code of Wartime Practices for the American Press and Radio* [May 15, 1945], 3.

172. On the *Ferdinand Magellan,* a "rolling fortress" designed with many security features, see Carolanne Griffith-Roberts, "Back on Track in Miami," *Southern Living,* June 1992, 24; Bob Withers, "When Ike Went to The Greenbrier," *Trains,* February 1990, 38–39.

173. Winfield, *FDR and the News Media,* 181–82; David Brinkley, *Washington Goes to War* (New York: Knopf, 1988): 165–71; Koop, *Weapon of Silence,* 221–33; "FDR Ignores Protest of Trip Censorship," *E&P,* October 10, 1942, 4, 50; Price, Memoir, 3 (sec. 3): 364. For a sampling

of journalists' reactions, see "Editors Fear Public Distrust from Too Strict a Censorship," *E&P*, October 10, 1942, 3, 46

174. Price, Memoir, 3 (sec. 1): 211, 227; "FDR Says He Will Make Other Censored Trips," October 17, 1942, 6.

175. Winfield, *FDR and the News Media*, 182. To the dismay of Eleanor Roosevelt, Lucy Mercer Rutherford was with Franklin Roosevelt when he died at Warm Springs, Georgia. She quickly departed. Irwin F. Gellman, *Secret Affairs: Franklin Roosevelt, Cordell Hull, and Sumner Welles* (Baltimore: Johns Hopkins University Press, 1995), 8–9, 343, 373–75; *Closest Companion: The Unknown Story of the Intimate Friendship between Franklin Roosevelt and Margaret Suckley*, ed. Geoffrey C. Ward (Boston: Houghton Mifflin, 1995), xvi, 287–88, 322–25, 349–53, 412–19.

176. "Presidential Secrecy," *E&P*, July 29, 1944, 32; Price, Memoir, 3 (sec. 1): 228.

177. Koop, *Weapon of Silence*, 3–15, 58, 77–144; *Report on the Office of Censorship*, 43–54.

178. "Censors Clip *L. A. Times* at Post Office," *E&P*, February 21, 1942, 6; Raymond Clapper, "Dispatches Going Abroad," in Mott, *Journalism in Wartime*, 53–54. For a brief description of the censorship of racial and labor problems, see Chafee, *Government and Mass Communication*, 1: 456.

179. Koop, *Weapon of Silence*, 42, 64–70; Pratt, "How the Censors Rigged the News," 98–99.

180. Chafee, *Government and Mass Communication*, 1: 457; "What British Correspondents Think about U.S. Censorship," *E&P*, November 28, 1942, 9; Arthur Krock, "In Wartime What News Shall the Nation Have?" *New York Times Magazine*, August 16, 1942, 25.

181. Alex Faulkner, "How Tough Is American Censorship?" *Harper's*, April 1943, 502–9.

182. Price, "The American Way," 23, 30, 31. See also Price, "Censorship and Free Speech," 17–22.

183. Jacques Barzun, "The Counterfeiters," *Atlantic Monthly*, May 1946, 129.

184. Koop, *Weapon of Silence*, 27, 70–71.

185. Robert C. Mikesh, *Japan's World War II Balloon Bomb Attacks on North America* (Washington, D.C.: Smithsonian Institution Press, 1973); Koop, *Weapon of Silence*, 198–204; Wallace B. Eberhard, "From Balloon Bombs to H-Bombs: Mass Media and National Security," *Military Review* 61 (February 1981): 2–8; John McPhee, "Balloons of War," *New Yorker*, January 29, 1996, 52–60.

186. Sheldon Harris, *Factories of Death: Japanese Biological Warfare 1932–45 and the American Cover-Up* (New York: Routledge, 1994); Peter Williams and David Wallace, *Unit 731: The Japanese Army's Secret of Secrets* (London: Hodder and Stoughton, 1989); Nicholas D. Kristof, "Japan Confronting Gruesome War Atrocity," *NYT*, March 17, 1995, A1 (national edition).

187. Koop, *Weapon of Silence*, 262–63; Price, Notebooks, 1 (pt. 2): 76, 79–81; Price, "Nation's Press Has Complied with Censorship Code," 318–19; Byron Price to William D. Leahy, March 1, 1945, Notebooks, 4: 342.

188. *Proceedings, Twenty-second Annual Convention, American Society of Newspaper Editors* (n.p.: American Society of Newspaper Editors, 1944), 153–56; Price, "Nation's Press Has Complied with Censorship Code," 319.

189. Brad Lynch, "Ad Council Marks 50 Years of Crusades," *Media History Digest*, Spring–Summer 1992, 52; James P. S. Devereux, "This Is How It Was," *Saturday Evening Post*, February 23, 1946, 10; Karal Ann Marling and John Wetenhall, *Iwo Jima: Monuments, Memories, and the American Hero* (Cambridge: Harvard University Press, 1991).

190. *Regulations for Correspondents Accompanying U.S. Army Forces in the Field* (Washington, D.C.: Government Printing Office, 1942), 1, 2, 4, 6, 7, 10; Forrest C. Pogue, *United States Army in World War II, The European Theater of Operations: The Supreme Command* (Washington, D.C.: Office of the Chief of Military History, Department of the Army, 1954), 91, 524.

191. Pogue, *United States Army in World War II,* 523, 525, 527–28; Cecil Brown, *Suez to Singapore* (New York: Random House, 1942); Eric Sevareid, "Censors in the Saddle," *Nation,* April 14, 1945, 415–17.

192. Andrew Mendelson and C. Zoe Smith, "Part of the Team: *LIFE* Photographers and their Symbiotic Relationship with the Military During World War II," *American Journalism* 12 (Summer 1995): 276–89.

193. Pogue, *United States Army in World War II,* 89–90; Dwight D. Eisenhower to General Bradley and General Devers, March 14, 1945, in Harry C. Butcher, *My Three Years with Eisenhower* (New York: Simon and Schuster, 1946), 771; Dwight D. Eisenhower to the PRD, March 10, 1945, in Butcher, *My Three Years,* 772. On soldiers being upset by the lack of reality and of recognition in reporting, see Paul Fussell, *Wartime: Understanding and Behavior in the Second World War* (New York: Oxford University Press, 1989), 73, 155–56, 267–68, 285–88.

194. Stephen E. Ambrose, *D-Day, June 6, 1944: The Climactic Battle of World War II* (New York: Simon and Schuster, 1994), 148–49.

195. Dwight D. Eisenhower, *Crusade in Europe* (New York: Doubleday, 1948), 58–59, 300. On the political censorship CBS broadcasters encountered in World War II, see Stanley Cloud and Lynne Olson, *The Murrow Boys: Pioneers on the Front Lines of Broadcast Journalism* (Boston: Houghton Mifflin, 1996), 122–240.

196. Andy Rooney, *My War* (New York: Times Books, 1995), 56–59, 90, 93, 188.

197. "War News Role of Press Most Vital—MacArthur," *E&P,* September 26, 1942, sec. 2, 37; William Manchester, *American Caesar: Douglas MacArthur, 1880–1964* (Boston: Little, Brown, 1978), 311, 358–63, 413, 471, 498, 510–11, 524; Fred W. Friendly, "When War Comes, Whither the First Amendment?" *Arizona Law Review* 33 (1991): 274.

198. "Asks Wire Services to Seek Reform of Censorship," *E&P,* November 6, 1943, 16; Matthew S. Klimow, "Lying to the Troops: American Leaders and the Defense of Bataan," *Parameters* 20 (December 1990): 48–60; Geoffrey Perret, *Old Soldiers Never Die: The Life of Douglas MacArthur* (New York: Random House, 1996), 74, 76, 295, 325–26, 396; Frederick S. Voss, *Reporting the War: The Journalistic Coverage of World War II* (Washington, D.C.: Smithsonian Institution Press for the National Portrait Gallery, 1994), 29–32; Pratt, "How the Censors Rigged the News," 99–100; "Censors Scored," *E&P,* October 13, 1945, 13.

199. John Mueller, "Pearl Harbor: Military Inconvenience, Political Disaster," *International Security* 16 (Winter 1991–1992): 172–203; Thomas B. Allen, "Pearl Harbor: A Return to the Day of Infamy," *National Geographic,* December 1991, 75–76.

200. Raymond Fielding, *The American Newsreel, 1911–1967* (Norman: University of Oklahoma Press, 1972), 263–64, 295; Susan D. Moeller, *Shooting War: Photography and the American Experience of Combat* (New York: Basic Books, 1989), 234–35.

201. George H. Roeder Jr., *The Censored War: American Visual Experience During World War Two* (New Haven: Yale University Press, 1993), 21.

202. Knightley, *First Casualty,* 272–74; Elmer Davis, "Report to the President," [1945] ed. Ronald T. Farrar, *Journalism Monographs,* no. 7, August 1968, 14–15. For a comparison of coverage by a national newspaper in Tokyo, the *Asahi Shimbun,* and the *New York Times,* see Rei Okamoto, "Pearl Harbor and the Enemy Media," *Media History Digest,* Fall–Winter 1991, 15–19.

203. Gentry, *J. Edgar Hoover,* 278; Theoharis, "The FBI, the Roosevelt Administration, and the 'Subversive' Press," 6; Erwin D. Canham, "The Battle for News," in Mott, *Journalism in Wartime,* 47, 48.

204. Jim A. Richstad, "The Press under Martial Law: The Hawaiian Experience," *Journalism Monographs,* no. 17, November 1970; Alf Pratte, "The Honolulu *Star-Bulletin* and the 'Day of Infamy,'" *American Journalism* 5 (1988): 5–13.

205. Duncan v. Kahanamoku, 327 U.S. 304, 308–9, 313–24.

206. Robert W. Desmond, *Tides of War: World News Reporting, 1931–1945* (Iowa City: University of Iowa Press, 1984), 215–16; Koop, *Weapon of Silence,* 161–63; Press Conference No. 767, September 5, 1941, in *Complete Presidential Press Conferences of Franklin D. Roosevelt* (New York: Da Capo Press, 1972), 18: 146–47.

207. Stephen Bates, *If No News, Send Rumors: Anecdotes of American Journalism* (New York: Holt, 1991), 132–33; Palmer Hoyt, "The Use and Abuse of Restraints," in Mott, *Journalism in Wartime,* 39.

208. Lloyd J. Graybar, "Admiral King's Toughest Battle," *Naval War College Review* 32 (February 1979): 38–47.

209. Koop, *Weapon of Silence,* 191–96; Davis, "Report to the President," 14–18; "Tokyo Raid Was First Long-Range Censorship Test," *E&P,* May 1, 1943, 32; Albin Krebs, "James Doolittle, 96, Pioneer Aviator Who Led First Raid on Japan, Dies," *NYT,* September 29, 1993, B10 (national edition); Price, Notebooks, 1 (pt. 2): 82.

210. Davis, "Report to the President," 16; for examples of problems with Navy news, see 19–22.

211. Price, Memoir, 3 (sec. 2): 312–15; Price, Notebooks, 2: 202–7. When Winston Churchill was at the Admiralty during World War I he held bad news on the hope of obtaining offsetting good news. Harold D. Lasswell, *Propaganda Technique in World War I* (Cambridge: MIT Press, 1971), 109–10.

212. Voss, *Reporting the War,* 26–28; Tom Hanes, "Says Navy Officers Are Tired of Rigid Censorship," *E&P,* September 25, 1943, 19; Congress, House, 77th Cong., 2nd sess., *Congressional Record* (November 16, 1942), vol. 88, pt. 10, A3965–67; "The Seven Hundred and Ninetieth Press Conference—the First Wartime Press Conference (Excerpts)," December 9, 1941, in Rosenman, *Public Papers of Franklin Roosevelt,* 1941: 519–21; Davis, "Report to the President," 22–26.

213. Rooney, *My War,* 94–95, 169, 225; Roeder, *Censored War,* 1–25; Peter Maslowksi, *Armed with Cameras: The American Military Photographers of World War II* (New York: Free Press, 1993), 6; 29–30, 80–83; Moeller, *Shooting War,* 113–15, 204–8; Mendelson and Smith, "Part of the Team," 276–89; George H. Roeder Jr., "A Note on U.S. Photo Censorship in WW II," *Historical Journal of Film, Radio and Television* (October 1985), 191–98.

214. Fussell, *Wartime,* 288. See David Perlmutter, "Face-Lifting the Death's Head: The Calculated Pictoral Legacy of the Waffen-SS and Its Modern Audience," *Visual Anthropology* 4 (June 1991): 217–45.

215. *The Japan/America Film Wars: World War II Propaganda and Its Cultural Contexts,* ed. Abé Mark Nornes and Fukushima Yukio (Chur, Switzerland: Harwood Academic Publishers, 1994); John W. Dower, *War without Mercy: Race and Power in the Pacific War* (New York: Pantheon Books, 1986).

216. Conrad C. Crane, *Bombs, Cities, and Civilians: American Airpower Strategy in World War II* (Lawrence: University Press of Kansas, 1993), 120–21.

217. Douglas MacArthur, *Reminiscences* (New York: McGraw-Hill, 1964), 146–47. For background, see Dower, *War without Mercy,* 48–52.

218. Fussell, *Wartime,* 285–87; Dower, *War without Mercy,* 61–71; Knightley, *First Casualty,* 294, 323–28; Rooney, *My War,* 93, 178; Eric Sevareid, *Not So Wild a Dream* (New York: Knopf, 1946), 388–89, 390–91; Edgar L. Jones, "One War Is Enough," *Atlantic Monthly,* February 1946, 49.

219. Studs Terkel, *"The Good War": An Oral History of World War Two* (New York: Pantheon Books, 1984), 381–82; Mark Hertsgaard, "The Question Bush Never Got Asked," *Harper's,* September 1993, 44–45; John Steinbeck, *Once There Was a War* (New York: Viking Press, 1958), xi–xiii. For an account of Steinbeck's experiences with censorship, see Roy Sim-

monds, *John Steinbeck: The War Years, 1939–1945* (Lewisburg, Penn.: Bucknell University Press, 1996), 177, 198, 203, 210.

220. *Ernie's War: The Best of Ernie Pyle's World War II Dispatches*, ed. David Nichols (New York: Random House, 1986); Knightley, *First Casualty*, 326–27; Steinbeck, *Once There Was a War*, xv; Mack Morriss, "Pyle Goes Home," *Yank*, October 6, 1944, 11; Voss, *Reporting the War*, 104.

221. Voss, *Reporting the War*, 109–17; Bill Mauldin, *The Brass Ring* (New York: Norton, 1971), 245–64; Martin Blumenson, *The Patton Papers, 1940–1945* (Boston: Houghton Mifflin, 1974), 624.

222. Kent Cooper, *The Right to Know: An Exposition of the Evils of News Suppression and Propaganda* (New York: Farrar, Straus and Cudahy, 1956), 203–7.

223. Voss, *Reporting the War*, 191–96; Desmond, *Tides of War*, 401–12; Cooper, *Right to Know*, 211–36; Edward Kennedy, "I'd Do It Again," *Atlantic Monthly*, August 1948, 36–41.

224. Kennedy, "I'd Do It Again," 36, 37–40; Cooper, *Right to Know*, 235.

225. Voss, *Reporting the War*, 196; Desmond, *Tides of War*, 410–12; Cooper, *Right to Know*, 223–24, 225–26, 230–33, 235; Kennedy, "I'd Do It Again," 39–41.

226. Patrick S. Washburn, "The Office of Censorship's Attempt To Control Press Coverage of the Atomic Bomb during World War II," *Journalism Monographs*, no. 120, April 1990; Harry S. Truman, *Memoirs*, vol. 1, *Year of Decisions* (Garden City, N.Y.: Doubleday, 1955), 419; Barton J. Bernstein, "The Atomic Bombings Reconsidered," *Foreign Affairs*, January–February 1995, 138–39.

227. Koop, *Weapon of Silence*, 272–91.

228. Crane, *Bombs, Cities, and Civilians*, 113–19; Statement by the President Announcing the Use of the A-Bomb at Hiroshima, August 6, 1945, in *Public Papers of the Presidents of the United States, Harry S. Truman . . . 1945* (Washington, D.C.: Government Printing Office, 1961), 197.

229. For the view that "precision bombing" was a "comical oxymoron" except to "the home folks reading *Life* and *The Saturday Evening Post*," see Fussell, *Wartime*, 13–19.

230. Bernstein, "Atomic Bombings Reconsidered," 146–48.

231. Dennis D. Wainstock, *The Decision To Drop the Atomic Bomb* (Westport, Conn.: Praeger, 1996), 1–14; Crane, *Bombs, Cities, and Civilians*, 1–11, 120–47. See also Murray Sayle, "Did the Bomb End the War?" *New Yorker*, July 31, 1995, 40–64.

232. United States Strategic Bombing Survey, *Summary Report (Pacific War)* (Washington, D.C.: Government Printing Office, 1946), 26; Wainstock, *Decision To Drop the Atom Bomb*, 121–32; Gar Alperovitz, *The Decision to Use the Atomic Bomb and the Architecture of an American Myth* (New York: Knopf, 1995), 3–4, 321–65, 623–68.

233. Robert Jay Lifton and Greg Mitchell, *Hiroshima in America: Fifty Years of Denial* (New York: Putnam, 1995). For the conclusion that Americans were "systematically misled," see Alperovitz, *Decision To Drop the Atom Bomb*, 627.

234. War Department statement, as quoted in Koop, *Weapon of Silence*, 285; Harry S. Truman statement, September 14, 1945, as quoted in Lifton and Mitchell, *Hiroshima in American*, 55; Eric Barnouw, "The Hiroshima-Nagasaki Footage: A Report," *Historical Journal of Film, Radio and Television* 2 (March 1982): 91–100.

235. William Lawren, *The General and the Bomb: A Biography of General Leslie R. Groves, Director of the Manhattan Project* (New York: Dodd, Mead, 1988), 270–71; Paul Boyer, *By the Bomb's Early Light: American Thought and Culture at the Dawn of the Nuclear Age* (New York: Pantheon Books, 1985), 181–95, 303–18; Wilfred Burchett, *Shadows of Hiroshima* (London: Verso, 1983); George Weller, "Back in Nagasaki," in *How I Got That Story*, ed. David Brown and W. Richard Bruner (New York: Dutton, 1967), 209–27.

236. Congress, Senate, Special Committee on Atomic Energy, *Hearings . . . Pursuant to S. Res. 179,* 79th Cong., 1st sess., November 28, 1945, pt. I, 37.

237. Alperovitz, *Decision To Drop the Atom Bomb,* 609–22; John W. Dower, "The Bombed: Hiroshimas and Nagasakis in Japanese Memory," *Diplomatic History* 19 (Spring 1995): 275–95.

238. *Reports of General MacArthur* (Washington, D.C.: Center for Military History, 1994), 1 (supp.): 236.

239. Monica Braw, *The Atomic Bomb Suppressed: American Censorship in Occupied Japan* (Armonk, N.Y.: M. E. Sharpe, 1991).

240. Thomas Powers, "Was It Right?" *Atlantic Monthly,* July 1995, 23.

241. Truman, *Memoirs,* 417; Barton J. Bernstein, "A Postwar Myth: 500,000 U.S. Lives Saved," *Bulletin of the Atomic Scientists* 42 (June–July 1986): 38–40.

242. "The Fortune Survey," *Fortune,* December 1945, 305. The poll showed that 35.3 percent thought Japan would have held out less than six months without the atomic bombings, and 53.2 percent said that the war would have lasted for six or more months (309).

243. Henry L. Stimson, "The Decision to Use the Atomic Bomb," *Harper's,* February 1947, 106.

244. J. Samuel Walker, "History, Collective Memory, and the Decision to Use the Bomb," *Diplomatic History* 19 (Spring 1995): 319–28. See also Paul Boyer, "Exotic Resonances: Hiroshima in American Memory," *Diplomatic History* 19 (Spring 1995): 297–318.

245. John Hersey, *Hiroshima,* new ed. (New York: Knopf, 1985). The first edition of Hersey's book appeared in 1946. For background on *Hiroshima* and its impact, see Boyer, *By the Bomb's Early Light,* 203–10.

246. For one of the few attempts in mainstream journalism to survey the scholarship on Truman's action fifty years after the end of World War II, see John Kifner, "Hiroshima: A Controversy That Refuses to Die," *NYT,* January 31, 1995, C19 (national edition).

247. Tom Engelhardt, "Fifty Years under a Cloud," *Harper's,* January 1996, 71–76; Tony Capaccio and Uday Mohan, "Missing the Target," *American Journalism Review,* July–August 1995, 18–26; Karen De Witt, "Smithsonian Scales Back Exhibit of Plane in Atomic Bomb Attack," *NYT,* January 31, 1995, A1 (national edition); Barton J. Bernstein, "Hiroshima, Rewritten," *NYT,* January 31, 1995, A11 (national edition).

248. For one of the more striking defenses of Truman's decision, see Paul Fussell, *Thank God for the Atom Bomb and Other Essays* (New York: Summit Books, 1988), 13–37.

249. Koop, *Weapon of Silence,* 290, 291.

250. Tim Weiner, "Pentagon Book for Doomsday Is To Be Closed," *NYT,* April 18, 1994, A1 (national edition); Ted Gup, "The Doomsday Blueprints," *Time,* August 10, 1992, 32–39; Ted Gup, "Doomsday Hideaway," *Time,* December 9, 1991, 26–29. President Eisenhower participated in nuclear attack drills that included his declaring martial law. He was involved in one of the exercises at a top-secret underground command post in 1960 when the news of the American U-2 spy plane crash in the Soviet Union arrived. Michael R. Beschloss, *Mayday: Eisenhower, Khrushchev and the U-2 Affair* (New York: Harper and Row, 1986), 45–46.

251. Congress, House, Foreign Operations and Government Information Subcommittee, *Government Information Plans and Policies, Hearing Before a Subcommittee of the Committee on Government Operations,* 88th Cong., 1st sess., June 5, 1963, pt. 2, 177–218.

252. Congress, House, Foreign Operations and Government Information Subcommittee, *U.S. Government Information Policies and Practices—Problems of Congress in Obtaining Information from the Executive Branch, Hearings Before a Subcommittee of the Committee on Government Operations,* 92nd Cong., 2nd sess., May 12, 1972, pt. 8, 2939–94. For a summary of the program and its background, see David Wise, *The Politics of Lying: Government Deception, Secrecy, and Power* (New York: Random House, 1973), 134–140.

Chapter 7

1. NSC-68, A Report to the National Security Council, April 14, 1950, *Naval War College Review* 27 (March–April 1975): 59–60; Robert J. Donovan, *Tumultuous Years: The Presidency of Harry S. Truman, 1949–1953* (New York: Norton, 1982), 158–61, 176, 242, 244, 247.

2. For introductions to the subject, see Stephen F. Knott, *Secret and Sanctioned: Covert Operations and the American Presidency* (New York: Oxford University Press, 1996); Richard E. Morgan, *Domestic Intelligence: Monitoring Dissent in America* (Austin: University of Texas Press, 1980); Tyrus G. Fain, ed. and comp., *The Intelligence Community: History, Organization, and Issues* (New York: Bowker, 1977); Victor Marchetti and John D. Marks, *The CIA and the Cult of Intelligence* (New York: Knopf, 1974); Harold D. Lasswell, *National Security and Individual Freedom* (New York: McGraw-Hill, 1950).

3. "News Cooperation Asked by M'Arthur," *NYT*, July 3, 1950, 1, 4 (late city edition); "War News Code Approved," *NYT*, July 5, 1950, 29 (late city edition); James J. Butler, "Defense Sec. Johnson Okays 'Voluntary,'" *E&P*, July 22, 1950, 6; "MacArthur Praises Self-Censorship Rule," *E&P*, 6, 45.

4. Marguerite Higgins, *War in Korea: The Report of a Woman Combat Correspondent* (Garden City, N.Y.: Doubleday, 1951), 95.

5. Higgins, *War in Korea*, 67–109; Ray Erwin, "Censorship, Communications Worry 200 K-War Writers," *E&P*, July 22, 1950, 7; "Miss Higgins Going Back," *NYT*, July 19, 1950, 18 (late city edition); "M'Arthur Cancels Ban on Reporters," *NYT*, July 16, 1950, 7 (late city edition); "Press Censorship Wavers into Sight," *NYT*, July 11, 1950, 3 (late city edition);

6. "Varieties of Censorship," *NYT*, July 17, 1950, 20 (late city edition).

7. "Tight Censorship Pushed in Capital," *NYT*, August 13, 1950, 8 (late city edition).

8. Press representatives to Douglas MacArthur, December 18(?), 1950, and Douglas MacArthur to *Editor & Publisher*, January 18, 1951, in "MacArthur Says Press 'Demanded' Censorship," *E&P*, January 20, 1951, 7. For background, see D. Clayton James, *The Years of MacArthur*, vol. 3, *Triumph and Disaster, 1945–1964* (Boston: Houghton Mifflin, 1985), 566–67; "8th Army Censors Subject Press to Court-Martial," *E&P*, January 13, 1951, 7.

9. James, *Years of MacArthur*, 567–68; Melvin B. Voorhees, *Korean Tales* (New York: Simon and Schuster, 1952); John Davies Jr., "'The Truth about Korea,'" *Nieman Reports*, January 1952, 13–14; "MacArthur Says Press 'Demanded' Censorship," 7; "8th Army Censors Subject Press to Court-Martial," 7, 9.

10. "Censorship," *E&P*, January 13, 1951, 40. For the text of MacArthur's reply to this editorial, see "MacArthur Says Press 'Demanded' Censorship," 7.

11. "MacArthur Says Press 'Demanded' Censorship," 7; "8th Army Censors Subject Press to Court-Martial," 7, 9; "Censorship," 40. For the text of the censorship code, see "Newsmen Subject to Military Control . . . Wide Area of Reporting is Forbidden," *E&P*, January 13, 1951, 8–9.

12. Voorhees, *Korean Tales*, 108.

13. Robert C. Miller, "News Censorship in Korea," *Nieman Reports*, July 1952, 4.

14. William M. Hammond, "The Army and Public Affairs: Enduring Principles," *Parameters* 19 (June 1989): 69.

15. Phillip Knightley, *The First Casualty: From Crimea to Vietnam: The War Correspondent as Hero, Propagandist, and Myth Maker* (New York: Harcourt Brace Jovanovich, 1975), 351–52.

16. Bruce W. Nelan, "Lost Prisoners of War: 'Sold Down the River'?" *Time*, September 30, 1996, 45; Philip Shenon, "U.S., in 50's, Knew North Korea Held American P.O.W.'s," *NYT*, September 17, 1996, A5 (national edition).

17. Miller, "News Censorship in Korea," 5, 6.

18. The memos are reprinted in Herbert Lee Williams, *The Newspaperman's President: Harry S. Truman* (Chicago: Nelson-Hall, 1984), 111–13.

19. Congress, House, 82nd Cong., 1st sess., *Congressional Record* (April 5, 1951), vol. 97, pt. 3, 3380; Harry S. Truman, *Memoirs*, vol. 2, *Years of Trial and Hope* (Garden City, N.Y.: Doubleday, 1956), 440–50.

20. Truman, *Memoirs*, 197–98, 381–84, 439–50. For a detailed description of the deteriorating relationship between MacArthur and Truman, including Truman's suspicions about MacArthur seeking office, see Donovan, *Tumultuous Years*, 258–59, 315–16, 340–62.

21. Explaining his decision to retire in 1952, Truman said, "If you don't like the heat, get out of the kitchen." "The Answer Man," *Time*, April 28, 1952, 19.

22. The President's News Conference of November 30, 1950, in *Public Papers of the Presidents of the United States, Harry S. Truman . . . 1950* (Washington, D.C.: Government Printing Office, 1965), 724–28.

23. Later in the day, the White House issued a press release saying that only the president could authorize use of the atomic bomb, that no such authorization had been given, and that "the military commander in the field would have charge of the tactical delivery of the weapon." The President's News Conference of November 30, 1950, in *Public Papers of Harry Truman . . . 1950*, 727 n. 3.

24. For a description of the events of late November and early December 1950, see Donovan, *Tumultuous Years*, 300–312.

25. Truman's outburst was reprinted in "The Letter," *Time*, December 18, 1950, 17.

26. Proclamation 2914: Proclaiming the Existence of a National Emergency, December 16, 1950, in *Public Papers of Harry Truman . . . 1950*, 746.

27. *Journals of the Continental Congress, 1774–1789*, ed. Worthington C. Ford (Washington, D.C.: U.S. Government Printing Office, 1904–1937), 5: 789; *Annals of Congress*, 8th Cong., 1st sess., 1190–91.

28. Ch. 20, art. 5, 2 Stat. 359, 360 (1806). For background, see Frederick Bernays Wiener, "Courts-Martial and the Bill of Rights: The Original Practice II," *Harvard Law Review* 72 (December 1958): 267–69.

29. This estimate is given in Joseph W. Bishop Jr., *Justice under Fire: A Study of Military Law* (New York: Charterhouse, 1974), 157. For examples, see U.S. v. Howe, 17 C.M.A. 165 (1967); Michael R. Gordon, "General Ousted for Derisive Remarks about President," *NYT*, June 19, 1993, 9 (national edition).

30. Douglas MacArthur, *Reminiscences* (New York: McGraw-Hill, 1964), 385–96; Henry Kissinger, *Diplomacy* (New York: Simon and Schuster, 1994), 484; Congress, Senate, *Military Cold War Education and Speech Review Policies, Hearings before the Special Preparedness Subcommittee of the Committee on Armed Forces*, 87th Cong., 2nd sess., 1962, pt. 1, 7.

31. See, for instance, Alan L. Gropman, "On Nonconformity," *Air University Review* 37 (September–October 1986): 100–101; William S. Lind, "Reading, Writing, and Policy Review: The Air Force's Unilateral Disarmament in the War of Ideas," *Air University Review* 36 (November–December 1984): 66–70.

32. Internal Security Act, ch. 1024, 64 Stat. 987 (1950). The Immigration and Nationality Act, ch. 477, 66 Stat. 163 (1952), known as the McCarran-Walter Act, placed broad restrictions on entry into the United States by individuals with subversive political beliefs. See Elizabeth Hull, *Taking Liberties: National Barriers to the Free Flow of Ideas* (New York: Praeger, 1990).

33. For background, see Stephen J. Whitfield, "Civil Liberties and the Culture of the Cold War, 1945–1965," in *Crucible of Liberty: 200 Years of the Bill of Rights*, ed. Raymond Arsenault (New York: Free Press, 1991), 52–72.

34. Veto of the Internal Security Bill, September 22, 1950, in *Public Papers of Harry Truman . . . 1950*, 645–53; Truman, *Memoirs*, 272–73, 499.

35. Exec. Order No. 9835, 12 Fed. Reg. 1935 (1947). For a brief history of federal employee loyalty programs from 1939 through 1952, see Jeff Broadwater, *Eisenhower and the Anti-Communist Crusade* (Chapel Hill: University of North Carolina Press, 1992), 7–17.

36. For accounts of Truman's political calculations in dealing with communists and the results, see Margaret A. Blanchard, *Revolutionary Sparks: Freedom of Expression in Modern America* (New York: Oxford University Press, 1992), 230–54; Richard M. Fried, *Nightmare in Red: The McCarthy Era in Perspective* (New York: Oxford University Press, 1990), 59–119; Stanley I. Kutler, *The American Inquisition: Justice and Injustice in the Cold War* (New York: Hill and Wang, 1982); Michal R. Belknap, *Cold War Political Justice: The Smith Act, the Communist Party, and American Civil Liberties* (Westport, Conn.: Greenwood Press, 1977), 35, 50–51.

37. Truman, *Memoirs*, 291–92.

38. Such laws included the Administrative Procedure Act of 1946, ch. 324, 60 Stat. 237. For background, see Peter Hernon and Charles R. McClure, *Federal Information Policies in the 1980's: Conflicts and Issues* (Norwood, N.J.: Ablex, 1987), 52–59.

39. Exec. Order No. 10290, 16 Fed. Reg. 9795 (1951); Blanchard, *Revolutionary Sparks*, 271–74; Arthur M. Schlesinger Jr., *The Imperial Presidency* (Boston: Houghton Mifflin, 1973), 331–76; David Wise, *The Politics of Lying: Government Deception, Secrecy, and Power* (New York: Random House, 1973), 62–66; David H. Morrissey, "Disclosure and Secrecy: Security Classification Executive Orders," *Journalism Monographs*, no. 161, February 1997; Kathleen L. Endres, "National Security Benchmark: Truman, Executive Order 10290, and the Press," *Journalism Quarterly* 67 (Winter 1990): 1071–77. The Reagan administration was particularly notable for drastic measures. See Richard O. Curry, ed., *Freedom at Risk: Secrecy, Censorship, and Repression in the 1980s* (Philadelphia: Temple University Press, 1988); Robert C. Toth, "President Orders Lie Detector Tests," *Los Angeles Times*, December 11, 1985, 1; Walter Karp, "Liberty under Seige," *Harper's*, November 1985, 53–58, 60–67; Margaret Genovese, "Reagan Administration Information Policies," *Presstime*, April 1985, 14–21. Reagan said the measures were necessary because of a left-wing bias in the press on national security matters. Leonard R. Sussman, *Power, the Press and the Technology of Freedom: The Coming Age of ISDN* (New York: Freedom House, 1989), 132.

40. Statement by Direction of the President Clarifying His News Conference Remarks on Security Information, October 4, 1951, in *Public Papers of the Presidents of the United States, Harry S. Truman . . . 1951* (Washington, D.C.: Government Printing Office, 1965), 563; The President's News Conference of October 4, 1951, in *Public Papers of Harry Truman . . . 1951*, 554, 556; J. R. Wiggins, "The Right to Know," *Nieman Reports*, July 1952, 27–33; Campbell Watson, "Protest to Truman Voted on Censorship," *E&P*, October 6, 1951, 12.

41. Special Message to the Congress Reporting on the Situation in the Steel Industry, April 9, 1952, in *Public Papers of the Presidents of the United States, Harry S. Truman . . . 1952–53* (Washington, D.C.: Government Printing Office, 1966), 251; Brief for Charles F. Sawyer, Secretary of Commerce, in *Landmark Briefs and Arguments of the Supreme Court of the United States: Constitutional Law*, ed. Philip B. Kurland and Gerhard Casper (Arlington, Va.: University Publications of America, 1975–), 48: 704, 706; U.S. v. Curtiss-Wright Export Corp., 299 U.S. 304, 320 (1936). For the view that the *Curtiss-Wright* decision was badly reasoned and based on inaccurate historical evidence, see Louis Fisher, *Presidential War Power* (Lawrence: University Press of Kansas, 1995), 57–59.

42. The frequent and bogus use of the *Curtiss-Wright* cite is discussed in Harold Honju Koh, *The National Security Constitution: Sharing Power after the Iran-Contra Affair* (New Haven: Yale University Press, 1990), 72–73, 93–95, 136–41, 144, 146, 211–12.

43. The President's News Conference of April 17, 1952, in *Public Papers of Harry Truman . . . 1952–53*, 269.

44. The President's News Conference of April 24, 1952, in *Public Papers of Harry Truman* . . . *1952–53*, 290–91, 293–94. For Truman's original statement on the possibility of seizing the news media, see The President's News Conference of April 17, 1952, in *Public Papers of Harry Truman* . . . *1952–53*, 273. In 1951 Governor Thomas Dewey of New York had proposed a state law that would have allowed the governor to seize communication facilities in the event of an enemy attack. The bill, which was based on a model law written by federal civil defense officials, was so questionable that Dewey himself admitted it was "repulsive." "Defense Plan Provides for Orders to Press," *E&P*, January 13, 1951, 9; "Repulsive," *E&P*, 40.

45. Harry S. Truman to Harold Moody, May 21, 1952, as quoted in Williams, *Newspaperman's President*, 193.

46. Internal Security Act, ch. 1024, 64 Stat. 987, 987 (1950).

47. U.S. House of Representatives, *The Steel Seizure Case*, H. Doc. 534, 82d Cong., 2nd sess., 1952, pt. 1, 371.

48. Letter to C. S. Jones in Response to Questions on the Steel Situation, April 27, 1952, in *Public Papers of Harry Truman* . . . *1952–53*, 301.

49. Youngstown Co. v. Sawyer, 343 U.S. 579, 589 (1952). For a detailed history of the case, see Maeva Marcus, *Truman and the Steel Seizure: The Limits of Presidential Power* (New York: Columbia University Press, 1977).

50. Youngstown Co. v. Sawyer, 343 U.S. at 640–41, 642, 643–44.

51. Truman, *Memoirs*, 472, 473, 475, 476, 477, 478.

52. For Truman's description of the National Security Act of 1947 and the origins of the CIA, see Truman, *Memoirs*, 55–60.

53. Christopher Andrew, *For the President's Eyes Only: Secret Intelligence and the American Presidency from Washington to Bush* (New York: HarperCollins, 1995). For a Senate committee's report, see *Alleged Assassination Plots Involving Foreign Leaders* (New York: Norton, 1976).

54. Christy Macy and Susan Kaplan, comps., *Documents* (New York: Penguin Books, 1980), 22, 23; Dwight D. Eisenhower to the Secretary of Defense, May 17, 1954, in *Freedom of the Press from Hamilton to the Warren Court*, ed. Harold L. Nelson (Indianapolis: Bobbs-Merrill, 1967), 385; Memorandum, [January 17, 1962], in Fain, *Intelligence Community*, 707–715; U.S. v. Curtiss-Wright Export Corp., 299 U.S. 304, 320 (1936).

55. Blanche Wiesen Cook, *The Declassified Eisenhower: A Divided Legacy* (Garden City, N.Y.: Doubleday, 1981); Stefan D. Schindler, "Deconstructing Eisenhower," *Lies of Our Times*, February 1991, 14–15. For an examination of Luce's philosophies and his promotion of Eisenhower, see James L. Baughman, *Henry R. Luce and the Rise of the American News Media* (Boston: Twayne, 1987).

56. Earl Warren, *The Memoirs of Earl Warren* (Garden City, N.Y.: Doubleday, 1977), 5–6.

57. Craig Allen, *Eisenhower and the Mass Media: Peace, Prosperity, and Prime-Time TV* (Chapel Hill: University of North Carolina Press, 1993), 10–20; Broadwater, *Eisenhower and the Anti-Communist Crusade*, 209–12; Fried, *Nightmare in Red*, 123–24, 132, 135–36; Edwin R. Bayley, *Joe McCarthy and the Press* (Madison: University of Wisconsin Press, 1981; New York: Pantheon Books, 1982).

58. Turner Catledge, *My Life and The Times* (New York: Harper and Row, 1971), 225–236.

59. Stephen J. Whitfield, *The Culture of the Cold War* (Baltimore: Johns Hopkins University Press, 1991), 153–63.

60. Donald Kagan, *On the Origins of War and the Preservation of Peace* (New York: Doubleday, 1995), 452–66; Erik Barnouw, *Tube of Plenty: The Evolution of American Television*, 2nd rev. ed. (New York: Oxford University Press, 1990), 290–98; Arthur M. Schlesinger Jr., *A*

Thousand Days: John F. Kennedy in the White House (Boston: Houghton Mifflin, 1965), 206–97; James Reston, "The President and the Press—The Old Dilemma," *NYT*, May 10, 1961, 44 (late city edition).

61. Arthur M. Schlesinger Jr. to John F. Kennedy, April 10, 1961, as quoted in Richard Reeves, *President Kennedy: Profile of Power* (New York: Simon and Schuster, 1993), 85.

62. The President's News Conference of April 21, 1961, in *Public Papers of the Presidents of the United States, John F. Kennedy . . . 1961* (Washington, D.C.: Government Printing Office, 1962), 312–13; *NYT*, May 10, 1961, 44 (late city edition).

63. Pierre Salinger, *With Kennedy* (Garden City, N.Y.: Doubleday, 1966), 154–55.

64. "The President and the Press," Address before the American Newspaper Publishers Association, April 27, 1961, in *Public Papers of John Kennedy . . . 1961*, 336.

65. Salinger, *With Kennedy*, 158–60; "Kennedy Pledges Free News Access," *NYT*, May 10, 1961, 3 (late city edition).

66. Clarence R. Wyatt, *Paper Soldiers: The American Press and the Vietnam War* (New York: Norton, 1993), 24–50; Louis M. Lyons, "Press and President," *Nieman Reports*, December 1962, 2; Clark R. Mollenhoff, "Managing the News," *Nieman Reports*, December 1962, 3–7.

67. "U. S. Aide Defends Lying to Nation," *NYT*, December 7, 1962, 5 (late city edition); *Kennedy and the Press: The News Conferences*, ed. Harold W. Chase and Allen H. Lerman (New York: Crowell, 1965), 393. For journalists' comments on Kennedy administration news management, see *Problems of Journalism: Proceedings of the 1963 Convention, American Society of Newspaper Editors* (New York: American Society of Newspaper Editors, 1963), 225–27; "The News Management Issue," *Nieman Reports*, March 1963, 3–15.

68. For catalogs of Kennedy's presidential and personal misdeeds, see Seymour H. Hersh, *The Dark Side of Camelot* (Boston: Little, Brown, 1997); Reeves, *President Kennedy*.

69. Salinger, *With Kennedy*, 149–51. Salinger later became known as a purveyor of government conspiracy theories. Christopher Dickey and Mark Hosenball, "A Conspiratorial Turn of Mind," *Newsweek*, November 25, 1996, 93.

70. James T. Patterson, *Grand Expectations: The United States, 1945–1974* (New York: Oxford University Press, 1996), 492–509; Michael R. Beschloss, *The Crisis Years: Kennedy and Khrushchev, 1960–1963* (New York: HarperCollins, 1991), 5–6, 374–93, 411–12, 418, 544, 549–51; James McCartney, "Rallying around the Flag," *American Journalism Review*, September 1994, 40–46; Jane Franklin, "Operation Mongoose Revisited," *Lies of Our Times*, November 1992, 25–26; Fedor Burlatsky, "Castro Wanted a Nuclear Strike," *NYT*, October 23, 1992, A17 (national edition); Robert S. McNamara, "One Minute to Doomsday," *NYT*, October 14, 1992, A19 (national edition); Gilbert Cranberg, "What the Hell Went on in Miami?" *ASNE Bulletin*, July–August 1978, 9–11.

71. Patterson, *Grand Expectations*, 505–9; Beschloss, *Crisis Years*, 564–68.

72. Athan Theoharis, *Spying on Americans: Political Surveillance from Hoover to the Huston Plan* (Philadelphia: Temple University Press, 1978); Victor Lasky, *It Didn't Start with Watergate* (New York: Dial Press, 1977); David Wise, *The American Police State: The Government against the People* (New York: Random House, 1976).

73. Theoharis, *Spying on Americans*, 170; Hanson W. Baldwin, "Managed News: Our Peacetime Censorship," *Atlantic Monthly*, April 1963, 53–59.

74. Peter Arnett, *Live from the Battlefield: From Vietnam to Baghdad, Thirty-five Years in the World's War Zones* (New York: Simon and Schuster, 1994), 90, 106, 109–10, 116–19, 213–14; Wyatt, *Paper Soldiers*, 117–19; Salinger, *With Kennedy*, 319–29.

75. William Prochnau, *Once upon a Distant War* (New York: Times Books, 1995); John M. Newman, *JFK and Vietnam: Deception, Intrigue, and the Struggle for Power* (New York: Warner Books, 1992); Kathleen J. Turner, *Lyndon Johnson's Dual War: Vietnam and the Press* (Chicago: University of Chicago Press, 1985).

76. See, for example, Arnett, *Live from the Battlefield,* 169. For background on American reliance on weaponry and phony attrition statistics, see Robert Buzzanco, *Masters of War: Military Dissent and Politics in the Vietnam Era* (New York: Cambridge University Press, 1996), 282–85; Jeffrey J. Clarke, *United States Army in Vietnam,* vol. 4, *Advice and Support: The Final Years, 1965–1973* (Washington, D.C.: Center for Military History, United States Army, 1988).

77. Harry G. Summers Jr., *On Strategy: A Critical Analysis of the Vietnam War* (Novato, Calif.: Presidio Press, 1982), 31, 33–40, 174–75, 185–86, 197–98. On the impact of *On Strategy* within the military, see Michael Massing, "Conventional Warfare," *Atlantic Monthly,* January 1990, 32.

78. David Halberstam, *The Making of a Quagmire* (New York: Random House, 1964), 72, 191–92, 268. See also Neil Sheehan, *A Bright Shining Lie: John Paul Vann and America in Vietnam* (New York: Random House, 1988).

79. Arnett, *Live from the Battlefield,* 132, 140–44, 169–70, 212–13, 249, 255–58, 259–60, 267. For Johnson's anger at CBS coverage, see Barnouw, *Tube of Plenty,* 388, 402.

80. Arnett, *Live from the Battlefield,* 89, 140, 215; William M. Hammond, *Public Affairs: The Military and the Media, 1962–1968* (Washington, D.C.: Center of Military History, United States Army, 1988).

81. Wyatt, *Paper Soldiers,* 159–60; Daniel C. Hallin, *The "Uncensored War": The Media and Vietnam* (New York: Oxford University Press, 1986; Berkeley: University of California Press, 1989), 128–29; Peter Braestrup, *Background Paper, Battle Lines: Report of the Twentieth Century Fund Task Force on the Military and the Media* (New York: Priority Press Publications, 1985), 64–66, 73; Knightley, *First Casualty,* 403; W. C. Westmoreland, "Report on Operations in South Vietnam, January 1964–June 1968," in *Report on the War in Vietnam (As of 30 June 1968)* (Washington, D.C.: Government Printing Office, n.d.), 273–74.

82. Liz Trotta, *Fighting for Air: In the Trenches with Television News* (New York: Simon and Schuster, 1991), 119.

83. For a biography of Chapelle that discusses her views and her difficulties in dealing with the military, see Roberta Ostroff, *Fire in the Wind: The Life of Dickey Chapelle* (New York: Ballantine Books, 1992). Chapelle was one of the dozens of journalists who were killed in Vietnam.

84. Dickey Chapelle to Lincoln White and Arthur Sylvester, August 8, 1962, in Georgette Meyer ("Dickey") Chapelle Papers, State Historical Society of Wisconsin, Madison; Dickey Chapelle, "Helicopter War in South Vietnam," *National Geographic,* November 1962, 729.

85. Dickey Chapelle to Robert Prentiss, March 4, 1962, Chapelle Papers, State Historical Society of Wisconsin, Madison.

86. Ostroff, *Fire in the Wind,* 82; Dickey Chapelle to Daniel Mich, July 9, 1942, as quoted in Ostroff, *Fire in the Wind,* 82.

87. Wyatt, *Paper Soldiers,* 147–48.

88. Fred W. Friendly, "When War Comes, Whither the First Amendment?" *Arizona Law Review* 33 (1991): 275–76.

89. Morley Safer, *Flashbacks: On Returning to Vietnam* (New York: Random House, 1990), 85–97.

90. Arnett, *Live from the Battlefield,* 169, 170, 173–75, 185, 214–15, 249; Wyatt, *Paper Soldiers,* 157; Safer, *Flashbacks,* 95; Hammond, *Public Affairs,* 190.

91. Harrison E. Salisbury, *A Time of Change: A Reporter's Tale of Our Time* (New York: Harper and Row, 1988), 136–69.

92. Phil G. Goulding, *Confirm or Deny: Informing the People of National Security* (New York: Harper and Row: 1970), 53, 92; for Goulding's lengthy critique of Salisbury's series, see 52–92.

93. Salisbury, *A Time of Change*, 167–68; Gay Talese, *The Kingdom and the Power* (New York: New American Library, 1969), 449; Karen Rothmyer, "75 Diamond Years of the Pulitzers," *Media History Digest* 10 (Fall–Winter 1990), 56.

94. Hallin, *"Uncensored War,"* 3 n.

95. Wyatt, *Paper Soldiers*, 206–8; Knightley, *First Casualty*, 390–97; Seymour M. Hersh, *Cover-Up* (New York: Random House, 1972); Seymour M. Hersh, *My Lai 4: A Report on the Massacre and Its Aftermath* (New York: Random House, 1970).

96. Laurence I. Barrett, " 'Always Attack, Never Defend,' " *Time*, September 23, 1991, 23.

97. Pub. L. No. 88–408, 78 Stat. 384 (1964); Schlesinger, *Imperial Presidency*, 177–82; The President's News Conference of August 18, 1967, in *Public Papers of the Presidents of the United States, Lyndon B. Johnson . . . 1967* (Washington, D.C.: Government Printing Office, 1968), 794.

98. A Conversation with the President about Foreign Policy, July 1, 1970, in *Public Papers of the Presidents of the United States, Richard Nixon . . . 1970* (Washington, D.C.: Government Printing Office, 1971), 546–47, 552–53; William H. Rehnquist, Authority of the President to Permit Incursion into Communist Sanctuaries in the Cambodia-Vietnam Border Area, May 14, 1970, in *From: The President, Richard Nixon's Secret Files*, ed. Bruce Oudes (New York: Harper and Row, 1989), 138–39.

99. Schlesinger, *Imperial Presidency*, 188.

100. "200,000 Rally in Capital to End War," *NYT*, April 25, 1971, 1 (late city edition).

101. Richard Nixon, *RN: The Memoirs of Richard Nixon* (New York: Grosset and Dunlap, 1978), 497, 513.

102. Richard Nixon to H. R. Haldeman, May 9, 1971, in Oudes, *From: The President*, 251–52.

103. Eugene McCarthy, *Up 'Til Now: A Memoir* (San Diego, Calif.: Harcourt Brace Jovanovich, 1987), 37–41. As chairman of the Commission on Bicentennial of the United States Constitution, Burger quoted Blackstone on the meaning of press freedom and suggested "there are certainly some amendments that we could have done without." Warren E. Burger, "Bicentennial Considerations on America's Bill of Rights," *Presidential Studies Quarterly* 22 (Fall 1992): 663–66; Warren E. Burger, "America's Bill of Rights at Two Hundred Years," *Presidential Studies Quarterly* 21 (Summer 1991): 453–57.

104. Warren E. Burger to Richard Nixon, May 10, 1971, in Oudes, *From: The President*, 254–55; Richard Nixon to Warren E. Burger, May 12, 1971, in Oudes, *From: The President*, 257.

105. Seven years earlier, Supreme Court *dicta* had regarded the Sedition Act as unconstitutional *ab initio*. New York Times v. Sullivan, 376 U.S. 254, 276 (1964).

106. David Rudenstine, *The Day the Presses Stopped: A History of the Pentagon Papers Case* (Berkeley: University of California Press, 1996), 1–300; Nixon, *RN*, 508–15. The various editions of the documents include *The Pentagon Papers as Published by the New York Times* (New York: Quadrangle Books, 1971). *Times* attorneys disagreed about the unsettled legal question of whether publication of the classified documents would violate espionage laws. The paper was not prosecuted after the Supreme Court denied an injunction. Rudenstine, *Day the Presses Stopped*, 48–65, 343.

107. Brief for the United States in Kurland and Casper, *Landmark Briefs*, 71: 122–46.

108. Brief for the Petitioner in Kurland and Casper, *Landmark Briefs*, 71: 47, 52–57; see also Oral Argument of Alexander Bickel, 232–41.

109. John Cary Sims, "Triangulating the Boundaries of *Pentagon Papers*," *William and Mary Bill of Rights Journal* 2 (Winter 1993): 341–453; the secret portion of the government's brief is reprinted at 441–53.

110. New York Times Co. v. U.S., 403 U.S. 713, 714 (1971).

111. For the concurring opinions of Justices Brennan, Stewart, White, and Marshall, see New York Times Co. v. U.S., 403 U.S. at 724–48.

112. New York Times Co. v. U.S., 403 U.S. 713 at 714–20; for the concurring opinion of Justice Douglas, see 720–24.

113. For the dissents of Justices Burger, Harlan, and Blackmun, see New York Times Co. v. U.S., 403 U.S. at 748–63.

114. New York Times Co. v. U.S., 403 U.S. at 761 (Blackmun, J., dissenting).

115. Congress, Senate, 92nd Cong., 1st sess., *Congressional Record* (June 22, 1971), vol. 117, pt. 16, 21307–8; Rudenstine, *Day the Presses Stopped,* 323–38.

116. Anthony Marro, "A Case for National Insecurity," *CJR,* July–August 1996, 57.

117. Erwin N. Griswold, *Ould Fields, New Corne: The Personal Memoirs of a Twentieth Century Lawyer* (St. Paul, Minn.: West, 1992), 309, 312; Daniel Ellsberg, the leaker, did not turn over the most sensitive documents (300–301, 309).

118. Compilations of such actions by Nixon include Joseph C. Spear, *Presidents and the Press: The Nixon Legacy* (Cambridge, Mass.: MIT Press, 1986); William E. Porter, *Assault on the Media: The Nixon Years* (Ann Arbor: University of Michigan Press, 1976). On the use of the Internal Revenue Service by Nixon and other presidents to harass the press and political opponents, see David Burnham, *A Law unto Itself: Power, Politics, and the IRS* (New York: Random House, 1989).

119. Robert MacNeil, *The Right Place at the Right Time* (Boston: Little, Brown, 1982), 285; for an insider's view of Nixon's attacks on public broadcasting, see 279–96.

120. For examples of the grudges Nixon and his aides held and their efforts to put pressure on the news media for better coverage, see Patrick J. Sloyan, "The Place is Forever Duller without Him," *American Journalism Review,* June 1994, 12–13; "Richard Nixon: By the Press Obsessed," *CJR,* May–June 1989, 46–51.

121. H. R. Haldeman, *The Haldeman Diaries: Inside the Nixon White House* (New York: Putnam, 1994), 405; Debra Gersh Hernandez, "Nixon and the Press," *E&P,* June 25, 1994, 82.

122. "Enemy Mine," *American Journalism Review,* June 1994, 13.

123. Alex Butterfield to Gertrude Brown, August 20, 1971, in Oudes, *From: The President,* 311; Daniel Schorr, *Clearing the Air* (Boston: Houghton Mifflin, 1977), 65–90.

124. Marvin Kalb, *The Nixon Memo: Political Responsibility, Russia, and the Press* (Chicago: University of Chicago Press, 1994), 199–212.

125. J. Anthony Lukas, *Nightmare: The Underside of the Nixon Years* (New York: Viking Press, 1976), 41–65.

126. United States v. United States District Court, 407 U.S. 297, 318–20, 321 (1972).

127. A number of theories have been advanced to explain the motives for the Watergate break-ins. Joan Hoff, *Nixon Reconsidered* (New York: Basic Books, 1994), 301–28.

128. For evidence that the *Pentagon Papers* case and fears about the 1972 election set in motion Nixon's downfall, see Rudenstine, *Day the Presses Stopped,* 252–56, 343–48.

129. U.S. v. Nixon, 418 U.S. 683 (1974); Brief for the respondent, cross-petitioner Richard M. Nixon, U.S. v. Richard M. Nixon, in Kurland and Casper, *Landmark Briefs,* 79: 576.

130. Nixon interview with David Frost, as quoted in John Orman, *Presidential Accountability: New and Recurring Problems* (New York: Greenwood Press, 1990), 33–37.

131. Oriana Fallaci, *Interview with History,* trans. John Shepley (New York: Liveright, 1976), 37, 41.

132. See John R. MacArthur, *Second Front: Censorship and Propaganda in the Gulf War* (New York: Hill and Wang, 1992); John Fialka, *Hotel Warriors: Covering the Gulf War* (Washington, D.C.: Woodrow Wilson Center Press, 1991); Micah L. Sifry and Christopher Cerf, eds., *The Gulf War Reader: History, Documents, Opinions* (New York: Times Books, 1991).

133. Nation Magazine v. U.S. Department of Defense, 762 F. Supp. 1558 (S.D.N.Y. 1991) (determination left for future when controversy is more sharply focused); Flynt v. Weinberger, 588 F. Supp. 57 (D.D.C. 1984), *aff'd per curiam but opinion vacated,* 762 F.2d 134 (D.C. Cir.

1985). The district courts in the *Nation* and *Flynt* cases appeared willing to recognize a limited First Amendment right of access to battlefields subject to a balancing with reasonable safety and security needs of the military. Those courts and the court of appeals that affirmed the dismissal of Flynt's claim as moot agreed that the issue would have to be handled on a case-by-case basis in the future.

134. "Pentagon Adopts Revised Media Pool Rules," *News Media & the Law*, Spring 1993, 25; Debra Gersh, "Hard-Line Stand," *E&P*, December 12, 1992, 11–12; Winant Sidle, "A Battle behind the Scenes: The Gulf War Reheats Military-Media Controversy," *Military Review* 71 (September 1991): 52–63; Eligibility Criteria for News Media Membership in the DoD National Media Pool, 57 Fed. Reg. 43,645 (1992).

135. Courts and commentators have often recognized that constitutional protections extend beyond the nation's borders, but a court may find little or no protection for expression that involves safety, national security, or foreign affairs. In *Haig v. Agee*, for instance, the Supreme Court said it was "[a]ssuming, *arguendo*, that First Amendment protections reach beyond our national boundaries," but the opinion upheld the secretary of state's revocation of a former CIA agent's passport for making disclosures about intelligence operations and revealing the names of undercover intelligence agents. 453 U.S. 280, 307–9 (1981).

136. H. Norman Schwarzkopf, *It Doesn't Take a Hero* (New York: Bantam Books, 1992), 257–58; Larry Speakes, *Speaking Out: The Reagan Presidency from Inside the White House* (New York: Scribner's, 1988), 150–63; Joseph Metcalf III, "The Press and Grenada, 1983," in *Defence and the Media in Time of Limited War*, ed. Peter R. Young (Portland, Ore.: Frank Cass, 1992), 168–74; Roger W. Pincus, "Press Access to Military Operations: Grenada and the Need for a New Analytical Framework," *University of Pennsylvania Law Review* 135 (March 1987): 813–50.

137. Congress, Senate, 98th Cong., 1st sess., *Congressional Record*, vol. 129, no. 145, daily ed. (October 29, 1983), S14957.

138. Speakes, *Speaking Out*, 159–60; Metcalf, "Press and Grenada," 174; John Norton Moore, "Address: Do We Have an Imperial Congress?" *University of Miami Law Review* 43 (September 1988): 150. A poll showed 51 percent of the American public approving the use of troops in Grenada and 37 percent opposing. David Shribman, "Poll Shows Support for Presence of U.S. Troops in Lebanon and Grenada," *NYT*, October 29, 1983, 9 (late edition).

139. Robert J. Beck, *The Grenada Invasion: Politics, Law, and Foreign Policy Decisionmaking* (Boulder, Colo.: Westview Press, 1993), 23, 164–65; Speakes, *Speaking Out*, 161–62; "Secrets from the Reagan Years," *Newsweek*, October 30, 1995, 6; William Schaap, "Remembering Grenada," *Lies of Our Times*, June 1994, 16–17; Stuart Taylor Jr., "In the Wake of Invasion, Much Official Misinformation by U.S. Comes to Light," *NYT*, November 6, 1983, 20 (late edition); Richard Bernstein, "U.N. Assembly Adopts Measure 'Deeply Deploring' Invasion of Isle," *NYT*, November 3, 1983, A21 (late edition); Richard Bernstein, "U.S. Vetoes U.N. Resolution 'Deploring' Grenada Invasion," *NYT*, October 29, 1983, A1 (late edition). Some of the students felt threatened and others thought that their presence was simply an excuse to invade Grenada. Robert D. McFadden, "From Rescued Students, Gratitude and Praise," *NYT*, October 28, 1983, A1 (late edition).

140. For the position that each of Reagan's unilateral military involvements was lawful, see David Locke Hall, *The Reagan Wars: A Constitutional Perspective on War Powers and the Presidency* (Boulder, Colo.: Westview Press, 1991). For Reagan's reliance on the Lincoln-Berns view, see Theodore Draper, *A Very Thin Line: The Iran-Contra Affairs* (New York: Hill and Wang, 1991), 581. For the narrow view of First Amendment freedoms that Berns had developed, see Walter Berns, *The First Amendment and the Future of American Democracy* (New York: Basic Books, 1976).

141. Berns quoted Hamilton as saying "[The powers needed for the common defense] ought to exist without limitation." Hamilton, however, was not talking about general "powers"

that were "needed," but rather about the specific, unlimited authority given to Congress to make defense expenditures and military rules and for the president to direct the armed forces. Walter Berns, "Constitutional Power and the Defense of Free Government: The Case of Abraham Lincoln," in *Terrorism: How the West Can Win*, ed. Benjamin Netanyahu (New York: Farrar Straus Giroux, 1986), 150; Hamilton, "The Federalist No. 23," in *FED*, 147.

Berns quoted Locke's definition of prerogative, "the power to act according to discretion for the public good, without the prescription of law and sometimes even against it," without noting that Locke at the same time said prerogative could be limited by "declared *limitations*" made by the people. The press clause is a declared limitation that applies to all branches of government. Berns, "Constitutional Power and the Defense of Free Government," in Netanyahu, *Terrorism*, 151; John Locke, *Two Treatises of Government*, 2nd ed. (Cambridge: Cambridge University Press, 1967), 392–98.

142. Berns, "Constitutional Power and the Defense of Free Government," in Netanyahu, *Terrorism*, 151–53. The Berns quote of Lincoln is not exact. See Abraham Lincoln to Erastus Corning and Others, [June 12], 1863, in *WAL*, 6: 266–67. The quote was also appreciated within the Nixon administration. Patrick J. Buchanan to Richard Nixon, November 18, 1971, in Oudes, *From: the President*, 341.

143. Draper, *A Very Thin Line*, 587.

144. Christopher Hitchens, "A Few Questions for Poindexter," *Harper's*, January 1990, 70–75; Dave Lindorff, "Oliver's Martial Plan," *Village Voice*, July 21, 1987, 18; Alfonso Chardy, "Reagan Advisers Ran 'Secret' Government," *Miami Herald*, July 5, 1987, 1A, 15A; Congress, *Iran-Contra Investigation, Joint Hearings before the Senate Select Committee on Secret Military Assistance to Iran and the Nicaraguan Opposition and the House Select Committee to Investigate Covert Arms Transactions with Iran*, 100th Cong., 1st sess., 1987, 122, 187–88; Richard O. Curry, *An Uncertain Future: Thought Control and Repression during the Reagan-Bush Era* (Los Angeles: First Amendment Foundation, 1992), 89; Oliver L. North with William Novak, *Under Fire: An American Story* (New York: HarperCollins, 1991), 163–64, 165–66.

145. Fred S. Hoffman, "The Panama Press Pool Deployment: A Critique," in *Newsmen and National Defense: Is Conflict Inevitable?* ed. Lloyd Matthews (Washington: Brassey's [US] 1991), 91–109; Peter Schmeisser, "Shooting Pool," *New Republic*, March 18, 1991, 22; Charles B. Rangel, "The Pentagon Pictures," *NYT*, December 20, 1990, A19 (national edition); George Garneau, "Panning the Pentagon," *E&P*, March 31, 1990, 11–12; William Boot, "Wading around in the Panama Pool," *CJR*, March–April 1990, 18–20; Stanley W. Cloud, "How Reporters Missed the War," *Time*, January 8, 1990, 61.

146. Sandra H. Dickson, "Understanding Media Bias: The Press and the U.S. Invasion of Panama," *Journalism Quarterly* 71 (Winter 1994): 809–19; Sonia Gutierrez-Villalobos, James K. Hertog, and Ramona R. Rush, "Press Support for the U.S. Administration during the Panama Invasion: Analyses of Strategic and Tactical Critique in the Domestic Press," *Journalism Quarterly* 71 (Winter 1994): 618–27.

147. George Klay Kieh Jr., "Propaganda and United States Foreign Policy: The Case of Panama," *Political Communication and Persuasion* 7 (April–June 1990), 61–72; James LeMoyne, "U.S. Won't Reveal Noriega Payments," *NYT*, May 22, 1990, A1 (national edition).

148. Francisco Goldman, "What Price Panama?" *Harper's*, September 1990, 73; Douglas Waller and John Barry, "Inside the Invasion," *Newsweek*, June 25, 1990, 28–31.

149. Address to the Nation Announcing United States Military Action in Panama, December 20, 1989, in *Public Papers of the Presidents of the United States, George Bush, 1989* (Washington, D.C.: Government Printing Office, 1990), 2: 1722–23.

150. Tom Wicker, "Overkill in Panama," *NYT*, April 5, 1990, A15 (national edition); Gilbert Cranberg, "A Flimsy Story and a Compliant Press," *Washington Journalism Review*, March 1990, 48.

151. Waller and Barry, "Inside the Invastion," 31.

152. "An Accident-Prone Army," *Newsweek*, November 5, 1990, 7. For examples of the debate over Panamanian deaths and related issues, see Independent Commission of Inquiry on the U.S. Invasion of Panama, *The U.S. Invasion of Panama: The Truth behind Operation "Just Cause"* (Boston: South End Press, 1991); Goldman, "What Price Panama?" 72; Tom Wicker, "Panama and the Press," *NYT*, April 19, 1990, A11 (national edition); Wicker, "Overkill in Panama," A15.

153. Barbara Ehrenreich, "Who Wants Another Panama?" *Time*, January 21, 1991, 74; Ricardo Chavira, "Meanwhile, Back in Panama," *Time*, November 26, 1990, 38; Mark A. Uhlig, "Panama Drug Smugglers Prosper as Dictator's Exit Opens the Door," *NYT*, August 21, 1990, A1 (national edition).

154. Pub. L. No. 102–1, 105 Stat. 3 (1991); Adam Clymer, "Congress in Step," *NYT*, January 14, 1991, A11 (national edition); Richard Lacayo, "On the Fence," *Time*, January 14, 1991; Maureen Dowd, "President Seems to Blunt Calls for Gulf Session," *NYT*, November 15, 1990, A1 (national edition); Neil A. Lewis, "Sorting Out Legal War Concerning Real War," *NYT*, November 15, 1990, A8 (national edition).

155. MacArthur, *Second Front*, 37–77; Arthur E. Rowse, "How to Build Support for War," *CJR*, September–October 1992, 28–29.

156. For the evolution of the rules and guidelines and appendices where they are reproduced, see Jacqueline E. Sharkey, *Under Fire: U.S. Military Restrictions on the Media from Grenada to the Persian Gulf* (Washington, D.C.: Center for Public Integrity, 1991). Relevant documents are also available in Congress, Senate, *Pentagon Rules on Media Access to the Persian Gulf War, Hearing before the Committee on Governmental Affairs*, 102nd Cong., 1st sess., 1991.

157. Michael R. Gordon, "The Press Corps in the Desert: Lots of Sweat but Little News," *NYT*, August 28, 1990, A1 (national edition); Alex S. Jones, "News Executives See Pool Hamstrung by Rules of Coverage," *NYT*, August 17, 1990, A6 (national edition).

158. "Pentagon Manipulates War Coverage," *News Media and the Law*, Winter 1991, 2–3.

159. Pete Williams, Memorandum with Operation Desert Shield Ground Rules and Guidelines for News Media dated January 14, 1991, January 15, 1991, reproduced in Sharkey, *Under Fire*, Appendix D, Exhibit 6.

160. Douglas Kellner, *The Persian Gulf TV War* (Boulder, Colo: Westview Press, 1992); MacArthur, *Second Front*, 3–36, 146–98; Fialka, *Hotel Warriors*; Pete Williams, "The Press and the Persian Gulf War," *Parameters* 21 (Autumn 1991): 2–9; "Military Obstacles Detailed," *E&P*, July 13, 1991, 8–10; Chris Hedges, "The Unilaterals," *CJR*, May–June 1991, 27–29; Schmeisser, "Shooting Pool," 21–23; Richard L. Berke, "Pentagon Defends Coverage Rules, While Admitting to Some Delays," *NYT*, February 21, 1991, A6 (national edition); Richard Zoglin, "Jumping out of the Pool," *Time*, February 18, 1991, 39; Edith Lederer, "Press Pool Hassles," *E&P*, February 16, 1991, 10; R. W. Apple Jr., "Correspondents Protest Pool System," *NYT*, February 12, 1991, A8 (national edition); R. W. Apple Jr., "Press and the Military: Old Suspicions," *NYT*, February 4, 1991, A6 (national edition).

161. See Michael Kammen, *A Machine That Would Go of Itself: The Constitution in American Culture* (New York: Knopf, 1986), xvii, 399.

Chapter 8

1. See, for example, James E. Wentz, "Should America Have a 'War Press Act'?" *Naval War College Review* 36 (November–December 1983): 65–67. For a government lawyer's argument that the news media have no constitutional right of access to military operations, see Marshall

Silverberg, "Constitutional Concerns in Denying the Press Access to Military Operations," in *Defense Beat: The Dilemmas of Defense Coverage*, ed. Loren B. Thompson (New York: Lexington Books, 1991), 165–75.

2. Some law journal articles have suggested that war correspondents could be subject to reasonable "time, place, and manner" restrictions. See, for example, Mark C. Rahdert, "The First Amendment and Media Rights during Wartime: Some Thoughts after Operation Desert Storm," *Villanova Law Review* 36 (November 1991): 1551–53; Roger W. Pincus, "Press Access to Military Operations: Grenada and the Need for a New Analytical Framework," *University of Pennsylvania Law Review* 135 (March 1987): 847–49. Such restrictions, however, could be used by the military in unconstitutional ways to control content.

3. Eric Carlson, as quoted in Johanna Neuman, *Lights, Camera, War: Is Media Technology Driving International Politics?* (New York: St. Martin's Press, 1996), 10–11. The Marines were more accommodating to the media than the Army, but they provided an offshore diversion and were not involved in the main attack. John J. Fialka, *Hotel Warriors: Covering the Gulf War* (Washington, D.C.: Woodrow Wilson Center Press, 1991), 6–8.

4. See, for instance, Erik Barnouw, *Tube of Plenty: The Evolution of American Television*, 2nd rev. ed. (New York: Oxford University Press, 1990), 366–77; Bosah Ebo, "War as Popular Culture: The Gulf Conflict and the Technology of Illusionary Entertainment," *Journal of Popular Culture* 18 (Fall 1995): 19–25.

5. Russell Watson, "When Words Are the Best Weapon," *Newsweek*, February 27, 1995, 36–37, 39–40.

6. Ithiel de Sola Pool, *Technologies of Freedom* (Cambridge: Harvard University Press, 1983).

7. Susan J. Douglas, *Inventing American Broadcasting: 1899–1922* (Baltimore: Johns Hopkins University Press, 1987), 274.

8. A. M. Sperber, *Murrow: His Life and Times* (New York: Bantam Books, 1987), 157–200; Fred W. Friendly, "When War Comes, Whither the First Amendment?" *Arizona Law Review* 33 (1991): 274.

9. Stephen L. Vaughn, *Holding Fast the Inner Lines: Democracy, Nationalism, and the Committee on Public Information* (Chapel Hill: University of North Carolina Press, 1980), 203–11; Raymond Fielding, *The American Newsreel, 1911–1967* (Norman: University of Oklahoma Press, 1972), 92–96, 109–10, 115–25, 263–64, 273–74, 288–96, 297; James R. Mock and Cedric Larson, *Words That Won the War: The Story of the Committee on Public Information* (Princeton: Princeton University Press, 1939), 138–42.

10. *Regulations for Correspondents Accompanying U.S. Army Forces in the Field* (Washington, D.C.: Government Printing Office, 1942), 6–7.

11. W. C. Westmoreland, "Report on Operations in South Vietnam, January 1964–June 1968," in *Report on the War in Vietnam (As of 30 June 1968)* (Washington, D.C.: Government Printing Office, n.d.), 273, 274; William C. Westmoreland, *A Soldier Reports* (New York: Dell, 1980), 555.

12. Robert Elegant, "How To Lose a War: Reflections of a Foreign Correspondent," *Encounter*, August 1981, 73.

13. Mark R. Levy and Michael Gurevitch, preface to *Defining Media Studies: Reflections on the Future of the Field*, ed. Mark R. Levy and Michael Gurevitch (New York: Oxford University Press, 1994), 8; Herbert J. Gans, "Reopening the Black Box: Toward a Limited Effects Theory," in Levy and Gurevitch, *Defining Media Studies: Reflections on the Future of the Field*, 276.

14. See Sam C. Sarkesian, "Soldiers, Scholars, and the Media," in *Newsmen and National Defense: Is Conflict Inevitable?* ed. Lloyd Matthews (Washington: Brassey's [US] 1991), 61; Bernard E. Trainor, "The Military and the Media: A Troubled Embrace," in Matthews, *Newsmen and National Defense*, 121–22; Richard Halloran, "Soldiers and Scribblers Revisited: Working

with the Media," in Matthews, *Newsmen and National Defense*, 132–33. A survey conducted in 1994 and 1995 found that 64 percent of military respondents agreed that media coverage harmed the war effort in Vietnam. Frank Aukofer and William P. Lawrence, *America's Team; The Odd Couple—A Report on the Relationship between the Media and the Military* (Nashville, Tenn.: Freedom Forum First Amendment Center, 1995), 31.

15. Henry Kissinger, *Diplomacy* (New York: Simon and Schuster, 1994), 667–73.

16. For brief accounts of the events and reactions, see Barbara W. Tuchman, *The March of Folly: From Troy to Vietnam* (New York: Knopf, 1984), 348–56; David Halberstam, *The Powers That Be* (New York: Knopf, 1979), 510–14.

17. Richard Nixon, *No More Vietnams* (New York: Arbor House, 1985), 88–93; Peter Braestrup, *Big Story: How the American Press and Television Reported and Interpreted the Crisis of Tet 1968 in Vietnam and Washington*, abridged ed. (New Haven: Yale University Press, 1983); Bill Monroe, "Rusk to John Scali: 'Whose Side Are You On?' " *Washington Journalism Review*, January–February 1991, 8.

18. Kissinger, *Diplomacy*, 670; Nixon, *No More Vietnams*, 89, 93.

19. Rodney A. Smolla, *Suing the Press* (New York: Oxford University Press, 1986), 232; Daniel C. Hallin, *The "Uncensored War": The Media and Vietnam* (New York: Oxford University Press, 1986; Berkeley: University of California Press, 1989), 168–69, 173; Kathleen J. Turner, *Lyndon Johnson's Dual War: Vietnam and the Press* (Chicago: University of Chicago Press, 1985), 219, 234–36; Philip E. Converse, Warren E. Miller, Jerrold G. Rusk, and Arthur C. Wolfe, "Continuity and Change in American Politics: Parties and Issues in the 1968 Election," *American Political Science Review* 63 (December 1969): 1092.

20. John E. Mueller, *War, Presidents and Public Opinion* (New York: Wiley, 1973), 65, 167.

21. William M. Hammond, *Public Affairs: The Military and the Media, 1962–1968* (Washington, D.C.: Center of Military History, United States Army, 1988), 387, 388.

22. Michael J. Arlen, *Living-Room War* (New York: Viking Press, 1969), 8. See also Clarence R. Wyatt, *Paper Soldiers: The American Press and the Vietnam War* (New York: Norton, 1993), 216–17.

23. On this point, see Sidney Blumenthal, "McNamara's Peace," *New Yorker*, May 8, 1995, 66–70.

24. Robert S. McNamara, *In Retrospect: The Tragedy and Lessons of Vietnam* (New York: Times Books, 1995). McNamara was among those who tried to ignore or silence widespread warnings about military involvement. Louis G. Sarris, "McNamara's War, and Mine," *NYT*, September 5, 1995, A13 (national edition).

25. Clark Clifford, *Counsel to the President: A Memoir* (New York: Random House, 1991), 404, 405, 474.

26. James L. Baughman, *Henry R. Luce and the Rise of the American News Media* (Boston: Twayne, 1987), 186–92; Philip Knightley, *The First Casualty: From Crimea to Vietnam: The War Correspondent as Hero, Propagandist, and Myth Maker* (New York: Harcourt Brace Jovanovich, 1975), 379–81; David Halberstam, *The Making of a Quagmire* (New York: Random House, 1964), 269–74.

27. Melvin Small, *Covering Dissent: The Press and the Anti-Vietnam War Movement* (New Brunswick, N.J.: Rutgers University Press, 1994).

28. Hallin, *"Uncensored War,"* x–xi.

29. Lawrence W. Lichty, "Comments on the Influence of Television on Public Opinion," in *Vietnam as History: Ten Years after the Paris Peace Accords*, ed. Peter Braestrup (Washington, D.C.: Woodrow Wilson International Center for Scholars and University Press of America, 1984), 158; Oscar Patterson III, "An Analysis of Television Coverage of the Vietnam War," *Journal of Broadcasting* 28 (Fall 1984): 397–404.

30. On the message films of the 1960s and early 1970s, including those that disparaged war and the military, see David Manning White and Richard Averson, *The Celluloid Weapon: Social Comment in the American Film* (Boston: Beacon Press, 1972), 185–259.

31. Peter Braestrup, *Background Paper, Battle Lines: Report of the Twentieth Century Fund Task Force on the Military and the Media* (New York: Priority Press Publications, 1985), 65.

32. Susan D. Moeller, *Shooting War: Photography and the American Combat Experience* (New York: Basic Books, 1989), 19; for the stories behind the monk and prisoner photographs, see 376–77, 377–78.

33. Moeller, *Shooting War,* 377; Knightley, *First Casualty,* 379. After this incident, authorities in South Vietnam realized the impact of photographs and tried to confiscate the film of later protests. Moeller, *Shooting War,* 363. The secret police put journalists under surveillance. Knightley, *First Casualty,* 379.

34. "Viet War Photo Is Challenged," *Washington Post,* January 19, 1986, A3.

35. George Judson, "2 Prisoners of History Meet Camera's Captors," *NYT,* October 11, 1995, B1 (national edition).

36. Judith Coburn, "The Girl in the Photograph," *Los Angeles Times Magazine,* August 20, 1989, 8.

37. Arthur A. Humphries, "Two Routes to the Wrong Destination: Public Affairs in the South Atlantic War," *Naval War College Review* 36 (May-June 1983): 57; Joseph Metcalf III, "The Press and Grenada, 1983," in *Defence and the Media in Time of Limited War,* ed. Peter R. Young (Portland, Ore.: Cass, 1992), 168; Michael K. Deaver with Mickey Herskowitz, *Behind the Scenes* (New York: Morrow, 1987), 147.

38. See Edward N. Luttwak, "Is Intervention a Thing of the Past?" *Harper's Magazine,* October 1994, 15–17; Jacqueline Sharkey, "When Pictures Drive Foreign Policy," *American Journalism Review,* December 1993, 14–19.

39. H. Norman Schwarzkopf, *It Doesn't Take a Hero* (New York: Bantam Books, 1992), 468–70.

40. See, for example, E. L. Pattullo, "War and the American Press," *Parameters* 22 (Winter 1992–1993): 61–69.

41. Harry F. Noyes III, "Like It or Not, The Armed Forces Need the Media," *Army,* June 1992, 32–34.

42. Roger Cohen and Claudio Gatti, *In the Eye of the Storm: The Life of General H. Norman Schwarzkopf* (New York: Farrar Straus Giroux, 1991), 269; Fialka, *Hotel Warriors,* 59; Jason DeParle, "Keeping the News in Step: Are the Pentagon's Gulf War Rules Here to Stay?" *NYT,* May 6, 1991, A5 (national edition); Tom Mathews, "The Secret History of the War," *Newsweek,* March 18, 1991, 32; Russell Watson and Gregg Easterbrook, "A New Kind of Warfare," *Newsweek,* January 28, 1991, 19.

43. Gregg Easterbrook, "Operation Desert Shill," *New Republic,* September 30, 1991, 42.

44. Guidelines for News Media, January 14, 1991, reproduced in Jacqueline E. Sharkey, *Under Fire: U.S. Military Restrictions on the Media from Grenada to the Persian Gulf* (Washington, D.C.: Center for Public Integrity, 1991), Appendix D—Exhibit 6.

45. Ken Jarecke, "The Image of War," *American Photo,* July–August 1991, 41, 44, 46, 120; William H. Schaap, "The Images of War," *Lies of Our Times,* July–August 1991, 6; "Editors Criticize Curbs on Photos," *NYT,* February 21, 1991, A6 (national edition); "War Photos 'Pretty Tame,'" *NYT,* February 1, 1991, A5 (national edition).

46. Michael Griffin and Jongsoo Lee, "Picturing the Gulf War: Constructing an Image of War in *Time, Newsweek,* and *U.S. News and World Report,*" *Journalism and Mass Communication Quarterly* 72 (Winter 1995): 813–25.

47. Colin L. Powell, "Remarks to the National Newspaper Association," Washington, D.C., March 15, 1991, copy in possession of author.

48. Michael Emery, *On the Front Lines: Following America's Foreign Correspondents across the Twentieth Century* (Washington, D.C.: American University Press, 1995), 289; Robert D. Kaplan, "Fort Leavenworth and the Eclipse of Nationhood," *Atlantic Monthly*, September 1996, 80–82.

49. Neuman, *Lights, Camera, War*, 13–40, 92–100; Armand Mattelart, *Mapping World Communication: War, Progress, Culture*, trans. Susan Emanuel and James A. Cohen (Minneapolis: University of Minnesota Press, 1994).

50. Warren P. Strobel, *Late-Breaking Foreign Policy: The New Media's Influence on Peace Operations* (Washington, D. C.: U. S. Institute of Peace, 1997); Warren P. Strobel, "The CNN Effect," *American Journalism Review*, May 1996, 32–37.

51. Debra Gersh Hernandez, "The Media's Impact on the Military," *E&P*, May 13, 1995, 14, 46.

52. Michael R. Gordon, "Pentagon's Haiti Policy Focuses on Casualties," *NYT*, October 6, 1994, A5 (national edition).

53. Mueller, *War, Presidents, and Public Opinion*, 167; Jonathan Alter, "Does Bloody Footage Lose Wars?" *Newsweek*, February 11, 1991, 38. On public rallying during the Gulf War, see Douglas M. McLeod, William P. Eveland Jr., and Nancy Signorielli, "Conflict and Public Opinion: Rallying Effects of the Persian Gulf War," *Journalism Quarterly* 71 (Spring 1994): 20–31.

54. Douglas Waller, "Onward Cyber Soldiers," *Time*, August 21, 1995, 38–44; Richard L. Garwin, "Secret Weapons for the CNN Era," *Harper's Magazine*, October 1994, 17–18; John Barry, "Soon, 'Phasers on Stun,' " *Newsweek*, February 7, 1994, 24–26.

55. See, for example, Aukofer and Lawrence, *America's Team*, 158; *The Military and the Media: The Continuing Dialogue*, ed. Nancy Ethiel (Chicago: Robert R. McCormick Tribune Foundation, 1993), 18, 49; Richard H. Sinnreich, "The Changing Face of Battlefield Reporting," *Army*, November 1994, 30–34; John W. Spelich, "In the Crossfire: A Reporter's Right of Access to the Battlefield in Time of War," *Detroit College of Law Review* 1992 (Winter 1992): 1083–86; Charles D. Cooper, "Media, Give Us a Break," *Retired Officer Magazine*, March 1991, 4; M. L. Stein, "Persian Gulf Coverage and the 'Vietnam Hangover,' " *E&P*, February 23, 1991, 18.

56. William J. Broad, "In Era of Satellites, Army Plots Ways to Destroy Them," *NYT*, March 4, 1997, B9 (national edition); William J. Broad, "Private Ventures Hope for Profits on Spy Satellites," *NYT*, February 10, 1997, A1 (national edition).

57. Dennis D. Wainstock, *The Decision to Drop the Atomic Bomb* (Westport, Conn.: Praeger, 1996), 13; Conrad C. Crane, *Bombs, Cities, and Civilians: American Airpower Strategy in World War II* (Lawrence: University Press of Kansas, 1993), 51, 133–34.

58. Douglas Waller, "Secret Warriors," *Newsweek*, June 17, 1991, 24; "psy-ops" also dropped approximately twenty-nine million leaflets urging surrender (24). The Pentagon released sensitive information on deployments to intimidate Iraq during a later confrontation. Bruce W. Nelan, "How the Attack on Iraq Is Planned," *Time*, February 23, 1998, 42.

59. John Tierney, " 'The Press Was Here,' but Not the Enemy," *NYT*, September 20, 1994, A8 (national edition).

60. High-tech combat has required the development of offensive and defensive "information warfare" techniques. Steve Lohr, "Ready, Aim, Zap," *NYT*, September 30, 1996, C1 (national edition); "Gunning for Bytes," *Newsweek*, June 10, 1996, 11.

61. Mark Thompson, "Wired for War," *Time*, March 31, 1997, 72–73; Kaplan, "Fort Leavenworth and the Eclipse of Nationhood," 78; Mathews, "Secret History of the War," 36.

62. Easterbrook, "Operation Desert Shill," 38, 40. See also Aukofer and Lawrence, *America's Team*, 45–46; Fialka, *Hotel Warriors*, 8.

63. On determining factors in war, see Richard Overy, *Why the Allies Won* (New York: Norton, 1995).

64. Aukofer and Lawrence, *America's Team,* 25.

65. John Barry, "The Battle over Warfare," *Newsweek,* December 5, 1994, 27–28.

66. Schwarzkopf, *It Doesn't Take a Hero,* 394–95, 439–40.

67. Gregory L. Vistica, *Fall from Glory: The Men Who Sank the U.S. Navy* (New York: Simon and Schuster, 1995), 316; Cohen and Gatti, *In the Eye of the Storm,* 268, 276; Fialka, *Hotel Warriors,* 28; Mathews, "Secret History of the War," 38; Easterbrook, "Operation Desert Shill," 39. Schwarzkopf later denied deliberately misleading the press. Aukofer and Lawrence, *America's Team,* 30, 102–3, 156.

68. Robert Leckie, *George Washington's War: The Saga of the American Revolution* (New York: HarperCollins, 1992), 316–18; J. Cutler Andrews, *The South Reports the Civil War* (Princeton: Princeton University Press, 1970), 528; James G. Randall, "The Newspaper Problem in Its Bearing upon Military Secrecy during the Civil War," *American Historical Review* 23 (January 1918): 311, 312, 314.

69. Emmet Crozier, *Yankee Reporters, 1861–65* (New York: Oxford University Press, 1956), 191–94.

70. Hodding Carter, *Their Words Were Bullets: The Southern Press in War, Reconstruction, and Peace* (Athens: University of Georgia Press, 1969), 30–31; John L. Offner, *An Unwanted War: The Diplomacy of the United States and Spain over Cuba, 1895–1898* (Chapel Hill: University of North Carolina Press, 1992), 195–96; Howard Bray, "Fast Boats, Slow Censors," *Washington Journalism Review,* March 1988, 19.

71. Ralph O. Nafziger, "World War Correspondents and Censorship of the Belligerents," *Journalism Quarterly* 14 (September 1937): 229, 238; Paul Fussell, *Wartime: Understanding and Behavior in the Second World War* (New York: Oxford University Press, 1989), 45–48; Lawrence C. Soley, *Radio Warfare: OSS and CIA Subversive Propaganda* (New York: Praeger, 1989); Lawrence H. McDonald, "The Office of Strategic Services: America's First National Intelligence Agency," *Prologue* 23 (Spring 1991): 7–22.

72. Alexander S. Cochran, "ULTRA, FORTITUDE, and D-Day Planning: The Missing Dimension," in *D-Day 1944,* ed. Theodore A. Wilson (Lawrence: University Press of Kansas, 1994), 63–79; Charles Cruickshank, *Deception in World War II* (New York: Oxford University Press, 1980); Jock Haswell, *D-Day: Intelligence and Deception* (New York: Times Books, 1979).

73. Andy Rooney, *My War* (New York: Times Books, 1995), 185–88.

74. Norman Polmar and Thomas B. Allen, *Spy Book: The Encyclopedia of Espionage* (New York: Random House, 1997), 79.

75. Cold War: Lawrence C. Soley and John S. Nichols, *Clandestine Radio Broadcasting: A Study of Revolutionary and Counterrevolutionary Electronic Communication* (New York: Praeger, 1987); William Preston Jr., and Ellen Ray, "Disinformation and Mass Deception: Democracy as a Cover Story," in *Freedom at Risk: Secrecy, Censorship, and Repression in the 1980s,* ed. Richard O. Curry (Philadelphia: Temple University Press, 1988), 203–23; Douglas Waller, "For Your Disinformation," *Time,* November 13, 1995, 82; Tim Weiner, "Lies and Rigged 'Star Wars' Test Fooled the Kremlin, and Congress," *NYT,* August 18, 1993, A1 (national edition). Gulf War: Ramsey Clark, *The Fire This Time: U.S. War Crimes in the Gulf* (New York: Thunder's Mouth Press, 1992), 141; Everette E. Dennis et al., *The Media at War: The Press and the Persian Gulf Conflict* (New York: Gannett Foundation Media Center, 1991), 20, 30–31, 73–74; John Chancellor, "War Stories," *NYT,* April 1, 1991, A11 (national edition); Richard Zoglin, "It Was a Public Relations Rout Too," *Time,* March 11, 1991, 56–57; "Exaggerated," *Newsweek,* February 18, 1991, 10; Debra Gersh, "Tracking Iraqi Disinformation," *E&P,* February 9, 1991, 11, 39.

76. Garry Wills, *Nixon Agonistes: The Crisis of the Self-Made Man* (Boston: Houghton Mifflin, 1970), 122–23; Andrew Clymer, "A-Test 'Confusion' Laid to Eisenhower," *NYT,* April 20, 1979, A1 (late city edition). See Fred I. Greenstein, *The Hidden-Hand Presidency: Eisenhower as Leader* (Baltimore: Johns Hopkins University Press, 1994).

77. Michael R. Beschloss, *Mayday: Eisenhower, Khrushchev and the U-2 Affair* (New York: Harper and Row, 1986); The President's News Conference of May 11, 1960, in *Public Papers of the Presidents of the United States, Dwight D. Eisenhower, 1960–61* (Washington, D.C.: Government Printing Office, 1961), 403–4.

78. Richard M. Nixon, *Six Crises* (Garden City, N.Y.: Doubleday, 1962), 309–12.

79. Robert A. Caro, *The Years of Lyndon Johnson*, vol. 2, *Means of Ascent* (New York: Knopf, 1990), 40–53.

80. Louis Fisher, *Presidential War Power* (Lawrence: University Press of Kansas, 1995), 114–18; Julie H. Blissert, "Guerilla Journalist: I. F. Stone and Tonkin," *Journalism History* 23 (Autumn 1997): 102–13; Turner, *Lyndon Johnson's Dual War*, 81–85.

81. See, for example, Fireside Chat on National Defense, May 26, 1940, in *Nothing to Fear: The Selected Addresses of Franklin Delano Roosevelt, 1932–1945*, ed. B. D. Zevin (Cambridge, Mass.: Houghton Mifflin, 1946), 203–13; Address on Hemispheric Defense, October 12, 1940, in Zevin, *Nothing to Fear*, 223–30; Radio Address on Selective Service Registration Day, October 16, 1940, in Zevin, *Nothing to Fear*, 230–32; Campaign Address at Madison Square Garden, October 28, 1940, in Zevin, *Nothing to Fear*, 242; Fireside Chat on National Security, December 29, 1940, in Zevin, *Nothing to Fear*, 247–58.

82. Richard N. Smith, *The Colonel: The Life and Legend of Robert R. McCormick, 1880–1955* (Boston: Houghton Mifflin, 1997), 415–19; Thomas Fleming, "The Big Leak," *American Heritage* 38 (December 1987): 64–71; Chesly Manly, "F.D.R.'s War Plans!" *Chicago Tribune*, December 4, 1941, 1.

83. Robert Buzzanco, *Masters of War: Military Dissent and Politics in the Vietnam Era* (New York: Cambridge University Press, 1996), 17–19; Peter J. Roman, *Eisenhower and the Missile Gap* (Ithaca: Cornell University Press, 1995); Donald Kagan, *On the Origins of War and the Preservation of Peace* (New York: Doubleday, 1995), 449–51, 458; Edwin M. Yoder Jr., *Joe Alsop's Cold War: A Study of Journalistic Influence and Intrigue* (Chapel Hill: University of North Carolina Press, 1995), 168–74; Fisher, *Presidential War Power*, 115–18; Joan Hoff, *Nixon Reconsidered* (New York: Basic Books, 1994), 208–19; James McCartney, "Hoodwinked!" *American Journalism Review*, March 1996, 22–24; Sidney Lens, "On the Uses and Abuse of Secrecy," *Progressive*, March 1980, 46. For Johnson's cautiously worded statement, see Remarks in Manchester to the Members of the New Hampshire Weekly Newspaper Editors Association, September 28, 1964, in *Public Papers of the Presidents of the United States, Lyndon B. Johnson . . . 1963–64* (Washington, D.C.: Government Printing Office, 1965), 2: 1164.

84. Debate between the President and Former Vice President Walter F. Mondale in Kansas City, Missouri, October 21, 1984, in *Public Papers of the Presidents of the United States, Ronald Reagan, 1984* (Washington, D.C.: Government Printing Office, 1987), 1602, 1606; Interview with Editors of the Hearst Corporation, October 30, 1984, in *Public Papers of Ronald Reagan, 1984*, 1696; Tina Rosenberg, "The Authorized Version," *Atlantic Monthly*, February 1986, 26, 28, 30. For a summary of later criticism of the Strategic Defense Initiative, see Sharon Begley, "A Safety Net Full of Holes," *Newsweek*, March 23, 1992, 56–57, 58.

85. A poll taken before the 1992 election showed that only 34 percent of registered voters were satisfied with Bush's explanation of his role in the Iran-Contra arms deal. Bill Turque, "Was Bush Really 'Out of the Loop'?" *Newsweek*, October 5, 1992, 43.

86. Peter Kornbluh and Malcolm Byrne, eds., *The Iran-Contra Scandal: The Declassified History* (New York: New Press, 1993); Scott Armstrong, "Iran-Contra: Was the Press Any Match for All the President's Men?" *CJR*, May–June 1990, 31, 33.

87. See, for example, David Johnston, "A Secret Memo Puts Bush Close to Hostage Deals," *NYT*, October 23, 1992, A15 (national edition); David Johnston, "Cable Says Bush Endorsed Secrecy for Hostage Affair," *NYT*, October 21, 1992, A11 (national edition); "What the President Knew," *NYT*, October 19, 1992, A14 (national edition). George Shultz, who was

secretary of state in the Reagan administration, waited until shortly after Bush left office to make his revelations about Bush's role in the scandal. David Johnston, "Shultz's Iran-Contra Account Poses Stiff Challenge for Bush," *NYT,* February 2, 1993, A6 (national edition).

88. Janice Castro, "Don't Want to Talk about It," *Time,* October 12, 1992, 23; United States of America v. Caspar W. Weinberger, Indictment, October 30, 1992, in Kornbluh and Byrne, *Iran-Contra Scandal,* 368–73; Evan Thomas, "Pardon Me," *Newsweek,* January 4, 1993, 15; George Bush, Presidential Pardon of Caspar Weinberger, Elliot Abrams, Duane Clarridge, Alan Fiers, Clair George, and Robert McFarlane, December 24, 1992, in Kornbluh and Byrne, *Iran-Contra Scandal,* 374–76; Lawrence Walsh, Response to Presidential Pardons, December 24, 1993, in Kornbluh and Byrne, *Iran-Contra Scandal,* 377.

89. "Legally, Nixon's acceptance of the pardon was an admission of guilt for unspecified crimes," said an article at the time of his death, "and it was the only confession he ever made." Tom Morganthau, "The Legacy of Richard Nixon," *Newsweek,* May 2, 1994, 29.

90. William Shawcross, *Sideshow: Kissinger, Nixon and the Destruction of Cambodia* (New York: Simon and Schuster, 1979); Kissinger, *Diplomacy,* 698–700.

91. Henry Kissinger, *White House Years* (Boston: Little, Brown, 1979), 253.

92. United States v. United States District Court, 407 U.S. 297 (1972).

93. Seymour M. Hersh, *The Price of Power: Kissinger in the Nixon White House* (New York: Summit Books, 1983), 83–88. For a description of the wiretap program and the secrecy surrounding the Cambodia bombing, see Walter Isaacson, *Kissinger: A Biography* (New York: Simon and Schuster, 1992), 174–77, 216–17, 226–27.

94. Schwarzkopf, *It Doesn't Take a Hero,* 119, 178, 253, 258, 344.

95. Reynold A. Burrowes, *Revolution and Rescue in Grenada: An Account of the U.S.-Caribbean Invasion* (New York: Greenwood Press, 1988), 80; Steven A. Holmes, "Office in Grenada Closing, U. S. Says," *NYT,* May 2, 1994, A1 (national edition); Easterbrook, "Operation Desert Shill," 36; Gilbert S. Harper, "Logistics in Grenada: Supporting No-Plan Wars," *Parameters* 20 (June 1990): 50–63; B. Drummond Ayres Jr., "U.S. Concedes Bombing Hospital in Grenada, Killing at Least Twelve," *NYT,* November 1, 1983, A1 (late edition); "Pentagon Account of Attack," *NYT,* November 1, 1983, A16 (late edition).

96. John R. MacArthur, *Second Front: Censorship and Propaganda in the Gulf War* (New York: Hill and Wang, 1992), 172–78; David H. Hackworth, "Killed by Their Comrades," *Newsweek,* November 18, 1991, 45; Easterbrook, "Operation Desert Shill," 36–42; Patrick E. Tyler, "Iraq's War Toll Estimated by U.S.," *NYT,* June 5, 1991, A5 (national edition). For discussion of the changes after Grenada, see Donald R. Baucom, "Military Reform: An Idea Whose Time Has Come," *Air University Review* 38 (January–March 1987): 79–87.

97. On access being more of a problem than censorship in the Gulf War, see Dennis, *Media at War,* 26–37.

98. Helio Fred Garcia, "On Strategy and War: Public Relations Lessons from the Gulf," *Public Relations Quarterly* 36 (Summer 1991): 29–32; Ann McDaniel and Howard Fineman, "The President's 'Spin' Patrol," *Newsweek,* February 11, 1991, 31.

99. "The Early Bird Scores Big," *Time,* November 4, 1991, 18; Esther B. Fein, "The Schwarzkopf Strategy Works in Bookstores, Too," *NYT,* January 11, 1993, C6 (national edition).

100. Mark Fitzgerald, "War Boosts Readership," *E&P,* May 11, 1991, 7–8; Lou Prato, "War Showed That Radio Listeners Want News," *Washington Journalism Review,* May 1991, 54; "The Path to (Ratings) War," *Harper's,* April 1991, 20, 22.

101. Michael Hoyt, "Jon Alpert: NBC's Odd Man Out," *CJR,* September–October 1991, 44–47; David Astor, "Anti-Gulf War Cartoonists Got Reader Flak," *E&P,* May 18, 1991, 44–45; "Our Wartime Press," *CJR,* May–June 1991, 19–20; Mark Fitzgerald, " 'Free Press' Group Wants a Not-So-Free Press," *E&P,* April 6, 1991, 13; M. L. Stein, "Reporter Fired Over Gulf-

Related Story," *E&P*, March 23, 1991, 18; Richard Zoglin, "Just Whose Side Are They On?" *Time*, February 25, 1991, 52–53.

102. W. Lance Bennett and David L. Paletz, eds., *Taken By Storm: The Media, Public Opinion, and U. S. Foreign Policy in the Gulf War* (Chicago: University of Chicago Press, 1994); Norman Solomon, "The Media Protest Too Much," *NYT*, May 24, 1991, A15 (national edition); Lewis H. Lapham, "Trained Seals and Sitting Ducks," *Harper's*, May 1991, 10–15.

103. Michael Oreskes, "Bush Regains Record Rating in Crisis," *NYT*, August 22, 1990, A10 (national edition); Debra Gersh, "The Public, the Press and War Coverage," *E&P*, March 30, 1991, 11, 39; William Boot, "The Press Stands Alone," *CJR*, March–April 1991, 23–24; Zoglin, "Just Whose Side Are They On?" 52–53; Alex S. Jones, "Military Control of News is Backed in a Poll," *NYT*, January 31, 1991, B4 (national edition).

104. Tim Weiner, "'Smart' Weapons Were Overrated, Study Concludes," *NYT*, July 9, 1996, A1 (national edition); Seymour M. Hersh, "Missile Wars," *New Yorker*, September 26, 1994, 86–94, 96–99; Jennifer Weeks, "Patriot Games," *CJR*, July–August 1992, 13–14.

Eric Schmitt, "A Tally of Iraqis in War Is Doubted," *NYT*, April 24, 1992, A6 (national edition).

Douglas Waller, "Spies in Cyberspace," *Time*, March 20, 1995, 63.

Charles R. Shrader, "Friendly Fire: The Inevitable Price," *Parameters* 22 (Autumn 1992): 29–44; Eric Schmitt, "U.S. Seeks to Cut Accidental War Death," *NYT*, December 9, 1991, A7 (national edition); Hackworth, "Killed by Their Comrades," 45; Bruce van Voorst, "They Didn't Have To Die," *Time*, August 26, 1991, 20. Problems leading to "friendly fire" casualties had been spotted two years earlier, but not acted upon. Thomas E. Ricks, "Army Devises System To Decide What Does, and Does Not, Work," *Wall Street Journal*, May 23, 1997, A1.

David C. Hackworth, "War and the Second Sex," *Newsweek*, August 5, 1991, 29.

After years of denials, the Pentagon acknowledged in 1996 that chemical weapons were detected during the Persian Gulf War. The report ruled out a chemical attack by Iraq but suggested that the source may have been fallout from coalition bombing of Iraqi facilities. Philip Shenon, "New Report Cited on Chemical Arms Used in Gulf War," *NYT*, August 22, 1996, A1 (national edition).

105. Lewis J. Paper, *Empire: William S. Paley and the Making of CBS* (New York: St. Martin's Press, 1987), 158–59; Sperber, *Murrow*, 345–48; Friendly, "When War Comes," 276–77; "Situation Not Normal," *Newsweek*, September 25, 1950, 61.

106. Stanley Cloud and Lynne Olson, *The Murrow Boys: Pioneers on the Front Lines of Broadcast Journalism* (Boston: Houghton Mifflin, 1996), 300–313.

107. Paper, *Empire*, 303–4; Daniel Schorr, *Clearing the Air* (Boston: Houghton Mifflin, 1977), 198, 201–4, 274–80. For additional details on the CIA-CBS relationship, see Nancy E. Bernhard, "Ready, Willing, Able: Network Television News and the Federal Government, 1948–1953," in *Ruthless Criticism: New Perspectives in U.S. Communication History*, ed. William S. Solomon and Robert W. McChesney (Minneapolis: University of Minnesota Press, 1993), 303–7.

108. Beschloss, *Mayday*, 342; Barbara Matusow, *The Evening Stars: The Making of the Network News Anchor* (Boston: Houghton Mifflin, 1983), 58–59. For an account of Sarnoff's longstanding ties to the military, see Kenneth Bilby, *The General: David Sarnoff and the Rise of the Communications Industry* (New York: Harper and Row, 1986), 139–70.

109. Some of the earliest and loudest objections to Cold War secrecy came from the Committee on Freedom of Information of the American Society of Newspaper Editors and the committee's chairman, James S. Pope, managing editor of the Louisville *Courier-Journal*. The organization retained First Amendment lawyer Harold L. Cross, who, along with California Congressman John Moss, pushed for federal legislation. In 1966 Congress passed the Freedom of Information Act in an attempt to improve access to federal records. The act is Pub. L. No.

89–487, 80 Stat. 250 (1966). For examples of public warnings, see James Russell Wiggins, *Freedom or Secrecy*, rev. ed. (New York: Oxford University Press, 1964); Harold L. Cross, *The People's Right to Know: Legal Access to Public Records and Proceedings* (New York: Columbia University Press, 1953); James S. Pope, "The Cult of Secrecy," *Nieman Reports*, October 1951, 8–10; James S. Pope, "The Suppression of News," *Atlantic Monthly*, July 1951, 50–54.

110. For examples, see Evan Thomas, *The Very Best Men: Four Who Dared: The Early Years of the CIA* (New York: Simon and Schuster, 1995), 104–6, 117, 123–24, 159, 277. For examples of John F. Kennedy's deniability on national security matters, see Richard Reeves, *President Kennedy: Profile of Power* (New York: Simon and Schuster, 1993), 71, 104, 141, 262, 310, 337, 365, 473, 519, 577, 617–18, 638.

111. See Stephen F. Knott, *Secret and Sanctioned: Covert Operations and the American Presidency* (New York: Oxford University Press, 1996), 169–70; Michael R. Beschloss, *The Crisis Years: Kennedy and Khrushchev, 1960–1963* (New York: HarperCollins, 1991), 308–9, 514–15.

112. Christopher Andrew, *For the President's Eyes Only: Secret Intelligence and the American Presidency from Washington to Bush* (New York: HarperCollins, 1995), 299–301; Roger Hilsman, *To Move a Nation: The Politics of Foreign Policy in the Administration of John F. Kennedy* (New York: Delta, 1968), 217–24. Scali's efforts are downplayed in Beschloss, *Crisis Years*, 514–15.

113. Lawrence Van Gelder, "John A. Scali, 77, ABC Reporter Who Helped Ease Missile Crisis," *NYT*, October 10, 1995, A13 (national edition).

114. Martin A. Lee and Norman Solomon, *Unreliable Sources: A Guide to Detecting Bias in the News Media* (New York: Carol Publishing Group, 1990), 110–14; David Astor, "They Moved from Politics to Punditry," *E&P*, March 30, 1996, 34; A. M. Rosenthal, "Making of Buchanan," *NYT*, February 16, 1996, A17 (national edition).

115. Lee and Solomon, *Unreliable Sources*, 116; Stuart H. Loory, "The CIA's Use of the Press: 'A Mighty Wurlitzer,'" *CJR*, September–October 1974, 10.

116. Nathan Miller, *Spying for America: The Hidden History of U.S. Intelligence* (New York: Paragon House, 1989), 244, 315.

117. Stansfield Turner, *Secrecy and Democracy: The CIA in Transition* (Boston: Houghton Mifflin, 1985), 99–105; Debra Gersh Hernandez, "Journalists as Spies," *E&P*, August 10, 1996, 16–17, 36; "No Press Cards for Spies," *NYT*, March 18, 1996, A10 (national edition); Debra Gersh Hernandez, "Posing as Journalists," *E&P*, March 2, 1996, 8–9, 22; Frank Smyth, "My Spy Story," *NYT*, February 22, 1996, A15 (national edition); "The C.I.A., the F.B.I., and the Media," *CJR*, July–August 1976, 37–42.

118. Dwight D. Eisenhower, *Crusade in Europe* (New York: Doubleday, 1948), 169–70.

119. Frederick S. Voss, *Reporting the War: The Journalistic Coverage of World War II* (Washington, D.C.: Smithsonian Institution Press for the National Portrait Gallery, 1994), 202–6; William L. Laurence, "The Greatest Story," in *How I Got That Story*, ed. David Brown and W. Richard Bruner (New York: Dutton, 1967), 189–202.

120. Martin Blumenson, *The Patton Papers, 1940–1945* (Boston: Houghton Mifflin, 1974), 328–42; Knightley, *First Casualty*, 320–21; Eisenhower, *Crusade in Europe*, 182–83; Edward Kennedy, "Patton Struck Soldier in Hospital, Was Castigated by Eisenhower," in *Reporting World War II* (New York: Library of America, 1995), 1: 665–71; S. J. Monchak, "Censorship Backfired on Gen. Patton Story," *E&P*, November 27, 1943, 7, 32.

121. For a list of examples of the *Washington Post* talking to officials before deciding to publish a story, see Don Oberdorfer, "The First Amendment and National Security," *University of Miami Law Review* 43 (September 1988), 76–77.

122. Kathryn S. Olmsted, *Challenging the Secret Government: The Post-Watergate Investigations of the CIA and FBI* (Chapel Hill: University of North Carolina Press, 1996), 1–39, 59–85, 161–67, 183–85; Kati Marton, *The Polk Conspiracy: Murder and Cover-up in the Case of CBS News Correspondent George Polk* (New York: Farrar Straus Giroux, 1990); Edmund Keeley, *The*

Salonika Bay Murder: Cold War Politics and the Polk Affair (Princeton: Princeton University Press, 1989).

123. James Reston, *Deadline: A Memoir* (New York: Random House, 1991), 324; Beschloss, *Mayday*, 234–35.

124. Douglas Stanglin, Susan Headden, and Peter Cary, "Secrets of the Cold War," *U.S. News and World Report*, March 15, 1993, 30, 32–36.

125. Reeves, *President Kennedy*, 82–84; Reston, *Deadlines*, 324–27; Tad Szulc, "The *New York Times* and the Bay of Pigs," in Brown and Bruner, *How I Got That Story*, 315–29; Daniel D. Kennedy, "The Bay of Pigs and the *New York Times*: Another View of What Happened," *Journalism Quarterly* 63 (Autumn 1986): 524–29.

126. R. W. Apple Jr., "James Reston, a Journalist Nonpareil, Dies at 86," *NYT*, December 8, 1995, B15 (national edition).

127. Tom Reilly, " 'The War Press of New Orleans,': 1846–48," *Journalism History* 13 (Autumn–Winter 1986): 92; Donald A. Ritchie, *Press Gallery: Congress and the Washington Correspondents* (Cambridge: Harvard University Press, 1991), 69.

128. Adolph O. Goldsmith, "Reporting the Civil War: Union Army Press Relations," *Journalism Quarterly* 33 (Fall 1956): 480.

129. See, for example, J. Cutler Andrews, *The North Reports the Civil War* (Pittsburgh: University of Pittsburgh Press, 1955), 332; Robert S. Harper, *Lincoln and the Press* (New York: McGraw-Hill, 1951), 181. At times reporters helped Lincoln analyze the news. See, for instance, L. A. Gobright, *Recollections of Men and Things at Washington During the Third of a Century*, 2nd ed. (Philadelphia: Claxton, Remses, and Haffelfinger, 1869), 335–37.

130. Henry E. Wing, *When Lincoln Kissed Me: A Story of the Wilderness Campaign* (New York: Abingdon Press, 1913).

131. Eisenhower, *Crusade in Europe*, 299, 300–301.

132. Westmoreland, *A Soldier Reports*, 556, 558.

133. For examples of President Kennedy not being informed about failures, see John M. Newman, *JFK and Vietnam: Deception, Intrigue, and the Struggle for Power* (New York: Warner Books, 1992), 229–31.

134. Bill Monroe, "Peter Arnett: Anti-Hero of Baghdad," *Washington Journalism Review*, March 1991, 6; Walter Goodman, "CNN in Baghdad: Danger of Propaganda v. Virtue of Reporting," *NYT*, January 29, 1991, B1 (national edition).

135. William F. Buckley Jr., "Who's Right on Arnett?" *National Review*, March 18, 1991, 70–71; "Group Launches Campaign To 'Pull Plug' on CNN's Arnett," *Broadcasting*, February 18, 1991, 61; Goodman, "CNN in Baghdad," B1.

136. Peter Arnett, *Live from the Battlefield: From Vietnam to Baghdad, 35 Years in the World's War Zones* (New York: Simon and Schuster, 1994), 408–10; Andrew Arnett, "The Truth about My Family," *NYT*, March 13, 1991, A15 (national edition); Robin Toner, "Senator, Press and Crossed Swords," *NYT*, February 12, 1991, A8 (national edition).

137. "Saddam Hussein: The Old Tack," *Harper's*, October 1990, 21; Michael Hoyt, "A Chat with Iraq's Hussein," *CJR*, September–October 1990, 50.

138. Jonathan Alter, "When CNN Hit Its Target," *Newsweek*, January 28, 1991, 41.

139. Neuman, *Lights, Camera, War*, 216; Noyes, "Like It or Not," 38.

140. Neuman, *Lights, Camera, War*, 1–2, 217. In Iraq only a handful of top officials had access to CNN. "Peter Arnett, from Baghdad," *Newsweek*, February 11, 1991, 37.

141. George J. Church, "An Exquisite Balancing Act," *Time*, September 24, 1990, 45.

142. "Live, from Baghdad!" *Newsweek*, September 24, 1990, 6.

143. William A. Henry III, "History as It Happens," *Time*, January 6, 1992, 24. Intelligence agencies and the Pentagon responded to their information shortcomings in the Gulf War by establishing an encrypted computer system, Intelink, for users with secret or top secret security

clearances. Waller, "Spies in Cyberspace," 63–64; "A Network That Guarantees Scoops," *Time*, December 16, 1991, 15.

144. Walter Goodman, "A Day of Good News; Then Urgency," *NYT*, January 18, 1991, A13 (national edition).

145. Mathews, "Secret History of the War," 31.

146. Shannon E. Martin, *Bits, Bytes, and Big Brother: Federal Information Control in the Technological Age* (Westport, Conn.: Praeger, 1995), 74–79.

147. Schwarzkopf, *It Doesn't Take a Hero*, 336–37, 344–45, 439–40, 461; Cohen and Gatti, *In the Eye of the Storm*, 203.

148. The poster reached its pinnacle during World War I. See Walton Rawls, *Wake Up, America: World War I and the American Poster* (New York: Abbeville Press, 1988). During World War II approximately half of all the cartoons made were war-related, and the major American animators were under contract to produce shorts for the military. Norman M. Klein, *Seven Minutes: The Life and Death of the American Animated Cartoon* (London: Verso, 1993), 186.

149. Robert C. Miller, "News Censorship in Korea," *Nieman Reports*, July 1952, 5.

150. J. W. Fulbright, *The Pentagon Propaganda Machine* (New York: Liveright, 1970); F. Leslie Smith, " 'Selling of the Pentagon' and the First Amendment," *Journalism History* 2 (Spring 1975): 2–5, 14; F. Leslie Smith, "CBS Reports: The Selling of the Pentagon," in *Mass News: Practices, Controversies, and Alternatives*, ed. David J. Leroy and Christopher H. Sterling (Englewood Cliffs, N. J.: Prentice Hall, 1973), 200–210.

151. Lee and Solomon, *Unreliable Sources*, 105.

152. Evan Thomas, "The Art of the Techno-Thriller," *Newsweek*, August 8, 1988, 60–65.

153. See Lawrence H. Suid, *Guts and Glory: Great American War Movies* (Reading, Mass.: Addison-Wesley, 1978); Stewart Lytle, "The Military Cultivates Its Hollywood Connection," *The Press* 8 (August 1980): 9.

154. Richard Schickel, *D. W. Griffith: An American Life* (New York: Simon and Schuster, 1984), 227; White and Averson, *Celluloid Weapon*, 11–16.

155. Thomas Schatz, *The Genius of the System: Hollywood Filmmaking in the Studio Era* (New York: Pantheon Books, 1988), 37.

156. Frank T. Thompson, *William A. Wellman* (Metuchen, N.J.: Scarecrow Press, 1983), 58–65; William A. Wellman, *A Short Time for Insanity: An Autobiography* (New York: Hawthorn Books, 1974), 164–65.

157. David Culbert and Martin Loiperdinger, "Leni Riefenstahl's 'Tag der Freiheit': The 1935 Nazi Party Rally Film," *Historical Journal of Film, Radio and Television* 12 (1992): 12–15.

158. Robert Lindsey, " 'Top Gun': Ingenious Dogfights," *NYT*, May 27, 1986, 20 (national edition).

159. Gregory L. Vistica, "A Snakebit Squadron," *Newsweek*, February 12, 1996, 34. On the fighter's problems, see Vistica, *Fall From Glory*, 206–9; Philip Shenon, "Inquiry into F-14's Looks at Afterburners," *NYT*, April 4, 1996, A15 (national edition); "Navy Grounding All F-14's After Third Crash in a Month," *NYT*, February 23, 1996, A1 (national edition).

160. Clayton R. Koppes and Gregory D. Black, *Hollywood Goes to War: How Politics, Profits, and Propaganda Shaped World War II Movies* (New York: Free Press, 1987; Berkeley: University of California Press, 1990), 113–14; Edward de Grazia and Roger K. Newman, *Banned Films: Movies, Censors and the First Amendment* (New York: R. R. Bowker, 1982), 62.

161. Koppes and Black, *Hollywood Goes to War*, 15, 17–47.

162. Koppes and Black, *Hollywood Goes to War*, 31–32, 35; Gerald Gardner, *The Censorship Papers: Movie Censorship Letters from the Hays Office, 1934 to 1968* (New York: Dodd, Mead, 1987), 123–27, 209, 211.

163. Thomas Doherty, *Projections of War: Hollywood, American Culture and World War II* (New York: Columbia University Press, 1993), 36–59; Koppes and Black, *Hollywood Goes to*

War, 32–34; Richard W. Steele, "The Great Debate: Roosevelt, the Media, and the Coming of the War, 1940–1941," *Journal of American History* 71 (June 1984): 69–92.

164. The producers of *The Story of G.I. Joe* (1945), for instance, wanted to convey the realities of combat, but the Hays Office insisted that the vulgar language in the script be eliminated. *Ernie's War: The Best of Ernie Pyle's World War II Dispatches*, ed. David Nichols (New York: Random House, 1986), 35. On the use of profanities by real soldiers, see Fussell, *Wartime*, 79–95, 251–67.

The Hays Office insisted that soldiers who had been subjected to torture not be shown directly in *Objective, Burma!* (1945). Only the legs of a tortured soldier begging to be killed were shown. Bernard F. Dick, *The Star-Spangled Screen: The American World War II Film* (Lexington: University Press of Kentucky, 1985), 228.

165. Suid, *Guts and Glory*, 10.

166. George H. Roeder Jr., *The Censored War: American Visual Experience during World War Two* (New Haven: Yale University Press, 1993), 102–3; for a discussion of the relationship between the government and the movie industry, see 19–25.

167. Bob Herbert, "Bullet to the Heart," *NYT*, March 11, 1996, A11 (national edition).

168. Koppes and Black, *Hollywood Goes to War*, vii–viii, 65–72, 125–26, 134–41, 142–221, 287–90; Theodore F. Koop, *Weapon of Silence* (Chicago: University of Chicago Press, 1946), 43–44; Clayton R. Koppes and Gregory D. Black, "What to Show the World: The Office of War Information and Hollywood, 1942–1945," *Journal of American History* 64 (June 1977): 87–105.

169. Department of the Air Force, Standard Operating Directive for Cooperation with Motion Picture Companies, [1947], in *1945 and After*, ed. Lawrence H. Suid, vol. 4 of *Film and Propaganda in America: A Documentary History*, ed. David Culbert (New York: Greenwood Press, 1991), 192. For a later policy statement, see DoD Instruction 5410.16, "DoD Assitance to Non-Government, Entertainment-Oriented Motion Picture, Television, and Video Productions," January 26, 1988. Military advisers do help film crews avoid inaccuracies in the technical details of their movies. John M. Glionna, "Navy's Top Gun in Hollywood," San Diego *Union-Tribune*, April 17, 1989, C1.

170. Dick, *Star-Spangled Screen*, 135.

171. Suid, *Guts and Glory*, 150–62, 167–74.

172. Frank J. Wetta and Stephen J. Curley, *Celluloid Wars: A Guide to Film and the American Experience of War* (New York: Greenwood Press, 1992), 16, 17; Larry Suid, "Carter Nixes Coppola Aid," *More*, July–August 1977, 6.

173. Walter Goodman, "Using History To Serve Politics on TV," *NYT*, October 7, 1991, B2 (national edition).

174. Mark J. Eitelberg and Roger D. Little, "Influential Elites and the American Military after the Cold War," in *U.S. Civil-Military Relations: In Crisis or Transition?* ed. Don M. Snider and Miranda A. Carlton-Carew (Washington, D.C.: Center for Strategic and International Studies, 1995), 43–45; Karen Breslau, "Last Action President," *Newsweek*, July 21, 1997, 67; "The Screen Berets," *Harper's*, August 1996, 15–17.

175. See Richard D. MacCann, *The People's Films: A Political History of U.S. Government Motion Pictures* (New York: Hastings House, 1973).

176. Richard Wood, ed., *World War I*, vol. 1 of David Culbert, ed., *Film and Propaganda in America: A Documentary History* (New York: Greenwood Press, 1990); Larry W. Ward, *The Motion Picture Goes to War: The U.S. Government Film Effort during World War I* (Ann Arbor, Mich.: UMI Research Press, 1985); Michael T. Isenberg, *War on Film: The American Cinema and World War I, 1914–1941* (Rutherford, N. J.: Fairleigh Dickinson University Press, 1981); Vaughn, *Holding Fast the Inner Lines*, 203–11; Mock and Larson, *Words That Won the War*, 131–53.

177. Marion T. Marzolf, *Civilizing Voices: American Press Criticism, 1880–1950* (New York: Longman, 1991), 106–18; Garth S. Jowett and Victoria O'Donnell, *Propaganda and Persuasion* (Newbury Park, Calif.: Sage, 1986), 97–102; Harold D. Lasswell, *Propaganda Technique in World War I* (Cambridge, Mass.: MIT Press, 1971); Ericka G. King, "Exposing the 'Age of Lies': The Propaganda Menace as Portrayed in American Magazines in the Aftermath of World War I," *Journal of American Culture* 12 (Spring 1989): 35–40.
178. "This Is What the Soldiers Complain About," *Life*, August 18, 1941, 17–19.
179. MacCann, *People's Films*, 153–59; Frank Capra, *The Name above the Title: An Autobiography* (New York: Macmillan, 1971), 325–37; Jessica A. Meyerson, "Theater of War: American Propaganda Films during the Second World War," in *Propaganda*, ed. Robert Jackall (New York: New York University Press, 1995): 238–46; Laurence W. Mazzeno, "Getting the Word to Willie and Joe," *Military Review* 67 (August 1987): 70–71; Richard W. Steele, " 'The Greatest Gangster Movie Ever Filmed': *Prelude to War*," *Prologue* 11 (Winter 1979): 221–35. According to one estimate, Capra had to get approval from as many as fifty government agencies before releasing a "Why We Fight" film. *World War II*, pt. 1, ed. David Culbert, vol. 2 of *Film and Propaganda in America: A Documentary History*, ed. David Culbert (New York: Greenwood Press, 1990), xi.
180. Carl I. Hovland, Arthur A. Lumsdaine, and Fred D. Sheffield, *Experiments on Mass Communication* (Princeton: Princeton University Press, 1949), 3: 255–56.
181. F. H. Osborn, "Information and Education Division," *Military Review* 24 (December 1944): 22–26.
182. Mazzeno, "Getting the Word to Willie and Joe," 69–82.
183. Jerome S. Bruner, "OWI and the American Public," *Public Opinion Quarterly* 7 (Spring 1943): 129. See also Richard W. Steele, "News of the 'Good War': World War II News Management," *Journalism Quarterly* 62 (Winter 1985): 712.
184. Tag Gallagher, *John Ford: The Man and His Films* (Berkeley: University of California Press, 1986), 214–16; Andrew Sinclair, *John Ford* (New York: Dial Press/James Wade, 1979), 114, 118; Robert Parrish, *Growing Up in Hollywood* (New York: Harcourt Brace Jovanovich, 1976), 144–51; Meyerson, "Theatre of War," 231–38; James M. Skinner, "*December 7*: Filmic Myth Masquerading as Historical Fact," *Journal of Military History* 55 (October 1991): 507–16; Robert Parrish, "Directors at War: John Ford," *American Film* 10 (July–August 1985): 22, 27, 28, 63.
185. Lawrence Grobel, *The Hustons* (New York: Scribner's, 1989), 250–53, 262–63; John Huston, *An Open Book* (New York: Knopf, 1980), 107–26; Meyerson, "Theater of War," 250–56; Memo for the Record, Charles S. Stodter, November 16, 1944, in *World War II*, pt. 2, ed. David Culbert, vol. 3 of Culbert, *Film and Propaganda in America* (New York: Greenwood Press, 1990), 277. One of the reasons for the suppression of *Let There Be Light* may have been that the documentary took the unusual approach of showing black and white soldiers together without racial differentiation. Greg Garrett, "It's Everybody's War: Racism and the World War Two Documentary," *Journal of Popular Film and Television* 22 (Summer 1994): 73.
186. Claudia Springer, "Military Propaganda: Defense Department Films from World War II and Vietnam," *Cultural Critique* 1 (Spring 1986): 151–67.
187. Robert W. Chandler, *War of Ideas: The U.S. Propaganda Campaign in Vietnam* (Boulder, Colo.: Westview Press, 1981).
188. Fred Kaplan, "*Vietnam! Vietnam!*" in Suid, *1945 and After*, 415–18.
189. On the forces that can shape the quality of journalism, see Dan Berkowitz, ed., *Social Meanings of News: A Text-Reader* (Thousand Oaks, Calif.: Sage Publications, 1997).
190. John Steinbeck, *Once There Was a War* (New York: Viking Press, 1958), xvii.
191. Wyatt, *Paper Soldiers*, 145; Friendly, "When War Comes," 276.
192. Malcolm W. Browne, *Muddy Boots and Red Socks: A Reporter's Life* (New York: Times Books, 1993), 349.

193. William Prochnau, *Once Upon a Distant War* (New York: Times Books, 1995).

194. *Ibid.*, 219–23.

195. See Ken Silverstein, "Follow the Leader," *American Journalism Review*, November 1993, 30–36.

Conclusion

1. On the marketplace of ideas concept, see Jeffery A. Smith, *Printers and Press Freedom: The Ideology of Early American Journalism* (New York: Oxford University Press, 1988), 31–41; W. Wat Hopkins, "The Supreme Court Defines the Marketplace of Ideas," *Journalism and Mass Communication Quarterly* 73 (Spring 1996): 40–52; William P. Marshall, "In Defense of the Search for Truth as a First Amendment Justification," *Georgia Law Review* 30 (Fall 1995): 1–39.

2. See Barbara Ehrenreich, "The Warrior Culture," *Time*, October 15, 1990, 100; Michael S. Sherry, *In the Shadow of War: The United States Since the 1930s* (New Haven: Yale University Press, 1995).

3. Sissela Bok, *Secrets: On the Ethics of Concealment and Revelation* (New York: Pantheon Books, 1982), 194–96.

4. Remarks and a Question-and-Answer Session with the American Society of Newspaper Editors, April 13, 1994, in *Public Papers of the Presidents of the United States, William J. Clinton, 1994* (Washington, D.C.: Government Printing Office, 1995), 686, 687.

5. Ingrid Detter De Lupis, *The Law of War* (New York: Cambridge University Press, 1987), 278.

6. Harry F. Noyes III, "Like It or Not, The Armed Forces Need the Media," *Army*, June 1992, 30–31, 33.

7. On the causes listed by Thucydides and how they can be observed in case studies, see Donald Kagan, *On the Origins of War and the Preservation of Peace* (New York: Doubleday, 1995).

8. Thomas S. Langston, *With Reverence and Contempt: How Americans Think About Their President* (Baltimore: Johns Hopkins University Press, 1995), 96.

9. Benjamin I. Page and Robert Y. Shapiro, *The Rational Public: Fifty Years of Trends in Americans' Policy Preferences* (Chicago: University of Chicago Press, 1992), 2–3, 170–74, 221, 382–98.

10. See Stephen Holmes, *The Anatomy of Antiliberalism* (Cambridge: Harvard University Press, 1993), 4, 262.

11. Seth Shulman, *The Threat at Home: Confronting the Toxic Legacy of the U.S. Military* (Boston: Beacon Press, 1992); Bruce Van Voorst, "A Thousand Points of Blight," *Time*, November 2, 1992, 68–69.

12. Frederick Palmer, *With My Own Eyes: A Personal Story of Battle Years* (Indianapolis: Bobbs-Merrill, 1933), 300, 366; George Creel, *How We Advertised America* (New York: Harper, 1920), 17; Byron Price, Memoir, Byron Price Papers, State Historical Society of Wisconsin, Madison, 3 (sec. 1): 213; Elmer Davis, "Report to the President," [1945] ed. Ronald T. Farrar, *Journalism Monographs*, no. 7, August 1968, 16; Pierre Salinger, *With Kennedy* (Garden City, N.Y.: Doubleday, 1966), 329.

13. See Richard E. Neustadt and Ernest R. May, *Thinking in Time: The Uses of History for Decision Makers* (New York: Free Press, 1986).

14. Ritchie P. Lowry, "Toward a Sociology of Secrecy and Security Systems," in *Secrecy: A Cross-Cultural Perspective*, ed. Stanton K. Tefft (New York: Human Sciences Press, 1980), 308. An argument for easily obtained satellite reconnaissance is the hope that aggression can be deterred by advance warning of military movements. William J. Broad, "Private Ventures Hope for Profits on Spy Satellites," *NYT*, February 10, 1997, A1 (national edition).

15. Eric Sevareid, "Censors in the Saddle," *Nation*, April 14, 1945, 417.

16. Johanna Neuman, *Lights, Camera, War: Is Media Technology Driving International Politics?* (New York: St. Martin's Press, 1996), 185–201. Repressive governments, of course, do take countermeasures against the flow of information. Tim Zimmermann, "All Propaganda, All the Time," *U.S. News and World Report*, November 11, 1996, 48–49.

17. Eric B. Easton, "Closing the Barn Door after the Genie is Out of the Bag: Recognizing a 'Futility Principle' in First Amendment Jurisprudence," *DePaul Law Review* 45 (Fall 1995): 1–64.

18. Martin Kitchen, *Nazi Germany at War* (New York: Longman, 1995), 282–83; Nathan Stoltzfus, "Dissent in Nazi Germany," *Atlantic Monthly*, September 1992, 87–90, 92–94.

19. Daniel Jonah Goldhagen, *Hitler's Willing Executioners: Ordinary Germans and the Holocaust* (New York: Knopf, 1996); Primo Levi, *Survival in Auschwitz* and *The Reawakening: Two Memoirs*, trans. Stuart Woolf (New York: Summit Books, 1986), 381.

20. Levi, *Two Memoirs*, 377–81; Howard Andrew G. Chua-Eoan, "War in Europe," *Time*, December 2, 1991, 68.

21. David Bankier, "German Public Awareness of the Final Solution," in *The Final Solution: Origins and Implementation*, ed. David Cesarani (New York: Routledge, 1994), 215–27.

22. *The Army Almanac: A Book of Facts Concerning the United States Army*, 2nd ed. (Harrisburg, Penn.: Stackpole, 1959), 353; Davis, "Report to the President," 25.

23. Tim Weiner, "Lawmaker Tells of High Cost of Data Secrecy," *NYT*, June 28, 1996, A9 (national edition).

24. Tim Weiner, "A Spy Agency Opens Some Dusty Secret Files," *NYT*, April 5, 1996, A16 (national edition). In 1995 President Clinton signed an executive order generally requiring that classified documents be made public after twenty-five years. Some exceptions can be made by agency heads with the approval of an appeals panel. Douglas Jehl, "Clinton Revamps Policy on Secrecy of U.S. Documents," *NYT*, April 18, 1995, A1 (national edition).

25. John Wicklein, "Foiled FOIA," *American Journalism Review*, April 1996, 38; "Harper's Index," *Harper's*, August 1994, 11.

26. R. W. Apple Jr., "Government is Overzealous on Secrecy, Panel Advises," *NYT*, March 5, 1997, A11 (national edition).

27. Tim Weiner, "For First Time, U.S. Discloses Budget on Spying: $26.6 Billion," *NYT*, October 16, 1997, A17 (national edition).

28. Tim Weiner, "C.I.A. Chief Backs Secrecy, in Spending and Spying, to Senate," *NYT*, February 23, 1996, A6 (national edition); Robert Pear, "Congress Imposes New Restrictions on Secret Funds," *NYT*, October 31, 1990 (national edition).

29. Douglas Waller, "The Vision Thing," *Time*, December 11, 1995, 48; Gregory Vistica, "Psychics and Spooks," *Newsweek*, December 11, 1995, 50.

30. Arlen Specter, chairman of the Senate intelligence committee, as quoted in Evan Thomas, "Cleaning Up 'The Company,'" *Newsweek*, June 12, 1995, 35. CIA estimates of Soviet strength supported a costly American arms buildup in the 1980s that was unnecessary and apparently not the reason for the collapse of communism. Tim Weiner, "C.I.A. Admits Failing To Sift Tainted Data," *NYT*, November 1, 1995, A1 (national edition); Richard Ned Lebow and Janice Gross Stein, "Reagan and the Russians," *Atlantic Monthly*, February 1994, 35–37; George F. Kennan, "The G.O.P. Won the Cold War? Ridiculous." *NYT*, October 28, 1992, A15 (national edition); Leslie H. Gelb, "Who Won the Cold War?" *NYT*, August 20, 1992, A19 (national edition); Michael Kinsley, "Just Why Did Communism Fail?" *Time*, November 4, 1991, 98.

31. For a list of examples, see "My Country for a Rolex," *Time*, March 7, 1994, 16. On the sloppiness of supervision, see Jeff Stein, "The Mole's Manual," *NYT*, July 5, 1994, A15 (national edition); Douglas Waller, "How Ames Fooled the CIA," *Newsweek*, May 9, 1994, 24–25.

32. Norman Polmar and Thomas B. Allen, *Spy Book: The Encyclopedia of Espionage* (New York: Random House, 1997), 21–22; Tim Weiner, "C.I.A. Remains in Darkness on Extent of Spy's Damage," *NYT*, August 25, 1995, A1 (national edition); David Wise, "The Ames Spy Hunt," *Time*, May 22, 1995, 54–61; Tim Weiner, "Spy's Intrigues Were a C.I.A. Disaster," *NYT*, April 29, 1994, A8 (national edition). For eight years the CIA evaded disclosing the Ames-related problems to Congress as required by law. Tim Weiner, "C.I.A. Is Criticized for Failing To Report Lapse in Mole Case," *NYT*, December 1, 1994, A9 (national edition).

33. "Excerpts from Statement by C.I.A. Officer Who Pleaded Guilty in Spy Case," *NYT*, April 29, 1994, A8 (national edition).

34. Rick Marin and T. Trent Gegax, "Conspiracy Mania Feeds Our Growing National Paranoia," *Newsweek*, December 30, 1996–January 6, 1997, 64–66, 71.

35. Evan Thomas, "Who Shot JFK?" *Newsweek*, September 6, 1993, 14–17. One of the better efforts to refute the conspiracy theories is Gerald L. Posner, *Case Closed: Lee Harvey Oswald and the Assassination of JFK* (New York: Random House, 1993).

36. David Ellis, "Did J.F.K. Really Commit Suicide?" *Time*, April 13, 1992, 64–65.

37. Glenn Campbell, "Groom Lake: The Base That Isn't There," *CovertAction Quarterly*, Spring 1995, 34–37, 40; Mark Farmer, "Not So Secret Weapons," *CovertAction Quarterly*, Spring 1995, 38–39; Terry Allen, "National Security's Wasting Illness," *CovertAction Quarterly*, Spring 1995, 41, 47; "Off Base," *Newsweek*, April 24, 1995, 4; Donovan Webster, " 'Area 51,' " *New York Times Magazine*, June 26, 1994, 32–35, 44; "The Mystery at Groom Lake," *Newsweek*, November 1, 1993, 4.

38. See H. Bruce Franklin, *M.I.A., or Mythmaking in America* (Chicago: Lawrence Hill Books, 1992); Jack Colhoun, "Inside the POW/MIA Lobby," *Lies of Our Times*, June 1993, 5–7; Robert C. Doyle, "Unresolved Mysteries: The Myth of the Missing Warrior and the Government Deceit Theme in the Popular Captivity Culture of the Vietnam War," *Journal of American Culture* 15 (Summer 1992): 1–18.

39. William V. Kennedy, *The Military and the Media: Why the Press Cannot Be Trusted To Cover a War* (Westport, Conn.: Praeger, 1993), 31; Ed Offley, "Unhappy Alliance: Military and the Media," *Presstime*, January 1993, 35.

40. Daniel C. Hallin, Robert Karl Manoff, and Judy K. Weddle, "Sourcing Patterns of National Security Reporters," *Journalism Quarterly* 70 (Winter 1993): 753–66.

41. See Douglas Waller, "Arms Deals," *Time*, April 14, 1997, 48–50; Mark Thompson, "Why the Pentagon Gets a Free Ride," *Time*, June 5, 1995, 26–27; David Futrelle, "Pentagon Pork," *Utne Reader*, January-February 1995, 32, 34; John Barry, "The Battle over Warfare," *Newsweek*, December 5, 1994, 27–28; Seymour M. Hersh, "Missile Wars," *New Yorker*, September 26, 1994, 93; Richard J. Barnet, "Still Putting Arms First," *Harper's*, February 1993, 59–65; Ann Markusen, "The Politics of Peacetime Conversion," *Harper's*, October 1992, 25–26, 28; David H. Hackworth, " 'You in Congress, Listen Up,' " *Newsweek*, June 8, 1992, 30.

42. Matthew L. Wald, "Cost of U.S. Nuclear Arms is $3.9 Trillion, Study Says," *NYT*, July 13, 1995, A12 (national edition).

43. Adam Walinsky, "The Crisis of Public Order," *Atlantic Monthly*, July 1995, 48, 53.

44. Seymour Melman, "Preparing for War (against Ourselves)," *NYT*, June 26, 1995, A11 (national edition); Miles Harvey, "Eco-Warriors," *Utne Reader*, January–February 1993, 17–18.

45. Fred Ritchin, "The March of Images," *NYT*, June 10, 1991, A11 (national edition); Robert Goldberg, "TV: The Antiseptic Tube," *Wall Street Journal*, March 4, 1991, A7.

46. For a collection of such stories, see *Reporting World War II* (New York: Library of America, 1995).

47. Eric Sevareid, *Not So Wild a Dream* (New York: Knopf, 1946), 390.

48. Frank Aukofer and William P. Lawrence, *America's Team; The Odd Couple—A Report on the Relationship Between the Media and the Military* (Nashville, Tenn.: Freedom Forum First Amendment Center, 1995), 11, 16.

49. Debra Gersh Hernandez, "The Media's Impact on the Military," *E&P*, May 13, 1995, 14.

50. For sets of policy suggestions for the military and the media, see Aukofer and Lawrence, *America's Team,* 53–55; Jacqueline E. Sharkey, *Under Fire: U.S. Military Restrictions on the Media from Grenada to the Persian Gulf* (Washington, D.C.: Center for Public Integrity, 1991), 157–71. For the view that a specialized court should be established to review disputes between the press and military, see Rana Jazayerli, "War and the First Amendment: A Call for Legislation to Protect a Press' Right of Access to Military Operations," *Columbia Journal of Transnational Law* 35 (Winter 1997): 131–73.

51. Statement of DoD Principles for News Media Coverage of DoD Operations, 32 C.F.R. ch. 1 pt. 375 app. B (1995). The statement was later removed from the Code of Federal Regulations as unnnecessary for inclusion, but was reissued under DoD Directive 5122.5, "Assistant to the Secretary of Defense for Public Affairs," March 29, 1996, 61 Fed. Reg. 18,083 (1996).

52. Principles of Information, 32 C.F.R. ch. 1 pt. 375 app. A (1995).

53. James P. Terry, "Press Access to Combatant Operations in the Post-Peacekeeping Era," *Military Law Review* 154 (October, 1997): 1–26; Aukofer and Lawrence, *America's Team,* 197–99; Debra Gersh, "New Guidelines for War Coverage in Place," *E&P*, June 6, 1992, 17, 72–73, 86; "Pentagon, Journalists Agree on Most Coverage Rules," *News Media and the Law,* Spring 1992, 21–22.

54. Debra Gersh Hernandez, "No Media Pool in Bosnia," *E&P*, December 16, 1995, 9; John H. Cushman Jr., "Who Reports What on Iraq: Pentagon Eases Reins a Bit," *NYT*, September 9, 1992, A4 (national edition); "Navy Officials Back Off on Security Review Plan," *E&P*, October 17, 1992, 29. For interviewing restrictions in Bosnia, however, see Debra Gersh Hernandez, " 'Embedding' Leads to Restrictions," *E&P*, May 25, 1996, 10–11.

55. Walter Cronkite, "What Is There To Hide?" *Newsweek*, February 25, 1991, 43.

56. John Chancellor, "From Normandy to Grenada," *American Heritage* 36 (June–July 1985): 33.

57. When pilot Scott O'Grady was rescued in 1995 after six days in Bosnia, Air Force public affairs officers seemingly wanted secrecy *after* the rescue. O'Grady was treated as a hero in the extensive media exposure he received, but apparently was coached to say very little about what was actually an embarrassing incident. Kevin Fedarko, "Glomming on to a Hero," *Time*, June 26, 1995, 31–32.

58. David Wise, *The Politics of Lying: Government Deception, Secrecy, and Power* (New York: Random House, 1973), 150.

59. For the view that the Pentagon building is "a vast factory of policy" where facts are distorted to avoid losing funds, see Kennedy, *Military and the Media,* 31.

60. *Complete Report of the Chairman of the Committee on Public Information* (Washington, D.C.: Government Printing Office, 1920), 13.

61. Davis, "Report to the President," 24.

62. See, for example, Debra Gersh Hernandez and Bill Schmitt, "SPJ Approves Ethics Code," *E&P*, October 19, 1996, 22, 51.

63. William T. Sherman, *Memoirs of General W. T. Sherman* (New York: Library of America, 1990), 899.

64. Thomas I. Emerson, "National Security and Civil Liberties," *Yale Journal of World Public Order* 9 (April 1982): 81, 111; Rodney A. Smolla, *Free Speech in an Open Society* (New York: Knopf, 1992), 320; Pennsylvania Assembly: Reply to the Governor, [November 11, 1755], in *The Papers of Benjamin Franklin*, ed. Leonard W. Labaree et al. (New Haven, Conn.: Yale University Press, 1959–), 6: 242.

Index